Azerbaijan
Since
INDEPENDENCE

Svante E. Cornell

Azerbaijan Since Independence offers a comprehensive introduction to modern Azerbaijan, a post-Soviet republic located on the western shore of the Caspian Sea. This small country has outsized importance due to its strategic location at the crossroads of Europe and Asia, its energy wealth, and its historical experience as an early modernizer in the Muslim world.

The book begins with six chapters on Azerbaijan's history from pre-Soviet times to the present, with an emphasis on the past twenty years. The next four chapters are thematic, covering the conflict over Karabakh, the political system, the oil-dominated economy, and societal changes and trends including the role of Islam. The remainder of the book surveys Azerbaijan's foreign relations, with an analysis of the foreign-policy-making context complemented by chapters on relations with Iran, Russia, Turkey, and the West. The book closes with a brief epilogue discussing the country's future.

Studies of Central Asia and the Caucasus

Books in this series are published in association with the Central Asia–Caucasus Institute of the Johns Hopkins University's Paul H. Nitze School of Advanced International Studies, under the editorship of S. Frederick Starr.

Azerbaijan

Since

INDEPENDENCE

SVANTE E. CORNELL

M.E.Sharpe
Armonk, New York
London, England

Library of Congress Cataloging-in-Publication Data

Cornell, Svante E.
  Azerbaijan since independence / by Svante E. Cornell.
    p. cm. — (Studies of Central Asia and the Caucasus)
  Includes bibliographical references and index.
  ISBN 978-0-7656-3002-5 (cloth : alk. paper) — ISBN 978-0-7656-3003-2 (pbk. : alk. paper)
  1. Azerbaijan—Politics and government—1991– 2. Azerbaijan—Foreign relations—1991–
  3. Azerbaijan—Economic conditions—1991– 4. Azerbaijan—Social conditions—1991–
  I. Title.

  DK697.68.C6 2011
  947.5608´6—dc22   2010042749

Printed in the United States of America

The paper used in this publication meets the minimum requirements of
American National Standard for Information Sciences
Permanence of Paper for Printed Library Materials,
ANSI Z 39.48-1984.

VG (p)   10   9   8   7   6   5   4   3   2   1

For Anna

Contents

Preface

This book seeks to introduce the reader to a small but fascinating country at the crossroads of Europe and Asia, the Republic of Azerbaijan. My interest in the country, and the wider region of the Caucasus, dates to the early 1990s, when I lived in Turkey and attended the Middle East Technical University in Ankara during eventful years that featured the collapse of the Soviet Union and the wars in the South Caucasus, as well as the Gulf war and Turkey's own Kurdish insurgency. Among my classmates were a dozen students from the newly independent Soviet republics, Azerbaijanis prominent among them—epitomizing the fact that a large area that had previously been all but closed was now opening up to the world.

My knowledge of Turkish helped me acquire a proficiency in Azerbaijani with relative ease, something that proved a valuable asset in understanding a society that most others had to approach through intermediary languages—Russian, or even English.

Throughout the years of my acquaintance with the region, I have often been struck by the lack of comprehensive studies covering the Caucasus and its countries. This led me to compile, ten years ago, a study of the conflicts of the Caucasus, entitled *Small Nations and Great Powers*. The present volume aims to focus in more detail on one of these small nations, which is also the largest and arguably most important country of the Caucasus: Azerbaijan.

If Azerbaijan had to be defined by a single word, that word would have to be "crossroads"—an observation made by the perhaps greatest historian of Azerbaijan, Tadeusz Swietochowski. Azerbaijan epitomizes the fact that being at a crossroads, it does not have to choose between identities—in fact, it cannot choose between them. Azerbaijan is both European and Asian at the same time.

Azerbaijan's importance is much greater than its small size. Located at the crossroads of Europe and Asia and endowed with substantial energy reserves, Azerbaijan cannot escape being at the center of the high politics of Eurasia in the early twenty-first century. But Azerbaijan is more than an area of geo-political confrontation and intrigue. It is a fascinating culture, which stands out in the Muslim world for its progressive nature and accomplishments.

Not only was Azerbaijan host to the first democratic and secular republic of the Muslim world, it was also leading in terms of modern literary works and cultural accomplishments, including the first opera produced in the Muslim world. As such, the future of Azerbaijan matters much more than its size on a map would indicate.

The structure of this book seeks to combine a chronological and thematic approach, in order to grasp the complexity and interrelated character of all the domestic and external issues that are included in this book. Thus, this book has three parts. Chapters one through six form a chronological narrative of Azerbaijan's development from the pre-Soviet period to the present—and as the reader will see, the attention to detail grows incrementally as the narrative nears the present. This first part provides the context for the following, thematically organized chapters. Chapters seven through ten constitute the book's second part, and discuss the domestic affairs of present-day Azerbaijan. First among these, the focus of chapter seven, is the unresolved conflict over Nagorno-Karabakh, which more than anything else has made an imprint on the country. Chapter eight attempts to go behind the veil of Azerbaijan's opaque political system, while chapters nine and ten, respectively, study Azerbaijan's oil-led economy and its society in rapid evolution. The third and final part of the book, chapters eleven through fifteen, focus on Azerbaijan's foreign relations. After a chapter on the context of foreign policy-making in Azerbaijan, attention turns in sequence to the country's relations with Iran, Russia, Turkey, and the West.

I would not have been able to devote time to research and write this book had it not been for the support of several sponsors. The Swedish Ministry for Foreign Affairs and the Smith Richardson Foundation have provided generous institutional support for the Stockholm and Washington offices, respectively, of the Central Asia-Caucasus Institute & Silk Road Studies Program Joint Center. I am also grateful for the additional support provided by the U.S.-Azerbaijan Chamber of Commerce for this project.

This book is a project fifteen years in the making, and my gratitude is due to scores of people that have in some way contributed to my quest to understand Azerbaijan. Most important among these are those Azerbaijanis that have shared their knowledge and time with me, and have provided their various perspectives on their country, in turn enriching my own.

Fariz Ismailzade has been an especially close friend and associate in a number of joint projects, and numerous ideas and arguments in this book are a result of our joint writings on Azerbaijan and the Caucasus. With Elin Suleymanov, I have shared countless lengthy conversations on every conceivable aspect of Azerbaijan over the past decade. I have also benefited greatly from the friendship and insights of Eldar Ismailov and Seymour Khalilov.

My thanks go also to Hafiz Pashayev, Elmar Mamedyarov, and Araz Azimov, as well as Tofiq Zulfugarov, Niyazi Mehdi, Chingiz Sultansoy, Galib Mammad, Taleh Ziyadov, and Tair Faradov.

During my trips to Azerbaijan over the past decade, a number of Azerbaijani politicians have been very generous with their time. First and foremost, I am grateful to President Ilham Aliyev and First Lady Mehriban Aliyeva for receiving me on several occasions. I would also like to thank Isa Gambar, leader of the Müsavat party, and Ali Kerimli, leader of the Popular Front Party, for generously receiving me over the years.

A word of thanks also goes to those few but notable western scholars of Azerbaijan whose works, written long before I took an interest in the country and in much more difficult circumstances, have inspired my own research. Historians Tadeusz Swietochowski and Audrey Altstadt, and writer Thomas Goltz stand out among them. Zeyno Baran, Jonathan Elkind, and Brenda Shaffer have all read parts of this book and provided valuable comments. S. Frederick Starr, Chairman of the Central Asia-Caucasus Institute, has been tireless in his encouragement for this project, and I owe him a debt of gratitude.

At the Joint Center, I am especially grateful to Alec Forss, whose help in editing and layout was crucial to produce this book. The manuscript also benefited greatly from the arduous style editing by Vincent Ercolano. The cover of the book was designed by Anna Starr Townsend, featuring a Karabakh rug in the author's possession. Dena Barmas, Rena Efendi, and Tim McNaught also graciously provided some of their photographs for the illustrations to this book, as did Betty Blair. Any remaining errors, which I am sure readers are bound to find in this book, are my own.

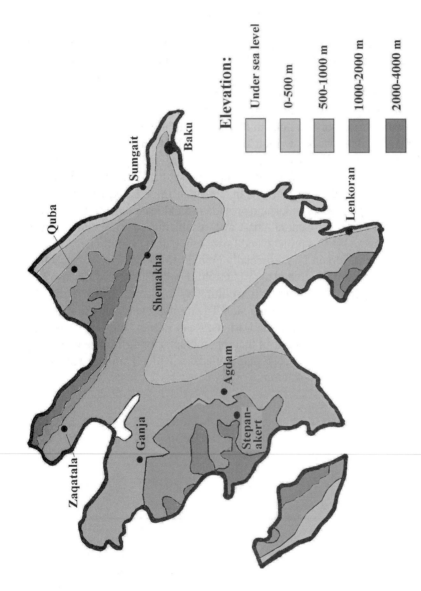

Elevation:

Under sea level

0–500 m

500–1000 m

1000–2000 m

2000–4000 m

Topographic Map of Azerbaijan (Central Asia–Caucasus Institute)

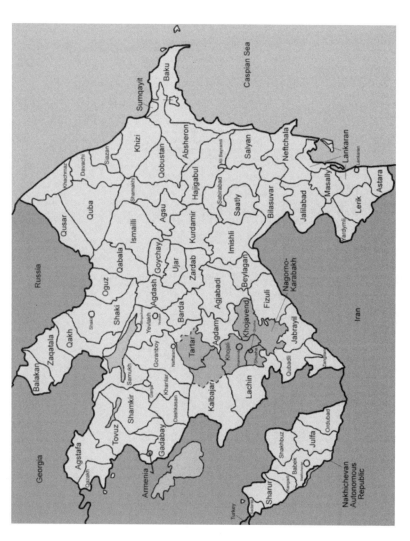

Administrative Map of Azerbaijan (Wikimedia Commons)

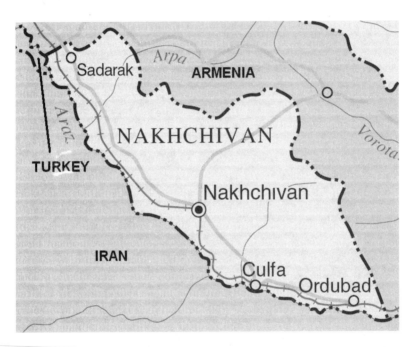

Nakhchivan Exclave of Azerbaijan (Central Asia-Caucasus Institute)

Lines of Control in Armenian-Azerbaijan Conflict, May 1994
(Central Asia-Caucasus Institute)

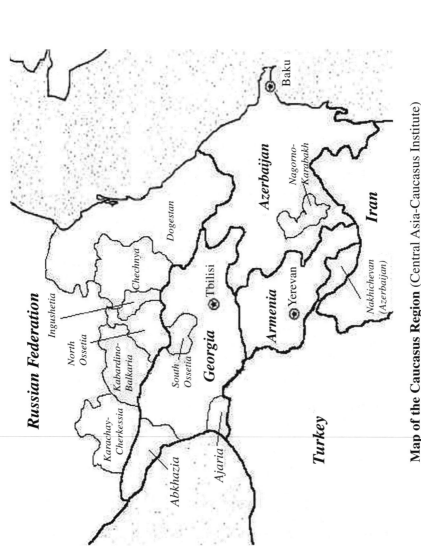

Map of the Caucasus Region (Central Asia-Caucasus Institute)

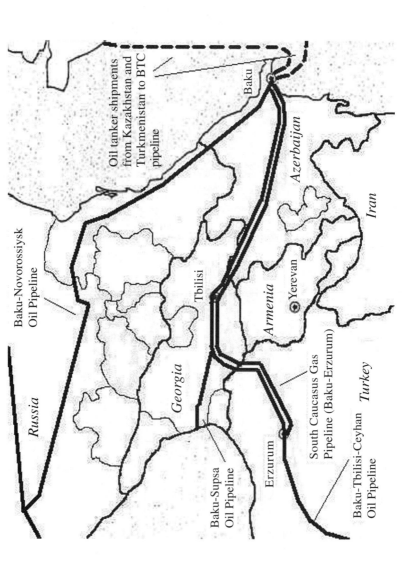

Oil and Gas Pipeline Infrastructure in the South Caucasus (Central Asia-Caucasus Institute)

Memmed Emin Rasulzade

Nariman Narimanov

Heydar Aliyev as leader of Soviet Azerbaijan in 1979

Abülfez Elçibey

Heydar Aliyev as President of Azerbaijan, 1997

Ilham Aliyev in 2008

Heydar Aliyev, Ilham Aliyev, and Heydar Aliyev Jr.

Baku at the Turn of the Twentieth Century

Baku in 2010

Baku's Historic Old Town

Baku's Maiden Tower

(Courtesy of BP/AIOC)

The West Azeri platform, developed and operated by BP/AIOC
in the Azerbaijani sector of the Caspian Sea

(Courtesy of Tim McNaught)

A View of the Greater Caucasus near Zaqatala in Early Spring

The Besh Barmaq (Five Finger) mountain in northern Azerbaijan

Mud Volcano in the Gobustan State Preserve

Displaced Persons from the war with Armenia

Azerbaijan
Since
INDEPENDENCE

1

Azerbaijan Before Soviet Rule

If Azerbaijan's history from the earliest times to the present were to be characterized by a single word, the most appropriate would be *crossroads*. Situated between Europe and Asia, Azerbaijan is marked by major routes of migration, conquest, and trade that transit the country from east to west and north to south. This circumstance has shaped Azerbaijan's history and demography, not least its complicated and contested ethnographic history. Evidence of protohuman activity dating back more than a million years has been discovered in Azerbaijan, with the first traces of agriculture found in Nakhichevan.[1]

Azerbaijan can be geographically defined in at least two ways. On the one hand, its territory can be understood as constituting that of the Republic of Azerbaijan, which was defined as a nation-state in 1918 and, with a slight loss of territory, as a Soviet republic from 1922 to 1991, and, since 1991, as an independent state. But a historic definition of Azerbaijan—and an ethnographic one, if the country is understood as the territory populated mainly by Azerbaijani Turks—encompasses a considerably larger area including parts of neighboring countries, most prominently a large portion of northwestern Iran. Indeed, until the decisive division of Azerbaijan between the Russian and Persian empires in 1828, there was little rationale for making distinctions between the lands north and south of the Araks River (which forms much of the present-day border between Azerbaijan and Iran).

Azerbaijan From Antiquity to the Turkic Invasions

For much of human history, the focus of settlement and the emergence of states in the region occurred mainly south of the Araks River, that is, in present-day Iranian Azerbaijan (also referred to as southern Azerbaijan). This circumstance was due in large part to the area's proximity to Mesopotamia, an early center of intense social, commercial, and political development. The northern part of what is now the independent state of Azerbaijan experienced political development somewhat later, with human settlement concentrated mainly in the fertile delta at the confluence of the Kura and Araks rivers.

Atropatena and Caucasian Albania

Two states that existed in antiquity have been especially crucial to the historiography of Azerbaijan. The first is Atropatena, which existed south of the Araks River in the first centuries BCE. Atropatena was named after a satrap of Alexander the Great, and provides one of several possible origins for the term *Azerbaijan*. An alternative explanation is that the name derives from the combination of *azer*, Persian for "fire," and *baygan*, Persian for "protector." This definition is closely connected to the role played by Azerbaijan in the emergence of the Zoroastrian religion. Southern Azerbaijan is believed by some scholars to be the birthplace of Zoroaster, though many present-day scholars dispute that claim, suggesting instead a Central Asian location.[2] The second crucial historical state is Caucasian Albania, also known as Aghvania. This entity, unrelated to the Albania of the Balkans, developed north of the Araks River in the fourth century BCE, in a territory roughly coterminous with the present-day state of Azerbaijan. Especially since the early Soviet period, Azerbaijani scholars have emphasized their people's direct link to Caucasian Albania, arguing that the present-day Azerbaijani population derives from Albania's population, which was later intermixed with Turkic tribes and became linguistically Turkified. Building on the works of Strabo and Ptolemy, among others, these scholars have identified Albania as the land between the Caucasus Mountains and the Araks River, and between "Iberia" (Georgia) and the Caspian—making it an ideal fit with the territory of northern Azerbaijan post-1828.

Azerbaijan's history up to the seventeenth century is a bewildering tale of innumerable short-lived principalities, competing empires, and sequences of settlers, conquests, and migrations. Such a tumultuous history undoubtedly caused large-scale, continuous suffering on the part of the land's population. The few periods of peace and development that occurred seldom lasted more than several decades.[3] The Sumerians, Lullubians, Akkadians, Kutians, Cadusians, Caspians, Zamoans, Mannaeans, Assyrians, Urartians, Medians, Scythians, Armenians, and Alans are only some of the peoples who ruled parts of Azerbaijan in the centuries that preceded the Arab—and later, the even more significant Turkic—invasions. The Arab invasions of the eighth century spelled the beginning of the end of the Albanian state, as they led to the Islamization of Azerbaijan. As a result, the Albanian church—a monophysite church very similar to the Armenian but independent from it—gradually was incorporated into the Armenian one. Presently, great historical debate surrounds this issue, as Azerbaijani scholars claim that ancient Christian monuments in Karabakh are Albanian, not Armenian, something vigorously contested by Armenian scholars.

Most of Azerbaijan gradually came to adopt the Shia version of Islam, in great part because of its greater tolerance of mysticism, which was more suitable to the syncretism that had evolved (as in many other Turkic lands) among Zoroastrian, Christian, and shamanistic practices. But on the slopes of the Caucasus Mountains in northern Azerbaijan, in part because of their proximity to the staunchly Sunni North Caucasus, Sunni Islam remained dominant.

The Arrival of the Turks

While Turkic tribes certainly ventured south of the Caucasus Mountains long before, it was really in the ninth and tenth centuries that a significant Turkic element established itself in Azerbaijan. The process began with warrior clans entering the service of the Sassanid dynasty of the Persian Empire, and gained impetus in subsequent centuries with the emergence of the Oghuz Turks' Seljuk dynasty, which gradually established its suzerainty over much of the Islamic world, making distant Baghdad its capital. Azerbaijan may have been a crossroads, but it was also a backwater for both the Seljuk dynasty and the Byzantine Empire, which before the battle of Manzikert in 1071 controlled Anatolia to Azerbaijan's west. As a result, imperial control was weak and inconsistent, depending on changes in the relative strength and interest of the two empires at a given time. One consequence of this situation was instability and constant competition for local power among native as well as nonnative princes and vassals. Native principalities developed, the most significant being the Shirvanshahs, who originally had their seat at Qabala but were dislocated by the Arab invasions and moved to Baku a few hundred miles to the southeast, then only a village. The Shirvanshahs developed a remarkable capability for survival, allying themselves most often with the victorious empires that projected their influence into Azerbaijan. Hence, through "resilience and adaptability," they were able to survive the destruction of both the Mongol invasion of 1235 and the Timurid invasions 150 years later.[4]

If native Caucasian, Iranian, and Turkic populations—among others—dominated Azerbaijan from the fourth century CE onward, the Turkic element would grow increasingly dominant in linguistic terms,[5] while the

Persian element retained a strong cultural and religious influence. Turkic tribes of the Oghuz lineage began arriving in Azerbaijan probably as early as the sixth and seventh centuries CE. An Oghuz presence in pre-Islamic Azerbaijan is suggested by one of the most important Oghuz Turkic historical documents, the *Book of Dede Korkut*, which was probably written in the ninth century, though the final version is several centuries more recent.[6] The dominance of the Oghuz Turkic tribes, of which the Seljuks constituted a part, provided for the development of a Turkic vernacular language that would eventually become the present-day Azerbaijani language. Azerbaijani Turkish is closely similar to the Turkish spoken in Turkey and the Turkmen of both Turkmenistan and Iraq, but also has a strong Persian influence in its vocabulary. In fact, Persian retained its status as the language of culture among Azerbaijanis for centuries. Azerbaijan's most famous and venerated poets, such as Nizami Ganjevi, wrote mainly in Persian. Following the Seljuk great power period, the Turkic element in Azerbaijan was further strengthened by migrations during the Mongol onslaught of the thirteenth century and the subsequent domination by the Turkmen Qara-qoyunlu and Aq-qoyunlu dynasties.

From Safavid to Russian Rule

Throughout Asia, Turkic dynasties played a central role in the building of statehood and empire, dominating India, the Middle East, Asia Minor, and parts of Europe for the better part of the second millennium CE. The Ottomans came to dominate Asia Minor and eastern Europe, the Mamluks left their mark on Egypt, the Ghaznavids and Moghuls ruled the Indian subcontinent, and the Seljuks controlled the Middle East. Likewise, in the sixteenth century, a dynasty with roots in Ardebil in southern Azerbaijan emerged as the leading force in the building of the modern Iranian state: the Safavids.

The Safavid Dynasty

The Safavid dynasty—which was based on a mystical Sufi order—was founded by Shah Ismail Khatai, who is best known for establishing Shia Islam as the state religion of Iran. The Safavids stood out in comparison to the Ghaznavids and other Turkic conquerors by being a local, not an invading, dynasty. Established in 1501, the Safavids fought to evict the Ottoman rule that had been imposed on parts of the region. Historians indeed argue that one reason Shah Ismail imposed Shia Islam on his state was to sharpen the differences between his rule and that of the ethnically and linguistically closely related—but Sunni—Ottomans. Shah Ismail himself wrote poetry in the Azerbaijani Turkish vernacular, which remained the court language of the early Safavid rulers. Azerbaijani Turkish developed into a literary language in a form close to that used today, as is shown by remarkable works of the time such as the prose and poetry of Muhammad Fuzuli.

The long tenure of the Safavid dynasty helped integrate Azerbaijan into the Persian world while giving the Azerbaijanis the distinction of being the only Turkic people that is predominantly Shia. As Brenda Shaffer observes, this "contributed to the formation of their distinctive and common Azerbaijani identity."[7]

From its capital in Tabriz, the Safavid court gradually moved its seat southward in the face of Ottoman attacks. In 1592 Isfahan became the capital, and would remain so until 1795. The seventeenth century saw the gradual disintegration of Iranian power, beginning in earnest with the collapse of the Safavid dynasty in the face of an Afghan invasion in 1722. The Safavids were gradually replaced by the equally Turkic Qajar dynasty after a short stint in power by Nadir Shah. One of the most direct results of the weakening of Iranian central power was the growing independence this granted to the khanates of both northern and southern Azerbaijan. Most powerful among them after the destruction of the Shirvanshah khanate by the Safavids was the khanate of Quba, ruled by Fath Ali Khan; other khanates included Shamakha, Sheki, Gandja, Baku, Talysh, Nakhichevan, and Yerevan.

Russian Conquest

The late eighteenth century also saw the emergence of a new, powerful actor in the politics of the South Caucasus. This was Russia, which benefited greatly from the weakness of both the Ottoman and Iranian empires. Peter the Great sent an initial expedition down the Caspian coast past Baku in the 1720s, but business on the European side of the empire prevented Russia from focusing on the Caucasus until the 1780s. In 1783, under attack by both Iranians and Ottomans and receiving no support from the European powers in spite of continuous pleas, King Irakli II of Georgia signed the Treaty of Georgievsk with Russia, effectively making his realm a Russian protectorate and giving Russia a foothold south of the Caucasus. In return, Russia made three promises, none of which would be kept: Irakli and his descendents would be guaranteed the Georgian throne; the Georgian Orthodox Church would retain its independence; and Russia would defend Georgia from any attack from Turkey or Iran attributable to the treaty. In 1801, the eastern Georgian kingdom of Kartli-Kakheti was annexed to Russia, becoming the Tiflis Gubernia, and nine years later western Georgia was conquered. Also in the first decade of the nineteenth century, Russia extended its reach from Georgia into the rest of the South Caucasus, conquering the Shirvan and Karabakh khanates in 1805.

These expansionist moves led to two successive Russo-Persian wars, one fought from 1812 to 1813 and another from 1827 to 1828. Russia emerged victorious from both, cementing its control over the South Caucasus by means of the treaties of Gulustan (1813) and Turkmanchai (1828). Much of the fighting was done not by armies deployed from central Iran but by the local khans and their subjects, who often strenuously resisted the Russian onslaught.[8] To this day, the border delimiting Azerbaijan and Armenia from Iran is the one devised under the Treaty of Turkmanchai, which led to the division of Azerbaijan between the Russian and Iranian empires.

Once in control of the South Caucasus, Russia moved to administer its new territorial gains. This generated a debate on how best to deal with the conquered lands. One option was to maintain colonial rule over them, and hence not incorporate them outright into the Russian state. That would follow the general model of the Western colonial powers, with some exceptions such as French Algeria or Portuguese colonies. The other option was to designate the territories of the South Caucasus as provinces of the Russian Empire like any other. Russia first tilted toward colonial status, which would be less costly because it would permit local rulers to handle internal matters as long as their loyalty to the czar was unquestioned. But by the 1840s, Russia had reversed this policy and began to impose direct rule over the South Caucasus, which in practice meant maintaining a Russian administration and spreading the use of Russian as the official language.[9]

Direct rule was imposed through the creation of various provinces or *gubernii*, whose composition and delimitation changed over time. The one thing they had in common was their artificial character, having little relationship with local conditions and loyalties or preexisting entities.

Russian rule meant the imposition of Russian law, and a concomitant onslaught on the role of religion and the clergy as they had existed in Azerbaijan. With brief exceptions, Russian rule was heavily anti-Muslim. Religious properties were confiscated, and Azerbaijanis were proselytized to convert to Orthodox Christianity. On the other hand, the Georgians and Armenians retained numerous privileges, especially as far as religious properties and government staffing were concerned. Armenians, in particular, came to play an important role in the administration of the Caucasus region. As Tadeusz Swietochowski has observed, the Armenians played a role for Russia similar to that of the Lebanese Maronites for the French: "a strategic foothold in the Middle East with the large proportion of Christians as the mainstay of the colonial rule."[10] Simultaneously, Russia tried to co-opt segments of the local elites, focusing in particular on the increasingly powerless beys and aghas, providing them with opportunities for civil service careers and granting them title to land—the latter measure constituting the introduction of private landownership in Azerbaijan.[11]

One important consequence of Russian rule, particularly with the gradual centralization of power in the second half of the eighteenth century, was the unification of the former khanates of northern Azerbaijan in both economic and political terms. Though three *gubernii* (Baku, Elizavetpol, and Erivan) covered the area populated by Azerbaijani Turks, Russian rule imposed a uniform system of administration, provided for a single currency and an increasingly monetarized economy, removed tariffs and other impediments to trade among the khanates, and standardized weights and measurements.[12] But as Swietochowski has noted, though it brought one portion of Azerbaijan under European rule, Russian conquest was a case of one pre-industrial society conquering another. Hence, until the industrialization of the 1870s, it therefore had only limited economic impact. In fact, the lack of attention to maintaining irrigation systems set Azerbaijan back and indirectly provided the basis for the large migrations to Baku that were to follow.[13]

Industrialization and the Baku Oil Boom

While the oil boom did not arrive until the 1870s, the area around Baku had been known for its oil resources since the ninth century, when Arab travelers noted the use of oil for heating purposes in the Apsheron Peninsula. Marco Polo wrote of Baku's oil being exported to Middle Eastern destinations, and two British travelers in the mid-sixteenth century described Baku as follows: "Which town is a strange thing to behold, for there issueth out of the ground a marvelous quantity of oil, which serveth all the country to burn in their houses. This oil is black and is called 'nefte.'"[14]

The oil industry developed gradually over the course of the nineteenth century, with the production of kerosene and distillation of oil. But the boom came following an 1872 law that changed the prevailing system of state-granted oil concessions to long-term commercial leases. This attracted businessmen to Baku from both the Russian Empire and abroad; the most important of these were the Nobel brothers, who would eventually come to control more than half of Baku's production. The Nobel company and other foreign investors such as the Rothschilds brought not only capital to the industry but also new technologies, many of which were tested first in Baku before spreading across the world. The first oil-carrying steamer, the *Zoroaster*, was built by the Nobels in 1877; in 1883, the Rothschilds built the Caucasus Railway, which transported oil from Baku to the Black Sea port of Batumi; In 1907, the world's first oil export pipeline was built, also running between Baku and Batumi. By 1898, Baku was producing more oil than the United States. But as so often occurs in the Russian context, the industry developed in an inefficient way, leading to declines in productivity but, more important, an environmental disaster across the Apsheron Peninsula that is plainly visible to the contemporary visitor but is only beginning to be addressed.

Baku's role in the oil industry began a slow but steady decline around the time of the aborted Russian revolution of 1905. This decline would last until the early 1990s, with the renewal of international investment and participation in the oil industry. The oil boom had immense implications for Azerbaijan, and specifically for Baku. As always, Swietochowski's observations are to the point:

> The overall result of the "oil revolution" was a dichotomy not uncommon in a colonial situation: a generally traditional but lopsided economy, with a single rapidly growing industry based on mineral resources rather than on manufacturing, geared to external markets, owned largely by foreign investors, and operated by nonnative skilled labor. Typical also was the contrast between the city rising out of the industrialization and the countryside unshaken from its timeless pattern of existence.[15]

Yet Azerbaijan remained overwhelmingly rural, as the immigration into Baku did not come primarily from the adjacent countryside. While the number of Azerbaijani Turks in Baku stayed relatively stable from 1897 to 1913, the Russian population increased more than 100 percent, surpassing the native population in size by about 1900. The number of Iranians in the city (presumably mainly southern Azerbaijani Turks) almost tripled, while the population of Armenians doubled, making them practically as numerous as the natives. Hence, industrialization helped make Baku increasingly cosmopolitan, thereby creating the gulf between the metropolis and the countryside that remains a key issue in present-day Azerbaijan.[16] As shown in the next chapter, it would take until the 1950s for Baku to become a truly Azerbaijani city in ethnic terms.

The oil boom affected the different ethnic groups in Azerbaijan vastly differently. With the exception of a few notable native self-made industrialists such as Zeynalabdin Taghiev, Musa Naghiev, and Shamsi Asadullayev, Azerbaijani Turks either remained peasants in the countryside or became involved in unskilled labor in the oil industry. Among Armenians, the urbanized portion was prominent in administration, skilled labor, and trade. Also, a large number of the industrialists were Armenians: at the turn of the century, a third of industrial companies belonged to Armenians, while less than a fifth belonged to Azerbaijanis. Russians dominated administration and were prominently represented among technicians and skilled labor. But the various groups did not mix: within Baku, they lived mostly in separate quarters, which grew increasingly homogeneous after local riots associated with the 1905 revolution.[17] But despite being gradually outnumbered, the Azerbaijani Turks were native to the land and commanded informal networks and ties to the countryside that the settling communities did not. Hence, it would be wrong to conclude that they were being marginalized; rather, with the help of native industrialists who supported education, publishing, and the arts, the Azerbaijani Turks were gradually acquiring a voice.

As Audrey Altstadt has observed, a crucial corollary of the emergence of the oil industry for Azerbaijan's future was the formation of a native working class.[18] This led Azerbaijan to become one of the few Muslim areas where some, albeit marginal, support for socialist ideologies was to be found and subsequently exploited by the Bolsheviks. Meanwhile, among Armenians, national sentiment found an outlet in the radical Dashnaktsutiun, the Armenian Revolutionary Federation (ARF). Drawn equally to socialism and nationalism, the ARF grew in strength in parallel with a short-lived attempt by the czarist authorities to curry favor in the Azerbaijani community. Meanwhile, the tensions between the Armenian and Azerbaijani communities had grown due to a mix of factors. A prominent one was a competition for resources and economic profit that developed along ethnic lines, with different sectors of the economy dominated by one or the other ethnic group. Also, as Kari Strømmen has observed, the Western oil barons controlled a lot more of the oil industry than the Armenians did; but not being locals, the Westerners were not perceived as an impediment to the ambitions of Azerbaijani Turks seeking to establish themselves in the oil industry—while Armenians, supported by discriminatory Russian policies, were.[19]

As Altstadt concludes, "The root of conflict must be sought in historical differences manipulated over decades by tsarist colonial policies meant to incite jealousy, perhaps violence, as a means of control."[20] In 1905, with the temporary relaxation of state control that followed the failed revolution, tensions between Azerbaijanis and Armenians exploded across the South Caucasus—both in rural areas, including Nakhichevan, Yerevan, and the Karabakh Mountains, and in Baku. Between 3,000 and 10,000 people were killed in the clashes. As would happen again almost a century later, the fighting often pitted well-organized Armenian groups against less disciplined and spontaneously formed assemblages of Azerbaijanis. Overall, the Azerbaijanis were clearly on the losing end of this confrontation—which one Armenian observer called an "unqualified victory."[21] As would be the case in the 1990s, Russian soldiers stood by and watched the violence, ordered not to intervene. In another clear parallel with the 1990s, the conflict contributed to intensified political activity and greater unity in the Azerbaijani community.

The Formation of Azerbaijani National Identity

The Russian and European education provided to the native elite formed the seed of the development of an Azerbaijani intelligentsia in the nineteenth century.[22] As Shaffer has noted, the early Azerbaijani thinkers and writers displayed three major trends: first, the development of a supranational Islamic identity; second, the development of liberal values and the rejection of authoritarianism, which these proponents sought to wed to pan-Islamic thought; and third, the gradual growth of local Azerbaijani nationalism stressing the Turkish cultural identity of the Azerbaijanis.[23] By the early twentieth century, the intelligentsia would become the major force in Azerbaijani nation building.

The Early Intelligentsia

In the Azerbaijani context, the term *intelligentsia*, as Swietochowski has noted, does not refer simply to an educated elite, but is more specific: it denotes the secular, modern intelligentsia, and hence excludes the religiously trained elite.[24] Hence, in practice this select group was limited to Azerbaijanis who had served in the Russian civil service or had been trained in Russian institutes of higher education.

The acknowledged founder of modern literary Azerbaijani Turkish is Mirza Fath Ali Khan Akhundzade. A translator employed by the Russian viceroy, Akhundzade published in Azerbaijani and, from 1850 to 1855, wrote the first Western-style plays ever published in the Muslim world.[25] A critique of the superstition and ignorance of native society, his work emphasized the importance of building up secular education. A key issue in debates among the early intelligentsia was education, in particular the reform of Muslim schooling, hitherto mainly focused on boys and consisting of religious education as well as limited rote instruction in writing, reading, and basic mathematics. The literacy rate among Azerbaijanis was 10 percent in Baku, and far less in the countryside, especially for girls.[26] In this context, Azerbaijani intellectuals were drawn to a reform movement originating in Tatarstan called the *Jadid*, literally meaning "New method," an agenda for the modernization of Muslim education that discouraged rote memorization and introduced new methods of learning and new subjects, including foreign languages.[27] In Azerbaijan, a leading proponent was Abdulrahim Talebzade, who set up the first Muslim school of the Jadid type, emphasizing secular education, in Baku.[28]

Aside from education, identity was a major question, in which Azerbaijani intellectuals displayed a variety of tendencies. The main vehicles for debate and discussion were the various newspapers and other periodicals that emerged, printed in Azerbaijani, Ottoman Turkish, Persian, and Russian. Among the intellectuals, many sought a larger community of which the Azerbaijanis could be part, making Pan-Turkism and Pan-Islamism powerful ideologies.[29] Pan-Turkism was influenced by Pan-Slavist ideas that Azerbaijanis and other Turkic peoples of the Russian Empire were exposed to, and contributed to the emerging Young Turk movement in the Ottoman Empire. In fact, there were close connections between Turkish and Azerbaijani intellectuals at the time. Somewhat opposed to Pan-Turkism was the call for Pan-Islamism, a striving for the unity of the Ummah (the Muslim community of believers) that in Azerbaijan was often connected to views favoring Iran over Turkey. Nevertheless, while Pan-Turkists emphasized the primacy of the ethnic bonds of Turkic origin, the fact that almost all Turkic peoples are Muslim (except for small groups such as the Christian Chuvash and Gagauz and the Jewish Karaims) made Pan-Islamism acceptable to Turkic nationalists under certain conditions. Likewise, Pan-Islamists disillusioned with Iran could accept the ideas of Pan-Turkism. Hence, Ali Huseynzade, a Turkist writer, articulated the joint principles of "Turkify, Islamize, and Europeanize," unifying three concepts that could otherwise seem at odds.[30] This slogan was adopted by the leading ideologist of Pan-Turkism, Ziya Gökalp, in his *Principles of Turkism*.[31] On the other hand, former Pan-Islamist Ali Aghaoghlu, initially highly critical of the Ottoman Empire, gradually gravitated toward Turkism, realizing that Turkey represented a much better hope than Iran of unifying Muslim lands.[32]

Yet proponents of a distinct Azerbaijani identity also grew in number, indicating the growing independence of thought in Azerbaijan and the reluctance to be subsumed under either a Persian or a Turkish ideology. (This attitude would resurface in the 1990s.) The concept of self-identification as an "Azerbaijani Turk" first emerged in the newspaper *Keshkul* in 1891.[33] In Altstadt's words, this conception managed "in one stroke [to convey] a distinction between religious and national identity while marrying the idea of Turkishness to the Azerbaijan land."[34] Part of this movement involved the rejection of forthright adoption of the Ottoman Turkish written language; instead, Azerbaijanis would codify and standardize the vernacular Azerbaijani dialect, a task undertaken by several newspapers. In its new form as a written language, Azerbaijani was increasingly put to practical use in both book publishing and the theater.

The late czarist period, ca 1890–1915, was a formative and creative one in Azerbaijan's history, and the country's cultural richness and progressive social and political nature were unique in the Muslim world at the time. The first indigenously composed and staged opera in the Muslim world, Uzeyir Hacibeyli's *Leila and Majnun*, premiered in Baku in 1908, and the first women's college in a Muslim country was established by the industrialist Taghiyev in 1896.[35] At this time, Azerbaijan established its position as a mediator between East and West. It learned from the West, and emulated the progressive nature of European civilization, but it did so without losing its connection to its Islamic and Turkic origins. This trend, which continues to this day, is paralleled in the politicization of the Azerbaijani intelligentsia, which was characterized by the same moderation and progressiveness that guided its attitude toward culture. Azerbaijani political life, which experienced its culmination in 1918 with the establishment of the Muslim world's first secular and democratic republic, saw a generally cordial atmosphere—especially for the time—develop between its socialist and nationalist components that generated a culture of compromise and gradualism. As is related in subsequent chapters of the present volume, this culture of compromise did not survive the Soviet Union's onslaught on Azerbaijan's society and intelligentsia, and its absence is notable in the country today.

The Politicization of Azerbaijani Intellectuals

In the years between 1905 and the Russian Revolution, the Azerbaijani intelligentsia became increasingly politicized. The collapse of Russian rule in 1917 eventually led the intelligentsia to step in to create the independent state of Azerbaijan. But the Russian Revolution was not the only moment-ous event of the time. The other two powers that Azerbaijani intellectuals oscillated between also experienced political convulsions: in Iran, the constitutional revolution of 1906, and in Turkey, the Young Turk revolution of 1908[36]; both upheavals took place in "cultures and societies with which the Azerbaijanis identified themselves incomparably closer than with Russia."[37] Still, it was the events of 1905 that left the deepest mark on Azerbaijan.

The events of 1905. particularly the inter-communal riots, shook the Azerbaijani community deeply. If "the Muslims at first maintained their splendid isolation of indifference toward the turmoil in the world of the infidel,"[38] the intercommunal clashes changed this—not only as far as Azerbaijanis' attitudes toward Armenians were concerned, but indeed concerning their attitudes toward the Russian Empire. As would, remarkably, occur again in 1988 and 1990, the Russian police and military forces failed to intervene during the 1905 riots, apparently under orders to let the communal fighting continue. In 1905, as eight decades later, this led the Azerbaijanis to conclude that the Russian authorities were perfectly happy with—and perhaps had even instigated—the unrest in order to divide and rule, to keep Caucasian peoples busy with one another instead of turning against Russia. Following the riots, Russia reinstated the position of viceroy of the Caucasus. This was followed by a return to pro-Armenian policies, and soldiers were explicitly ordered to fire at Muslim armed groups, though not at groups of armed Armenians; in addition, the Armenian Orthodox Church was given back the property the Russian government had seized from it a few years earlier.[39] As Naki Keykurun, a resident of the Gandja khanate and later a leading figure in the Azerbaijani Popular Republic, wrote in his memoirs, "The cooperation between the Russians and Armenians during the conflict induced our people to think about the future consequences."[40]

The twin revolutions in Iran and Turkey also involved Azerbaijanis and affected Azerbaijan greatly. During the 1906 constitutional revolution in Iran, the self-made leader Sattar Khan of Tabriz became a revolutionary hero by galvanizing support for withstanding two royalist sieges of Tabriz, and subsequently refusing to disarm when urged to do o by the new government A brief condition of civil war ensued in southern Azerbaijan. Azerbaijani intellectuals, especially the subsequent leader of the Musavat party Mämmädemin Räsulzadä, played a leading role among left-wing intellectuals in the period that followed. As for Turkey, the 1908 coup by the Committee for Union and Progress (CUP; Ittihad ve Terakki Cemiyeti) was more decisive than developments in Iran, as it rapidly changed the political climate in the Ottoman Empire. Most important, whereas nationalism of any type, including Turkish, had been repressed under the Ottoman Sultan Abdülhamit II, the Young Turk movement that now dominated Turkey's political landscape encouraged Pan-Turkism. Azerbaijanis were among the leading and most influential thinkers behind Pan-Turkism, not least the secularist playwright Akhundzade. The Azerbaijani intelligentsia was remarkable not least because of its continued exposure to—and role in—developments in the three large empires of Russia, Turkey, and Iran in the period from 1905 to the First World War.

Back home, the Azerbaijani intellectual leadership was faced with a dilemma very much related to its cosmopolitan nature. Being increasingly hostile toward czarist rule, Azerbaijani intellectuals were nevertheless undecided whether to build a separate Azerbaijani nationalism or join revolutionary or reformist forces in cooperation with other peoples of the Russian Empire, even Russians. Indeed, as Shaffer has put it, the Azerbaijani intelligentsia had an ambivalent relationship with Russia. Russia was still regarded as a force that had brought European modernism to Azerbaijan, and independence—an existence totally separate from the Russian orbit—was seen as infeasible, much as it would seem to Ayaz Mutalibov during 1991–92. This understanding led Azerbaijanis to seek other ways of reconstructing their relationship with Russia. An important characteristic of the Azerbaijani political movements was, with few exceptions, their moderation and progressive outlook. As Shaffer observes, "In almost all movements they joined, the Azerbaijanis continued to be at the forefront of Muslims advocating the adoption of liberal values and enlightenment. One example of this is the insistence on the emancipation of women advocated by political parties in both north and south Azerbaijan."[41] Hence, whether nationalist in orientation, like the Difai and Müsavat, or leftist, like the Hümmät, Azerbaijani groupings eschewed radicalism and were oriented toward compromise—a trend that would lead to the remarkable political system that was set up in 1918 with creation of the Azerbaijan Popular Republic (commonly known as the First Republic).

In contrast to cosmopolitan Baku, Gandja emerged as a center of the nationalist movement. It was in Gandja that the first rebellious nationalist organization, Difai, (Defense), was formed in the fall of 1905. It blamed Russia for the bloodshed, while maintaining an ambivalent attitude toward Armenian groups, in fact seeking to counter the perceived Russian policies of divide and rule by exploring ways to bury the hatchet with the Armenians and work for an independent Transcaucasia that could be possible only through cooperation among Armenians, Azerbaijanis, and Georgians.

Political activity in Baku was much less inclined toward separatism. Instead, two chief branches developed: the socialists and the Muslim liberals. The earliest political organization of note was the leftist Hümmät, created in 1904. Hümmät was formed in response to neglect of the Azerbaijanis by Russian leftist movements. It would become linked to the Russian Social Democratic Workers' Party, which would later produce the Bolsheviks, but stood out by being the only native socialist grouping allowed by Lenin to retain a status separate from the party. Hümmät was much more moderate than most leftist groupings in Russia at the time—indeed, it was not even operating on the basis of a Marxist class perspective, focusing mainly on the inequalities created by foreign rule rather than on class cleavages. This was symptomatic of a larger fact: the weakness of class consciousness in the Caucasus compared to ethnic nationalism. Workers hardly ever allied across ethnic boundaries against the capitalists; neither did the bourgeoisie unite across national lines.[42] The importance of Hümmät as a native socialist movement was considerable, as it attracted members from both northern and southern Azerbaijan. It is considered the seed from which both the Azerbaijani and Iranian communist parties evolved.

Two figures in Hümmät were of particular importance: Mämmädämin Räsulzadä and Nariman Narimanov. Räsulzadä would play an important role in the First Republic, and Narimanov in the establishment of Soviet power in Azerbaijan, a legacy that is discussed in detail in chapter 2 of the present volume. Mämmedämin Räsulzadä was born in 1884 in Novkhanä, outside Baku, and got involved in social democratic movements at an early age. He became a writer published in numerous legal and illegal publications and a founder of Hümmät. In one of history's twists, Räsulzadä developed a personal relationship with the young Joseph Stalin, actually saving his life in 1905, a favor Stalin would return upon the sovietization of Azerbaijan in 1920. In 1907, a crackdown on Hümmät led to the arrest of many members and the exile of others, including Räsulzadä, to Iran. He continued agitating there, and was exiled from Iran under Russian pressure in 1912, this time to Istanbul, where he became active in Turkish nationalist circles.[43] Returning to Azerbaijan when an amnesty was declared in 1913, he joined a newly created political party, Müsavat, and rapidly became its leader. Müsavat had begun as a Pan-Islamic modernist party seeking to liberate and modernize the wider Islamic world. But with Räsulzadä at its helm, it drifted increasingly in a Turkist direction.

The liberals, for their part, participated in the first Congress of Muslims of Russia in August 1905, which staked out a course that lay emphasis on gaining equal rights for Muslims and turning Russia into a constitutional monarchy—a platform close to that of the Russian Constitutional Democrats.[44] Within this grouping, Fatali Khan Khoisky emerged as a leading figure. Born in 1875 of a noble family that had been the khans of Khoy, in Iran, Khoisky graduated from the Moscow Faculty of Law in 1901 and subsequently worked as a lawyer and judge. He was elected to the second Duma in 1907, as a member of its Muslim section. After the Duma was dissolved the same year, Khoisky went back to practicing law until the February 1917 revolution.

War and the Collapse of Czarist Russia

From 1912 to 1917, Azerbaijani loyalty to the Russian Empire would be further tested, as the Balkan wars of 1912–13 and, subsequently, the First World War brought Russia into direct conflict with Turkey.[45] In the Balkan wars, Müsavat unequivocally took the Turkish side, castigating Russia for fomenting an attack on Turkey.[46] The first months of World War I were less problematic. But when war was declared between Turkey and Russia, the Turkish armies led by Enver Pasha attacked Russia on the Caucasus front. The attack was clearly motivated by Pan-Turkic ideology, as the CUP saw the opportunity to build a Turkic empire in the east to replace its collapsing European holdings. Undefended Tabriz was briefly taken by a small Ottoman contingent in January 1915, before Russian forces took it back. The CUP at this point also sought to undermine Russia by cultivating the ARF. In spite of the November 1914 Armenian uprising in Van, the CUP sought to remove this obstacle to its eastern aspirations by offering an arrangement in which Armenia would be unified under Turkish rule and autonomous within an expanded Turkic state—an offer the ARF refused. Instead, Armenian irregulars joined the Russian counterattack in the spring of 1915, helping the Russians move as far west as Erzincan on the Anatolian plateau.[47] This action would prove to be the starting point for the deportations and massacres of eastern Turkey's Armenian population. Ajarians and other Muslims who had risen up against Russian rule as Turkish armies advanced were also massacred when czarist forces took back these territories.

A combination of factors muted the Azerbaijani intelligentsia in this complex and unpredictable situation; four are particularly noteworthy. The first was the Russian military advances; the second was the fear inspired by the massacres of rebellious Muslims in the southwestern Caucasus; a third was Azerbaijani reluctance to be engulfed in a Turkish state that had failed to specify the status it intended to grant Azerbaijan.[48] Indeed, as would be the case in 1918 and again in the 1990s, many Azerbaijanis resented the big-brotherly and intermittently condescending attitude that Turks adopted toward them in spite of what Azerbaijanis considered their equal or even higher level of culture. Fourth, and typically for Russian policy, Moscow relaxed its pressure and even sought to appease the Azerbaijani elite, allowing more room for Azerbaijani publications, which returned the favor by focusing on social and economic demands. The socialist environment in which the Baku intelligentsia operated contributed to this stance, whereas the Gandja elite, unaffected by socialism, was considerably more nationalistic.[49] As a result of the more liberal political climate, "the Azerbaijanis were sinking deeper into their complacent apathy, from which they were to be awakened suddenly by the outbreak of a new revolution in Russia."[50] Moreover, Muslims were not conscripted into the military, and because of the need to keep pumping oil out of Baku, other nationalities were also relatively less affected by the draft.[51]

The First Republic: Defining the Nation-State

The collapse of the Russian Empire that resulted from the two revolutions of 1917 left the Caucasus practically ungoverned. Officially, a "Transcaucasian Special Committee" (known by its Russian acronym "Ozakom") was formed by the Provisional Government in order to assume government functions in the region. Yet this body was weak and did not constitute a priority for the Petrograd government. Furthermore, its composition revealed a disconnection from the peoples and political forces with real influence in the Caucasus.

The Russian Revolution and Independent Transcaucasia

Into the vacuum stepped several influential organizations. Georgia was dominated by the Menshevik wing of the Russian Social Democratic Workers' Party in Georgia, which asserted its influence over the Tiflis socialist movement in Georgia.[52] In Armenia, the nationalist but also socialist-leaning ARF held sway, and in Azerbaijan the Turkist national forces, gradually represented mainly within the enlarged Müsavat party, increasingly asserted control. But the situation in Azerbaijan was more complicated, due in part to Baku's specific situation. Being a multiethnic city with a significant worker population, Baku was the only place in the Caucasus where the Mensheviks did not completely dominate the socialist movement, and where instead Social Revolutionaries and Bolsheviks were dominant. If in Tiflis the Mensheviks were the most powerful, in Baku the Social Revolutionaries—mainly composed of Russians and, to a lesser degree, Armenians—were the principal component of the Soviet of Workers' Deputies (which had been organized March 7, 1917), with Mensheviks and Bolsheviks playing second and third fiddle. The Baku Soviet was dominated by the Bolshevik leader Stepan Shaumian. The native population was practically excluded, and neither Hümmät nor Müsavat was represented.[53] Hümmät consequently was temporarily marginalized among the socialist forces. On the other hand, this pushed Müsavat away from the leftist bloc and closer to nationalism, and brought it into cooperation with a nationalist movement emerging in Gandja, the Türk Adäm-i-Märkäziyat Firqäsi, or Turk Decentralization Party, a successor to Difai that for all practical purposes ruled the city.[54] A "Muslim Congress of the Caucasus," held in April 1917, helped to consolidate Müsavat and the Turk Decentralization Party as a single bloc; the two parties officially merged the following month.[55] While the party ideology moved closer to that of the more nationalistic Gandja grouping, the short name of the merged unit continued to be Müsavat. In elections to the Baku Soviet in October 1917, the party won a plurality of votes, far more than any of the socialist parties—which was a likely reason why the socialists had the results invalidated.[56] Equally important is that the election showed the primacy of ethnicity over class even in Baku. As one historian put it, all attempts to unite workers of different ethnic origins in Baku toward an understanding of common interests failed.[57]

If power in Russia proper was characterized by *dvoevlastie*, or the twin and parallel powers of the Provisional Government and the soviets, the picture was even messier in Azerbaijan. Aside from the Ozakom and the Baku and Gandja soviets, there was also an Executive Committee of Social Organizations, the Baku Duma, and the National Committees, the latter of which had been created to defend the rights of the Azerbaijani population in Baku and most larger towns in Azerbaijan. Rival centers of power and influence, representing different population segments, hence emerged in the chaotic months after the February revolution. The success of Müsavat in winning the loyalty of both Muslim workers and peasants, as well as that of the intellectual elite, was met with alarm by the socialist forces, since it dealt a strong blow to the validity of the socialist claims of class struggle.[58] The rise of Müsavat set the divergent course that history would take in Baku compared to the rest of Azerbaijan. When the Bolsheviks ignited the October revolution, promulgating the freedom of the subject nations of the Russian Empire and pledging to end Russia's involvement in the Great War, the Caucasus was one of the most affected areas. Paradoxically, Müsavat and the Bolsheviks had common tactical interests, including approval of the Treaty of Brest-Litovsk, which ended Russia's involvement in the First World War, something all other parties opposed. But by early 1918 the Bolsheviks, led by Shaumian, had gradually won control of the Baku Soviet, and were working to transfer all power to it. This development exacerbated relations with Müsavat, which lacked representation in the soviet.

Meanwhile, soldiers crossing the Caucasus on their way home from the front were drawing the interest of every political faction, given that the power vacuum had left the use of force as a major determinant of power. National Committees across Azerbaijan sought, to the extent possible, to disarm Russian soldiers and send them back to Russia.[59] In this atmosphere of insecurity and increasing antagonism, each political faction acquired arms and ethnic tensions spiraled, leading to a breakdown in relations among Müsavat, the ARF, and the Baku Soviet. In March 1918, the fragile peace broke down when the soviet's forces disarmed the Azerbaijani crew of the *Evelina*, a ship hired by an Azerbaijani regiment from Lenkoran to transport officers to a funeral in Baku. This was in all likelihood a provocation to rally all non-Muslim forces around the Baku Soviet, and it ceeded.[60] Müsavat proposed a tactical alliance to the ARF, but the latter declared itself neutral, only to suddenly join the Bolsheviks in battle on the night of March 31.[61] Most socialist forces also aligned with the Bolsheviks against the Müsavat-led Muslim forces that had just returned from the front, and the next day, Muslim residential areas were systematically shelled. Müsavat's forces surrendered the next day, but the fighting then degenerated into a massacre, as the ARF detachments "looted, killed, and burned" in the Azerbaijani parts of the city, leaving several thousand dead and prompting an exodus of Azerbaijanis.[62] As Baberowski observes, "Shaumian, the leader of the Baku Bolsheviks, was Armenian. Even if he was not an Armenian nationalist, he apparently did let his political decisions be guided by resentment against the Muslim population. The decision to use force against the Muslims of the city was clearly not taken in Moscow…. Even Lenin saw himself forced to criticize the anti-Muslim course of the Soviet. Shaumian and his followers wanted to hear nothing of it."[63]

If Baku had been a multiethnic city, its native component was now drastically reduced as natives fled to the countryside and the Bolsheviks reigned supreme. The Baku Commune had been created, and the Azerbaijani state would have to form its first capital in Gandja.

The Creation of the Azerbaijan Popular Republic

In February 1918, the Transcaucasian parliament, the Seim, convened in Tiflis. The largest factions were the Georgian Mensheviks and the Müsavat, closely followed by the ARF. Other factions were marginal, making the parliament a three-way and increasingly ethnic affair, as the interests of the three peoples' representatives gradually grew more divergent.[64] Faced with Turkish advances once the front had collapsed, the South Caucasus was in limbo. This situation was exacerbated by the Brest-Litovsk Treaty, signed by the Bolsheviks in March, which handed the cities of Batumi, Kars, and Ardahan to Turkey without so much as a consultation with Caucasian leaders. Most of the parliament was reluctant to separate from Russia, but there was an overwhelming need to determine Transcaucasia's legal position in negotiations with the advancing Turkish armies. The Bolshevik takeover of Baku, just days before Batumi fell to the Turks, was another factor pressing Transcaucasia to resolve its status.

On April 9, 1918, "without fanfare, in a reluctant and muddled fashion, Transcaucasia became an independent country."[65] The Azerbaijanis were the strongest—in fact, practically the only—adherents of independence, whereas the Georgians and Armenians were either reluctant toward or outright hostile to the idea of separating from Russia. The most direct reason for this divergence was obviously the Turkish advances, welcomed by the Azerbaijanis but dreaded by Georgians and especially Armenians, given the massacres of recent years, in which the Armenians had mostly and tragically been on the losing end. But the divergences in national interests and external orientation were wider. Georgians sought German support: tactically this made sense, given that Germany was the only power able to influence the Ottoman leadership. The Armenians, for their part, pursued two equally bleak prospects: seeking continued protection from Russia, then reaching out to the Allied powers, especially France and Britain, for succor. But Russian forces withdrew, and the Allies would have been unable to come to Armenia's support even if they had so desired. As for the Azerbaijanis, their loyalty to the Transcaucasian state was dubious. As

Kazemzadeh observes, "The Azerbaijanis were closer to the enemy than to the state of which they formed a part."[66] In fact, relations between Armenians and Azerbaijanis had deteriorated significantly following the March massacre in Baku; the Azerbaijanis' eagerness to see Turkish forces in the Caucasus was much related to this. In retrospect, the Transcaucasian republic was as doomed an entity as it was an unnatural one, lasting only six weeks. On May 26, the Seim dissolved itself; that same day, the Georgian National Council declared Georgia independent and obtained promises of support from Germany. With no other option than to follow suit, Armenia and Azerbaijan both declared independence—in Tiflis—two days later. The Azärbaycan Khalq Cumhuriyäti (Azerbaijan People's Republic, a more correct translation than the often used "Azerbaijan Democratic Republic") formed a government at Gandja on June 15 (Baku was still under Bolshevik control). The jurist Fatali Khan Khoisky was elected prime minister.

The Caucasus had now irrevocably fractured along ethnic lines, with little preparation or demographic basis for the creation of nation-states. While not unproblematic, Georgia's borders could be delimited on the basis of reasonably discernable settlement patterns. But Armenians and Azerbaijanis did not live in distinct areas. The largest Armenian concentrations, and the bulk of Armenian cultural life in the Caucasus, were found in Baku and Tiflis, with large Armenian populations in Gandja and other towns and villages across the territory of Azerbaijan. By contrast, a substantial portion of the population of Yerevan region's (that would become Armenia) population was Muslim, consisting of Azerbaijanis and Kurds. This demographic pattern made a division of the South Caucasus along ethnic lines practically impossible without considerable population exchanges, conflict, or ethnic cleansing. Unfortunately, communal relations had deteriorated into mutual fear and suspicion to such an extent that a peaceful division was impossible. Instead, territorial conflict would become a major and inescapable aspect of independence for the three Caucasian nations, weakening them, preventing their recognition by the world community, and facilitating their reabsorption into Russia.

Making the Republic Work

The Azerbaijan People's Republic was the first republic ever created in the Muslim world, predating the Turkish republic by five years. This fact is not only of historical importance: the new state's form of governance created differences between the Azerbaijani elite and the Ottoman armies, still representatives of a sultanate that had not embraced secularism, and whose legitimacy in fact ultimately rested on religion. Moreover, the remarkably progressive spirit and moderation of the Azerbaijani elite did not remain on paper: with reservations for the circumstances of the time, these traits were reflected in the activities and behavior of the political elite during this brief period of independence, which lasted only twenty-three months. The National Charter of the Republic proclaimed the state a democratic, parliamentary republic. Its fourth article stated that the republic "guarantees to all its citizens within its borders full civil and political rights, regardless of ethnic origin, religion, class, profession, or sex."[67]

An Azerbaijani parliament was constituted on the basis of the National Council, the Azerbaijani delegation to the now-dissolved Seim. Once reconvened in Baku in November, it adopted the name "Parliament" and passed a law on elections to a constituent assembly that would have replaced it, which were to be held on the basis of proportional representation with universal suffrage—giving women the right to vote long before many western European countries did. Owing to the chaotic character of the republic's existence, the elections were never held. Nevertheless, the Parliament immediately worked to expand its membership by including new groups and giving representation to minority representatives.[68] Out of a total of 120 seats, 21 were allocated to Armenians. Russians were granted 10, in recognition of their long-standing presence within the territory of the new republic.

The democratic nature of the Azerbaijan People's Republic can be said to have been more beneficial in principle than in actual fact. Its ambition to have all major political groups represented did ensure that most politics took place in Parliament rather than in the streets, but it made decision making difficult as Parliament turned out to be fragmented into numerous factions. Müsavat held two fifths of the occupied seats (some Armenian deputies conducted a boycott) and dominated proceedings. But a right-wing party, Ittihad; the socialists, including Hümmät; the liberal Ahrar faction; and Armenians, including members of the ARF and independents, all held around ten seats each, making coalition governments necessary. Though it endured for less than two years, the state saw five different cabinets. The Azerbaijan People's Republic was a parliamentary republic par excellence, having no presidency: the head of Parliament was the head of state. It also displayed the main shortcoming of the parliamentary form of government: the weakness of the executive, which was exacerbated by interference by a series of foreign powers—first Turkey, then Britain, and finally the Soviet Union. Parliament was a great venue for political activity, with 145 sessions and more than 250 legislative proposals during its brief existence. It sought to initiate many reforms, with education being a pet issue. A comprehensive reform was enacted, making instruction in the Azerbaijani language obligatory in all schools as well as replacing the teaching of Russian history with that of Azerbaijan.[69] A key accomplishment was the establishment of a state university in Baku in 1919, teaching in Azerbaijani.

Yet the domestic and international situations prevented the republic from focusing on internal reform, especially its implementation. Economic troubles were a leading cause, stemming mainly from the termination of trade with Russia due to the war in the North Caucasus, where the counter-revolutionary White forces led by General Anton Denikin were fighting the Bolsheviks.[70] Although, thanks to its oil, Azerbaijan fared somewhat better fiscally than its neighbors, revenue amounted only to two thirds of expenditures in 1919. This gap created inflation and also debt, as Azerbaijan was able to attract credit thanks to the promise of future oil sales.

The Azerbaijan Parliament failed in one important respect: land reform, one of the most important issues for the population. This was largely because of the country's informal power structures, which exercised authority behind the scenes. Kazemzadeh argues that "Azerbaijan was ruled not so much by its parliament as by a combination of forces, including the Müsavat, the fabulously rich owners of the Baku oil fields, and the feudal landowners of western Azerbaijan."[71] Clearly, the newly created Parliament, with no experience in government, weak institutions, few financial resources, and a chaotic domestic environment, was unable to supersede the existing informal power structures. The landlords, naturally, opposed land reform and managed to have consideration of this issue postponed several times in spite of Müsavat's attempts to deal with the issue, providing socialist groups with a rallying cry and generating unrest in the countryside.

The Republic and the Great Powers

The Azerbaijan People's Republic did not live in a void: to the contrary, it existed in a volatile and completely unpredictable external environment. At its founding, Turkish armies were carrying its government to power in Baku while contemplating a new empire in Asia; less than six months later, the Ottoman Empire had capitulated to the Allies, leaving Azerbaijan alone and isolated. To the north, the fate of Russia was uncertain, with Whites and Reds fighting over command of the state, both equally determined to reassert control over the Caucasus and especially over Baku's black gold.

As has already been observed, Azerbaijan's relations with Turkey were complicated—perhaps too close for comfort. The Ottoman peace treaty of 1918 recognized Georgia, but *not* Azerbaijan, as an independent state. This offended the Azerbaijani leaders, who envisioned their country as an independent state closely allied with Turkey, but not as a part of the Ottoman Empire. Enver and Nuri Pasha, the half-brothers who led the Ottoman forces in the Caucasus, thought differently—for them, securing Azerbaijan was the most logical first step in reconstituting a Turanian Empire in the East as a replacement for the collapsing Middle Eastern and European Ottoman Empire. Though with hurt feelings, the Azerbaijani leadership quickly swallowed its pride. When Nuri Pasha interfered in the formation of a government, Prime Minister Khoisky compromised by redrawing his cabinet in a manner more to the Pasha's liking. If Azerbaijan did so for pragmatic reasons, the Ottoman attitude nonetheless broke many illusions of brotherhood. Furthermore, as Swietochowski observes, Ottoman interference served to "reinforce the trend toward Azerbaijanism within the republic's ruling elite: Azerbaijan's relations with Turkey would henceforth be tainted with resentment and distrust, while Pan-Turkism would be reduced to a purely cultural doctrine."[72]

But without Ottoman support, there was no chance of taking back Baku. In preparation for the march toward Azerbaijan's designated capital, the remnants of the "Savage Division," the Muslim volunteer army that had taken part in the First World War, merged with Azerbaijani general Ali Agha Shihlinski's Muslim National Corps and the Ottoman Fifth Infantry Division, creating the so-called Army of Islam. Its very name indicates the Ottomans' domination of the force, and thereby of the newly created republic.

As Turkish and Azerbaijani forces built strength in Gandja in June 1918, Shaumian, the head of the Baku Commune, led attacks on the forces of the republic, apparently in the delusional assumption that the peasants of Azerbaijan would rise up for socialism against their new "bourgeois" leaders.[73] Of course, nothing of the sort happened. While Shaumian's armies advanced at first, the four-day Battle of Gökçay ended their progress, and opened the road to the fall of the Baku Commune. The twenty-six commissars escaped by ship to present-day Turkmenistan, where they would meet their death, executed in the desert by the local government, which was led by the Social Revolutionaries. In their place, the Social Revolutionaries created the Central Caspian Dictatorship in August 1918 with the support of the British army, which was eyeing the Caucasus from its base at the Iranian Caspian port of Enzeli. From there, General Lionel C. Dunsterville landed in Baku in mid-August 1918 to complicate further the bewildering array of forces in the Caucasus. Dunsterville described himself as "a British general on the Caspian, the only sea unploughed before by British keels, on board a ship named after a South African Dutch president and whilom enemy, sailing from a Persian port, under the Serbian flag, to relieve from the Turks a body of Armenians in a revolutionary Russian town."[74] Dunsterville nevertheless left Baku after a month, considering the battle for the city lost. The Russian and Armenian defenders succumbed to the Army of Islam, which exacted vengeance for the massacres of March of that year, killing several thousand Armenians.

The collapse of Turkey's western front and the Armistice of Mudros, signed October 30, 1918, which ended hostilities between the Ottoman Empire and the Allies, forced Turkish forces to withdraw from Azerbaijan, leaving it exposed and without a protector. As the Turks left, a new British force entered the Caucasus, led by General William Thomson. The Azerbaijani government had accepted the British presence on condition that White Russian units would not be allowed in the city.[75] The British force was accepted reluctantly, as it reduced the sovereignty of the Azerbaijani government; but on the whole, it must be regarded as a benign factor. It stayed in Baku, and Thomson granted Azerbaijan jurisdiction over Karabakh. Thomson's presence also helped support order in Baku. Though wary at first, Thomson warmed to the democratic credentials of the Azerbaijan People's Republic, and came to recognize it as the legitimate government of Azerbaijan. The British forces left in August 1919, leaving the republic completely sovereign for the nine months that remained before the Soviet invasion. As an aside, Azerbaijan nearly experienced control by yet another foreign power in the meantime, as Italy was awarded a mandate over the country in the Treaty of Versailles. Only a change of government in Rome prevented Italian troops from landing in the Caucasus.[76]

To the south, Iran's government saw Azerbaijan as an Ottoman creation and feared its aims in regard to southern Azerbaijan. Indeed, fears of offending Iran prompted Baku to refer to the nascent republic as "Caucasian Azerbaijan." Generally, Azerbaijan had no easy task in dealing with its neighbors. It was in a constant state of conflict with Armenia, as both claimed the areas of Zangezur and Nakhichevan. In the face of the common Russian threat, Azerbaijan managed to conclude an alliance with Georgia, though the affiliation of the Zaqatala district, in Azerbaijan's northwestern corner, was a bone of contention.

Like its neighbors, Azerbaijan desperately sought Allied support and recognition at the Paris Peace Conference, sending some of its most senior statesmen to the negotiations. But the constant bickering of the Armenian, Azerbaijani, and Georgian delegations, and their inability to present a united front, terminated any remaining hope that the war-weary European powers would take on responsibility for a faraway region still understood as a part of Russia. Only when the White forces led by General Denikin were irreversibly routed by the Bolsheviks in early 1920 did the Allies extend de facto recognition to Azerbaijan, in a vain last hope of averting a Bolshevik takeover of the Caucasus.

The Fall of the First Republic

On February 2, 1920, Soviet commissar for foreign affairs Grigory Chicherin sent a note to Prime Minister Khoisky, which Swietochowski aptly terms "the opening salvo in a war of nerves."[77] Commissar Chicherin demanded that Baku concede to a military agreement to accelerate the defeat of the White armies. Khoisky refused. Learning of this development at the Paris Peace Conference, the Allies now belatedly understood that the Azerbaijan People's Republic was the chief factor preventing a Soviet invasion of the entire South Caucasus. The Allied Supreme Council hence recognized Azerbaijan, and a decision was made to send military aid to the South Caucasus. Of course, it was too late. Chicherin took matters one step further two weeks later, denouncing Azerbaijan's intransigence and repeating his demands. Khoisky failed to budge, demanding that Soviet recognition of Azerbaijan precede any agreement. But by this time, Khoisky no longer had the full backing of the diverse Azerbaijani governing elite. While the right-wing Müsavat was behind him, a number of other groups and individuals—perhaps realizing that no one would come to Azerbaijan's rescue—advocated appeasing Soviet Russia in order to secure the republic's survival. Chief among these was Memmed Hasan Hajinski, at that time interior minister. Hajinski was replaced and moved to a less central cabinet position, but continued to advocate close relations with Russia, basing his position in part on an economic rationale—that is, by supplying oil to the Soviets, Azerbaijan could buy its own survival. By March, Räsulzadä and his Müsavat followers had been swayed by this line of reasoning. As Swietochowski puts it, "The Azerbaijani ruling elite realistically and prudently began preparing for the inevitable."[78]

On March 23, an Armenian uprising broke out in Karabakh, prompting almost the entire Azerbaijani military to rush to the region. A harbinger of things to come seven decades later, the uprising also prevented the Azerbaijani military from putting up a serious fight against the Bolsheviks a month later. In retrospect, given the Bolshevik tendency to punish peoples that resisted their invasion, Karabakh's uprising may paradoxically have prevented the useless spilling of blood for a hopeless cause. At the very same time, the 70,000-strong Bolshevik Eleventh Army was occupying the North Caucasus, including Dagestan, positioning itself for the next target: Baku. There is little doubt the Bolsheviks saw taking Baku as a high priority, not least because of the city's oil resources. Lenin himself at this time emphasized the point to Georgian Bolshevik leader Sergo Orzhonikdze, noting that it was "extremely important to take Baku."[79] To facilitate this endeavor, the Kavburo, or Caucasian bureau of the Bolshevik Party, was created. While underscoring the importance Moscow accorded to capturing the South Caucasus, the existence of the Kavburo also illustrates the weakness of local Bolshevik groups and their lack of popular following in the South Caucasus at the time—even in industrial Baku, the city potentially most likely to harbor Bolshevik sympathizers.

With Soviet troops massing on the border, the government collapsed, with many of its leading figures escaping to Tiflis and on to Turkey and the West. On April 27, the first armored trains crossed into Azerbaijan, in a variation from Moscow's standard routine of waiting for a local Bolshevik coup and responding to the Bolsheviks' request for succor. The newly created Azerbaijani Communist Party issued a declaration that the equally new Azrevkom, the Provisional Azerbaijan Revolutionary Committee, was the land's only legitimate authority. The next day, an Azerbaijani Sovnarkom, or Soviet People's Commissariate, was created, consisting mainly of former Hümmät members and led by Nariman Narimanov.[80]

Since there were few Soviets around Azerbaijan, the sovietization of the country had to be undertaken from above: through the instigation of revolutionary committees, often composed of one official sent to a given region who in turn recruited members.

The Red Army moved on toward its next target, Georgia. The Bolsheviks thought they could subdue that country as easily as they had conquered Baku, but resistance to their progress through rural Azerbaijan was so strong that they had to postpone their plans for Georgia for almost a year. Indeed, resistance in the countryside continued for years and proved ferocious in many places. In particular, the military campaign to regain territory lost to Poland in the Great War forced the Bolsheviks to make a priority of securing their advances rather than pressing onward in the Caucasus. Though Baku had fallen relatively easily, this did not signal the easy sovietization of Azerbaijan.

The first uprising occurred with the mutiny of the Gandja garrison, which seized the Muslim area of the city on May 28, the second anniversary of Azerbaijan's independence. Only after heavy fighting and great losses were the Bolsheviks able to take the city back. Smaller revolts followed in Shusha, Lenkoran, Quba, and Zaqatala. But as Swietochowski noted, the resistance occurred mainly spontaneously, conducted by isolated groups with little organization—and was therefore doomed to failure.[81] Though the unrest continued until 1924, Azerbaijan was now thoroughly in Soviet hands.

The Azerbaijani People's Republic may have lasted only twenty-three months, but it left a crucial mark on Azerbaijani and Caucasian history. As the first republic built on democratic principles in the Muslim world, predating the Turkish republic by five years and providing an important stimulus for it, it proved early on the inherent compatibility of Islamic culture and democratic values. It did so not only in its declarative acts—such as extending suffrage to women long before many Western countries did—but through its civilized form of government, with political matters being decided by means of successive coalitions in Parliament rather than by violence. Moreover, the First Republic set an undeniable precedent that the newly independent Azerbaijan of the 1990s would look back to for legitimacy and inspiration. In this it would enjoy an advantage that the former Soviet republics of Central Asian states would not. The fact that Azerbaijan had been—for its time—a democratic republic would strengthen the hand of progressive forces in the 1990s, and proved an effective antidote to retreat into full-blown authoritarianism.

2

Soviet Azerbaijan

After the fall of the First Republic, Azerbaijan was technically an independent Soviet state. In this guise, it was used by the Soviet powers to spread the revolution to Muslim lands beyond the borders of what had been czarist Russia, and to improve relations with the newly established Republic of Turkey, led by the staunchly reformist secularist Kemal Atatürk. There was even an Azerbaijani diplomatic representation in Ankara. Moreover, in September 1920 Baku hosted a "Congress of the Peoples of the East," which brought together communists and representatives of Asian national liberation movements with a view—from the Bolsheviks' perspective, anyway[1]—of undermining imperialism worldwide. But these gestures toward autonomy constituted only a brief experiment; by the end of the 1920s Azerbaijan would be gradually integrated into the Soviet Union, its independence gone. Sovietization would thoroughly change Azerbaijan's society, economy, and mentality, and create a rift between northern and southern (Iranian) Azerbaijan that continues to this day.

The Sovietization of Azerbaijan

In September 1920, Azerbaijani Communist authorities ceded most important functions of statehood, including defense and finance, to the Russian Soviet Federated Socialist Republic, confirming de jure what was already the de facto reality: Azerbaijan was now ruled from Moscow. In the initial years of Soviet rule, two key issues stood out: the territorial delimitations of the South Caucasus and the role of the titular nationality in the governing of the republic. A key role in these issues was played by Azerbaijan's Communist leader, Nariman Narimanov. Born in 1870 in Tiflis (now Tbilisi), Narimanov became part of the emerging Azerbaijani cultural intelligentsia. He began his professional life as a schoolteacher in the 1890s, but he also wrote plays, including the first Azerbaijani historical drama, *Nadir Shah*, which he completed in 1894.[2] His political career began with the Hümmät movement, discussed in the previous chapter, and intensified when he traveled to Odessa to study medicine. He joined the Russian Social Democratic Workers' Party in 1905, when he was 35. One of his strongest political motivations appears to have been opposition to Russification of the subject nations of the czarist empire. He was jailed in Tiflis in 1908, then exiled to Astrakhan, in Russia, the next year. Returning to Baku in 1917, he became one of the leading intellectuals of the national movement that emerged there, in close interaction with the would-be leaders of the First Republic. He nevertheless chose the Bolsheviks' line in their dispute with the more gradualist Mensheviks and like the other Hümmätists initially backed the Baku Commune. Narimanov was the only Azerbaijani Turk in the Baku Soviet of 1917–18; as a leader with both socialist and national credentials, he was a wise choice as leader of the Provisional Azerbaijan Revolutionary Committee (Azrevkom) in 1920.

Soviet Nationality Policy and Korenizatsiia

The Bolshevik policy on nationalities, closely following the ideas of Lenin and Stalin, was composed of two rather contradictory principles. One main determinant was the conviction that socialism would make nationalism obsolete. The end of class struggle would remove the support base of nationalism in society. In a socialist society, nations would first grow closer (*sblizhenie*) in order to eventually merge (*slianiie*). Given that this was understood as a historically inescapable fact, the ruling socialists saw no danger in speeding up this process by granting all national groups full rights to develop their own culture and language, even to the extent of acknowledging a right of secession. The more concessions made to national demands, it was thought, the sooner nationalism itself would vanish.[3] Hence, a policy was implemented that actively and aggressively "nativized" the minority areas, bringing locals to positions of power and creating actual intellectual elites. This policy was especially appropriate for the Muslim subject nations, since emphasizing national identity was instrumental in weakening religious identity, the main Bolshevik nemesis.[4]

In spite of the successful military reconquest of areas that did exercise the right to secession, such as the South Caucasus, the Soviet state was being built in marked conformity with Lenin's ideas. Indeed, the Soviet Union developed an ethnically based territorial structure paralleled by that of no other state in history, amounting to what Terry Martin calls an "affirmative action empire." The Soviet state evolved, in effect, into a hierarchically organized ethnic federation. As Martin puts it, "New national elites were trained and promoted to leadership positions in the government, schools, and industrial enterprises of these newly formed territories. In each territory, the national language was declared the official language of government. In dozens of cases, this necessitated the creation of a written language where one did not yet exist."[5]

Immediately after having won the civil war and begun to consolidate its rule in the early 1920s, the Bolshevik government launched the policy of *korenizatsiia* (nativization). The doctrine of self-determination evolved into a concept of nation building, which in practice implied central support for the consolidation of the various ethnic groups in the Soviet Union. As Gerhard Simon writes, it became official party policy to help the non-Russian peoples "catch up with the better-developed Central Russia ... develop a local-language press, schools, theaters, clubs, and cultural and educational facilities altogether; to establish and further a network of courses and schools for ... education in local languages."[6]

Lenin managed to force through his position that the Soviet Union be composed of equal republics, of which Russia would be one—though Stalin argued against this. The Soviet Union was from the beginning created as a hierarchical federation of ethnically defined territories. Though the number of such territories varied until the annexation of new lands in the Second World War, eventually there were more than fifty of them, each with a functional governmental structure. Significantly, of the more than 100 ethnic groups identified in the Union of Soviet Socialist Republics (USSR), 53 at some point were the titular nation of an ethnically determined administrative unit.[7]

The primary units in this elaborate federal system were the soviet socialist republics (SSR), eventually fifteen in number, which were constructed in the manner of independent states that were joined in a federation to form the USSR. Second in the hierarchy were the autonomous soviet socialist republics (ASSR), of which there were more than fifteen, including Nakhichevan; third, and fewer in number, were the autonomous provinces, or oblasts (including Mountainous Karabakh), and finally a few autonomous areas, or *Okrugi*. These autonomous formations were subject to the jurisdiction of one of the SSRs, not directly to that of the central authorities. Officially, SSR and ASSR status was to be given to ethnic groups with a developed sense of national consciousness, whereas less "advanced" ethnic groups were to be assigned the lower level of self-rule of an autonomous region, which did not have its own constitution and was not intended to have political and economic self-determination at the level enjoyed by an ASSR. At all levels of the autonomous hierarchy, the local languages and cultures were aggressively promoted throughout the 1920s.

In numerous cases, the Soviet authorities created alphabets and written languages for peoples that had not used their language in writing. Written languages were developed for forty-eight ethnic groups, which until then had had no literature in their own spoken language. This meant the introduction of native languages in public life, replacing Russian. This policy was not merely cosmetic; indeed, it formed a most remarkable example of social engineering that benefited the separate identities of the minority groups within the Soviet Union. As Simon notes, "Support for and development of non-Russian languages was one of the most visible signs of the policy of nation-building."[8]

At the creation of the Soviet Union in 1922, the Communist Party was dominated by Russians and a few other ethnic groups. Russians constituted 72 percent of party members (compared to roughly half of the population as a whole), while Jews were heavily overrepresented relative to their share of the population. Poles, Armenians, and Georgians were also well represented. On the other hand, Ukrainians, Belorussians, and especially Muslim peoples were practically absent from the party. In the higher echelons of the party, this structure was even more pronounced. Throughout the 1920s and early 1930s, however, a dramatic shift in the party and state structures developed. In the ten years from 1922 to 1932, the percentage of Ukrainians in the Ukrainian party structures went from 24 percent to 59 percent, while native representation in Uzbekistan and Kyrgyzstan went from practically zero to 57 percent. In Armenia, the percentage of Armenians was already high, at almost 90 percent, and stayed there, while in Georgia it increased slightly, from 62 percent to 66 percent. These were the only titular nations that were consistently well-represented in the party structures compared to their proportion of the population.[9] As for Azerbaijan, it had a much higher rate of native participation than any other Muslim republic, though it lagged behind Armenia and Georgia.

Perhaps because of his origins in the Caucasus and his experience in that region, Stalin seemed considerably less convinced than Lenin of the transient nature of nationalism. This perception grew stronger with time, and Stalin in his mind ever more departed from the conviction that class consciousness would necessarily and automatically surpass national consciousness. As Simon notes, Stalin "did not share Lenin's optimism that the revolution had in principle ended nationalism and separatism or that the best way to neutralize these movements would be to make national concessions."[10] Stalin agreed with Lenin that in the time of civil war, national concessions were necessary from a purely pragmatic perspective. While realizing the objective need to grant autonomy to the minorities and espouse the theoretical concept of self-determination, Stalin early on favored the equal bestowal of autonomous rights on all minorities within the Russian state, rather than the gradual, hierarchically differentiated federal status granted to different non-Russian groups.

Stalin also saw the very concept of nationhood in a more realistic and less ideologically determined way than most Bolsheviks, including Lenin. He "considered relations between nations to be similar to relations between classes, that is, to be determined by force rather than by education or understanding."[11] By the late 1920s, Stalin's rhetoric had changed with the introduction of the term "socialist nations." He argued that the nation building of the USSR had helped the oppressed nations to blossom, which was a necessary stage in the historical process that would eventually lead to the merger of nations (*slianiie*).

Practically speaking, during the 1930s and later Stalin strengthened the centralized character of Soviet rule. It should be recalled that the Soviet Union's federative structure was not mirrored in the organization of the Communist Party. The party had always been a highly centralized institution directed from the center in Moscow. This lever was constantly available to regulate the level of actual self-rule by the indigenous elites in the ethnic units of the Union. As Audrey Altstadt has noted, the party-state divide was paralleled in Azerbaijan by an ethnic divide: the state apparatus of the Azerbaijani Republic very soon came to be filled by Azerbaijani Turks, whereas the Communist Party was dominated by non-natives for many years, reflecting the nonindigenous nature of the communist ideology.[12]

In 1934, Stalin began dismantling institutions that promoted nativization or the rights of minorities in various cities, autonomous republics, and regions, such as the Presidium of the Council of Nationalities. Especially in the economic realm, the centralization of the state was accelerated, a process that began with the onslaught of collectivization in 1929, when the administration of agriculture was centralized in Moscow. Economic and political power was concentrated at the SSR level, and increasingly at the level of the Union authorities, who gained the ability to overrule republic-level decisions in most matters of importance. Hence, by the mid-1930s the autonomy extended to the ethnic republics was gradually being reduced. Stalin, however, was careful not to touch the symbolic status of the ethnic republics: centralization did not mean the abolition of autonomous units. This corresponded well with Stalin's dictum "National in form, socialist in content." Similarly, at the center, the Council of Nationalities was expanded in size and standing; however, its presidium, which had been intro-

duced against Stalin's wishes in 1923, disappeared upon the promulgation
of the constitution of 1936, which clearly indicated the move toward centralization.

Issues of Territorial Delimitation

Following the sovietization of Armenia at the end of 1920 and of Georgia
in early 1921, the Bolshevik leadership rejuvenated—mainly on economic
grounds—the 1918 idea of a South Caucasian federation. This jurisdiction
took the form of the Transcaucasian Soviet Federated Socialist Republic
(Transcaucasian Federation), which would be a constituent member of the
Soviet Union, still in formation at that point. The federalization of the
South Caucasus was vigorously resisted by Narimanov and other Azerbaijani Communists, but to no avail. Narimanov was nevertheless lucky
enough to be promoted away from Baku to Moscow, as one of the four
mainly ceremonial chairmen of the Central Executive Committee of the
USSR. He died a natural death in 1925. Azerbaijan was amalgamated into
the Transcaucasian Federation, which controlled most aspects of administration, including budgeting, commerce, the distribution and use of land
and natural resources, and judicial as well as educational issues. There was
little left for Baku to decide: in many ways, with the seat of the federation
in Tiflis, the situation was reminiscent not only of the Transcaucasian Federation of 1918 but of the czarist viceroyalty of the Caucasus. As Altstadt
writes, "Azerbaijan found itself back in the 'prison house of peoples,' with
new and zealous jailers."[13]

Territorial delimitation nevertheless remained an issue, and a central
one. At stake was the status of Nakhichevan, Mountainous Karabakh, and
Zangezur. Armenia and Azerbaijan both claimed these areas, which had all
been part of the First Republic. The deliberations, mainly managed by
Moscow, with the personal involvement of Stalin, were not completed until
March 1924. By that time, Zangezur had been granted outright to the Armenian Republic. Zanzegur had no form of territorial autonomy. On the
other hand, both Nakhichevan and Karabakh were made special territories.
Even though Nakhichevan was separated from the rest of Azerbaijan by
Zangezur, it was made an autonomous republic within Azerbaijan; whereas
the mountainous, largely Armenian-populated parts of Karabakh were
given the lower status of an autonomous province—but also within Azerbaijan, though with an ethnic Armenian majority, and an Armenian party
elite administering the area. This decision was to take on momentous importance in the latter part of the Soviet period, as Armenian nationalists

considered the granting of Karabakh to Azerbaijan to be a historic injustice. They felt similarly about the disposition of Nakhichevan, even though it had an Azerbaijani majority. Azerbaijani scholars, for their part, lamented the loss of Zangezur and of the Derbent area of Southern Dagestan, which they considered historically Azerbaijani. They also questioned the reason for providing autonomy to Karabakh, given its small population and the fact that its residents were a national minority that already had a homeland, Armenia. Indeed, the territorial delimitation deviated from Leninist principles, which normally granted territorial autonomy only to peoples without a homeland. Karabakh and Nakhichevan were in fact the only two autonomous units of the Soviet Union that were named after a geographic area and not a people. Karabakh was also the only autonomous region in the USSR whose titular nationality also was the titular nation of a union republic. As a jurisdiction Nakhichevan was even more bizarre, an Azerbaijani autonomous unit within the Azerbaijani Republic. Its autonomy was hence solely motivated by its geographic exclave status; then again, Kaliningrad was an exclave of Russia and had only the status of a regular Russian province.

In 1936, the newly promulgated Soviet constitution spelled the end of the Transcaucasian Federation. Each republic now constituted a nominally independent soviet socialist republic in voluntary union with its counterparts in the USSR. This new arrangement removed the federation level between Moscow and Baku, and confirmed Azerbaijan's nominal right to secession.

The Great Terror: Lives—and Collective Memory—Lost

In the first years of sovietization, Azerbaijan in several respects had fared well. The country's borders were largely resolved, with Nakhichevan, Karabakh, and Zaqatala confirmed as parts of Azerbaijan. Most of its leaders from the independence era were allowed to live, and some, like Mämmädemin Räsulzadä, were even taken into the Soviet administration. *Korenizatsiia* allowed for the emergence of a new, Azerbaijani class of professionals in the administration—something unthinkable in czarist times. But after these initial advances, the situation quickly deteriorated up to the time of the Second World War. As elsewhere in the Soviet Union, Stalin's repression intensified, threatening the very foundation of the nation's intellectual life.

As Altstadt has noted, the "Great Terror" in Azerbaijan consisted of three main phases.[14] The first, in the early 1920s, was the crushing of initial opposition to Soviet rule and of specific class enemies such as religious leaders and kulaks. The second, in the late 1920s and early 1930s, targeted the "national communists" across the Union, specifically Müsavat members in the case of Azerbaijan. The third and most serious, in the late 1930s, targeted a broader group, including Azerbaijan's old Bolshevik leaders and the republic's entire cultural elite and their works. The purges were directed by "Azerbaijan's Stalin," Mir Jafar Baghirov, commissar for internal affairs until 1933 and subsequently first secretary of the Communist Party of Azerbaijan until Stalin's death in 1953.

Repression from the early days of Soviet rule onward focused primarily on Müsavat supporters. This campaign reached its heyday during 1927–28, as Soviet propaganda sought to vehemently counter the émigré publications coming out of Turkey and Western Europe, and rounded up for exile or death people associated with Müsavat in the pre-Soviet era. Religious leaders experienced their share of the repression as well. In the early 1920s, Soviet leaders had mainly built on the native secularism that had been the trademark of the First Republic. In 1927, however, the *hujjum* (an attack on religion in the Muslim areas of the USSR) was launched, focusing on the emancipation of women and the forced removal of the veil. The *hujjum* was soon followed by the mass closure of mosques and harassment of ams.[15] The collectivization of agriculture during 1929–30, which included the formation of hundreds of kolkhozy (collective farms), brought with it an onslaught on the kulaks (landowning peasants). Stunningly, the "dekulakization" proceeded on an assumption of how many kulaks would on average exist in a locality, followed by a demand that village soviets produce that number of kulaks for deportation and exile. But inaccurate population data made these assumptions faulty and led to the deportation to Siberia of many peasants of poor or modest means who simply opposed collectivization.[16]

Coinciding with the abolition of the Transcaucasian Soviet Federated Republic, the period from 1936 to 1938 was particularly horrific for the old Communists of Azerbaijan, in fact those who had established Soviet power in the republic. Lumped together as "Trotskyite-Zinovievite riffraff," pan-Islamists, pan-Turkists, Müsavatists, German spies, or generally as anticommunists, many of the members of the old elite were eliminated. In spite of his closeness to Stalin, Narimanov (who had died in 1925) was now vilified as a nationalist, and his time generally and pejoratively referred to by the derogatory term of "Narimanovshchina." Baghirov himself survived, in all likelihood because of his close personal relationship with Lavrentii Beria, the head of the Soviet secret police who maintained an iron grip on his native Caucasus.

The Great Terror coincided with a new phase in the Soviet Union's development. The national differentiation of the various nations, especially Muslim ones, had progressed to the level where Moscow could dispense with "horizontal" relations among the different republican capitals, and replace them with direct, vertical relations between Moscow and each republic, what Tadeusz Swietochowski calls "the crowning act in the Stalinist policy of promoting local particularisms by splitting cultural, linguistic, or regional entities."[17]

Doing away with relations among the republics, Moscow sought also to isolate each national group within the Soviet Union, and hence to prevent contacts with the outside world—in the case of Azerbaijan, specifically Iran and Turkey. This not only meant severing Azerbaijan from its kin but also from its own history. A threefold strategy was developed to accomplish this objective. First, the people itself was renamed: whereas the Turkic inhabitants of Azerbaijan had been registered as "Turks" in the 1926 census, in 1936 they became "Azerbaijanis," with any reference to their Turkic origin removed. Second, the alphabet was once again changed: having exchanged the Arabic alphabet for the Latin one in 1926, they now had to abandon the Latin for the Cyrillic. In one stroke, this policy made most of the population illiterate, as they had barely had the time and exposure to get used to Latin, and it cut off Azerbaijan from cultural links to Kemalist Turkey, which had adopted the Latin alphabet shortly after (and with inspiration from) Azerbaijan. Finally, an onslaught on the literary and cultural intelligentsia of the country was launched, which in fact amounted to an attempt to eradicate the collective memory of the Azerbaijani people. Of 70,000 people reported killed in the purges that followed, a full 29,000 were listed as part of the intelligentsia.[18] The estimates of the total number of people killed during 1937–38 alone are higher, at around 120,000. But as Altstadt observed writing in 1992, "The more enduring impact was blackening the memories of national and cultural leaders, distorting their words and misrepresenting their intentions, confiscating published writings, and manipulating the content of literature and school curricula. These policies reached beyond the lives of the destroyed individuals to affect later generations in ways that the present generation is only beginning to grasp."[19]

Azerbaijan During and After World War II

The German attack on the Soviet Union had the Caucasus and specifically Baku's oil as one of its chief military objectives. The Nazi onslaught extended no further than the northern tip of Ingushetia, however. Because German forces never crossed the main Caucasian ridge, Azerbaijan was spared the material destruction of war. But given the high number of Azerbaijanis drafted into the Soviet military, Azerbaijan's people did not go unaffected. This is indicated by pre- and postwar population figures. In 1940, the year before Germany attacked the Soviet Union, Azerbaijan had an official population of 3.2 million (a figure that, according to Altstadt, was almost certainly inflated, given the collectivization, famines, exile, and purges of the preceding decades[20]). In 1946, the year after the war ended, Azerbaijan's population was officially listed as being 2.7 million, a loss of about half a million, though the real decrease was likely smaller given the high probability that the prewar population had been overstated. Though statistics are unreliable, Azerbaijan evidently sent more than half a million soldiers to the war. Most never made it back.[21] This staggering figure illustrates the treatment of the non-Russian peoples in the Soviet army. Central Asian and Caucasian peoples constituted three times as large a proportion of the military as they did of the general population; in battles such as Stalingrad, where Soviet soldiers perished as cannon fodder by the thousands, Central Asians and Caucasians may have made up half of the fighting force.[22] On the other hand, Azerbaijanis also figured among the "Eastern Legions" created among the Soviet prisoners of war by the Germans. Some joined voluntarily, others less willingly—given the low chances of survival in German prisoner-of-war camps, joining the Eastern Legions must have seemed, more than anything, a potential ticket to survival to many such enlistees. Swietochowski has estimated the number at 25,000 to 35,000.[23] Meanwhile, Germany was courting the Müsavatist exile community in Europe. Räsulzadä was invited to Berlin, but chose to leave the city rather than cut a deal with Nazi Germany.

A short-lived corollary to the war was the need for Moscow to secure internal peace for the duration of the fighting. While anecdotal evidence indicates that Stalin contemplated deporting the population of Azerbaijan, much as he deported Chechens, Ingush, and other peoples considered unreliable, this has not been proven. What is clear, however, is that the Russification policies briefly gave way to patriotic propaganda emphasizing the defense of the homeland and digging into Azerbaijani cultural history. While this practice was reversed immediately after the war, peace also provided renewed links with southern Azerbaijan: the Soviet occupation of northern Iran and the brief Soviet support for the creation of an Azerbaijani state there brought many northern Azerbaijanis in contact with the Soviet-occupied areas in Iran. The fall in 1946 of a nascent south Azerbaijani republic, led by Jafar Pishevari, ended such relations, and brought numerous refugees to Soviet Azerbaijan from the south.[24]

In the decade that followed, which coincided with Mir Jafar Baghirov's last years in power, Russification and the accompanying onslaught on Azerbaijani cultural identity accelerated. Historical resistance to Russian occupation was denounced, and Turkic epics such as *The Book of Dede Korkut* were banned. Baghirov himself began praising Russia and the Russian language with increasing fervor. This only came to an end with Stalin's death in 1953, which was followed by Lavrentii Beria's short-lived attempt to use the nationality question to enable his succession to Stalin.[25] Beria himself was killed shortly thereafter, but the resurgence of the non-Russian peoples and a reversal of Russification and centralization followed. Indeed, by 1954, Nikita Khrushchev, by then first secretary of the Communist Party, had increased the economic power of the union republics and permitted a restoration of the position of the indigenous languages. Baghirov was removed from his position as first secretary of the party in Azerbaijan in July 1953, four months after Stalin's death, and "Azerbaijan's Stalin" was sentenced to be executed three years later.

Baghirov's successors, plant geneticist Imam Mustafayev and medical doctor Vali Akhundov, were considerably less dominant leaders. Under their rule, the Communist Party was characterized more by group leadership and consensus politics than by the strongman methods Baghirov had used before them and Heydar Aliyev would later. Mustafayev nevertheless led the rehabilitation of Narimanov, who would even be honored as a founding father of Soviet Azerbaijan. He also diligently advocated official status for the Azerbaijani language, promoted the economic autonomy of the republic, and encouraged the migration of Azeris to Baku, starting, in earnest, the process that would gradually transform the city from a multiethnic city to an Azerbaijani one. Under Akhundov, Azerbaijanis became a majority in the Azerbaijani Communist Party for the first time.[26]

In the early 1960s, toward the end of the Khrushchev era, the thaw nevertheless was again reversed, in one of the many changes of direction in Soviet nationality policy, and the antireligious campaign was reinvigorated. But the 1960s brought another development of great economic significance for Azerbaijan: the discovery of immense oil fields in western Siberia and the gradual loss of Soviet interest in Azerbaijan's oil. Investment and assistance from the center consequently dwindled, and Azerbaijan dropped to last place among Soviet republics in terms of industrial growth.[27] The emphasis on oil and cotton in the Azerbaijani economy meant a structural imbalance that fixed Azerbaijan as a producer of raw materials, providing more to the Soviet economy than it got in return.[28]

The Aliyev Era

In July 1969, Heydar Aliyev acceded to the post of first secretary of the Azerbaijani Communist Party, marking the beginning of one man's remarkable domination of the republic's political scene, which would last for more than three decades. Aliyev was born to a family of modest origins in Nakhichevan in 1923 or possibly earlier, and graduated from the Nakhichevan Pedagogical Institute in 1939. He then made a career in the Azerbaijani security services, beginning with the People's Commissariat of Internal Affairs, and joined the Communist Party in 1945. He returned to Baku in 1950, working in the Ministry of State Security. In 1957, while working with apparent success in the Committee for State Security (KGB) of Azerbaijan, he acquired a degree in history from Baku State University, writing a thesis on the Turkic nationalist Committee for Union and Progress movement of the early twentieth century.[29]

Aliyev rose rapidly through the ranks, becoming deputy head of the Azerbaijani KGB in 1964. His more specific activities in the security services are the subject of much speculation. Many sources point to his work in the Azerbaijani KGB's Eastern Division, whose jurisdiction included Iran (where Aliyev may have worked during the short-lived Azerbaijani republic there) and the Middle East. Aliyev became a close associate of and deputy to Semyon Tsvigun, Leonid Brezhnev's brother-in-law, who headed the Azerbaijani KGB until 1967. When Tsvigun was promoted to head of the Soviet KGB, Aliyev replaced him. Only two years later, he was appointed head of the Communist Party of Azerbaijan. Aliyev's rise did not end there: in 1976, he became a candidate member of the Politburo, the highest decision-making authority in the Soviet Union, but retained his position in Azerbaijan. When Yuri Andropov succeeded Brezhnev as Soviet leader in 1982, Aliyev became a full member of the Politburo and a deputy prime minister of the Soviet Union—the third-highest position in the empire. At the time, Western media speculated that Aliyev was given this position as a result of the Soviet Union's growing interest in the Muslim world. However, most evidence indicates that his elevation had little to do with foreign policy and more to do with Soviet elite politics. Aliyev himself told Thomas Goltz in no uncertain terms that "Andropov was insistent [that I go to Moscow] because he wanted to have his own people [in Moscow] and I was one of his people."[30] A close Andropov associate, Aliyev retained his high-ranking positions until 1987, when Mikhail Gorbachev, as part of his efforts under perestroika to recentralize power and rein in the national republics, removed Aliyev from power.

Aliyev's governance style and relationship with Brezhnev were indicative of a larger trend in the Soviet Union. With Brezhnev, the fundamental dynamic of center-periphery relations changed, as a more or less explicit compact was established. Republican leaders such as Aliyev and Eduard Shevardnadze, and Central Asian leaders such as Sharaf Rashidov and Dinmuhammed Kunaev, provided absolute loyalty, kept internal order, and delivered economic goods to the Union. In return, they were more or less free to run their affairs as they saw fit: as Georgi Derluguian has put it, "the Soviet state simply failed to penetrate there."[31] This arrangement led, for most of the 1970s and into the 1980s, to the most stable and arguably most locally grounded period of leadership in the Soviet era, though the new balance that was allowed to form inevitably resulted in a consolidation of patronage structures that produced groups of haves and have-nots.

One of the main reasons Aliyev came to power was his reputation (like that of Eduard Shevardnadze in Georgia) as a man of action, who could root out the widespread corruption and nepotism that had contributed to the stagnation of Azerbaijan in prior decades. Almost immediately, Aliyev cleaned up the state structures and put the republican machinery to work, staffing government offices with new people. The new hires were portionately individuals with backgrounds in the security services or in Aliyev's native Nakhichevan. Economically, Aliyev focused on agriculture, and specifically on two major crops: cotton and grapes. Cotton production doubled in the 1970s from the previous decade, and grape cultivation increased several times faster than that, making Azerbaijan the largest producer in the USSR. Between 1976 and 1980, Azerbaijan had the highest rate of industrial growth in the Soviet Union, 47 percent. This economic revival led to higher living standards, if official statistics are to be believed. By the late stages of Aliyev's tenure, Azerbaijan's standard of living was still below the Soviet median; nonetheless, its per capita income had improved from 62 percent of the Union average in 1970 to 80 percent in 1980.[32] But in typical Soviet style, economic growth took place at the cost of reliance on a small number of sectors, and with considerable environmental destruction resulting from oil spills, overuse of pesticide, and inefficient irrigation. At the same time, a substantial transformation of the rural economy occurred: in fact, a form of de-collectivization, as farmers across Azerbaijan switched from government-mandated crops to grow fruits and flowers that were shipped to Russian cities and sold at markets. This required the tacit approval of local Soviet authorities, who obviously profited from the developing gray market economy through extracting bribes from the farmers and traders.[33]

For the intelligentsia, Aliyev's reign coincided with a relaxation of pressure on writers and academics, a situation that led to a rebirth of patriotic literature and indeed to the re-creation of an Azerbaijani intelligentsia that had largely been physically destroyed during Baghirov's tenure. By the late 1970s and early 1980s, literature—especially poetry—with strong national-patriotic overtones was being published ever more openly in the official journals of the Azerbaijani academy of writers.[34] Discussion of the accomplishments of the Azerbaijan People's Republic grew, and Mämmädemin Räsulzadä was gradually rehabilitated.[35] As Altstadt observes,

> During the early 1980s a pattern of increasingly frank and substantive discussions of cultural and intellectual issues was established.... The implications of the internal discussions in the Azerbaijani Turkish community were momentous. Yet this movement, for it seems to bear the marks of a coordinated and conscious effort, developed under the rule of Heydar Aliyev, a man who vigorously articulated Moscow's line and freely replaced party cadres. Because Aliyev cannot be regarded as weak, uninformed, lax, or tuse, it can be supposed that he permitted, perhaps encouraged, this upsurge of national self-investigation, this exploration of historic identity, and this expression of national pride.[36]

Others have gone further. In a rare and largely approving biography of Aliyev, Turkish journalist Irfan Ülkü argued that Aliyev consciously acted as a protector of the emerging Azerbaijani intelligentsia. Ülkü, who spent time with Aliyev in 1991 in Nakhichevan, said that Aliyev joined the security services with the explicit intention of contributing to Azerbaijanis' efforts to take control of their own republic.[37] Once he was in power, it is clear that this is precisely what Aliyev did, in fact making a return to the early policies of *korenizatsiia*. As Swietochowski says, Aliyev was "consolidating the native nomenklatura and upgrading it through an infusion of the element of technocracy. Of his thirty-five chief clients and protégés, almost all were Azeris."[38] Aliyev continued the rehabilitation of Narimanov, in fact using the latter's relationship with Lenin to justify the erection of a Narimanov bust in Ulyanovsk (now Simbirsk), Lenin's birthplace, in addition to the large Narimanov statue overlooking Baku.[39] He also managed to bring home the remains of Javid Hüseyin, the Azerbaijani poet and victim of Baghirov's purges, and to tell foreign journalists in 1982 that he hoped for the unification of northern and southern Azerbaijan.[40]

Yet at the same time, Aliyev in his official proclamations was steadfast in his proclamations of loyalty to Leninist nationality policy and to the importance of the Russian language. Indeed, even as Baku was gradually becoming ethnically more Azerbaijani, with an Islamic religious revival occurring in the 1970s and ethnic Russians beginning to leave the republic in the 1980s, the Azerbaijani capital in particular was subjected to linguistic Russification. A type of double culture evolved, with the Azerbaijani Turkish language being confined to the home and social interactions, and Russian increasingly taking over the domains of officialdom, science, and technical language. Aliyev's record, much like his personality, hence remains complex. Though he became the most senior Azerbaijani in the Soviet Union, and for that matter its most senior official of Muslim origin, Aliyev was without doubt a champion of his republic's rights, and both oversaw and endorsed a national revival whose results would determine the republic's future in the late 1980s.

3

The National Revival and the Road to Independence

When *perestroika* and *glasnost* appeared in the official Soviet vocabulary in 1986, there were political activists in both Armenia and Georgia who were well positioned, both intellectually and organizationally, to use the new freedom represented by these concepts to mobilize public support for nationalist purposes. In both republics, movements led by elite figures and intellectuals had been in place since the 1960s, and had significant following among students and the general public. In Azerbaijan, however, it took somewhat longer for dissident forces to coalesce into what would eventually become the Azerbaijani Popular Front (APF). Indeed, the rise of Azerbaijani nationalism—previously a notion entertained mainly by the intelligentsia—was very much an awakening spurred by conflict in Mountainous Karabakh and a response to the threat of Armenian expansionism. At the same time, Azerbaijan experienced a national revival to a much higher degree than its fellow Muslim republics in Central Asia.

Although it proceeded more slowly than in neighboring republics or among those of the Baltic region, a national revival had begun to gather momentum in Azerbaijan in the 1970s. This stemmed in part from the gradual increase in freedoms and relaxation of repression, but also from a reaction to the increasing Russification of Azerbaijan. Indeed, especially in cosmopolitan Baku, the use of the Azerbaijani language among youth had dwindled by the late 1970s. An Azerbaijani intellectual related how hearing children speak Russian among themselves on the streets in the early 1980s made many patriotically minded Azeris seriously worried about the survival of their nation. The same intellectual related how the discovery of a package of Turkish-made spaghetti in a local supermarket lifted his spirits: if a food package could travel from Turkey to Azerbaijan, there was hope for breaking the cultural isolation from its ethnic kin that Azerbaijan was experiencing.[1]

Although the political climate did not permit the coalescence of politically active interest groups, an Azerbaijani intelligentsia with an agenda to protect the Azerbaijani Turkish ethnic identity had emerged to replace the layer killed off during the Stalinist purges. And although Heydar Aliyev did not overtly betray such tendencies, it is clear that he exercised increasing leniency and tolerance toward this agenda in the intellectual community. In 1978 Azerbaijani was confirmed as the state language of the republic, and efforts to put Russian on a par with Azerbaijani were foiled.

As elsewhere in the Soviet Union, dissident elements took advantage of the human rights movement and the Helsinki Accords of 1975 to advance their cause, although doing so still had its perils. For instance, Abulfez Elçibey, who later would become a Popular Front leader and then president, was jailed for several years for his dissident writings and activities.

By the early 1980s, Azerbaijani intellectuals were beginning to publish books and articles in literary magazines focusing on the language, culture, and national heritage of Azerbaijan, as well as the origins of the Azerbaijani nation and its relationships with Caucasian Albania and various Turkic tribes. The issue of reunification with the Azerbaijanis living in Iran was also increasingly discussed.[2] Azerbaijani writers could now—in the Azerbaijani-language press, and in the late 1980s in the Russian-language press as well—discuss the importance of native-language education and deplore the widespread use of Russian and the steady loss of the native language among the young. As one leader of what would become the Popular Front put it, "A national spirit had developed," and there was a notable increase in freedom and a relaxation of repression.[3] By 1987, cultural organizations to protect architectural heritage, establish contact with coethnics abroad, and study Azerbaijani history had been formally established, such as Yurd, Veten, and Çanlibel. By early 1988, a small intellectual grouping with more overtly political objectives emerged called Varliq, named after an Iranian Azerbaijani journal published since 1978. This organization included future leading members of the Popular Front such as Elçibey and Sabir Rustamhanli.

Mountainous Karabakh

Nothing did more to mobilize Azerbaijan's population and spur the Azerbaijani national movement than the issue of Mountainous Karabakh. But if Karabakh had been a recurring preoccupation in Armenia during the Soviet era, it was a nonissue for most Azerbaijanis in the mid-1980s. But the freshening of the political atmosphere in the Soviet Union under President Mikhail Gorbachev led to a rapid increase of nationalist momentum in Armenia. There, emerging groups were directing their attention to securing the transfer of both the autonomous oblast of Mountainous Karabakh and the autonomous soviet socialist republic of Nakhichevan to Armenia. It is notable that organized Armenian claims on Karabakh began very shortly after Heydar Aliyev fell from grace with the Gorbachev regime in 1987. It seems likely that these claims would have been difficult to voice while Aliyev retained substantial influence in Moscow. His political demise, on the other hand, left Azerbaijan very much unrepresented in Moscow, while Armenia's influence grew, in part because of ethnic Armenian Abel Aganbeyan's status as one of Gorbachev's leading advisers.

In August 1987, a petition requesting the transfer of Karabakh and Nakhichevan was prepared by the Armenian Academy of Sciences, sparking the official rekindling of the dormant topic in Armenia. In October, Armenians in the village of Chardakli in northwestern Azerbaijan rejected the appointment of an ethnic Azerbaijani director for a state farm (*sovkhoz*). This challenge resulted in a crackdown by the local authorities. As news of these developments reached the Armenian capital, Yerevan, demonstrations there advocating the closing of polluting industries were quickly politicized and turned into nationalist manifestations demanding the transfer of Karabakh to Armenia.[4] During the fall of 1987 speculation mounted that the Soviet leadership would approve such a transfer, spurred in part by Aganbeyan's statement in November to that effect, published in the French communist newspaper *L'Humanité*.[5] But although Gorbachev was reportedly sympathetic to the Armenian cause, his memoirs show a strong belief in the sanctity of internal Soviet borders, probably the main reason he did not approve the transfer.[6]

Following the events in Chardakli, anti-Azerbaijani sentiment grew rapidly in Armenia, leading to the systematic harassment of ethnic Azerbaijanis living there; many were forced to leave their homes. The first refugee waves, consisting of tens of thousands of people, reached Baku and the surrounding towns and villages at the beginning of 1988. Two more waves of refugees reached Baku before the end of February, and several thousand were resettled in Sumgait, a run-down industrial city 30 kilometers from the capital. In Karabakh itself the local parliament quickly radicalized, and a docile party leader was replaced with a more outspoken Armenian nationalist. On February 20, the Karabakh Soviet in Stepanakert adopted a formal appeal to the central government of the Soviet Union, as well as to the leadership of Armenia and Azerbaijan, that it be transferred to Armenian jurisdiction. This action provided the impetus for the formation of a "Karabakh Committee" in Yerevan, and large demonstrations in support of the appeal were held there. Gorbachev met with Armenian intellectuals, and asked for a one-month moratorium on protests to consider the issue, spurring speculation that Moscow was ready to give in. This raised the level of militancy in Stepanakert, as leaders of the Armenian Groong movement, an informal organization formed to spearhead the advocacy for Karabakh to be turned over to Armenia, seemed to think that a final push would make Moscow accept Armenia's claims.

On February 26, rumors reached the Azerbaijani city of Agdam that violence in Stepanakert had led to the death of an ethnic Azerbaijani. A mob formed and reached Askeran, on Karabakh's border, where clashes ensued between the Azerbaijani mob and Armenian villagers and police, leaving two Azeris dead. News of these deaths was then cabled across Azerbaijan together with reports that Armenian leaders were proclaiming victory after their meeting with Gorbachev, and reached activists and refugees in Sumgait. In the days that followed, uncontrolled Azerbaijani mobs went on a rampage, looting and seeking out and killing ethnic Armenians. Estimates of the number of dead range from the official figure of 32 to the several hundred cited by Armenian sources. The mob action occurred despite the presence of a significant contingent of Soviet Interior Ministry troops in and around Sumgait, who did not intervene until the third day of the riots, in spite of the fact that Soviet deputy interior minister Nikolai Demidov later admitted being in Sumgait during the riots.[7] As the *Washington Post* reported, "Despite the heavy presence of armed militia, the protests and riots went largely undeterred until March 1, when troops and tanks were dispatched."[8]

The inaction of Soviet Interior Ministry forces, at odds with their trigger-happy reputation, prompted speculation about the roots of the unrest and the role of the central government; in particular, the troops' failure to intervene led to accusations that Moscow at the very least saw the riots as conveniently serving to support a divide-and-rule policy in the Caucasus. Given that no mobilized Azerbaijani nationalism was in place in early 1988, and that events in Armenia and Karabakh had just begun to get the attention of the wider population in Azerbaijani cities, the events in Sumgait remain a mystery. What it clear, however, is that Sumgait was a turning point in the Azerbaijani-Armenian conflict. It seemed to confirm the worst Armenian prejudices against Azerbaijanis, and projected the conflict into a new phase that made a peaceful resolution all the more unlikely.

Even before 1988, Karabakh had been a focal point of concern for nationalist intellectuals in Azerbaijan. While the Armenian claims to Karabakh went unnoticed among the wider population, intellectuals were aware of these claims and the growing campaign by Armenian intellectuals across the Soviet Union for the transfer of the territory to Armenian rule. Likewise, it was the events in Karabakh in the late 1980s that gradually awakened a strong sense of national belonging in Azerbaijan; they were also the main issue prompting the emergence of the movements that would coalesce into the Azerbaijani Popular Front.

The Azerbaijani Popular Front

The beginnings of a truly popular movement in Azerbaijan date to November 1988, when large-scale demonstrations began on Baku's Lenin Square (present-day Freedom Square). Even Soviet media reported that tens of thousands of people joined these demonstrations, where intellectuals and workers' leaders made crowd-stirring appearances. The demonstrations focused on a number of issues on which the Communist government of Azerbaijan was faulted, primarily the Karabakh issue and the refugees coming in thousands from Armenia, but also environmental issues and other concerns. The demonstrations spread beyond Baku to Nakhichevan and Gandja, where clashes between the military and the crowds led to several deaths and dozens of injuries. The Soviet authorities allowed these events to continue for days, seeking to gradually weaken the demonstrations by mixing threats with promises that the protestors' demands would be met. In early December, the remaining protesters, including several dissident leaders, were jailed. However, the increased general participation in protests formed the basis for the dissident leaders to try to institutionalize the emerging popular movement. The impetus for this was further strengthened in January 1989, when Moscow moved to assert control over the Karabakh situation, instituting direct rule over the region without consulting Azerbaijani authorities. In Baku, fears mounted that direct rule would be only a step toward transferring the territory to Armenia outright, as the move in fact removed Karabakh from Azerbaijani jurisdiction, and as such undermined the republic's sovereignty.

The protests in Azerbaijan often illustrated how mobilization around the Karabakh issue was catalyzed by refugees from Armenia, but also how anti-Armenian feelings were quickly coupled with anger toward the Soviet authorities. In Gandja, for example, unrest mounted in November 1988 upon news that a manufacturer operating out of Armenia would be building an aluminum plant in Topkhana, a historic nature preserve in Karabakh revered by Azerbaijanis. A crowd surrounded the municipal Communist Party committee building, throwing stones at officials and soldiers arriving to secure the facility as well as at least one grenade, which killed three soldiers, indicating the level to which the protestors' hostility had risen.[9] The construction of the plant was subsequently halted, and the party chiefs of Gandja and Nakhichevan were fired.[10] Another example of the twin grievances the Karabakh issue created in Azerbaijan is the refusal by printers in Baku to print *Izvestiya* during several days in November, citing the newspaper's failure to give space to the events in Baku and the aluminum plant issue.[11] Hence, and probably inevitably in a centralized state such as the Soviet Union, frustrations at a local level quickly turned toward the center, in reaction to the power wielded by Moscow but also because of a lingering distrust of imperial domination.

By late 1988 secession from the Soviet Union had already become a rallying cry, especially for more nationalistically minded leaders such as Nemet Panakhov. A metalworker who joined the mainly intellectual circle of leaders of what would become the Popular Front, Panakhov had become one of the most popular and charismatic leaders, rousing crowds with his calls for Azerbaijan's independence.[12] This intense appeal was the main reason why, whenever he was arrested, Panakhov would be kept in custody longer than most dissident leaders.

The November 1988 disturbances led to considerable violence against Armenians, and was paralleled by anti-Azerbaijani riots in Armenia. As a result, that month saw the first large population exchange between the two republics, with more than 150,000 people fleeing in each direction, inevitably fueling nationalist sentiment in both republics with accounts of their experiences.

The spring of 1989 saw the coalescing of various forces and individuals into a broad-based movement with roots across the republic, the Azerbaijani Popular Front. As Audrey Altstadt noted,

> The APF... embodied the politicization of a long process--clarifying cultural and social issues that had been reflected in Azerbaijani Turkish publications in previous decades.... This educated, articulate elite, sometimes related by blood or marriage, was united by a singleness of purpose and efforts reminiscent of the same coordinated and nationally conscious secular elite active at the turn of the century. Now as then, political organizations are fluid, with cooperation among some groups and with some individuals belonging to various groups simultaneously.[13]

The Popular Front stood out the relatively strong initial consensus among its founders on the need to coalesce into a single national movement, but also on the future course of Azerbaijan. While there were variations in the level of emphasis put on Turkic identity and nationalism, there was broad agreement on Azerbaijan's future as a democratic and secular society respecting the rights of every citizen, including ethnic and religious minorities. The consensus among the APF's founders was largely attributable to their ambition to reconnect to the pre-Soviet Müsavat party and the legacy of the 1918–20 period, which supplied the ideological foundation of the movement.[14]

In July 1989, the Popular Front held its founding congress, formulating a program that focused on turning Azerbaijan into an advanced democratic society and a state based on the rule of law.[15] It kept open the possibility that Azerbaijan could remain in a reformed Soviet Union, but failing that, achieving full independence would be the objective. Equally significantly, the APF sought to reconnect to the legacy of the First Republic, demanding the restoration of the tricolor flag and coat of arms of the short-lived state, its national anthem, and the observance of May 28 as independence day. The program also foresaw full respect for the cultural autonomy of ethnic minorities, but did not include language indicating a respect for the Soviet form of territorial autonomy. The founding congress chose Abulfez Elçibey as its chairman.

Elçibey was born Abülfez Kadirgül oğlı Aliyev in 1938, in the village of Keleki, near Ordubad in Nakhichevan. In 1957 he began studying Arabic philology at Baku State University, where he also was part of a small group of dissident thinkers. After graduating he worked as an interpreter in Egypt from 1963 to 1964, then took a faculty position in history at Baku State University. In this milieu, Elçibey became involved in the anti-Soviet student movements that emerged in the early 1970s. This led to his arrest in 1975 for defaming the Soviet Union. After spending 18 months in jail, Elçibey worked as a researcher for the Azerbaijani Academy of Sciences and wrote numerous works on history and philosophy, specializing in the Turkic Tulunid dynasty, which ruled Egypt in the ninth century. Elçibey built a reputation as an honest and uncompromising nationalist, with an aura of incorruptibility that was a great asset in his election to lead the Popular Front.

The APF quickly grew as a force to be reckoned with, one that the Azerbaijani Communist Party authorities could not ignore—if for no other reason because of its capacity to cripple the economy and humiliate the government by starting as well as terminating strikes. As a result, the government of Azerbaijan had little choice but to accede, in October 1989, to the Popular Front's main demand: to be officially registered as an organization. Meanwhile, the APF saw its first important split—between liberals seeking an evolutionary and peaceful path toward independence on the one hand,

and radicals working for an immediate and forceful secession, on the other. The split threatened to undo the organization, and forced the convening of an extraordinary congress in December 1989.

But before that could happen, the situation was again overtaken by developments regarding Mountainous Karabakh. On November 27, Moscow simply ended its direct rule over Mountainous Karabakh and returned the territory to Azerbaijan's jurisdiction. While this was ostensibly a victory for the Azerbaijani side, its joy was short-lived, thanks to Armenia's decision on December 1 to annex the province—directly challenging Moscow—and its promulgation a month later of a budget for Karabakh. Passions mounted in Azerbaijan as Communist Party first secretary Abdurrahman Vezirov's government deferred to an increasingly paralyzed central government in Moscow rather than take the initiative to safeguard its interests. In fact, the Baku Communist leadership took several days to condemn the move. As a result, protests began spreading in the country, managed mainly by Popular Front activists—but not always coordinated or approved by the central APF leadership. In Nakhichevan, locals dismantled border installations and fortifications separating them from their ethnic kin across the border in Iran, enabling them to reestablish contact and to reclaim land along the Araks River that had been turned into a no-go military zone. In Lenkoran and Jalal-Abad, where a disposition toward violence against the Soviet authorities had been simmering, the Popular Front, for most practical purposes, began to replace the state authorities.

The developments of late 1989 made it clear that across Azerbaijan, the Popular Front enjoyed an increased popular loyalty, while the government's ability to control the flow of events was rapidly waning. In September, the Front successfully imposed a rail embargo on Armenia in order to force it to relinquish claims on Karabakh. On September 13, Vazirov was forced to sign a protocol with the Front, registering the organization and acceding to many of its demands, including convening the republic's parliament to pass a declaration of sovereignty. As The *New York Times* put it, "Of all the nationalist movements that have sprung up in the Soviet Union, none has moved from obscurity to power quite so quickly as the Azerbaijani Popular Front."[16]

But events nevertheless also posed problems for the APF. In a harbinger of things to come once they gained power, the leaders of the Popular Front failed to exert control over their local branches, in spite of being fully aware of how Moscow could interpret events in Lenkoran and Jalal-Abad, and hardly six months after a notorious episode in April 1989, in which Soviet troops brutally dispersed a peaceful rally in Tbilisi, killing more than twenty protesters with shovels. Indeed, Popular Front demonstrations had already seen the participation of groups of youths who refused to obey leaders' orders, and who were likely provocateurs sent out by the security forces to sow unrest. As records show, APF leaders were also aware of the need to contain mounting anti-Armenian sentiments inflamed by arriving refugees, and sought to prevent these feelings from turning violent. Already, on December 30, 1989, the Popular Front newspaper *Azadliq* had warned its readers of impending provocations intended to destabilize the city by targeting Armenians, and urged APF activists to refrain from involvement in such activities. By this time, republic's authorities were doubly powerless: while unable to control the Popular Front's growing popularity, they were in no position to affect, let alone challenge, Moscow's role in the situation.

January 20

Anti-Armenian riots broke out in Baku January 13–14, 1990, in spite of the Popular Front's active attempts to calm passions and prevent bloodshed. The government, on the other hand, did little. Repeating their performance in Sumgait two years earlier, local militia forces stood on the sidelines and watched the violence escalate. Leading APF representatives pleaded with republican authorities to deploy Interior Ministry forces to restore order, but military officials made it clear that they had received orders not to intervene.[17] Instead, as Azerbaijani refugees from Armenia led mobs evicting Armenians from apartments and taking these dwellings for themselves, the APF organized escorts for Armenians leaving the city. The Popular Front's efforts helped end the violence on January 15. By this time, of course, most Armenian residents of Baku had left under duress, thus contributing to Baku's deepening loss of diversity. From having been a multiethnic, cosmopolitan city, the Azerbaijani capital was increasingly becoming an ethnic Azerbaijani community. In this sense, Baku's development paralleled that of Istanbul several decades earlier. The combination of mass migration from the countryside into the city and occasional bouts of violence toward minorities (to which authorities turned a blind eye) made both cities increasingly homogeneous.

The same day that the violence ended, Moscow ordered thousands of troops to the South Caucasus. While a state of emergency was declared in Karabakh and troops moved into Armenia as well, the primary objective of the forces was to be Baku. A news blackout accompanied the Soviet deployment, and as troops slowly made their way toward Baku from the north, the Popular Front frantically sought to negotiate with Soviet representatives to prevent the invasion of the city.[18] What followed was a well-planned effort to end the growing restiveness in Azerbaijan by brutal use of force directed primarily at the civilian population. Tanks rolled into Baku after midnight on January 20, crushing civilians, ambulances, and cars, and randomly spraying residential compounds with bullets. Residents were not informed of the state of emergency that had been imposed on the city until the next morning, however. By that time, more than 100 people had been killed and more than 700 wounded, and Soviet troops were in full control of the city. A particular focus was the APF headquarters, which was among the first buildings attacked without warning. Most of the Popular Front's leaders were arrested, and the Soviet leadership variously cited interethnic unrest and the need to defend against purported Islamic fundamentalism as the reason behind the intervention.

Black January, as the crackdown became known in Azerbaijan, was striking both for its character and its implications. There is little doubt that the authorities willfully refrained from intervening in the ethnic clashes in Baku the week before the crackdown, then used the same clashes as a justification for intervention. It is also apparent that the Soviet leadership felt that the Azerbaijani Communist Party was losing control over the republic due to what Mark Saroyan called "the politics of party paralysis,"[19] and that something had to be done to avoid losing this strategic republic. The Popular Front's popularity and the paralysis of the Azerbaijani Communist Party formed a trend most disturbing to Moscow. The open challenges posed to Soviet rule in Lenkoran, Nakhichevan, and Jalal-Abad may well have been the turning point. The severity of the crackdown, even compared with the murderous suppression of protestors in Tbilisi in April 1989, nevertheless indicates that Moscow either wanted to establish a precedent to halt the slippage of its power across the Soviet territory or felt especially worried that a Muslim republic was for the first time in a real position to rise up against Moscow, with potential consequences for the relatively peaceful situation in Central Asia. A high-level Soviet military officer even admitted that the crackdown was ordered "to crush the Azerbaijani drive for greater sovereignty in order to discourage similar movements where."[20] Soviet defense minister Dimitri Yazov, for his part, stated that "the military occupation of Azerbaijan's capital was designed to prevent the Azerbaijan Popular Front from seizing power from the Communist Party."[21] Either way, and as would be the case with so many of Moscow's subsequent policies in the Caucasus, the move would prove enormously counter-productive. The most immediate effect was to spur rebelliousness in the hinterlands, mainly Nakhichevan and Gandja, where declarations of secession were made but order restored after undoubtedly dire ultimatums from Soviet authorities.[22]

Perhaps the most serious consequence of the Soviet intervention was the long-term effect: Black January made the alienation of Azerbaijan from the Soviet Union—and for that matter, from Russia—final and irreversible. Whereas the Popular Front was increasingly powerful, and nationalist sentiments were rising, mainly on account of Karabakh, the wider Azerbaijani public had not previously been uniformly and irretrievably anti-Soviet. Indeed, few Azerbaijanis, even within the Popular Front, thought seriously of independence from the USSR. But with January 20, the emotional link between Azerbaijan and the Soviet Union took a mortal blow. As in Tbilisi in April 1989, the Communist Party lost its chance of regaining the loyalty of the population, although it was (in the short term) able to remain in power. As Altstadt put it, the intervention broke "whatever bonds of limited trust remained between the rulers in Moscow and their subjects in Azerbaijan."[23] This was most obvious from the wave of people dropping the Russian "–ov" ending from their names and changing them to Turkic endings. Gambarov became Gambar, Mehdiyev became Mehdi, while some added endings like the Turkic "-beyli" or the Persian "-zade" to their newly truncated last names.

In order to reinvigorate the Azerbaijani Communist Party, Moscow sought to reverse its slippage under the weak leaders who had ruled the republic since Heydar Aliyev's removal from power. Abdurrahman Vezirov was therefore dismissed as president, and replaced by the 52-year old Ayaz Mutalibov, an engineer by training, who had served as chairman of the Council of Ministers of the Republic.[24] Mutalibov's rise to power proved a mixed blessing: on the one hand, his major challenger, the Popular Front, had been significantly weakened as its leaders were thrown in jail after the January 20 intervention. But on the other hand, the challenge of rebuilding even a modicum of legitimacy was substantial. As the population resigned en masse from membership in the Communist Party, Mutalibov moved quickly to improve his credentials as a defender of Azerbaijan's interests.

Most important, Mutalibov managed to secure a deal to conduct joint military operations with the Soviet Interior Ministry in western Azerbaijan. This stemmed in part from Armenia's increasingly strong secessionist policies; as Armenia developed into one of the most anti-Soviet republics of the Union, Moscow stayed true to its policies of divide and rule, and tilted towards Azerbaijan's position in the conflict between the two republics.

The result was far-reaching cooperation between Soviet interior ministry troops and the local Azerbaijani counterparts, in the form of operation "Ring."[25] The operation was aimed at disarming Armenian paramilitary forces that had emerged mainly in the Armenian-populated areas north of Karabakh and in the autonomous region itself. These paramilitaries had emerged partly as a reaction to blatant failure of Soviet forces to intervene against persecutions of Armenians in Baku and elsewhere. The joint operations temporarily put pressure on the Armenian forces in Karabakh, thereby supporting Mutalibov's attempts to ingratiate himself with the population there. Yet the operations were seen by Armenians as indicative of Soviet culpability in the ethnic cleansing of Armenians from these territories, after numerous Armenian villages were emptied, their inhabitants forced to move to Armenia. As such, the operations furthered Armenia's alienation from the Soviet Union. Neither did they succeed in disarming the Armenian forces: increasingly, supplies for the paramilitary groups, including weaponry, were flowing from Armenia into western Azerbaijan. Clashes escalated during the summer of 1990, as Soviet and Azerbaijani forces found themselves in outright firefights with Armenian paramilitaries, and the situation continued until Soviet forces were withdrawn after the August 1991 coup in Moscow.

Mutalibov understood the need to appeal to growing nationalism in Azerbaijan. After he had himself elected president of the Supreme Soviet of Azerbaijan, his first decision was to reinstitute May 28 as a public holiday, called, significantly, "the Day of Azerbaijani Statehood." The Communist Party also adopted a new program, much closer to the views of the APF, and in August 1990 abolished the Nagorno-Karabakh Autonomous Province. However, the concomitant radicalization of the Popular Front and the cosmetic character of Mutalibov's attempts to negotiation with APF leaders made these moves ring hollow. For all the rhetoric, the Azerbaijani leadership remained slavishly loyal to Moscow. In the elections to the Supreme Soviet held in fall 1990, the Communist Party failed to hold on to power in both Armenia and Georgia, and nationalist forces instead took power. But in Azerbaijan, electoral fraud and repression enabled the Communists to secure a near-total domination of the legislative body. As a result, in spite of protests and calls for a boycott by the Popular Front, Azerbaijan took part in the March 1991 all-Union referendum on a new Union treaty, unlike Armenia and Georgia. While official figures showed 95 percent of the electorate supporting the treaty, the APF claimed that only 20 percent of the eligible voters had participated. Mutalibov nevertheless had to agree with the Popular Front on the creation of a smaller body, the National Council, composed of fifty representatives—twenty-five each from the government and the opposition. While that body would gain tremendous importance later, it did not at first have any particular official function.

Yet Armenia's increasing estrangement from the USSR tilted Moscow in Mutalibov's favor. Soviet military forces and Azerbaijani Interior Ministry forces initiated "Operation Ring," which disarmed and resettled (i.e., evicted) several thousand Armenians living to the north of Mountainous Karabakh. The move was widely seen as Moscow's punishment of Armenia and reward to Azerbaijan; the Popular Front termed it trading "freedom for land."[26] His uncompromising attitude further polarizing politics, Mutalibov missed the opportunity to use his accomplishments to thaw his frosty relations with the APF.

The APF, for its part, held a congress in July 1991, which focused on adjusting the Popular Front's priorities and positions relative to the developing realities. Elçibey noted that the Soviet Union was in the process of collapsing; he also emphasized the need to build true independence and democracy for Azerbaijan, and denounced the authoritarian character of Mutalibov's rule. The congress also paid increasing attention to Iranian Azerbaijan, and the general viewpoint in the Popular Front was to regard Azerbaijan's reunification as a natural future development.[27] The APF decided to postpone a scheduled second session of the congress until September. But events in Moscow would overtake that plan.

Independence

When the August 19, 1991, putsch in Moscow got under way, Ayaz Mutalibov was in Tehran on a state visit. Due to poor judgment and perhaps even worse information, Mutalibov praised the coup makers and condemned Gorbachev. His calculus may well have been that since the hardliners had helped him organize Operation Ring, their coming to power would help Azerbaijan settle the Karabakh issue in its favor and help him stay in power as a national hero. Of course, matters turned out differently. When, within three days, the coup collapsed, the Soviet Union began its gradual slide toward oblivion, making it painfully evident that Mutalibov had placed all his eggs in a basket that, for all practical purposes, no longer existed.

On August 30, 1991, the Supreme Soviet of Azerbaijan declared its intention to restore the country's independent statehood. This declaration was followed by a constitutional act on October 18 and a referendum on

December 29, in which over 95 percent of the electorate voted in favor of independence for Azerbaijan. An independent state was thus (re)born, but the conditions were far from auspicious. Azerbaijan entered the community of independent nations in a state of escalating military conflict with its neighbor Armenia; with a comatose planned economy that was coming apart despite the country's latent mineral wealth; and with rulers who had neither sought nor desired independence, and who lacked popular legitimacy. Worst of all, in the military conflict with Armenia, the Azerbaijani leadership had hedged its bets on Moscow and failed even to build an army—a mistake Armenia had not made. Together, these factors would make Azerbaijan's first years of independence a roller-coaster ride.

4

The Rise and Fall of the Popular Front

As in 1918, the collapse of Russian power in the South Caucasus in 1991 left a vacuum in which Azerbaijan found itself free without actually having fought a war of independence. However, in 1991 an independence movement had existed, brought to life mainly by the conflict over Mountainous Karabakh and the January 20 massacre. In 1991, as in 1918, it was the Azerbaijani intelligentsia that moved in to administer the new state. On both occasions, this led to the same advantages and drawbacks. On the positive side, the intelligentsia left a strong mark on the principles of statehood. If the events of 1918–20 had put Azerbaijan on the map as the first secular and democratic republic in the Muslim world, the 1992–93 experience of the Azerbaijani Popular Front (APF) was a unique instance of true democrats taking control of a post-Soviet Muslim state. But both experiences were short-lived, and for the same reasons: the intelligentsia was simply not sufficiently trained or experienced to actually administer a state, and the internal and external challenges—such as conflict with Armenia, building a state without trained staff, internal elite dissent, and dealing with vestiges of the old regime—were more than the democratic but novice forces could manage.

Coming to Power: The Reluctant End of Communism

In 1992, Azerbaijan was faced with building or reforming communist state institutions into democratic institutions in both form and action. This was a momentous task: it included drafting and passing a new constitution; creating a new parliament to replace the Supreme Soviet; building a judiciary that was independent, and not simply a tool of the Communist Party elite; and distributing power to the various state bodies while determining the balance of power among them. The most challenging aspect of the task was that all these reforms, which were needed to build a functioning democratic state, had to be enacted while the country dealt with a failing economy and the need to build a military force from scratch to counter Armenia's armed advances. Indeed, unlike Azerbaijan, Armenia had completed its political and military transition even before the Soviet Union collapsed. To make matters worse, during the first few months of independence, Azerbaijan was ruled by a government that saw little need to reform anything. President Ayaz Mutalibov had declared independence, but like the leaders of the new states of post-Soviet Central Asia, he sought to reinvent himself as a national leader without introducing meaningful political reform. In this spirit, he had himself elected president in September 1991 without allowing opposition candidates to run.

But two things made Azerbaijan different from the Central Asian republics, and eventually spelled the end of Mutalibov's career. The first was the existence of an increasingly assertive political opposition, motivated by rekindled nationalism, which had actually sought to replace the Azerbaijani Communist Party in various localities as early as 1990. The second was the problem of Mountainous Karabakh, which, to the detriment of his already weak popular legitimacy, Mutalibov was unable to handle.

In January 1992 the Popular Front held a congress, ten days after two different drafts of an agenda for the new state had been published in the APF mouthpiece, the *Azadlıq* newspaper.[1] While both drafts stressed the aim of creating an independent, secular, and democratic republic based on the rule of law, they displayed the continued division between the APF's nationalist/conservative and liberal wings. The program adopted on January 26 was a synthesis of the two drafts, and defined the role of the Popular Front not as a political party but as a movement in the spirit of Müsavat and the First Republic, within which independent parties could coexist. It aspired to remove the remnants of totalitarian rule and to create a multiparty political system while fighting separatism and safeguarding Azerbaijan's territorial integrity.[2]

The Khojaly Trauma and Mutalibov's Fall

The unsuccessful August 1991 coup against the government of President Mikhail Gorbachev was a defining moment in the conflict over Mountainous Karabakh. The three days of the coup are said to be the only three days of 1991 when no gunshots were heard in Karabakh—an indication of the fears of what the coup might bring in terms of repression.[3] But once Azerbaijan proclaimed independence, so did the Mountainous Karabakh oblast Soviet on September 2, 1991, laying claim, in the process, to the district of Geranboi (in Armenian, Shaumyan), to the north of the autonomous province. Azerbaijan responded by seeking to restore control over Karabakh. All military hardware in the republic was nationalized, and Azerbaijani conscripts were recalled from the Soviet military. Yet the Azerbaijani forces were powerless compared to the much more organized and better-equipped Armenian forces that gradually established military control of village after village in Karabakh. With its hold on the province rapidly slipping, the Azerbaijani Parliament made a largely symbolic decision on November 26 to abolish Karabakh's autonomous status.

On February 25 and 26, 1992, the small Azerbaijani-populated town of Khojaly in Mountainous Karabakh was overrun by Armenian forces, supported by the Russian army's 366th Infantry Regiment. Khojaly had strategic value, as it controlled the airport of Stepanakert, the nearby Karabakh capital. The attack was timed, in all likelihood not coincidentally, to occur on the anniversary of the Sumgait killings of Armenians four years earlier. The combined forces of ethnic Armenians and the Russian infantry regiment attacked the town from three sides, leaving a funnel through which the population might escape. But as the fleeing residents of Khojaly reached the outskirts of a nearby village, Nakhjivanli, they were met by "a gauntlet of lead and fire."[4] More than 600 civilians were killed, and several hundred more went missing. Autopsies by the International Committee for the Red Cross indicated that numerous dead bodies were mutilated.[5] Although Khojaly was the sole instance of a premeditated massacre of this scale recorded during the conflict over Karabakh, it had a great impact, since the killings spared the Armenian forces the trouble of evicting civilians from the Azerbaijani regions they subsequently conquered in and outside Karabakh. Thereafter, when Armenian forces moved in, civilian Azerbaijanis invariably had already fled, fearful of being massacred should they decide to stay. Creating this kind of fear was probably an objective of the Khojaly killings, which, unlike the massacres in the Bosnian war, have yet to be investigated. While pro-Armenian authors have put forward the claim that the civilians were killed by Azerbaijanis themselves, no one other than current Armenian president Serzh Sargsyan in an interview with British author Thomas De Waal seems to make the narrative clear:

> Before Khojali, the Azerbaijanis thought that they were joking with us, they thought that the Armenians were people who could not raise their hand against the civilian population. We were able to break that [stereotype]. And that's what happened.[6]

Khojaly made headlines in the West only gradually, as the event flew in the face of the ready-made Western picture of the conflict, in which Armenian diasporas had successfully managed to portray Karabakh Armenians as the victim of Azerbaijani aggression. The Azerbaijani government's attitude did not help, either. Mutalibov infamously tried to downplay the situation in Karabakh during the events, obviously understanding the impact that his inability to manage the situation would have on his weakening position. But of course, this was a futile attempt: the magnitude of the massacre ensured that news quickly spread to Baku and, eventually, to the rest of the world, through the reporting of journalists such as Thomas Goltz, Anatol Lieven, and Hugh Pope. The Popular Front sought to prevent demonstrations, as anti-Russian feelings were mounting on account of the 366th Infantry Regiment's involvement in Khojaly, and there were fears of anti-Russian rioting in the city. The only protest events were silent demonstrations by the Azerbaijani Writers' Union calling on Mutalibov to resign; they drew several hundred people.[7] The National Council called an emergency meeting of the Supreme Soviet on March 5, which attracted thousands of protestors demanding Mutalibov's resignation. Parliament elected a new speaker, Yaqub Mamedov, known mainly by his nickname, "Dollar," allegedly derived from his preference for that currency when accepting favors as rector of Baku's medical university. Against the wishes of the former Communist Party members of the Supreme Soviet but on the urging of the crowd outside and Khojaly's mayor, Mamedov allowed the screening of video footage of Khojaly shot by the late Azerbaijani journalist Chingiz Mustafayev.[8] As Thomas Goltz, present at the meeting, stated, the shocking footage of the dead "changed the history of the country."

> A literal wake of stiff, dead bodies trailed back into Karabakh. Many had their hands raised as if shot after having surrendered. Others were mutilated, with fingers cut off and eyes gouged out. Some were apparently scalped.... Then the film was over. But the reaction had just begun: groans and sighs and whispers welled up from the chamber floor as the magnitude of the event began to penetrate ... the deputies. Something big had broken, and there was no going back. New scapegoats were needed and heads had to roll.[9]

The next day Mutalibov resigned, making "Dollar" Mamedov the acting president of Azerbaijan. Mamedov was in no sense one of the heavyweights of the political system, and real power instead shifted to the appointed prime minister, Hasan Hasanov, who had been one of the most powerful politicians in the country in the late Soviet period.[10] Hasanov initiated talks with Popular Front leader Abulfez Elçibey, and a coalition government including three APF figures was created. Parliament had earlier resolved to hold presidential elections on June 7, 1992, providing the APF with a distinct goal in its effort to come to power. Nevertheless, the Popular Front was more interested in parliamentary elections—the only way to put the country on the path to a new constitution and a rebuilt political system not tailored to the Soviet model. Parliamentary elections nevertheless would only be held in 1995, long after the Popular Front's fall from power. At a session of Parliament in which the APF's demands for parliamentary elections were denied, Elçibey made one of his most prescient statements:

> Now you are in a rush to elect a new president—elect him! But the president you elect in three months will be overthrown in a year. And this is natural. Because today the state that we live in is only deserving of a president who can be kept in power by force ... we need to create structures that can protect a president and prevent him from turning into a dictator. This requires institutions ... if we fail to create such counterbalancing structures, whoever you elect as president will destroy himself or be destroyed by those nearest to him because there is no institutional structure.[11]

Little did Elçibey know that his prediction would come true almost to the day, and that he would be that president.

Mutalibov's Return and the Election of Elçibey

A presidential campaign developed in the spring of 1992 that made it abundantly clear that Mamedov had little or no chance to win the election. The war in Mountainous Karabakh was not going well, in spite of efforts to enlist Iran as a mediator.[12] On the other hand, Mutalibov began preparing the ground for a comeback, counterintuitively drawing on the support of demonstrations in Baku by the Iran-leaning Islamic repentance society.[13]

On May 9, Azerbaijan's last remaining stronghold in Karabakh, the citadel town of Shusha, from which Azerbaijani forces had shelled the Karabakh capital of Stepanakert, was overrun by Armenian forces. Ten days later, the Armenians overran the Lachin corridor, ending Karabakh's status as an enclave within Azerbaijan and providing a channel for Armenian supplies and troops.

The fall of Shusha caused pandemonium in Azerbaijani politics, as it once again exposed the total chaos in the nascent military and the political leadership's inability to do something about it. The fragile relationship between the old and new elites broke at its first test. Mamedov, the acting president, blamed the Popular Front–appointed defense minister, Rahim

Gaziyev, for "selling out" Shusha, while Gaziyev returned the favor. Things got serious on May 14, however, when Mutalibov suddenly reappeared in Parliament, seeking to make use of the fall of Shusha to recast himself as a dictator. Despite the lack of a quorum—the presence of two-thirds of the deputies was necessary to approve a decision—the old guard in parliament reinstated Mutalibov, who took up his old job as if nothing had happened. Swiftly, he announced his readiness to step in "if the country needs a dictator," and promised to take Azerbaijan into the newly founded and Russia-led Commonwealth of Independent States, which, until his final downfall, he regarded as the cure-all solution for Azerbaijan's problems.[14]

The Popular Front would not concede defeat that easily. Elçibey and his firebrand militia leader Iskender Hamidov—who regarded himself as second only to Turkish nationalist leader Alparslan Türkeş as a pan-Turkist leader—had other ideas. On May 15, the day after Mutalibov was returned to power, the Popular Front took forceful action. Making use of the manpower of Hamidov's nationalist followers and a few tanks and armored personnel carriers Hamidov had acquired, the APF feigned an attack on the presidential palace while sending an armored column to capture the undefended parliament building, which was taken with hardly a shot fired.[15] The troops defending the presidential palace fled, and Mutalibov, in turn, escaped to Moscow, where he remains to this day.

The Popular Front was now practically in power. But significantly, its leaders sought to cloak the developments of recent weeks in legality, seeking to approximate, under the conditions, the best possible semblance of the rule of law. Because Mutalibov had been reinstated without a quorum, the APF had grounds for invalidating the process. But the lack of a quorum also threatened to incapacitate the Popular Front, until the force of an angry crowd outside the parliament building compelled a sufficient number of deputies to assemble and elect Isa Gambar, head of the Musavat party and Elçibey's right-hand man, to the position of speaker of parliament and acting president.

In the June 7 election, Abulfez Elçibey was elected president of Azerbaijan with slightly less than 60 percent of the vote. The turnout was just under 80 percent of the electorate. Elçibey's entirely plausible majority was a refreshing departure from the near-unanimous mandate claimed by Mutalibov in September 1991, not only quantitatively but qualitatively. Indeed, the June 1992 vote was probably as good an election as was possible in the chaotic circumstances of a war-torn former Soviet state early in its transition from communism. The volatile nature of the situation was best illu-

strated by the strong performance of an unknown candidate, Nizami Suleymanov, a scientist who ran an unabashed populist campaign promising
to slash the cost of meat, bread, and butter, and to solve the Karabakh crisis
within three months, using a secret plan. Amazingly, Suleymanov received
close to a third of the vote. The threat posed by populism to an inexperienced electoral democracy could hardly be better illustrated. But Suleymanov was not a loner. Shortly after the election, Suleymanov made no
secret that the first thing he would have done as president was ask Heydar
Aliyev to return to Baku to lead the country.[16]

Indeed, Aliyev was not idle during this period. He had fallen victim to a
Gorbachev-era law prohibiting anyone over 65 years of age from standing
for presidential election. Having just turned 70, he was disenfranchised,
even though—or, more likely, because—he still commanded a strong following in the country. It was abundantly clear that the Popular Front had
no interest in removing this specific constitutional clause in the name of
fairness or democracy.

Heydar Aliyev had launched his return to politics in January 1990, following the Soviet military intervention in Baku. He demanded answers
regarding the Black January massacre, and briefly stopped in Baku in spite
of Mutalibov's efforts to prevent him, before going to his native Nakhichevan, where he settled in his sister's modest apartment and was subsequently elected speaker of the autonomous republic's supreme soviet[17] Once in
office, Aliyev built his modest but stable power base—technically, his
position also made him second deputy speaker, ex officio, of the Azerbaijan Supreme Soviet, a feature of the system that would facilitate his return
to power in 1993. With the national government's hands full during the
tenures of both Mutalibov and the Popular Front, Aliyev ran the Nakhichevan Autonomous Republic much like an independent state, conducting
diplomacy with both Iran and Turkey. In the case of Iran, these efforts
served to provide Nakhichevan with a secure source of energy in the form
of Iranian gas, and in the case of Turkey to deter an Armenian attack. Naturally, such dealings also built up Aliyev's underlying support. He showed
his determination to return to national politics in May 1992, when he upstaged the planned celebration of the anniversary of the founding of the First
Republic by inviting Turkish president Suleyman Demirel to Nakhichevan.
Of course, this forced the entire government to swallow its pride and attend
the celebration hosted by Aliyev.[18]

Building A State in Chaos

The Azerbaijani Popular Front's time in government echoed the First Republic's short lease on life. It was characterized by well-meant reforms that never had a chance to be thoroughly implemented, and by war in Mountainous Karabakh. It also repeated the First Republic's accomplishment of laying an indelible foundation for the future state of Azerbaijan. But it differed from the experience of eighty years earlier in one crucial way: Azerbaijan, like Georgia, narrowly avoided being swallowed up by a resurgent Russian empire—something its neighbor Armenia accepted for all practical purposes as the cost of conquest in Karabakh. Instead, Azerbaijan would grow increasingly independent in the coming years.

Democracy: From Theory to Practice

The Popular Front government tried hard to build a democratic state in an inhospitable environment, but suffered greatly from its narrow elite following and lack of personnel when it came to implementing reforms. Its first task was to halt the disintegration of the state structures and particularly law enforcement across the country, especially as far as the interior and national security ministries were concerned, and to reverse the proliferation of local private militias that had resulted.[19] Related to this undertaking, of course, was the larger issue of state structure. Like all post-Soviet states, Azerbaijan had inherited the legacy of twin centers of power: a centralized ruling party where all real power lay, and formal state institutions that were in effect subordinated to the Communist Party and therefore not staffed with the best human resources. Independence and the abolition of the party hence had removed one of the pillars of the system. While the Popular Front realized the need to revamp the entire system through a new constitution, the conditions of war and economic collapse led it to postpone parliamentary elections and the drafting of this new constitution. Hence, the APF government was stuck in the half-collapsed mold of the Communist power structures in Azerbaijan. As a result, it proved unable to free itself from the formal as well as informal power brokers in the republic, or to take the initiative and lay down new rules of the game. As it lost the initiative it undeniably had possessed in the first few months of its rule, the small Popular Front elite increasingly became mired in the quicksand of the larger postcommunist system around it.

That said, the accomplishments of the Popular Front government are undeniable. To begin with, the country's news media and political system were free, for the most part, during the APF's brief tenure. More than twenty political parties were created—including Heydar Aliyev's New Azerbaijan Party—and more than 500 periodicals were founded.[20] Everyone in the APF was not a liberal, of course: a case in point was Iskender Hamidov, interior minister and leader of the Turkic nationalist paramilitary Gray Wolves forces (Bozkurt). Hamidov twice showed up during live television broadcasts to physically assault people who spoke against him, indicating his limited respect for freedom of expression. But Hamidov was the exception to the rule and an indication of hot spirits rather than systematic repression.

Elçibey announced that 1993 would be the year of state building. In his plans, parliamentary elections would be held, a new constitution would be drafted, and crucial reforms would be undertaken. A constitutional drafting committee was set up, but the reform effort's loss of momentum kept the committee from achieving its objective. By contrast, a judicial reform package was passed that sought to strengthen the Justice Ministry. In addition, important basic laws were enacted to provide a basis for the transition from a planned to a market economy. Azerbaijan managed to gain membership in a number of international organizations and to receive support from the World Bank.[21] In August 1992, a national currency, the manat, was introduced, and laws establishing a banking sector, including a national bank, were put in place. In early 1993, the government put in place the legal bases for privatizing the economy and welcoming foreign investment, especially in the oil industry. With these laws, it also became increasingly clear that Azerbaijan was economically—not only politically—distancing itself from Russia, and orienting itself toward the West in action, not just words.[22]

One of the government's biggest problems in the field of economics was the lack of trained staff.[23] Indeed, in spite of the fact that the APF sought to replace the Communist-era staff in government offices, it simply did not have enough cadres, let alone properly trained cadres with managerial skills and training in market economics. A minimum of eight thousand officials are considered necessary to run Azerbaijan's government offices in the center and provinces; the Popular Front had less than a tenth of that. As a result, it was forced to keep large numbers of recalcitrant former Communist officials in place. They obviously did not like what was going on, and knew they would be the first to go once state building got under way. Consequently, they delayed the implementation of reforms.

Cultural policies was one of the Popular Front government's favorite fields. Its ambition was no less than to reverse the significant Soviet and Russian influence on Azerbaijan's language and culture. The first thing to go was the Cyrillic alphabet, replaced at least on paper by a Latin-based one that had been devised by the pre-1918 intelligentsia and used in the 1920s and 1930s. As Goltz has noted, the widely held view that Azerbaijan adopted the Turkish alphabet is erroneous, since the First Republic adopted a Latin-based alphabet long before Turkey did. The Azerbaijani alphabet also includes characters absent in Turkish such as X, Q, and ∂.[24]

While restoration of the modified Latin alphabet was popular, the government decision to change the designation of the national language from "Azerbaijani" to "Türk" was not. Rather, this move opened the festering can of worms of Azerbaijani self-identification. By politicizing this issue, Elçibey and Gambar seemed to side with the Pan-Turkists, who appeared to want to make Azerbaijan more or less a Turkish province. That may not have been a fair assessment, since it was partly based on the misconception that the language had been changed to "Turkish"—the concept of *Türk dili* could be taken to mean both "Turkish" and "Turkic," and the government implied the latter. But the relabeling did mean that Elçibey and Gambar were implicitly challenging the very existence of a distinct Azerbaijani language, instead settling for the vague concept of a wider Turkic language—with the obvious implication that Azerbaijani was thus a dialect of Turkic, not a language.[25] Azerbaijan was not ripe for that move, and it was one of the first things Aliyev would reverse once he was back in power.

The Popular Front government also made the native tongue the required language for all state communications, and passed a law for the de-Russification of the last names of Azerbaijanis.[26] (Unlike Georgians and Armenians, who were allowed to keep their distinct last names in the Soviet period, most Azerbaijanis, like other residents of Muslim Soviet nations, had had to acquiesce in the addition of the ubiquitous Russian "–ov" to the end of their family names, in cases where they had any.) As a result of the de-Russification law, many politically conscious people applied to have their last names changed. This created problems, not least with military service records, given the lack of technology to keep current data on the citizenry. Yet it is significant that Azerbaijan was the only Muslim republic of the former USSR where the process of de-sovietizing last names took place until President Emomali Rahmonov of Tajikistan dropped the "–ov" from his name fifteen years later, in 2007.

Diplomatic Relations: The Triangle Drama

Geopolitically stuck between Turkey, Iran and Russia, the Popular Front government sought to build international relations in a very unfavorable climate. Russia was increasingly siding with Armenia and directly seeking to subvert the APF's position in power; Iran was hostile; and in the West, Azerbaijan was unfairly perceived as the "bad guy" in the conflict over Mountainous Karabakh, thanks not only to Armenian lobbying efforts but also to the near-automatic stigma attached to being Turkic and Muslim in the European press. Foreign relations are specifically addressed in later chapters, but it is necessary to observe here that the Popular Front's foreign policy was largely a failure. This was the case not so much because of its general directions, though these were problematic; it had more to do with the presentation of policy, and the inexperienced and unprofessional way in which the leadership went about it.[27]

The foreign policy perspective of the APF itself was built on ideology and principle, not pragmatism. As much as it can be lauded for its Western orientation and generally liberal attitudes, it was inadequate to meet the needs of Azerbaijan at the time and was not built on realistic calculations of cost and benefit. To begin with, the inordinately warm public embrace of Turkey and Turkism generated shock waves across the region. Aside from alienating non-Turkic minority populations within Azerbaijan, it put both Iran and Russia on high alert, added a geopolitical vector to the conflict over Karabakh, and strengthened the hands of the forces in Moscow and Tehran who thought that support for Armenia served their interest in weakening Azerbaijan. Elçibey's personal role in inflaming Russian and Iranian feelings was a crucial element in this. Known for his activism on the issue of southern Azerbaijan, Elçibey on several occasions blasted Iran as a doomed state, castigated Tehran for the cultural repression of Azerbaijanis in Iran, and predicted that within five years Azerbaijan would be reunified.[28] As for Russia, Elçibey's principled decision in late 1992 to withdraw from the Commonwealth of Independent States is understandable (Mutalibov had signed up Azerbaijan for membership in December 1991); in retrospect, the CIS was then and has continued to be a catatonic organization with the sole purpose of halting the loss of Russian influence in the former Soviet Union. But the consequences of this move were devastating in light of Azerbaijan's political and military realities. The withdrawal from the CIS prompted Moscow to strengthen its political and military support for Armenia; this translated into crucial support for the Armenian military offensive, as well as international cover for this act of aggression.

Elçibey refused to sell his soul for the country's gain—or even to let the Russians think he would sell his soul while actually crafting long-term strategies to build independence, which is what Aliyev after him would do. In all fairness, the Elçibey government's hand was weak and its chances of success limited. Russia had decisively taken the Armenian side at the time of the Khojaly massacre and the fall of Shusha, months before Elçibey was even president. Indeed, Moscow's simple ambition was to get Elçibey out of power by whatever covert means possible, and there was little, short of a total surrender, that could have changed its mind.

In relations with the West, the situation was not much better. Azerbaijan got a late start in its European diplomacy, losing almost half a year because of the tumultuous transfer of power. By the time Elçibey was elected president, the Armenian lobby in the U.S. Congress had already managed to hijack the Freedom Support Act, the main vehicle for U.S. aid to former Soviet republics. Indeed, Armenia's supporters, led by Senator John F. Kerry, had inserted text that prohibited U.S. government assistance to the Azerbaijani government because of its "aggression on Karabakh." As bewildering as this legislation would appear only months later, when Armenia held the entire territory of Karabakh and had engaged in the ethnic cleansing of other Azerbaijani provinces, Azerbaijan was officially designated as the aggressor by Congress in a law that would remain in force despite opposition by every successive U.S. president. Only with Azerbaijan's support for America after 9/11 were its requirements waived, though not rescinded. Given the generally pro-Armenian Western media and the outspoken Armenian diaspora, Azerbaijan's diplomatic struggle in 1992 was a long, steep, uphill battle that Elçibey's government was neither organized nor trained to handle.[29]

Even in the case of Turkey, the sole voice speaking up for Azerbaijan in international forums, the government's expectations were not matched by reality. Elçibey and the Azerbaijani elite did not fully comprehend the many constraints on Turkish foreign policy stemming from Ankara's membership in the North Atlantic Treaty Organization, its involvement in the long-running Cyprus dispute, and Armenian allegations of genocide in the massacres of 1915. Turkey turned out to be powerless in its attempts to prevent further Armenian military attacks on Azerbaijan, effectively counterbalanced by a resurgent Russia whose resolve Turkey could and would not challenge. The pro-Turkish vector in Azerbaijan's foreign policy thus failed to deliver what Elçibey hoped it would.

Karabakh: Initial Advances

Immediately after Elçibey came to power, his attempts to pool resources and put together an army did have at least one effect: once the voluntary formations that had arisen were subjected to the most rudimentary coordination by the Defense Ministry, Azerbaijan had the semblance of an army with a somewhat higher morale, and was able to up the ante in Mountainous Karabakh. The release of large amounts of weaponry from former Soviet military depots within Azerbaijan also helped provide a new beginning in the military field. In a June 1992 counteroffensive, Azerbaijani forces first took control of the Shaumyan region north of Karabakh, then crossed into Karabakh itself, where they captured most of the northern province of Mardakert, also known as Agdere. Stemming Armenian counteroffensives, the Azerbaijani forces approached Stepanakert and were beginning to plan ways to cut off Karabakh's link to Armenia via the Lachin corridor. But at this point, the command-and-control structure started to crack. The problem lay with defense minister Rahim Gaziyev, a Popular Front member who had developed surprisingly good personal relations with Russia, and Surat Huseynov, a factory boss turned guerrilla fighter who had used his wealth to assemble a private army and had taken to calling himself a colonel. Huseynov had 2,000 to 3,000 armed men who were not really involved in major battles, but were important because they held large tracts of the military front—especially in Kelbajar Province, the only part of the territories between Karabakh and Armenia that remained under Azerbaijani control. Events would soon confirm suspicions about the true loyalties of both Gaziyev and Huseynov.

The Downward Slide

February 1993 was the turning point for the Popular Front government. It was in that month that the government decisively began to lose its monopoly over the use of force, the most basic element of statehood. The slide began physically in Mountainous Karabakh, with the government losing control over its forces on the front.

Losing the Monopoly over the Use of Force

In early February 1993, an Armenian counteroffensive took back most of Mardakert Province, which had recently been reconquered by Azerbaijan.

Meanwhile, Armenian forces attacked Kelbajar Province, west of Karabakh—but the attacks came primarily from the west, that is, from Armenian territory, not from Armenian-held areas in Karabakh. This marked the
increasingly blatant involvement of the Armenian state in the war. At this
time, Surat Huseynov, who had been appointed presidential envoy in Mardakert and commander of the front in northern Karabakh, stopped taking
orders from Baku and pulled back heavy artillery from the front line.
Threatened with insubordination and apparent treason, Elçibey fired both
Huseynov and defense minister Gaziyev, whose loyalty had long been in
doubt.[30] But the pair did not simply resign. Gaziyev made a halfhearted
attempt to seize the Baku television tower, and Huseynov left the front with
his forces—making it painfully obvious that his soldiers were loyal to him
personally and not to the country. Huseynov returned to his stronghold at
Gandja, where the local head of administration was also fired for insubordination.[31] Armenians forces then rapidly rolled back all Azerbaijani advances in northern Karabakh and overran Kelbajar Province from east and
west, cleansing it of its mainly ethnic Kurdish population by early April.
Meanwhile, the Armenians began shelling another homogeneously Azerbaijani area outside Karabakh, Fizuli Province.[32]

   Azerbaijan now rapidly lost Karabakh and all lands to its west. The army
Elçibey had pieced together had fallen apart, due to the lack of a command
structure and the disloyalty of its highest officers. Moreover, the second-
largest city in the country, Gandja, was slipping from government control.
The remaining military formations collapsed like a house of cards, allowing Armenian forces in the following months to conquer the four provinces
connecting Karabakh to Iran almost without a fight and forcing 700,000
more Azerbaijanis to flee their homes. But this was not all: the government
itself began to crumble. Interior minister Iskender Hamidov continued his
practice of vendettas, personally beating up the editor of an opposition
newspaper in April. More worryingly, perhaps, the government's control
over law enforcement structures began to crumble. The regular police were
gradually returning to old Soviet practices, and Minister Hamidov's personal militia was an increasingly independent and unruly force.[33] By late
April, Elçibey gave in to pressure to fire the obviously unstable Hamidov,
and soon enough also his state secretary, Panakh Huseynov. Increasingly
isolated in a rapidly failing state, Elçibey himself turned increasingly passive and introverted.

Corruption and Mismanagement

For all the criticism leveled against Elçibey then and later, one thing is clear: his integrity has never been doubted. He was a true man of principles, who continued to live in his brother's apartment rather than move into the official residence he was entitled to. Strangely, in this he resembled Heydar Aliyev, likewise a native of Nakhichevan, who lived in his sister's apartment.

Unfortunately, Elçibey's government was not comparably principled; nor was the remainder of Azerbaijani officialdom during his administration. The advent of the market economy and Azerbaijan's opening to the world created many opportunities for personal gain; being in government provided the best vantage point from which to profit from these developments. Many did, not least those connected with the military such as the deposed interior minister Gaziyev, accused of embezzling millions of dollars. With no accountability, no judicial system, and no rule of law, the state degenerated into a free-for-all of corruption. By mid-1993, even international aid to the refugees fleeing the advancing Armenian forces was being diverted into the black market, with profits going into the pockets of officials.[34] Elected with great popular hopes, the Elçibey government was rapidly losing the benefit of the doubt once granted by its noncommunist, nationalist, and democratic credentials. If the Popular Front government was incapable of defending Karabakh and inept at setting up a functioning economy, that was bad enough in the eyes of the Azerbaijani public. But that the behavior of its ministers was deteriorating into a bad comedy, and an increasingly corrupt one at that, was unforgivable.

In the economic sector, as in many areas, the government displayed no clear strategy and changed policies frequently. Though a new national currency had been introduced, privatization laws had been enacted, and an influx of imported consumer products had begun, the regime paid a stiff penalty in public opinion for its failure to control inflation, which increased from an annual rate of 616 percent in 1992 to 1130 percent in 1993.[35] Price hikes, the loss of savings accounts and salaries, and other problems familiar from economies in transition took a hard toll on Azerbaijan's population. Meanwhile, social inequality grew rapidly as a clique of racketeers, officials, and businessmen made fortunes in no time. This likely brought back to mind the Communist propaganda about what capitalism led to in terms of economic exploitation.[36]

The Challenge of Ethnic Minorities

Corruption was not Elçibey's only problem: the ethnic issue was also becoming a distinct concern. Despite its strong tendency toward Azerbaijani nationalism, the Popular Front regime had kept its promises on minority policy, according full cultural autonomy to ethnic minorities such as the Lezgins and Talysh. Yet the combination of Turkist nationalist tendencies within the Popular Front and centrifugal forces among Lezgins and Talysh, supported by forces in Russia and Iran, respectively, led to increasing tensions between the government and ethnic minorities. Lezgins refused to be drafted into the military for the war effort in Mountainous Karabakh, and a Lezgin nationalist movement called Sadval emerged.[37] In the south, the ethnic Talysh colonel Alikram Humbätov had, by early 1993, stopped taking orders from Baku and began declaring his intention to create an autonomous "Talysh-Mugam" republic along the Iranian border.

It is difficult to determine what level of popular following these would-be breakaway groups had. Since little unrest existed either before or after the late Popular Front period, there is little that indicates the existence of strong separatist tendencies, particularly among the Talysh. As such, the movements were very much elite led, and inspired by foreign backers to weaken the government. But the minority populations were at least as dissatisfied as the rest of the Azerbaijani population, if not more so, because of the widespread identification of the government with Pan-Turkist forces. The fact that the (eventually disgraced) interior minister Gaziyev was a proud Pan-Turkist nationalist was certainly not lost on them. In an environment of collapsing state authority, it was hence easy for leaders appealing to ethnic sentiments to build a political platform, however tenuous this would turn out to be once the state was being rebuilt.

The Fall of the Popular Front Government

Late in spring 1993, the troubled Elçibey government received a sign of hope for the future: Prime Minister John Major of Britain invited President Elçibey to come to London in late June to sign an agreement on large-scale investments in the oil industry. This prospect meant several things. Most immediately, the government could receive advance payments on investments, which would help its cash-strapped budget and perhaps even enable it to turn the tables in Mountainous Karabakh. The war was being fought with such rudimentary weapons that even comparatively small upgrades in equipment or forces, such as the addition of a few fighter jets, could make a difference. Indeed, Azerbaijan had already enlisted help by bringing in several hundred Afghan mujahideen. These men made a difference on the battlefield, and the promise of millions of petrodollars could have helped Azerbaijan acquire modern equipment and professional assistance if properly utilized. The mujahideen deployment was nevertheless unsuccessful, because the Afghans posed more problems than they helped resolve. To begin with, the culture clash was too great between the hard-drinking Azerbaijani soldiers and commanders and the pious Afghans—aside from the inherent suspicion the devoutly Sunni Afghans felt toward the Shia Azerbaijanis. Second, because the Azerbaijani military command structure had collapsed, no one really controlled the Afghans. Third, an ill-advised decision had been made to bring in Afghans from clans that did not get along well. A purportedly true anecdote tells of an incident in which the front line suddenly came alive with gunfire, even though neither the Azerbaijani nor the Armenian side was shooting—a fact that was ascertained as the two opposing commanders made contact with one another. It was the Afghans, shooting at each other—which led to a cease-fire between Armenian and Azerbaijani forces that lasted as long as it took to pack up the Afghans and get them away from the front.[38]

If quick monetary gain was to be an outcome of the London meeting, more important perhaps was the shift in Western attention that would likely result from the event. Oil was the only real foreign-policy tool Azerbaijan had, but Baku had been unable to use it. Western oil investment would in time generate a lobby for Azerbaijan in Western corridors of power (and with it a vested interest in the country's future), and would restore some balance in the Western view of the conflict with Armenia. Most of all, it would provide the government with the opportunity to build up its oil industry independently from Russia and acquire a serious source of long-term income over which Moscow had no say. Bluntly, Western investments in oil would cut the proverbial umbilical cord that tied Azerbaijan's economy and politics to Moscow. All of this was to happen, but not rapidly enough to save the Elçibey government or keep Karabakh in Azerbaijani hands.

It may seem counterintuitive that Azerbaijan was the first former Soviet republic to become free of Russian military forces—achieving this status even before Germany and the Baltic republics. But that is indeed what happened, though, as one might very well intuit about the period, the immediate outcome was not a happy one for Baku. On May 24 and 25, 1993, the Russian 104th Infantry Regiment left its base at Gandja and headed north back to Russia, half a year ahead of schedule. This event was indeed unique: other states had to go through excruciating negotiations, forced delays, diplomatic tricks and pressure, and the payment of subventions to remove Russian military installations from their territories. There was a catch, of course. The Russians "forgot" to bring their military hardware along—or to leave it to the Azerbaijani government, as the treaty concluded between the two states had provided. Instead, they left the equipment to Surat Huseynov, garrisoned with his private army less than a mile away from the 104th Infantry Regiment's freshly vacated barracks.[39]

After a botched attempt by Elçibey to take control of the weaponry, Huseynov capitalized on the incident by accusing the government of attacking his forces, starting a civil war, and killing more than sixty people. In reality, fewer than four people were killed in the confrontation.[40] But it did constitute yet another proof of the government's ineptitude, led to three high officials and hundreds of troops being taken hostage, and provided an excuse for Huseynov to advance political demands. He insisted on the resignation of the speaker of the Parliament, Isa Gambar, and of Panakh Huseynov, now prime minister, and declared that he would march on Baku. As his forces started out, they met no resistance from the military: not wanting a repeat of the civil war that had broken out in Tbilisi when Georgia's first president, Zviad Gamsakhurdia, was ousted in January 1992, Elçibey had ordered the troops not to fire. But Huseynov raised the stakes: he would no longer be satisfied with anything less than the president's resignation. As his troops moved closer to Baku, the total collapse of the state and its takeover by a warlord seemed increasingly plausible—just as had occurred in Georgia in early 1992, when criminalized militia leaders seized power from a discredited, increasingly paranoid nationalist leader with a dissident background. Apart from Elçibey being much more of a democrat than Gamsakhurdia, the parallels were striking.

Aliyev Intervenes

On June 9, Elçibey called Heydar Aliyev in Nakhichevan, asking him to come to Baku to help resolve the crisis. The next day, Aliyev arrived in Baku aboard a Turkish government jet. After again refusing the post of prime minister and speeding to Gandja to meet Surat Huseynov, Aliyev was named speaker of Parliament following Gambar's hasty and reluctant resignation. The grounds for Aliyev's appointment were tenuous, but had a veneer of legality given his position as speaker of Nakhichevan's parliament, which made him, ex officio, second deputy speaker of the Azerbaijani Supreme Soviet. On June 18, with Huseynov's forces at Baku's gates, Elçibey left the capital for his native village of Keleki in Nakhichevan, where he would spend the next several years in internal exile. He did not resign from the presidency, however, even though he was stripped by Parliament of most of his powers on June 24. At the end of the month, Aliyev struck a deal with Huseynov, appointing the warlord prime minister, in charge also of the ministries of defense and interior. This appeared to be a capitulation, but as Goltz observed, it actually meant giving Huseynov responsibilities he could not handle: "Surat had just been given a long, oily rope with which to hang himself."[41] Aliyev soon had his elevation to the presidency confirmed by a referendum of no confidence in Elçibey, held in late August. While the percentage of the anti-Elçibey vote was obviously inflated, there was no doubt that the vast majority of the population, perhaps more than three-quarters, according to observers, voted against the incumbent president. The restoration of Aliyev, in spite of its doubtful legality, clearly had public legitimacy, as did the unseating of the Popular Front.

The evidence that Surat Husyenov's coup was engineered in Moscow is as incontrovertible as it gets. The Elçibey government was doing a pretty good job of destroying its public legitimacy by its own actions, but the Russian government helped it on its way. In fact, Moscow slowly strangled the Popular Front government. Russia responded to every refusal to accede to the CIS or to accept a long-term Russian military presence on Azerbaijan's soil by disbursing a little more weaponry to Armenia; spreading disinformation through the Russian media about Azerbaijani attacks in Mountainous Karabakh when it was the Armenians who were on the offensive; cranking up support for Lezgin or Talysh separatist forces; and undermining the Azerbaijani economy, all the while making it perfectly clear that all this would stop if Azerbaijan would just return to the fold. And Azerbaijan was not alone: Georgia under President Eduard Shevardnadze was being subjected to exactly the same treatment at exactly the same time.[42] But Moscow had time, and was roasting Elçibey slowly—that is, until the news of his impending visit to London, which meant that the plug needed to be pulled on the Popular Front government lest it reverse its fortunes with foreign help. Thus the troops were withdrawn, Huseynov was activated, and the government crumbled.

Given Heydar Aliyev's personal history with the KGB in the days of the Soviet Union, the general assumption in retrospect was that he was part of Moscow's plan. But it rapidly became clear that this was far from the truth. Moscow's plan was in all likelihood to have Mutalibov returned to power, an intention that seemed all the more likely a year later when Huseynov attempted a coup against Aliyev but fled to Russia, where he immediately joined forces with Mutalibov. Heydar Aliyev was not part of the plan: he had stolen the coup from Huseynov. If there was a foreign hand behind Aliyev, it was in Ankara. For several months, Turkish president Süleyman Demirel had tried to convince Aliyev to return to Baku to help President Elçibey put Azerbaijan back on track. Elçibey had agreed to offer Aliyev the post of prime minister, but Aliyev had refused at least twice.[43] Perhaps things had to get even worse before Aliyev could return as the country's savior.

Once returned to the presidency, Aliyev in no way became a pushover: he developed into as a staunch a defender of Azerbaijan's independence as Elçibey had been, only more tactful and pragmatic in his implementation of that ideal. He joined the CIS, a move that cost Azerbaijan little, and promised to discuss Russian military bases and border guards with Moscow. But the Russian forces were out of Azerbaijan, and would never return. Indeed, Moscow's dissatisfaction with Aliyev would grow so much that in October 1994, Huseynov, again in the context of an impending international oil contract, would try to overthrow him.

Conclusions

The Azerbaijani Popular Front government came to power under inauspicious conditions. Indeed, its inability to assert control over the institutions of the state led to corruption and mismanagement—most blatantly the debacle in the war with Armenia—and consigned the Elçibey administration to failure. It proved incapable of meeting the challenges facing the nation and thus lost popularity—and the war—within less than a year. This in turn led to the end of the "democratic interlude" in Azerbaijan's transition to independence, a process paralleled in all the other southern republics of the former Soviet Union that had experienced the liberalization of their political system at independence. Armenia, Georgia, and Tajikistan likewise witnessed a strengthening tendency back toward authoritarianism after democratization came to be identified with civil war, economic collapse, and general misery.

But the Popular Front should also be remembered for several important achievements. Despite the challenge of balancing political reform with national defense and state building, Azerbaijan managed to hold presidential elections in June 1992 that, given the circumstances, were reasonably free and fair. Once in power, the APF generally put its liberal and democratic principles into practice: as chaotic as it was and despite its failures and disappointments, the year the Popular Front spent in power was one of political freedoms that Azerbaijan had never known before. In retrospect, it was something that Azerbaijan's political culture was unable to live up to and to sustain. Yet it provided an indelible experience that would remain in the public memory.

Had Mutalibov stayed in power, Azerbaijan might have resembled the political systems of Central Asia; but the mark of openness and pluralism left by the Elçibey era meant that, throughout the subsequent Aliyev era, Azerbaijan would remain a pluralistic if not democratic polity. The foundations of pluralism and openness had been laid; these principles would challenge the Aliyev government from within, and empower progressive forces both within and outside the government to push back against the remaining autocratic tendencies of the old ruling class.

5

The Aliyev Era: Restoring Stability

Heydar Aliyev's return to power was greeted with great expectations: things would go back to normal. And order, indeed, is what Aliyev brought Azerbaijan. Within two years, he had consolidated power and built a political system tailor-made to his own personality. He had sued for a cease-fire in Mountainous Karabakh while moving aggressively to take advantage of Azerbaijan's oil resources. Finally, he had launched a successful campaign to elevate the country's place in the world. These accomplishments did not come without cost, however. What was lost was the fledgling democracy the country had begun to enjoy. Of course, *enjoy* would be the wrong term: to most Azerbaijanis (just like most Russians or Georgians), democracy had come to be perceived as synonymous with political anarchy, massive theft of state property, and internal disorder.

Consolidating Power

In the conditions of Azerbaijan in 1993, Aliyev's consolidation of power meant at least five things. First and foremost, it meant reassertion of control over the state, and, by implication, reinstatement of a system of control over the informal structures of power—the country's entrenched economic, regional, and functional interest groups. Second, consolidation meant the restoration of a monopoly on power through the removal of disloyal elements within the system that could threaten Aliyev's position. The third element was ending the largest distraction to state building, the war with Armenia, which had brought down the presidencies of both Ayaz Mutalibov and Abulfez Elçibey. Fourth, consolidation meant building a formal system of power, that is, the legal foundations of political power such as a constitution, a parliament, and political parties. Fifth, and finally, it implied legitimizing power externally—that is, winning the acceptance of Azerbaijan's neighbors and the international community, chiefly the West.

Rebuilding the Aliyev Political Network

Referring to the selection of Heydar Aliyev to lead Soviet Azerbaijan in 1969, John Willerton noted that "Aliev's selection signaled the application of a particular set of solutions to the stagnating republic: a set of solutions grounded in the reestablishment of discipline within the hierarchy of party and state bodies."[1] Had those words been written in reference to Aliyev's 1993 comeback, they would have been equally true. This time, there was no Soviet Union and Aliyev was beholden to absolutely nobody for his power. But if Aliyev had stepped into a stagnating Soviet republic in 1969, in 1993 he was taking the reins of a collapsing newly independent state. On both occasions, within the constraints that were present, Aliyev's priority was to rebuild a functioning state that delivered public order and economic growth.

The constraints on both occasions were obvious and, moreover, the same: in the political and economic entity known as Azerbaijan, powerful informal institutions, loyalties, and networks matter at least as much as formal political institutions. This reality goes far back: czarist officials in the nineteenth century had struggled hard to dismantle the regionalism and vested interests ensconced in the rival khanates; during 1918–20, the First Republic had faced the dilemma of handling the very real power of the large landowners; and Soviet Azerbaijan became notorious, to an even greater extent than Georgia or the republics of Central Asia, for the resilience of informal kinship and regional ties that were sustained under the communist surface and penetrated deep into Soviet institutions. By 1969, these relationships had managed to bring Azerbaijan's progress to a grinding halt. But in that year, Aliyev came to power with an explicit mandate to clean up the rampant corruption, nepotism, and mismanagement that had made the Azerbaijan of his predecessors, Imam Mustafayev and Vali Akhundov, one of the worst-performing republics in the Soviet Union.

Aliyev executed this reform mandate by purging state institutions, filling positions of authority with people whose loyalty he absolutely trusted. In many cases these were people with managerial skills and discipline, or people he had personally supervised in Nakhichevan, or, like himself, people with experience in the security services. Moreover, people in positions of power were frequently rotated geographically and functionally to prevent them from building personal fiefdoms that would challenge both the efficiency of the state and institutional loyalty to Aliyev.

In sum, Aliyev built his own patronage network to replace the old one; but he built one that ran on time and delivered economic progress and political stability. Clearly there were winners and losers, and Aliyev's former KGB colleagues and the Nakhichevani and Yeraz elites were most prominent among the winners. But the system delivered, to such a surprising extent that Aliyev was promoted to the highest offices in the Soviet Union.

In 1993, the task was to restore the basic functioning of government institutions in a near-failed state where the advent of market economics without institutional constraints was rapidly creating an ungovernable kleptocracy. This meant getting the government to deliver the basic functions of statehood to the population, and to assert control over state institutions. In 1993, economic production stood at less than 40 percent of 1990 levels, and government officials received the equivalent of a few dozen dollars a month in pay. That meant that the resources necessary to build a professional, noncorrupt, and efficient state were simply absent, as was trained staff with modern skills. Corruption was a fact, and could not be wished away. Rather, it had to be tamed.

Aliyev's recipe was an adaptation of his old, tested model of authoritative as well as authoritarian rule, reconciling the reality of informal structures of power with the needs of a modern state. This implied building a patronage system that actually *supported* the building of a state, rather than undermining the state by creating anarchy. In other words, corruption had to be tolerated but also brought under control—anarchic and uncontrolled corruption had to be replaced by a form of controlled, structured, almost feudal relations. The key concept here is control: in a collapsed economy, what is known in the West as corruption is an instrument without which the government cannot keep the state together. In the absence of loyalties based on ideology or respect for law, and without resources to pay officials a salary they can live on, corruption serves as a legitimizing factor and a way to maintain the support of the elite and power ministries, a necessity if the ruler's position is to be stable. In more than one respect, this arrangement resembles a feudal system, in which the ruler delegates certain economic functions to a baron or bureaucrat in exchange for loyalty. The crux, of course, is how to change a system running on informal transfers of money and influence into one in which these exchanges are formalized and occur within the law. That issue would be dealt with later; in 1993 Aliyev restored the now half-dismantled system of power he had built up in the 1970s, which rested upon his personal authority and intimate knowledge both of the country and of the officials he would bring back to power.

Removing the Challengers

The monopoly on the use of force had collapsed to such a degree that power in 1993 was roughly commensurate with the number of armed men a person controlled. Personnel in the armed units nominally belonging to the state were, as a rule, loyal not to the state but to their individual commander, from whose pocket their pay normally came, often as a result of involvement in illegal business of some sort.[2] One of Aliyev's key priorities was therefore reestablishing the state's monopoly on the use of force. It should be recalled that Aliyev had not come to power with the help of militia groups, nor did he control any of his own. But others did, such as Surat Huseynov, the paramilitary commander who had been largely responsible for the removal of Aliyev's predecessor, Elçibey. Such men posed a serious challenge to Aliyev's power base while making him vulnerable to the influence of the warlords and, by extension, their external backers.

Aliyev's first challenger was Aliakram Humbatov, a renegade militia commander in the southern Lenkoran Province. Humbatov was a self-proclaimed representative of the Talysh minority group, which numbers several hundred thousand in Lenkoran and adjacent regions of Azerbaijan. Generally speaking, the Talysh are well integrated into Azerbaijani society and heavily intermarried with Azeris. Colonel Humbatov took the opportunity of unrest in the summer of 1993 to declare an independent Talysh-Mugan republic on August 7, and attempted to fortify its borders. The name drew on the pro-Bolshevik Mugan Soviet Republic, which existed briefly from March to June 1919 in opposition to the First republic. The idea of independence nevertheless failed to gain popularity among most Talysh people, and seemed closely linked to political games that had occurred in Baku at the time of the June coup. Humbatov was allied with Huseynov, and his bid may have served to weaken Aliyev's position. But Aliyev, understanding the lack of popular support for the uprising, urged the people to take action against Humbatov. Crowds gathered around Humbatov's offices, and soon his republic was no more—without the government having to make a serious effort to intervene. Humbatov fled to Iran but was soon extradited to Azerbaijan. He was sentenced to death for high treason in 1996, but was pardoned in 2004 and moved into exile in the Netherlands.

In the year that followed Humbatov's gambit, Aliyev took several steps to build up his power: settling the open warfare in Mountainous Karabakh, conducting a referendum on his deposed predecessor's presidency, and building international relations based in great part on oil. Moreover, under the newly appointed minister of the interior and Aliyev loyalist Ramil Usubov, the government sought to bring to heel various semi-independent armed factions and put away their leaders, such as former defense minister Rahim Gaziyev.

But in September 1994, a crisis erupted. Not surprisingly, it was linked to oil diplomacy. On September 20, Aliyev and a consortium of Western energy multinationals signed a thirty-year production-sharing agreement covering the Azeri, Chirag, and Guneshli oil fields. The deal, worth US$8 billion, was soon dubbed the "contract of the century."[3] The very next day, four high-profile prisoners on trial for treason, including Humbatov and Gaziyev, "escaped" to Moscow from the Azerbaijani security service's detention facilities in Baku, something said to be impossible. Aliyev, who should know, said as much the next day, and fired his national security minister. A few days later two high officials, including a deputy speaker of Parliament, were assassinated, and members of Parliament began receiving anonymous phone calls telling them to veto the contract lest they be next.[4] Three members of the OMON, the special-purpose police forces, were arrested for the murders. The OMON, in particular a crack unit of 200 especially well-trained personnel, were controlled by a deputy minister of the interior, Rovshan Javadov. On October 2, Javadov's forces stormed the prosecutor general's office and freed the three arrested men; government forces surrounded the building, and the army was called out to protect strategic installations. A spokesman for the Ministry of Defense found it necessary to make a televised announcement stating the full loyalty of the army to the president. Aliyev declared a state of emergency and negotiated with Javadov, who after a brief firefight had retreated to his base on the outskirts of Baku.

Meanwhile, reports of unrest in Gandja had surfaced. Huseynov's troops had apparently cordoned off the city and seized strategic installations.[5] Aliyev now made a passionate appeal to the people of Azerbaijan on national television, asking young and old alike to assemble at the presidential palace in order to protect the independence of the country. He blamed unnamed foreign forces, obviously implying Russia, of seeking to undermine the country's independence. Aliyev assumed he had the people's support, and gambled that they would turn out both to shield him against any possible attack and to send a clear message to his internal and external rivals that the time when a band of armed men could take over the country was over. Reportedly, Aliyev then nervously waited in his office, constantly checking his watch.[6]

He did not have to wait long. Within minutes crowds began to assemble, swelling to several thousand people within an hour. Javadov then softened his stance, claiming loyalty to the president but demanding that a number of leading figures be fired. Appearing at the scene, he pledged full support for Aliyev.[7] The next day, Aliyev presided over an even larger popular gathering in Freedom Square on Baku's Caspian Sea shoreline. Flanked by Surat Huseynov, Aliyev denounced the uprising in Gandja and announced what had become clear to everyone: that elements in the government were involved in a coup against the head of state, together with Ayaz Mutalibov and the former head of the KGB of the Azerbaijan Soviet Socialist Republic, Vagif Huseynov (no relation to Surat Huseynov). Aliyev then delivered the coup de grâce, directly accusing Surat Huseynov of complicity in a coup against the legitimate government of the country—a government that, ironically, Prime Minister Huseynov himself nominally headed.[8] Within days, Huseynov was placed under house arrest, removed from his post, and stripped of his parliamentary seat. He then escaped to the Russian-controlled Qabala radar station in northern Azerbaijan, from which he was airlifted by Russian security services to a military base in the North Caucasus, and from there to Moscow.[9]

If the external links of the September coup were no surprise to either Aliyev or anyone else, the coup attempt that took place only six months later, in March 1995, did not fit the mold. This time, Rovshan Javadov took advantage of Aliyev's absence from the country to make another bid for power. Javadov's call for members of the Azerbaijani Popular Front and Chechen groups in Baku to rise up and support the coup indicated the different connections Javadov had built on. But Chechen president Jokhar Dudayev instructed all Chechens to stay at home, and only a few scattered former Popular Front officials responded, while the masses stayed home.

Javadov's OMON forces had gradually degenerated into a criminal group, involved in various types of smuggling and cooperating with elements of Turkish far-right nationalist organizations. These groups' connections to organized crime and elements of the Turkish state were uncovered in the aftermath of an infamous car crash in Susurluk in western Turkey, which gradually led to the uncovering of police and state ties to organized crime in the country. Aliyev's efforts to get the law enforcement agencies under control had begun to put pressure on these types of forces, which, in response, hatched a plot to remove him from office. Unlike earlier coups, moreover, this one clearly was aimed at killing the president. Elements of the Turkish intelligence services, and possibly the Turkish embassy in Baku, appear to have been involved in the planned coup. In any event,

Aliyev was convinced that this was the case, as is Turkish journalist Irfan Ülkü, who detailed the episode in his 2000 book on Azerbaijan.[10]

Javadov had planned to have Aliyev assassinated immediately upon the president's return from a summit in Copenhagen of the OSCE. But in an action that made the Turkish connection seem even more complex, Aliyev was reportedly tipped off by Turkish president Süleyman Demirel, as the Turkish intelligence services had begun to unearth the plot. This last-minute warning prompted Aliyev to leave for Baku early on March 16. He ordered an assault on Javadov's headquarters that ended the revolt and led to Javadov's death from injuries incurred during the shootout. The episode made it clear that Aliyev, who had shown remarkable leniency regarding Huseynov's coup attempt against him, drew the line when a coup plotter meant to assassinate him. Javadov's was the last armed revolt in Aliyev's Azerbaijan, and the turning point after which the government regained its monopoly on the use of force.[11]

The two coups had profound implications for Azerbaijan's foreign relations. Aliyev for good reason had not trusted Russia, but his erstwhile affinity with Turkey took a beating with the March 1995 coup. It was only his personal relationship with President Demirel that prevented him from making the affair public at the time; the details only appeared almost three years later in the Turkish media. Shortly after the events, Aliyev made his famous speech to the Turkish Parliament in which he delineated the principle of *Bir millet, iki dövlet* ("One nation, two states"). Azerbaijan's relationship with Turkey remained cordial, but had lost the emotional feeling of kinship and trust that had earlier made it a truly "special relationship." Practically, this made Azerbaijan a rather lonely member of the international community: already at war with Armenia, it faced meddling in its internal affairs, including the sponsoring of uprisings, by Russia, Iran, and now elements in Turkey. Aliyev's decision to build strong, direct ties to the West, not least the United States, may very well have received significant impetus from this experience.

The Tabling of Karabakh

The third imperative for consolidating power and building the state was to bring the war in Mountainous Karabakh to a halt. Armenia had rapidly exploited the rare opportunity provided by Azerbaijan's chaos and anarchy. As had happened at every juncture of the war in Karabakh, Azerbaijan lost territory during the summer and fall of 1993 because all attention was focused on power struggles in Baku. By June 28, 1993, Mardakert Province, in northern Karabakh, was securely in Armenian hands. Seeing the disarray of the Azerbaijani forces on the eastern and southern fronts, the Armenians moved on July 4 to besiege Agdam, a strategic town just east of Karabakh from which Azerbaijani forces had shelled Armenian positions, including Stepanakert. Agdam fell on July 23, and was burned and looted.

The Armenians next turned to the city of Fizuli, to the southeast of Karabakh. This move indicated that Armenia had decided to conquer the entire swath of land connecting Karabakh to Iran, where more than half a million Azerbaijanis lived. Doing so would provide Armenia with an easily defensible border and spare it the problem of having a southern front in Karabakh. With Azerbaijani forces in total disarray, Fizuli fell on August 23, followed days later by neighboring Jebrail.

The Armenian forces then slowly moved west, having secured the gateway to Karabakh but left a short strip of territory as an escape route for the fleeing masses of Azerbaijanis. After a short unilateral cease-fire by the Armenian forces, to regroup and allow for new supplies of troops, arms, and equipment to be delivered from Armenia proper, the campaign restarted. In short order, Zangilan on the Iranian border and Qubatli south of the Lachin corridor also fell, as did the town of Huradiz, south of Fizuli. That cut the escape route for the remaining several thousand civilians in encircled Zangilan, who had resolutely refused to leave their homes, even at the risk of a new Khojaly massacre. Adding to the half-million refugees already expelled from these areas, the last remaining civilians were forced to swim over the Araks River to Iran; hundreds drowned.

Armenia's blatantly expansionist moves were too much for the international community to stomach. Despite overwhelming evidence to the contrary, Armenian officials said they had nothing to do with the attacks, yet justified the expulsion of 700,000 people in the name of the security of the perhaps 120,000 Armenians living in Karabakh.[12] But this rationalization did not placate the international community, whose patience with the Armenian advances was running out. For their part, regional powers began to show unease as well. Both Turkey and Iran threatened to intervene, generating a crisis that also concerned Russia. With tensions at their highest level yet, Turkey massed 50,000 troops on the Armenian border. Also mobilizing its armed forces, Iran threatened Armenia with intervention, impelled at least in part by the refugee crisis in Azerbaijani-populated northern Iran, which was rapidly making the Iranian government's neutral stance toward the conflict highly unpopular at home. Even Russia issued a threat, informing Armenia that the invasions of Azerbaijani territory would harm bilateral relations.[13] The crisis gradually dissipated as Armenian advances came to a halt. By late 1993 Aliyev had joined the Commonwealth of Independent States, thereby meeting one of Moscow's long-standing demands on Azerbaijan. As if by magic, this action resulted in the release of additional Soviet-era weaponry and may have induced the Russian government to make some military advisers available. Soon thereafter Azerbaijan counterattacked, prompting the Armenian national army to cross the border into Azerbaijan on a larger scale than ever before to defend its newly achieved territorial gains. Azerbaijan managed to take back some territory, but at great cost, and within a short time the conflict was at a stalemate. Armenia had bitten off much more than it could chew, while Aliyev had no real army to fight back with. It was time to sue for peace, at least for the time being.

The OSCE's so-called Minsk Group had long been working on a cease-fire deal, but it was upstaged on May 16, 1994, when Russian defense minister Pavel Grachev managed to secure an agreement signed by President Aliyev and his Armenian counterpart, Levon Ter-Petrossian. The cease-fire remained in force in 2009, though small-scale yet lethal violations had regularly occurred over the years. Some of the largest violations took place in March 2008, immediately after Armenia's disputed elections, when over 20 soldiers on both sides were killed.[14]

With Azerbaijan having been roundly defeated, Aliyev now focused on building the state, turning to diplomatic means to resolve the conflict. He nevertheless vowed from the outset to keep the military option open for a later day should diplomacy fail.

It is ironic that had Armenia stopped at conquering Karabakh and perhaps securing the Lachin corridor, it might have gotten away with it in the court of international public opinion. After all, rightly or wrongly, the Armenians of Karabakh had come to be seen as victims in the conflict, and Azerbaijan conceivably may have adapted to the new reality, though it would hardly have accepted it. But the conquest of an additional 10 percent of Azerbaijan's territory and the expulsion of nearly three-quarters of a million people from their homes constituted such a humiliation that it became impossible for any Azerbaijani leader to concede the loss of Karabakh. Aliyev, or any other Azerbaijani leader, had no choice but to promise that all territories, including Karabakh, would be returned to Azerbaijan. Moreover, the conquests of 1993 marked the zenith of Armenia's international position. Up to that point, protestations that Armenia was the victim of the conflict, mainly on the grounds that Armenians are generally victims and Turks generally aggressors, had played well in the West. But with the facts on the ground being clear, and pictures spreading across the world of the ethnic cleansing of southwestern Azerbaijan and the ensuing humanitarian disaster, the traditional image of Armenia not only rang hollow but was exposed as an outright lie. From that moment, Azerbaijan began its uphill but eventually successful struggle to turn world opinion around.

The 1995 Constitution: Institutionalizing Presidentialism

The fourth objective in Aliyev's consolidation of power was to legitimize the formal underpinnings of his position. This meant first and foremost legitimizing his accession to the highest office in the land, and, in the longer run, establishing a presidential system of government by means of a new constitution and parliamentary elections.

Aliyev began the process with a referendum on the fate of former president Elçibey. The vote, conducted on August 30, 1993, produced a thundering verdict of no confidence. The outcome was so obvious that Aliyev's election officials hardly needed to do much to inflate the anti-Elçibey margin. But a precedent was nevertheless set for future elections in Azerbaijan. Whether because of the zeal of low-level officials, the demands of the presidential office, or a combination of both, victory margins would be inflated even when the outcome was clear. Consequently, Azerbaijan's international reputation was gratuitously tarnished. Such tampering would mar the 1993, 1998, 2003 and 2008 presidential elections, and the 2000 and 2005 parliamentary elections.

On October 3, 1993, Aliyev was elected president with a reported 98.8 percent of the vote and an official 96 percent turnout—distinctly Brezhnevian numbers—with only two unknown politicians allowed to contest the vote. Parliamentary elections were scheduled for November 12, 1995; in the meantime, a legislative framework was being built.

President Aliyev convened a Constitutional Commission in June 1995 to replace the redundant 1978 Soviet constitution that remained in force. The Commission presented a first draft in October, and the final version was approved by referendum after having been publicly available for only six days on November 12.[15] The Constitution provided for separation of powers, including an independent judiciary and an elected parliament with considerable responsibilities; nevertheless, the emphasis was clearly upon the extensive powers granted to the office of the president. The Constitution's article 109 outlines a broad list of 32 paragraphs of powers given to the president. These include appointing or dismissing the prime minister and the cabinet members, as well as the prosecutor general, judges, and high-ranking military officers. Aside from this and many other rights and responsibilities, the president can also "form special security bodies." Clearly, Heydar Aliyev intended Azerbaijan to be a presidential republic, tailored to his own vision of state-building.

An electoral law was put in place in August 1995, stipulating that 100 of Parliament's 125 representatives would be elected in single-member constituencies, while the remainder were to be chosen on party lists. Parliamentary elections would coincide with a referendum on the constitutional draft, prepared by a commission headed by Aliyev.

In a tightly controlled environment, several opposition parties were prevented from running, as were 60 percent of the candidates in single-members constituencies. The elections produced resounding approval of the constitution, but also a Parliament totally dominated by the ruling Yeni Azerbaijan Party (YAP; also referred to as "New Azerbaijan"). Small numbers of seats were won by the Azerbaijani Popular Front, now led by Elçibey's deputy, Ali Kerimli, and the Azerbaijani National Independence Party, led by Etibar Mamedov (no relation to Yaqub Mamedov). The elections were characterized as neither free nor fair by international observers, but they did provide a formal legal basis for the political institutions of post-Soviet Azerbaijan, correcting one of the largest blunders of the Popular Front government. Following the 1995 elections, however, the opposition was gradually given greater representation in Parliament through by-elections, eventually coming to control more than a quarter of the seats. This was a trend that would be repeated in each parliamentary election: the government would win big, the opposition and foreign observers would protest, and as a result a few more opposition figures would be allowed to take seats in order to keep peace and avoid international condemnation. In a sense, this trend dated to the rule of Ayaz Mutalibov, who had agreed to equal government and opposition representation in the fifty-member National Council carved out of the 350-member Supreme Soviet of Azerbaijan in 1991.

The Quest for International Legitimacy

Finally, Aliyev needed to legitimize his position internationally. This was done partially through the formal, nominally democratic procedures of elections and constitutions, but mainly through diplomacy. Oil was a key element in this process, as Aliyev astutely used international interest in the country's oil riches as a way to foster relations with foreign leaders. He built the oil consortium mainly with Western multinationals, including American companies such as Amoco, Unocal, Exxon, and Pennzoil, as well as European companies such as Norway's Statoil and the consortium's operator, British Petroleum. (BP's share doubled after its acquisition of Amoco.) Others were also invited, including Japan's Itochu, the Turkish Petroleum Corporation, and Saudi Delta Oil. Aliyev then gladly cut up Azerbaijan's own 20 percent share and provided half of that to Russia's Lukoil, in a measure to placate Russian objections to the deal. In the process, he drove a wedge between Russian energy interests (which wanted a share) and the Russian Foreign Ministry (which had sought to stop the deal). Aliyev also initially promised Iran a 5 percent share, but U.S. pressure eventually forced him to renege, at great diplomatic cost.

Most of all, aside from oil, it was the pragmatist and experienced diplomat in Aliyev that built his international legitimacy. A senior statesman by any standard, Aliyev deployed his personal charisma and to some extent his Soviet- era fame in winning access to the corridors of power in Western capitals. Not least among these was Washington, where a constituency of interest in the Caucasus and Caspian region was growing, related not only to oil but to U.S. geostrategic interests. By 1997, Aliyev had managed to assemble a significant constituency of support in the U.S. capital, including former high-level officials such as Zbigniew Brzezinski, Brent Scowcroft, John Sununu, Richard Cheney, Lloyd Bentsen, James Baker, Richard Armitage, and Lawrence Eagleburger. Aliyev's efforts gradually turned the tide in the West, earning Azerbaijan status as a strategic partner of the United States by the late 1990s.[16]

Muddling Through: 1997–2003

By 1997, Heydar Aliyev had effected a remarkable turnaround in Azerbaijan. The country was now both politically and economically stable. Billions of dollars were flowing into the oil industry, beefing up the country's macroeconomic indicators but generating few jobs, something that disappointed some of the population's expectations. Nevertheless, the chaos of the early 1990s had generated a national desire for stability and order that gave Aliyev room to maneuver in the face of popular demands for democracy and freedom and helped him manage the political opposition. In all this, as the next chapter shows, he was aided—in fact, until his death and beyond—by the utter inability of the opposition groups to admit their failure of 1992–93 and reform themselves accordingly.

Politics and Society: Semiauthoritarianism in Practice

Azerbaijan under Heydar Aliyev's rule is best described as a semiauthoritarian society, a concept defined by Marina Ottaway as an "ambiguous system that combines rhetorical acceptance of liberal democracy, the existence of some formal democratic institutions, and respect for a limited sphere of civil and political liberties with essentially illiberal or even authoritarian traits."[17] Indeed, the Azerbaijani population at large felt no particular repression, as freedom of speech was generally respected. Urban dwellers could pick up an opposition newspaper and read grave accusations, bordering on slander, against government officials, and political parties functioned openly, though they were occasionally subjected to official harassment. In the countryside, hierarchical social structures that had survived the Soviet Union remained, steeped in respect for authority. As such, Azerbaijani society in the 1990s returned to a structure characterized by clearly defined social classes, an arrangement that was not paralleled, for example, in much more egalitarian and individualistic Georgia. Only genuine political activists and journalists, and the radical opposition, found themselves systematically in officialdom's line of fire.

As Daniel Heradstveit and Kari Eken Strømmen have shown, Aliyev's conception of his own position was that of a benevolent autocrat, a father figure who had saved the country from destruction.[18] From this understanding flowed his long-term ambitions, as well as his view of the opposition as political small fry. During his absence from power, from 1987 to 1993, the country self-destructed, undoing—as he saw it—the progress he had presided over during 1969–83, for which he took personal credit. The Popular Front government had alienated and isolated him; then it presided over a collapse of the country, only to escape, as Aliyev would put it, "like a mother who abandons her children"—a telling analogy, since it strengthens the impression of his paternalistic conception of the people of Azerbaijan as his children. Yet the opposition was now back, shamelessly claiming a right to wield power and to influence decisions—daring to tell Aliyev how to run the country.[19]

A recurring feature of Aliyev's own view was that democracy might be a long-term goal, but immediate introduction of its procedures and trappings was not necessarily the means to stable representative government. He tirelessly reminded Western interlocutors of the centuries it took them to build democracy, and that Azerbaijan only a few years earlier had lived in chaos and anarchy. Building democracy, he said, was the goal; but it would be achieved gradually, through the building of institutions, a market economy, and political culture. In the meantime, the country needed stability and control, which Aliyev was happy to provide. One of his most famous statements, from a 1997 speech in Washington at Georgetown University, illustrates this viewpoint:

> Some people think we should be able to establish democracy in a short time, but that is impossible. Azerbaijan is a young nation and democracy is a new concept. The United States has been advancing on the path of democracy for a long time—more than 200 years. You have achieved a lot, but you are still working on it. Democracy is not an apple you buy at the market and bring back home.[20]

This worldview, in which a domestic challenger to his own personality and authority was tantamount to unthinkable, governed Aliyev's rule. Indeed, while perhaps viewing democracy as an ideal end state for Azerbaijan, Aliyev repeatedly said that he was bequeathing the remainder of his life to the nation. Leaving office during his lifetime was, it seems, simply not something that occurred to Heydar Aliyev—or that he would have taken seriously if the idea had been submitted to him. That said, Aliyev's government was always responsive to international criticism and recommendations: there was a sense that when issues reached his attention, he acted on them. For example, the widespread corruption in the operations of Baku's international airport grew out of control in 1998, eventually forcing even Pakistan International Airlines to stop serving the city. Once this problem appeared on Aliyev's personal radar screen, he called an emergency meeting and successfully cracked down on it. After this incident, the airport largely operated professionally. Aliyev responded in similar fashion in 2001, a year of crisis for independent journalism in Azerbaijan. The government was breaking up demonstrations violently and accusing the opposition media of "undermining the statehood of the country" by reporting on these acts of suppression. In December, Aliyev held an unprecedented and frank three-hour meeting with the press. He condemned the statements by his own party representatives and subsequently signed a decree liberalizing the mass media law.[21] The following year saw a drastic decrease in media-related problems.[22]

The Vexing Relationship Between Elections and Democracy

Largely because of the Western focus on elections rather than the arduous process of building governance and rule of law, Azerbaijan makes headlines in the West mainly at voting time. This situation is unfortunate, since it strengthens the equation of democracy with elections, whereas the mechanical event of elections is just the outer manifestation of a functioning democracy. Of course, there is a good reason for this: for the media, elections are potentially dramatic events and make a good story, which, for example, judicial reforms might not. But more important, elections constitute the main legally sanctioned challenge to the government's position, and conversely the main legal chance for the opposition to gain power, or alternatively to expose to the world the democratic deficits of the country. Elections have hence been major determinants of Azerbaijan's political development.

Azerbaijan achieved important progress in democratization in the late 1990s. Significant legislative reform prepared the ground for elections, press censorship was abolished, and opposition media functioned, albeit with difficulty. The country developed an increasingly pluralistic political environment, and it is no exaggeration to argue that of the three Caucasian states, Azerbaijan had gone furthest toward developing a multiparty system with relatively stable political parties. These positive developments, together with the regime's responsiveness to international criticism and advice, generated hope for improvement in the conduct of elections as well. But such improvement would only come gradually, and with occasional setbacks.

Ahead of the 1998 presidential election, both the OSCE and the opposition rejected the electoral law proposed by the government, and the opposition decided to boycott. In response to the OSCE's criticism and after dialogue with the opposition, Aliyev reformed the electoral law, among other things abolishing press censorship. These changes won the OSCE's approval, and several opposition candidates, including the Azerbaijani National Independence Party's Etibar Mamedov, decided to run. But Müsavat, led by Isa Gambar, and Ali Kerimli's Azerbaijani Popular Front regarded the reforms as insufficient and stood by their choice not to participate. But Mamedov's decision to run wrecked the boycott, providing the vote with much-needed legitimacy, both internally and externally.

In the 1998 election, Aliyev fell into a trap of his own making. Back in 1993, convinced of his sky-high popularity, he had inserted a clause in the election law implying that a presidential election would be won in the first round only if the winner gathered more than two-thirds of the votes—not the usual 50 percent plus one. But as election day approached, it became clear to the presidential staff that Mamedov, by virtue of being the sole true opposition candidate, was resonating with a significant portion of the population. Mamedov was running a professional campaign, and large numbers of people were attending his rallies. This forced Aliyev, somewhat belatedly, to hit the campaign trail—something he had originally not considered necessary. The campaign was visibly hard on the seventy-six-year-old president, who went to the United States the following spring for coronary bypass surgery in a Cleveland hospital. Indeed, this episode is considered the time when Aliyev truly realized that he could hardly manage yet another presidential campaign, and that he needed to begin to prepare his succession.

On election day 1998, there is little doubt that Aliyev gathered far more votes than his main challenger. Official results gave Aliyev 76 percent of the vote, far ahead of Mamedov's 11 percent, thus averting a runoff. But international observers reported major irregularities both in the election process (such as ballot stuffing) and in the counting of votes.[23] Independent assessments on election day indicated that Aliyev had indeed won, but had received "only" 50 to 60 percent of the vote, with Mamedov's votes exceeding 25 percent. In any Western election, Aliyev's victory would have been considered a landslide. But though he likely would have won a runoff as well, holding one was out of the question, because it would have dimmed Aliyev's image as father of the nation. Therefore, his share of the vote had to be "helped" across the two-thirds threshold by a sound margin.

In retrospect, the effect of this electoral manipulation was the opposite of what was intended. It substantially weakened Aliyev's popularity and boosted the divided opposition. This was true especially for Etibar Mamedov and his National Independence Party, which hitherto had run significantly behind Isa Gambar's Müsavat. On the other hand, the opposition parties that boycotted the election, especially the Popular Front and Müsavat, grudgingly came to realize that sitting it out, which had been interpreted by large parts of the population as a sign of weakness, had been a mistake.

In Azerbaijan, as in most postsocialist states, presidential and parliamentary elections are widely different things. To begin with, the personality-centered political culture of the Caucasus makes parliamentary elections far less of a focus; the presidentialism of the region's political systems only strengthens this tendency. For an incumbent, this can be dangerous: even if he easily wins a presidential election, parliamentary votes can develop into shows of popular dissatisfaction even where the population does not necessarily hold the opposition in particularly high esteem. This was the case with the 2000 parliamentary elections, which were heralded as a great opportunity to provide Azerbaijan with a truly representative legislature, bringing politics into Parliament from the streets.

As had also been the case in 1998, concerns about the composition and functions of the Central Electoral Commission (CEC) were a major issue in 2000. In May, Mazahir Panahov, the chairman of the physics department at Baku State University, was appointed the CEC's new chairman. Panahov was not associated with the Soviet-era nomenklatura, and his appointment was interpreted as a positive development. In June, after heavy international pressure, Parliament reformed the electoral law and adopted a new law on the CEC that gave the opposition the ability to block a quorum in the central, district, and precinct electoral commissions. After the opposition boycotted the CEC's first three meetings, incapacitating the body, Parliament revised the law in July to remove the opposition's de facto veto power, and to allow the ruling party to appoint commission chairmen at all levels. The OSCE and other international organizations nevertheless concluded that the law provided "a comprehensive legislative framework for the conduct of elections" and represented a significant improvement over the previous law.[24] But the CEC initially rejected the applications of eight of thirteen parties that had intended to run candidates in the proportional elections (including Müsavat and the Azerbaijani National Independence Party) and half of the candidates in single-member constituencies. Aliyev eventually reversed the ban on the eight parties, but not on most rejected candidates in single-member constituencies.

In an election plagued by numerous irregularities, the governing party declared victory, claiming more than 60 percent of the proportional vote and a sweep of the single-member constituencies. While the latter assertion was somewhat credible, given the advantages of local potentates in rural areas, the proportional results were not, given that in-country observers unanimously concluded that while the ruling party may have emerged with the greatest representation it had won far less than a majority. And while Müsavat clearly emerged as the largest opposition party, official results gave it less than 2 percent. But two small parties that most likely had drawn far fewer votes, Civil Solidarity and the Communists, as well as the reasonably strong Popular Front, were declared to have surpassed the 6 percent threshold for representation. While this outcome ingeniously brought two nominal opposition parties into Parliament, the results did not conform with the reality of voting patterns.[25] Indeed, they differed so much as to be obviously implausible.

The 2000 parliamentary elections taught several lessons. The most obvious was that the population was politically apathetic. Hardly a third of the electorate cast ballots, the claims of the CEC notwithstanding. (Indeed, the voter turnout figures were even more heavily doctored than the results.) Another intriguing finding was how poorly the elites in both the government and the opposition gauged their respective parties' public support. For example, Müsavat chairman Isa Gambar repeatedly stated that his party had polled close to 50 percent—an implausibly high figure. Moreover, personal meetings with Gambar and his closest associates, even long after the elections, convinced the present author that the Müsavat leadership actually believed it had received about half the votes. Conversely, the vehemence with which the government's representatives maintained that the ruling party had received a majority was equally indicative that the information that had been sent up to the leadership from the grassroots was overly optimistic. With both the government and the main opposition party—each of which may have plausibly polled a quarter of the vote—believing they commanded the support of half the country, the stage was set for an increasingly polarized and uncompromising political system as the succession to Aliyev approached and all eyes turned to the 2003 presidential election.

Society and Economics: A Changing Country

The stability of the Aliyev era allowed Azerbaijan's society and economy to begin to integrate with the rest of the world. The end of hostilities, macroeconomic stabilization programs, and foreign investments helped revive economic growth in 1996. In 1995, the economy had bottomed out around 40 percent of 1989 production levels. Agricultural production began to increase again in 1996, with industrial production joining the upward trend in 1997. Gross domestic product, in free fall in the early 1990s, stabilized in 1996 and grew by 5.7 percent in 1997. Subsequently, Azerbaijan experienced a multiyear period of annual double-digit growth, with the only exception occurring in 1999, when the Russian economic crisis affected the country, albeit relatively mildly.[26] Inflation rates stayed under 3 percent until 2004. This economic growth was focused in the oil industry, but spread to the rest of the economy as well. By 2000, economic stability began to yield results in terms of increased salaries and real incomes, and decreasing poverty rates.

Aside from the economy, Azerbaijani society was now exposed to the world like never before. As is discussed in a later chapter, this new level of exposure widened economic and cultural gaps in society, especially between rural and urban areas. Particularly in Baku, this implied a widening of the population's mental horizons from the narrow prism afforded by the Soviet monopoly on telecommunications and media. In Baku, middle-class youth now grew up in an environment where the cultures of Islam and the secular West both converged and clashed. Distinct subcultures mixing local and foreign influences emerged: a prominent example is the nationalistically and religiously minded rap music community that became very popular with the younger generation. Other, less benevolent influences, such as religious radicalism, criminal gangs, and drug abuse, also developed, though these generally remained contained. Azerbaijan irrevocably distanced itself from the Soviet era, which paradoxically had been deeply colored by tradition and Islamic values—sustained, ironically, by the very isolation Soviet communism had imposed on the land.

Where Azerbaijani society was heading was less clear. The older generation had had to adjust to a totally different world whose functioning and principles they mostly failed to understand. As for young people, they were faced with determining their response to the changing times, choosing a way of life under the influence of the various forces seeking to seduce them—all at a time when contrasts were developing in society as never before. The younger generation's choices could manifest themselves in the growing and decidedly Western consumerism—with its attendant social mores—of the young Baku middle class, but also its direct opposite, the Islamic backlash to such changes that was strengthening within the exact same community. As in so many other areas, Turkey was an important influence, as it had dealt with similar challenges to collective and individual identity since the 1930s, if not earlier.

Under the surface of Azerbaijan's changing society and economy lurked the oft-repressed reality of Mountainous Karabakh. While not always talked about, it was always present, in the shape of the humiliation of defeat, frustration with the perceived double standards of the outside world, and the masses of refugees lingering in camps only a few hours from the lights of the capital or looking for work in the downtrodden industrial suburbs.

September 11: The Caucasus Moves West

For Azerbaijan, like the rest of the world, things would never be the same after the terrorist attacks of September 11, 2001. Western leaders, particularly those in Washington, now began to understand what Azerbaijanis in general and Aliyev's circle in particular had been arguing for years. The Caucasus was no longer merely an oil-rich backwater; it was a crucial piece of real estate linking Europe (and thereby the North Atlantic Treaty Organization) to the new theaters of conflict in Afghanistan and elsewhere in Central Asia. And more quickly than most, Heydar Aliyev grasped the importance of the events of September 11. On that very day, several advisers urged patience, a wait-and-see approach that would allow Baku to gauge Russia's reaction. Aliyev dismissed such counsel, fully understanding the magnitude of what had just happened. The only response that would do was to proclaim full and unequivocal support for the United States, and express Azerbaijan's readiness to support America with all the means at its disposal. So rapid was Aliyev's calculation that Azerbaijan was one of the first countries to extend a blanket offer of support to the United States. This strategy clearly paid off, leading to a waiver of section 907a of the Freedom Support Act of 1992 (which had prohibited direct assistance from the U.S. government to the government of Azerbaijan) in early 2002 and a much-upgraded security cooperation arrangement between Azerbaijan and the United States.

But the changes in global politics and economics that followed *indirectly* from September 11 also altered Azerbaijan's position. For Azerbaijan, these changes were initially overwhelmingly positive; for the incumbent regime, mainly so. To begin with, the war in Afghanistan cemented Azerbaijan's geopolitical importance—it is, after all, the only country bordering both Russia and Iran, and therefore is key to the establishment and maintenance of any west-to-east corridor to Central Asia. But the global war on terrorism—of which the Afghanistan war was a basic part—also increased Azerbaijan's strategic importance, in both tangible and intangible ways. It did so most tangibly through a new international appreciation of the energy resources of the country at a time of increasingly unstable oil markets. Less tangibly, Azerbaijan's symbolic value as a moderate, Western-looking, and potentially democratic Shia Muslim nation was a key asset to those in the West who understood it. Both of these factors heightened sensitivity to Azerbaijan's economic and security interests among the democracies of North America and the European Union. While this benefited the Azerbaijani people as well as their government, the sharpening focus on democracy in the Muslim world prompted by the wars in Afghanistan and, later, Iraq constituted a challenge to the government. Of course, Western attention to the region would later falter. As progress in the U.S.-led war effort in Iraq ground to a halt between 2003 and 2007, the Americans' attention span in regard to the Caucasus shrank dramatically and had not returned as of 2009. But Heydar Aliyev would not live to see that.

Succession Politics

From the late 1990s until 2003, succession was the buzzword in the Caucasus. The sheer strength of personality that Eduard Shevardnadze and Heydar Aliyev brought to bear in ensuring stability in their respective countries, and the patriarchal character of their rule, were considered so strong that it was widely believed that their demise might well result in instability or, even worse, civil war. The advanced age of the two presidents—especially Aliyev, born in 1923, five years before Shevardnadze—made the question of succession particularly pressing. Discussions of succession scenarios intensified in late 1999 after the entourage of Russian president Boris Yeltsin skillfully engineered the designation of an almost unknown figure, Vladimir Putin, to succeed him as president, keep order, and ensure that the elite remained in place. The "Putin model" was obviously workable, but it proved dangerous. Putin soon turned on the oligarchs who had brought him to power, eliminating them one by one. Shevardnadze, having unsuccessfully groomed a sequence of potential successors, more or less gave up as they all turned on him and went into opposition. Indeed, the troika that led Georgia's "Rose Revolution" in 2003—Mikheil Saakashvili, Zurab Zhvania, and Nino Burjanadze—had all been, at one time or another, Shevardnadze's handpicked protégés.

The question of the heir apparent therefore became a favorite subject around kitchen tables and in newspapers in Azerbaijan and beyond. Gradually all eyes focused on Ilham Aliyev, the president's son. While Ilham kept a generally low profile, he was increasingly derided by the opposition as a playboy and gambler, among other less-than-flattering appellations—a clear indication of the opposition's fear that he would be picked as his father's successor.

Born in Baku in 1961, Ilham Aliyev lived in Moscow during his father's time in the Soviet government, and obtained a Ph.D. from the prestigious Moscow State Institute of International Relations, where he also taught for five years. Upon the breakup of the Soviet Union he briefly went into business, then returned to Azerbaijan in 1994, a year after his father's comeback. The same year, he was appointed vice president of the State Oil Company (SOCAR), and later promoted to first vice president. in 1995, he was elected to Parliament. As the 1990s drew to a close, Ilham seemed to be growing less wary of the spotlight. In 1997 he was chosen to head the Olympic Committee of Azerbaijan, an assignment he took seriously, infusing funds into athletics by building sports complexes across Azerbaijan and supporting the development of athletes. His efforts paid off: with Ilham cheering on site, Azerbaijani athletes won three gold medals at the 2000 Sydney Olympics. True to the state broadcast media's unreformed style, Azerbaijani television crews focused their cameras on Ilham a lot more than on the athletes themselves. Nevertheless, the Olympic victories— associated with Ilham's management of sports—generated considerable pride in the country and boosted his image as a successful manager, a "doer."

Meanwhile, Ilham continued to collect positions. In 1999 he was elected one of the five deputy chairmen of the ruling party, and was promoted to first deputy chairman in 2001. It was his smiling face that adorned most of the ruling party's campaign posters in the 2000 parliamentary elections, which carried the slogan *YAP xalqdan Ilham alir*. Literally, this meant "YAP [the ruling Yeni Azerbaijan Party] takes inspiration from the people," given that *ilham* means "inspiration" in Azerbaijani. Of course, the slogan also made clear to the population that Ilham was the designated successor. Ilham also made sure to build his international exposure and connections. Aside from his trips abroad on behalf of SOCAR, he headed Azerbaijan's delegation to the Parliamentary Assembly of the Council of Europe. Two years later, he was elected one of PACE's deputy chairmen. Ilham Aliyev was slowly but surely emerging as one of the country's leading politicians.

The End of Heydar Aliyev's Reign

In spite of Ilham Aliyev's increasing prominence, doubts remained in the minds of both Azerbaijani and foreign observers as to whether he really was the designated successor. These doubts stemmed from several factors. The first was intraregime politics. As in any political system, the ruling party, the Yeni Azerbaijan Party (New Azerbaijan Party), included numerous potential aspirants to the presidency. In fact, YAP was an odd coalition of forces whose main common denominator was a desire to retain power— something that can be said about many political forces. By 2001, the party seemed increasingly split between the older, formerly Communist nomenklatura and a younger group of reformers. Ilham Aliyev was increasingly identified as the leader of the reforming wing, generating resistance and opposition from strong figures in the administration's "old guard," those figures whom Thomas Goltz called the "crocodiles" in his 1998 book *Azerbaijan Diary*. Most prominent among the "crocodiles" was Jelal Aliyev, Ilham's uncle, who was a powerful figure in the old guard and reputedly controlled his own small band of racketeer militia. Second, there was—and remains—no consensus that Ilham himself actually actively sought the office. Neither before nor after his election did he display the same urge for and love of power and politics that his father constantly radiated. Observers close to Ilham Aliyev as president have spoken of his frustration with the incompetence and vested interests that, from the outset, he perceived as surrounding him and limiting his freedom of action. A third source of questions about Ilham's status was the concern that even if he got YAP squarely behind him, he would find it difficult to gain acceptance in Azerbaijan's political culture.

Shortly before his eightieth birthday—on April 21, 2003—Heydar Aliyev addressed a crowd of 2,000 at Baku's military academy. In the middle of his speech, he suffered chest pain and subsequently collapsed in front of his horrified audience. Though he was back at work the next morning, it was clear that Aliyev was not well—and that he would not do much campaigning for the presidential election scheduled for October. He was flown to the Gülhane military hospital in Ankara, Turkey. From the Turkish capital, he was transported by a medical plane dispatched by President Putin to a clinic in Cleveland, Ohio, where he had undergone bypass surgery in 1999 and subsequently received yearly checkups. This cooperation between three of the four major players in Caucasian politics was an illustration of the role they accorded to Aliyev, but also of the more cooperative atmosphere that had developed in the late 1990s, but which was not to last. Heydar Aliyev personified stability in Azerbaijan, and no one wanted instability.

Once he was in Cleveland, President Aliyev was diagnosed with congestive heart failure and a kidney failure related to this condition. When he returned to Azerbaijan, it was to be laid to rest, on December 15, 2003. He had died three days earlier, in Cleveland. The Heydar Aliyev era in Azerbaijani politics was over.

6

Ilham Aliyev's Azerbaijan

An era ended when Heydar Aliyev took his leave from Azerbaijan in the summer of 2003. Small countries rarely produce such outsized leaders. Indeed, in Azerbaijan—as throughout the Caucasus—Aliyev loomed larger than life. This meant that the force of his personality dominated the country to the extent that other political personalities were prevented from developing. As Elin Suleymanov observed, the simultaneous departure from power of Aliyev and Georgian leader Eduard Shevardnadze meant the end of the "long" 1990s for the Caucasus—the decade that had brought the end of the Soviet Union, independence, war, and other tumultuous changes.[1] By his training, experience, and age, Aliyev was quintessentially a product of the Cold War, beginning his career during World War II and subsequently rising to the top of the Soviet system. He was thus a master geopolitician, whose understanding of global politics remained razor sharp in spite of the fundamental changes that took place in the post–Cold War world. He was a chess player on a global scale, and achieved strategic wonders given the conditions that existed when he took power in an independent Azerbaijan. Domestically, he stabilized the country and brought it back to economic and political functioning. But if his understanding of international politics was first-rate even in the early twenty-first century, his view of domestic politics had not quite kept up with the major developments in the world. Indeed, the reactive and reluctant attitude toward demands for internal reform he exhibited during his rule showed that the norms governing domestic politics in the world had changed considerably more than those governing international politics. Keeping up with that change was a challenge for Aliyev—exactly because his perspective went far beyond Azerbaijan's domestic affairs. His passing brought to power a leader who, even though he was Aliyev's own son, had had very different formative experiences, espoused a different worldview, and took very different approaches to being the nation's ruler. But he would also come to power at a time that coincided with the culmination of the West's power and influence in the post-Cold War world. Indeed, Ilham Aliyev's first term as president coincided with a rapid decline in the West's global power and prestige, which had far-reaching implications for Azerbaijan. In a period running from the 2003 Iraq war to the 2008 global financial crisis, the West's domination of world politics waned, while the power and influence of non-Western and often authoritarian powers grew. This, coupled with the near-disengagement of America and Europe from the South Caucasus, would weaken the gravitational pull that the West had previously exerted on Azerbaijan both in terms of geopolitics and political organization.

A Transition Not Quite According to Plan

With President Heydar Aliyev ailing in a Cleveland hospital, it was increasingly obvious that he would not be able to run for president in October 2003. He had left Azerbaijan on August 6 to seek medical care in the United States, and would die there December 12 without ever seeing his homeland again. The ruling elite faced a distinct challenge on how to proceed. Aliyev appears to have planned to achieve reelection one last time, then gradually and peacefully transfer power to his son, Ilham. But this was no longer possible.

In contrast to earlier occasions, the Azerbaijani government had begun to develop the legal setting for elections more than a year ahead of the 2003 presidential vote. The government worked with the OSCE, the Council of Europe, and the International Foundation on Election Systems, leading to several improvements over earlier election laws. However, nongovernmental organizations receiving foreign funding were prohibited from election monitoring, and, most important, the composition of the election commissions at the central, regional, and local levels remained under the control of the ruling Yeni Azerbaijan Party (YAP). Nevertheless, the country's three major opposition leaders—Isa Gambar, Ali Kerimli, and Etibar Mamedov—all got registered without problems, although the two main opposition figures in exile, former speaker of the Parliament and Azerbaijani Democratic Party chairman Rasul Guliyev and Soviet-era leader Ayaz Mutalibov, who apparently had not given up his ambition to return, were denied registration.

We All Have Our Fathers: Ilham Aliyev's Awkward Position

On June 28, an "initiative group" from Nakhichevan nominated Ilham Aliyev for president; YAP had nominated Heydar Aliyev.[2] On August 4, Ilham was appointed prime minister, which made him first in the line of succession should his father not live to see the election. These two measures are perhaps indicative of the controversy within YAP over Ilham's appointment, as there would hardly have been a need to name him prime minister otherwise. The campaign developed awkwardly, with Ilham Aliyev at pains to explain why he was a candidate against his ailing father, who finally pulled out of the race two weeks before the election, endorsing Ilham.

The confusion in the governing bloc was a golden opportunity for the opposition parties, which had eagerly awaited this chance finally to come to power. The situation could hardly have been better for them: there was an unwell president, obvious confusion, and political machinations within a divided governing bloc. But the opposition proved unable to capitalize on this tactical advantage.

Four leaders were in a position to pose a serious challenge to the incumbent administration: Etibar Mamedov, of the Azerbaijani National Independence Party (ANIP); Ali Kerimli, of the Azerbaijani Popular Front (APF); Isa Gambar, of Müsavat; and Rasul Guliyev, of the Azerbaijani Democratic Party (ADP). All of these parties had existed for a considerable time, had well-known leaders with high name recognition, and shared a general center-right political profile, a pro-Western foreign policy, and a stated adherence to liberal democratic values. Their histories were nevertheless different: the Popular Front and Müsavat had shared power during Elçibey's rule, while Guliyev's ADP had begun as a splinter group from the governing bloc after a falling-out in 1996 between Aliyev and Guliyev while Guliyev was speaker of the Parliament. As for Mamedov, his ANIP had been in opposition to every Azerbaijani government since independence.

Finding a unity candidate became the opposition's priority. The past had showed that the opposition's lack of unity was its main liability, something that Aliyev had masterfully used by playing one opposition leader against another. A decade of political sclerosis among the opposition parties had, in combination with public distaste for their internal bickering, gravely damaged the opposition's credibility as an alternative to the Aliyev regime, and created a sense, even in friendly Western circles, that little could be done to help it. During the summer of 2003, Kerimli proposed to resume deadlocked talks on a unity candidate, even offering to step down in favor of a consensus nominee. The four made a much-publicized trip to London for negotiations, but failed to come to an agreement. Kerimli then withdrew and publicly endorsed Mamedov, realizing that doing so would build his own long-term legitimacy. Intense discussions followed between Mamedov and Gambar, the opposition leader with the strongest public following at

the time. A deal was struck only days before the election whereby Mamedov would endorse Gambar in exchange for the post of prime minister
should Gambar be elected. Yet for unknown reasons, Gambar reneged on
the deal at the last minute, choosing instead to offer the same arrangement
to Guliyev. This move was a bad fit with Gambar's image of honesty and
anticorruption platform, given that Guliyev was well known for having
been accused of siphoning huge sums from the sale of oil from state-owned
refineries in the early 1990s. Therefore, no unity candidate materialized,
and the opposition entered the election with both Gambar and Mamedov on
the ballot.

In the election campaign, local authorities created constant obstacles to
opposition campaigning—breaking up rallies, intimidating local party
branches, denying permission or venues for rallies, and preventing opposition members from traveling. Moreover, media coverage was highly
slanted toward the ruling party.

Official figures released late on election day, October 15, gave Ilham
Aliyev 76 percent of the vote, with Gambar taking only 14 percent, a result
fervently contested by the opposition. International observers recorded
numerous irregularities during elections procedures, especially the counting and tabulation of votes, but the most concern was expressed over the
level of intimidation and unequal conditions for candidates during the
campaign.

The election was problematic enough, but the real damage was done by
postelection violence and the numerous arrests and instances of intimidation of opposition activists that followed. When the opposition refused to
recognize the election results, about 5,000 of the most radical members of
Müsavat and ADP clashed with government forces during unauthorized
rallies. Scores were injured on both sides, and there was at least one fatali-
ty. Police used tear gas to disperse crowds that raged on to break shop and
car windows. In the government crackdown, Gambar was put under house
arrest and his deputies were detained.

As in 2000, both Aliyev's and Gambar's entourages were genuinely
convinced their candidate had won. In the Georgian parliamentary elections two weeks later, parallel vote tabulation and exit polls quickly
showed the divergence between the official results and reality, but no such
tabulations were conducted in Azerbaijan. The U.S. Embassy concluded
that widespread fraud had taken place, and that this put the legitimacy of
the election in doubt.[3] Most available information suggests that Aliyev
really did receive the largest number of votes, though less than the official
results. But there was little way of knowing whether this was indeed the

case or whether massive fraud had been committed. Ilham Aliyev was duly inaugurated, but the violence surrounding the election would remain a bitter aftertaste for the new president. The disturbances and their harsh suppression fed into the preconceived image of him presented by the Western media—and fueled by the Azerbaijani opposition—emphasizing the "dynastic" elements of the succession and his father's KGB background.

Thus, the stereotype that Ilham Aliyev most wanted to avoid was being strengthened—though perhaps unfairly so. Indeed, while his accession to power was the result of a carefully prepared if somewhat hurried plan, it was in retrospect no different from how Vladimir Putin had gained power in Russia in 1999. Putin was handpicked by Boris Yeltsin's entourage, installed as prime minister, made de facto ruler when Yeltsin resigned, and backed as the representative of the "party of power" in an election that he probably did win, but which failed to meet international standards. That is almost exactly the sequence that made Ilham Aliyev president of Azerbaijan. Yet the Yeltsin-Putin transfer of power received little of the kind of Western criticism that was directed at the Aliyev succession, even though Putin already had the blood of thousands of Chechens on his hands. The only difference between the two successions, of course, was that Ilham Aliyev was Heydar Aliyev's son.

Azerbaijan and Georgia, Fall 2003: An Unhelpful Comparison

One reason for the West's relatively harsh criticism of the transfer of power in Azerbaijan may have been the contrast between developments in Azerbaijan and the Georgian succession, which happened only days later.

The first and foremost difference between the two countries was the degree of opposition unity. Although the three Georgian opposition leaders were known for their internal rivalries, they managed to form an alliance in good time before the elections. This fact was crucial in generating a critical mass of public support for the opposition. Georgian opposition leaders, moreover, were characterized by dynamism, enthusiasm, and a sense of public expectation. They articulated a clear vision of Georgia as a modern democratic state moving toward European institutions and battling corruption, and Mikheil Saakashvili had his experience as mayor of Tbilisi to back up his claim that he could run the country if elected. By comparison, Azerbaijan's opposition parties had failed to present concrete, coherent party platforms in terms of either domestic or foreign policy, and thus failed to make a credible case that they could do a better job than the incumbent government. Their failure to join forces led to disappointment so acute that it was not rare to come across pro-opposition supporters who had decided to vote for Aliyev as a result of this debacle.[4]

Second, in organizational and financial terms, the Azerbaijani state was considerably stronger than its Georgian counterpart, a result of the financial capacity generated by oil revenues. In spite of its shortcomings, the Azerbaijani government did provide a minimum level of public goods to the population, including improvements in civil servants' salaries, road construction, and energy provision. Conversely, the Georgian government had abdicated most responsibilities of a state, failing to exert control over the country's territory and its own bureaucracy.

Third, civil society and independent media were significantly more restricted in Azerbaijan. The Georgian opposition was able to form a youth movement, "Kmara!," modeled on the Serbian *Otpor!* movement that brought down Slobodan Milošević in 2000, something that never developed in Azerbaijan because civil society was too weak. Georgia also had independent television stations such as Rustavi-2, which broadcast the opposition's viewpoints, it's message to reach the population at large.

As a consequence of these factors, the international community's attitude diverged toward the two countries. In Georgia, the contrast between a united opposition and a collapsing state made the prospect of regime change both real and desirable. As Charles Fairbanks concluded, "the U.S. was in the throes of its most consistent and serious attempt ever in a ex-Soviet republic to secure free and fair balloting and ensure the effectuality of the people's verdict,"[5] and huge amounts of aid poured into parallel vote tabulation, exit polls, and support for civil society groups. But in Azerbaijan, the significant efforts spent to get the Azerbaijani opposition to unite failed, dampening international interest and leading to a much smaller international electoral observation mission than in Georgia.

Why the discrepancy in international interest? Oil is often stressed as the reason, particularly by frustrated Azerbaijani opposition members, who accuse the West of betraying their righteous cause. While Western economic interests may have played a role, that is an insufficient explanation. The international community acted in Georgia based on a conviction that the country's stability and development could only be secured through support for democratic elections. In Azerbaijan, the opportunity was dashed by internal squabbles that damaged the opposition's external and domestic legitimacy. Conversely, the government's position was strong and civil society was weak, making support for the type of measures taken in Georgia both less attractive and less feasible. Finally, cultural factors—

mainly Georgia's Christian religion—may have generated greater Western interest in Georgia than in Azerbaijan.

Setting Up Shop: Change and Continuity

Once in power, Ilham Aliyev faced a distinct dilemma. He was president and formally had supreme powers, given Azerbaijan's hyperpresidential form of government. But as is discussed in chapter 8, power in Azerbaijan derives not from formal positions but from a host of informal factors including economic, regional, and kinship ties.

The Perils of Being a Designated Successor

As a designated successor, Ilham Aliyev was unable to craft an independent platform. Given the traditional values that dominate Azerbaijani society, it would have been unthinkable for him to distance himself from his own father, or to advocate policies that differed significantly or involved widespread change. Such conduct would have been considered disloyal, while also unsettling to the ruling elite. Instead, it was Heydar Aliyev who implicitly delivered the message of change from his Cleveland hospital bed. In a letter endorsing Ilham, he called his son a man of "high intellect, pragmatic thinking, and a fine understanding of contemporary world politics and economics."[6]

With no team of his own, Ilham Aliyev was forced to rely on his father's cabinet, composed mainly of men from another generation, and whose loyalty had been to his father personally rather than to the office of the presidency. These power brokers were entrenched, with their own fiefdoms and interests; their loyalty to Ilham could not be taken for granted. Further, Ilham's youth (he was 41 when elected president) implied that he commanded little natural authority with his cabinet. The veneration of age is a traditional Azerbaijani value, and the equation of age with authority permeates society. In extended families in Azerbaijan, powerful but younger individuals are often treated almost like children by the older generation. Hence, Ilham commanded little natural authority among the firmly rooted septuagenarians in his entourage, and had to build his own personal authority gradually and meticulously. Ilham did possess several advantages. First of all, internal stability was not a major problem. The monopoly over the use of force was never in question, as the "power ministries" were all under firm government control and no active paramilitary groups existed. This represented a world of difference from the situation in 1993. Moreover,

Azerbaijan had secured its independence and achieved a place for itself in international politics. Except for the usual jockeying among regional powers, Azerbaijan faced no acute foreign policy challenges. September 11 and the Iraq war controversy were in the past, and Azerbaijan had decisively taken America's side on both occasions. In addition, Ilham had gained power just as serious oil revenues were about to begin accruing, with construction having begun in late 2002 of the Baku-Tbilisi-Ceyhan pipeline, which connected Baku with the Turkish Mediterranean port of Ceyhan. In other words, the Russian-orchestrated distractions that would take up so much of President Saakashvili's time in Georgia were of less concern to Ilham Aliyev.

Because Ilham had been unable to define his own political profile, his aims, goals, tactics, and methods were unknown—and his political acumen was underestimated. His opponents maligned him, the foreign media ridiculed him, and many of his older cabinet members looked at him as an upstart. But as much as these issues were liabilities, Ilham may have seen them as assets in consolidating power and building his own base.

Publicly, Ilham consistently pledged continuity with his father's legacy, highlighting its obvious successes such as domestic stability, oil revenues, and foreign policy advances. But he also appeared deeply aware of the structural problems in the Azerbaijani state machinery, and of the need to adapt the country to contemporary economic realities. Here was one major difference between Heydar and Ilham: a younger man, Ilham was compelled to think in the long term. He thus had a much stronger incentive to reform Azerbaijan into a country where the people were satisfied and he remained reasonably popular. Therefore, Ilham saw Azerbaijan's future through an economic prism. When asked about his top priorities for Azerbaijan, without hesitation he would cite the need to make Azerbaijan "a normal country," where people's living standards improved and laws were observed.[7]

Ilham was well aware that the economy was his greatest asset. During the 2003 electoral campaign, he once observed that governments that preside over seven consecutive years of double-digit growth in gross domestic product (GDP) usually win elections. The impending completion of the Baku-Tbilisi-Ceyhan pipeline and increasing oil prices ensured that once Ilham was in power, he would be able to use the inflow of revenue to improve Azerbaijan's economy. With the rise in oil prices that lasted into 2008, billions of dollars accumulated in the state oil fund. The situation put Ilham in the happy position of having to figure out how best to direct the flow of money, which was amounting to more than US$10 billion per year by late in the decade.

From the outset, Ilham made clear that the government was going to use the oil fund to finance infrastructure development, develop housing and improve living conditions for refugees from the conflict in Mountainous Karabakh, and transfer monies to the state budget to raise salaries and improve government functioning in general. In 2006, expenditures from the oil fund actually exceeded revenues. Of course, with the world's highest rate of GDP growth from 2006 to 2009 (reaching 30 percent in 2007), the means existed for increased expenditures. By raising living standards and laying the groundwork for a prosperous Azerbaijan, Ilham made his plan for Azerbaijan's social contract obvious: make the people happy, and stay in power.

Earning Reformist Credentials

The major challenge for Ilham Aliyev's presidency would be the managing of oil wealth. Would it be squandered on short-term projects, as had occurred in so many other oil-producing countries? Or would it be used to sustain lasting growth, particularly in the non-oil sector? As is discussed in chapter 9, large inflows of cash provide many opportunities, but at least as many challenges. The oil industry produces only a handful of jobs, but creates large income gaps and inequalities. Hence, the way funds would be used was crucial, especially given Azerbaijan's narrow window of opportunity: dozens of billions of dollars would flow into the economy in a short time, but failing new major discoveries, the flow was expected to decrease at some point between 2015 and 2020. Ilham Aliyev's presidency therefore would determine the economy and politics of Azerbaijan for the period *after* the era of Big Oil.

This circumstance made the questions surrounding Ilham Aliyev's presidency all the more important. Would he be a progressive leader in charge of a state on the reform track, or a weak leader succumbing to the narrow self-interests of oligarchs and clans? The answer to that question would largely determine the condition of Azerbaijan twenty years hence. While history would be the judge, the picture that emerged from the young president's first term in office (2003–8) was that of a determined but cautious leader.

In 2003, Ilham Aliyev's main task was to consolidate power vis-à-vis his father's old guard. In the immediate aftermath of his election, they were too powerful to be fired either collectively or individually. To supplant the old guard, Ilham had to have a replacement for a system that actually worked, in spite of all its flaws and corruption. It kept the president in power, and the country in order. He began by slowly building a support base of his own among newly appointed, young, and often reform-minded officials, and by circumventing structures not considered loyal—creating and empowering parallel ones rather than reforming old ones. In this sense, reform and the consolidation of power became mutually reinforcing goals. This shift was quickly discerned among the old guard, and as a result, overt tensions among the ruling elite emerged, which intermittently reached the public through media outlets used by various members of the elite to attack one another.

In a tightly knit political system, cadre policies become the most obvious external sign of change. And in changing official personnel at the highest levels, Ilham moved at an excruciatingly slow pace, taking months to appoint his first new minister. Cadre changes centered first on personnel changes on the second tier (at the deputy minister level); later, the focus shifted higher, to a few ministers without strong clan links or economic bases of their own. Notable among the young deputy ministers President Aliyev appointed was a U.S.-educated lawyer, Mikayil Jabbarov, who formerly had run the foreign investment foundation. Jabbarov was appointed deputy minister for economic development under the oligarch minister, Farhad Aliyev (unrelated to Ilham). At the ministerial level, the president started with two weak ministries with high visibility: Foreign Affairs and Communications and Information Technologies. He acted most forcefully in bringing changes to the derelict Foreign Ministry, appointing a dynamic career diplomat, Elmar Mamedyarov, to the top post, but also by putting Vagif Sadihov, a former ambassador to Austria and well-respected technocrat, in charge of personnel and the day-to-day affairs of the ministry.[8] Ilham's new minister of communications and information technologies, Ali Abbasov, replaced Nadir Ahmadov, a member of the old guard known for running one of the most inefficient, corrupt, and red tape–plagued ministries in the government. The next to go was the minister of national security, Namik Abbasov, another old-guard stalwart who was replaced by a young Aliyev loyalist, Eldar Mahmudov, significantly without a past in the KGB. Following the 2005 parliamentary elections, President Aliyev reshuffled a dozen of provincial representatives of the central government, known as executive committee heads. These appointees were the main power base of the head of the presidential administration and informal leader of the old guard, Ramiz Mehdiyev.

Other changes in late 2005 and early 2006 confirm the picture of gradual reform that brought in younger, professional people and ousted the more corrupt members of the old guard. In November, following accusations of collusion with opposition member Rasul Guliyev and plans to foment a coup, Minister of the Economy Farhad Aliyev was fired and arrested, as was Minister of Health Ali Insanov. Insanov's removal was the most surprising: his official post was of little relevance, but he was thought to be practically untouchable, given that he was the much-reviled and much-feared head of the Yeraz clan. Indeed, the 2005 parliamentary elections coincided with the main change in the power balance during Ilham's first term: the fall from grace, and power, of the old-guard leadership of the Yeraz clan, with roots in what is now Armenia, which constituted the second most powerful group in the Heydar Aliyev administrations behind the Nakhichevanis.

Aside from Insanov, the main loser was Speaker of Parliament Murtuz Aleskerov. His own constituency had been among the most controversial in the elections—he lost the seat according to exit polls—and Aleskerov failed to be reelected to the post of speaker in spite of the ruling party's continued control over Parliament. Instead, three young officials with close ties to the business community took over the post of speaker and deputy speakers of Parliament. In addition, the Ministry of Energy and Industry was strengthened at the expense of the dysfunctional state oil company.

All these cadre changes show a distinct pattern: slow but gradual changes of personnel that in practically all cases removed old-guard figures and replaced them with younger ones, predominantly individuals from the business community with managerial experience. The problem was not the direction of change, but its slow pace. Indeed, following the reshuffles of 2005–6, the pace slowed further. This may have resulted from shifts in the ruling elite caused by the purge of the Yeraz clan, which made Aliyev increasingly dependent on the elite's Nakhichevani core. But Foreign relations are likely to have played a key role. In fact, the most striking trend during Ilham Aliyev's first term was the weakening of the West and the concomitant strengthening of Russia in the region. This trend was highly visible since 2005, culminating with the Russian invasion of Georgia in August 2008, and created an environment decidedly unfriendly to reform. In fact, it is generally accepted that Western assistance and support—not least promises of membership in NATO and the EU—made possible the speedy democratic transitions in Central and Eastern Europe in the 1990s.

That carrot had never been present in the Caucasus, but western presence remained a powerful force for reform. When Western presence receded and Russia's influence grew in the past decade, this affected domestic politics in countries such as Azerbaijan powerfully. The forces defending the status quo were strengthened, while the reformists were increasingly isolated.

Elements of Aliyev's foreign relations display the same mixture of independence and caution. Even though he faced few crises and challenges in his first years as president, his response to Ukraine's "Orange Revolution" of late 2004 testifies to the precarious balance Baku sought to maintain. Through the regional association GUAM (for Georgia, Ukraine, Azerbaijan, Moldova), the Azerbaijani government had developed close ties in the 1990s to the government of Ukrainian president Leonid Kuchma, who had first been elected in 1994. Aliyev came under heavy Russian pressure to support the tainted victory of Kuchma's designated successor, Viktor Yanukovich, and to congratulate the latter on the occasion—all as part of the Kremlin's fevered effort to legitimize the stolen election. Moscow managed to convince the presidents of the Central Asian republics to do so, as well as Armenian president Robert Kocharyan, much to the latter's embarrassment when the election was rerun and Viktor Yushchenko won power. Yet in spite of both Russian pressure and sentiment within his own government, which feared that the Orange Revolution would create a precedent for the upcoming Azerbaijani elections less than a year later, Aliyev refused to go along. Instead, he waited out the crisis and thereby improved his international credibility, also gaining goodwill with the new Yushchenko administration in Ukraine.

In general, Ilham Aliyev sought to build on his father's accomplishment of making Azerbaijan the only truly independent state in the South Caucasus. Armenia was dependent on Russia, and Georgia on the United States, but Azerbaijan managed to make itself a country that maintained independence in the formulation of its foreign policy. Despite Washington's cold shoulder after his controversial election, Ilham and his government were nevertheless cautious enough not to succumb to the charm offensive launched by Vladimir Putin's government to seduce Baku into a closer alliance with Russia. In 2009, when Turkey's Justice and Development Party government changed the regional balance by normalizing relations with Armenia without taking Azerbaijan's interests into consideration, Aliyev again refrained from allowing Russian courting to sway him from his course.

The 2005 Parliamentary Elections: Politics Turn Local

Azerbaijan's 2005 parliamentary elections followed the series of "color revolutions" in Georgia, Ukraine, and Kyrgyzstan. Flawed elections had catalyzed peaceful and orderly popular uprisings in the Georgian and Ukrainian cases that brought regime change, but in Kyrgyzstan the outcome had been a successful coup. All three actions led to the demise of unpopular and corrupt regimes. Meanwhile, Azerbaijan's strategic value to the West had increased, due not only to the country's significant oil resources but to its role in the international antiterrorist coalition, as the West's strategic access route to Afghanistan and the states of Central Asia. While this was to the benefit of Ilham Aliyev's government, the George W. Bush administration's increased emphasis on democratization in the greater Middle East was not. Indeed, Azerbaijan's geopolitical importance and energy resources became as much a liability as an asset, since Azerbaijan came to be seen as a test case for the so-called Bush doctrine: would Washington stick to its principles in case of a fraudulent election, or stand by a strategic though authoritarian ally? Accusations of the Bush administration's chummy relations with Big Oil directed additional attention to the issue. As a result, the U.S. administration took on a much more active role in Azerbaijan's electoral politics than on earlier occasions. There was significant media interest, with Baku crowded by reporters hungry for a new revolution.

But no Western support for regime change was forthcoming. The West's diffidence was built on the sound premise that Azerbaijan differed strongly from Georgia, Ukraine, and Kyrgyzstan, three states with numerous commonalities. All three had had widely unpopular governments whose leaders had lost most of their legitimacy, with economic stagnation creating broad dissatisfaction. Moreover, the opposition was united in all three states, led by former high-level government officials who were well known and respected. Law enforcement structures were demoralized, refusing to intervene to uphold the incumbent regime in the face of public protests. Finally, especially in Georgia and Ukraine, the opposition was organized and enjoyed strong external support.

Azerbaijan met none of these criteria. Curiously, the Azerbaijani opposition failed to understand what had caused the color revolutions to succeed. Kerimli and Gambar once again allied with the notorious Guliyev; moreover, they tended to focus more attention on the Western powers and on talk of revolution than on the electoral campaign. The opposition's decision to feature the color orange in its demonstrations was symptomatic of this. In

October 2005, Kerimli said in no uncertain terms that the opposition's aim was to emulate Ukraine and achieve peaceful regime change.[9]

On the other hand, sensitive to the impact of Ukraine's Orange Revolution and the increasingly strong U.S. emphasis on democracy, the Azerbaijani government realized the need to speed up the reform process and ensure a greater degree of Western acceptance of the parliamentary elections. Aliyev appeared to understand that a more inclusive political system would reduce the risk of a color revolution. Given Azerbaijan's economic performance and his own popularity, he had reason to be confident that a gradual political liberalization would not seriously threaten his position in power. In the popular view, he actually succeeded in portraying himself as a reformist figure hindered by the old guard. The number of ordinary citizens expressing this perception of Azerbaijan's politics was surprisingly high.

Wiser for his 2003 experience, Aliyev also understood the importance of elections to foreign relations. In an October 2005 interview, he stressed that Azerbaijan's integration into Europe would depend primarily on his country's own performance.[10] Hence, in two decrees (one issued as early as May 2005) and several public speeches, Aliyev held out a commitment to democratic improvements in the electoral process, in effect putting his personal credibility at stake.

Of the many demands made by international organizations, many were adopted, though some only at the last minute. This time, practically all candidates were easily registered, including Rasul Guliyev and Ayaz Mutalibov. The government also observed provisions on granting candidates airtime on public television, and improved voter registration lists. The government eventually accepted the inking of voters' fingers, and lifted the ban on foreign-funded NGOs' observation of the elections. But the composition of electoral commissions remained the same, empowering the government to override all opposition in the Central Electoral Commission—a sizable obstacle to free elections. Moreover, in spite of the president's executive orders, local executive bodies continued their pattern of interference in the campaign, going unpunished until election day. The level of tolerance toward unauthorized demonstrations also remained very low.

The election marked a significant change in the way political forces affected its conduct. The balloting itself was orderly; there was little evidence of endemic Soviet practices such as ballot stuffing, voter intimidation, multiple and carousel voting, and inflated turnout figures. Exit polls, conducted for the first time, covered about half of the 125 single-mandate districts. In over 80 percent of districts surveyed, official results concurred with those of an exit poll sponsored by the U.S. Agency for International

Development. Results in nine districts (including speaker Aleskerov's) showed substantial divergences from exit polling.

The counting and tabulation of votes remained very problematic. The electoral administration system suffered from being managed by elderly school officials, an arrangement dating back to Soviet times. Since the Communist era, these officials had been tasked with delivering suitable outcomes in elections, creating a familiar but not particularly neutral atmosphere for election administration—a cultural impediment that only a generational change or a total reform of the electoral administration could possibly overcome. Indeed, the vote count was at the center of international criticism, as the international observer mission found that the elections "did not meet a number of OSCE commitments and Council of Europe standards and commitments for democratic elections."[11]

The government moved fairly quickly to address some of the most pressing concerns voiced by the international observer mission. In a televised address the day after the election, President Aliyev acknowledged that irregularities had taken place, in particular the interference of local executive bodies with the electoral process. He pledged to investigate allegations of fraud, to cancel results if necessary, and to hold officials accountable. The government then invalidated the results in numerous districts. Reruns were announced; they would be held in ten districts in May 2006. A few days after the election, two executive committee heads and several functionaries were fired and subsequently detained on charges of electoral fraud, as were several more in the weeks after the election. This marked a watershed in Azerbaijani politics and ended the climate of impunity for election fraud that previously had been pervasive.

If Ilham Aliyev wanted the elections to receive a passing grade from international observes, why the debacle on election night? The answer is that, in an indication of the complexities of Azerbaijan's political climate, the 2005 elections were not simply a struggle between government and opposition. Candidates who were aligned with different interest groups within the ruling elite—as well as different opposition blocs—faced off in many districts. On numerous occasions, independent candidates aligned with one or another government figure won races against the ruling party's official candidate. The most illustrative example is that of Elmira Akhundova, who was Heydar Aliyev's official biographer, a fact that made her government credentials impeccable. Akhundova won the race in District 71 in Masalli, near the Iranian border, with 29 percent of the vote. But more important, she did so running against not one but two candidates who represented the ruling party, Ali Azizov and Mirbaba Shukurov. These candidates, in turn, alleged fraud in a race that essentially had pitted three pro-government candidates against one another.

This example illustrates the multiple splits within the ruling elite, and underscores that the fundamental dividing line that is often assumed to exist in Azerbaijani politics—that of the government versus the opposition parties—is so oversimplified as to be a caricature. Indeed, splits between various forces in the government are often more important to an understanding of Azerbaijani politics than the traditional government-opposition split. Indeed, opposition politician Asim Mollazade has pointedly referred to Azerbaijani politics as "Jurassic Park": dinosaurs in both the government and opposition camps prevent the rise of younger, modern figures—again in both camps.

This has two important implications. First, fraud in an election may originate either at the central or the local level. Fraud that favors a local candidate may emanate not from the central government but from the local authorities and power-brokers.[12] This possibility would shed light on the president's decision to fire and punish some local officials involved in electoral fraud. Against this background, it may have been more than a way of sacrificing lower-level officials in order to respond to Western pressures; it may have constituted punishment of insubordination.

Ilham Aliyev's reforms should be seen in the light of a complex political environment where cross-cutting linkages of an ideological, regional, and economic nature create a web of interactions that makes running the country and implementing reforms of any kind a challenge, including democratic reform of the electoral system. In fact, the gradual liberalization of the political system in the country also decentralized authority and appears to have made the presidential office less rather than more able to control the electoral process, at least in local and parliamentary elections that, as in British and American legislative races, are based on the first-past-the-post system. During Heydar Aliyev's rule, power was strongly centralized and deviations from central policies were swiftly punished. Under Ilham Aliyev's government, ultimate power remained with the president, as indicated by his firing and arrest of some highly influential ministers in 2005. But that said, power nonetheless became more decentralized. Hence, influential figures within the ruling elite and local potentates benefited from the increasingly liberal atmosphere, in that it enabled them to seek to influence elections for their own narrow goals, irrespective of and sometimes in conflict with the objectives of the president. Competition and struggles within the governing elite were hence an important element of Azerbaijan's political situation, and arguably played a larger role than the government-opposition split in the country's political life.

This, of course, is a reality that the international media failed to take into account. Rather, their coverage, especially during election cycles, was based on the assumption that Ilham Aliyev and his government were illegitimate by virtue of being the government, and that the opposition was virtuous and democratic simply by virtue of being the opposition. An Associated Press story of November 10, 2005, seems to have let this sentiment creep into the headline: "Protest in Azerbaijan Disappoints." In the text of the story, it was further noted that the demonstrations did not lead to "an unstoppable momentum."[13]

Toward Consolidation of a "Hybrid Regime"

Ilham Aliyev's image on the international scene had begun to change by 2006. Emissaries from most Western countries were bringing back surprising news to their governments: the media depiction did not do justice to the well-spoken, articulate, and knowledgeable leader with an obvious understanding of Western economic and political principles. Aliyev became an increasingly frequent visitor to Western capitals, making his first official visit to Washington in spring 2006. Azerbaijan also signed various memoranda on cooperation with the European Union, both in the energy sphere and in broader contexts, most notably joining the Eastern Partnership, an EU initiative launched in 2008 to improve multilateral relations with former Soviet republics within continental Europe, in May 2009.

Yet by the end of Ilham Aliyev's first term, Azerbaijan's political system remained governed by informal networks, codes, structures, and rules. The changes necessary for the country to combat corruption and build the rule of law and a modern economy—i.e., changes to the very nature of the country's political system—had yet to come. Rather, from 2006 to 2009 the government was fully occupied with coping with the energy windfall income that had made Azerbaijan's economy the world's fastest growing for four years in a row. Indeed, it is well proven that rapid economic growth is a strong disincentive to reform. For instance, former Russian prime minister Yegor Gaidar was once quoted as saying that reform in Russia would only take place if oil stayed below $25 per barrel. Oil windfalls also made the government complacent; a slowing of personnel changes could be observed from 2007 onward, and more important, the continuous crackdowns on journalists and press freedom has not relented. In the 2005 elections, journalists were routinely targeted and beaten by police when covering opposition demonstrations. In 2006, as will be discussed in detail in chapter 10, a series of editors and journalists critical of the government—particularly those publicizing corruption among officials—were kidnapped and beaten, often by unknown civilian-clothed men. The oppositional Turan news agency and *Azadliq* newspaper were evicted from their offices that year, and the country's most independent TV station, ANS, was briefly closed down. But lately, government officials have in particular used laws on libel and defamation to target journalists, imposing jail sentences as well as massive financial penalties for criticism against officials. In 2009, moreover, the broadcast of western radio stations such as the BBC, Radio Liberty and Voice of America on Azerbaijani airwaves was prohibited.

As a result of this, Azerbaijan in 2009 ranked 150th out of 173 countries on the press freedom ranking of reporters without borders.[14] The Committee to Protect Journalists called the country's record "disastrous."[15] The higher echelons of the government were apparently unwilling or unable to prevent or address this counterproductive and largely unnecessary blemish on Azerbaijan's international credentials. President Aliyev repeatedly pardoned journalists, and in a communication with OSCE officials in April 2009 agreed that defamation laws to target journalists were not in line with European standards.[16] Nevertheless, they remained on the books by 2010, indicating the lack of will on the part of the leadership to seriously address the issue.

The oil windfall, coupled with the consolidation of statehood, indeed increased the self-confidence of Azerbaijan's leaders. Other developments contributed to making the Azerbaijani leadership more confident and less apologetic in defending its political and economic systems. Two factors were key: the already mentioned decline of the West's influence in the former Soviet space, and the troubles experienced by Georgia and Ukraine. The United States got bogged down in Iraq, and the EU failed to digest its twelve new members through its inability to devise a functional internal mechanism to run what was now a twenty-seven-member body. And the United States had hardly achieved a sense of stability in Iraq before the debacle of Russia's 2008 invasion of Georgia followed. Here, the West proved thoroughly unable to react effectively to a premeditated Russian move to amputate territory from the leading pro-Western country in the former Soviet Union.

Russian stirrings in Ukraine further brought home the point that democratization in the former Soviet Union was not only difficult but dangerous, as Russia's leadership appeared to see the process as an affront to itself.

Moreover, the problems of Georgia and Ukraine were not only of Russia's making. Ukraine, in particular, gradually got bogged down in political instability following the collapse of the "Orange Coalition." In Georgia, Mikheil Saakashvili was more successful in bringing lasting change to the political system and fighting corruption; yet by 2007, mounting opposition to his government had also made his country increasingly unstable. If Azerbaijan had appeared on the losing side of post-Soviet history in 2005, the heyday of the color revolutions,, by 2008 its self-proclaimed model of gradual reform appeared more palatable even to some Western audiences. In spring 2009, it was even leaked that NATO officials viewed potential Azerbaijani membership in NATO more favorably than Ukrainian or Georgian accession, indicating the full circle that the reasoning in some western circles had come.[17] Fatigue with the travails of Georgia and Ukraine did not bode well for liberal reforms in Azerbaijan, but it did imply a more comfortable international situation for Aliyev's administration.

Hence, Ilham Aliyev's reelection in October 2008 itself was uneventful—the main opposition leaders refused to participate, thereby partially allowing younger opposition leaders to pick up their mantle. But no one disputed the results this time, as the country's great economic progress would likely have made Aliyev's return to office a foregone conclusion even in a totally free and fair environment. International observers found that the 2008 presidential election "marked considerable progress, but did not meet all of the country's international commitments."[18] More controversial was the scrapping of constitutionally mandated presidential term limits, a change approved in Parliament in early 2009. A constitutional amendment was pushed through rapidly and with little debate, making it possible for Aliyev to remain in power beyond 2013. While the move was understandably decried by democracy supporters, the speed with which it was enacted following Aliyev's reelection and soon after the war in Georgia suggests a more complex rationale behind the decision. Indeed, if unchecked, insecurity regarding succession would constitute a major vulnerability for the Azerbaijani leadership, both internally and externally. nally, various leaders within the government would be susceptible to beginning to jockey for position against one another with an eye to 2013; similarly, foreign powers such as Russia, Iran, and Turkey would all have an excellent opportunity to interfere in Azerbaijan's internal affairs by playing favorites. The abolition of term limits effectively put an end to such prospects, something that was reportedly considered urgent given the growing Russian assertiveness following the war in Georgia.

In sum, at the beginning of Ilham Aliyev's second term, Azerbaijan was no longer a country in transition but one in which a form of government was consolidating. This was not a Western liberal democracy; nor was it a regular dictatorship such as Belarus or most Central Asian republics. Azerbaijan had evolved into an excellent example of what political scientists term "hybrid regimes" or "semiauthoritarian states": systems that mix elements of authoritarianism with elements of pluralism and liberal democracy.[19]

That conclusion could inspire either disappointment or hope, depending on one's viewpoint. Indeed, most democracy supporters would balk at the prospect of a consolidating semiauthoritarian regime, in which elections may be free but not fair, and where the odds are heavily stacked in favor of the ruling elite; where the rule of law is implemented selectively at best; and where governing institutions lack popular accountability and are characterized by informal power networks. Yet on the other hand, a series of Western authors have recognized the historical fact that rapid transitions to electoral democracy tend to fail to bring about sustained democratization. States experiencing such transition succumb either to what Fareed Zakaria has termed "illiberal democracy" or to populist and nationalist elected regimes that end up undermining democracy itself, as happened in Russia and Venezuela.[20] Instead, these authors argue, the record shows that the most successful and sustained democratization processes have taken place in countries—mainly in East Asia but also elsewhere—where liberal-minded authoritarian regimes have presided over social and economic development, the creation of a middle class, and eventually the liberalization of the political sphere as well. That model is one that Azerbaijan's authorities officially embrace, though it remains to be seen whether their actions will lead in that direction. Nevertheless, realistically speaking, this is the optimistic scenario for Azerbaijan in the coming decade. Azerbaijan's economic growth could make the country a leading candidate for such an evolutionary scenario. The main cloud on the horizon, even in this interpretation, is that few resource-dependent economies have traveled that route. Yet Azerbaijan's position on the periphery of Europe and its gradual integration into Euro-Atlantic institutions are also conditions that no resource-dependent economy has experienced; once again, Azerbaijan is in uncharted territory.

Conclusions

Under Ilham Aliyev's rule, Azerbaijan came face to face with a multitude of challenges likely to become only more pressing with each year of continued economic development. First among these was the conflict in Mountainous Karabakh. In 2006 and 2009, mediators repeatedly announced imminent breakthroughs in the negotiation process. But the talks repeatedly failed to bring notable results. Azerbaijan's dynamic economy ensured that the capability gap between Azerbaijan and Armenia would keep widening, increasing the risk of a new war. From his first day in office, the ticking time bomb of Karabakh hung like a dark cloud over Ilham Aliyev's presidency.

A second challenge was that as it approached the start of its second decade, the political system of independent Azerbaijan continued to be governed by informal networks, codes, structures, and rules. Well into his administration, the changes Ilham Aliyev would be willing and able to bring about remained in question; in the meantime, the task for foreign observers was to gain a greater understanding of the political system that did exist in the country.

Third, Azerbaijan's remarkable oil-driven economic progress actualized the question of how the oil wealth could be used to generate long-term stability and prosperity. Would Azerbaijan be able to avoid the economic monoculture that eventually enthralls almost all oil-producing countries?

Fourth, as the initial decade of the twenty-first century drew to a close, Azerbaijan was undergoing an extremely rapid social transformation. Stuck between its Soviet past and Islamic heritage and the overwhelming Western popular culture, the nation displayed enormous generation gaps and an ideological and indeed ideational vacuum that would only grow as the national economy and culture, energized by petrodollars, became increasingly globalized. With Western, Russian, Turkish, and Islamic orientations mixing, the very identity of the future Azerbaijan was now in play. Would a harmonious and positive, distinctively Azerbaijani approach to the nation's multiple contradictions of identity emerge? Or would the country be divided among segregated groups with fundamentally diverging understandings of themselves and the ideal society?

Fifth, and finally, Azerbaijan is situated in a corner of the world that long has witnessed and surely will continue to witness many crises whose impact the country cannot avoid being affected by. Building its place in the world and managing the converging and conflicting interests of its neighbors and the great powers while delineating and fulfilling its own interests will be a major challenge for Azerbaijan in the twenty-first century.

7

The Shadow over Azerbaijan: Karabakh

Less inquisitive foreign visitors to Azerbaijan, and especially the great number who never leave the capital, Baku, will certainly not get the feeling that they are visiting a country at war. They will see a maddening construction boom, a rapidly developing city, opulent wealth in the midst of poverty, and the omnipresence of the oil industry. But for the entire period of its independence, Azerbaijan has indeed been at war. Under a cease-fire in effect since 1994, no major resumption of hostilities has occurred, but neither has a political solution to Azerbaijan's conflict with Armenia materialized. The struggle over Mountainous Karabakh has hence come to be known as one of the "frozen conflicts" of the post–Cold War era. But as catchy as this term may be, it provides a false sense of security by indicating that so long as the conflict is kept in the freezer, business can go on as usual. Indeed, casual visitors to Baku may feel that the war that was fought nearly two decades ago a few hundred miles to the west has been forgotten. But as events in neighboring Georgia have showed, the conflicts of the South Caucasus have never been frozen. Rather, they have been dynamic processes that have gotten more, not less, dangerous with every year that passes without their resolution. In Georgia, President Mikheil Saakashvili's assertive efforts to build up the state and to restore its territorial integrity eventually led Russia to invade the country in 2008.[1] Azerbaijan is not Georgia, but the episode showed the centrality of the unresolved, caged in, but by no means frozen conflicts that plague the Caucasus. Indeed, the development, stability, and national identity of the states of the Caucasus are hostage to these conflicts.

Between the three unresolved irredentist conflicts in the south Caucasus, the one pitting Azerbaijan against Armenia is as large a threat to peace and security in the South Caucasus—and perhaps in the wider region—as the Russian-Georgian war and the two conflicts that were its catalysts and focal points. Moreover, because of the humiliation and frustration caused by Azerbaijan's defeat even as the country was developing its oil industry and easily outpacing Armenia in economic expansion, the failure to find a negotiated solution perpetuates a decade-old status quo that has become increasingly revolting to both Azerbaijan's elite and its general population. For every year the conflict goes unresolved, the risk of renewed war actually increases rather than decreases. Thus, the analogy of a frozen conflict is erroneous.

The present chapter is not a study of the Karabakh conflict per se; rather, it is about the Karabakh conflict's significance for Azerbaijan's state and society since independence.[2] Hence, the chapter is concerned with the conflict's impact on Azerbaijan, the realities behind the conflict, and the efforts to negotiate a solution. These issues are taken up with a focus on the Azerbaijani side of the problem.

Karabakh's Impact on Azerbaijan

For each year that the status quo remains in place, the unresolved conflicts of the Caucasus charge the region's countries a high price. To understand the human toll of the Karabakh conflict, one only has to go to the Shehidler Khiyabani (Martyrs' Lane), on a hill overlooking the Baku bay, across the street from Parliament. Here, near the eternal flame flaring in the wind under a high dome, lie several hundred of the many thousand untrained, unequipped, and very young soldiers who were killed in the Karabakh war. This is only the largest and most imposing war cemetery: smaller versions of Martyrs' Lane can be found, with fresh flowers adorning many of the graves, on the outskirts of most settlements of some size in Azerbaijan.

For another glimpse of the human cost of the war, one need only go to the outskirts of Baku, where refugees (or "internally displaced persons," in the correct international lingo—an important distinction, since the international community considers itself unobligated to help refugees who did not cross an international border) from the fighting search for day jobs in construction whose wages, low as they are, will nonetheless help them feed themselves and their families—those who have not already left to toil as legal or illegal guest workers in Russia, the Gulf states, or Turkey, that is. But to fully comprehend the human toll exacted on the population of Azerbaijan, one had to travel to the many decrepit refugee camps that remained for a decade and a half before the government acquired the resources to provide better facilities for the camps' unfortunate residents. United Nations statistics indicate that for many years no country had a larger percentage of displaced people in its national population than Azerbaijan—as late as 2009, more than one in every ten Azerbaijanis was a refugee.[3] The camp at Saatli, perhaps the best known in Azerbaijan, was laden with symbolism: there, just a few hours' drive southwest of Baku, refugees lived in train cars that got scorching hot in summer and freezing cold in winter. But because the cars were on railroad tracks, they were always ready to roll right back to the occupied territories from which their inhabitants had been expelled more than a decade earlier.

The comprehensive economic costs of the Karabakh conflict have never been estimated—not only the destruction caused by the war, but the loss in production caused by the transformation of one-sixth of Azerbaijan's population into refugees—people who had been living and working on some of the country's richest agricultural land. The available data nonetheless make it obvious that the "internally displaced" have been a heavy burden on a country that already had high levels of poverty, and indeed provide at least a partial explanation for the precipitous drop in economic production that occurred in the early 1990s. Ever since, though no exact figures are available, the absence of these people's labor and production has likely subtracted several percentage points from the Azerbaijani economy's annual growth rate. This loss has been compounded by declines in investment and tourism income caused by the war. Aside from those interested in the oil industry, most international investors shied away from the Caucasus in the 1990s, choosing for understandable reasons to invest in countries unshadowed by the prospect that a suspended war would flare up anew. Left for the future is the immense cost of the reconstruction that will be necessary once Azerbaijan recovers the occupied territories, most of which not even Armenia disputes will one day be returned to Azerbaijani rule. For, as eyewitnesses relate, there is little for the displaced residents of Karabakh to come back to. As is shown by the work of Belgian photographer Michel Ivor, who snuck into areas such as Fizuli Province, houses were looted of everything valuable, from refrigerators to windows and furniture, with the abodes themselves left to rot. Even if one does not take into account the mine clearing that will be necessary even before reconstruction can begin, many settlements likely will need to be rebuilt from scratch. This will cost the equivalent of hundreds of millions of dollars.

On a political level, the war was arguably the major reason the Azerbaijani Popular Front (APF) government's democratic experiment failed in 1993. To begin with, the war prevented the Popular Front government from focusing on economic transition and the consolidation of a democratic system of government. Inexperienced as it was, and burdened by the unenviable legacy left to it by its predecessor, the government of Ayaz Mutalibov took power facing grim prospects in any field where it hoped for success. The war also put enormous pressure on the APF leadership, exacerbating the divisions that existed within it. Moreover, the conflict formed the major instrument for Russia's ambition to undermine and overthrow any democratically minded, pro-Western government in the Caucasus. Georgia may have been the chief victim of Moscow's ambition, but Azerbaijan by no means was spared. Through protégés such as onetime defense minister Rahim Gaziyev and rebel army commander Surat Huseynov, Moscow used the Karabakh conflict to undermine the Popular Front government. As related in chapter 4 of the present volume, Huseynov first withdrew forces from the front, a move that led to the loss of Azerbaijani control of Kelbajar Province and the end of Azerbaijan's rather successful 1992 counteroffensive. Later, Huseynov marched on Baku to unseat the Popular Front government, thus precipitating Azerbaijan's total military collapse. Thus, the devastation caused by the war, which exacerbated the Popular Front's weaknesses and accelerated the breakdown of the economy, also fed the population's disillusionment with democracy, which came to be associated in the popular mind with chaos and anarchy. Conditions thus became ripe for the more authoritarian rule that would characterize the regime of Heydar Aliyev.

The Popular Front government's collapse, moreover, gave shape to a political landscape that would grow sadly familiar in Azerbaijan: by propelling the APF into opposition, where it split into rival factions, the events of 1993 ensured that the damaged Popular Front leadership would be cemented into position at the forefront of the opposition forces. Too weak to effectively challenge the government, the Popular Front and Müsavat, together with the perennial opposition Azerbaijani National Independence Party, were able to install a relatively stable opposition structure that prevented the emergence of new opposition leaders unassociated with the 1993 debacle. The sole exception was Rasul Guliyev, who defected to the opposition camp from the government. Yet Guliyev's subsequent exile meant that he never functioned as a true opposition chief, while the de facto leaders of his Azerbaijani Democratic Party on the ground were always correctly understood to be surrogates. Yet if in the short term the fallout from the Karabakh conflict led the government to turn to authoritarian behavior, in the longer term it forms any Azerbaijani government's Achilles heel. Failure to solve the problem of Karabakh can be used as a sign of a government's lack of initiative, while steps toward a compromise can be immediately jumped on by the political opposition as a sellout. In this sense, any Azerbaijani government—be it an Aliyev-run regime or one led by someone else—is destined to be caught between a rock and a hard place in domestic politics as far as Karabakh is concerned. Hence, any government must ponder which would cause the greatest political damage: accepting the status quo or trying to achieve a solution.

Aside from these concrete human, material, economic, and political consequences, the Karabakh conflict has had deeper implications for the collective identity and psyche of Azerbaijani society. Azerbaijani nationalism, demands for independence from the Soviet Union, and the very concept of Azerbaijani national identity that emerged in the late 1980s developed in tandem with the Karabakh conflict and were deeply affected by it. It is no exaggeration to say that the conflict accelerated the concretization of Azerbaijani identity, in the sense that it provided the concept of Azerbaijani nationalism with a concrete content and agenda, and not least an enemy that increased nationalism's appeal among a population that had not been significantly politicized. Karabakh, more than anything, has shaped the development of national consciousness and a sense of purpose among a large segment of Azerbaijani youth, not least those who go abroad not only to seek higher education but also to raise awareness in the outside world of their country's plight.

Conceptually, frustration and humiliation epitomize the Karabakh conflict's effect on Azerbaijan. In spite of its larger population, Azerbaijan lost the war against much smaller Armenia. But unlike Georgia, it not only lost control of disputed territory; it also lost much larger adjacent territories, in Azerbaijan's case areas outside the autonomous province of Mountainous Karabakh that were home to few if any Armenians. These provinces had been homogeneously Azerbaijani, or in some cases, such as the provinces of Lachin and Kelbajar, partly Kurdish. This meant that Azerbaijan's military defeat was much more extensive, and much more costly in human terms, but also in terms of damage to national pride and identity.

As Azerbaijan developed its oil industry, built itself a place in regional and world politics, and increasingly laid the foundation for a functioning state, the status quo appeared ever more unfair, illogical, and frustrating. Paradoxically, the expansionist spree that the Armenian forces engaged in during the Azerbaijani military collapse in the autumn of 1993 came to backfire on Armenia. Armenia took advantage of the chaos in Azerbaijan to acquire additional territories that, it hoped, would serve as a bargaining chip and security buffer. But because Armenia failed induce Azerbaijan to accept Karabakh's unification with Armenia in exchange for the occupied territories, the bargaining chip lost its value. Had Armenia limited itself to asserting control over Karabakh and perhaps the corridor linking it to Armenia, a larger number of Azerbaijanis might have been inclined to accept the idea of letting Karabakh go in one way or another. But the loss of much larger Azerbaijani territories fueled a strong sense of humiliation, which led to frustration, which in turn led to growing revanchism in all strata of Azerbaijani society. Moreover, Armenia's occupation of these territories effectively made a mockery of its claim to be the victim in the conflict. Indeed, the occupation clearly showed Armenia to be the aggressor, damaging its relatively good standing on the international scene, reducing the goodwill it had initially enjoyed with the major powers, and, ironically, undermining its prospects of winning sufficient international support to force Azerbaijan to accept the loss of Karabakh. In turn, the sense that Azerbaijan could make a very good case for itself as the aggrieved party strengthened its determination to achieve the return of its territories—and that meant *all* of the lost territories, not just the occupied territories.

The sense of humiliation in Azerbaijan also led to the creation of a pernicious culture of victimization. To military defeat, Azerbaijani observers have added a largely understandable frustration over the perceived double standards of the West. Articulation of this perspective goes something like this: the West liberated Kuwait after it was invaded by Saddam Hussein, but when a fifth of Azerbaijan's territory was invaded, the international community did nothing. UN resolutions did not even name an aggressor, and no sanctions were ever levied on Armenia. Instead, the United States slammed the victim of aggression, Azerbaijan, with sanctions that were not lifted until 2003. The West intervened against Serbian leader Slobodan Milosevic, but treats the Armenian leadership, which presided over ethnic cleansing, as a respected member of the European family. The West spends large diplomatic efforts and use strong pressure to get Armenia and Turkey to open their border, to Azerbaijan's detriment; but do not have a comparable interest in getting to a resolution of Karabakh. Indeed, Azerbaijanis say, they perceive that Armenians, being Christians, are treated with considerably more warmth by the European powers, whereas being Turkic and Muslim, Azerbaijan is given the cold shoulder. President Ilham Aliyev himself professed to perceive such a difference in the treatment of Armenia and Azerbaijan in his experience working in European organizations.[4] Europe's treatment of Turkey in the early 2000s furthered the sense in Azerbaijan that a cultural, civilizational factor might be at work that would explain what they perceived as bias on the part of the West. As correct as this perception might be, its consequence could in the longer term be a mental process in which a sense of victimhood developed, in the best case taking away initiative and in the worst case legitimizing the infliction of suffering on others because of the suffering endured. Ironically, one can argue that this is precisely what happened in Armenian society starting in the 1960s.

As Tabib Huseynov wrote, "Azerbaijani society is experiencing trends in public consciousness—similar to those experienced earlier in Armenian society—stemming from a 'defeat complex,' unachieved national aspirations and the perceived 'victimization' of the nation."[5] Former Armenian presidential advisor Gerard Libaridian termed the Karabakh victory an event that, for the Armenian nation, "held a universal appeal as historical vindication for a victimized nation."[6] With every passing year of conflict, mirroring Armenia, Azerbaijan appears to itself go down the road of victimization, feeding yet another generation of frustration that could explode in a new war.

The Situation on the Ground

The 1994 stalemate and subsequent cease-fire put in place the basis of all subsequent negotiations. The war was brought to an end by a confusing mixture of competing Russian and international mediation efforts, and established a military reality that could only be interpreted as a major Azerbaijani defeat. The cease-fire, which has held in spite of numerous notable but minor violations, never saw the insertion of peacekeeping forces, chiefly because Russia would accept nothing less than a Russian-dominated force, and neither Azerbaijan nor the international community was ready to accept that. As a result, the two armies have stayed eyeball to eyeball along a line of contact running for several hundred miles, a major factor in the frequent cease-fire violations that by 2010 had killed hundreds of soldiers on both sides.

The military situation on the ground at the time of the cease-fire led to the creation of a de facto republic of Karabakh, with ties to Armenia so close that the administrative separation of these two territories appeared in many ways to be a smoke screen.

The Cease-Fire

The cease-fire that ended major military operations was signed under Russian auspices on May 16, 1994. It is significant that the international efforts to bring an end to the conflict had two parallel tracks. The international body that had been given the task of mediating the conflict by the United Nations was the Conference (later Organization) on Security and Cooperation in Europe (CSCE/OSCE). The United Nations remained on the periphery of the conflict, limiting its role to issuing Security Council resolutions condemning fighting in general and affirming the territorial integrity of "all states in the region," thus abstaining from defining an aggressor although it demanded the withdrawal of unnamed occupying forces from Azerbaijan's territory.[7] Clearly, the veto power enjoyed by Russia in the Security Council was a major factor affecting these resolutions. The United Nations delegated the mediation and resolution efforts to the CSCE, which in March 1991 formed an eleven-member committee to handle the conflict. It only got involved in a serious manner once the Soviet Union had collapsed, thereby making the conflict an international issue and not an internal matter of the USSR. The CSCE envisaged an eventual peace conference in Minsk in mid-1992, something that never materialized, as the organization was unable to stop the Armenian advances into Azerbaijani territory or to handle the Russian role in the conflict. Nevertheless, the negotiating team became informally known as the "Minsk Group," with Russia a member but by no means a dominant power. The name has stuck ever since.

The CSCE efforts began in 1992, when Russian foreign policy was still in a formative phase and strong forces in Moscow were pushing for integration into European structures. By 1993, neoimperialist forces had begun to assert themselves in the Russian government. It became increasingly clear that Russia would not allow an international organization to supplant its role as regional arbiter and otherwise impinge upon its interests in the Caucasus. Moscow in fact actively undermined the efforts of the Minsk Group by conducting parallel, unilateral mediation attempts without either informing or coordinating with the Minsk Group negotiators. It is illustrative that the final May 16, 1994, cease-fire occurred at a time when Swedish diplomat and later president of the UN General Assembly Jan Eliasson, then chairman of the Minsk Group, was in the region to promote the CSCE peace plan. Even though he was in the region at the time and despite Azerbaijani requests that he be a party to the talks, Eliasson was not invited to take part in the Russia-led cease-fire negotiations. Russia's stance was so blatantly uncooperative that the United States representative to the CSCE, John Maresca, later strongly condemned it:

> At first, Russia fully supported the Minsk group. But in 1993 Russia reactivated its earlier independent mediation effort.... Russia wished to reestablish its dominance in the region and to exclude outsiders, namely the U.S. and Turkey... To accomplish these aims, Russia has been pressuring Azerbaijan to accept the reentry of Russian troops as border guards.... For leverage, the Russians have used an implicit but dramatic threat: If Azerbaijan does not comply, Russia will step up its backing for Armenia... with disastrous military results for the Azeris.[8]

The existence of multiple tracks to end the war led to what is known as "forum shopping," in which the parties could play one mediation track against another to obtain the most advantageous terms. Initially, there were not only the CSCE and Russian formats, but also unilateral Iranian as well as Turkish attempts at mediation. Eventually, with increasing Russian pressure, it became clear that the CSCE mediation team had too little clout compared to the Russian one, which benefited from being neither impartial nor neutral. In control of many levers that it did not hesitate to use to achieve its interests, Moscow managed to undermine and sideline the Minsk Group.

The Balance of Forces

The war ended in unmitigated defeat for Azerbaijan. This reality has led to the assumption that Azerbaijan's military forces were and have continued to be vastly inferior to Armenia's, and that Azerbaijan's chances of taking back Karabakh by military means are slim. Very much because of their military victory, Armenia and the Karabakh Armenians have been said to have the most professional military forces in the Caucasus, and even among the most professional in the entire former Soviet Union.[9] There may be some truth to this statement, especially as far as discipline and motivation are concerned. With the Karabakh armies dug in for almost two decades, Azerbaijan would clearly be fighting an uphill struggle—literally and figuratively—and would require immensely stronger firepower if it decided to try to retake the region by force. Nevertheless, the assumption that Azerbaijan lost the war because of Armenia's superior martial power does not hold up to scrutiny. The poor state of the Azerbaijani forces, painfully illustrated by Thomas Goltz's firsthand accounts from the Azerbaijani side of the front, played a key role. But the fact is that Azerbaijan did not lose the war on the battlefield: it lost it in Baku.

The history of the conflict shows that all major Azerbaijani losses followed upheavals in the government or struggles for power in Baku. These either diverted the leadership's attention from the front or meant that there was no leadership at all to direct the military effort. Either way, these convulsions led to a profound loss of morale on the front. The provinces of Lachin and Shusha fell in spring 1992, just after the Mutalibov regime had been ousted and during the weak interim regime that eventually brought the Popular Front to power. Kelbajar Province fell in early 1993 because of Huseynov and Gaziyev's machinations and the ensuing collapse of the command structure. Agdam Province fell in July 1993, immediately after the collapse of the Popular Front government, and was followed by the southern provinces of Fizuli, Jebrail, Qubatli, and Zangilan, which all fell before Heydar Aliyev was able to take the reins of power. By contrast, at the few times when Azerbaijan had a somewhat functioning government and a united command structure, Azerbaijani forces were actually able to roll back the Armenian advances. This was the case in the late summer of 1992, when the ragtag forces of the Popular Front had taken control over the northern half of Karabakh and were threatening the capital, Stepanakert. It was the case again in late 1993, when Aliyev had consolidated power and restored some order to the army. Indeed, a large-scale December 1993 counteroffensive along the entire front succeeded in recapturing some territories, being beaten back only by the full-scale intervention of Armenia's national army, crossing over the border into Azerbaijan once again to save the Karabakh Armenians from defeat.[10]

Karabakh's De Facto Integration into Armenia

Following the war, the territories that fell under Armenian control, in particular Mountainous Karabakh itself, were slowly but steadily integrated into Armenia. Officially, Karabakh and Armenia remain separate political entities, but for most practical matters the two entities are unified. Part of Armenia's national budget is spent on Karabakh, and any visitor to Yerevan since the mid-1990s can observe the presence of Karabakh military personnel in full uniform on the streets of the capital. Great expenditures of effort and resources have been made to improve communications between Karabakh and Armenia. In the absence of regular rail or air links, the road through the Lachin corridor connecting Stepanakert to Armenia has become the enclave's main lifeline. In the 1990s the Armenian diaspora funded a $11 million project to make this winding mountain road safer and capable of carrying larger amounts of goods.[11] Armenia has repeatedly asserted that it can neither control nor vouch for Karabakh officials, but the image of free association between Yerevan and Stepanakert has mainly been a fig leaf put in place to ward off international sanctions for occupying another state's territory. Immunity to sanctions has also been facilitated by pro-Armenian positions taken by Russia in the UN Security Council and other multilateral bodies.

If the link between Karabakh and Armenia is obvious, the direction in which power flows is less clear. As outspoken Armenian observers have increasingly contended, the Armenian government has long been controlled by an elite rooted in Karabakh. Given the crucial role played by the Kara-

bakh question and the subsequent war effort in the shaping of an independent Armenian state, Karabakhi leaders were placed in a unique position to
gain prominence in Armenian politics. The hold of a Karabakhi elite was
boosted by the gradual appointments of Karabakhi officials to the Armenian government—most obviously the appointment of Karabakh president
Robert Kocharyan as prime minister of Armenia in 1997 and his subsequent election to the presidency in 1998, following a dispute over Karabakh with President Levon Ter-Petrossian that ended with Ter-Petrossian's
resignation. Since 1997 Armenia has been dominated by two politicians
from Karabakh: Kocharyan and his successor as president, Serzh Sarkissian. Sarkissian served as head of Karabakh's defense forces before being
appointed Armenian defense minister in 1993. As Vicken Cheterian observed, the appointment created the potential for a situation in which "Karabakh's security preoccupation hijacks the political agenda and future
development of Armenia."[12]

Following the October 27, 1999, assassination of Prime Minister Vazgen
Sarkissian (unrelated to Sezh) and Speaker of Parliament Karen Demirchian—who had no roots in Karabakh—this is exactly what happened. The
country came to be dominated by an elite that seemed to determine the
national interest of Armenia based on their understanding of the interests of
Karabakh—unlike former President Ter-Petrossian, who in 1997 had concluded that Armenia's long-term interests required a compromise on the
status of the occupied enclave. Indeed, the dominance of the Karabakh
lobby in Armenian politics gradually became more overt, before finally
breaking into the open as a major divisive issue in 2008. The primary impetus for this development was the succession to Robert Kocharyan, and
the elite's evident intention to ensure that the presidency remained in Karabakhi hands. In June 2004, Kocharyan's national security adviser, Garnik
Isagulian, publicly declared that Armenia's next president should be from
Karabakh, as that area was crucial to Armenia's national interests.[13] This
was interpreted as an official indication that Minister of Defense Serzh
Sarkissian, with his close ties to the Russian defense structures and strong
influence over Armenia's economy, would be the designated successor.
Indeed, that became clear by 2006, two years ahead of the 2008 presidential election. That election finally put on full display the endemic resentment in Armenian society over the Karabakhis' domination of Armenian
political life, and was the first instance in which this issue became a rallying cry for the opposition, led by former president Ter-Petrossian. In what
the opposition called a case of rampant fraud, Sarkissian was declared the
winner of the presidential election. At least eight people died in riots that

followed demonstrations protesting the outcome. The post-election violence further deepened the division in Armenian society.

When Kocharyan had come to power in 1998, most observers saw it as a setback for the chances of a settlement in Karabakh, given his past leadership role there. Nevertheless, hope was expressed that Kocharyan would be another Yitzhak Rabin or even Ariel Sharon, that is, a hard-liner with impeccable nationalist credentials who would sue for peace for the sake of the nation's future. Indeed, it was thought that Kocharyan would be the leader who would be able not only to sign a peace agreement, but to deliver one. Such hopes did not materialize in the 1990s, but they were voiced again when Sarkissian came to power in 2008. His stance appeared more constructive than Kocharyan's, but the serious legitimacy crisis surrounding his election seemed bound to weaken his domestic stance when it came time to make concessions, just as Ter-Petrossian had been weakened by his own questionable election in 1996, which paved the way for his removal from office two years later. The domestic reaction to Sarkissian's efforts to mend ties with Turkey in 2009 showed this conundrum in practice, making it unlikely that Sarkissian could preside over painful compromises on Karabakh.

Negotiations over Karabakh

The negotiations over Karabakh have been ongoing since the international community first became engaged in the conflict, even before a cease-fire was in place. Throughout the decade and more that have followed, a number of different formats for negotiations and several different models for a solution have been discussed.

The Negotiating Format

The negotiations over Karabakh began in the rather large format of the Minsk Group, which comprised eleven countries. At first, small and disinterested states took a leading role in the negotiations. For reasons of their neutrality, which made them acceptable to Russia, Sweden and Finland initially played important roles chairing the Minsk Group. This had both a positive and a negative aspect: the mediation process was trusted by all parties as impartial, since countries such as Sweden or Finland had few interests in the South Caucasus. But they could only act as mediators in the true sense of the word; they possessed no incentives, no carrots or sticks to convince the belligerents to adopt a more compromising attitude. As pointed out by John Maresca, the Minsk Group itself was "too large and too low level for serious negotiation, [having] no way of guaranteeing that the much larger CSCE itself would either agree or actually produce a peacekeeping force."[14] Meanwhile, Russia was undermining the Minsk Group's work. At its Budapest summit of December 1994, the institution now known as the Organization for Security and Cooperation in Europe (OSCE) resolved to integrate its mediation process with the Russian one. This was a setback in terms of the organization's authority, but also a success, as it removed the possibility of forum shopping. As a result, the Russian mediator was given the post of permanent cochairman of the Minsk Group, alongside the rotating OSCE cochairman, a position first held by Sweden and then by Finland. During this period of negotiations, few actual steps toward a resolution were achieved, although the mediation process was instrumental in upholding the cease-fire. According to Finnish Minsk Group cochairman Heikki Talvitie (who subsequently became the European Union's first special representative to the South Caucasus), the main accomplishment of his mediation period was to establish confidence between the Russian and OSCE mediation tracks.[15] As such, however, the Minsk process became not mainly a forum for negotiations between the parties but, in Gerard Libaridian's words, a "propaganda forum for both sides."[16]

In December 1996, Finland's tenure in the cochairmanship was expiring, and both France and the United States expressed a desire to follow Finland—a sign of the increasing interest of the great powers in the region. A solution was reached whereby the United States would have a permanent chair, like Russia, with France filling the rotating position held by Finland. Hence a "troika" format emerged, and France became, de facto, a permanent co-chair as well: no rotation occurred in the fourteen years subsequent to 1996. The Minsk process was thus given a higher profile, effectively acquiring a three-country format with the others members of the Minsk Group becoming sidelined. The three cochairs focused on agreeing among themselves—no easy task given the three countries involved—and negotiating with the parties. What did not change, however, was the level of the diplomatic representatives in the Minsk Group. Far from being senior diplomats with experience in high-level conflict resolution, the cochairs continued to be junior ambassadorial appointees. The role of the Minsk Group in the negotiation process, by contrast, has gone through various phases. From 1997 to 1999 it was relatively active, presenting a series of proposals. Then a period of direct negotiations between Presidents Aliyev and Kocharyan followed, which reduced the role of the Minsk Group. In the early

2000s, the negotiations remained direct but were downgraded to the foreign-minister or even deputy-minister level, before an upsurge in activity from 2004 to 2006. Since 2008, a growing Russian leadership, nominally in the name of the Minsk Group, has dominated the peace process, concomitant with Russia's growing assertion of dominance in the region.

The changing format for negotiations has highlighted the paradox of the Karabakh conflict. On the one hand, no peace deal was likely to be achieved without the involvement and support of Russia and the United States (and, to a lesser degree, Europe). This led to the involvement of these two powers in the mediation process, since it was preferable to keeping them outside the process, where they could act as spoilers unconstrained by any institutional mechanism. But on the other hand, the Minsk Group also turned into a forum where disagreements between the mediators clouded the prospects of the process. Indeed, the functionality of the Minsk Group depended largely on the mutual relations of the three mediator states.

Models and Principles of a Solution

A series of models have been proposed to resolve the Karabakh conflict. These models, which are summarized in the following sections of the present chapter, all fit within two general frameworks. The first, and dominant, framework is built on maintaining the borders of Mountainous Karabakh as they existed in 1991, and seeking a compromise solution based on recognizing Azerbaijan's territorial integrity while also securing the Karabakh Armenians' right to self-determination, the objective being to establish a federal or confederal solution that would satisfy the needs of both parties. Several major points of contention impede implementation of this framework, however, such as Karabakh's territorial status, the right of return of refugees and internally displaced persons, and the status of the Lachin corridor and Kelbajar Province. But an equally important problem has been the sequence of steps once the process of implementation begins. Azerbaijan has refused to discuss the status of Karabakh until its occupied territories are liberated and refugees are allowed to return, preferring a phased or "step-by-step" solution to the conflict. Armenia, by contrast, has retained Azerbaijan's occupied territories as a bargaining chip, seeking a "package deal" in which all outstanding issues would be resolved in a single document. Only with the 2005–06 idea of a framework agreement, interim status and phased implementation of the agreement was the problem of sequencing moving toward a resolution.

The major alternative to this general framework was the so-called swap deal, under which the two sides would do away with complicated territorial and federal constructs by simply trading land. Armenia would be granted Karabakh and the Lachin corridor; in exchange, Azerbaijan would take control of a corridor of Armenian land linking Azerbaijan to the exclave of Nakhichevan. The deal would give Armenia a net gain in territory, but this would be offset by the strategic benefits Azerbaijan would receive by becoming territorially contiguous with Nakhichevan and, as a consequence, Turkey, as well as by eliminating the common border between Armenia and Iran. As is discussed below, exasperation with the first framework briefly shifted the spotlight to the land swap alternative. It did not survive serious scrutiny, however, and all the major concerned parties soon enough returned to the original framework, though in modified form.

1996: Lisbon and the International Community's Bottom Line

At the OSCE's December 1996 Lisbon summit, the international community was faced, in a prominent setting, with outlining the major elements of a solution to the Karabakh conflict. A draft statement prepared by the Minsk Group had been approved or at least accepted by all nonparty OSCE states. The document called for a settlement of the conflict based on Azerbaijan's territorial integrity, a legal status for Karabakh giving it the highest degree of self-government within Azerbaijan, and security guarantees for Karabakh's population. This was the first serious indication that Armenia was failing in its effort to convince the international community of the primacy of the right of self-determination for the Karabakh Armenians. The strength of the international principles of sovereignty and territorial integrity was finally being felt by the government in Yerevan—certainly not a moment too soon, from the perspective of Azerbaijan.

Faced with unanimous opposition from the other OSCE member states, Armenia finally used its right under the procedural rules of the organization to veto the language to be included in the summit's final document, which would have upheld the territorial integrity of Azerbaijan. Armenia argued that the resolution, if approved, would have prejudiced the negotiations over Karabakh by predetermining their outcome.[17] A typically diplomatic solution to the crisis was found: a separate "chairman's declaration" on the conflict, which made clear the position of all OSCE member countries, save one, on the inviolability of the principle of territorial integrity. Technically, Armenia had been able to make its veto stick, but Lisbon was nonetheless an Azerbaijani diplomatic victory, in that it ended a trend generally favoring Armenia in international opinion. Indeed, the Lisbon summit broadly accepted the Azerbaijani position. Conversely, Armenia resisted the OSCE's insistence that negotiations follow the Lisbon principles, to the point of considering the Lisbon principles the main impediment to resolution of the conflict.[18]

1997: Step by Step

In September 1997, the newly created Minsk Group troika put forward a peace proposal for Karabakh, based on a step-by-step solution. A first set of talks would deal with troop withdrawals from Armenian-occupied territories, the return of refugees, the lifting of economic embargoes and obstacles to trade, and the deployment of peacekeepers. The issue of Karabakh's status would be left for a second set of talks.[19] This proposal was predictably endorsed by Azerbaijan. From Yerevan, President Ter-Petrossian accepted the main principles of the plan, but the Karabakh Armenian leadership immediately rejected the proposal, as it would restore Karabakh to Azerbaijani sovereignty.[20] Ter-Petrossian now showed the degree to which the thinking among Armenia's leadership had changed: he claimed it was "not realistic" to demand Karabakh's unilateral secession from Azerbaijan.[21] The Armenian president's view was based on a differentiation of the national interests of Armenia from the interests of Karabakh. A pragmatist, Ter-Petrossian realized that the achievement of international recognition for Karabakh or its attachment to Armenia was not going to happen, and that time was not on Armenia's side. Azerbaijan's international standing was rapidly rising, as were its prospects for economic wealth based on an expanding oil industry. From Ter-Petrossian's perspective, Armenia needed to settle its differences with Azerbaijan before its bargaining position deteriorated even further. While he believed that the "silent and sensible majority"[22] supported his conciliatory position, in the expectation that peace would help improve Armenia's disastrous economic situation and low living standards, he ran into harsh resistance not only from the political opposition but even from his chief aides. In the end, perhaps he was wrong about the silent majority, or maybe they simply remained *too* silent. In February 1998, a "palace revolt" led by the three men who had been his closest allies—Robert Kocharyan, Serzh Sarkissian, and Vazgen Sarkissian—forced his resignation, and opened the way for Kocharyan to take power. Ter-Petrossian's legitimacy was already strongly eroded, given that he had had to resort to both electoral fraud and violence against protestors to secure reelection in 1996. To what degree the people refused to support him personally as opposed to his views on Karabakh will never be known, but the takeover nonetheless showed that a weakened leader could not deliver serious concessions. However, Kocharyan's assumption of power marked the onset of the gradual marginalization of the leadership in Stepanakert, something that would make the negotiations with Azerbaijan less complicated. With his own background in Karabakh, Kocharyan clearly saw himself as representing both Armenia and Karabakh, and as a result paid less attention to the views of the Stepanakert leadership, which itself was increasingly subdued.

1998: The "Common State" Approach

November 1998 saw a new OSCE proposal that came to be known as the "common state" approach. This signaled the abandonment of the phased approach in favor of the package solution, which had the virtue of seeking to avoid the use of value-laden terms such as *autonomy* and *territorial integrity*.[23] The proposal envisaged that Karabakh and Azerbaijan would form a "common state" in which there would be no "vertical" relations between Baku and Stepanakert. In practice, this amounted to a confederation between two equal parties. The "common state" concept was a brainchild of then–Russian foreign minister Yevgeny Primakov, and had been used by Russia in brokering negotiations over the breakaway regions of Transnistria and Abkhazia. Separatist leaders in both Transnistria and Abkhazia had interpreted the principle as entitling them to separate statehood first and to negotiating the "common state" later, as equal parties with, respectively, Moldova and Georgia. The Moldovan and Georgian governments, by contrast, had interpreted the concept as *precluding* full independence of the breakaway regions, although entitling them to full autonomy within a single state. As these widely divergent readings show, the "common state" approach was just too vague, defeating its own purpose by preventing a clear and mutual understanding. In the case of Karabakh, as Vladimir Socor noted, the "common state" proposal "deepened the stalemate, postponed the resolution of conflicts, and maximized Russia's leverage upon all parties as arbiter."[24]

The proposal implied that the OSCE had stepped back from the Lisbon principle. This prompted Armenia to endorse the main points of the proposal, as did the Karabakh authorities.[25] Azerbaijan, on the other hand, almost immediately refuted it. According to a published report, the Azerbaijani government said the plan "departed from the OSCE's own norms, blindsided Baku virtually on the eve of the OSCE's year-end conference, and appeared designed to shift onto Baku the blame for the mediators' ineffectiveness."[26] Presidential adviser Vafa Gulizade singled out several major problems with the OSCE's abrupt shift. First, the ambiguous concept of a "common state" was an inherently contentious and unstable basis for any settlement. Second, the OSCE's lurch from insistence on "territorial integrity" to an opposite principle undermined the organization's own influence. Third, the sudden repositioning rewarded Armenia's intransigent elements, signaling that the overthrow of Ter-Petrossian had paid off.[27] Indeed, Kocharyan himself stated that "the change of leadership in Armenia played a great role in securing these gains for the Armenian side." It is nevertheless doubtful whether the OSCE espoused an principle opposite to territorial integrity. The problem with the "common state" approach was not that it denied the Lisbon principle, but that by refraining from mentioning it, it represented a deviation from the original approach, which held territorial integrity central to any solution. That led Yerevan to rejoice, but for Azerbaijan, it was a setback.

1999–2000: Direct Negotiations and the "Swap Deal"

In spite of two failed proposals, the talks continued. By the spring of 1999, efforts to break the deadlock grew as Washington sought a larger role in the peace process. The United States hosted a one-to-one meeting between Presidents Aliyev and Kocharyan in Washington on April 26.[28] On July 16, the presidents had an unmediated meeting in Geneva, and a new type of optimism could be seen in the declarations made by the two leaders, who nevertheless refused to communicate the exact topics of discussion or the agreements they had reached. Two more meetings took place, again in Geneva on August 22 and at Sadarak, on the border between Armenia and Nakhichevan, on October 11. The public language had changed to one of greater understanding of the other side's concerns and reiteration of the need for "mutual compromise."[29] Speculation was rife that a deal was almost ready, and would be presented at the OSCE summit in Istanbul in November (which, mediators subsequently confirmed in private, was indeed the plan).

But a lot more than Karabakh negotiations was going in the Caucasus that year. Indeed, the fall of 1999 may have been one of the defining periods in the region's post-Soviet history.[30] Russia's new prime minister, Vladimir Putin, had embarked on a mission to restore order and government control in Russia, and the security services, which formed Putin's power base, were quickly gaining control over the Russian state. The launch of the renewed war in Chechnya stands out as the symbol of the quest to restore Russia's great-power status; this quest applied to foreign policy as well, as Putin increasingly turned his attention to Georgia, which was soon subjected to the heaviest external pressures since independence.[31] Moreover, Iran had resumed its encouragement of resistance to the Aliyev government, giving safe haven to and otherwise supporting Mahir Javadov, the surviving brother of onetime anti-Aliyev plotter Rovshan Javadov.[32] In the economic sphere, the fall of oil prices forced a much-needed but painful reshuffling of actors in Azerbaijan's oil industry, with smaller players leaving the scene.

Meanwhile, the U.S. government was engaging in intensive shuttle diplomacy concerning Karabakh. Secretary of State Madeleine Albright had corresponded with the presidents of Armenia and Azerbaijan, and a high-level delegation led by Deputy Secretary of State Strobe Talbott visited Baku and Yerevan on October 26 and 27 to make the final push for a peace deal, to be concluded in Istanbul. Notably, this was a more-or-less unilateral U.S. effort, with other Minsk Group cochairmen not directly involved.

The specifics of the peace deal were kept shrouded in secrecy. Even Azerbaijan's foreign minister at the time, Tofiq Zulfugarov, was somewhat in the dark. As he wrote in 2005, "Even today it is difficult to say precisely what the proposal involved or who authored it."[33] Whatever was known of the proposal was apparently so revolting to the immediate community of Heydar Aliyev's closest circle that both Zulfugarov and the president's closest adviser, Eldar Namazov, resigned on October 24—just ahead of the arrival of the Talbott-led U.S. delegation. Aliyev did not waver, but the upheavals did not end there. On the afternoon of October 27, Armenian prime minister Vazgen Sarkissian escorted Deputy Secretary of State Talbott and his delegation to the Yerevan airport, concluding Talbott's visit to the Caucasus. Sarkissian returned to Parliament and was addressing a plenary session when a mysterious group of five gunmen with no apparent connection to anyone managed to get through the multiple security checks at the parliament building, reach the plenary session, and open fire, killing Prime Minister Sarkissian, Speaker of Parliament Demirchian, and five other leading legislators.

No Karabakh peace deal was signed at the OSCE's Istanbul summit two weeks later, as the political earthquake in Armenia had catapulted the country into what would be a long period of political instability. President Kocharyan's position was undermined by unproven allegations of his and Russia's involvement in the killings, and a long and ultimately futile investigation in which parts of his administration were charged with obstruction of justice. The vigorous if sometimes contentious triumvirate that Kocharyan, Vazgen Sarkissian, and Demirchian had formed gave way to the weakened leadership of a damaged president, increasingly reliant on Minister of Defense Serzh Sarkissian's support. Meanwhile, in Azerbaijan, President Aliyev stomached the departure of his main advisers and large opposition demonstrations against a plan that no one quite seemed to know the details of, though everyone had made up their minds that its basic precepts were unacceptable. It became painfully clear that the secret negotiations—the question of their outcome notwithstanding—had aroused a degree of popular unease and fear that Presidents Aliyev and Kocharyan had not expected and could not handle.[34]

What, then, was the 1999 deal about, which would likely have been signed had Armenia's parliamentary leadership not been brutally murdered? The details remain shrouded in secrecy, but it was clear that the two presidents had departed markedly from earlier negotiations and that the deal on the table was a territorial swap. The core of the plan was simple but daring: Karabakh would be removed from Azerbaijani sovereignty—incorporated outright into Armenia, or with a status that made it independent in everything but name. Armenia would receive full sovereignty over the Lachin corridor, while Azerbaijan would gain sovereignty over the so-called Meghri strip, the southernmost part of Armenia's Zangezur Province. This would make Nakhichevan contiguous with the rest of Azerbaijan and eliminate the border between Iran and Armenia. The deal would once and for all remove any imperative for Azerbaijanis and Armenians to live together, make complicated constitutional systems function, or build mutual trust. A distinct border would be drawn, and the two countries would go their separate ways. But what seemed a good deal on paper, especially to Western observers, did not go down well in the region.

To Armenians, giving up sovereign territory in the Meghri area for the right to territory Armenia already controlled was anathema. Moreover, by losing its link to Iran, Armenia would consign itself to increased dependence on Azerbaijan and Turkey, while giving these two countries an opportunity to link their respective mainland territorially—a prospect decried as a strategic threat to Armenia's security. In Azerbaijan, large segments of both the elite and the general population thought it unacceptable to give up both Karabakh and the Lachin corridor, the latter being sovereign Azerbaijani territory that had been neither autonomous nor Armenian populated, in spite of the prospect of a connection to Nakhichevan and Turkey. The territory gained would be much less than the territory lost, an outcome that would later force Aliyev to demand parallel and reciprocal territorial concession that Kocharyan was in no position to deliver. Aliyev, for his part, seems to have been tempted by the geopolitical gains to be made. By giving up Karabakh, a territory that would be disloyal and generally troublesome if ever returned to Azerbaijan, Aliyev saw himself making a chess move of historic proportions: he would manage to first of all restore Azerbaijan's physical unity with his home province of Nakhichevan, but much more important, he would give mainland Azerbaijan a connection to Turkey, which would provide Ankara with an uninterrupted corridor of Turkic land all the way to the Caspian Sea and from there into Central Asia. In terms of Azerbaijan's future security, this was a great prize that Aliyev may well have regarded as worth the loss of Karabakh. Yet, feeling the pulse of the nation, his advisers disagreed, believing that this deal was not only wrong but could rock the entire regime. They wanted nothing to do with it. As Zulfugarov put it, he resigned as foreign minister "in protest at the admissibility of even discussing such a project."[35]

Larger powers were worried, too. Most of all, Iran was incensed by the prospect of losing its land border with Armenia, because that would mean the realization of its greatest fear: the reconnection of the two halves of the Turanian world—heretofore wedged apart quite usefully by Armenia—since this development would tie Azerbaijan to Turkey and break the north-south axis consisting of Russia, Armenia, and Iran that was so wholeheartedly supported by Tehran. Moscow was equally worried, as it had no desire for either Turkic unity or any resolution of the Armenian-Azerbaijani conflict that was not arbitrated by Russia. Indeed, the deal not only sidelined Russia but was U.S.-brokered, and epitomized what had been happening since Chechen separatist forces defeated Russia in August 1996, and what President Putin had vowed to stop: the gradual but rapid erosion of Russian influence in global politics in general, and among the republics of the former Soviet Union in particular. Georgia and Azerbaijan had reasserted their independence, pushing for oil exportation outside Russia's control and even considering the pursuit of membership in the North Atlantic Treaty Organization (NATO). Only Armenia remained tractable, and a Karabakh peace deal brokered by the United States could lead Russia to lose its last bastion in the South Caucasus. Small wonder, then, that the mysterious carnage in the Armenian Parliament led observers both in and outside the Caucasus to point fingers at Moscow. The "lone gunman" theory made little sense, as the ringleader did not behave like a madman; nor did he put forward a good reason for the killings. Indeed, the entire episode seemed reminiscent of the tactics of the Russian secret services. Many well-placed observers in the Caucasus believed that Russian military intelligence had failed to detect the seriousness of the upcoming peace deal, or to head it off through the usual means of diplomatic pressure on Armenia's leaders. Perhaps, as some suggested, trusted men such as Vazgen Sarkissian had started looking to the United States instead. With only days left until the OSCE summit, the argument goes, there was only one way to stop the peace deal.

Whether this account of events is true or not will probably never be known. The late KGB colonel Aleksandr Litvinenko, a high-level defector who was infamously killed by the Russian secret services by polonium poisoning in London in 2006, claimed that this was exactly what happened: "The 1999 shootings in the Armenian parliament were organized by Russia's GRU [Main Intelligence Directorate] to prevent the signing of a peace agreement resolving the Nagorno-Karabakh conflict."[36] Whether or not this was actually the case, leading policymakers in both Azerbaijan and Georgia, and some in Armenia, were and remain convinced that this was the case, and drew their own lessons from it. Most obviously, any leader seeking peace would henceforth look over his shoulder more than once, fearing the "dark forces" that might seek to prevent a solution. The incentive structure now became even more tilted toward the status quo, since the risks of compromising and reaching a solution had just passed from the political to the existential.

In subsequent talks, the United States, ostensibly assisted by the other Minsk Group cochairs, kept pushing for a solution based on the land swap, believing that strong pressure on the two presidents would close the deal. As part of a high-level U.S. initiative launched as George W. Bush took office; Presidents Aliyev and Kocharyan met in Key West, Florida, in April 2001, with Secretary of State Colin Powell taking an active role in the proceedings. Perhaps because the West had accepted the "lone gunman" explanation for the October 27 killings—which leaders in the South Caucasus had not—the U.S. government persevered in an approach that had lost its appeal in the region. Severely weakened at this point, Kocharyan backpedaled. As Gerard Libaridian has noted, the Armenian president now "offered passageway rights to Azerbaijan through or over Meghri in return for full sovereignty over the disputed territory. Aliyev had had enough trouble selling the initial exchange and was not in a position to accept the revised formula."[37] If the Key West talks were heralded as a chance for peace, that was a fundamental misreading of both the regional situation and the domestic position of the two presidents. Following the collapse of the talks, the co-chairs of the Minsk Group, led by Ambassador Carey Cavanaugh of the United States, concluded that the presidents were "ahead of their people."[38] This was true in the sense that nothing had been done to inform civil society, opposition groups, or the population at large of the contents of the talks. There seemed to be a good reason for this: the international mediators had tried to pull off a deal in spite of the firm opposition of the respective publics. The fact was that the territorial swap had touched too many raw nerves in Azerbaijan, Armenia, Iran, and Russia to be a workable proposition.

The failure of Key West sent the Karabakh negotiations into a downward spiral for half a decade. In Armenia, Kocharyan needed to rebuild his position, while in Azerbaijan, Aliyev's health was worsening and he was becoming increasingly occupied with the succession issue. Having failed to resolve the Karabakh conflict, Aliyev would be, much against his wishes, forced to leave it to his son. With this unappealing prospect very much in mind, the Azerbaijani president made a last effort to break the deadlock. In August 2002, he met Kocharyan at the Nakhichevani-Armenian border, and offered the restoration of economic links, conditional on Armenia's withdrawal from four of the seven occupied territories to the south of Karabakh. This was the first time Azerbaijan delinked the restoration of economic ties from the status of Karabakh, which would seem to fit Armenia's interests.[39] Nevertheless, Kocharyan refused the offer out of hand.

Kocharyan's refusal to discuss Aliyev's offer seemed to strengthen the widespread view in Baku that Armenia's leadership was not interested in a negotiated solution—even one that many considered tantamount to a sellout on Aliyev's part. Azerbaijani officials, Ilham Aliyev foremost among them, began increasingly to stress that a military solution would not be excluded as an option of last resort to restore the country's territorial integrity and enable refugees to return to their homes. Once in power, Ilham began using oil revenues to increase Azerbaijan's defense budget. From an estimated $150 million in 2004, it reached $2.4 billion in 2009.[40] As he publicly noted, Azerbaijan's defense budget was now equivalent to the entire state budget of Armenia, and growing.[41]

2006: A Framework Agreement and Interim Status

Peace talks remained on the back burner between 2003 and 2005, as domestic politics dominated the concerns of the two states. Kocharyan focused on getting returned to office in Armenia's March 2003 presidential election, and only months after that, attention focused on the succession in Azerbaijan, the revolution in Georgia, and the Armenian opposition's subsequent failed attempt to lead a copycat revolution in Yerevan in 2004. By late 2004, Ilham Aliyev had consolidated his position enough to take the risk of entering renewed peace talks, while Kocharyan had easily weathered the recent storms of political opposition. During this time, the Minsk Group had planned for a push for peace. Noting the problem of domestic distractions during election years, it concluded that the window of opportunity for a solution would open in 2006. The expected accession of Serzh Sarkissian to the Armenian presidency would begin to preoccupy Yerevan sometime in mid-2007, with Kocharyan's second term coming to an end in early 2008.

For a deal to be implemented, a simple handshake would not be enough: arrangements for peacekeeping forces would have to be in place and an international donors' conference for reconstruction would have to be held. All this would take up to a year, and the international community, having lived through so many false alarms, would not commit to such measures unless the two presidents first agreed to a rudimentary framework agreement that would provide a basis for these steps and, of course, for further talks. Given this timeline, this deal had to be reached in the first half of 2006. Hence, a series of meetings began in Prague in August 2004 that came to be dubbed the "Prague process." The Minsk Group pressed for high-level talks in early 2006, to be held at the Rambouillet castle, outside Paris.

With the swap deal discarded, the negotiators now returned to an amended version of the earlier concept, this time trying to mix the phased and package approaches. The plan called for a general agreement on the basic principles of a solution. It foresaw the liberation of the occupied territories to the east and south of Karabakh, with the status quo inside Karabakh itself accepted for the time being. Some form of interim status would be granted to Karabakh, with a final resolution of the status issue deferred to some unspecified later time. This arrangement appealed to both parties, even though it signified movement on the Armenian side toward the phased approach. The main problem, from the Armenian standpoint, was how the status of Karabakh could be guaranteed. To that end, Armenia sought to include the promise of a referendum on independence even if it would only be held many years in the future. To the Armenian side, that would guarantee independence, since no one thought that Karabakh, even given Azerbaijan's oil wealth, would vote to remain inside Azerbaijan. Azerbaijan was wary of the referendum idea, but did not dismiss it out of hand—the question would be, of course, who would get to vote in such a referendum. Other issues were more problematic to Baku, chief among them the status of Kelbajar Province, which Armenia did not want to cede until a Karabakh referendum had taken place. The idea seemed to be to retain Kelbajar as security against the prospect that the status of Karabakh would be left in limbo. Kelbajar's continuance in Armenian possession remained anathema to Azerbaijan, although Baku had seemingly accepted that it would not regain full control over the Lachin corridor. Baku also seemed to waver between positions, apparently interpreting Armenian concessions as signs of weakness that should be met by stronger demands by Azerbaijan. This irritated both the Armenian side and the mediators. But the Armenian side could be just as exasperating. For instance, its insistence on a referendum (whose results, if confined to Karabakh itself, would be entirely predictable) seemed tantamount to going back to demanding Karabakh's independence in exchange for the return of territories, something Baku had always rejected.

Until a week or two before the Rambouillet meeting, an upbeat atmosphere dominated among the Minsk Group cochairs as well as the Armenian and Azerbaijani foreign ministers—much as it had prior to the ill-fated Key West talks. Azerbaijan's Foreign Minister Elmar Mamedyarov, in particular, was optimistic that a document of some sort would be signed. But at the last minute, it became clear that something had changed in Yerevan. Shortly before the talks, President Kocharyan adopted a defensive, almost negative tone. Contrary to the generally accepted feelings in Armenian society, Kocharyan told this author that "if I want to be a hero [at home], I should just say no to everything," adding that he felt resentment toward the optimism of the Western representatives who were "trying to force us to a deal."[42] Once at Rambouillet, Kocharyan stuck to his hard line, announcing that there was no point in talks since Armenia's maximum position had been laid down and was not negotiable. The meeting subsequently led nowhere, dashing the earlier expectations. Whereas seven of nine points in a framework agreement had been agreed on, two apparently remained outstanding—the status of Karabakh and the related matter of the referendum, as well as the phasing of the Armenian withdrawal from the occupied territories west of Karabakh, particularly Kelbajar Province.

The Madrid Ministerial and the Russian Invasion of Georgia

At the OSCE ministerial in Madrid in November 2007, the three mediating powers raised the prominence of the Karabakh question by proposing a set of principles for its resolution. Significantly, the push was made not by the cochairs of the Minsk Group but by high-level officials, the foreign ministers of Russia and France and the U.S. undersecretary of state. The "Madrid

Principles" built on the Rambouillet negotiations, essentially reasserting the prevalent model on which negotiations had been built: the liberation of the five occupied territories to the south and east of Karabakh and the return of internally displaced persons, while Karabakh itself would remain in legal limbo pending a referendum on its final status. Kelbajar would be liberated a number of years after the other provinces, possibly pending progress on the status of Karabakh, and a portion of the Lachin corridor—possibly a 20-mile-wide zone—would be allowed to function as a link between Armenia and Karabakh. Finally, an international peacekeeping mission would be deployed on the ground during implementation of the agreement.

During 2008, however, the regional situation in the South Caucasus changed drastically. The Russian invasion of Georgia in August shook the region deeply, and brought home the weakness of the West compared to Russia's relative strength in the region. It also prompted a flurry of Turkish activity, with a rapid, though uneasy, rapprochement between Ankara and Yerevan that altered the decade-long balances that had more or less endured in the South Caucasus. Russia seized on the moment to push for a resolution to the Karabakh conflict. Moscow sought to act on the heels of its show of force in Georgia to impose a solution on the two belligerents that would cement its own position as arbiter of the peace, including the deployment of Russian peacekeepers. Second, the Kremlin undoubtedly sought to repair some of the damage to its international standing suffered in Georgia by appearing interested in regional peace. Nevertheless, this bid also failed, as a November 2008 summit yielded only a watered-down resolution signed by Presidents Serzh Sarkissian and Ilham Aliyev, along with President Dmitry Medvedev of Russia. Several additional meetings between the presidents were organized during 2009, with the other members of the Minsk Group gradually regaining a greater role in the Russian-led process. Moreover, the high-level attention shown by the mediators was reinforced by a joint statement issued by the French, Russian, and U.S. presidents at the sidelines of the July 2009 Group of Eight (G–8) summit in L'Aquila, Italy. The statement urged "the Presidents of Armenia and Azerbaijan to resolve the few differences remaining between them and finalize their agreement on these Basic Principles, which will outline a comprehensive settlement."[43]

To the Azerbaijani side, Madrid and the ensuing process reinforced the emphasis on the step-by-step solution and the immediate return of most of the occupied territories and the right of return of internally displaced persons; to the Armenian side, the inclusion of a referendum in Karabakh was taken as a boost to the principle of self-determination for the Karabakh Armenians.[44] Moreover, Armenian de facto control over Karabakh itself until the date of a referendum would be recognized in the framework agreement envisaged by the mediators. That would cement Armenian control over Karabakh, but possibly delay indefinitely a formal decision on the status issue. That might, in the end, be a way to allow both Baku and Yerevan to begin a process of normalization of relations between the two countries. Baku gradually came to accept the basic outlines of such a deal under the right conditions, but that only made the importance of the Lachin and Kelbajar aspects of a solution more pressing. If a long-term freeze on the status question appeared likely, Baku would need to secure guarantees that Kelbajar, in particular, would be liberated even in the absence of a deal on Karabakh's status.

Hence, by late 2009 the modalities of a solution to the Armenian-Azerbaijani conflict were clearer than ever. Nevertheless, what had not changed were the geopolitical implications of the conflict, and the fact that negotiations were more than ever affected by great-power politics rather than local concerns.

Negotiators and Mediators

In spite of the ups and downs of the mediation process, the general contours of a settlement to the problem became increasingly clear over time. The trick was to find a solution that put Karabakh outside Baku's jurisdiction (i.e., there would be no "vertical relations") while keeping it legally part of Azerbaijan (in conformance with Baku's pledge never to allow the independence of Karabakh). Hence, Azerbaijan's territorial integrity would be preserved while the Karabakh Armenians would enjoy self-determination. This led to the often mentioned de jure–de facto formula, under which Karabakh would have de facto independence but remain, de jure, part of Azerbaijan. In fact, status itself was not always the main problem: Karabakh's link to Armenia, security guarantees, and not least the status of the territories between Karabakh and Armenia provided equally hard nuts to crack. Eventually, it seemed that any solution would require the Lachin corridor to at least be outside the de facto control of the Azerbaijani government, whether that meant, as Armenia desired, Armenian control over the corridor, or demilitarization and international supervision, which would be more acceptable to Azerbaijan. Given Kelbajar's strategic position between Karabakh and Armenia, Yerevan sought a similar status for that province, but that seemed too much for Azerbaijan to stomach.

Baku instead wanted Kelbajar to be returned at the same time as the other occupied territories, with the prospect of demilitarization held open.

If the outlines of a deal were fairly well known, and negotiators appeared close to a settlement on several occasions, why did negotiations drag on for years without reaching fruition? Gerard Libaridian has noted that a negotiated solution ultimately will depend on three factors: a sense of urgency on the part of the parties; sufficient domestic political capital; and the combined and determined support of regional and international players.[45] All three factors appear problematic. Both parties have exhibited a lack of a sense of urgency, stemming from diverging understandings of the effects of an extension of the status quo. Likewise, the level of political capital has fluctuated. Although Ilham Aliyev appeared by 2009 to be in a sufficiently strong position to deliver a deal, the same might not have been true for Serzh Sarkissian, deeply weakened in the wake of the violence that followed the presidential election of 2008. As for the regional powers, their role had been less than engaged, or in Russia's case, deeply equivocal: Moscow had made clear it would only support a deal that consolidated its dominance over the South Caucasus, something irksome not only to outside powers but to the two belligerents, most of all Baku, which would likely prefer the status quo to a peace that would imply the presence of Russian soldiers on its territory. In addition to Libaridian's factors should be noted the inherent fallacies of the Minsk Group format itself, discussed in a subsequent section.

Time Is on Whose Side?

A leading problem in the search for a solution has been the temptation on the part of both parties to think that time is on *their* side, and that by waiting, they will be able to win a better deal. Baku has the most obvious case for thinking along these lines: with oil revenues beginning to flood the country, Azerbaijan has since 2005 had the opportunity to rapidly build and equip its armed forces. With every year that its military budget doubles, Baku sees its negotiating position improve, and hence its chances of getting an acceptable settlement. Should negotiations fail, Azerbaijan could retake Karabakh militarily, having spent a decade amassing declarations by foreign powers accepting it as part of Azerbaijan. Azerbaijan's template would be Operation Storm, the August 1995 military action that restored Croatia's control of a breakaway region, the self-proclaimed Republic of Serbian Krajina. But such an operation would entail great risks. First, the Russian invasion of Georgia showed Moscow's readiness to intervene militarily in the South Caucasus. Indeed, the 2008 invasion made clear that Moscow could very well intervene against Azerbaijan should Baku seek a military solution to the Karabakh conflict without obtaining Russian approval. Moreover, a military action in Karabakh would bring the wrath of the international community down on Azerbaijan. As the Georgian move on South Ossetia in 2008 demonstrated—even though it was primarily defensive—it is unlikely that Baku could conduct such an operation without committing considerable human rights violations, which experience has shown the Armenian side to be highly skilled at exploiting for propaganda purposes. Attacking Serbs in 1995 was a relatively low-risk enterprise given the revulsion Serbian policies had stirred in Europe. But Armenia has managed to largely escape the stigma and international isolation suffered by the Serbs in the 1990s, and would hence be in a position to benefit from international condemnation and perhaps even sanctions directed against Azerbaijan. Western oil interests in Azerbaijan would be unlikely to prevent that.

Thus, time does not work only in Azerbaijan's favor. With every year that the Armenian occupation of Karabakh continues, the two populations become more distant. Prejudices and mutual hatred are further entrenched, and the possibility for peaceful coexistence is further reduced. Indeed, the situation in Karabakh has begun to resemble the scenario in Cyprus, where time has served only to widen the gap between the communities. As such, time could make the prospect of compromise ever more distant, as fewer and fewer people remember the times when Azerbaijanis and Armenians coexisted peacefully. Aside from this, of course, is the fact that every year without a solution means a year of continued hardship and suffering for the refugees from Karabakh and the occupied territories, and deeper inculcation of the victim mentality in Azerbaijani society.

For its part, Armenia's leadership has been more divided on the issue of time. President Ter-Petrossian obviously had accepted the fact that the balance between the two countries was shifting fast in Azerbaijan's favor. The OSCE Lisbon summit in particular proved an eye-opener, convincing Ter-Petrossian that Armenia was rapidly slipping from its advantageous position on the international scene. Meanwhile, economic advances such as the opening in 1998 of an oil pipeline linking Baku and Georgian Black Sea port of Supsa, the subsequent completion of the Baku-Tbilisi-Ceyhan pipeline, and the construction of a rail link between the western Turkish city of Kars and the eastern Georgian city of Akhalkalaki underlined Armenia's self-inflicted isolation from regional development. Georgia and Azerbaijan's ever closer relations with NATO had a similar effect, prompting the Armenian leadership by 2002 to rapidly but discretely jump onto the train of NATO cooperation, so as not to be left behind. A sizable portion of the Armenian intelligentsia hence grew worried that Armenia was losing its chance for a favorable settlement. Ilham Aliyev's confident strides to bring his military budget far past the level of Armenia's state budget only served to deepen Armenian concerns. However, the Karabakh-born Armenian leadership and Robert Kocharyan in particular never bought into this perspective. Instead, they argued, Azerbaijan had far to travel before it could challenge Armenia's position on the ground. Moreover, even if Azerbaijan's international position improved, Armenia has enough allies in Russia and the Armenian diaspora to counter such a change. Armenian leaders further argued that international processes seemed to be breathing new life into the principle of self-determination, citing the examples of independence being achieved through referendum in Eritrea and East Timor, and, closer to home, the cases of Montenegro and Kosovo. In February 2006, Kocharyan gave voice to this view: "Today, in conflict settlement much more attention is paid to the principle of nations' self-determination.... Examples we have today, undoubtedly, give an opportunity to the Armenian party to work more effectively in this direction."[46] In particular, Kosovo's declaration of independence in 2008 had the effect of strengthening Armenia's resolve, as it meant the creation of a second Armenian state in the Balkans—a potential precursor to a second Armenian state in the Caucasus.

In the final analysis, Gerard Libaridian's assessment seems apt: "Time is on neither side."[47]

The Russia Factor

A maxim in the Karabakh peace talks has been that no solution is possible without Russia. The 1994 cease-fire talks and the botched 1999 attempt at U.S.-led mediation both underlined this reality. And if Russia was more of a troublemaker than a help in the 1990s, when Russian diplomat Vladimir Kazimirov was Russia's Minsk Group co-chair, the official Russian policy evolved toward a much more constructive stance after 1999. Some heralded this as a result of Moscow's realization that peace in the South Caucasus was in Russia's interest, and the Western powers generally took a Russian change of heart at face value until proven wrong. What many regional analysts were at a loss to understand was why Russia would have had a change of heart concerning Karabakh even as it was ratcheting up pressure on Georgia that would culminate in a military invasion to uphold

Russian domination of the region. Long before the August 2008 war, Russia imposed a discriminatory visa regime on Georgia that exempted South Ossetia and Abkhazia, then illegally began handing out Russian citizenship to the near-totality of citizens in these breakaway areas—only to claim later that it had the right to protect the rights of "Russian citizens" in these areas. Russia then increasingly openly subsidized their governments, armed their militaries, and staffed their government offices with personnel from the Russian Federal Security Service (FSB). Moscow cut economic ties with Georgia to cripple the Georgian economy, and engaged in subversion to destabilize its government and in military incidents to intimidate it. Clearly, Russia was not working for peace in Georgia's separatist regions, a sign that Russian geopolitical zero-sum thinking was still in full vigor.

Why, then, would Karabakh be different? One possible explanation would be the changed atmosphere in Russian-Azerbaijani relations. When Vladimir Putin came to power, a bond developed between the onetime KGB colonel and Heydar Aliyev, a former KGB general. The two found a common language, Putin professed his admiration for Aliyev, and relations improved dramatically. Personal relations should not be underestimated in this corner of the world, and they did matter in changing Russian policies toward Azerbaijan, to Armenia's great worry. Putin also wholeheartedly endorsed Ilham Aliyev's election—not unexpectedly, either for shrewd geopolitical reasons or because he had come to power in much the same way. But more cautious analysts, especially those who are prone to believe that Russia was involved in the 1999 assassinations in Armenia, noted that the killings had obliterated chances for a resolution of the Karabakh situation anytime soon. Russia hence had no need to appear hostile; as long as no peace deal was imminent, there was no risk in playing along with the Western powers; indeed, some incidental goodwill might accrue. In this context, it may be significant that Kocharyan's change of heart ahead of the Rambouillet talks occurred eerily soon after Russian defense minister Sergei Ivanov's visit to the region in late January 2006. Moscow's renewed push for a deal, in 2009, took place at the time of unprecedented strengthening of Russia's position in the region. Clearly, Moscow was seeking a deal that would lock in its much-improved strategic situation and exclude the West from a meaningful role.

In the final analysis, Russia has long followed an increasingly obvious anti-Western campaign, penalizing pro-Western states such as Georgia and Ukraine and seeking to squeeze the United States out of Central Asia, going so far as to jealously speak out against the European Union's innocuous Eastern Partnership initiative. Such policies make Moscow's strategic intentions relatively clear. With respect to the stalemated conflicts of the South Caucasus, Russia has provided abundant evidence that it finds the status quo convenient, and does not desire a resolution of the Armenian-Azerbaijani conflict unless Moscow can be the arbiter of a deal that would strengthen its dominance of the region.

The Minsk Group: Fit for Its Purpose?

The Minsk Group format for negotiations has been problematic, to the point that its usefulness can seriously be questioned. Several difficulties should be noted.

The first is its complex structure, with three cochairs representing influential countries that are often at odds. Indeed, as a former U.S. secretary of defense privately noted in bewilderment, how could those countries resolve a complicated international conflict when they could hardly agree on anything themselves? This question may have been somewhat unfair, as the cochairs of the Minsk Group have often labored to develop solutions. But the problem of reconciling three co-chairs with different interests has been a constant one, especially given lingering doubts about Russia's commitment to peace. France's role has provided a further complication. The idea of turning the French cochairmanship into an EU cochairmanship has been repeatedly advanced, and received support from the two other cochairs and the parties, since it would bring a greater European interest and potential financial resources to the process of resolution. The only country opposing this move has been France, a jealous guardian of its high-level international engagements.

Second, the Minsk Group has not stuck to a firm set of principles, such as those established at the OSCE Lisbon summit. By moving away, in 1998, from a phased approach to implementing an agreement, the Minsk Group led the parties to believe that no clear boundaries existed within which a solution must be found. Especially from the perspective of Azerbaijan, the Minsk Group failed to uphold the inviolability of its sovereignty and territorial integrity, a cornerstone of OSCE principles.[48] Indeed, this wavering on principle contributed to a futile search for innovative but unworkable solution models, such as the land swap deal, and hence to the loss of time and political capital in the 1999–2001 period. Since 2005, however, a more stable and focused agenda has developed, somewhat alleviating this problem.

Third, just as the mechanisms that have existed for conflict resolution in Moldova and in Georgia (up to 2008), the Minsk Group dates back to a situation in the early 1990s reflective of an entirely different geopolitical reality than the present one, and one in which Russia had a totally dominant regional position. The Minsk Group process has proven more prone to change than the other mechanisms, as the inclusion of the United States in a prominent capacity in 1997 showed. Yet the format ignores the entry of other actors in the region such as the European Union, which could play a much more constructive role. The process has hence served foreign policy goals of its members unrelated to the conflict. Indeed, at times it has even appeared to serve as an excuse for inaction on the part of the international community. Far from systematically assigning its best diplomats to the Minsk Group, the member states have on occasion made it a short-term repository for diplomats awaiting a promotion. As a result, several co-chairs have served only two years, and the posts have even been sometimes left unfilled, or combined with other positions. The high rate of turnover and occasional vacancies among the three co-chairs have made it impossible for the group to work coherently. An added problem has been the occasionally unconstructive attitude of individual cochairs. For example, French cochair Henry Jacolin told this author in 2004 that "you cannot force a donkey to drink."[49] Apparently seeking to find an idiomatic way of expressing the unwillingness of the parties to come to a solution, Jacolin said more about the co-chairs' attitudes than about the parties' intransigence. In the same defensive manner, Russian cochair Nikolai Gribkov said in 2002 that "we do not have magic wands."[50] It should be noted that the 2001–04 period was the low point in the Minsk Group's history: not a single proposal was made, and hardly any other activity occurred. But in 2004, the process was re-energized: Stephen Mann was appointed U.S. special negotiator in the former Soviet Union, an assignment that included the co-chairmanship of the Minsk Group. Mann had served as a U.S. special representative for Caspian Sea energy issues and had done a stint in Iraq, and his appointment indicated Washington's rediscovery of the conflict. Soon enough, Bernard Fassier was appointed to succeed Jacolin on France's behalf. (Russia had appointed Yuri Merzlyakov in fall 2003.) This new cast of characters laid the foundation for an uptick in activity in 2005 and 2006. The United States named Deputy Assistant Secretary of State Matthew Bryza its Minsk Group co-chairman in 2006. Already a high-ranking State Department official who had extensive experience in the South Caucasus, this was a positive step. However, Bryza took on the Karabakh portfolio *in addition* to his regular responsibility for all aspects of U.S. diplomacy toward the entire region; that raised the prospect that, able as he was, he would not be able there would be no way he could give the issue his full attention.

The apparent failure of the Minsk Group calls into question the usefulness of its very concept, which requires that mid-level diplomats of major powers with many different policy prerogatives hammer out serious proposals, often in isolation from their political leadership. Indeed, the Minsk Group process precludes the appointment of high-level negotiators from key states that could work intensively on the conflict. Hence the process has received high-level backing only fitfully—for example, when Secretary of State Powell participated in the Key West meetings, or when President Jacques Chirac got involved in the proceedings at Rambouillet. Showing a higher profile in the negotiations, as the United States did when President Bill Clinton appointed Richard Holbrooke to help resolve the Balkan conflicts of the mid-1990s, will probably be necessary if the conflict is to be resolved. Indeed, the appointment of an experienced, high-level U.S. official as presidential representative was advanced as an option in a 2004 paper by S. Frederick Starr.[51] An appointee of comparable stature from the European Union would complement this move, and contribute further impetus toward a solution. Such steps would address the increasingly evident need to bypass or significantly revamp the Minsk Group format if real progress toward settlement of the conflict is to occur.

Azerbaijan's Prospects in Karabakh

For more than a decade, Azerbaijan has sought to walk the path of negotiation to redress the injustice inflicted on it in the early 1990s. As this process has led to repeated cycles of hope and disappointment, the Azerbaijani leadership has gradually become disillusioned with negotiations. Of course, Azerbaijan has its share of the blame for the failure of the talks. For years, Azerbaijan stated its readiness to give the Karabakh Armenians the "highest degree of self-rule and autonomy," claiming that it would be "less than independence but more than autonomy."[52] But Baku's stance remained an abstraction, as there was a marked inability or unwillingness to articulate what was actually meant by this formula. This in turn led the Armenian side to doubt the good faith of the Azerbaijani leadership's proposition.[53] In the early years of the negotiations, this had very much to do with a lack of experienced diplomats. At other times, the Azerbaijani negotiating position has shown a tendency to waver, mostly in the direction of demanding additional concessions. For many years, Azerbaijan's insistence on the phased solution may have also been an impediment to a solution. But as a whole, the problems on the Azerbaijani side seemed dwarfed by the problem of the Armenian government's unwillingness—particularly during Robert Kocharyan's presidency—to seriously consider even deep-reaching concessions from the Azerbaijani side, a posture that repeatedly generated doubt that the Armenian side was at all interested in a solution, and suspicion that Yerevan was stalling for time, taking part in negotiations mainly to extract maximum concessions from the Azerbaijani side.

Ilham Aliyev's reaction to the failure of the 2006 Rambouillet talks indicates that he had drawn just that conclusion. In a lecture to the Second Congress of World Azerbaijanis, on March 16, 2006, Aliyev drew the conclusion that had not yet been uttered:

> For twelve years, Azerbaijan has lived under a cease-fire regime, but no peace has been achieved. Peace talks go on. But for how long? Azerbaijan's patience is running out. This situation cannot go on forever. We are interested in the peace talks, but if we see that Armenia's involvement is a mocking of negotiations, and that Yerevan is not honestly involved but seeks to appease the international community, then we will leave the negotiations.[54]

The speech indicates that Rambouillet had confirmed Aliyev's suspicion that the Kocharyan government was not interested in a deal, but engaging in talks merely to keep from alienating the international community. To Aliyev, who reportedly showed a significant degree of flexibility at Rambouillet,[55] this implied that participation in the talks would play into Kocharyan's stalling tactics.

This situation displayed strong similarities to the Israeli-Palestinian peace process. At Camp David in July 2000, Ehud Barak offered Yasir Arafat more than he probably could have delivered, only to be rebuffed, which led Israel to conclude that Arafat was not interested in peace at all, but in extracting maximum concessions.[56] A comparable feeling was especially keen in the Azerbaijani government after Aliyev offered in 2002 to end the Azerbaijani economic embargo on Armenia, Baku's main bargaining chip, without demanding either the return of all seven occupied provinces or of Karabakh itself as a precondition. The Azerbaijani leadership at this point felt that it had now gone out of its way twice, the first time being during the ultimately unsuccessful talks at Key West, when Armenia backtracked on the Meghri strip, in effect offering Azerbaijan nothing more than an elevated highway to Nakhichevan in exchange for Karabakh and the Lachin corridor. During 2005–06, after having watched the talks from the sidelines during his father's tenure, Ilham Aliyev decided to embark on serious talks for himself, if only to confirm this lingering suspicion for himself.

Ilham Aliyev hence faced the dilemma, as he saw it, of an international community whose interest in the conflict was lukewarm at best, and an Armenia that had no intention of settling, but which had gotten away with keeping peace talks running on low fire for more than a decade. The conclusion, from Aliyev's perspective, was clear. Azerbaijan needed to improve its negotiating position. This could be done only by multiplying defense expenditures to make the military option credible, while simultaneously calling Yerevan's bluff by threatening to walk out of the talks. The problem, given the limited nature of U.S. and European attention to the problem even after the war in Georgia showed the danger posed by the conflicts in the South Caucasus, remained what Azerbaijan would do if a settlement was not realistically on the horizon.

8

Politics and Power in Azerbaijan

The fall of the Soviet Union in December 1991 meant the collapse of institutions of government that had existed and been built upon since the 1920s. But in contrast with the states of Central Europe or the Baltics, Azerbaijan had precious little history or tradition of independent statehood to fall back on. Its first taste of freedom, the First Republic period (1918–20), fulfilled a symbolic purpose that the new post-Soviet leadership could reconnect to and pledge continuity with. But in real political terms, that two-year interval of independence offered little in terms of insights, precedents, or practical guidance on how to set up an Azerbaijani polity in the 1990s. This lack of guidance, coupled with the economic collapse and state of war that plagued the country's first years of independence, put Azerbaijan face-to-face with state failure by early 1993. At this time, the state had practically abdicated some of its most central tasks such as taxation, defense, payment of salaries to officials and pensioners, maintenance of public order, and control of the monopoly over the use of force. Instead, many of these functions were effectively privatized. A parallel system of economic distribution emerged, which can be characterized as institutionalized corruption, or, more accurately, neofeudalism. The point is that this system emerged for a reason: the collapse of the socialist system for distributing economic resources and the absence of a new system to take its place. Likewise, the provision of order and national defense had been privatized, with this essential state function being taken over by more-or-less autonomous fighting forces, over which the government held little sway.

As has been detailed in chapters 5–6, Azerbaijan has since come a long way toward institutionalizing state authority and formalizing the institutions of power and governance. Nevertheless, the formative years of the early 1990s created vested interests and forms of social and political interaction that have yet to be undone and that continue to determine the function of political relations in the country. These forms of interaction reflect the continued predominance of informal networks of power. As in most developing and postsocialist states, it is not purely institutions that determine what constitutes power in a polity. This is true of developed states as well, but to a much lesser extent. To put it simply, a person's power is not simply a function of what is printed on his or her business card—that only indicates the official position a person holds in a government hierarchy. Indeed, whether a country is developed or developing, a host of other factors are relevant to the determination of power. These include personality, economic and kinship ties, and ideology, among many other attributes of groups or individuals. For example, Dick Cheney's unprecedented influence during the George W. Bush administration was not based solely on his position as vice president of the United States, but on informal structures and networks in America's political system. Any country will have what S. Frederick Starr calls "politics A" and "politics B"—the former implying the overt, formalized political system and the latter the informal relations and factors that are not usually seen in public but that operate behind the scenes.[1]

Such informal networks and structures will be particularly strong in developing countries with little experience of independent politics, inadequate social cohesion, limited acceptance of the principle of state authority, and weak institutions. Understanding the politics of a country, especially one with multiple cross-cutting linkages and underdeveloped state institutions, such as Azerbaijan, requires understanding the factors that determine power in that country—that is, the bases of power, and the *nature* of power. Without such an understanding, it will be difficult for any outside observer to comprehend the context of Azerbaijani politics, or for that matter to understand what measures can be applied to bring about participatory government.

The Nature of Power in Azerbaijan

The basis of power in any political system is conditioned by a number of factors, which can range from the appeal of ideologies to the use of brute force, and include personal charisma as well as other claims on loyalty to a leadership based on ethnicity, religion, region, tribe, or descent. In Azerbaijan, a society in rapid transformation, there has been a relatively rapid transition in terms of the elements of power that are most important and relevant. The character of these elements, moreover, changes in conjunction with a country's process of integration with the world community, as it sheds an old system while simultaneously facing the challenge of building a new one—often without a thoughtfully realized conception of what this new system is going to be. The following paragraphs provide a catalog of potential factors of power and their relative importance.

Ideology

Political ideologies are the cornerstone of the Western model of government, with its left-right spectrum as the norm for the development of political parties. In a sense, however, this form of government assumes that political ideologies are at the center of political loyalties in a given country—which may not be the case. In Azerbaijan, ideology played an important role in the period straddling the end of the Soviet Union and the first years of independence, roughly 1988–93. Nationalism and liberal democracy were important elements in the Azerbaijani Popular Front's revolution against the former Communist leadership. At that time, a group with little in terms of financial resources was able to successfully challenge the entrenched leadership, partly because the latter was demoralized and lacked Moscow's support, but also because nationalism had a wide popular following and mobilized large segments of the population. With the collapse of the Popular Front government in 1993, and the nationalists' propensity for extremism and lack of pragmatism, nationalism took a political beating. It subsequently reemerged in a different shape among younger Azerbaijanis, manifesting their frustration over the unresolved conflict with Armenia. Indeed, a surprising element in Azerbaijani politics is the consensus that reigns in terms of ideological questions. The hegemonic position, which both the government and the main opposition forces claim to adhere to, is a commitment to the building of a secular, liberal, democratic republic where citizenship is the basis for membership in the national community.

Fascist or ultranationalist parties or groups in Azerbaijan are marginal. The ultranationalist Gray Wolves were a factor in the early 1990s. Led by then-interior minister Iskender Hamidov, they offered a platform of Pan-Turkic nationalism and Turkic supremacy. After a focused crackdown undertaken by Heydar Aliyev once he took power, the group became largely inactive, although its leader was eventually released from prison. Socialist parties exist, but have never posed much of a threat to the ruling elite, whose erstwhile Communists successfully transformed themselves into "new democrats." Social democrats were united around former president Ayaz Mutalibov, who remained in exile in Russia and became known for his pro-Russian orientation and left-wing ideology. It is unclear whether Mutalibov was a true left-wing politician or merely resorted to left-wing ideology as the only available means of staying in the public eye. Azerbaijani society has proven markedly unanimous when it comes to its foreign policy orientation. Opinion polls show that roughly 85 percent of the people support a pro-Turkish and pro-Western orientation, whereas 10 percent, chiefly in the older generation, support a pro-Russian orientation and 5 percent, primarily in southern border areas, support a pro-Iranian stance. The major opposition parties advocate market reforms, freedom, human rights, democracy, and civil society, and support the country's integration into Euro-Atlantic political, economic, and security institutions. In terms of overt political agendas, they are hence no different from the ruling Yeni Azerbaycan Party (New Azerbaijan Party).

Indicative of general regional trends and a natural reemergence of previously oppressed religious identity, an increasingly popular ideological basis for the pursuit of political objectives has been Islam. The Islamic Party of Azerbaijan is one of the better-known forces that have tried to use the renewed interest in Islam to engage citizens frustrated with the government, poverty, cultural demoralization, and Westernization. The party's reputation has been severely damaged, however, by its affiliation with various Iranian establishments. The government, for its part, has shown an official commitment to Islam by building mosques and respecting Islamic values, and the nation's top cleric, Sheikh-ul-Islam Allahshukur Pashazade, has been a loyal ally of both Presidents Aliyev and has worked against extremist forces. Yet by the early 2000s, radical Islamists had begun to set up rival, unofficial Islamic structures. Unofficial Islamic groups sought to use aspects of Islam to mobilize the population and establish the foundations for a future political struggle. Nevertheless, as is shown in chapter 10 of the present volume, by 2010 Islam was still far from being a strong factor in political mobilization, though isolated instances of Islam-based mobilization could be observed.

Azerbaijani nationalism, in and of itself an ideology, has the potential for greater popularity deriving from rising separatist feelings in Azerbaijani areas of northern Iran and, in particular, the unresolved conflict in Mountainous Karabakh. The majority of Azerbaijanis feel humiliated by their defeat in the Karabakh war, and any would-be leader who succeeds in tapping into this feeling could find himself in possession of a political trump card. Most crucially, the possible synthesis of Azerbaijani nationalism with some form of Islamic ideology is a distinct possibility, especially if a feeling of estrangement from the Western community of nations persists and grows. Unlike Turkey, Azerbaijan does not have the powerful ideological legacy of secularism, and the decline of Turkish secularism under the Islamic conservative Justice and Development Party (AKP) government also has had repercussions in Azerbaijan. While the founder of Turkey's secular republic, Kemal Atatürk, is widely admired, and his principles widely respected in the country, the conflict with Armenia has bred frustration that is increasingly being answered by a combined Islamic and nationalist sentiment, especially among younger people. This has become evident in the emerging youth culture in Azerbaijan.

On the whole, ideology is not a leading influence on power relations in Azerbaijan. The experience with communism and the disappointing performance of the Popular Front—both partially regarded as failures of ideologically motivated politics—have acted as ideological turnoffs for many Azerbaijanis.

Violence and Paramilitary Forces

With the decline of the Soviet central government and the growing conflict with Armenia over Karabakh, Azerbaijan became an arena for the competition of paramilitary forces. Especially until 1995, armed groups strongly influenced decision making, and precipitated several attempts, some successful, to overthrow the legal government of the country.

Some of the paramilitary groups were connected to forces fighting the Armenians, while others were based in Baku, for example, Iskender Hamidov's Gray Wolves, whom the Popular Front interior minister used against his political rivals in the capital. Hamidov had also led the Popular Front groups that overthrew the Mutalibov regime in 1992, organizing a march toward Parliament and capturing key state institutions. During 1993–94, it was Surat Huseynov's control over military forces that gave Huseynov sufficient strength to force Popular Front standard-bearer Abulfez Elçibey out of the presidency and into internal exile. Indeed, Huseynov had no ideology and no strong regional backing, although he became a de facto chieftain in the Gandja-Yevlakh region. He was propelled to power through Russian support and money, but mainly by his control over armed men. In 1995, the OMON (special-purpose police) forces led by Rovshan Javadov revolted against Heydar Aliyev, intending his overthrow. This time, President Aliyev used army and police forces against Javadov, crushing the rebellion. The numerous casualties included Javadov himself. This was the last open fighting involving paramilitary groups in Azerbaijan and become a turning point in the nation's history of violent confrontations. As discussed in chapter 5, armed movements were used not only by politicians with national ambitions, but also by minority ethnic groups to weaken the authority of the central government. Aliakram Hümbatov's abortive attempt to declare an independent Talysh-Mugan republic testifies to the crucial role played by paramilitary force in the early 1990s.

The year 1995 was indeed the turning point. President Aliyev effectively cracked down on all armed groups that were not under the control of the central authorities, and succeeded in establishing a state monopoly over the use of force. The army, police, and border guards were centralized under a single command, and through 1998 the government conducted a massive campaign of confiscating illegal arms from the public and reclaiming the streets from gangs. Today, there is at least on the surface no challenge to the monopoly over the use of force. However, the resilient power of strongmen in the law enforcement sector should not be underestimated. Interior Minister Ramil Usubov, for example, is not believed to be one of President Aliyev's favorite ministers; but his powerful influence over the police forces may be one reason that has kept him in his seat since April 1994. Likewise, the power of Emergency Situations Minister Kemaleddin Heydarov is based in part on that ministry's paramilitary forces. The degree to which armed formations in these ministries are loyal to the state or to their ministers would only be clarified if the minister were asked to leave his post. That has yet to happen.

It is hard to say, of course, whether some future weakening of central authority, political instability, or a change in government could lead to the emergence of new claimants to the means of force—for example, through a fractionalization of the police and armed forces. But it is clear that the governing structures learned an important lesson from the early 1990s: that the monopoly over the use of force had to be jealously guarded by the government, certainly influencing intra-elite reslationships.

Regionalism

For a system based, in part, on relationships of trust between individuals, regionalism has achieved a unique position in power politics, because the foundation for trust within elite circles has traditionally been based largely on regional identities. Being from a particular region or town can either foster the rise of political hopefuls up the rungs of the government ladder or preclude their success in politics from the onset.

Regionalism in Azerbaijan is a result of the country's historical fragmentation into rival khanates, which fostered the growth of local allegiances and delayed the development of national identity until the twentieth century—a process no different from that experienced in Italy and Germany, which each became unified only in the second half of the nineteenth century. As a result, a person's place of origin is an important element in the characteristics ascribed to that person in society, given the prevailing tendency to stereotype people based on their geographic origin. Geographic origin is understood to be a determinant of a person's culture, traditions, and family networks. Added to this are the differences in dialect among the regions of Azerbaijan, which remain significant despite the country's small size.

The contestants in the struggle for political power in modern Azerbaijan are connected, in many cases, with one of a number of regionally associated networks, often referred to as "clans." Five regions are most closely associated with these: Nakhichevan, present-day Armenia (the ancestral home of many members of the "Yeraz" clan), southeastern Georgia (the ancestral home of the "Graz" clan), Karabakh, and the Baku-Shirvan area. (With the exception of Baku-Shirvan, all of these areas have been, at one time or another, home to communities of "diaspora Azerbaijanis.") As for the southern Talysh networks, they have failed to become a significant force in politics, but instead dominate the religious hierarchy in the country.

In the 1960s, a decade that culminated in Heydar Aliyev's rise to power as a Soviet leader, the Azerbaijani Communist leadership worked to "Azerify" cosmopolitan Baku by inciting thousands of Azerbaijanis from the outlying regions to move to the capital. Accommodating people from rural regions is the role of a metropolis in a time of economic growth anywhere, but in Azerbaijan's case the process was sped up for political reasons. Migrants brought with them elements of their own culture as well as their own personal networks that remained based in their regions of origin. As a result, regionally based networks of influence developed in both the economy and politics of the country. Interestingly, the groups that were the most successful at imposing their influence on the politics of the country were the diaspora Azerbaijanis living along the western edge of Azerbaijani-populated areas: the Nakhichevani, Yeraz, and Graz communities. The experience of being surrounded by an alien and occasionally hostile environment was instrumental in helping these groups gain the upper hand in the political domain.

Most prominent of all were the Nakhichevanis. As Heydar Aliyev himself came from Nakhichevan, he mainly used Nakhichevanis as his power base, appointing natives of the region to governmental and academic positions because anticipations of regional loyalty made it more likely that he could trust them. This ensured Aliyev's own political survival and strengthened the resilience of his political base, and indeed was a key factor allowing him to return to power and consolidate his rule in the mid-1990s. The people he had once appointed were still in government, and welcomed back their former benefactor, while his opponents had not yet been able to replace the Communist-era cadres.

During its short tenure in power, the Popular Front government claimed to work against regionalism, appointing ministers from throughout the country. However, President Elçibey as well as many other members of the Popular Front were natives of Nakhichevan or were Yerazi. Isa Gambar and Ali Kerimli, however, hailed from the greater Karabakh region. After Aliyev returned from Nakhichevan to take power in 1993, he used the support of Nakhichevanis and Yerazi to consolidate power. Nakhichevani power brokers included the Head of the Presidential Administration, Ramiz Mehdiyev, erstwhile speaker of Parliament Rasul Guliyev, national security minister and onetime Azerbaijan KGB chief Namik Abbasov, and Minister of Social Welfare and Labor Ali Nagiyev. The Yeraz grouping was led by Minister of Health Ali Insanov and Speaker of Parliament Murtuz Aleskerov. Nevertheless, many ministers, including those controlling power ministries, were not part of either group, including the powerful minister of the interior, Ramil Usubov, who hails from Karabakh but served in Nakhichevan in the 1980s, and Minister of Defense Safar Abiyev, from the Lezgin north of the country. While the government has been more balanced than publicly acknowledged, it goes without saying that the "real" positions of power within it have been related more to clan membership than to a position at the helm of a bureaucratic unit.

By the end of 1990s, as the ruling power and economic resources of the country became dominated by the Nakhichevani and Yerazi groupings, a rivalry between them gradually emerged. Heydar Aliyev skillfully played upon this rivalry, promoting and punishing each side at different times and thus preventing the rise and consolidation of either clan. In the absence of an institutional division of power, the two clans in many ways provided a system of "checks and balances." That changed in 2005, however, when Ilham Aliyev, undoubtedly believing the Yerazi leaders were part of a plot against him, fired and jailed Ali Insanov and prevented Aleskerov from being re-elected as Speaker of parliament. Since then, the balance in the system has gradually slipped, allowing the Nakhichevani leadership to consolidate its influence.

Regionalism is not solely an attribute of the government: some opposition parties function within the same framework. The long-time leader of the Azerbaijani National Independence Party, Etibar Mamedov, is Yerazi, and consequently his party was known for its strong Yeraz character. Regionalism can transcend the government-opposition divide: during the 1998 election, government officials of the Yeraz clan allegedly covertly supported Mamedov's presidential candidacy because they felt marginalized by their Nakhichevani rivals. The Azerbaijani Democratic Party (ADP), headed by Rasul Guliyev, is based on a strong cadre from Nakhichevan. From exile in the United states, Guliyev appointed Nakhichevanis to most of the prominent positions in the party. Former president Mutalibov is popular chiefly among residents of his own native Baku and the Apsheron Peninsula, which explains the otherwise counterintuitive support he enjoys from the Islamist groups centered in Nardaran, a village on the peninsula's north side. Support for Mutalibov is often based on deep antagonism toward the Nakhichevanis and Yeraz, who are perceived as having come to Baku and taken power from the Baku elite. Müsavat, on the other hand, is led by people from the greater Karabakh area, most notably Isa Gambar. But Müsavat is less affected by regionalism than the other opposition parties, and Gambar has consciously built his political platform on opposition to the Nakhichevani clan and in opposition to regionalism.

Though regionalism is entrenched, it should not be regarded as an all-purpose explanation for the country's politics. It is only one among several factors, and one that appears to be in retreat, given the gradual homogenization of Azerbaijani society and the reduction of regional differences in an age of national integration and globalization. Moreover, compared to his father, Ilham Aliyev appears less driven by regionalism. Ilham Aliyev grew up not in Nakhichevan in the 1920s but in Baku in the 1960s, and later in Moscow. Hence, his formative experiences were more cosmopolitan and multicultural. Indeed, he has shown himself more inclined to staff his government with young, business-oriented politicians than with individuals chosen simply on the basis of regionalism. However, for much of the "old guard" that remains influential, regionalism is clearly a chief determinant.

Personality

Strong personal authority has been an important characteristic of politics in Azerbaijan since medieval times, when kings and khans dominated the political arena and practically no democratic institutions existed. As a political factor, personality grew in importance during Heydar Aliyev's tenure, for the simple reason that his overwhelming and charismatic personality dominated the country.

Both the ruling party and the opposition parties were united around strong leaders in the 1990s. Azerbaijan's political parties are in no sense democratic, instead being led by more-or-less charismatic figures who control their party structures as hierarchically run fiefdoms. As was seen in

2005, when Etibar Mamedov floated the idea of retiring from politics, only to see his party immediately begin to crumble, most of the country's political parties would probably collapse without their leader. The leader is usually the primary financier of the party as well as the ideologist behind the party platform, if there is one. In such an environment, ideological platforms and issue-based programs have a hard time gaining traction. The sway of personalism is such that people often refer to a party by its leader's name rather than by the name of the party itself. For instance, in the 2000 parliamentary elections, when party lists still existed, the election staff counting the ballots witnessed by this author in Baku's industrial district would say "one Isa" or "one Rasul," using the first names of party leaders Isa Gambar or Rasul Guliyev rather than their respective parties' names: Müsavat and the ADP. Since Ali Kerimli's replacement of Abulfez Elçibey as head of the Popular Front after the latter was forced from the presidency and into exile in 1993, no major political party in Azerbaijan other than New Azerbaijan has experienced a change of leadership.

It will likely be a long time before the political situation in Azerbaijan changes in such a way that people will vote on the basis of party platforms and not simply in support of a particular leader. For this to happen, parties will probably need to survive several leadership cycles, and make a concerted effort to introduce their platforms to the voting public. In the meantime, the government's decision in 2003 to replace the party list system for parliamentary elections with the single-mandate constituency system will continue to have the effect of impeding that process, in that it empowers individual candidates—and thereby, personality—at the expense of political institutions.

Ilham Aliyev's succession to his father's office and the aging of the first generation of opposition politicians may nevertheless have weakened the force of personality in Azerbaijani politics. Given Ilham's relative youth in a cabinet dominated by elder statesmen from his father's tenure, the advent of his administration necessarily implied a shift toward the vesting of power in the institution of the presidency rather than the personality of the president. Likewise, by the late 2000s the old guard of the opposition, many of whom had held their party posts since 1993, were facing growing challenges to their authority. As younger forces assert themselves in the political opposition, it remains to be seen whether they will grow to prominence on the basis of personality politics or by building party institutions.

External Players

Azerbaijan, like the rest of the states of the South Caucasus, is a small country located at a strategically vital regional crossroads surrounded by regional and great powers. This means that the Azerbaijani political scene has always been sensitive to political changes in Russia, Turkey, Iran, and, to a lesser extent, the United States. But this is not merely a matter of geographical proximity. Further complicating the situation are the facts that Azerbaijan is a former Soviet republic and that a large portion of northern Iran is populated by ethnic Azerbaijanis. In the early days of independence, external influence meant direct interventions and covert support for various groups with clear ties to patrons abroad. More recently, external influence has taken on different forms. Under Heydar Aliyev, Azerbaijan established itself as a relatively independent player in the region. By comparison with Armenia, heavily dependent on Russia, and Georgia, heavily dependent on the West, Azerbaijan has a much more independent standing and an ensuing freedom of movement in its foreign policy, as is detailed in chapter 11. This means that although elements of foreign interference remain, the focus on the part of external powers has shifted to promoting one's agenda through domestic groups and trying to achieve domestic legitimization of that agenda. Moscow, for instance, began in 1999 to significantly tone down its belligerent rhetoric toward Azerbaijan; instead, it began to woo the incumbent government and simultaneously to work hard to develop domestic groups with a broadly pro-Russian orientation. This was done partly through education, though much less than in the Soviet days; through the continuation and expansion of Russian-language broadcasts to Azerbaijan (until they were curtailed in 2007); and by means of a growing economic presence in the country. Moreover, the large numbers of Azerbaijani migrant workers in Russia proved to be an important instrument of influence for Moscow. Transfers from these migrant workers to their families became a major factor in Azerbaijan's economic growth, a development that has given Moscow leverage.

In spite of strong pro-Turkish sentiment among many Azerbaijanis, and close cultural and linguistic links between their country and Turkey, Ankara has failed to achieve its full potential for a strong Turkish presence in Azerbaijan. Azerbaijanis perceive a lack of interest and effort on the part of Turkey, but also point to policies that have led them to feel badly treated by the Turks—especially the frequent big-brotherly attitude. It should be noted, though, that Turkey has helped train and otherwise develop the Azerbaijani military's officer corps and has increased access to broadcasts of Turkish television in Azerbaijan (which has had the incidental effect of making the Azerbaijani language more closely resemble Turkish). Yet politically, Ankara's ill-advised rapprochement with Armenia in 2009 hurt its position with Azerbaijan significantly (see chapter 14). Moreover, Turkish influence is not homogeneous: Turkish religious groups, such as the Fethullah Gülen community, have developed a constituency in Azerbaijan that may be in line with the interests of the AKP, but not with earlier Turkish governments.

Iran has been much more active, both applying direct military pressure and seeking to develop an Azerbaijani domestic constituency. Tehran, of course, is investing in strengthening the influence of ideology, specifically Shiite Islamic radicalism. Areas with a strong presence of Iranian preachers and schools, such as Azerbaijan's conservative south, already see the emergence of religiously motivated conservatism, not least in the social opinions recorded by pollsters in these areas. Most visibly, however, Tehran showed its influence by injecting a strong dose of Shiite radicalism into the violent confrontation in 2002 between the government and the residents of Baku's suburb of Nardaran. The disturbances in Nardaran clearly marked Iran as one of the external players working to influence Azerbaijani politics through domestic groups.

While the United States and the Western bloc more broadly have invested in Azerbaijan both by economic means and through educational exchanges and support for civil society, the Western presence nevertheless remains much less prominent than Western observes would normally like to believe. There are no Western TV stations available in Azerbaijan for the general public, and the West's impact on basic education, an area where Russia and Turkey are active, has been miniscule.

Although the more-or-less open endorsement of Ilham Aliyev by Turkey and Russia was a significant element in the symbolic politics of the 2003 presidential campaign, foreign forces are not as prominently on the minds of the voters as they were in the 1990s. One of the results of the stability established in Azerbaijan has been that politics has turned somewhat inward. The factor of external influence in Azerbaijani politics thus continues to be present, but is itself changing, reflecting the changes in Azerbaijan's domestic political thinking.

The Population

Azerbaijan's people are often considered a secondary force in the politics of the country. On a superficial level and under normal conditions, such an assessment appears correct. Their votes have never been permitted to determine the outcome of an election or to remove an incumbent from office; nor does the population participate in politics to a great extent. Yet at turning points in the history of Azerbaijan, the people have influenced political outcomes either by acting or, equally important, by failing to act. In the spring of 1992, it was popular support for the Popular Front against the widely unpopular Communist Party under Ayaz Mutalibov that ensured the transfer of power that put an end to Mutalibov's rule. It was the same people's total disillusionment with President Elçibey and the Popular Front that only a year later allowed an illegitimate and externally supported maverick commander, Surat Huseynov, to march on Baku unhindered to unseat the government. In 1994, when the same maverick commander tried to unseat President Aliyev, it was the people showing up in thousands on the streets outside the presidential palace that prevented the coup from succeeding, precipitating Huseynov's demise.

The level of the public's participation and interest in political developments is therefore the most crucial determinant of the people's power. In this sense, implicit public legitimacy is an important factor in the politics of Azerbaijan. The opposition parties during Heydar Aliyev's rule were severely tarnished by memories of their brief and ineffective period in government, although some leaders seemed able to gradually remodel themselves. But the disunity among the opposition, and its lack of an alternative political program, was a severe liability and led to popular disillusionment. In 1998, Ali Kerimli told this author that the opposition would never come to power unless and until it made peace with the mistakes of its time in government and moved on. This did not happen in the subsequent decade, even though Kerimli, the leader most cognizant of the problem, put his belief into action by ending his 2003 campaign for president for the sake of a unity candidacy that, in the end, never quite materialized.

By the same token, the widespread conviction that the ruling elite is hopelessly corrupt has led to broad popular disillusionment with the government. This implies, in the short term, that less than popular political figures are competing against one another; it also means that a political figure who commanded loyalty and was able to give hope to large segments of the population could fill a huge vacuum and mobilize public support into a powerful force.

Ilham Aliyev and most of the opposition have both failed to attract popular enthusiasm. Despite what the opposition anticipated when he came to power, Aliyev does not lack legitimacy and popularity. Indeed, he has been able to build a relatively strong popular following, a task facilitated by windfall oil revenues, but he does not generate widespread enthusiasm either. In recent years, only Isa Gambar has proved capable of pulling crowds numbering in the tens of thousands of people, and then did so only at the very end of the 2003 presidential campaign as it became apparent that he was the only credible opposition candidate. Yet Gambar's association in the public perception with postelection violence greatly reduced his public appeal. By using means of pursuing power that were widely seen as illegitimate, Gambar undermined his own standing, especially given the fact that his tactics recalled his involvement with the 1992–93 Popular Front debacle.

Financial Resources

Control over financial resources has been one of the most important factors of power in Azerbaijan since independence. The generally low level of income in the country, compounded by a high level of corruption, a large black market, and a lack of transparency in the country's financial sector, facilitated a concentration of wealth, particularly in the hands of government officials and people with close government connections, who later used that money in the struggle for power.

The most vivid example of this phenomenon is former speaker of Parliament Rasul Guliyev. At the beginning of the 1990s, Guliyev was the director of Azerbaijan's largest oil refinery, and thus had access to millions of petrodollars. With the collapse of the Soviet Union, the central planning system collapsed as well, thus creating additional opportunities for Guliyev to accumulate wealth, which he used in part to finance various political groups within the Popular Front and, later, among Heydar Aliyev's supporters. He was soon promoted to deputy prime minister and in 1993 became speaker of Parliament. While in the latter position, Guliyev used his wealth for patronage purposes, buying gifts for parliamentary deputies and government officials, thereby creating a network of supporters. He developed an aura of generosity, and sponsored scholarships for athletes, students, and artists. With his influence growing, largely due to his expanding support base, he began to openly challenge President Aliyev, who forced him to resign in 1996. Guliyev then moved to the United States, where he has lived ever since, positioning himself in opposition and creating the ADP. The Azerbaijani government opened criminal proceedings against Guliyev in 1997, accusing him of embezzling up to $80 million in government funds, though his personal fortune was believed to be several times larger.

Guliyev channeled his gains to the ADP in order to weaken the regime, and thus eventually to come to power. With its relatively ample financial resources and a core group of die-hard supporters who could be counted on to turn out for antigovernment demonstrations, as they did during the 2003 election, the ADP carved out a niche among the other opposition parties on the political landscape. In the 2003 presidential election, Guliyev's origins in Nakhichevan helped calm the fears of government officials of what could happen should the opposition take over, but the ADP's financial clout was likely the main reason Isa Gambar allied with him instead of Etibar Mamedov in the run-up to the election. Guliyev has deployed his wealth strategically: while the ADP remains his main political vehicle in Azerbaijan, he is known to have contributed funds to other political parties in the opposition. Despite his lack of political sophistication and the widespread public perception that he has engaged in corrupt deals, the fact that Guliyev remained a central political player more than a decade after he left Azerbaijan is testimony to the power of money in Azerbaijani politics.

Transparency International and World Bank surveys routinely classify Azerbaijan's level of corruption as among the highest in the world. In Transparency's 2009 survey, Azerbaijan ranked 142nd of 180 countries. Indeed, corruption has become endemic in almost every sphere of life, from industry to education, health, and social services. Its root causes are well known: low salaries, lack of accountability and transparency, the absence of strict government control or an efficient system of punishment, gaps in legislation, and excessive bureaucracy in licensing procedures, as well as a general lack of respect for law.

Corruption is nothing new: it flourished during Soviet times and during the Popular Front period. Neither Aliyev administration has done much to suppress it. On the other hand, unlike the administration of Eduard Shevardnadze in Georgia (1993–2003), corruption became centralized and kept within a narrow elite network. Critics often argue that this was due to the Aliyev cronies' appetite, that explanation is simplistic. In fact, in a collapsed economy, corruption becomes a feudal-style alternative system for keeping the state together. In the absence of loyalties based on ideology or respect for law, the redistributive effect of corruption serves as a legitimizing factor and a way to maintain the support of the elite and the power ministries. As in a feudal system, certain economic functions are delegated under the control of a bureaucrat in exchange for loyalty. Heydar Aliyev's driving force was always power and never money, and control over legal as well as illegal financial flows became instrumental to his acquisition and maintenance of political power. Indeed, ministers making political use of an independent financial base were, and continue to be, systematically targeted by the government. Guliyev was forced out in 1996; so was Hasan Hasanov, a former foreign minister and prime minister who headed the Graz clan. More recently, Ilham Aliyev deposed and jailed the powerful oligarch and minister of the economy Farhad Aliyev (no relation) in 2005.

Consequently, corruption at the highest levels of politics fulfills a political rather than an economic purpose: simply put, controlling the country would be impossible without control over the largest flows of money in the country. Moreover, the government under Heydar Aliyev in particular showed a capacity to crack down on corruption when and where that proved necessary. For example, in 1998 reports of runaway corruption at Baku's international airport led President Aliyev to call an emergency meeting and subsequently to crack down on airport corruption (see chapter 5). A similar situation occurred in 2002, when Aliyev moved against corruption in the field of licensing for small and medium-size enterprises. What these specific examples highlight is the propensity of the Azerbaijani government to use anticorruption measures as a tool periodically required to improve the country's international reputation, to ensure the functioning of important state institutions, and to prevent the emergence of (or to discredit) rival centers of wealth. This logic has led the government to file several corruption suits against government officials, and subsequently punish them by either firing them, forcing them into exile, or imprisoning them. This happened to Guliyev and to Hasanov, who in 1998 was accused of embezzling funds for the construction of diplomatic buildings; in 2003, former Baku deputy mayor Eldaniz Lahijev received an eleven-year prison sentence for embezzling nearly $600,000 in U.S. Embassy funds. The funds had been designated as compensation for the residents of apartment buildings on property purchased by the embassy.

The government appears to view corruption as a threat when it challenges political power. Thus, it seeks to exercise tight control over financial flows, especially those from other states, most notably Russia and Iran, but also the West. This is also why Azerbaijan's casinos were closed in 1997: they represented a convenient vehicle for moving large sums of money undetected within the country. The government has also been known to pressure entrepreneurs believed to be involved in dubious enterprises to invest illicit funds in legitimate projects, where financial transactions are easier to control.

In the later days of Heydar Aliyev's tenure, however, a more lax approach to high-level officials gained ground. Rather than keep the cabinet in an iron fist, Aliyev allowed his barons to consolidate their fiefdoms.

That did not change under Ilham Aliyev, who has removed only a few of these barons—most visibly in his 2005 crackdown, but hardly any since then. Indeed, these barons have been able to operate their fiefdoms, and associated patronage networks, with little or no oversight from the presidential administration. It should not be assumed that the latter is even fully aware of the machinations that take place in various sectors of the economy, or that it can easily intervene to address them. Rather, there appears to be an unwritten rule that such feudal-style systems are tolerated as long as complete loyalty to the president is assured, and as long as the baron in question does not become too powerful.

At a lower level, the fight against corruption remains mostly inactive, despite sporadic anticorruption drives initiated for external consumption and to keep the government functioning. The problem of corruption has reached a critical stage in the armed forces and law enforcement, to the point of becoming a hindrance to the efficient development of the Azerbaijani internal and external defense and policing systems. Education is also rife with corruption, to the particular detriment of future generations, as are the science professions. Most important, corruption has become the social norm. At the same time, money, often illegally accumulated, has become a vital factor of power, determining the strength of potential political candidates. For this reason, the ruling party has successfully cut off the opposition from financial resources simply by threatening or punishing businessmen who are known to fund opposition parties.

Uprooting the problem of corruption would hence be very difficult even assuming that the political will to do so was present, since corruption forms the power base of the many potentates who individually and collectively constitute political forces that cannot be ignored. Threatening the networks of corruption would immediately undermine the president's position; seeking to exercise indirect control over these networks may hence the best the government can do, unless it is willing to challenge the entire neo-feudal system in the way that Mikheil Saakashvili did in Georgia, a much smaller country with considerably lower stakes involved. Especially when the country's economy was only slowly recovering from the post-Soviet collapse, when tax revenues were nonexistent and oil revenues merely a hope, little of substance could be done to eradicate corruption. But as Azerbaijan develops, entrenched corruption networks will be a major impediment to development and especially to the diversification of the economy, as well as a source of discontent that could pose the single largest challenge to President Ilham Aliyev's popularity and popular legitimacy. President Aliyev has repeatedly indicated that he understands this problem. First of all, the creation of a "State Oil Fund," described in more detail in the next chapter, is an example: Aliyev realized that the billions of dollars that were to come into the economy could not be allowed to be disbursed and divided among hungry government officials. Allowing that would have led to chaos, as it would have bred rivalries among the leading oligarchs, allowed them to threaten the ruling circle's position, and to provoke substantial popular frustration. As such, a tightly monitored oil fund regularly audited by international companies was instituted. In addition, to the surprise of the West, Azerbaijan was one of the first countries to join the Extractive Industries Transparency Initiative, sponsored by British prime minister Tony Blair; it even became a pilot state in that initiative. As it happens, the interests of the president and those of transparency coincided. The downside is that the transparency only functions in the inflow of money: once money is transferred from the oil fund to the regular budget, it is exposed to the corrupt practices prevalent within the regular government ministries and agencies.

The Evolution of the Nature of Power

The interplay among the many elements that make up political power in Azerbaijan puts certain tendencies on plain display. First and foremost, personal authority and financial resources are leading factors that are unlikely to lose importance anytime soon. Personality remains an important political factor even in more horizontally structured Western societies, and the continuing focus on personality in countries with a level of development and social structure roughly comparable to that of Azerbaijan— Turkey, to name only one rather more developed example—indicates that personalities will remain more important than political programs over the foreseeable future. Personal authority is relevant in various ways, however. It is a crucial element in attracting a public following; moreover, because it is taken here to mean more than simply rhetorical ability, it is important in the establishment and sustenance of a political network, while it matters significantly in the cultivation of the foreign contacts so important to a small and crucially located state such as Azerbaijan.

In recent years, financial resources have gained crucial significance in Azerbaijan's politics, as the collapsed Soviet-era planned economy gave way to an energy-dominated market economy that created grotesque income disparities even as it generated great wealth. The ensuing economic dynamics have strengthened the importance of patron-client relationships (often in forms that warrant use of the term *corruption*) in shaping society, a development that implies that control over large sums of money—not just liquid assets but payrolls—will remain a crucial determinant of political power absent the emergence of a more balanced form of income distribution. While important in terms of determining power at the level of high politics, money is even more crucial in determining the interests of high- and middle-level bureaucrats. These players almost always have important roles in larger patron-client relationships, and assign their primary loyalties to their role in this type of network (which may or may not be connected to regionalism) rather than to their official positions in government structures. Sustaining their role in these networks is also dependent in great part on their ability to ensure the effective functioning of the channels of economic redistribution over which they preside.

The importance of financial resources in turn favors the individuals and political groupings that control state institutions, and explains the continued marriage of economic and political power in post-Soviet states, specifically in Azerbaijan. This is the case not only because incumbents receive media coverage and can deploy administrative resources to their advantage, but because control over state institutions is instrumental to control over economic resources—as it implies control over what is by far the largest network of patron-client relationships in the country. By contrast, regionalism is becoming a less reliable factor of power. As Azerbaijan develops, the strengthening of its common national identity and the improvement of communication among its various urban centers are likely to make regional origin less crucial politically, even though it is likely to remain an important factor in understanding the informal networks that uphold the power bases in the country. The trend away from regionalism is likely to accelerate if and when the young generation of foreign-educated Azerbaijanis gain prominent positions in politics and the bureaucracy. But for the time being, regionalism is a conducive or catalyzing factor, though in no sense a dominating one, in determining political allegiances.

Even more than regionalism, violence is a factor decidedly on the decline in Azerbaijani politics. While in the early 1990s paramilitary forces were a more-or-less legitimate factor of power, given the weakness of state institutions and the general unruliness of those times, it no longer seems likely that successful bids for power will result from the use of violence, especially if those who resort to it are obviously lacking in political legitimacy. This does not mean that violence will no longer be used—for example, by the government, to fend off a political challenge, either preemptively or in response to an emerging threat. Nevertheless, the political climate in Azerbaijan has changed decidedly. External intervention has also become less relevant than it was earlier. Azerbaijan's statehood has consolidated significantly since the days in 1993 when an armed rebellion instigated by Moscow managed to unseat the government of the country. The ability of the Heydar and Ilham Aliyev governments to consolidate control over Azerbaijan's territory, bureaucracy, economy, and means of violence has given external actors less room to influence politics, while the state's ability to respond to externally backed challenges has strengthened. This means that while *direct* external efforts are unlikely to be a major factor of power, external forces can prove *indirectly* important in legitimizing a political actor. In this sense, the support of America and Europe provides some democratic and international legitimacy, though the importance of that factor was diminishing along with the overall standing of the West in the region as the first decade of the twenty-first century draws to a close. Ties with Russia and Turkey still provide some political legitimacy, though not without some liabilities. Links to Iran are clearly more a liability than an asset.

Ideology is a kind of dark horse, as it has lost tremendously in popular appeal since the early 1990s. It should not be written off, however. Specifically, the unresolved Karabakh conflict and the frustration it generates could at some point be used to boost a nationalist leader. This is especially likely if socioeconomic conditions fail to improve in Azerbaijan, and in that case the possible union of nationalism and religion is also a possibility.

The final element that plays an implicit but central role is the people of Azerbaijan. While this observation should not be taken to mean that the country is democratic, Azerbaijan is in no sense a totalitarian country either. The elements of power in Azerbaijan have been and are likely to continue to be determined by implicit public legitimacy. This means that a way of achieving power that is considered illegitimate by the people is unlikely to last. Azerbaijani society and the values that dominate it are gradually changing, and the political figures who best follow the moods of the people are also likely to be the most successful. This reality is an important one, as it limits the freedom of movement of either a ruling or opposition force. Just as the opposition is likely to be discredited if it uses paramilitary-type violence overtly, a government that is less popular among the people than that of its political opponents is unlikely to retain power. Maintaining an aura of popular legitimacy is hence crucial for any leader in Azerbaijan.

Prospects for Political Development

Given the intricate nature of power in Azerbaijan, what are the prospects for the growth of participatory politics and democracy? The chances of achieving real democracy through revolution are evidently slim. Indeed, revolutionary change could be achieved only if the forces promoting change had a dramatically different view of politics than the incumbent elite, which is not the case in Azerbaijan. Alternatively, evolutionary change, though possible, would depend largely on the agenda of the ruling elite.

The Opposition: Revolutionary Dreamers or Serious Opposition?

A comparison of the three so-called color revolutions that shook the post-Soviet space between November 2003 and March 2005 shows that their accomplishments varied, in large part on the basis of the character of the revolutionary leadership in each country and its degree of determination to bring about real change. Perhaps the most genuinely systemic change occurred in Georgia. There, the government was taken over by a group of people clearly different from their predecessors. They were young, Western educated, and possessed of a dramatically different perspective on life than that of the autocratic Shevardnadze government. In spite of continued problems with nepotism and centralization of power, the new Georgian leadership showed an authentic determination in the struggle against corruption and in the building of a functioning state. By 2010, Georgia ranked ahead of several EU members in corruption indices.

In Ukraine, it rapidly became obvious that the change was less radical. Even if Viktor Yushchenko's democratic credentials were far better than those of the discredited clique surrounding Leonid Kuchma, the change in Ukraine can only be considered gradual and tentative. The rivalries among elites that broke the Orange Coalition only several months after it triumphantly took over power testified to the continued salience of narrow group thinking. Even so, as James Sherr has pointed out, Ukraine has changed so thoroughly that "there is no authoritarian alternative to [democracy] on offer and none with any foreseeable legitimacy."[2] Indeed, in early 2010 Ukraine experienced something unique in the post-Soviet space: a presidential election where no one knew for sure who would turn out to be the winner.

At the other extreme, Kyrgyzstan saw a distinctive deterioration in its political development after the upheaval there in March 2005, which was more of a coup d'état than a velvet revolution. The opposition did not so much lead as follow the rage of public opinion, and arrived in power more or less inadvertently. It had no program, and no common ideology or determination to change the basic system on which the state was based. Instead, it soon fell back into rivalries among various elite groups, with domestic politics becoming flavored by the influence of organized crime kingpins.[3] In 2010, Kyrgyzstan for the second time in five years saw a crowd of a few thousand able to oust a government, and the country was sliding toward state failure.

Where does Azerbaijan stand in this comparison? Clearly, it is not comparable to the Kyrgyz case, as its opposition eschewed the involvement with organized crime that characterized both sides of the Kyrgyz political struggle. But it should be painfully clear from previous chapters that the career of the Azerbaijani opposition more closely resembles that of its Ukrainian counterpart than that of its Georgian one. Furthermore, the Azerbaijani opposition has lacked a charismatic leader along the lines of Viktor Yushchenko, let alone Mikheil Saakashvili. Indeed, Azerbaijan's opposition has failed to achieve the two most crucial elements that could have made it a serious challenger to the incumbent leadership. First, it has failed to attain a credible semblance of unity. The debacle ahead of and after the 2003 presidential election indicated how little had changed since 1993, and suggested the truth in Ali Kerimli's observation that the opposition would not come to power unless it acknowledged its past mistakes and managed to show that it had moved on. Müsavat in particular gradually set aside issue-based politics, making a practice of blaming the Aliyev regime for all the ills of the country. Indeed, during a meeting with foreign students that this author organized in 2002, Isa Gambar made the basis of his political platform quite clear, saying that the only real problem in Azerbaijan was the Aliyev regime, and when it would go, the problems would be resolved. While perhaps an unfair representation of Gambar's many public speeches and intelligent arguments, this sound bite encapsulates the problem at the core of the Azerbaijani opposition: leaders who once worked on party programs and fielded strategies for dealing with corruption, the economy, or the Karabakh problem gradually stopped doing so, instead engaging in pure power politics. Under the authoritarian rule of Heydar Aliyev, this perhaps was understandable: the rules of the game were not fair, and the opposition had no real chance of coming to power or even of gaining meaningful representation in Parliament. Abandoning the drafting of redundant political programs perhaps came naturally in such an environment, especially as the political culture of the country was so focused on personality rather than ideology. Nevertheless, the opposition experienced a very evident decline between the late 1990s, when all major leaders still discussed the issues, and the 2000s.

In the latter period, only Kerimli's Azerbaijani Popular Front showed a potential to rise above the petty politics of the opposition. The Popular Front actually used its representation in Parliament to draft legislative proposals, to seek a dialogue with elements in the government, and to move politics into discussion of actual problems. In 2003, Kerimli's efforts to reach a compromise on a unified opposition candidate and his decision to unilaterally withdraw his candidacy garnered him much appreciation both among the population and outside the country. For the first time in elite politics in Azerbaijan, a politician had stepped back in deference to another. This also meant that in the period between the 2003 presidential and 2005 parliamentary elections, the balance of power in the opposition had shifted. Kerimli was now the leading figure in the opposition and in the "democratic bloc" that was created jointly with Müsavat and the ADP. Symptomatically, even this bloc did not succeed in presenting a unified opposition, as rival blocs and parties campaigned independently. The abolition of the party list system in 2002, which had partially been applied to Parliament, in favor of a legislature elected entirely on the basis of single-member constituencies, also affected the opposition: it further strengthened the importance of individuals at the expense of political parties and ideologies, since parties were not technically involved in parliamentary elections anymore; it also enabled the government to cut deals with individual opposition politicians. Nevertheless, this reform paradoxically made it easier for opposition parties to cooperate, since they were no longer directly challenging each other for first place on a list. Hence, among the democratic bloc, a seat adjustment program was agreed upon that prevented candidates from the three parties from running in the same district.[4]

But with the onset of the 2005 elections, Kerimli seemed to slip back into more confrontational politics. There was good reason for this: seeing him as its single most worrisome threat, the government had focused its efforts on discrediting the Popular Front leader. First, it transferred control of the Popular Front's party registration from "the reformers," a grouping controlled by Kerimli, to a rival faction known as the "classics," who followed Abulfez Elçibey's line. Also, in 2005 a smear campaign was started alleging that the married family man Kerimli was gay, an allegation that is particularly damaging in conservative societies such as Azerbaijan. When he landed at the Istanbul airport shortly before the 2005 elections, Kerimli was welcomed by a flag-waving group of people identified in media reports as gay. Predictably, Azerbaijani state television gave extensive coverage to the event, adding credence to Kerimli's own assertion that the provocation had been sponsored by the government. This smear campaign seems to have been too much for Kerimli, whose composed mien now gave way to a more visceral attitude toward the regime. Indeed, Kerimli's live television reply to the allegations illustrate this: "If anyone has doubts about my manliness, let them send me their wives and they will become convinced of my prowess for themselves."[5] Even on election day, Kerimli's district in a Baku suburb—which he clearly carried—was the one marked by the most direct government efforts to disrupt pro-opposition voting. The interference was so blatant that the government was later forced to cancel the district's results altogether.

This defamation strategy was borrowed from similar—and successful—campaigns in Russia and Belarus. It changed Kerimli, formerly so willing to work within the system, into the 2005 election's most virulent and uncompromising opposition leader. Indeed, after the election the tables were turned: it was Müsavat and Isa Gambar who urged caution and agreed to take up seats in the new Parliament, while Kerimli defied government orders on demonstrations and refused to participate in the election rerun in May 2006. Kerimli's rage may be understandable on a personal level, but it played right into the government's hands—and provided yet another display of the opposition's vulnerability to government manipulation. With Kerimli going down, Gambar saw his chance to regain his position as undisputed opposition leader.

In the 2005 elections, the opposition adopted orange as the color of its alliance. This choice was symptomatic, in that it indicated that the opposition simply planned to copy developments in Ukraine a year earlier by using the same color adopted by Yushchenko's group. Georgia had its rose and Ukraine its orange, while Kyrgyzstan's opposition claimed to have yellow as its color and to have carried out a "Tulip Revolution," although few tulips were seen in that uprising. But Azerbaijan's opposition had neither a color nor a flower of its own. Its campaign was more focused on the revolution than on the elections, which the opposition seemed to regard as nothing more than an instrument for sparking a revolution that would be achieved through street power. Moreover, the campaign was directed as much at the foreign media as at Azerbaijan's voters. As the opposition failed to bring substantial numbers to the streets, the planned revolution died out. By the time of the presidential election three years later, the main opposition leaders were so disillusioned and disheartened that they refused even to take part, facing an incumbent regime buoyed by the world's highest rates of economic growth.

The experience of electoral politics in Azerbaijan in the first decade of the twenty-first century, taken together with the experience of the three "color revolutions," implies that true revolutionary change can only be a credible prospect if a major change in the opposition's character occurs—and even then, the travails of Georgia, Ukraine, and Kyrgyzstan show the inherent difficulties of revolutionary change itself. Only an opposition leadership that is able to put turf wars aside and unite around a common political purpose would stand a chance of fundamentally challenging the hegemony of the ruling elite.

Nonetheless, especially given the largesse that has spread through the government as oil revenues have skyrocketed, the country is in dire need of a credible, issue-based opposition that functions as a serious watchdog, limiting the freedom of movement of the government and exercising the functions of checks and balances. As the first decade of the century drew to a close, an embryonic "new" opposition seemed possibly to be emerging, one example of which was the Azerbaijan Democratic Reforms Party, led by Asim Mollazade, a former deputy head of the Popular Front who was elected to Parliament in 2005. But until a generational change takes place in Azerbaijani politics, the opposition is unlikely to command the enthusiasm of the masses. In the late 1990s, the opposition had many ardent supporters among the people. By the late 2000s, political apathy was rife; it was not uncommon to meet ordinary citizens who expressed hope that the government would remain in power—not out of any love for the incumbents, but paradoxically exactly because, as popular thinking went, the regime's officials had engaged in corruption and lined their pockets for so long that they must be relatively satisfied. If new figures would come to power, the argument went, they could be expected to enter office with deep, empty pockets to fill.

The realities of Azerbaijani politics circa 2010 seemed to indicate that whatever progress was to take place would be dependent on the policies of, and rivalries within, the government bloc, as well as the attention and attitudes of Western institutions. For the time being, anyway, the opposition would remain sidelined.

The State: From Semifeudalism Toward a Real State?

If the Azerbaijani opposition displays numerous impediments to functioning as a successful force for political development, the same can be said for the government. Indeed, the weakness of Azerbaijani state institutions has allowed the development of a peculiar form of patrimonialism, in which politics and economics are so tightly intertwined that, at a certain level, they are impossible to dissociate from one another. The seeds of this de facto system of government were planted in the late Communist era,. It grew during the Popular Front's tenure and attained its present extent during the decade of Heydar Aliyev's rule.

The system operates on at least two levels: visible on the surface are the official state institutions, with their business cards and other appurtenances; below the surface lie the informal structures and loyalties. As has been discussed in the present chapter, these often have little to do with the official purposes of government offices, or even with the government-opposition divide, and more to do with alignments based on mutual loyalties or mutual interests, whether related to economic profit or regional origin. Of course, such an arrangement is not unique to Azerbaijan, rather being a feature of post-Communist government. Turkey, too, has its share of the problem, which became known as the *deep state* in the mid-1990s following a scandal that unearthed the shady connections between the state, law enforcement agencies, and organized crime. The Turkish scandal had connections to Azerbaijan as well: in shady business dealings involving Turkish organized crime, Azerbaijan's casinos were used for money laundering, in which Azerbaijani government officials became implicated.

Throughout the 1990s, the state in Azerbaijan was not sufficiently institutionalized to preserve or develop any meaningful autonomy from the political and economic forces that had come to dominate society. The disparate group of individuals that made up the ruling elite did not primarily think of themselves as a state, or, if they did, they saw the state as an instrument to other ends. The same holds true for the ruling Yeni Azerbaycan Party. Devoid of any real ideology, the party is held together mainly by the fact that it holds power. Indeed, true to his typical style, upon becoming president Heydar Aliyev made this very clear to the assembled delegates of the party congress, reminding them that the primary stipulated reason for the party's creation and its existence had been precisely to bring him to power. Now that this objective had been achieved, Aliyev asked a rhetorical question: "What purpose did the party have?" This comment was intended to remind the delegates of their utter lack of power, but it did suggest the important point that the Yeni Azerbaycan Party is not a political party but a party of power. Indeed, it has long been characterized by internal dissent and rivalries. Had it not been for the one factor of being in power, it would almost certainly have fragmented into an array of forces at least as diverse as the opposition. In the absence of a common ideology, principle, political objective, or background, holding power is the only factor keeping together the oligarchs and kingpins who nominally belong to the ruling party. Power, in turn, is only partly an end in itself, and partly an instrument for achieving influence, prestige, and most of all wealth, since the control of political offices is crucial in sustaining the fiefdoms that provide the oligarchs with their sources of income and economic clout.

If the nature of power in Azerbaijan contributes to this skewed incentive structure for the individuals in power, where does this leave the state? The most obvious implication is that the state is left under-institutionalized and that the country is undergoverned. If a health minister is preoccupied primarily with skimming money from the system and with engaging in power politics as the head of a regional-based clan, as was the case with Ali Insanov, the health–care system in Azerbaijan is unlikely to function well. The same can be said for the education system. Indeed, both the health–care and education sectors have been plagued by neglect and corruption since independence. In the last few years of his life, Heydar Aliyev either allowed, tolerated, or was unable to prevent this type of administration by fiefdom from consolidating—especially in institutions that were not crucial to the state's cohesion. Corruption and feudal behavior were tolerated only up to a point in the ministries controlling the use of force, as a monopoly over the use of force was a keystone of Heydar's presidency. Likewise, the offshore oil industry remained off limits to the designs of Azerbaijan's oligarchs: this was Heydar Aliyev's tool for building Azerbaijan's foreign relations. The land-based oil fields, less lucrative, were an entirely different story.

The emergence—in the 1990s—and eventual prevalence of a system of governance that operated primarily as a collection of pyramid-structured semifeudal entities with a mixed political-economic function became the glaring deficiency of the Azerbaijani state. Such a development was perhaps inevitable, given the need to replace the defunct Soviet system and the absence of functioning institutions or the rule of law. As Heydar Aliyev grew older and his iron grip on the country weakened, the rotation of key power brokers lost speed, allowing the consolidation of fiefdoms into bastions. In a sense, the patriarchal style of government of Heydar Aliyev came back to haunt Ilham Aliyev's administration: the state system was built on one man's control over the entire political system, and when that control waned, the second tier of power brokers were able to entrench themselves. The continued prevalence of this system also implied that no election was by itself likely to magically change the way the country was run; only a reordering of priorities at the very helm of the state could change the incentive structure among officials, limit corruption, and reorient ministers and functionaries to the job they were actually supposed to be doing. In practical terms, this meant building the institutions of a state, but that, in turn, meant encroaching upon the powerful bastions that had consolidated their positions as much as Ilham Aliyev had consolidated his own.

For such institutional development, several factors must be in place. The first factor is stability and order, which has been less of a problem since the late 1990s. Second, there is a need for economic means to build the state. This is crucial, because the redistributive semifeudal system of fiefdoms emerged partly because of the collapse of the state's ability to pay its employees. Only if the state is able to pay its employees a salary on which they can feed their families will it be possible to change their incentive structure. In other words, if a state is to fight corruption, stop the consolidation of fiefdoms built on the misuse of government institutions, and develop professionalism and meritocracy, the bottom line is that employees have to be paid. Azerbaijan's heavy inflow of oil revenue in recent years has certainly facilitated the objective of putting the compensation of the government workforce on a rational basis.

A third prerequisite for effective state institutions is a *capacity* on the part of the highest officeholder in the country to do away with the semifeudal system. This could be understood as a contradiction in terms, since by definition the individual at the helm of the state is also automatically at the helm of the semifeudal system of informal relations that was grafted onto the state and, for most practical purposes, came to replace it. Hence true state building requires, paradoxically, that a president undermine the very system his power rests on, in order to develop a tenuous alternative. For this to be possible, the president of the country must be entrenched in power and be the undisputed ruler. Azerbaijan's constitutional system provides for this formally through the extensive authority given to the presidency. But precisely because of the salience of informal structures and networks in determining power in the country, the president also needs to be in absolute control de facto, and not only de jure, in order to be able to reform the central features of the political system—lest he risk losing power. When Ilham Aliyev came to power, his position in the informal hierarchies of power did not provide such a position. Indeed, only gradually and methodically was he able to establish himself in this position among the influential, wealthy, and well-connected members of the ruling elite. But it became gradually clear that his grip on the machinery of power was tightening. This implies that the capacity of the president to reform the system grew.

Finally, there needs to be not only a capacity but a *willingness* on the part of the highest leadership to make state building a priority. With other factors in place, this is the main unresolved question. Ilham Aliyev has made it abundantly clear that he is a realist, very different from his neighbor Mikheil Saakashvili in terms of temperament, emotions, and priorities. Aliyev is no activist, ideologue, or firebrand speaker, but a calm and composed pragmatist who hardly ever allows his emotions to shine through the neutral surface, which almost seems to suggest indifference. The art of politics as practiced by Ilham Aliyev has involved capitalizing upon being underestimated through the use of dry, methodical calculation. Being increasingly secure in his position of leadership, he has also been able to tighten his grip on power. The steps he has taken have been well planned, cautious, and gradual, commensurate with both his own character and his analysis of the position in which he found himself when elected. In this sense, Ilham Aliyev should not be expected to implement dramatic changes. Any change in Azerbaijan during his tenure is likely to be gradual, methodical, and unannounced, unfolding over a period of years.

The initial days of his tenure did not give much reason to cheer, as it started with an exceptionally harsh crackdown on opposition demonstrations as well as the countrywide organizations of the two major opposition parties that had challenged his election, the ADP and Müsavat. Yet in the years that followed, a more positive record emerged. President Aliyev gradually removed some of the most corrupt and reform-resistant kingpins of the old guard and replaced them with persons with backgrounds as serious managers, often from business enterprises. From the foreign ministry to the communications ministry and other offices that have seen a change of leadership, significant improvements in the levels of professionalism and honesty have been recorded.

The emphasis placed on loyalty by Ilham Aliyev also merits notice. Like his father, he has shown little or no tolerance of disloyalty. This was most obviously the case in the harsh measures employed again his former associate Farhad Aliyev, the deposed minister of economics. Following the latter's ouster, President Aliyev related a surprisingly mundane version of what had transpired: he claimed to have twice gone directly to Farhad Aliyev and confronted him with the reports about his funding of the opposition, whereupon the latter swore his loyalty on everything holy. Upon obtaining what was apparently incontrovertible evidence to the contrary, the president then showed no mercy, very clearly making Farhad Aliyev's case a warning to all other potentially disloyal officials. Likewise, the president's decision to punish officials who had engaged in solo acts of election interference to promote their personal interests not only broke the tradition of being able to practice election fraud with impunity, which had been the hallmark of old-style electoral politics, but showed that he would not tolerate insubordination.

Yet the large inflows of oil money that started in 2006 slowed implementation of the cautious reform agenda the president had put in place. Indeed, being awash in oil revenues seemed to lead to complacency and self-confidence; the sense that reforms were necessary for the sake of the country's future no longer seemed so urgent. In both the political and economic fields, stagnation set in, a development that, not coincidentally, occurred in parallel with the gradual disengagement of the West from the South Caucasus in general and Azerbaijan in particular.

Does Reform Mean Democracy?

In spite of a trend toward stagnation, the Azerbaijani state has clearly become a more efficient institution than it was at the start of the new century. For the great majority of citizens, this implies an improved ability to receive the services of a state and to seek recourse to it for problem solving and other needs. But will the construction of a more efficient state in tandem with economic development and the emergence of a middle class also lead to political reform of a magnitude that will bring Azerbaijan into the community of democracies? The answer to that question is by no means obvious, not least because there is no prior case of a resource-dependent developing country making such a political transition. Indeed, Azerbaijan is torn between strong forces—both domestic and external—pulling it simultaneously toward democracy and authoritarianism. The domestic and international forces, moreover, are interconnected, as the authoritarianism-inclined domestic forces favor relations with authoritarian powers such as Russia, while the more progressive forces depend on their country's relations with the West. Unfortunately, in neither the domestic nor the international realm are the progressive forces currently on the advance. To the contrary, the disengagement of the West from the region has made the task of the progressive elements in the Azerbaijani state all the more complicated.

Internally, Azerbaijan carries the authoritarian traditions of the khanates, the Russian Empire, and the Soviet Union, as well as the strongly hierarchical social structures of established communities of agrarian Muslims.

Added to this is rapid state-controlled economic development that could tempt the government to believe—perhaps correctly—that it can buy the loyalty of the population by delivering order, stability, and prosperity. No matter how many ministers Ilham Aliyev removes, entrenched vested interests will remain, for whom the stakes are high and giving up power is tantamount to giving up everything. But on the other hand, survey after survey shows a level of support for democratic principles in the population that makes Azerbaijan seem more similar to the countries of Central and Eastern Europe than to Russia. Indeed, Azerbaijan can lay claim to the longest indigenous tradition of liberal democratic thinking in the Muslim world, as well as the experiences of two democratic-minded—albeit abortive and ultimately unsuccessful—governments that espoused liberal and democratic ideologies: the First Republic of 1918–20 and the Popular Front government of 1992–93. This experience prevented Heydar Aliyev from exerting total control over Azerbaijani society, as his understanding of the need for implicit public legitimacy prevented him from outlawing opposition or restricting press freedom completely. Azerbaijan remains a pluralistic country, with not only a political opposition but a strong democratic constituency—represented by increasingly vocal nongovernmental organizations, modern-minded businessmen, a cultural intelligentsia, and not least progressively minded individuals and groups in the middle levels of the bureaucratic hierarchy. These are all increasingly connected to the globalized world and to a significant degree educated in the West. The fact that the government itself publicly commits itself to democratic development also generates a self-fulfilling momentum that is difficult to halt, let alone overturn.

Geographically speaking, Azerbaijan is located on the outskirts of the community of democratic states, and the political developments around the country are not auspicious, as developments in Russia and Iran suggest. The 1990s were the years of democratization in the republics of the former Soviet Union, and of a general belief in the transition paradigm: what Thomas Carothers has called "an analytic model of democratic transition [which] democracy promoters extended as a universal paradigm for understanding democratization," and whose core assumption is that "any country moving away from dictatorial rule can be considered a country in transition toward democracy."[6] Nevertheless, as Carothers has put it,

> As they arrived at their frameworks for understanding democratization, democracy aid practitioners did not give significant attention to the challenge of a society trying to democratize while it is grappling with the reality

of building a state from scratch or coping with an existent but largely non-functional state.[7]

By the early 2000s, it was apparent that not all postsocialist transitions had ended in democracy, or were even heading that way. Transition—understood as a systemic shift from one system of government to another—had come to an end in most former communist states, and what was taking place was normal political and economic transformation, which occurs everywhere. Central European and Baltic states had become consolidated democracies, in Freedom House's terminology, while several Central Asian states, Belarus, and Russia were moving toward consolidated autocratic systems of a new and different kind. The three states in the South Caucasus, Moldova and Ukraine were the only ones still hanging in the balance.

These states, including Azerbaijan, were pulled toward both the democratic European identity and the authoritarian Russian and Asiatic model. Beyond the former Soviet space, Azerbaijan's closest neighbors were equally divided. On the one hand, Iran's theocracy was recoiling from a liberal phase into a renewed hard-liner dominance represented by President Mahmoud Ahmadinejad and the Revolutionary Guards Corps. As for Turkey, under the Islamic conservative government of Recep Tayyip Erdoğan, the country at first implemented wide-ranging democratic reforms from 2002 to 2005, then began moving in a worryingly authoritarian direction from 2007 onward, with Islamic ideology becoming increasingly dominant. Simply put, Turkey was no longer a force for democratic change in the region.

While Ilham Aliyev was clearly glancing toward the East Asian development model, which suited his own temperament by putting much greater emphasis on economic development than on political reform, he was also unmistakably clear about his views on Europe. President Aliyev stated that for a country such as Azerbaijan, sandwiched between East and West, Europe was the only model for Azerbaijan's future development as a state.[8] In fact, starting with his father's time in office, Azerbaijan has been recognized as one of the post-Soviet states most responsive to the influence of Western governments and organizations. Azerbaijan's government has received recognition for taking into account the criticism and recommendations of Western institutions in its electoral legislation, reform process, and political life. In particular, Azerbaijan's membership in the Council of Europe since 2001 has given crucial, constant encouragement to the pro-democracy forces in the country by providing both the nagging voice of a

critic and the constructive force of technical assistance and concrete recommendations. The effect of this membership in a key European institution
should not be underestimated, especially as Ilham Aliyev himself served as
head of Azerbaijan's delegation to the council's parliamentary assembly
and was elected one of its deputy chairmen, a position Baku freely used at
home to highlight the president's international profile.

In spite of the short-term intoxication with oil money with the resulting
arrogance among elites, and Europe's gradual disengagement discussed in
chapter 15, Azerbaijan's European vocation is a reality, In turn, it stems
very much from the unattractive nature of any other option presented to the
country. Given the lack of Western attention to Azerbaijan, discussed in
greater detail in a chapter 15, it is remarkable how little Moscow has to
show for its efforts to court Baku and Ilham Aliyev personally. On the
other hand, it would be a mistake to draw parallels to Turkey too closely.
The two countries share many striking similarities, such as a tradition of
Western liberal democratic thought and secularism and a cautious present-
day alignment with Western institutions and ideals, which make them a
unique pair in the Muslim world.

Yet there has been something almost desperate about Turkey's European
vocation, as the Turkish republic's national identity appeared to be built to
a significant degree on the vision of full status as a European state. Europe,
however, has no comparable hold on the Azerbaijani national psyche.
Azerbaijan's identity is, in a sense, less dogmatic and more confident than
Turkey's, as it is less coherent and top-down, and less of an ideological
construct. The consequence is that Azerbaijan may be less willing than
Turkey to endure hardships caused by its Turkic ethnicity and Islamic culture for the sake of membership in European clubs. Again, Ilham Aliyev's
pragmatic attitude can be observed in his view of Europe. While making it
clear that he understands Azerbaijan's participation in Euro-Atlantic institutions being primarily dependent on its own performance, he has also
conceded his concern with the double standard with which Western powers
have treated Azerbaijan. From his Council of Europe experience, he gave
voice to a sense that Azerbaijan was always treated slightly differently than
either Armenia or Georgia. Hence, compared to that of Turkey, Azerbaijan's leadership has a more sober and pragmatic stance toward Europe, and
certainly lacks a determination to join it at any cost.

Azerbaijan's future could hold the prospect of a gradual democratization, in which case it would follow the "transition paradigm" and the model
of the countries of Central Europe, which gradually came to approximate
the Western European states and join the European Union and NATO. But

it could also become what has been called a "liberal autocracy": a state that maintains the formal institutions of democracy, holds elections, and allows critical media to exist; and where "rulers may eschew full-scale authoritarianism for a system that offers periodic openings in response to a variety of social, political, and strategic challenges [but where] all actors must agree to the rules promulgated by leaders who remain unaccountable."[9] Indeed, this is increasingly a model that states in Southeast Asia and some resource rich-countries elsewhere appear to be choosing, which puts them in the category defined by political scientists as "hybrid regimes." Indeed, such a model could end up suiting the interests of the Azerbaijani ruling elites relatively well. Through the provision of some political and economic pluralism, a semifree media, and a political opposition, the population is kept calm so long as the government delivers economically. Simultaneously, the freedoms remain limited and the ruling elite's grip on power remains unthreatened.

The designs of Azerbaijan's leadership and the development of internal political forces will be paramount in determining which road the country eventually travels. But the policies of the international community will also be crucial.

Western Assistance Policies: From a Focus on Elections to Building the Rule of Law

Western democracy assistance programs often see democracy not only as an end in itself, but also as the method by which it achieves itself. In other words, democracy is both the goal and the way to achieve that goal. But as less dogmatic observers such as Fareed Zakaria have discerned, this construct does not always correspond to reality.[10] Countries that in the early 1990s embarked on free elections without functioning state institutions rapidly spun into economic downturn, widespread corruption, and unrest, with the very basics of democracy subsequently becoming compromised. This scenario is fairly descriptive of what happened in the Caucasus in the early 1990s, and leads to the building of what Zakaria famously called "illiberal democracies."[11] But as Zakaria and others argue, stable democracies in the long term evolve not from snap elections but out of the long-term building of statehood and the emergence of economic prosperity and a middle class, which gradually works to limit the state's encroachment on its rights. Hence, the rule of law is gradually built while the state is technically the opposite of an illiberal democracy—a liberal autocracy, in which the state gradually and irrevocably loses its control over society, with political democratization the outcome. This is the East Asian model of democratization, which has yielded results that appear at least as promising as those offered by the electoral model. Of course, especially in resource-rich societies, the risk is that democracy never develops due to the consolidation of semi-authoritarian government.

This is where Western policies are relevant, particularly in a country such as Azerbaijan. Azerbaijan is unique in that it is both a resource-dependent economy and a country that aspires to membership in Euro-Atlantic institutions. The economic lifeline of its energy industry, and thereby of its sovereignty and independence, is the westward transportation of energy to European markets. Interestingly, this situation could work against the conventional wisdom that oil wealth has a negative impact on democracy: because Azerbaijan is in proximity to Europe and because the export of Azerbaijani oil intricately connects the country with European economics and politics, that link could eventually result in the full political and economic integration of Azerbaijan into institutions based on European values. This, in turn, would mean that oil could indirectly further the cause of democracy, good governance, transparency, and human rights. But this rosy scenario can only occur if the West manages to follow an articulate and balanced policy toward Azerbaijan based on a strategy that combines democracy promotion with recognition of Baku's economic interests and acknowledgment of its security concerns, something that appears increasingly unlikely.

In devising aid strategies for the states of the South Caucasus and Central Asia, the West made two missteps: first, it deliberately avoided engaging in unresolved conflicts, the region's main problem; second, it eschewed involvement with state building, instead preferring to build civil society. Both of these acts of avoidance show a fundamental misunderstanding of the politics of these regions, and explain why Western aid has largely failed to achieve its broader objectives.

Although regional ethnopolitical conflicts, including Karabakh, clearly pose the main threat to development and stability in the South Caucasus, development cooperation proceeded under the assumption that these conflicts could not be resolved with the resources at hand. This assumption led to a two-pronged approach. First, Western donors instituted "processes" that have come to serve mainly as an excuse for inaction on the part of the international community, certainly since about 2005. The implication was that Western agents of development would circumvent the conflicts. Development cooperation hence focused on everything but the conflicts: building civil society, improving governance, ensuring transparency, reforming agriculture, advancing gender equality, widening access to education, etc.

Second, donors concluded that the governing structures in the states of the region states were corrupted and unreformed. Hundreds of millions in any currency were spent on democratization and development—not primarily on building and reforming the state, but, rather, on building parallel structures, that is civil society. The idea was to lay the foundation for voluntary associations that could sustain themselves once they were created. Yet these efforts seldom created truly voluntary associations, instead building Westernized cultural elite groups created on a foundation of Western funds, whose members make a living out of positioning themselves as forces of perpetual opposition instead of working with governments. Aside from this, Western governments and organizations focused their attention on elections and not on state building. Armies of election observers were catapulted for a few days into countries they mostly had never visited in order to participate in observer missions; meanwhile, the more important but tedious work of continual institution building was given comparatively scant attention.

In particular, the security sector—specifically the military, police, interior ministry, and customs, as well as the judiciary—are the most unreformed, inefficient, and corrupt institutions in all post-Soviet states. The dysfunctional character of these institutions impedes the resolution of conflicts as the salience of private interests in the security forces creates narrow self-interests, including criminal ones, dedicated to sustaining the status quo. The lack of strict control over the armed forces, in conjunction with weak military hierarchy and discipline, increases the risk of outbreaks of armed violence, cease-fire violations, and the resumption of organized interstate or domestic hostilities. In addition, the weakness of the security sector impedes the building of democratic and accountable states across the region. Indeed, the primitive practices on the part of law enforcement and other government agencies have alienated many loyal citizens, exacerbating existing socioeconomic frustration.

Yet Western aid programs long focused their assistance instead on such sympathetic entities as unregistered political parties and nongovernmental organizations, and treated local officialdom and the police as unredeemable pariahs. Alienated from Western assistance, security sector forces did not improve their behavior; rather, they became even more unruly. Representing a powerful and backward-looking faction they became locked in struggle with reformist elements concentrated in other parts of the government. The strength of these forces implies that the presidents of these states cannot ignore or override them. In Azerbaijan, these agencies are widely corrupt and dysfunctional institutions that enjoy little or no support among the population, whose money is regularly being extorted by low-level officials.

Western disengagement from the security sector helped perpetuate the very practices that development cooperation has been intent on counteracting and rooting out. Against this background, it is clear that stable societies cannot be built in disregard of the security sector, or, for that matter, the legal system. Where 70 percent of the police force is corrupt, strengthening civil society will be futile. True development will take place only if support for civil society is balanced with efforts to build the state institutions that lie at the basis of, and are prerequisites for, a functioning and influential civil society in the first place. A society built on justice and equity—the rule of law—must be the foundation of any effort at democratic development.

9

Azerbaijan's Economy: The Primacy of Oil

Oil has been the driving force of post-Soviet Azerbaijan's economic development, as well as its foreign policy. In the first decade of the twenty-first century, as the country emerged from the collapsed economy of the war-torn post-Soviet Caucasus, it was oil that enabled Azerbaijan to experience what could be the fastest government revenue growth cycle in modern times. This provided the country's leadership with a tremendous opportunity to secure the long-term development of the country. But oil is reputed to be a curse as well as a blessing. The perils are well known and many. Oil generates huge revenues but few jobs. Rather than promote democratic governance, it tends to encourage autocracy and corruption, and has been linked to instability and warfare.[1] Azerbaijan's leaders have thus needed to face the dangers resulting from their economic dependence on oil, and have continuously stressed their awareness of the associated problems—and their determination to develop the non-oil sector of the economy. Yet Azerbaijan remains dependent on oil and gas. Azerbaijan's case could be all the more acute because the window of windfall oil revenues is so narrow. Whereas most oil-producing countries have the luxury of decades of opulence to squander their revenues, Azerbaijan's greatest profits are likely to accrue over a twenty-year period that is expected to end in 2025. Of course, new technologies may increase recovery rates, and new discoveries could change the picture entirely. Still, the country in all likelihood faces only a brief interval of secure and guaranteed revenues. In this context, how Azerbaijan manages and utilizes its oil and gas revenues will be perhaps the chief determinant of what the nation will look like a decade from the time of writing.

The Soviet Economic Heritage

Azerbaijan's economy, like its politics and society, has been and continues to be plagued by the Soviet legacy. As in other sectors, this legacy is mixed, though it tilts steeply toward the negative. The Soviet Union brought industrialization, infrastructure development, and a high level of education to Azerbaijan, all important assets as the country works toward securing its future in the world economy. Yet the Soviet legacy also ensured that the task of integrating the country into global economic activities would be a traumatic one. The command economy had led to ecological devastation and the persistence of ineffective industries manufacturing useless products, which following independence became known as LAOs, or "large abandoned objects"—big piles of rusting metal that lay scattered on the landscape for a decade, until the growing Chinese demand for base metals caused them to be gradually dismantled and sold as scrap. Moreover, the Soviet legacy created compartmentalized economies specialized in one or just a few sectors, and dependent for their survival on the intricate Moscow-devised system for exchanging goods between republics. In practice, individual republics were not allowed to engage in foreign trade independently, as all such commerce was controlled by the center. Even after independence, this system kept the economies of the former Soviet republics bound to each other, with Russia acting as arbiter of their economic relations not only with their erstwhile Soviet counterparts but with the rest of the world. This forced the new states to go through the painful process of reorienting their economies to historical trading partners to whom their crashed economies had little to offer—though with the notable exception of those fortunate enough to have abundant natural resources. The alternative—which some embraced for lack of a realistic alternative—was continued subservience to Moscow in both economic and political terms.

Aside from these very practical problems, the Soviet heritage included a less tangible element that proved equally resilient: its effect on the mentality and adaptability of the population. To begin with, the Soviet Union had enforced a mentality as far removed from entrepreneurship as imaginable. In its most damaging form, socialism led people to expect the delivery of social goods without seeing a connection to the individual effort such goods required. The popular saying that the state pretended to pay people while the people pretended to work was indeed true. Ordinary people simply did not understand the principles of a market economy. This is exemplified not least by the difficulty that former Soviet students, including Azerbaijanis, faced in grappling with introductory courses in economics in the 1990s. Their secondary education had been plagued by the relics of Marxism-Leninism; no one had prepared them to understand the nuts and bolts of economics. This delayed the building of a functioning economy and made the people vulnerable to unfair privatization schemes that benefited those in power or in control of enterprises, or simply those shrewd enough to benefit from the changing system. Related to this, the education provided by Soviet institutions of higher education, while of high quality in some areas, fit poorly with the requirements of the modern world—hence the contemporary phenomenon of an abundance of well-trained Soviet engineers unable to find jobs, and who fail to get new training in skills desirable in the modern economy.

Following World War II, Azerbaijan fared badly in comparison to other Soviet republics, with the partial exception of the (Soviet) era of Heydar Aliyev (1969–87), whose astute political skills drew greater investment and other forms of useful attention. In 1956, addressing the Twentieth Congress of the Azerbaijani Communist Party, First Secretary Imam Mustafayev called Azerbaijan "a republic of oil and cotton." A number of industrial enterprises were built in the 1950s, and while they provided employment, they also created a gigantic environmental problem, especially in areas such as Sumgait where chemical industries created an industrial waste-land.[2] First Secretary Mustafayev, who was later ousted for his nationalist tendencies, fought for Azerbaijan's economic autonomy—both creating an Azerbaijani oil ministry and keeping it under Baku's command despite Premier Nikita Khrushchev's efforts to assert central control over it.[3] The center did not accord great importance to Azerbaijan: the republic received only 61 percent of the average Soviet republics' level of economic investment between 1960 and 1978.[4]

During Heydar Aliyev's first round as head of state, official figures indicated healthy economic expansion. The production rates of cotton, wheat, and grapes were all said to have doubled between 1970 and 1980. Data on living standards signaled a less dramatic though still impressive improvement: the income level, pegged at 63 percent of the Soviet average in 1970, was reported to have reached 80 percent in 1980.[5]

The official figures on productivity, though rosy, were actually inflated, especially in the case of agriculture. Frequent shortages of food staples, and the ensuing breadlines, were a more reliable indicator of the true state of affairs in regard to output, not to mention the standard of living. These observations are not made with the purpose of singling out Azerbaijan; rather, they are applicable to practices and conditions at the time throughout the Soviet system.

During the Soviet period, Azerbaijan's oil industry experienced an agonizingly slow but steady decline. It was large, having produced the bulk of the Soviet Union's oil in World War II and kept Stalin's tanks running. In 1940, Azerbaijan produced a record 25.4 million tons of oil, or roughly half a million barrels per day—a record not surpassed until 2006.[6] But in the aftermath of the war, Moscow directed most investment to new production areas in Siberia and Kazakhstan.[7] Gradually, the lack of investment and declining production began to have a serious impact on Azerbaijan's economy, not least on its workforce. In 1980, Azerbaijan produced only three percent of the Soviet Union's oil.

Figure 9.1: Azerbaijan's Oil Production in Historical Perspective

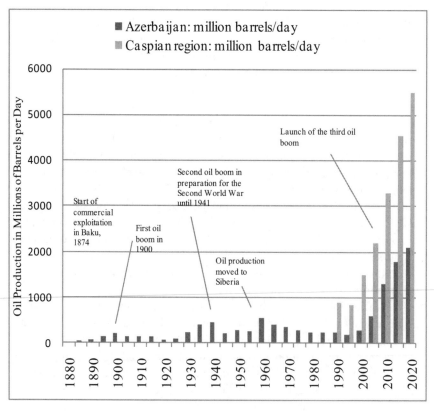

Source: Adapted from Juhani Laurila, *Power Politics and Oil as Determinants of Transition: The Case of Azerbaijan* [BOFIT Discussion Paper No. 10] (Helsinki: Bank of Finland, Institute of Economies in Transition, 1999), p. 14.

To make matters worse, the price at which this oil was sold was set by Moscow, and had little to do with economic reality. As one researcher has observed, Azerbaijan received 120 rubles per ton of oil produced, while the cost of extracting it was 130 rubles. Incidentally, the latter sum bought four kilograms of meat or a pair of shoes.[8] Because Baku did not have enough jobs for them, oil workers were forced to travel seasonally to the Siberian oil fields, where their expertise was in strong demand. Yet if they possessed skills that others did not, this did not endear them to their Russian colleagues. Indeed, the anti-Caucasian mood that prevailed in the Azerbaijanis' seasonal workplaces could be considered an important element of the nationalist revival of the late 1980s—which was significant in that it not only engaged the intellectual elite, but rapidly drew large numbers from every stratum of society. The long decline in the job-site conditions faced by Azerbaijan's oil workers, and their exposure to Russian xenophobia, surely contributed to this rebirth of national pride.

Between 1985 and 1991, Azerbaijan's gross domestic product (GDP) shrank by 17 percent. In 1990, Azerbaijan ranked tenth among the Soviet Union's fifteen republics in terms of the population's welfare, standing one third below the Union average.[9] Any economic gains made by Azerbaijan in the 1970s that had surpassed the Soviet average, so proudly reported by Heydar Aliyev to his superiors in Moscow, had been erased.

The Post-Soviet Economy: War, Downturn, and Recovery

If Azerbaijan's economy had suffered in the last decades of Soviet rule, the transition from Soviet rule made the era of Leonid Brezhnev (1964–82) look like a paradise. Azerbaijan shared the other problems of Soviet successor states: the shift to a market economy, the realization that its industries were producing low-grade goods at high cost, and dependence on the centrally controlled division of labor among republics, to name only a few. But in addition Azerbaijan was struck by war, which disturbed its economy far more than was the case for other former Soviet republics. Moreover, political instability from 1991 to 1995 prevented serious economic policies from being designed and implemented. However, the recovery that began in 1995 was as significant, if not as dramatic, as the downturn in the early 1990s. Buoyed mainly by oil revenues but also by serious economic policies widely lauded by the International Monetary Fund, Azerbaijan emerged as a leading economic performer in the former Soviet Union.

The Early 1990s: Economic Collapse

The collapse of the Soviet Union and the escalating war over Mountainous Karabakh severed Azerbaijan's economic ties to Armenia. The armed conflicts that broke out in Georgia had a similarly disruptive effect on economic relations with that country. The destruction of the Karabakh war took a substantial toll, not least as a tenth of the Azerbaijani population was forced to flee their homes. Coming mostly from the fertile southwestern farmlands, these internal refugees were no longer able to contribute to the economy, and instead became a burden that, in terms of size and duration, was not experienced by any other post-Soviet state. The wars in Karabakh and Georgia, along with fighting in Chechnya and elsewhere in the North Caucasus, had a negative economic effect that crossed borders throughout the region, and of course also impeded all forms of external investment in anything except the energy sector. Figure 9.2 on the following page illustrates the sharp downturn of the war economies of the republics of the former Soviet Union, including Azerbaijan.

Aside from the war, Azerbaijan also suffered from political instability— a rapid succession of short-lived governments that had little understanding of market economics, or skill in handling policies in the areas of budget, trade, taxation, and general reform—even on the rare occasions when these governments actually focused on such issues. Hence, in the first years of independence the economy was in free fall. By 1994 industrial production had declined to 38 percent of 1990 levels, and agriculture stood at 59 percent. Real average monthly wages were at a devastating 17 percent of the level five years earlier, with household consumption at 25 percent.[10]

Azerbaijan's economy effectively bottomed out in 1995, at around 35 percent of the level of economic production of 1989. Two-thirds of the country's economic production and four-fifths of household income had disappeared in half a decade—giving the concept of recession, liberally used in states with industrialized economies when growth turns negative as in 2008–09, a meaning that is difficult for citizens of industrialized economies to imagine. But with the rapid sequence of events following Heydar Aliyev's return to power in 1993, particularly the May 1994 cease-fire in the war with Armenia and the signing four months later of the oil field production-sharing agreement that became known as the "contract of the century" (see chapter 5), Azerbaijan gradually gained the political stability needed to rebuild the economy. In 1995, with support from the World Bank and the International Monetary Fund, the government embarked on a comprehensive stabilization and structural adjustment program. It focused on liberalization of trade and prices, and led to the rapid privatization of lan-downing and small enterprises.[11] A regulatory environment was put in place, the budget deficit was reduced to less than 2 percent of GDP, and the inflation rate was brought down close to zero, though it would increase again in the 2000s. Starting in 1996 the economy registered positive annual growth, and experienced continued expansion through the first decade of the twenty-first century on the basis of investment in the oil and gas sector. Indeed, Azerbaijan has been widely credited by international financial institutions for its favorable macroeconomic environment. The stability of the country's rapidly built economic foundation is perhaps best illustrated by the fact that it had little trouble weathering the Russian economic crisis of 1998 and the related steep drop in oil prices.

Figure 9.2: Changes in Gross Domestic Product (GDP) Among the Republics of the Former Soviet Union, 1989–2001 (1989 = 100%)

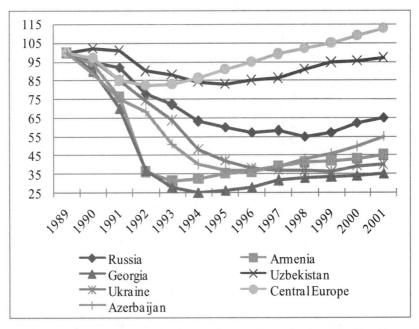

Source: Adapted from World Institute for Development Economics Research, "Ten Years of Transition," news release, 2001.

Table 9.1: Annual Changes in Gross Domestic Product (GDP), Azerbaijan, 1989–2006

Year	Change in GDP (%)
1989	4.4
1990	11.7
1991	0.7
1992	22.6
1993	23.1
1994	19.7
1995	11.8
1996	1.3
1997	5.8
1998	10.1
1999	7.4
2000	11.1
2001	9.9
2002	10.6
2003	11.2
2004	10.2
2005	26.2
2006	32.5
2007	24.7
2008	11.6
2009	9.3

The oil price collapse of 1998 gave Azerbaijan a significant though ultimately healthy scare. Moreover, it came after a succession of disappointing oil and gas test drillings. Until that time, foreign investors in Azerbaijan's oil sector had consisted of large multinationals with a number of smaller companies mixed in, including some out to make a quick killing. Moreover, by privatizing the State Oil Company of Azerbaijan (SOCAR), Baku hoped to lure foreign companies, which indeed invested heavily in privatization vouchers in the expectation that SOCAR eventually would be offered for sale—an expectation that, more than a decade later, remained unrealized.

The story of the "Pirate of Prague" is the most quixotic of these times. A Harvard-educated economist, Viktor Kozeny helped convince the Czech government to embark on a plan of privatizing enterprises through vouchers. Kozeny then created a business (named "Harvard Capital" in order to install confidence) that managed ordinary people's vouchers, offering huge future returns. Kozeny nevertheless extracted $300 million from the company and settled in the Bahamas. Kozeny then set his sights on the voucher privatization program in Azerbaijan. He raised $400 million from major American investors including AIG and Columbia University in a bid to assemble vouchers to buy SOCAR. U.S. prosecutors allege Kozeny conspired to bribe Azerbaijani officials with several hundred million dollars to ensure the privatization of SOCAR in a tender that only he could win.[12] But SOCAR was never privatized, in spite of suggestions that it might by government officials; and when the vouchers expired, the Western investors lost their money. Kozeny, however, stands accused of having created the scheme to bribe Azerbaijani officials.[13] In 2009, a New York court found his one-time associate guilty of the scheme, while Kozeny was at the time of writing fighting extradition in the Bahamas.[14]

In 1998, oil prices collapsed, and smaller companies, especially the more opportunistic ones, rapidly packed their bags and left Azerbaijan. The stakes they hurriedly disposed of were bought primarily by Chinese and Japanese companies—players with a long-term and strategic interest, which was a positive development, not least as it helped Azerbaijan diversify its political ties to include East Asia, a development well suited to President Aliyev's international strategy.

Oil-Led Growth in the Twenty-First Century

Oil prices recovered from the slump in 1998, attracting strong investment in the stabilizing oil sector. Development of the major Azeri, Chirag and Guneshli oil fields by the Azerbaijan International Operating Company (AIOC) went forward largely on schedule, and a pipeline between Baku and the Russian Black Sea port of Novorossiysk was refurbished, reversed, and brought into northbound operation in 1998. The Baku-Supsa early oil pipeline was completed in 1999. (*Early oil* is an industry term for oil that is piped in the period before large volumes enter the pipeline system.) The Baku-Tbilisi-Ceyhan pipeline—a much-derided enterprise in the late 1990s—was completed soon thereafter, a great achievement for Azerbaijan. Oil production picked up, and by 2005 Azerbaijan was enjoying world-leading rates of GDP and state revenue growth. Indeed, as Michael Ross has observed, the growth of revenue between 2005 and 2010, on the order of 600 percent, is estimated to be the greatest proportional increase in revenue over a five-year period by any country in the past half-century, even twice as great as China's rate of state revenue growth in its most hectic period of economic expansion, in the mid-1990s.[15] This obviously provided Azerbaijan with a once-in-a-lifetime opportunity to put itself on a fast track to modernization and wealth. But there were also great risks: the short duration of major oil revenues, the lack of strong political and legal institutions to guide the country as it absorbs the flood of wealth, and the systemic corruption likely to occur in such a turbulent situation.

As the government readily acknowledges, the recent growth has hardly addressed the deep-seated socioeconomic problems of the country, especially widespread poverty and rural underdevelopment. While President Ilham Aliyev has shown an understanding of the problems by prioritizing rural development and the building of the non-oil sector, the sheer dominance of the energy sector and its macroeconomic implications—such as the appreciation of the currency—are systemic factors that impede the development of the non-oil economy. Azerbaijan's task is challenging indeed: to avoid or minimize the problems that all economies dependent on a short list of primary resources have, to varying extents, experienced, and to do so in a tricky and unpredictable regional environment. The odds, in other words, are stacked against Azerbaijan becoming a success story in the long run.

That is not to say that the doomsday preachers will necessarily be right. Azerbaijan has taken several steps in the right direction, including the involvement of all sectors of the economy in economic growth. Especially crucial is the agricultural sector, which employs close to half the population and has long experienced annual growth rates close to 10 percent.[16] Nevertheless, it grew just 1 percent in 2006, an early signal of inflation, which is discussed in further detail below.[17]

By 2008 the country was experiencing a construction boom that was reshaping the capital city and, increasingly, other urban centers. The new construction provoked controversy, partly because of the resultant congestion and the substandard materials that were often used,[18] the latter a particular concern in the earthquake-prone South Caucasus. It was also widely believed that much of the development was fueled by the need to launder ill-gotten gains from the 1990s by using them to create legitimate assets. Yet the fact is that the construction boom created many new jobs; but the slump in 2009 again made these people jobless. In addition, the government began to direct a significant portion of oil revenues toward increases in public employee salaries, pensions, and other forms of social spending, which could help boost household demand and living standards as well as remedy the most egregious socioeconomic maladies of the country. Nevertheless, the reappearance of the specter of inflation as oil revenues grew threatened to eat up these increases. While economic theorists would have suggested a different course of action focused on investing proceeds abroad and improving the investment climate and creating a diversified economy, the socioeconomic realities of Azerbaijan made a rapid investment in pensions and salaries inevitable.

As concerns the management of oil revenues, Azerbaijan is a paradox. On the one hand, the country is routinely termed one of the worst affected by corruption in the region, and perhaps in the world. Such assertions are borne out by various indices. The onshore oil sector is seriously opaque, and SOCAR's murky operations are cause for serious concern. Yet at the same time the government has created the State Oil Fund of Azerbaijan, a vehicle for investing oil revenues that has been lauded internationally for its transparency, while Azerbaijan has also become a pilot member of the Extractive Industries Transparency Initiative, being the first country to launch its validation process.[19] The balance sheet, hence, is mixed. What is clear is that Azerbaijan's future will to a great extent be determined by its energy industry, and how it is managed. This is true for both the economy and society, as well as for Azerbaijan's place in the world.

Azerbaijan's Energy Resources in Regional and Global Perspective

The importance of Azerbaijan's oil and gas resources at independence seems apparent today. Yet these resources were by no means guaranteed to provide for an immediate flow of investments. Indeed, because Azerbaijan's oil industry had largely been neglected by the Soviet energy sector for decades, it was thought to be a thing of the past. The fact that it was so successfully revived is a story in its own right, and was contingent on a mix of circumstances in regional politics and the global economy.

Oil and Gas Resources

As is discussed in chapter 1, Azerbaijan's oil resources have been developed for centuries, and industrially since the late 1800s. But while the Apsheron Peninsula was the first place where an oil rig was used to pump oil from the seabed, nearly all oil production occurred onshore, where extraction was relatively easy. A short trip from the city center of Baku to the so-called Black City, where oil industries were concentrated, allows any visitor to see the ubiquity of the Apsheron Peninsula's onshore oil industry, not to mention the rusty old "nodding donkey" oil pumps around the capital that still tirelessly bring up gallons of black gold. Yet the rust on the rigs and the utter devastation of the peninsula itself are equally indicative of the fifty-year decay of Azerbaijan's onshore oil industry. It is true that the government and oil multinationals, supported by World Bank funding, began in 2005 to remove some of the decrepit infrastructure and to restore some of the damage wrought to the environment, but the degradation is such that it is likely to remain visible for decades. Soviet planners were aware of large deposits of oil under the Caspian seabed, and indeed built an entire artificial town, the *neft dashlari* ("oily rocks"), in the shallow waters thirty miles from Baku to extract some of these reserves. This structure was sufficiently unique to be immortalized in the 1999 James Bond movie *The World Is Not Enough*. But since the enormous onshore resources of western Siberia were both cheaper to explore and strategically better located than the shallow-water marine deposits near the Soviet Union's external borders, there was no major investment in exploring or extracting these resources, aside from the considerable mapping efforts that helped discover the Azeri-Chirag-Gunashli (ACG) oil fields. The true nature and size of Azerbaijan's offshore reserves hence remained unknown, and it took the arrival of Western multinationals in the early 1990s to begin their systematic mapping and exploration.

If onshore resources were gradually depleted, this does not mean that they lost their attraction. Especially with the invention of "enhanced oil recovery" technologies allowing the extraction of substantial additional resources from wells once considered depleted, many smaller investors have embarked on joint ventures with SOCAR to exploit these reserves.[20] Nevertheless, the onshore oil sector in Azerbaijan differs markedly from the offshore sector. The development of offshore oil is governed by Production Sharing Agreements (PSAs) carrying the force of law, providing insulation from Azerbaijan's fiscal system and the intrigues of regulators. Indeed, as far as the PSAs are concerned, Azerbaijan has generally honored the terms of the agreements. Investors in neighboring Russia and Kazakhstan have faced efforts to renegotiate deals that were deemed too advantageous to the oil companies (as in Kazakhstan) or simply to wrest majority ownership away from foreign investors, as Russia has cally done in recent years. The Azerbaijani government has refrained from such steps. But as above board as the offshore sector may be, onshore oil is another story, with considerably less transparency and openness. Here, the unreformed and largely nontransparent SOCAR runs the show, while investors in this sector need either strong and active backing from their home governments or very good connections and networks in order to avoid shady deals and corruption.[21] SOCAR was criticized in 2006 by local media on charges of corruption while purchasing an oil refinery and new office space in neighboring Georgia. The last several PSAs signed by SOCAR also raised eyebrows in Baku, as the selected partner companies were largely unknown offshore firms such as AZEN (Netherlands), the Caspian Energy Group (United Kingdom), and Noble Sky (Cayman Islands) with unknown beneficiary owners, and which are widely believed to be controlled behind the scenes by Azerbaijani minister-oligarchs. It should be noted that since the late 1990s some of the larger onshore joint ventures have been converted into PSAs, while a few new ones have been initiated as PSAs.

Nevertheless, it is the offshore reserves that have been the cornerstone of Azerbaijan's petroleum industry. These can be roughly divided into four major developments, though others are being explored. The first and most important is ACG, which came online in 1997 and produces mainly light crude oil of very high quality. It provided the foundation for President Heydar Aliyev's oil diplomacy, and for the building of the Baku-Tbilisi-Ceyhan pipeline. Second in importance is the Shah-Deniz deposit, containing mainly natural gas and gas condensate, which came online soon after ACG. Third, to the south, is the Araz-Sharq-Alov complex, which is also claimed by Iran, a complicating factor that effectively prevents any active exploration efforts. Finally, the fourth is the Serdar/Kyapaz field in the Central Caspian, which Turkmenistan also lays claim to. PSAs have been signed for a growing number of smaller oil fields, some of which are in operation, while others have failed to show evidence of commercially attractive quantities of oil or gas.

ACG is estimated to contain about 5.4 billion barrels of oil, or about 0.5 percent of proven world reserves, plus a significant quantity of associated gas and currently uncontracted deep gas. Azerbaijan's proven reserves of seven billion barrels are nevertheless sufficient to make them the twentieth largest in the world.[22] As for natural gas, Azerbaijan has recoverable proven reserves of about one trillion cubic meters, with the Shah-Deniz field believed to contain more than one tcm accessible by field development, with an additional 200 million tons of condensate. More important than its size, however, is the fact that Shah-Deniz consists of gas, not oil. When this was realized, it came as a more-or-less unanticipated, and at the time unwelcome, surprise, which led to a reshaping of Azerbaijan's energy industry into one based on two commodities rather than just one. The Araz-Sharq-Alov complex is estimated to contain about four billion barrels of oil or an equivalent amount of gas, but specific numbers will not be known until exploratory drilling has been undertaken—something that will remain impossible until the Iranian claims are resolved. The same is true for Serdar/Kyapaz, which is thought to be roughly the same order of size, but where prospects for resolution are better given the warming in Azerbaijani-Turkmen relations.

Benefits and Liabilities of Caspian Energy

Azerbaijan's energy resources are substantial, particularly given the size of the country. While they do not make the country a major oil producer on a global scale, they do make it one on a regional and—to some extent European—scale. The other states of the Caspian region can be similarly characterized, although Kazakhstan and Turkmenistan—which have considerably larger reserves than Azerbaijan—are situated in a less favorable position for exports, given that they are located east of the Caspian and thus at a greater distance from Western consumers. In spite of geography, not to mention regional turmoil, the states of the Caspian region—Azerbaijan in particular—have been the scene of one of the major oil booms of the post-Cold War era.

The oil industry in the Caspian region took off for a number of reasons, both economic and political in nature, and despite the initial doubts of numerous skeptics. In particular, the Baku-Tbilisi-Ceyhan pipeline has defied the predictions of a majority of industry analysts. But if the skeptics have been proven wrong, it has not been for lack of arguments. Indeed, the Caspian region's reserves of oil—as well as gas—could appear to an outsider to be some of the least attractive on the planet.

To begin with, when the current development boom began in the mid-1990s, the extent of reserves was very unclear. In 1996 and 1997, a series of exploration wells turned out to be dry, reducing hopes of major new finds. While dry holes are common, consisting of up to two-thirds of all exploration wells, the occurrence of so many dry holes in such a short period had a chilling effect on the regional oil industry. By contrast, Kazakhstan's supergiant Kashagan field, estimated at eighteen billion barrels of oil, possibly the largest single discovery in the world in the past two decades, was a significant bright spot. The extent of Turkmenistan's gas reserves remains unclear. Estimates ranged as low as three tcm until 2008, when an international firm's audit almost tripled that number. The government's own estimates stand at twenty tcm.

Another factor that gave analysts and potential investors pause was the uneven quality of Caspian oil. Whereas Azerbaijan's ACG fields produce light crude of very high quality, several Kazakhstani fields produce lower-grade heavy crude that fetches a lower price, as does some of Russia's oil. Another daunting factor was that exploring for Caspian oil brings with it numerous technological and logistical problems. The reserves lie under the Caspian seabed, which ranges in depth from a few dozen to several hundred meters. The exploration of these reserves therefore required the building of elaborate drilling rigs, which involved expensive high technology. Moreover, these rigs could not be easily built in the Caspian region, where there was no equipment, materials, or skilled labor to assemble such rigs. Even bringing in large components would be difficult: the Caspian is an inland sea, and Russia restricted use of the means of passage between it and the high seas, the Volga-Don Canal, which links the Caspian to the Sea of Azov. Consequently, the oil companies initially had to resort to revamping Soviet-era rigs, at great cost.

Once difficulties in exploration were overcome, the issue of exporting and marketing Caspian oil and gas remained to be addressed. The Caspian energy-producing states are surrounded by much larger competitors such as Russia and Iran. This implied that the Caspian states had limited prospects of finding consumers in their neighborhood except through limited swap deals. With the exception of Georgia, the countries of Central Asia and the Caucasus are all landlocked, and as a result oil or gas exports have to transit third countries to reach world markets. Adding to this, no route for the transportation of Caspian oil and gas has been cheap, easy, or uncontroversial. All options included financial as well as political drawbacks, and Azerbaijan was strongly desirous of avoiding dependence on either Russia or Iran for the movement of its exports. The most realistic options, to export via Georgia's Black Sea coast or the Turkish Mediterranean coast, would be very difficult and expensive to realize, with the cost of any main export pipeline exceeding $3.5 billion and the route itself traversing some of Eurasia's most unstable areas.

In the final analysis, bringing Caspian oil to market would be a risky business, a high-level, high-cost geopolitical game rife with unknown factors. By way of illustration, Saudi Arabia can bring a barrel of oil to a seaport for loading onto a tanker for $2–$3. For Norwegian North Sea oil the cost is considerably more, $5–$10, whereas for Caspian oil it is $10 or higher, depending on the field. This may seem less of a problem in recent years, with oil prices ranging from $50 to more than $100 a barrel, but considering that prices dropped below $10 in 1998, and that, as the 2008 economic crisis showed, weak energy markets still cannot be ruled out, the promise of Caspian oil was indeed doubtful. The situation for gas, historically a secondary commodity, was even more problematic: gas cannot be transported as easily as oil, and is normally piped directly to customers. As a result, the landlocked Caspian states, including Azerbaijan, themselves surrounded by the world's two largest gas producers, have had no easy time finding markets for their gas.

The Rationale of Multinational Companies and Western Governments

In spite of the many problems facing energy development there, oil companies and foreign governments both flocked to the Caspian region. In the case of Azerbaijan, the oil companies and the governments backing them shared a keen interest in the country's oil, though for very different reasons.

Oil companies live in an extremely competitive environment marked by fast-changing market conditions. On the other hand, a long-range perspective is essential: every investment normally operates on a time cycle of three to four decades. Consequently, a company seeking to maintain production levels must recognize that every well will go dry and must conduct exploration and development early, in order to replace that depleted well with new production. Since global demand is growing, maintaining market share implies increasing production, hence a need to acquire larger production capacities than those being depleted. Yet hydrocarbons are finite resources, usually located in politically difficult areas such as the Middle East. Moreover, the overwhelming majority of oil and gas resources in the world are owned by states, not companies. The era when Western companies controlled most of the world's oil is long gone—nationalization processes have handed ownership of oil reserves, especially in developing countries, over to states. This has significantly limited the access of the multinationals to many of the most lucrative markets, and concentrated their holdings in the developed world, where reserves are smaller and are becoming depleted faster. As a result, the world's largest private oil companies, known as the supermajors—Exxon Mobil, Lukoil, BP, Royal Dutch Shell, Chevron, and Total—control less than about 1 percent each of world proven reserves. By contrast, more than 90 percent of world oil reserves are controlled by state oil companies (see Table 9.2 on the following page).[23]

Table 9.2: Standing, in Reserve Holdings, of the Six Largest Private Oil Companies (the "Supermajors") Relative to Largest State-Owned Companies

Company (private companies in italics)	Oil and gas reserves*
Saudi Aramco	300
National Iranian Oil Company	289
Gazprom	168
Qatar Petroleum	162
Iraq National Oil Company	133
Abu Dhabi National Oil Company	124
Kuwait Petroleum Corporation	108
Petróleos de Venezuela S.A.	104
Nigerian National Petroleum Corporation	64
National Oil Company of Libya	47
Sonatrach (Algeria)	38
Chinese National Petroleum Corporation	31
Exxon Mobil	**22**
Lukoil	**20**
Petramina (Indonesia)	19
BP	**18**
Petronas (Malaysia)	18
Pemex (Mexico)	17
Turkmenneft	17
Royal Dutch Shell	**15**
Kazmunaigaz	15
Chevron	**11**
Total	**11**

* Billions of barrels of oil equivalent.

This reality is the main explanation for the keen interest private companies have shown in oil from Azerbaijan and elsewhere in the Caspian region. Indeed, the opening of the Caspian meant the addition of major new resources to a highly competitive market. Even if the risks were high, the tightness of the global oil market compelled the companies to get involved in the race for Caspian oil. In sum, they simply had no choice in case they wanted to continue as powerful, growing, healthy companies. As one American oilman put it, there were simply "not a lot of Caspians out there."[24]

To the supermajors, the smaller states of the Caspian, such as Azerbaijan, were by no means unfamiliar environments. These companies had long since learned to deal with political instability, weak states, authoritarian leaders, and civil wars—and to work profitably in spite of such problems. Moreover, the vulnerable geopolitical position of the Caspian states could in one way be seen as advantageous, as it led to a strong desire to improve ties to the Western powers. This was a task in which the companies were both directly and indirectly useful, and which in turn brought leverage to the companies that insulated them from threats of nationalization. Unfortunately, Russia became the painful exception to this rule during President Vladimir Putin's second term, as it gradually moved to take back control of large deposits.

In contrast to oil companies, which are driven primarily by the profit motive, foreign governments have focused primarily on strategic issues relating to Caspian oil and gas. These interests are related to considerations of European and global energy security, as well as to broader security interests in Eurasia. Against this background, it was not so much the size as the location of Caspian energy resources that mattered. In the 1990s, the main attraction was the emergence of oil resources that were outside the Middle East and not under control of the Organization of Petroleum Exporting Countries. Gradually, the Caspian's potential role as a gas producer for Europe, providing a possible alternative to dependence on Russian gas, also became important.

This dictated several of the main reasons for Western governments' interest. First, the West desired access for Western multinational companies to the oil sectors of the regional countries, including Azerbaijan—something that was forthcoming given these states' need for capital investment and technology inputs. Second, the West promoted the export of Caspian energy through westward routes, discouraging transport through Iran altogether and a Russian monopoly over pipelines. In this sense, Western interests corresponded well to those of Azerbaijan and Kazakhstan in particular—sometimes more than they corresponded to the interests of the companies, which sought the cheapest export routes and strove to position themselves for the anticipated, but as yet unrealized, opening of the Iranian market. But the Iranian option was not to be. U.S. sanctions on Iran played an important role, but were only one concern: others included Azerbaijan's shaky relations with Iran, and not least the desire among Western governments *not* to see another million or more barrels of oil per day shipped through the Strait of Hormuz, already perhaps the world economy's main chokepoint.

By the same token, an interest in Caspian oil and an interest in supporting the independence of the smaller regional states were mutually reinforcing: supporting these states' continued independence entailed opposing Russian monopolistic aspirations in the energy sector, and supporting the export of oil and gas westward without interference by hostile powers entailed support for their independence. These were the factors underlying American and European interests and policies in Caspian energy, more explicit in the case of the former and long implicit in the case of the latter.

Rebuilding Azerbaijan's Oil Industry

If reserves were significant and the Caspian Sea held great promise for the oil industry, this was not immediately obvious, nor was the Caspian—when its coast was still mostly within the Soviet Union—a prominent factor in the minds of most oil executives. Indeed, reinvigorating the Caspian oil industry would be a monumental task.

1989–94: Oil's Role During Perestroika and the Early Independence Period

Oil figured prominently from the outset in the Azerbaijani government's strategy for economic development and foreign relations. In fact, the revival of the oil industry predated independence, having already begun in the late 1980s. Mikhail Gorbachev's reforms made it possible for Western business interests to enter the Soviet Union, and one of the first to find Azerbaijan was Steve Remp, a self-made American oil executive based in Scotland who headed Ramco Energy, a once-small oil company that enjoyed significant growth during the North Sea oil boom of the 1970s. He arrived in Baku in 1989 as practically the first Western oilman in decades to take an interest in the country. He began networking with officials during the early bad years of the Karabakh conflict. Remp was selected by one of SOCAR's predecessor companies to represent Azerbaijan in contacts with Western oil companies, in practice kicking off the race for Baku among the companies as Remp presented data showing the sizable potential deposits in the ACG and Shah-Deniz fields.[25] BP and Norway's Statoil, which had long cooperated, soon moved into Azerbaijan, and were followed by several others, most prominent among them Amoco, which became a significant competitor as the majors began to wrestle for influence in Azerbaijan's emerging oil sector. In mid-1991, still within the Soviet period, a tender was announced for the "Azeri" deposit, which Amoco won.[26]

The political upheavals over the next few years blocked the progress of Azerbaijan's oil industry. Indeed, the toppling of Ayaz Mutalibov, independence, power struggles, and the descent into war with Armenia all meant a lack of direction and strategy in the country's leadership, which also affected the direction of the oil industry. The independent republic inherited a huge if somewhat decaying oil industry, extensively equipped with production and refining facilities and transportation systems—though everything was in pretty bad shape—as well as associated mechanical and petrochemical industries, and research centers that had played a leading role in the Soviet Union. The consolidation of all these elements took place during the rule of Abulfez Elçibey. In September 1992, President Elçibey decreed the creation of the State Oil Company of the Azerbaijan Republic, known as SOCAR. This umbrella company, much like its counterparts in other oil-producing states, took control of the entire oil industry in the country, and functioned as the main interlocutor for foreign oil companies seeking to invest there.

In spite of the upheavals during the Popular Front government, oil politics continued. In mid-1992, as the Popular Front appeared to consolidate its position, further deals were agreed upon, including one that gave BP and Statoil the concession to operate the Chirag and Shah-Deniz fields and another that provided Pennzoil with leadership in the Guneshli field. Given the geographical proximity of the ACG fields, these were gradually consolidated by agreement among the oil companies and the Azerbaijani government in late 1992, leading the way to the creation of a single consortium for their development. At roughly the same time the Turkish Petroleum Corporation (TPAO) was included in the consortium, as BP ceded part of its share—clearly in light of the wishes of pro-Turkish president Elçibey. Similar requests from Iran and Russia, among others, were rejected.[27] Negotiations proceeded, but were hindered by passage in the U.S. Congress of Section 907 of the Freedom Support Act of 1992 (which prohibited direct U.S. government assistance to the government of Azerbaijan). Another impediment was raised by manipulations within the Azerbaijani government, which, burdened by domestic turmoil and inexperience in international deal making, failed to handle the negotiations in a professional manner. Nevertheless, by the time of Surat Huseynov's coup in June 1993, the contract was ready to be signed, and a state visit to London for President Elçibey was planned. Before this could happen, however, Elçibey's government was toppled.

Following the fall of the Popular Front government, Heydar Aliyev dismissed the head of SOCAR, Sabit Bagirov, and in September 1993 appointed geologist Natiq Aliyev (no relation) to succeed him. Realizing its key role in the country's economy and politics, President Aliyev took a greater degree of control over SOCAR than his predecessor had. In 1994, he appointed his son Ilham vice president of SOCAR.

The return of Heydar Aliyev brought both change and continuity: continuity in the sense that the main outlines of foreign oil policy remained the same, but also change in many ways. To begin with, the president of the country was now directly supervising the negotiations, a signal that the oil companies now had a counterpart of an entire different caliber to deal with. Second, Aliyev was walking a tightrope in relations with both Russia and Iran and in the ongoing Karabakh war. He understood perfectly the interrelationship among oil politics, the Karabakh conflict, and regional geopolitics, and was determined to use these links to his and Azerbaijan's advantage. Hence, Aliyev interrupted the negotiations, citing irregularities in the process by which his predecessors had handled it, while also seeking to broaden the range of international contacts with a stake in the emerging consortium. Autumn 1993 thus saw intense shuttle diplomacy, in which Aliyev sought to strengthen the support he had received on the international scene from Great Britain and Turkey, counterbalance the Armenian lobby in the United States, mollify Russian opposition and interventionism by offering stakes in the contract, and acquire additional support through the inclusion of other partners, including French Elf Aquitaine and Saudi Arabia's Saudi Delta Oil. Aliyev made no qualms about his conviction that foreign states that were home to companies that sought to invest in Azerbaijan should be involved on a political level to support Azerbaijan in its time of crisis. Eventually a new constellation emerged, and intense negotiations ensued in locations ranging from Baku and Istanbul to Houston. On September 20, 1994, the contract that led to the creation of the Azerbaijan International Operating Company was signed at a ceremonial event in Baku with Aliyev presiding, and promptly dubbed the "contract of the century."

The agreement, valued at the time at $8 billion, was indeed a milestone in Azerbaijan's history. Forty percent of the stakes were held by American companies, including Amoco, Unocal, McDermott, and Pennzoil. European companies followed, most notably BP and Statoil, as well as Ramco. Turkey's TPAO, Russia's Lukoil, and Saudi Arabia's Saudi Delta Oil also held stakes in the contract.

The Legal Status of the Caspian

From the outset, the development of the Caspian's energy resources was clouded by a seemingly central issue: the unsettled legal status of the huge inland sea. Indeed, the ownership of the resources was highly controversial. The status of the Caspian had been unclear in Soviet times. While the Soviet Union nominally shared the Caspian with Iran, Soviet dominance of the sea was overwhelming. Treaties signed by the two states in 1921 and 1940 provided for arrangements of joint sovereignty over the Caspian, something that Russian and Iranian leaders have at various times used to advocate a condominium approach to the Caspian's status. However, as convincingly argued by Azerbaijan and Kazakhstan, the Soviet Union had, by the late 1940s, begun a systematic practice of developing energy resources in the Caspian unilaterally, without either informing or consulting with Tehran. For all practical purposes, the Soviets acted as if the Caspian were delimited into national sectors. Using the logic of this approach and building on legal arguments and practices elsewhere in the world, the Azerbaijani and Kazakhstani leaderships continuously argued for a division of the Caspian into national sectors.

Under a condominium regime, the five littoral states would jointly explore the energy resources and other assets of the Caspian, and split the earnings equally. Crucially, this would enable Russia and Iran—which have the smallest known energy reserves in the Caspian in their would-be national sectors—to benefit from the exploration of resources closer to the coastlines of Azerbaijan, Kazakhstan, and Turkmenistan, but also to acquire a say on the participation of foreign companies in oil and gas exploration. Conversely, if the Caspian were divided into national sectors, the exploration and export of energy resources would be a matter within the sovereignty of the respective states.

These legal issues have posed a significant problem, one that must be divided into several clusters of issues—some of which have explicitly or implicitly been resolved, and others that remain problematic. A first issue concerns the ownership of seabed resources; a second concerns the rights to the body and surface of water; a third concerns the issue of disputed deposits. No comprehensive multilateral solution has been found to the legal issues raised by the Caspian Sea. Nevertheless, this has not prevented a practice from emerging, as the local states and the multinational oil companies have charted their own course through this legal jungle—or are in fact ignoring many aspects of it.

At first, Iran and Russia both argued that the Caspian, actually being a lake and not a sea, was not subject to the 1984 Law of the Sea Convention. Hence, they argued, no littoral states could claim Exclusive Economic Zones. Instead, they advocated joint exploration of the resources under the seabed. This stance met with adamant resistance from Azerbaijan and Kazakhstan, which pointed out that nothing precluded the convention from being applied to inland seas or lakes. Moreover, lakes bordered by more than one state are typically not jointly controlled; indeed, most international lakes are demarcated and divided between the riparian states.[28]

Azerbaijan, Kazakhstan, and the oil companies in practice ignored this legal issue, not allowing the lack of a solid legal basis to prevent their exploration of energy resources. This was especially true of the deposits fairly close to the coastline, including the ACG and Shah-Deniz fields. When the "contract of the century" was signed in 1994, the Azerbaijani government and the oil companies simply assumed that these fields were the sovereign property of Azerbaijan. Aside from Turkmenistan, which claimed part of the Azeri field on rather fanciful grounds, the Russian foreign ministry objected, issuing a stern statement calling the contract null and void and ominously threatening that Russia would not be bound by it. But the threats rang somewhat hollow, not least because Russia's Lukoil itself had a 10 percent stake in the contract, and Russian prime minister Viktor Chernomyrdin—who was the champion of the energy industry—was quoted as saying that he had no objections to the deal.[29] Indeed, the diverging positions on this issue among the various forces vying for influence in Moscow undermined Russia's claims. The multinational companies, having secured the support of the British and U.S. governments, evidently felt that Russia or Iran would not force the issue.

This bold and potentially risky move clearly paid off. Amid occasional loud protestations from Moscow and Tehran, the Azerbaijani and Kazakhstani oil and gas deposits have gradually been developed and exported—with shipments even transiting Russian territory. Gradually, Moscow understood that its refusal to accept the de facto division of the Caspian seabed was detrimental to its own interests and had in fact become counterproductive. Instead of maximizing Russian influence over Caspian energy developments, it had marginalized Russia's role in the energy sector and pushed the energy-producing countries toward the West. By 1998, Russia had recognized the division of the seabed as a principle for resolving the Caspian Sea issue, but continued to argue for joint sovereignty over the body of water and the sea's surface. Kazakhstan rapidly grabbed this opportunity, signing a bilateral deal with Moscow in July 1998.[30] This was roundly condemned by Iran and Turkmenistan. Azerbaijan nevertheless continued to demand the division of the waters as well, clearly apprehensive of the fact that a deal like the one between Russia and Kazakhstan would legitimize the Russian navy's hegemony over the Caspian. In early 2001, however, President Aliyev in principle accepted the Russian viewpoint, and in September 2002 signed an agreement with Moscow along the lines of the one Russia had signed with Kazakhstan. The rationale was in all likelihood the lure of receiving formal Russian consent to Azerbaijan's unilateral exploitation of oil and gas in its sector of the Caspian. This document was complemented by a bilateral treaty between Azerbaijan and Kazakhstan in February 2003 and a trilateral Russian-Azerbaijani-Kazakhstani memorandum in May 2003 that upheld the three countries' respective treaties.[31] Hence, by 2003 the legal status of the northern half of the Caspian had effectively been resolved, at least as far as oil and gas deposits were concerned.

These bilateral agreements were important in at least two ways. Beyond legitimizing ongoing projects, they marked a movement away from attempts to find a comprehensive agreement among all littoral states on all issues relating to the Caspian, and instead toward the resolution of issues on a bilateral level. Second, they effectively killed the idea of a condominium approach to the ownership and exploitation of energy reserves.

In the southern half of the Caspian, efforts to resolve disputes have been far less successful. This is in part due to a simple fact of geology: significant oil and gas deposits are located in areas that straddle the potential dividing lines between national sectors, depending on which methodologies are used to delimit these. In the northern Caspian, the only such field of importance straddles the Kazakhstani-Russian border. In that case, the two countries reached an agreement under which they would jointly develop the field in question, with the profits being shared equally. In the southern Caspian, two specific areas are particularly disputed: the Araz-Sharq-Alov complex, in an area claimed by both Azerbaijan and Iran, and the Serdar-Kyapaz field, disputed between Azerbaijan and Turkmenistan, which has acquired growing importance as European interest in Turkmen gas has grown. There is also some potential for disputes between Iran and Turkmenistan.

Holding a losing hand by continuing to argue for the condominium approach, Tehran adjusted its policies following the bilateral agreements among Russian and the other former Soviet republics. Iran now claimed that if the Caspian was indeed to be divided, something that was clearly happening, it must be divided into equal-sized sectors. In other words, Iran rejected the standard international practice of delimiting maritime borders according to the length of a country's coastline. As the coastlines of the Caspian states vary greatly in length, Kazakhstan having the longest and Iran the shortest, Iran would stand to receive only around 13 percent of the Caspian if it were divided according to standard international practice. Iran instead took to claiming the right to 20 percent of the sea and of the seabed resources. Specifically, the Araz-Sharq-Alov complex, estimated to hold up to four billion barrels of oil equivalent, would fall in the Azerbaijani sector under standard international practice, but would belong to Iran according to Tehran's method of delimitation into equally large sectors.

Turkmenistan adopted a slightly different position. During Saparmurad Niyazov's presidency (1990–2006), Turkmenistan did not reject the delimitation along median lines per se; it just had a very peculiar method of defining median lines. Again, geography was the issue, since the considerable Serdar-Kyapaz field lies right in the middle of the Caspian, between the Turkmen and Azerbaijani coasts. The fact that Azerbaijan's Apsheron Peninsula protrudes far into the Caspian implies that the median line, if calculated according to normal practice from the actual shoreline of each country, would lie relatively far to the east. The Serdar-Kyapaz field would therefore straddle the median line dividing the Azerbaijani sector from the Turkmen sector. Therefore, Turkmenistan advocated a model that ignored the existence of the Apsheron Peninsula, thereby situating the field well within Turkmen waters, in addition to the eastern part of the ACG fields right outside Baku. Not wanting to be outdone, Azerbaijan advocated a solution of its own: calculating the median point from the *neft dashlari* ("oily rocks"), the artificial development in the Caspian waters east of Baku that Azerbaijan nonetheless considered to be an island, would place the Serdar-Kyapaz field squarely in Azerbaijani waters. While there were moves toward improvement of Turkmen-Azerbaijani relations during 2007–08, the dispute heated up again in 2009 as Turkmenistan threatened to take Azerbaijan to a court of international arbitration rather than seek a bilateral negotiated solution.

The net result of these disputes is that these field complexes remain trapped at the bottom of the Caspian—a boon for future generations, perhaps, but one that has soured relations among Turkmenistan, Azerbaijan, and Iran. All three have at various times sought to unilaterally exploit the reserves in the disputed areas, with warnings, threats, and incidents the result. Most dramatically, even as it adapted to the Russian-Azerbaijani agreement to divide the seabed bilaterally, Iran began in 2001 to exercise what it considered its sovereignty over the areas of the southwestern Caspian that it regarded as part of its 20 percent share. This led to a naval incident in August of that year in which an Azerbaijani vessel operated by BP that was surveying the Araz-Sharq-Alov field was forced out of the area by an Iranian gunboat. The incident was followed by recurrent Iranian violations of Azerbaijani airspace and the massing of Iranian troops on the Azerbaijani border. In subsequent years, there have been no attempts to explore either the Araz-Sharq-Alov field or the Serdar-Kyapaz field.

Hence, as the first decade of the twenty-first century was drawing to a close, the Caspian legal issue remained part resolved, part dormant. Azerbaijan was reasonably satisfied with the status quo, as the ACG and Shah-Deniz fields were, in the short term, bringing in more oil revenues than the country could handle. But when production in those fields begins to decrease, as is expected to happen before 2020, the prospect of tapping known but untouched reserves in the disputed sectors of the Caspian is sure to raise its head. The Azerbaijani-Iranian conflict appears much more difficult to resolve than the Azerbaijani-Turkmen dispute. One reason is the size differential between Azerbaijan and Iran, which makes it unlikely that the latter would readily back off from its position. Another reason is that Iran's huge oil supplies in the Persian Gulf free it from dependence on Caspian resources and would enable Tehran to use the Caspian fields as a bargaining chip—or lever—in any negotiation or confrontation with Baku. This would likely be true even if a change of government were to take place in Iran. But with Turkmenistan, the situation is different. Baku and Ashgabat have considerably larger common interests, especially as the prospect of a trans-Caspian pipeline began to make a comeback in 2006, with growing European interest in diversifying energy sources and looking to the Caspian for alternative supplies. The icy relations between Azerbaijan and Turkmenistan had to a considerable degree resulted from the sonal antipathy between Saparmurad Niyazov and Heydar Aliyev—with the latter viewing the former with some disdain. Following Aliyev's death, relations were not immediately improved, given Niyazov's growing self-imposed isolation. But Niyazov's death in December 2006 opened up new prospects. With a new Turkmen government reversing at least the most idiosyncratic elements of the deceased leader's rule, a gradual rapprochement between Baku and Ashgabat began. Then, in the summer of 2009, Ashgabat moved unexpectedly to take the matter of the division of Caspian resources to international arbitration, even though there was no arbitration court whose jurisdiction had been accepted by both countries. Nevertheless, the Turkmens did not appear to follow up on this issue.

The most logical way to resolve the issue would be the joint exploitation of the Serdar-Kyapaz field, with a pipeline carrying its output westward to link up with the South Caucasus (SCP) pipeline to Erzurum. Even short of that, gas or oil from the Petronas development off Turkmenistan's coast could be shipped toward the ACG platforms and onward. If this arrangement were used, it could be said that a portion of a trans-Caspian pipeline was, in effect, already in place.

Pipeline Politics and Economics in the 1990s

If the "contract of the century" put in place a system for the extraction of oil, there was one major missing element: a feasible plan to bring this oil to international markets. Azerbaijan is landlocked and surrounded by oil-producing countries, which means that large consumer markets are not to be found in its neighborhood. Turkey, lacking oil and gas resources, is the only possible exception. Azerbaijani oil would therefore have to be piped hundreds of miles to reach markets—just as had been the case a century earlier, when the world's first oil pipeline brought Baku's oil to the Black Sea port of Batumi. But because the Azerbaijan Soviet Socialist Republic had been an integrated part of the Soviet Union's energy system, all pipelines from Azerbaijan flowed north, toward Russia, denying Azerbaijan any direct infrastructure link to the outside world. Moreover, by 1991 the Soviet pipeline system was in disrepair, and nowhere near being capable of carrying a million barrels of oil per day.[32]

Consequently, once Azerbaijan gained independence, there followed years of speculation, scheming, planning, maneuvering, and the occasional engineering study regarding the pipeline route that would be chosen to export the bulk of the country's oil. There was no lack of contenders, nor of unsolicited opinions regarding the feasibility of any of the proposals under discussion. Over time, the myriad of pipeline projects for the delivery to market of Caspian oil and gas grew into a maze where only experienced observers could tell the serious from the ludicrous.

Despite some noteworthy drawbacks, four options stood out among the plethora of proposals: a northern route through Russia to the Black Sea coast, a southern route through Iran to the Persian Gulf, and two variations on a western route. The first would reinvigorate the century-old pipeline to Georgia's Black Sea coast, but this time not to Batumi but to the port of Supsa, to Batumi's north. The second envisaged the building of a much longer pipeline to Turkey's Mediterranean deep-sea port of Ceyhan-

Yumurtalik, an oil terminal that had already been built for the purpose of bringing Iraqi oil to market.

The Russian option looked good on paper, particularly since it was the least costly. It would reverse a Soviet-era pipeline and pipe Azerbaijani oil to Novorossiysk, on the Black Sea coast, a project that could be rather easily completed. To upgrade this route into a wide-diameter major export pipeline would require only limited investments of about $1 billion, considerably less than what would be required by the other proposed routes. Yet the Novorossiysk option had several disadvantages. The foremost was that it would provide Russia, the former regional hegemon that increasingly nurtured imperial designs on the Caucasus, with a monopoly over Azerbaijan's oil exports—and therefore its major source of income. Skeptics at the time have been more than vindicated by the Russian use of energy as a political tool in the 2000s. More important, Russia was in the mid-1990s strongly associated with Armenia's military victory over Azerbaijan. To Baku, Russia was Armenia's main backer; Moscow had played a direct role in the Karabakh conflict and in roiling Azerbaijan's domestic political situation. Even though relations would normalize somewhat beginning in 1999, Azerbaijan's political leadership did not want to increase the country's economic dependence on Russia. Neither, in fact, did the international oil companies, despite the temptation of the Russian option's smaller price tag. They had observed the difficulties Chevron encountered in building the U.S.-backed Caspian Consortium pipeline through Russia to the very same port of Novorossiysk. As one American oil executive said, "Russia had continually screwed [Chevron] over"; thus, the oil companies investing in Azerbaijan were exploring alternative options.[33]

Baku-Novorossiysk had four other major drawbacks. First, the Caspian Consortium pipeline would bring a million barrels of oil to Novorossiysk, raising the total oil volume transiting the Turkish straits to more than two million barrels per day at the beginning of the twenty-first century. There was a physical limit to the amount of oil that could traverse the narrow, difficult waters of the Bosporus, winding through the megalopolis of Istanbul, home to 12 million people. Turkey had a strong environmental case that moreover squared well with its political interests. Second, Novorossiysk suffers from regular wintertime operational problems, including fog and wind that complicate tanker loading. Since it is not a deepwater port, many tankers cannot use it. Third, the Russian option would not pipe Azerbaijani oil straight to Novorossiysk—it would combine Azerbaijani oil with lower-grade crude from Russia, with the resulting mix being sold as "Urals blend." As one energy expert explained,

Shipping oil north from the Caspian, through Russia's Transneft crude oil transport system, also has cost implications. Transneft does not operate a quality bank (a means of accounting for varied oil quality and compensating shippers according to the quality of the oil they ship); nor does Transneft use batching or other means of segregating cargoes to protect the market value of higher-quality crudes. This means that comparatively light, sweet crudes from the Caspian are mixed with all the other heavier, sourer grades in the Transneft system. Azeri Light crude that is shipped north from Baku, for example, arrives at the port as Urals blend, losing $4 to $5 per barrel of value in the process.[34]

Needless to say, Russia does not provide compensation for this loss, which not only costs Azerbaijan but also further enriches Russia, since the "Urals blend" can command a higher price than unadulterated Russian crude.

A third drawback of the Baku-Novorossiysk pipeline would be that it would go right through the Chechen capital, Grozny, where the eccentric general Jokhar Dudayev had declared independence—a red flag for many oil executives. Indeed, the Russian decision to invade Chechnya in late 1994 was made just after the signing of the "contract of the century"—and the latter event has often been stated as a reason for the timing of the invasion, implying a decision in Moscow to get ahead of a problem that could jeopardize its interests in the South Caucasus. The war in Chechnya did not go Moscow's way, thereby effectively killing Russia's hopes for Novorossiysk as the main export hub for Caspian oil.

Transit through Iran, the second option, was supported by many oil industry figures, who were suspected on more than one occasion of eyeing the Iranian market with a view to being well positioned when it eventually opened up to the international petroleum industry in a serious way. Iran pushed hard for a two-prong option, whereby the initial phase would see Azerbaijani oil exported to northern Iran for consumption there, while Iran would in turn sell the equivalent amount of oil on international markets on Azerbaijan's behalf. This was known as the "swap deal." In a second phase, a major export pipeline would be built through Iran to the Persian Gulf. This pipeline could be constructed at a cost of $2.0 to $2.5 billion. Popular though it was in the industry, this option failed not only because of the U.S. sanctions on Iran but also due to Azerbaijan's frosty relations with the Islamic republic and the strategic folly that would result from bringing another million barrels of oil a day to the Strait of Hormuz.

Third was the western route, with its two variations. Baku-Supsa was strongly promoted by the Clinton administration as a route for the smaller flows of early oil that would begin moving several years before the major volumes would come online. Some companies, notably BP, preferred the Novorossiysk pipeline for this purpose. In the end, AIOC decided to support both of these smaller-scale projects, giving birth to the concept of "multiple pipelines."

Yet as a means of shipping much larger quantities of oil, Baku-Supsa, while politically tempting to Azerbaijan and to Western nations, had a problem in common with Novorossiysk: it would bring the oil through the Bosporus. For this reason, a much longer pipeline was advocated by Turkey and well-placed segments of Azerbaijani society. Various configurations were proposed, all of them designed to bring Azerbaijan's oil to Turkey's Mediterranean coast, at Ceyhan. But this proposal had two major problems. The first was its huge projected cost, more than $3 billion, which made it by far the most expensive option. It should come as no surprise that most early advocates of the route to Ceyhan were political scientists or politicians, not economists or industry executives. The second major drawback was the routing problem. As mainland Azerbaijan has no border with Turkey, the pipeline would have to cross either Armenia, Iran, or Georgia to reach Ceyhan. The Armenian option was fancifully advocated in some circles, some proponents even dubbing it the "peace pipeline," in the vain hope that the prospect of a pipeline routed across Armenia would bring it together with Azerbaijan, its adversary in the war over Karabakh. In spite of renewed efforts by the Armenian lobby in the United States to this effect, the route across Armenia never got off the drawing board. The Iranian route was long entertained, but it suffered from problems with U.S. sanctions, and more importantly the realization that if Iran was to have a pipeline carrying Azerbaijani oil on its territory, it had little intention of that being intended for transit to Turkey.

When a route was finally assigned to the Baku-Ceyhan proposal—one crossing Georgian territory—it was not so much on the basis of economic merit as by default, the other options being even more impractical.

In the late 1990s, with the planned start-up date for production nearing, the problems impeding a northern or southern pipeline were not going away. Russian policies were growing increasingly imperial, and neither Iranian policies nor U.S.-Iranian relations were improving. In that context, the Baku-Ceyhan route emerged as the only feasible option. When the pipeline was eventually completed, in 2005—with a route that passed through Tbilisi—it was in large part the product of long-term strategic

thinking among Azerbaijani, Turkish, British, and not least American diplomats and executives. However, it must be noted that in no small measure,
Baku-Tbilisi-Ceyhan owes its existence to the discovery in 1999 of a deposit of natural gas of unprecedented size in the Shah-Deniz field. In the
meantime, SOCAR and AIOC settled on two complementary routes for
early oil: the refurbished Baku-Novorossiysk pipeline and the Baku-Supsa
pipeline—providing options, and satisfying both Russian and Western
political interests.[35]

Coming of Age: Shah-Deniz and the Building of the Twin Pipelines

While what became the Shah-Deniz project was being planned in the late
1990s, the U.S. government was lobbying hard for the export of Caspian
natural gas resources to the West. But Azerbaijan figured in these discussions mainly as a transit country: the real resources of natural gas were
across the Caspian, in the deserts of Turkmenistan. The country produced
up to ninety billion cubic meters of gas per year in the late Soviet period,
and was known to have substantial though unmapped additional deposits.
Through a trans-Caspian pipeline, Turkmen gas would be brought to Azerbaijan and then onward to Turkey.

The Shah-Deniz field was thought to contain up to three billion barrels
of oil, and additional gas resources.[36] The project was dominated by BP
and Statoil, which each acquired a 25.5 percent stake in the project. The
Russia-based LUKAgip, Total Fina Elf, and the Iranian National Oil Company each got a 10 percent stake, with Turkey's TPAO at 9 percent. But in
1999, the exploration well at the Shah-Deniz deposit about 100 kilometers
southeast of Baku struck natural gas, not oil. The deposit was one of the
largest accumulations of offshore gas to be discovered in about twenty
years. The field encompassed about 860 square kilometers (330 square
miles), and featured great variations in sea depth, ranging from 50 to 600
meters.[37] Recoverable reserves were estimated at more than one tcm, a
figure that was doubled a decade later in view of additional field development and new technologies.

In a flash, Azerbaijan turned into a producer not only of oil but also of
natural gas. This changed the outlook for the country's energy sector, creating headaches for the oil industry. To begin with, Shah-Deniz's output
could not be fed into the main oil export pipeline, as had been hoped. On
paper, this worsened the prospects of the Baku-Ceyhan project, still under
consideration at that time. Moreover, it meant that the industry had to find
separate export pipelines for gas. More worrying from a strategic perspec-

tive, the Shah-Deniz discovery changed the prospects for trans-Caspian pipelines generally. Azerbaijan was no longer just a transit country for gas, but also a producer and potential competitor with Turkmenistan. Logically, Azerbaijan thought the trans-Caspian pipeline project could be adapted to include Azerbaijani gas, by feeding Azerbaijani gas into the flow of Turkmen gas that was planned to cross the country's territory. But this would likely mean the reduction of Turkmen gas volumes to be exported by this route, This prospect further cooled the already frosty relations between the two states, and combined with a series of other factors to kill the project, at least for the following decade.

A solution to the export problems gradually matured. Building pipelines involves much more than laying pipes and constructing compressor stations: the pipeline company has to negotiate with literally thousands of landowners for the right-of-way across territory, a cumbersome and expensive process. If *two* parallel pipelines were built—one for oil and one for natural gas—economies of scale could be applied to the project and boost its commercial viability. This is an important factor that contributed to the willingness of the oil industry to get on board with the Baku-Ceyhan pipeline and that helped the consortium secure credits for the project.

The result was the development of a project that combined what had become the Baku-Tbilisi-Ceyhan pipeline with a parallel gas pipeline dubbed the South Caucasus pipeline. As oil development from ACG was scheduled earlier than gas development from Shah-Deniz, the pipelines were not physically built at the same time, but sequentially. While it was underway, in the early 2000s, this was one of the largest infrastructure projects in the world. And it was, and remains, controversial. As S. Frederick Starr has pointed out, "When the [Baku-Tbilisi-Ceyhan pipeline] was conceived, the burden of proof lay firmly on the side of anyone proposing that such a pipeline could be built."[38] Or that it should. Indeed, the project had to face a daunting set of interlocking challenges. First, it had to convince sponsors that it was feasible and economically viable despite its enormous cost. In spite of the gains of scale obtained by building twin pipelines, Baku-Tbilisi-Ceyhan would cost at least $3 billion and the South Caucasus gas pipeline another $900 million. Second, the consortium and its backers had to deal with continuous Russian and Iranian opposition, a delicate issue for both Azerbaijan and Georgia, but especially for oil companies that either held or hoped to acquire important interests in those countries. It was made clear to them that this project would not increase their chances in either country. Third, the project faced the problem of Armenian-Azerbaijani relations. As the "peace pipeline" project dream quickly died, it became clear that the route of the pipeline would cross Georgia, taking a northward turn and thus bypassing Armenia. This brought the project a powerful opponent: the worldwide Armenian diaspora. Fourth, the project faced loud protests from a wide spectrum of nongovernmental groups, a coalition so diverse as to generate speculation regarding its funding and support. It included environmental activists who thought that less and not more oil should be consumed in the world, and, more specifically, who worried of the consequences for the fragile ecosystems along the route, not least in Georgia's Borjomi area, home to the famous mineral water. Supplementing this charge, human rights activists accused the oil companies and host governments of neglecting the concerns of local communities, and even suppressing their expression. In particular, pro-Kurdish groups opposed the pipeline, claiming that it would run through Kurdish areas where nongovernmental organizations (NGOs) feared that local populations would be denied the opportunity to have their say. Finally, the pipeline opponents included a set of groups critical of international financial institutions in general and their policies on environmental and human rights issues in particular.

Eventually, in spite of these daunting challenges, a combination of economic and political factors came together to ensure that the pipeline would be built. Most important was the simple matter of time: with every passing day, the date when oil production would begin got closer, making the resolution of the pipeline issue increasingly urgent. The problems associated with the Russian and Iranian routes and a growing understanding of the Turkish straits problem eventually clinched the deal for the Baku-Tbilisi-Ceyhan route. Throwing further weight behind this choice was the decision by several companies active in Kazakhstan to acquire a stake in the pipeline, a move that enhanced prospects for its long-term economic viability. Construction of the pipeline would not have been possible, however, without the strong and consistent support given to the project by subsequent governments in the three local countries, the United States, and the United Kingdom. This convergence of support enabled the project to attract additional backing in the form of loans from the International Finance Corporation and the European Bank for Reconstruction and Development, as well as public guarantees from the Japanese Bank for International Cooperation, the U.S. Export-Import bank, and British Export Credit guarantees.

In October 2000, a $25 million basic engineering feasibility study was approved. Five months later, Chevron—which did not hold a stake in the ACG fields, but was invested in the Tengiz field in Kazakhstan and Azerbaijan's Absheron field—opted to join the project, leaving Exxon Mobil as the only major company to continue to oppose Baku-Tbilisi-Ceyhan.[39] In September 2002, construction of the pipeline began with a ceremony near Baku with Presidents Heydar Aliyev, Eduard Shevardnadze, and Ahmet Necdet Sezer in attendance, flanked by U.S. energy secretary Spencer raham.[40] On May 25, 2005, the completion of the pipeline was officially celebrated in Baku; the first tanker lifting Azerbaijani oil from Ceyhan was filled in June 2006. The Shah-Deniz pipeline was completed in mid-December 2006, and began to deliver natural gas to embattled Georgia in February 2007, greatly easing that country's energy situation.

Managing Revenues: The Oil Fund and the Budget

Under the PSA that provided the basis for development of the ACG fields and subsequent large contracts such as the Shah-Deniz consortium, the structuring of revenues between the Azerbaijani government and the energy companies was settled in a mutually beneficial way. In essence, the scheme envisaged that the companies would get a large portion of the revenues in the early years of production to compensate for their investments in the structures. Gradually, however, the bulk of the revenue would transfer to the government of Azerbaijan, whose share of the revenue would grow with time.[41] In total, the "contract of the century" is projected to result in Azerbaijan receiving about 80 percent of the total profits, including its share in the AIOC, taxes on the foreign companies' oil profits, bonuses, and royalties.

Table 9.3: Original Shareholders in the Azerbaijan International Operating Company (AIOC), September 20, 1994

Shareholder	Ownership share (%)
State Oil Company (Azerbaijan)	20.000
BP (United Kingdom)	17.127
Amoco (United States)	17.010
Lukoil (Russia)	10.000
Pennzoil (United States)	9.820
Unocal (United States)	9.520
Statoil (Norway)	8.563
McDermott International (United States)	2.450
Ramco (United Kingdom)	2.080
Turkish Petroleum Corporation (Turkey)	1.750
Delta-Nimir (Saudi Arabia)	1.680

Table 9.4: Shareholders in the Azerbaijan International Operating Company (AIOC), 2007

Shareholder	Ownership share (%)
BP (United Kingdom)	34.14
Unocal (United States)	10.28
State Oil Company (Azerbaijan)	10.00
INPEX (Japan)	10.00
Statoil (Norway)	8.56
Exxon Mobil (United States)	8.00
Turkish Petroleum Corporation	6.75
Devon Energy (United States)	5.63
Itochu (Japan)	3.92
Amerada Hess (United States)	2.72

The Resource Curse

Most projections show Azerbaijan receiving up to $120 billion in oil and gas revenues over the 2005–25 period. (Sharper estimates are not possible, given the fluctuations in oil prices.) The sheer size of these revenues raises important questions about how they will be used, and whether Azerbaijan will experience the familiar economic maladies of resource-rich countries, such as the "Dutch disease," the "resource curse," and the "paradox of plenty." Indeed, given that no country in modern times has experienced a flood of new revenues as great as the one now washing over Azerbaijan, there appears to be little reason why it should not encounter these problems.

The resource curse is an academic conception drawing on, and seeking to make coherent, the economic difficulties experienced by most resource-dependent countries. Indeed, academics discovered that resource-rich countries paradoxically have lower rates of GDP growth than their less affluent counterparts; hence the term, coined by Richard Auty, "resource curse."[42]

As it has developed, the concept of the resource curse encompasses several ailments suffered by oil-producing countries. A sequential examination of these problems makes clear that Azerbaijan was not immune, even though it had instituted some of the policies prescribed to reduce the potential for damage—but by no means enough of them to insulate the country from highly adverse effects.

First, the volatility of the prices of raw materials, particularly oil, results in equally volatile government revenues. This, in turn, creates the risk of sharp expansions and contractions in government spending. The Azerbaijani government has instituted the State Oil Fund of Azerbaijan to manage this problem, which is an important step. Nevertheless, the government does move a substantial part of the revenue into the state budget. This is only natural in the short term, given the need for investment in infrastructure and other projects; but if the trend continues, that would mitigate the very rationale of the oil fund.

Second, a large-scale influx of revenue can lead to appreciation of the local currency. This, in turn, harms the competitiveness of the non-oil economy, whose products become expensive on the international scene while imports become cheaper. This problem began to affect Azerbaijan as early as 2006, fueled by budget increases of 80 percent in 2006 and 50 percent in 2007. While the budget is unlikely to continue to grow at such a pace, the risk of continuously lax budgetary policies is present.

Third, like rents of any form, including foreign aid, oil revenues are known to create complacency in government circles, thereby removing incentives to conduct serious and needed reforms, and reducing the effectiveness of government or its perceived need to invest in infrastructure and education. In Azerbaijan's case, complacency may indeed become a growing risk: because the government is not beholden to foreign donors and partners, it believes that it has greater freedom of movement, a perception that may have the effect of hampering reforms. While infrastructure reform has progressed well, the education sector, crucial to Azerbaijan's post-oil future, is lagging badly, with little indication that something is being done to upgrade it.

Finally, the large influx of revenue facilitates corrupt practices, and provides the possibility for government figures to consolidate change-resistant fiefdoms of their own where they hold sway on the basis of the immense financial resources they command. This is indeed a serious problem in Azerbaijan today.

The State Oil Fund and EITI: Building Transparency

In dealing with the mounting flow of oil income into an economy marred by corruption and mismanagement, Azerbaijan has been widely lauded for two important steps it has taken—setting up an oil fund for the reinvestment of state oil revenues and joining the Extractive Industries Transparency Initiative (EITI). These actions have created a respectable level of transparency in terms of the income stream. That said, problems remain on the spending side—with the budget process and especially SOCAR being marred by great problems.

Moved to act by the prospect of growing amounts of oil revenues and recommendations from international financial institutions, the Azerbaijani government decided in December 1999 to establish the State Oil Fund of the Azerbaijan Republic (SOFAZ).[43] The statutory regulations of SOFAZ were approved on December 29, 2000. SOFAZ's executive director reports directly to the president. The oil fund is thus responsible not to Parliament but to the president, who appoints its director as well as its board. Hence, SOFAZ may be independent from the budgetary process, but not from the political leadership of the country. That said, SOFAZ was an entirely new institution in Azerbaijan's political and economic history and required a great deal of care in its establishment and management. Azerbaijan had never had experience with the receipt of large amounts of revenues over a short period of time, or with managing such revenues. SOFAZ's main goal was to accumulate revenues from the PSAs and invest them in interest-generating bonds and stocks. At the same time, SOFAZ serves as a tool for the prevention of the inflation that would likely result if the massive oil income went straight into the state budget. SOFAZ's funds are considered an investment opportunity for economic and social projects that will diversify the economy and build infrastructure so that the non-oil economy may develop.

SOFAZ's primary sources of income are bonus payments, royalties, revenues from the sale of crude oil and gas, rental and transit fees, revenues from joint activities with foreign companies, and revenues from investments and from the sale of assets. The accumulated revenues are kept offshore with internationally recognized and reputable financial institutions and fund managers. SOFAZ is often proudly referred to as one of the most transparent and noncorrupt institutions in Azerbaijan. From its first day of operation, it has been forthright with the local media and the NGO sector about its revenues, earned interest, and expenditures. This information has been shared with the public both through SOFAZ's website, *oilfund.az*, and regular press conferences, and the publication of periodic reports. In addition to the Parliamentary Chamber of Accounts, the international auditing firm Ernst & Young regularly conducts an audit of SOFAZ's activity.

By mid-2009, SOFAZ had attracted the equivalent of about $11.8 billion, up from $3.5 billion only two years earlier.[44] Large percentages of the oil fund's income were being transferred to the state budget—an amount equal to almost $10 billion since the fund's creation, with additional funds spent on various projects, chiefly housing for internally displaced persons and infrastructure projects focused on water supply and irrigation.

To those who thought of Azerbaijan as a hopelessly corrupt country, its decision not only to join but to become a pilot member of the EITI must have been greeted either with utter disbelief or as an extreme sign of cynicism. The EITI was launched by Prime Minister Tony Blair of Britain at the September 2002 World Summit on Sustainable Development, and aims to promote transparency in the oil, gas, and mining industries to ensure that revenues from these industries "fulfill their potential as an important engine for economic growth in developing countries, instead of leading to conflict, corruption, and poverty."[45] To the surprise of many, Azerbaijan became the first participant in the EITI to file a transparency initiative report, and several multinational oil and gas companies operating in the country committed to full disclosure of their monetary transfers to the Azerbaijani government.

Despite SOFAZ's general transparency, local and international organizations have continued to express concerns about the safety of the oil revenues and their most effective uses. For instance, the International Monetary Fund and other international organizations recommended to the Azerbaijani government that the role of primary decision maker for SOFAZ be passed from the president of the country to the Parliament—a step most observers would consider questionable given the nature of Azerbaijan's political system. More to the point are concerns that in spite of SOFAZ's transparency, the funds transferred into the state budget for public goods and services are susceptible to large-scale corruption and embezzlement. There is little public control or media or NGO monitoring of these funds. A local NGO, the Public Funds Monitoring Center, and Caspian Revenue Watch (a project initiated and funded by the Open Society Institute) so far have been the only initiatives from civil society to monitor oil and gas revenues. Indeed, once the funds leave SOFAZ and go to a regular government ministry or agency, there is no transparency in the ways the money is spent, though there is much anecdotal evidence on the broad corruption plaguing many agencies and ministries.

President Ilham Aliyev signed a presidential decree in September 2004 on "the long-term strategy on the management of oil and gas revenues."[46] This decree specified how oil and gas revenues would be managed for the period 2005–25, stipulating that they be directed toward seven areas:

- development of the non-oil sector, Azerbaijan's regions, and small and medium-size businesses

- large-scale development of infrastructure
- implementation of poverty reduction measures and other social projects
- stimulation of the intellectual and technological bases of the economy
- development of human capital
- strengthening of the nation's defense capacity
- redevelopment of the liberated territories and resettlement of internally displaced people

Some of these priority areas, such as the development of human capital, have been urged by the United Nations, opposition parties, and local NGOs. In 2003, the opposition Azerbaijan National Independence Party proposed to allocate $1 billion from SOFAZ funds to establish a scholarship program to enable Azerbaijani students to study abroad, a proposal that the government is implementing in modified form. Some members of Parliament have suggested spending 1 percent of SOFAZ revenues on the elderly and war veterans. The strengthening of the army has been also cited by President Aliyev as a regular focus for the expenditure of oil revenues.

Despite the presidential directive and other, more concrete planning, disagreement is rife on the use of oil and gas revenues. Some opposition parties have argued that the accumulation of the oil revenues in SOFAZ and their investment in foreign low-interest bonds and stock is not as productive as investment in the local economy would have been. A lack of loans for farmers and small business is often cited as a good example of this problem. A recurrent question has been why Azerbaijan borrows money from foreign banks and financial institutions at high interest rates to provide loans to farmers, when it could use its own oil revenues for the same purpose. On at least one occasion a government representative, state economic adviser Vahid Akhundov, expressed agreement with such concerns.

SOFAZ and the Transparency of the Budget

If SOFAZ and the EITI initiative have shown the Azerbaijani leadership's ability to ensure transparency in the revenue stream from the large oil and gas projects when political will is present, the picture is less bright on the spending side. Especially at times when major construction projects are being undertaken and major procurements are being made, opportunities for corruption are huge. Indeed, the government of Azerbaijan now transfers substantial amount of money from the oil fund into the regular budget for development work. Even worse is the situation in SOCAR itself, which, like many of its international counterparts, is much more than an oil company. SOCAR virtually runs a parallel budget, using its funds to build schools and other facilities, and doing so with even less transparency than is practiced with the general budget.

SOCAR has traditionally been perceived as the cash cow of the government, and is regularly called upon to contribute when some unexpected expenditure comes up. Examples include special fellowships for talented students, sports tournament sponsorships, organization of cultural events, funding of the construction of medical diagnostic centers, and humanitarian donations to refugees and internally displaced persons. In addition, SOCAR maintains an extensive benefits program for its own employees, totaling nearly 80,000 persons.

Oil and Governance

The overwhelming majority of countries where the energy sector dominates the local economy have experienced problems with democracy, human rights, governance, and corruption. Norway stands out as the exception that confirms the rule.[47] It remains to be seen whether in the years following the completion of the Baku-Tbilisi-Ceyhan pipeline and the export of "major oil" from Baku to Western markets, Azerbaijan will emulate the Norwegian model and significantly improve governance.

With completion of the pipeline still fairly recent, there are two ways to look at its impact on political developments in Azerbaijan: one optimistic, the other pessimistic. Those with an optimistic outlook claim that the proximity of Azerbaijan to Europe and the connection of Azerbaijan to the European economy through the Baku-Tbilisi-Ceyhan pipeline will eventually result in the full political and economic integration of the country into European institutions and Europe's system of values. This, in turn, will lead to improvements in governance, transparency, human rights, and the practice of democracy generally. Indeed, certain events in the first decade of the twenty-century support this argument. For instance, in 2001 Azerbaijan joined the Council of Europe, which has been a crucial factor behind reforms in the country, such as the passage of the law on the fight against corruption, the establishment of a public television station, the release of political prisoners, and amendments to the constitution, including one opening the way for ordinary citizens to appeal to the Constitutional Court. Some of these changes are still new to Azerbaijani society and lack proper mechanisms of implementation. Thus, it is not clear what the full ameliorative effects of these reforms will be. Yet the fact that these changes are being made provides hope for long-term development in the field of democracy and good governance. The Council of Europe continues to press the Azerbaijani government on other issues, such as reform of the electoral law, transfer of power and authority from local executive bodies to the municipalities, and the establishment of a strong civil society. Other international organizations also work on this front. With the help of the United Nations, the Azerbaijani government began in 2003 to develop and implement a state program on poverty reduction. The International Monetary Fund has been instrumental in working with the Azerbaijani government to establish a system of annual reports to Parliament on the activities of the executive branch.

Yet none of these improvements and reforms in the political sector are directly driven by oil and gas projects. In fact, those who take a pessimistic view of the impact of such gas projects argue that they seem to be impeding the development of democracy and human rights in the country. Following most elections since 2003, opposition figures and NGO activists regularly accused foreign governments and multinational oil companies of ignoring electoral fraud and supporting an authoritarian regime in the name of stability and security. Foreign powers and powerful energy companies are primarily interested in preserving long-term stability in the country in order to ensure the smooth continuation of the oil and gas projects. In effect, this requires that energy companies work with the incumbent regime. Indeed, in recent years the oil companies operating in Azerbaijan have developed strong partnership ties with the Azerbaijani government. Fearful of imperiling their contracts and business ties with the government, they have little incentive to finance opposition parties or civil society groups.

In the short term, the oil boom of 2006–10 at the very least appears not to have had any positive development on the governance situation in the country. If anything, it seems to have bred complacency regarding the need for reform in the country. Nevertheless, the oil boom has not taken place in isolation: it has been accompanied with a decreased Western engagement with the country, the factor that was always the leading force of positive change. Oil has, in the final analysis, been instrumental in helping Azerbaijan build a better-functioning state with governmental institutions that work considerably better than those of states in comparable socioeconomic situations, such as the countries of Central Asia. As argued by, among others, Francis Fukuyama, the building of functioning state institutions is a sine qua non for long-term political development and a durable democracy.[48]

Western policies will be crucial in determining oil's effects on Azerbaijan's political development. The country's integration into Europe will only happen if Western governments and institutions adopt a proactive policy of engagement with Azerbaijan and the broader region. However, since 2003 the opposite has been the case, with gradual Western dissociation from the region contributing to the stalling of reforms.

If anything, the cooling of Western attitudes toward Azerbaijan following the 2003 election tends to disprove the thesis that oil takes precedence over democracy in Western policies. Indeed, the completion of the Baku-Tbilisi-Ceyhan pipeline seems to have done little to alter the arm's-length state of relations between Washington and Baku that developed after the fall of 2003, when U.S. policy warmed up considerably to Georgia while maintaining a distance from Azerbaijan, in spite of the strong U.S. strategic interests in the country.

Building the Non-Oil Economy

Azerbaijan's energy sector produces close to a third of national GDP, but provides only one percent of employment in the country. This simple statistic illustrates the economic importance of the non-oil sector. If Azerbaijan is to avoid the fate of many other hydrocarbon-dependent countries, where industry subsidies, unfair distribution of wealth, and unemployment combine to generate explosive social situations, it will have to succeed in building a non-oil economy that generates jobs and helps the population live meaningful lives. But the very dominance of the oil sector makes the building of a non-oil economy difficult. To begin with, as oil pushes up the value of the national currency, it makes exports less competitive—a process that can already be observed in Azerbaijan. Of course, the oil sector also creates a surplus that induces short-term thinking in government bodies and a false sense of comfort: money is there, and money can solve problems.

Challenges to Building a Non-oil Economy

Azerbaijani government officials, including President Ilham Aliyev, have on numerous occasions stated that the country's economy should not rely solely on oil, but should, rather, diversify into other sectors primarily unrelated to oil. Oil and gas reserves from currently operational fields are likely to be depleted by 2025, and even if new fields are discovered, oil revenues will decrease considerably in a matter of two decades. This gives authorities a time window to use resources to develop the non-oil economy to ensure sustainable development. There are, however, serious impediments to the growth of the non-oil sector—some left over from the Soviet era, some newly created.

A first issue is infrastructure. Development of a sustainable non-oil economy will necessitate a solid infrastructural basis in the regions outside Baku. The requirements include roads and railways to transport goods, power stations to generate electricity for plants and factories, facilities to store and refrigerate agricultural products, and hotels and restaurants to attract tourists, among other improvements. At the time of independence, however, Azerbaijan's Soviet-era infrastructure was in a condition fit to evoke despair. After a long period of little improvement, the problem began to be addressed. In 2007, for example, Ministry of Transportation officials announced that the equivalent of more than $500 million had been or was being invested in road construction works, with plans being made for the further development of a regional road network.[49] Major highways such as the ones linking Baku and Quba (to the northwest), and Baku and Qazakh (to the far west) were renovated, and in Baku itself, roads were repaired and new bridges and tunnels were built to accommodate the rapid growth of traffic. A beltway around Baku was also being planned.

The government also began construction of gas-operated electricity generating stations in several regions of the country, which was expected to improve the availability of a stable and sustainable supply of power for the operation of industry. Many plants and factories in the food processing and light industry sectors have been opened in recent years, needing electricity but providing jobs. Tourism has also received a major boost, with the construction of hotels, restaurants, and recreational centers in various regions of the country.

Although most of the country still suffers from poor infrastructure, these measures show that the problem is slowly but steadily being addressed. This factor should gradually cease to constitute a major obstacle to the development of the non-oil economy However, it should be noted that most of the chemical and machinery factories such as those in Baku and Sumgait are hopelessly outdated. Because they use old equipment that is only profitable because of artificially low energy prices, they are in fact unsustainable. Thus, while infrastructure development is indeed helping the small and medium-size factories, the larger-scale metallurgy and chemical plants need extensive modernization if they are to return to competitiveness. A special state program to revive these sectors appears to be in order.

The second issue in the effort to build a non-oil economy is financial policy. A particular challenge is posed by the appreciation of the national currency, a well-known difficulty to economists familiar with the problems of oil-producing countries. Starting in 2005, billions of petrodollars not only began flowing into the country but set off rapid growth of the state budget, despite recommendations by international financial institutions that the government spend conservatively. As a result, the economy showed signs of overheating and inflation began to rear its head, jeopardizing people's savings and complicating the process of acquiring loans from banks. In 2006, the government appeared to lose control over inflation; experts funded by the U.S. Agency for International Development reckoned the inflation rate to have reached 14 percent, double the official figure.[50] By 2008, even the government acknowledged a 20 percent inflation rate.[51]

In addition, the appreciation of the manat makes life difficult for local producers, especially in the agricultural sector, who find themselves unable to compete with cheap foreign products. As a result, Azerbaijani consumers often find themselves buying Argentine fruit or Dutch roses instead of locally grown products. Unless the government takes measures to support export-oriented industries, it is likely that the Azerbaijani economy will lose much of its agricultural capacity. In 2006, for example, agriculture grew by only 1 percent. In recent years authorities have tried to support export-oriented industries by issuing loans to farmers, eliminating the farm tax, creating an Azerbaijan investment promotion fund, and several other measures, but these efforts have proven insufficient against the power of the oil revenues flooding the economy.

The third and perhaps biggest threat to development of the non-oil economy is the existence of local monopolies tied to government officials. Most of these monopolies have divided up sectors of influence in the economy and control their sectors with repressive policies supported by government patrons (mostly by means of tax and customs policies) to avoid competition from newly created companies. The most common examples of the monopolies are seen in the export-import sector of the economy. It is virtually impossible for a new player in the market to import foods and other products. Customs officers create so many hurdles for new businesses that, in the end, grocery products rot and the would-be importer goes bankrupt.

A similar situation is present in the construction materials market and even in services and light industry. Tax authorities and other government agencies use regulatory tools and policies to squeeze out competitors and capture the lion's share of the market for themselves. Various government ministers are known to control the major producers of many agricultural products, and to enjoy de facto monopolies in road building, the poultry industry, and general construction, to name only a few examples. This situation discourages the flow of foreign capital into the non-oil economy, and leads to the outflow of local capital. A fourth factor is human capital. The development of the non-oil economy will require high levels of education and knowledge if Azerbaijan and its people are to compete with foreign companies and other national economies. Although Azerbaijan's literacy rate remains very high, the quality of education has suffered significantly since independence. Schools and universities, notorious for pervasive corruption at every level, enroll thousands and thousands of students, but when these students graduate, they lack the training to be creative, to think independently, or to engage in critical analysis. Rather, they have been trained to be subordinate learners, memorizing the lectures of their teachers without making any new findings or experiencing fresh insights of their own. Indeed, the characterization of the education system by opposition leader Asim Mollazade as a "diploma market" is not far from the truth. The young people who emerge from such a system are ill positioned to prosper in a dynamic market economy. Consequently, despite the high level of unemployment in the country, many banks, government institutions, and private companies are unable to find job candidates with the skills and knowledge required in the modern professional workplace. The poor quality of education also hinders the marketing capacity of local companies. Most of them are unable to sell their products abroad because of poor packaging and a lack of the skills required for participation in international trade.

Government officials realize the importance of a cadre of highly qualified professionals to the development of the non-oil economy. For that purpose, in 2006 President Ilham Aliyev issued a decree establishing the Human Capital Fund, which began sending hundreds of Azerbaijani students abroad to study. Several efforts have also been made to upgrade the education system, prominent among them the construction of more than 130 modern secondary schools. A new computerization program of schools was also launched.

The Ministry of Education long blamed all problems on the lack of financial resources to pay higher salaries to teachers and upgrade the physical infrastructure of the schools. Nevertheless, the problem is much deeper, being in the very unreformed form of education being imparted.

Azerbaijan's New Economic Icons

During Soviet times, the non-oil economy was dominated by agriculture, light industry, and the mechanical and chemical industries. Most of these sectors now face serious challenges to their survival in the globally competitive environment. In response, the Azerbaijani government has decided to shift its non-oil economy away from these traditional sectors to two new areas of strategic interest: information technologies and a transportation hub.

The minister of communications and information technologies (IT) under Ilham Aliyev, Ali Abbasov, has been a driving force in this regard. He went as far as to state in February 2007 that revenues from the IT sector would equal those from the oil sector in fifteen years.[52] While this seems a rather sensational and ambitious statement, a closer look at recent developments in Azerbaijan's economy shows that something significant may be in the making. Both President Aliyev and Minister Abbasov have worked hard to get large American firms such as Microsoft, Cisco Systems, and Intel to invest in Azerbaijan. The development of the IT sector and the vision of making Baku the IT hub of the South Caucasus ans beyond has become the new icon of Azerbaijan's future economic model—one that will not depend on oil and gas.

Initial efforts focused on upgrading the domestic computer network. The number of computers and Internet users in the country rose rapidly, reaching 8 and 37 per hundred Azerbaijanis, respectively, by 2009.[53] A program to implement an e-government project (i.e., fuller integration of IT into services and other activities of government) was also launched, with South Korean support. The most ambitious step, however, was the creation of a regional innovation zone, which was being launched in 2009. The zone would consist of technology districts where small and medium-size companies would produce IT products for export.[54]

At the same time, the Azerbaijani government has been making significant efforts to turn the country into a regional transport hub. With the construction of the Kars-Akhalkalaki-Baku railway making a rail connection from Istanbul to the Caspian possible, and the addition of Kazakhstan's oil to the Baku-Tbilisi-Ceyhan oil pipeline, the plans to use Azerbaijan as a transit zone for regional trade are not unrealistic. The next challenge will be to lure natural gas producers in Turkmenistan into shipping their product through the Baku-Tbilisi-Erzurum gas pipeline. Clearly a step in the right direction, the development of IT and transportation sectors as part of the non-oil economy will nonetheless require support in the shape of new laws and other kinds of reform if the Azerbaijani economy is to have a vibrant and competitive counterpart to the oil sector.

Poverty Alleviation and the Distribution of Resources

Long before Azerbaijan became part of the Soviet Union, its population periodically suffered from malnutrition and widespread poverty brought on by chronic warfare in the region, including invasions by foreign powers, and a general lack of political and economic stability. After the Bolshevik Revolution and the subsequent fall of the Azerbaijan People's Republic, peasants and workers hoped that the new Soviet regime would eradicate poverty. But the chaos of 1920s and 1930s, followed by the Second World War, dashed those hopes. Just like other Soviet nationalities, Azerbaijanis greatly suffered from malnutrition and even starvation.

After the war, the rapid process of rebuilding the Soviet economy produced some short-term results, and poverty was substantially reduced by the mid-1970s. Although many Azerbaijanis were not making high wages, most earned enough to survive from paycheck to paycheck. It was only closer to the time of the Soviet Union's collapse that poverty again reappeared.

In the early 1990s, average monthly salaries in Azerbaijan were one-third below the Union average, and half of the level in the Baltic republics.[55] Considering the fact that wages made up almost 70 percent of the population's income, statistics for the period showed that over 35 percent of the population had incomes below the minimum subsistence level.

If poverty was ingrained at the time of independence, it grew rapidly in the years that followed. Many factors contributed: the Karabakh war and the ensuing occupation of Azerbaijani territories, the flood of refugees and internally displaced persons, the halving of GDP between 1990 to 1994, and the collapse of trade links, as well as mass unemployment and political chaos. Azerbaijanis experienced an unprecedented level of economic, political, and social hardship. Temporary measures taken by governments in the early 1990s such as doubling and tripling salaries did not prevent the rapid rise in the poverty rate.

During 1995–96, World Bank experts conducted several surveys, including a livings standards survey of Azerbaijan. Most of the population, 61.5 percent, was found to be living at or below the poverty level; 20.4 percent of the population was regarded as very poor. Not surprisingly, the poverty rate in Baku was slightly lower, 59.6 percent, though much higher among refugees and internally displaced persons (74.5 percent). The survey also showed the unequal distribution of poverty across the various regions of Azerbaijan. The exclave of Nakhichevan, which was under Armenian embargo, was the poorest of all (84.5 percent living in poverty), followed by the central regions (70.7 percent), whereas the northwestern regions ranked relatively well, though their poverty rate (49.0 percent) was still painfully high.[56] After Heydar Aliyev came to power in 1993, a number of poverty reduction measures were implemented. State expenditures on social needs were brought above 50 percent of total state budget expenditures, macroeconomic stability was established, inflation was reduced, and by 2000 more than 29,000 small and more than 1,000 medium-size enterprises had been privatized. Equally important, a comprehensive land reform led to the distribution of more than 1.3 million hectares of agricultural land among farmers. This was the first time in Azerbaijan's history that farmers were able to own their land. These measures, in addition to the liberalization of foreign trade and a number of other structural reforms, gradually began to produce results. From 1994 to 2000 GDP grew by 24.5 percent, and the contribution of the private sector to GDP reached 68 percent, compared to 29 percent in 1994. Within the agricultural segment of GDP, the private sector now accounted for virtually all production—99 percent. Yet at the same time, GDP growth did not automatically mean the eradication of poverty. As economists have long known, high levels of corruption and uneven distribution of resources can result in continued poverty even while GDP continues to grow.

In 2000, GDP per capita in Azerbaijan was $664. This indicator put Azerbaijan in 98th place among 189 countries, making it a poor country by UN standards. Average monthly wages of working people were $45, and the average monthly pension for the country's almost 1.2 million pensioners was $17.

Another factor that contributed to widespread poverty was the inefficiency and near-collapsed condition of the social protection system. The Azerbaijani Constitution provides citizens with broad social protections, but financial limitations had reduced these provisions to empty words. For instance, the minimum benefit per child was set at the level of $2 per month, and the minimum wage was only $6 per month. Pensions were also meager, mainly because of the low rate at which insurance premiums were collected for the Social Protection Fund.

Starting in 1999, international financial institutions such as the World Bank and the International Monetary Fund made nationally owned poverty reduction strategies the basis of their concessional lending. More than sixty countries became engaged in this strategy, including Azerbaijan. Azerbaijan's Poverty Reduction Strategy Paper was prepared by the government in July 2001, with the participation of civil society actors and international financial institutions, and approved by the World Bank and the International Monetary Fund. This was followed by the development of the State Program on Poverty Reduction and Economic Development (SPREAD), coordinated by the newly established SPREAD Secretariat at the Ministry of Economic Development. This was the beginning of a more comprehensive, coordinated, and planned effort to reduce poverty in the country.

Initially, SPREAD was planned to exist for a period of three years (2003–05), with the goal of revising it on an annual basis in line with monitoring of the implementation and effectiveness of envisaged policy measures. In a time when revenues from the oil contracts were starting to flow into the country, this coordinated effort to reduce poverty was especially important, as it showed a way to use oil revenues to create income generation activities and opportunities, improve the system of social protection, introduce targeted social assistance benefits to the population strata in greatest need, and increase the quality of education and health care, lifting in particular the living standards of internally displaced persons and other refugees.

In 2005, with the initial SPREAD concluded, the government initiated work on a second SPREAD, which would cover the ten-year period from 2006 to 2015. Partly because of SPREAD, but also partly due to skyrocketing oil revenues, the poverty level in Azerbaijan declined to 13 percent in 2009, less than a fourth of what it had been in the mid-1990s.[57] Azerbaijan's rapid growth had affected the general income of the people and the level of poverty in the country. SPREAD was renamed the State Program for Human Capital and Regional Development, a sign that its sponsors were lifting their ambitions beyond the objective of eliminating poverty.

Rising oil revenues and accelerating economic growth are very positive indications of the rapid development of the country. However, a frequent and legitimate question is whether these oil revenues trickle down to ordinary Azerbaijanis and have an impact on their lives.

While touring the regions in 2002, President Heydar Aliyev was confronted by a large crowd of local residents in Gandja, who managed to break through the security cordon to pass him letters of complaint. For the grandmaster of politics, it was a clear sign that things in the provinces were not going well. While increasing economic activity in the country was very much felt in Baku, the regions outside the capital continued to experience severe problems with utilities (electricity and gas), income, and job opportunities. Many young residents of these rural areas were migrating to Russia and other countries of the former Soviet Union in search for jobs. The angry Gandja crowd was a wake-up call for the political leadership: it had to start paying attention to the provinces. Mayors of several key towns—Gandja, Lenkoran, and Sumgait—were subsequently fired, and younger, more dynamic and reform-minded men were put in charge.

During his 2003 presidential campaign, Ilham Aliyev made regional development and the creation of job opportunities for Azerbaijanis his primary themes. His father had preached "stability" as his main message in the 1990s; now, he turned the message into "stability and development." During his campaign, he promised to create 600,000 new jobs during his first term as president.[58]

Immediately after his election, Ilham Aliyev signed a decree on the establishment of a state program for socioeconomic development of the provincial areas. This state program included a number of measures to develop the economy of the provinces, such as rebuilding roads, opening new factories and plants, developing infrastructure, building new electricity generation plants, repairing irrigation canals, opening new schools and health care centers, and introducing new investment and capital. A clear sign that Ilham Aliyev took the development of the provinces seriously was his frequent visits to those areas; practically on a daily basis, he could be seen inaugurating a school or factory.

In February 2007, the government reported that 520,000 new jobs had been created in the provincial areas.[59] Although some analysts were skeptical of this number and called it a deliberate exaggeration, it indeed indicated a clearly positive trend in Azerbaijan's provinces. Many of them had new governors who were engaging proactively in reconstruction efforts. Visitors to the provincial areas would find great changes compared a to five years earlier: where decrepit buildings and dirt roads had prevailed, towns now sport paved and cleaned streets, new parks, and new or renovated buildings. Ilham Aliyev has also informally put pressure the country's oligarchs to invest in the provinces. Thus, major holding companies such as ATA Holding, Gilan Holding, and Azersun Holding—known to be informally controlled by top cabinet officials—have begun operating in the provinces, and hundreds of new factories and food processing plans have been opened. Whether they stay open and productive, however, remains another question.

The government has also launched a new education program called the "New School for Modernizing Azerbaijan." This project is being implemented by the Heydar Aliyev Foundation, chaired by First Lady Mehriban Aliyeva; more than 130 secondary schools were built in 2006 alone. Health care services also receive special attention, with several modern medical diagnostic centers having been built in the provinces.

The banking sector also underwent major changes. Many banks opened branch offices in the provinces, while the government started providing microcredits to farmers through these banks for the development of agricultural lands. Related to this, a leasing system was established in 2005, and farmers now have access to agricultural equipment by means of a state leasing company.

Meanwhile, the social protection system has been completely changed. Universal benefits were eliminated, and targeted social assistance was established to help those most in need. The president repeatedly raised the salaries of state employees such as teachers, doctors, and scientists, and raised pensions and benefits to the families of those who had died in the Karabakh war.

Economic trends are thus positive and do indicate that a portion of the petrodollars are being put to constructive use. Ilham Aliyev seems to well understand the dangers of failing to use these revenues to develop the physical infrastructure of the country and raise living standards. If these improvements fail to be realized, crushed expectations for a better life could turn into the most destabilizing problem in the country, and constitute the most serious challenge to the president's power.

Significantly, the 2008 economic crisis, which did not spare Azerbaijan, did not generate widespread social discontent. Construction largely halted in Baku and the economy may be said to have received a much-needed cold shower reminiscent of the one that had doused it ten years earlier; but on the whole, thanks to oil revenues, Azerbaijan was relatively shielded from the crisis.

Azerbaijan in the Politics of Trade: The Silk Road and the East-West Superhighway

Continental trade and transportation is one area that could significantly boost Azerbaijan's prospects in the non-oil sector, and one where—for a change—Azerbaijan's location is a distinct asset. As has been noted a number of times in the present volume, one of the concepts that best epitomize Azerbaijan is that of a crossroads. Azerbaijan straddles Europe and Asia not only in cultural and political terms, but also in terms of trade. Lying at the intersection of developing east-west and north-south trade routes at a time when trade between Europe and Asia is growing at great speed, Azerbaijan stands to gain significantly.

The potential benefits to Azerbaijan are illustrated by the international movement of freight containers. It is expected that by 2015 the annual volume of global container traffic will reach ten million units, more than triple the volume in 2005 (three million units). The overwhelming majority of these containers, holding anything from cars, clothes, and computers to foodstuffs and toys, are being shipped by sea, crossing the Suez Canal and often also the Strait of Malacca. However, if a well-functioning land route were established as an alternative, it could reduce the time in transit by a third and the cost of transportation by a quarter. Simply put, there are huge potential advantages to reviving the traditional Silk Road through inland continental trade to complement the maritime container trade.[60] As Taleh Ziyadov has put observed, Azerbaijan is uniquely located to benefit from this development and to become a major transit country.[61]

Azerbaijan is located at the crossroads of both major rival continental transportation projects. The one with the greatest potential is often referred to as the "New Silk Road." As proposed, it would comprise an east-west transportation system that would include highways and railways (but also fiber-optic cable networks, electricity transmission lines, and oil and gas pipelines) and link Europe to China and India by means of a route across Turkey and the Black Sea, through the Caucasus, and across the Caspian Sea into Central Asia. This project is supported by the European Union through its TRACECA (Transport Corridor Europe-Caucasus-Asia) project, launched in 1993 but only gradually becoming a reality, and not mainly as a result of EU sponsorship but as the regional states take matters into their own hands. The rival project, supported by Russia and Iran, proposes to create a north-south transportation corridor, linking India through Iran and Azerbaijan or the Caspian Sea, to Russia and Europe. Azerbaijan is a key element in both projects. Baku hosted a large TRACECA summit in 1998, where a multilateral agreement to construct the transport corridor was signed; the Azerbaijani government joined the north-south corridor project in 2005.[62]

A great impediment to the building of these transportation networks is the legacy of the closed borders and closed economies of the Soviet period. Indeed, infrastructure linking former Soviet republics to their non-Soviet neighbors is often nonexistent or in disrepair. Large investments are needed for the construction of rail and road links, as well as to upgrade existing road and rail networks to international standards, a sine qua non if continental trade is to choose this route over the longer but simpler maritime routes. International financial institutions have made significant investments in these projects; nevertheless, it is only with the gradual economic recovery of the region since the late 1990s, in particular the impressive growth rates of Azerbaijan, the other South Caucasus states, and Kazakhstan, that extensive transportation networks are becoming a realistic prospect.

Indeed, Azerbaijan's infrastructure is far from ideally placed to handle fast-growing trade. In 2009, Azerbaijan still did not have a rail connection to Turkey or Europe; the only existing railway connecting the Caucasus to Turkey crossed the Turkish-Armenian border, and had been closed since the Karabakh war. Moreover, Azerbaijan refuses to let its export goods cross Armenian territory en route to Europe. Seventy-five percent of Azerbaijan's road network was characterized by the Asian Development Bank in 2005 as being in poor condition, including 61 percent of its east-west and north-south highways, although this problem is gradually being addressed.[63]

In terms of rail networks, the United Nations foresees development of a 7,000-kilometer railway linking China with Europe. The eastern terminus would be at the Kazakhstani-Chinese border, with the route going through the capital of Kazakhstan, Astana, to the Caspian port city of Aqtaū, across almost 4,000 kilometers of Kazakhstani territory. Railcar ferries would then link Aqtaū to Baku across the Caspian Sea. A railroad linking Baku to Turkey would complete the European connection.

For this vision to be realized, a thorough upgrade of the Soviet-era railway system will, of course, be necessary. Most of the railway is already in place, however. As it happens, the longest missing link on this 7,000-kilometer route is a 98-kilometer stretch from the eastern Turkish city of Kars to the southern Georgian city of Akhalkalaki. This gap is one of the most politically sensitive issues facing the transportation network, given that a rail connection dating back to the czarist era links Kars through the Armenian city of Gyumri to Tbilisi. That rail connection has not been in use for two decades, given the closure of the Turkish-Armenian border and Azerbaijan's adamant refusal to use any Armenian connection in its international trade. To close the gap, and because Turkey and Georgia lacked a direct rail connection, the Kars-Akhalkalaki railway project was conceived in the early 1990s to connect Turkey to Georgia—and thereby Turkey to Azerbaijan—by rail. Of course, this project also plays an important role in the wider development of Eurasian trade, as the unresolved conflict between Armenia and Azerbaijan would otherwise hold such trade hostage.

This project may seem to be in line with general Western policies for encouraging East-West trade. As it got under way, however, the United States refrained from supporting the project, in the hope of working instead to open the Turkish-Armenian border and avoid the further isolation of Armenia. Armenian-American organizations were successful in 2006 in getting a law enacted in the United States that prohibited the use of U.S. credit or funding toward construction of the railroad.

However, as would become clear in January 2007, such funding was not needed. Azerbaijan's new-found economic strength enabled it to push ahead with the project without external financing. Azerbaijan granted Georgia a $200 million loan at a nominal 1 percent interest rate for the building of the Georgian section of the railway, while Turkey would finance its own part. At a January 2007 ceremony in Tbilisi, the presidents of Azerbaijan and Georgia and the Turkish prime minister issued a declaration on the railroad and a series of other cooperative ventures, including the linking of their electricity networks. The project is expected to be completed by 2011.[64]

Azerbaijan scored a victory by showing its ability to override the Armenian opposition to its selected economic projects. The economic isolation of Armenia, however, is not necessarily in Azerbaijan's long-term interest if it compounds Armenia's militarization and its domination by a siege mentality. Nevertheless, the Kars-Akhalkalaki railroad may in the long term be of equal significance to the building of the Baku-Tbilisi-Ceyhan pipeline in terms of bringing home the point to Armenia that it was gradually losing the upper hand in its relationship with Azerbaijan.

Azerbaijan nevertheless faces a number of challenges before it can achieve the status of a major transit corridor. The building of adequate infrastructure is one such challenge. Other factors of importance include the state of the customs system, which is marred by systemic corruption, even to the highest levels. The successful completion of giant infrastructure projects in the energy field, in particular the Baku-Tbilisi-Ceyhan pipeline, was a precursor and perhaps a prerequisite to the development of greater international interest in rail and highway development, as well as other infrastructure projects in the region. And as Taleh Ziyadov has observed, as important as the economic aspects of continental trade may be, it is the strategic element that is of most importance to the Azerbaijani leadership— just as with the pipelines.[65] Integration with European communication arteries will bring Azerbaijan technical and administrative reform that will draw it closer to European standards of commerce and governance and deepen its engagement with European organizations. As such, it is a piece of Azerbaijan's foreign policy as much as it is a boon to the country's long-term economic prospects.

10

Azerbaijani Society: Identity, Modernity, and Tradition

The upheavals that buffeted politics and the economy in Azerbaijan in the 1990s also had a profound impact on society. But while the economic and political systems are gradually adapting to new realities, momentous developments such as the Soviet breakup, the war over Mountainous Karabakh, economic dislocation, the opening to the outside world, and the effort to build a nation-state have also had profound effects on Azerbaijani society. The very identity of the people and the way in which society has traditionally been organized have undergone particularly severe stress. Even before the onslaught of change that began with the Soviet collapse, the nation's demographic makeup had already been altered by the historic division of the nation along the border between the Soviet Union and Iran, as well as sovietization itself. Then, in the 1990s, came ethnic cleansing, migration both within and outside the country, and serious difficulties with the provision of health care and education.

The changes of the past two decades have encouraged strong and often contradictory tendencies in society. These concern basic identity issues: the respective roles and status of societal groups such as men and women, the young and the old, and the urban and rural populations. Fresh questions are being asked about the role of religion in society and, more generally, the lifestyle choices Azerbaijanis make.

Socioeconomic and Demographic Developments

The real social consequences of the Soviet breakup and its multiple attendant disasters in terms of war, forced migration, and economic collapse are best illustrated by changes in Azerbaijan's demographic composition since about 1990.

Azerbaijan was by no means in a leading position among the Soviet republics in socioeconomic terms. It ranked in the middle or lower middle on most indicators, being somewhat better off than the Central Asian republics, but lagging behind its two Caucasian neighbors and the more western republics. The state of affairs was particularly dire between the great purges of 1937 and the Aliyev era of the 1970s. Nevertheless, Azerbaijan developed greatly in socioeconomic terms during the Soviet era, acquiring basic infrastructure and modern health and education systems. These, it should be said, suffered from the common problems of the communist system—for example, the ideological slant and authoritarian nature of education, or the overuse of antibiotics in the health sector. Nevertheless, the Soviet era did bring considerable progress to a society that had been largely illiterate, patriarchal, and rural. One of the most significant accomplishments of the Soviet Union was to secure the secularization of Azerbaijani society, which had been an objective of the czarist rulers and of the secular Azerbaijani intelligentsia that preceded the Soviets. Another closely related accomplishment was the emancipation of women, and their inclusion in educational and professional life to an extent unseen in traditional or Muslim societies. Indeed, it is thanks to the Soviet experience that Azerbaijan exceeds Turkey, itself a forerunner in the Muslim world, on such indicators as both male and female literacy, and female participation in the workforce.

Azerbaijan's relatively impressive social development in the Soviet era was paralleled by a substantial increase in the national population: from 1.8 million inhabitants in 1897, about two decades before the czars gave way to the Communists, to almost 8 million in 1999, about a decade after the end of Soviet rule. In the twentieth century, Azerbaijan's population growth rate exceeded the global rate by 20 percent. Toward the end of the Soviet era, Azerbaijan also saw the majority of its population shift from being rural to urban dwellers.[1] In parallel, maternal and child mortality rates decreased and life expectancy increased as the population enjoyed the benefits of a developed health-care system.

The post-Soviet era has been a totally different story. To begin with, birthrates plummeted in the 1990s in both absolute and relative terms. About 183,000 births were recorded in 1990, but the figure for 1998 was down by almost a third, to about 124,000. While an alarming decline, this still kept the birthrate above the replacement level. More alarmingly, the collapse of the Soviet health-care system and the outbreak of the Karabakh war caused mortality rates to increase rapidly. Around 40,000 deaths, or about 6 per thousand residents, were recorded annually prior to the war. By contrast, the figures for 1992–94 exceeded 50,000 deaths per year, peaking at 54,900 in 1994 (7.4 per thousand). Following the end of the war, the death rate returned to about 6 per thousand. This indicates that the war indirectly or directly caused the deaths of more than 30,000 people, far more than the official figure of 18,000. Of course, the number of injured and disabled greatly surpassed the death toll, compounding the societal consequences of the war.

The increased fragility of life in Azerbaijan was not limited to the direct effects of the war. In the post-Soviet period, child mortality and maternal mortality rates increased rapidly, stabilizing at several times the level for developed countries in the late 1990s. The general decline of socioeconomic conditions is also illustrated by the fact that the mortality rate for men aged 20–60 years was double that of women, and that morbidity as a result of tuberculosis increased by a factor of five.[2]

Migration flows are another result of the combination of war and economic dislocation. These can be divided into three overlapping categories. First there were the forced migrations resulting from the Karabakh war: more than a million Azerbaijanis were forced to flee their homes in Armenia, Karabakh, and the occupied territories surrounding Karabakh. Second, rural Azerbaijanis—including refugees—left the poverty of the countryside in search of work in the cities, overwhelmingly with Baku as their destination. This in turn led to a depopulation of the countryside, particularly of working-age men, while Baku grew immensely. The wider Baku area now houses close to half of Azerbaijan's population, putting additional strain on the Apsheron Peninsula, whose environment is already severely damaged after centuries of oil production. Driving taxis or standing on the outskirts of the city in hopes of providing day labor to the construction sector, the migrants are ubiquitous around Baku. Third, the mass migration from the Azerbaijani countryside, including refugees from the Karabakh war, also had an international aspect, as hundreds of thousands of people, primarily men of working age, left the country for work in Russia, Turkey, or the Persian Gulf emirates.

Migration flows have both positive and negative consequences. Economically, they provide a vital source of income to rural communities. Yet, much as in the instance of oil, this comes is in the form of a "rent", not production. Moreover, these migration flows have contributed to the decreasing marriage rate in Azerbaijan, and the ensuing reduction in the birthrate. The number of recorded marriages fell almost by half from 1990 to 1998, decreasing by a factor of 1.8 even as the population was growing.[3]

These figures are all indicative of the social upheaval Azerbaijan went through after independence. All implications, of course, cannot be quantified. This is especially true regarding the psychological effect, not least on the young generation, which also includes the increased stress and anxiety visited upon parents unable to provide their sons and daughters with the standards of living they themselves had enjoyed. The fact that more than half of the country's population fell below the poverty level in the 1990s (as noted in chapter 9) has implications that also cannot be quantified. Many members of the current adolescent generation of Azerbaijanis likely have received inadequate nutrition and health care, with consequences that will affect their health for many years to come. Likewise, many young Azerbaijanis have received an inadequate education—either because they have had to work to supplement their family income, or because of declining education standards in the schools. Refugee children have been especially hard hit by these problems, and it remains to be seen whether they will indeed become what some have already called a "lost generation."[4]

These socioeconomic and demographic trends are not unique to Azerbaijan. Among the post-Soviet states, Azerbaijan is comparable to other societies ridden by conflict, such as Tajikistan, Georgia, and Armenia. Among these, Azerbaijan had the great disadvantage of not being granted substantial levels of development and humanitarian assistance, partly on account of its considerable oil-related income. Yet revenues from the oil industry were of little consequence to the people in the 1990s, and only started to make a substantial contribution to the state budget in the second decade of independence. While Azerbaijan's poor were mostly doing without international aid in the 1990s, Armenia and Georgia were receiving substantial support from foreign donors, and in Armenia's case the Armenian diaspora as well. Likewise, once its civil war was over, Tajikistan became a major recipient of international assistance, unlike Azerbaijan. But with the strong stream of oil revenues now helping to rapidly reduce poverty and raise living standards, Azerbaijan's leaders nonetheless bear a great responsibility, which brings with it a great risk: should the population conclude that the oil money is not being used to advance the common good, the government's very stability could be jeopardized.

A key problem has been government policy, or the lack thereof, in the fields of health care and education. The health and education ministries have been among the most dysfunctional in independent Azerbaijan, with high levels of corruption and low levels of reform. Indeed, while Azerbaijan transitioned to a new curriculum for its schools, the failure of the government to invest in education led to retention of the same, outdated methods of instruction used in Soviet times. A more modern curriculum, with modernized methods of instruction and teachers trained in these methods, remains sorely needed. The lack of funds in the education sector was dire in the 1990s and beyond—public spending on education in Azerbaijan in

1997 was 34 percent of 1992 levels.[5] Enrollment is also problematic: from 1989 to 1999, general secondary enrollment fell from 34 to 22.5 percent of the eligible population, while vocational and technical school enrollment fell from 28.8 to 10.1 percent.[6] The lack of funds contributed to widespread corruption, with teachers at all levels demanding money for admission or grades. While the practice was especially prevalent in higher education, 90 percent of parents of students enrolled below the university level reported in a 2006 survey that they had had to make informal payments. Most of these were for repairs and infrastructure, but almost 15 percent of parent reported having paid for grades, passing scores on examinations, or diplomas.[7]

While the lack of decent salaries may have given otherwise honest teachers little choice but to engage in corrupt practices, the effects of such practices on the emerging generation's values are still likely to be strongly negative. At the university level, students often have to pay both to get admitted and to graduate. The large-scale oil revenues provide the state with the financial resources needed to reform the education sector. Political will is nevertheless needed to accomplish this—breaking the pyramid of corruption that has developed in the education sector will go against entrenched interests, but such resolute action will be needed if Azerbaijan is ever to take its place among the developed nations of the world.

Identity and Values

The Soviet collapse unleashed a quest for identity that led to a competition between modernist (including Western) and traditional or, more precisely, neotraditional (including Islamic) self-images and lifestyle ideals. These forces had had only limited bearing on Soviet Azerbaijan. Indeed, the Soviet Union had been both radical and conservative at the same time. Its ideology and social engineering were radical, though in some areas disastrous—two prominent examples being the excesses of collectivization (especially in Ukraine and Kazakhstan) and the purges of the mid-1930s. Gradually, however, the Soviet leadership turned increasingly conservative. Already by the 1930s, any type of local initiative was either channeled through the top-down Communist Party apparatus or simply stifled. Hence, the Soviet Union kept a half-modernized society such as that of Azerbaijan in limbo, preventing it from progressing by its own devices, hindering it from interacting with the outside world, and restricting its knowledge about adjacent countries with which it shared culture and history. The Soviet Union's collapse can therefore be likened to the opening of a Pandora's box, as it removed artificial boundaries with the outside world but also dissolved the ideological glue of communism that had held the state together. When, in the early 1990s, the erstwhile Soviet republics found themselves on their own, their opening up to the rest of the world occurred in an ideological vacuum. Everywhere, this resulted in the forceful entry of Western consumerism, in competition—in Muslim areas—with a resurgent Islamic alternative.

Western lifestyles had a particular effect on the urban middle class, but most former Soviet citizens soon felt the impact of blue jeans, McDonalds, music videos, and the many other manifestations of consumerism. In Azerbaijan, this onslaught coincided with a war that greatly boosted the development of the country's separate national identity. Hence, the rapid evolution of lifestyle options coincided with a debate over the markers of the nation's identity, complicating matters further. This, in turn, had large implications for the structure of authority in society.

Azerbaijani Identity in Development

As discussed in chapter 2, a resurgence of patriotism and a quest for the markers of Azerbaijani identity occurred during Heydar Aliyev's tenure as leader of Soviet Azerbaijan in the 1970s and 1980s. When the Karabakh conflict broke out in 1988, this process was nevertheless limited mainly to the Baku intelligentsia and only nascent in the popular consciousness. Yet the conflict led to the rapid development of Azerbaijani nationalism, though what exactly this meant was ill defined. Whether Azerbaijani nationalism identified the nation to include non-Turkic ethnic minorities was unclear, as was what exactly defined the Azerbaijani nation. Indeed, the largest difficulties in the building of the political agenda of the Azerbaijani Popular Front (APF) were related to these questions of identity and national ideology. The people who make up Azerbaijan's majority population have in the past century gone by many names. Under the czars they were referred to simply as Muslims, or by the generic term "Tatar," which indicated a Turkic-speaking Muslim. Later, in the early Soviet era, they were referred to as Turks, which turned into "Azerbaijanis" after 1937. Meanwhile, the people themselves were never consulted on who they were. Were they best described as Azeri? Azerbaijani? Azeri Turks? Azerbaijani Turks? Or simply Turks?

The debates that followed independence regarding the correct ethnonym for the people inhabiting Azerbaijan illustrate this quandary. An influential current in the national movement held that there was no such thing as an

Azerbaijani nation or language. Azerbaijan, accordingly, was the name of a territory, but not of a people. The dominant population group was the Turks, and their language was Turkish or Turkic (two concepts that are not differentiated in Turkic languages). This rather narrow and exclusive concept of the nation stood against a much more inclusive and civic national idea, often called "Azerbaijanism," which heeds the Turkic heritage of Azerbaijan but is based on citizenship and common attachment to the territory rather than ethnicity; crucially, it includes the non-Turkic minorities in the definition of the national community. The former interpretation—the people of Azerbaijan as primarily Turkic—became state policy under President Abulfez Elçibey, upsetting not only the ethnic minorities but a large portion of the intelligentsia. Most Azerbaijanis, especially in Baku, were reluctant to fully embrace an ethnically based Turkic identity, which was often understood as tantamount to embracing Turkishness. This did not mean that they disliked Turkey; but they were not ready to define themselves in a way that they perceived as ignoring or neglecting their Caucasian geography, history, and culture, their links to Iran, or their Soviet past. Indeed, finding a consensus on what they were not—Persian, Russian, or even Turkish—was easier than defining what they actually were.

Elçibey's policies were reversed after Heydar Aliyev's return in 1993, as the nation, as well as the language, became defined as "Azerbaijani." This is important to note, since the Western press often uses the term "Azeri," which is not frequently used in Azerbaijan, certainly not in official documents. Indeed, the difference between these two terms merits some attention. The term "Azeri," used mostly by foreigners, has come to possess a narrower, ethnically based meaning, whereas the term "Azerbaijani" is understood to refer to residents within the territory of Azerbaijan, embracing the country's entire population. However, Azerbaijanis themselves refer their nation by the term "Azərbaycanlı," (Azerbaijani). By the same token, Azerbaijan's language was defined as "Azərbaycanca" (Azerbaijani), which implied that it was the state language of all citizens of Azerbaijan.

This definition has now been in use for more than a decade, and seems to represent the most acceptable notion to most of the population, in spite of objections from the Turkic nationalist fringe groups. Yet it does not mean that the definition of the Azerbaijani nation is settled; just as in any other modern nation-state, there is a continuing tug of war between civic and ethnic markers of identity. A nation's past is invariably built in great part upon the culture of its majority population, in this case a Turkic-speaking, mainly Shiite Muslim population. Yet many of the poets and writers who are hailed as the ancestors of Azerbaijani literature wrote mainly in Persian, while unquestionably being of Turkic origin. But those were the ironies of the time: one need only recall that Shah Ismail of Iran, an Azerbaijani Turk, wrote poetry in his Turkic dialect, while his contemporary, the Ottoman sultan Selim, wrote poetry in Persian. Language and ethnicity were simply not the determining features of identity in the Muslim world, and are therefore not necessarily a particularly powerful tool for understanding the building of identities.

Ethnic Minorities

No matter how the nation is defined, it remains a fact that the overwhelming majority of Azerbaijanis are ethnically and linguistically Turkic, while a sizable minority are not. Aside from Jews, Armenians, and Russians, the latter mainly located in the capital, this includes a number of Muslim minorities such as Lezgins, Talysh, and Kurds, as well as several North Caucasian ethnic groups. These mainly reside along the country's borders: the Talysh in the south, the Lezgins, Avars, and other North Caucasian peoples in the north, and the Kurds mainly in the west. These groups have historically been rather well integrated into Azerbaijani society, and levels of intermarriage are high. Consequently, estimates concerning their numbers vary greatly, as many Talysh, Lezgins, and Kurds are registered in official documents as Azerbaijani Turks. Nevertheless, it is generally estimated that about 200,000 Lezgins live in a compact area in the north of the country, near the Dagestani border. A slightly higher number of Talysh live near the Iranian border around Lenkoran and Astara, while the number of Kurds is harder to reckon. Kelbajar Province, situated between Armenia and Mountainous Karabakh and occupied by Armenia, was home to a significant Kurdish population that was evicted along with Azerbaijani Turks from the occupied territories.

Minority issues were a concern in the first years of independence, especially during the tenure of the Popular Front. Lezgins, in particular, reacted against the Turkic definition of the nation, and resisted military conscription. This led to tensions between them and the government, and to the formation of a nationalist group called Sadval. In all likelihood, Sadval received intermittent support from forces within the Russian government trying to undermine Azerbaijan, and was responsible for terrorist attacks on the Baku metro in 1994 that killed more than twenty people. Likewise, a renegade ethnic Talysh military commander tried to establish a fiefdom in southern Azerbaijan in 1993, but failed to gain popular support for the effort (see chapter 4). By the late 1990s, the minority situation had quieted considerably, in great part due to the inclusive policies of the Heydar Aliyev administration. Ethnic minorities are fairly well represented in Azerbaijani state institutions, including Parliament and the executive authorities. The level of inclusion of minorities is perhaps best illustrated by the criticism this draws from some corners in the Turkist opposition. Remnants of the erstwhile Popular Front, most notably Müsavat and its well-read party newspaper, *Yeni Müsavat*, regularly characterize the government as having been hijacked by non-Turkic people, raising allegations that leading politicians are of Kurdish, Talysh, or even Armenian origin.

A noteworthy aspect of social relations in Azerbaijan is the peaceful coexistence of the Jewish minority with the rest of society. Azerbaijan is home to a Jewish town, Krasnaya Sloboda, a twin city of the northern city of Quba, as well as a significant Jewish community in Baku. This community is relatively wealthy and well integrated into society, the Quba Jews speaking Azerbaijani rather than Russian. Though many Jews took the opportunity to migrate to Israel during the chaos of the early 1990s, the economic development of Azerbaijan, coupled with the troubles in the Middle East, has actually prompted Jews to return from Israel to resume residence in Azerbaijan.

The minority situation in Azerbaijan is relatively benign by regional standards, and certainly compared to that in both Iran and Russia, and even Georgia. However, by Western standards, Azerbaijan still has some difficulties. The government continues to deny any instance of discrimination against minorities, and sees little need to incorporate international minority-rights law, which it considers unnecessary given what it terms the lack of minority-related problems in the country.[8] Azerbaijan's relatively centralized form of government, for example, has the effect of limiting the political participation of minority populations at the local level. While the rest of the population faces similar limits, this condition resonates differently in minority areas, as it raises the possibility that minorities will perceive that the government wishes to discourage their involvement in the political realm. Likewise, the effort to widen use of the national language—commendable in itself, as the ability to communicate in Azerbaijani provides a means for minorities to participate in public life—has also meant that the protection of minority languages in education and media has weakened somewhat. It remains a challenge for Azerbaijan to balance its promotion of an inclusive Azerbaijani identity with the internationally recognized minority rights to which the state has assented.

Modernity Versus Tradition

The dramatic changes that have affected Azerbaijani society have brought with them completely new conditions of life for the young generation of today as compared to previous ones. Their mothers and fathers grew up under communism, as part of the enormous Soviet Union. They had stability and predictability, but suffered from a lack of freedom and information and from isolation from the rest of the world. Moreover, their identity was gradually being eroded. Patriotically minded Azerbaijanis were concerned, by the late 1970s, that their children's generation would be completely Russified and lose any sense of being Azerbaijani. Indeed, especially in Baku, visitors could still hear Russian being spoken among Azerbaijani youth as late as the mid-1990s. Yet even as Soviet society was pushing children away from their parents' linguistic heritage, it was also fundamentally conservative, permitting the older generations to exercise control over the younger ones and shielding the country from the influences of Western popular culture.

All this changed in the 1990s. The very rapid opening of the country to the world allowed for a variety of influences to affect Azerbaijan, and primarily, of course, the young generation. As in other post-Soviet states, the elder generations had tremendous difficulty adjusting to the change, often slipping into nostalgia for the good old Brezhnev era or simply being disoriented. The younger generations were exposed to Western popular culture, as well as its Western-inspired Russian counterpart. The Islamic world was also an influence, though quite a diverse one: Turkey had an impact both through its modern and secular culture, but also through its religious groups; so did theocratic Iran, and religiously conservative centers of influence in the Arab world.

Azerbaijani society stood out among its counterparts in the former Soviet republics, particularly neighboring Armenia and Georgia, in that it underwent a deeper identity crisis, complicated by the fundamental task of defining the national community. Moreover, its Muslim heritage added an important component to its development that was absent in Russia or its other two former Soviet neighbors. This Islamic element in Azerbaijani identity gradually gained influence in society. Yet simultaneously, Azerbaijan was immensely more influenced by Western culture than most other Muslim countries, such as those of Central Asia. Its proximity to the West, the oil industry, the strong influence of the Westernizing elements of Turkish popular culture, and its growing integration into Western institutions, not least through student exchanges, all contributed to this. As a result,

Azerbaijan is like a laboratory, in the process of developing a unique blend of its own traditions, with the Western and Islamic cultures mixed in.

This process is clearly a painful and complex one. Western-inspired youth culture is, as elsewhere, perceived as a threat both to re-emergent Islamic values and to Azerbaijani society in general, which is conservative, with firmly enforced societal norms, yet—thanks in large part to its Soviet legacy—devoid of explicit religious content. The sheer speed with which the new youth culture has permeated Azerbaijan has had an important side effect, seen first in the cities but increasingly also in rural areas: a generation gap that widely exceeds that typically observed in most societies. In many cases, the young people of today have very little in common with their parents in the way they think, their norms, their values and ideas, and their way of life. In Azerbaijan, this gap has been pushed wider by the shift to the Roman alphabet, which has brought the young generation closer to Turkey, the Internet and the West, but places a high barrier between the Cyrillic-raised generation of their parents and many of the benefits and other allures of modernity.

The resultant insecurities also help explain the very specific ways in which influences blend, and the cultural extremes that can result. On the one hand, as in every modernizing society, there is an urban youth culture that tries to be more Western than the West itself, its manifestations made even more outrageous by the nihilism and materialism that characterize Russia and other postcommunist societies. In turn, these excesses spark a backlash against Westernization that, at least among Azerbaijani youth, often takes the form of a gravitation toward Islamic culture, with its clearly defined, uncomplicated system of beliefs. But it is important to note that embracing Islamic values does not in itself constitute a return to tradition. Rather, it is in many cases a response to inducements from social and political movements that are often foreign based and, while doctrinally conservative, are technologically sophisticated and otherwise conversant with the trappings of modernity.

While the opening to the world in the first decade of independence enabled external influences to take a dominant role in Azerbaijani society, an exploration of Azerbaijan's own cultural and societal traditions may gradually emerge as an important countertrend. Indeed, with the progress in research and scholarship being made in an independent Azerbaijan, the nation is beginning to discover its history and interpret it in a new light. This is true not least for the study of Azerbaijan's pre-Soviet statehood, including the First Republic and the early communist era, as well as the purges conducted during the era of "Azerbaijan's Stalin," Mir Jafar Baghirov. This process of discovery started before independence. Later studies having followed this trend, including Nasib Nassibli's studies of the first republic, former foreign minister Hasan Hasanov's reinterpretation of Nariman Narimanov, the founder of Soviet Azerbaijan, and parliamentarian and historian Jamil Hasanli's study of the southern Azerbaijan crisis of 1946, which has also been published in English.[9]

As the fruits of this revival find their way into school curricula and as other projects to recover the national culture progress, it is likely that Azerbaijan will cultivate a stronger sense of itself both socially and culturally. As it develops its unique blend of Caucasian, Azerbaijani, Western, and Islamic cultures, Azerbaijan is following a similar path to the one Turkey has been so painfully traveling for the past half-century. Turkey's experiences will continue to be relevant, but Azerbaijan's specific secular traditions, its Caucasian culture, and the added ingredient—for better and for worse—of the Soviet experience will make Azerbaijani society and culture unique in their own right.

Corruption

Corruption is rife in Azerbaijan—politically, economically, and socially. If one accepts its most simple definition, the misuse of public office for personal gain, corruption includes not just high-level malfeasance but everyday practices such as informal payments to schoolteachers, doctors, and low-level officials by individual citizens. Businesses, which are likewise bedeviled by these routine activities, must also contend with higher-level corruption, such as the peddling of influence to their competitors by all-too-willing government regulatory institutions. Corruption also takes the form of ethically questionable practices between private actors in the business sphere, as well as the widespread practices of nepotism and cronyism, endemic to both government and the private sector. But it also includes much darker affairs, including the criminalization of elements of the state, often involving bewildering and violent rivalries within and between state institutions.

Measuring Corruption

Most international indexes rank Azerbaijan fairly low in world raknings when it comes to corruption. In Transparency International's Corruption Perceptions Index, Azerbaijan has regularly placed in the bottom cluster, though a slight improvement has been visible in recent years. For instance, in 2002, the country ranked 95th out of 102 countries. In 2008, however, Azerbaijan was ranked 143rd out of 180 countries, putting it marginally ahead of Russia, Ukraine, and all Central Asian states save Kazakhstan; but behind Moldova and Armenia, not to mention Georgia.[10] A 2000 World Bank study on anticorruption in "transition countries" disaggregated administrative corruption and state capture, and sought to measure actual experience of corruption in countries making the transition out of communism, rather than mere perceptions. In this survey, Azerbaijan ranked at the bottom of both indexes.[11] A much more detailed 2006 follow-up to this study showed that a turnaround had been experienced in many transition countries, with corruption receiving the attention it deserved and experienced corruption levels decreasing in many countries, notably including Azerbaijan's neighbor, Georgia. The report showed that corruption was now more problematic in seven countries, including Albania, the Czech Republic, and Kyrgyzstan, which all surpassed Azerbaijan's levels of corruption. Nevertheless, the report showed continuing growth of the magnitude of the problem in Azerbaijan. In other words, while a number of countries were beginning to effectively fight corruption, Azerbaijan had yet to reach that point.[12]

A detailed survey of corruption in Azerbaijan conducted by Transparency International and BP in 2004 concluded that "there exists conspicuous and systemic corruption in Azerbaijan. Only profound reform of the whole system of public administration as well as a mobilisation of public opinion, social institutions, and civil society can ensure the success of the fight against corruption in Azerbaijan."[13] The study, based on 1,000 interviews across the country, noted that almost 90 percent of respondents considered the level of corruption in the country to be rather high or very high, and that people had strong feelings against corruption. Interestingly, while half of respondents considered corruption to be direct extortion, more than a third regarded it as a voluntary form of reimbursement for "solving" a problem, and one in nine considered it something "prescribed by custom."[14] That said, only 11 percent of respondents considered corruption the country's main problem, a far smaller segment than those who assigned that status to unemployment or the Karabakh conflict. The study also provided some indication of the main sectors where corruption is rife. Health care and the highway police force topped the list, with more than 80 percent reporting that they experienced problems occasionally or often with these two institutions. Police protection, conscription issues, and the education and judicial sectors all followed, each cited by more than 70 percent of respondents. The figures were much lower for the executive authorities and religious bodies. More than half of respondents declared themselves willing to provide a bribe if necessary, with less than a third saying they would not—findings that led to the conclusion that "the general attitude of [Azerbaijani] society towards corruption is one of resignation rather than of active resistance."[15] Another significant finding of the study was people's level of trust toward various government institutions. The presidency and the Ministry of National Security fared best, with about three-quarters of respondents expressing trust in these two institutions. Courts, tax bodies, the health and education ministries, and customs were among the least trusted institutions, at about 30 percent, but all were surpassed by the odious highway police, trusted by less than one in six respondents.[16] The survey hence supports the view of a country where the president enjoys relatively strong support, but where the bulk of the state machinery, in particular the institutions that citizens most commonly encounter, does not.

From Corruption to Organized Crime

Corruption goes beyond paying officials taking bribes, however. While the typical form may be greasing a system through bribery, there are higher levels of sophistication—when corruption turns into collusion, meaning the systematic involvement of government officials in organized crime—i.e., not a passive taking of bribes to allow crime to occur, but the active facilitation of criminal enterprises by an institution or its leader. This problem has come to affect many developing and post-Communist states— especially those that are producers or transit zones for illicit drugs.[17] Indeed, there is ample evidence that criminal organizations seek to assert influence, if not control, over crucial government institutions in weak states. The judicial system and security, police and border structures, as well as the financial sector, are especially targeted.

Azerbaijan is not among the post-Soviet states most affected by this phenomenon, but it has not been spared either. The case of Haji Mammadov is instructive in this regard. Mammadov had been the director of the Crime Investigation Department of the Ministry of Interior, until arrested by the Ministry of National Security in 2005, and subsequently convicted in 2007, for having run a murder and kidnapping ring. He had, among others, abducted the wife of the director of the International Bank of Azerbaijan and the son of the State Insurance Company's director, as well as having had the head of the country's counter-narcotics unit murdered. He conducted at least some of these crimes on behalf of others, undoubtedly persons more powerful than himself.

That, in turn, gives pause for thought, and is another testimony to the opaque and murky nature of the informal groupings that wield power in Azerbaijan, and to what lengths they are prepared to go in order to safeguard or advance their interests. While Haji Mammadov was arrested and convicted, many of the people that used his services were not; and it is anyone's guess how many Haji Mammadovs there are in the country.

Understanding and Fighting Corruption

Several factors have contributed to the systemic corruption that plagues the country. Some are shared with other post-Soviet states, such as the impact of the economic downturn of the early 1990s and the legacy of corruption from the communist period. Yet corruption has clearly continued to grow, an indication that other factors have been at work. A first is the weakness of state institutions and the unrest accompanying the war with Armenia. It is known from most surveys that countries that experience war generally score higher on corruption. Aside from this, it is also clear that the strength of informal networks and structures in the country's political and economic systems, discussed in chapter 8, feeds corruption and nepotism, and undermines the building of state institutions and enforceable norms and laws. Finally, of course, corruption has been fed by the existence of a large oil and gas sector in the country and the lavish inflow of money that has accompanied the development of this area of the economy. However, it should be noted that corruption does not appear to have increased since the large inflow of money began in 2005. As illustrated in chapter 9, the State Oil Company is a particular locus of nontransparent and corrupt practices in the state apparatus.

Cultural factors are often cited as important, yet international comparisons and the evolution of corruption in numerous countries indicate that while culture may contribute to the spread of corruption, low living standards and a weak regulatory environment are much stronger factors. Georgia is a case in point. From having a worse corruption problem than Azerbaijan in the early 2000s, the later years of the rule of Eduard Shevardnadze, the country has, since the Rose Revolution of 2003, experienced a dramatic improvement: Transparency International now ranks it in 66th place in the world, just behind Italy and ahead of Greece, Bulgaria and Romania. This has had implications for Azerbaijan: following the Georgian success in ending corruption in the highway police force, the Azerbaijani government—cognizant of the harmful effect of widespread police corruption on its own image, both internally and externally—cracked down on this aspect of corruption, reducing but not eliminating the problem, and enacted an anticorruption law and other measures more expeditiously than had previously been the case.

Particularly since Ilham Aliyev came to power in 2003, the government has appeared to take the corruption issue more seriously, at least in terms of setting up a regulatory structure. This has been in line with the government's effort to attract foreign investment and counteract the country's corrupt reputation—hence the passage of the anticorruption law in early 2004, something the Council of Europe had long demanded. The law defined corruption, and instituted a department under the prosecutor general for combating it. Azerbaijan also joined numerous international conventions relevant to the issue, including the Council of Europe's Group of States Against Corruption and the UN Convention Against Corruption.[18] Perhaps most significant, nevertheless, was the Azerbaijani government's decision to become a pilot participant in the implementation of the Extractive Industries Transparency Initiative (see chapter 9).

If these steps indicate an interest on the part of the very top authorities of the country in improving the situation regarding transparency and anticorruption, the realization of these intentions has failed to keep pace with the growth of corruption in the country—undoubtedly to a large extent because of the strong vested interests in the state bureaucracy and the cabinet itself that overtly or covertly oppose and undermine all steps toward eradication of corruption. Thus (and as the Georgian experience illustrates), it appears that the problem of corruption can only be dealt with at the political level—at the risk of jeopardizing political stability. Yet the inescapable conclusion is that Azerbaijan's future development is contingent on the implementation of anticorruption measures.

Islam in Azerbaijan

The development of Azerbaijani society will depend to a great degree on the role Islam will play, both as a religion and as a social and political movement.[19] Most visitors to Azerbaijan since independence have been struck by the remarkably secular tone of life in Baku, and come away with the impression that the social atmosphere in the rest of the country is similar. Indeed, Azerbaijan has generally been considered among the most progressive and secular-minded areas of the Muslim world. As noted in chapter 1, this reputation predates the Soviet era: Azerbaijan took the lead in spectacular advances such as the first school for girls, the first Western-style theater plays, the first opera, and the first democratic, secular republic in the Islamic world. Among the former Soviet republics, Azerbaijan has again been standing out, with the consensus on secularism that has reigned in the country's political life and the absence of strong political movements advocating a dominant role for religion.

This has been the case in spite of social and economic conditions that are normally considered incubators of radicalism. Indeed, Azerbaijan has suffered the travails of economic collapse and reconstruction, along with a debilitating war that caused thousands of its people to become internally displaced. Worse yet, Azerbaijan was slammed with U.S. sanctions and witnessed a generally lenient Western attitude toward Armenian occupation of its territories. With halfhearted international efforts to resolve the conflict repeatedly failing, Azerbaijan's predicament became remarkably similar to those of Palestine, Kashmir, Afghanistan, and Chechnya—lands whose Muslim populations were forced into refugee camps as a result of wars with non-Muslims. Although in all other cases this kind of situation served to spread Islamic radicalism in the refugee populations as well as among the wider Muslim public, to date nothing of the sort has happened in Azerbaijan, which has instead stood out as a country where both the elite and the general population have continued to lean strongly toward the West. It is a safe country for Westerners to travel in, it has a model relationship with its Jewish population and with Israel, and its government has been among the staunchest allies of the United States in the Muslim world. Aside from being among the first states to offer support for the United States after 9/11, Azerbaijan is one of only three Muslim-majority countries (the others being Albania and Kazakhstan) to have sent troops to Iraq. It has also sent military personnel to Afghanistan.

Yet the situation in Azerbaijan is not as simple as it seems. The country is geographically surrounded by areas with strong Islamic movements, which have all sought an influence there. Of particular concern is Azerbaijan's powerful neighbor to the south, Iran, whose theocratic government has been eager to spread Shiite radicalism across its northern border. To the north, Dagestan and Chechnya, both centers of Sunni radicalism, have had growing influence. Turkish Islamic groups have also been active, increasingly unchecked by a Turkish state whose secular nature is changing under an Islamic-leaning government. Foreign terrorist groups, including Al Qaeda, have found the Caucasus, including Azerbaijan, an important area of operations, realizing just like the U.S. government the strategic location of the region between Russia, Turkey, the Middle East, and Central Asia. Over the past decade, direct influence from the Arab world has also grown.

These multiple influences have not failed to affect Azerbaijani society. They are felt in a country where the social upheavals of the past two decades have left a deep mark, and the population's hopes for Western support have faded. Politically, Azerbaijan has felt the same anti-American currents that are affecting diverse areas of the world, including, to varying degrees, Western Europe, Latin America, and the Middle East. Social frustration is increasing, while a post-Soviet identity crisis is troubling the country's youth. Hence, it should come as no surprise that a religious revival has taken place in Azerbaijan, as has been the case in Georgia, Armenia, and Russia, as well as in Central Asia. Opinion polls show a growing minority supporting the application of Islamic law in the country's politics and government. Visual observation over time shows an unmistakable increase in the wearing of Islamic attire. And ominously, the presence of both homegrown and foreign militant groups in the country has been recorded. The most dramatic example is the bombings of the U.S. embassies in East Africa in 1998: though these occurred far from Azerbaijan, it has been established that a fax message from Al Qaeda taking responsibility for the attacks was sent from Baku.[20]

Islam Returns—or Arrives in New Shapes

The issue of an Islamic upsurge was not taken seriously in the first decade of independence. Yet several years into the new millennium, a different picture emerged. Indeed, judging from a number of public opinion surveys, the observations of experts in the field, and visual and anecdotal evidence, a rise in Islamic values and sentiments was clearly evident in Azerbaijan. A 2001 study led by Tair Faradov concluded that "33.7 percent [of a representative sample] have changed their views in the direction of increasing the extent of religiosity, whereas 8.7 percent have indicated that 'they never believed before, but have become believers now.'"[21] The same survey found that more than 60 percent of survey respondents reported that they did not abide by religious commandments. Sixteen percent of Azerbaijanis reported saying the Namaz (prayer), while 27 percent said they observed the fast during Ramadan. Perhaps most significant, almost two-thirds said that they considered society's knowledge of Islam unsatisfactory. These findings point to a religious revival in the context of a post-Soviet society recovering from state-imposed atheism.

A comparative survey conducted by the local polling firm PULS-S from 2003 to 2005 came to conclusion that the "Islamic model of state-building and public life is drawing more interest, and the number of supporters of

Azerbaijan's strengthened relations with Islamic nations is also rising."[22] Similarly, a survey conducted by the Baku-based independent research center FAR showed that almost a quarter of the randomly selected 1,200 respondents favored Islamic governance in the form of Sharia. Another 29 percent welcomed the application of Sharia norms in some aspects of their daily life, such as family life.[23] Another Baku-based think tank, the Foundation for Azerbaijani Studies, came to a similar conclusion after its own survey, though its result were limited to the more conservative southern parts of the country: "Nearly 37 percent of the surveyed population in the south of Azerbaijan [near the Iranian border] favored Sharia governance."[24] To what extent the survey respondents had any knowledge of what Sharia means in practice was not apparent from the surveys. As such, the relatively high proportion of respondents favoring Sharia should not give undue cause for alarm—it should come as no surprise that many Muslims, when asked in general terms if they think religious edicts should be the basis for individual and societal life, answer in the affirmative.

Other anecdotal evidence confirms the trend. The increased prevalence of Islamic dress for both men and women, though concentrated in Baku and in the southern and the northern border regions, is noticeable throughout the country. A trained eye can observe the diverse influences displayed in this attire, with Turkish, Iranian, and Arab versions all present to varying degrees. A businessman who ran a large company in Azerbaijan in the 1990s related to this author an incident in 2006 in which he was approached by his successor, who wondered how to handle his staff's demands for a prayer room. Apparently, the number of people performing the Namaz during office hours had grown to such an extent that employees were insisting on an assigned space for the purpose—something no one in the 1990s could have dreamed would happen. Similar accounts, as well as anecdotes about secular families whose young members suddenly embraced religion, are abundant.

While it is clear that an Islamic revival is sweeping across Azerbaijan, the nature of this revival is less clear. Is it an attempt to return to traditions, or a fundamentally modern phenomenon? Is it a social phenomenon or increasingly also a political one? There is much to suggest that the current developments are not simply a return to Azerbaijani traditions. A significant element of the revival has distinct imprints of external influences, including contemporary social and political movements in Turkey, the Arab world, and the North Caucasus, as well as Iran. As such, the revival is a modern phenomenon in the globalized world of Islam.

Islam in Azerbaijan has mainly been a social phenomenon, and has failed to invade the political realm with any vigor. Yet the Islamic movement in the country being in its infancy, it is not unlikely that a political Islamic movement could gradually begin to make its voice heard. Attempts to this effect have occurred, though without success, in the two decades of the country's independence.

Factors in the Rise of Islam

With the collapse of communism, religious practice was no longer actively discouraged by the state. With its long history in Azerbaijan, Islam benefited from the quest for identity that was inevitable in the vacuum created by the demise of the Soviet Union. Religious freedom has combined with a yearning to return to the country's traditional culture and values to make Islam more attractive to many Azerbaijanis. Increasing numbers of people have started praying, fasting, attending mosques, and even making the hajj (the pilgrimage to Mecca.) In other words, Azerbaijani society is returning to a normal level of religiosity after a long period of unnatural conditions during Soviet rule. It is developing into a secular country with a significant number of believers, like the United States or Turkey. A related factor, discussed earlier in the present chapter, is the change in social mores—and the attendant identity crisis—that has been affecting Azerbaijan. Specifically, there was no clear precedent for establishing the role religion would have in Azerbaijani identity, aside from its status as a cultural heritage. In this sense, Azerbaijan's close links to both Turkey and Iran were a complicating factor: socially and linguistically, Azerbaijan resembled secular Turkey, and indeed emulated it. Yet historically and through bonds with the much larger ethnic Azeri population of Iran, Azerbaijan was also tied to its neighbor to the south, which had repudiated secularism and promoted a theocratic state. An overwhelming majority of Azerbaijanis continue to reject this form of statehood, but its existence was bound to affect the country. Since 2002, the rise of Islam in the society and politics of Turkey has also contributed to Islamicization in Azerbaijan.

The arrival of Western culture has been another factor in the rise of Islam. Western culture did not fill the identity vacuum following the Soviet collapse; indeed, as is the case with all rapid shifts in societal norms, it provoked a conservative backlash, which in the Azerbaijani context took on a religious character. Islamic values emerged partly as a reaction to the perceived excesses of the West, which large segments of society did not see as congruent with the Azerbaijani way of life. This is an important issue, which the modern, secular surface of life in Baku often obscures from foreigners' cognizance. As Mark Elliot notes in his excellent guide-book to Azerbaijan, visitors should not be fooled by the short skirts worn by local girls: most still have a nine o'clock curfew to make, lest they upset traditional family structures.[25] Traditional elements of Islamic belief, such as *namus*, a concept of honor that centers on female chastity, are still strong in Azerbaijani society, even in seemingly cosmopolitan Baku.[26]

Like almost all aspects of Azerbaijani life, the rise of Islam has been af-fected by the conflict over Karabakh. This impact has taken many forms. To begin with, the nationalism sparked by the war has taken on religious elements, though these have remained minor. But on a deeper level, Azer-baijani society has grown increasingly disillusioned with what it perceives as the double standards of the West. The lack of interest in the plight of Azerbaijani refugees shown by the West, its failure to uphold principles of international law, and not least the U.S. sanctions against Azerbaijan—which, though they had been waived annually since 2001, remained in U.S. law in 2010 even though Azerbaijan, not Armenia, was the country whose territory was occupied—contributed to this disillusionment with the idea of the West as an honest broker. The mainly Christian West was understood to be turning a blind eye to ethnic cleansing conducted by Christians against Muslims, and many Azerbaijanis asked the rhetorical question of whether the reaction would have been different had the tables been turned, that is, if Azerbaijan had occupied a fifth of Armenia's territory. These factors—compounded by American and to some degree European humani-tarian assistance to Karabakh—conform well to the image of the United States and Europe that radical Islamic groups are seeking to emphasize. This is the West that favors Christian Armenia over Muslim Azerbaijan; that is only interested in Azerbaijan's oil but is not ready to provide support to Azerbaijan in return; that is not interested in solving the Karabakh con-flict yet keeps sanctions on the books as a form of leverage to prevent Azerbaijan from straying too far from Western policies. Another, more recent factor has been a more general dissatisfaction with American and European policies toward the Muslim world, which have in turn actualized identity issues and cleavages as Azerbaijanis struggle to define an identity amalgamating elements of East and West. The U.S.-led war in Iraq was a most damaging factor in this regard. Azerbaijan contributed troops to the Iraq operation, yet, as in many other countries that did so, popular views of the war turned increasingly negative.

What makes Azerbaijan different from European countries that contri-buted troops is its Muslim heritage, specifically its Shiite majority. Media depictions of events in Iraq have led many Azerbaijanis to believe that the United States fought a war in Iraq not so much to prevent terrorism but to punish Muslims and acquire Iraqi oil. Whereas the preceding invasion of Afghanistan was largely understood as justified, the daily sufferings of ordinary citizens in Iraq, particularly in holy Shiite sites that are important to many Azerbaijanis, damaged America's image in Azerbaijan and fueled religious sentiment. The "cartoon scandal," which grew out of the publication in Denmark of demeaning cartoons of the Prophet Muhammad that were subsequently published elsewhere in Europe, contributed to religious sentiment and frustration with the West among Azerbaijanis, leading to the first Islamist demonstration seen in Baku.[27] This is not to say that anti-Western and anti-American thought has become ascendant; indeed, these sentiments are mild in Azerbaijan compared to most Muslim countries, including Turkey. What it does mean is that Azerbaijan's once rosily positive view of the West is gradually changing hue, with a minority of the population espousing a non-Western, pan-Islamic worldview.

As in other parts of the Muslim world, Islamist ideology is fundamentally a left-wing phenomenon, using rhetoric referring to social justice and denouncing corruption, authoritarian practices, mismanagement, and income disparities. Azerbaijan, meanwhile, suffers considerably from these ills. If living standards are improving, relative deprivation remains and income gaps are even growing. While most Azerbaijanis have recently been lifted out of poverty, the nouveaux riches of Baku display their wealth with impunity. The alienation generated by socioeconomic disparities is exacerbated by persistent problems with corruption and cronyism that the leadership is unable or unwilling to root out, especially as the inflow of petrodollars accelerates. This mix is exactly what may be fuelling Islamist sentiment. Much hinges on the government's ability to ensure that the windfall oil revenues are spread sufficiently across the general population so that at least some of the people's high expectations are met. Should this not happen, the political opposition will be energized, with the malaise of the secular opposition making it all the more likely that a rival ideology will emerge to fill the political void it has left. Islamist movements are likely to be among the primary contenders for this role.

Islamic Groups and Forces

A number of Islamic groups have emerged in Azerbaijan since independence. First among these are the government-sponsored clergy, who have little credibility, given that many of them are associated with the Soviet past. (The official clergy in Soviet times were widely known to cooperate with the KGB.) Alongside the official religious structures, unofficial movements have also emerged in society. But in contrast with the case in Central Asia, few of these appear overtly radical or extremist. Only the mysterious Jeyshaullah movement that emerged around 2000 could be taken as a homegrown militant organization ready to take up arms against the state; yet very little is known about the group and its origins. Azerbaijani officials have nevertheless foiled several plots by radical groups, though their level of organization or connections with external groups remains were not disclosed. In 2007, for example, Azerbaijan's Ministry for National Security foiled a plot by radical Sunni Islamists to attack the U.S. embassy in Baku, but it was not announced what particular group they belonged to.[28] In 2009, two Lebanese men were arrested along with four locals for plotting to bomb the Israeli embassy.[29] In sum, while there do not seem to be large, violent organized Jihadi groups in Azerbaijan, such elements, though marginal, are nevertheless present in the country.

The Islamic Party of Azerbaijan is the only organized political movement with an Islamic platform, but its role is limited and its influence weak. Instead, Islamic groups in Azerbaijan have organized themselves primarily as communities centered on individual mosques and religious leaders. This is the case both nationally and locally. The two most prominent examples of Baku-based religious communities are the Sunni Salafi Abu Bakr Mosque and the Shiite Juma Mosque community. Each is based on the charismatic leadership of an individual preacher.

As a secular state, Azerbaijan has been careful to separate religion and politics. Since Soviet times, religious activities have been administered by the Spiritual Board of Muslims of the Caucasus, headed since the late 1980s by Sheikh-ul-Islam Haji Allahshukur Pashazade. Officially known as the Spiritual Leader of Muslims of the South Caucasus, Pashazade controls a network of Shiite mosques and shrines in Azerbaijan and oversees the activities of imams and *akhunds* (religious clergy) in these mosques. He sustains their loyalty through control over the unaccounted donations and gifts made by visitors to these mosques. Although Pashazade is mistrusted by many believers, his strong clergy network gives him leverage to play an important role in the religious life of the country. Pashazade, himself from the southern part of Azerbaijan, mainly staffs the Spiritual Board of Muslims of the Caucasus with people from the Shiite and predominantly Talysh southern areas. He has been a ruling-regime loyalist since communist times, and has never threatened the secular government. While this is one of the main reasons he remains in his post, the other side of the coin is the unpopularity of the institution. Pashazade is no exception to the common view that former Soviet clerics are government stooges without religious legitimacy. Corruption within the Spiritual Board makes it even less popular, as do consistent allegations of Pashazade's personal impiety.[30] Antipathy is strongest among the segment of the population that understands Islamic norms better than the mainstream and wants to study Islam at a deeper level—that is, mainly among religiously inclined young people. A survey showed that only 4 percent of respondents expressed trust in Pashazade himself. On the other hand, almost two-thirds stated that they had no faith in any religious leader at all.[31] This apparent vacuum has left the playing field open for independent religious groups.

The Islamic Party of Azerbaijan was the first among these forces. A small leftist party, it reached the peak of its activity in the mid-1990s, a period when it enjoyed Iranian financial support. The party experienced its first crackdown during 1995–96, when it sought to establish its political positions and acquire paramilitary forces.[32] Following Islamist riots in the Baku suburb of Nardaran, the party's power base, party chairman Haci Alikram Aliyev was arrested and the party's registration was revoked. The party subsequently has not posed a serious threat to the system and is not the main driver of radical Islamist forces in the country. Until 2005 it was part of the left-wing "Pro-Azerbaijani Forces" alliance with the Social Democratic Party, which supports the former pro-Moscow president Ayaz Mutalibov. The alliance split in 2005. The Islamic Party of Azerbaijan regularly participates in opposition activities in Baku, but it has a weak regional network outside the capital. The party sticks to a strongly anti-Semitic ideology. The leader of the party in 2009, Hajiaga Nuriyev, has often made anti-Western speeches, and used the cartoon crisis to demand a boycott of Western goods. Indicative of the party's problems in the provinces is the refusal of the heads of several regional branches to recognize the authority of the chairman; they have also blamed him for creating an environment in which the party finds itself isolated, without international links, and dedicated solely to his personal ambitions.[33]

The center of unofficial Shiite Islam in recent years has been the Juma Mosque, and its imam, Ilgar Ibrahimoglu. Called the "Muqtada al-Sadr of Azerbaijan" because of his similarities to the radical young Iraqi Shiite cleric, he particularly resembles al-Sadr in his ability to capture the public mind. Ibrahimoglu became the imam of the Juma Mosque, located in Baku's old town district, after studying in Iran for several years. His passionate speeches and antigovernment rhetoric attracted numerous followers in a short period. Notably, Ibrahimoglu also spent time in Poland studying human rights and democracy. It is the combination of Islamic roots and modern democratic rhetoric that set him apart from other mullahs, and which allowed him to target young Azerbaijanis with secular minds. Ibrahimoglu nevertheless refused to distinguish religion from politics, and almost immediately got involved in opposition political activity. He thus came to pose a specific threat to the state because his involvement in politics formed a test case of the politicization of religion in Azerbaijan, thus threatening the secular but vulnerable political system. This made the crackdown on Ibrahimoglu and his Juma community inevitable. Following the presidential election of October 2003, the mullah was arrested and charged with using religious means to cross the line into politics and with participating in postelection violence. He was sentenced to a five-year suspended prison term, and his followers were evicted from the Juma Mosque on the grounds that the community was not officially registered and, perhaps less credibly, that the actual mosque building was an ancient, architecturally significant edifice in need of urgent repair work. Ibrahimoglu now calls himself a human rights activist, and leads an organization he has established, DEVAMM (Center for Protection of Religious Freedoms), in lobbying on Islamic issues such as overturning the ban on Azerbaijani women wearing Islamic head coverings when they have their passport photos taken. In spite of this focus on individual rights and freedoms, Ibrahimoglu was also in the forefront of the protests related to the Prophet Muhammad cartoons, organizing public discussions of the crisis and condemning the Western world for interfaith hostility. He also capitalized on discontent with the war in Iraq, denouncing the West and castigating Azerbaijani authorities for their silence on the matter, as well as demanding that Azerbaijani forces in Iraq be pulled out.

A novel phenomenon in the context of the Islamic upsurge in Azerbaijan is the growth of Salafi Sunni Islam. Known in Saudi Arabia, its country of origin, and elsewhere as Wahhabi Islam, Salafi is characterized by strict interpretation of the Qur'an and rigorous adherence to its tenets. Creation and expansion of Salafi communities has occurred both in Baku and in the country's traditionally Sunni north, close to the border with Dagestan, where Salafi Sunni Islam has a strong following. The Salafi phenomenon has no historical antecedents in Azerbaijan, having instead been imported by radical groups from the Arab Middle East and the North Caucasus. Azerbaijan's security services appear to have successfully infiltrated most of the foreign radical networks and closely monitor their activities, effectively preventing them from becoming involved in politics or militancy. Salafi activists have therefore concentrated on religious propaganda at the societal level, and not on politics. They have found an increasingly receptive audience among young, poor, and uneducated Azerbaijanis: Salafi sermons are populist and deal mostly with social injustice and other inequalities. Even though the Salafi ideology was a doctrinal import, communities of followers are almost uniformly Azerbaijani; few foreigners are involved. While the level of foreign funding for the Salafi groups and their proselytizing activities is unclear, such groups across Azerbaijan, as elsewhere in the world, possess significant assets that are unlikely to have come from Azerbaijani sources. If the experience of other countries is any guide, a money trail to the Persian Gulf is likely to exist.

The best-known Salafi group in Azerbaijan is based at the Abu Bakr Mosque, in Baku. The Abu Bakr Mosque was built in 1997 by the Azerbaijani branch of the Kuwait-based Society for the Revival of Islamic Heritage. The imam of the Abu Bakr mosque, Gamet Suleymanov, is a young, popular Saudi-educated preacher. He has a strong background in Islamic jurisprudence and is known for his rhetorical ability and his crowd-pleasing Friday sermons. Abu Bakr began to gather growing numbers of people around 2000. Visitors to the mosque, who number in the thousands on any Friday, can be roughly divided into two categories. The first consists of ordinary Azerbaijani youth, many of them educated and middle class. These young Muslims are less interested in the Salafi propaganda than in saying Friday prayers and listening to the imam's independent-minded sermons. The second category is made up of more dedicated members, who stand out by their long beards and Salafi dress, especially their shorter pants. They are also noted for displaying a strong sense of community. The government has apparently decided to let the Abu Bakr community exist, having permitted the mosque to reopen after briefly closing it. One likely reason is that Suleymanov refrains from involvement in political debate. He does not use antigovernment rhetoric in his speeches, although he continuously assails Western values. This lack of political content has apparently disappointed some radical-minded members of the Abu Bakr community, who appear to have left it.

Salafi Sunni Islam is also increasingly popular in northern regions of the country adjacent to Dagestan and Chechnya, particularly in towns such as Quba and Khachmaz. This is because for many years the more conservative families in northern Azerbaijani provinces such as Qusar sent their children for religious training to Salafi-operated madrassas in Dagestan. These students then return to promote their acquired values. Salafi adherence has also spread to other parts of the country. Deploring this trend, in 2006 a Shiite preacher in Gandja noted that "the number of Wahhabis is rapidly increasing. Especially, they are attracting our youth. They have lots of money."[34]

State authorities are concerned about the increasing sway of the Salafis, with their activities in the northern, Sunni parts of Azerbaijan attracting the most attention. Salafi teaching is very intolerant of both Shiite Islam and folk Islam, including of traditional native practices such as visiting holy shrines, which the Salafis consider heretical. Tensions and clashes between Salafis and Shia or traditional Sunni believers have already begun to occur, as is the case in Dagestan, where clashes and disputes between traditional Sunnis and Salafis have been going on since the late 1990s.

External Influences

The growth and politicization of Islam in Azerbaijan is intimately related to factors external to Azerbaijani society, in particular the influence of religious movements from abroad—mainly Iran, the Arab world, and Turkey. This influence takes several shapes. At the most basic level, Islamic movements in Azerbaijan are influenced by world events and by the ideology of foreign Islamic movements. Second, and more directly, an increasing number of emerging Azerbaijani religious figures have received training in core parts of the Islamic world, such as Iran and Saudi Arabia. Third, foreign Islamic movements and states sponsor and actively proselytize on behalf of political Islam in Azerbaijan. Finally, some militant groups have based some of their activities inside Azerbaijan without necessarily taking root or acquiring a local following. Concern over the impact of foreign religious groups grew so strong that the Azerbaijani parliament decided in mid-2009 to promulgate a law on religious freedom that among other banned individuals having received their religious education abroad from leading religious worship. As a result, most non-conformist preachers in Azerbaijan were banned from their pulpits.

Iran: Manageable, for Now

Iran has been a leading external factor, with the Iranian government and groups sponsored by it providing support for Islamic forces in Azerbaijan. These religious activities were initially conducted openly, and concentrated on the more conservative southern regions bordering Iran, including the southeastern provinces and Nakhichevan, but also several villages on the Apsheron Peninsula where Shiite Islam is traditionally influential. Iran has also been active in proselytizing among the refugees and internally displaced persons in the scattered camps that formed as a result of the Kara-bakh war. For religious propaganda, Tehran initially used Iranian mullahs and sponsored pro-Iranian mosques. Yet in the late 1990s, President Hey-dar Aliyev banned and expelled the Iranian mullahs. This did not stop Ira-nian religious activity, but resulted in a change of tactics. Tehran moved to using Azerbaijani mullahs sympathetic to the Iranian regime and often trained in Iran, as well as cultural and social organizations. Iran also bank-rolled the Islamic Party of Azerbaijan and to a limited extent supported Iran-connected groups of a more militant character. One of the other tools Iran uses to expand its influence in Azerbaijan is madrassas for young children. These religious schools target children who want to learn to read the Qur'an. But aside from teaching children how to read Arabic, the ma-drassas disseminate literature that glorifies Iran and its regime. In 2002, the Azerbaijani government shut down twenty-two of the madrassas, which had been operating in the country without proper documentations for more than six years.[35]

Tehran and pro-Iranian organizations in Azerbaijan also sponsor stu-dents who want to study Shiite theology in Iran. Iran's religious and cultur-al activities abroad are generally overseen by the Supreme Leader, Ayatol-lah Ali Khamenei, who uses so-called cultural bureaus to conduct his own foreign policy independent of official Iranian diplomatic institutions. The Islamic Propaganda Organization (sazeman-e tablighat-e eslam), the Hajj and Welfare Organization, and the Society for Reconciliation Among Is-lamic Sects (majma'-e jahani-ye baraye taqrib-e baine mazaheb-e eslami) are also a part of Khamenei's network.[36]

If left unaddressed, the Iranian influence in Azerbaijan's southern prov-inces is likely to strengthen, and could provide Tehran with substantial political leverage over Baku. Iran is likely to continue its religious activi-ties in Azerbaijan by sponsoring cultural and social events and supporting pro-Iranian Azerbaijani mullahs. As the economic welfare of Azerbaijanis improves and the last camps for internally displaced persons are disman-tled, Iran's ability to attract poor and alienated Azerbaijani citizens could very well diminish. However, Tehran's efforts will continue to bear fruit in more conservative areas such as villages around Baku and the southern regions of Azerbaijan. Iran will also remain a leading destination for stu-dents and scholars who want to pursue a religious education and, in par-ticular, study Shiite theology.

Political relations between Azerbaijan and Iran also affect Iranian reli-gious activity. In 2003, when relations were bad, Iran's Sahar television network, whose programming can be received in southern Azerbaijan, campaigned for opposition candidate Isa Gambar. But after President Ilham Aliyev sought a rapprochement with Tehran, proselytizing decreased, and in the 2005 parliamentary elections an Iranian diplomatic delegation went out of its way to support the ruling party. If Iran used to provide significant assistance to mosques across Azerbaijan, this seems to have decreased somewhat. As an official in a Gandja mosque put it in 2006, "They gave us carpets, books, praying supplies. They used to visit us a lot, but not lately."[37] Iranian officials have clearly made the point that refraining from proselytizing activity and support for subversive Islamic groups in Azerbaijan comes at a political price. Indeed, Iran seeks to use its restraint to prevent Azerbaijan from developing worrisomely close relations with ington. Should American influence be increased, Tehran could easily reopen the spigot of support for various political movements it has at its disposal.

Arab and Middle Eastern Actors: Potentially the Most Dangerous

If Iranian-sponsored activity has been a factor, it has been relatively manageable. On the other hand, Arab and Middle Eastern religious activities in Azerbaijan are considered potentially the most dangerous. Since 1991, wealthy Arab countries such Kuwait and Saudi Arabia have funded mostly Salafi religious groups and foundations in Azerbaijan. The ebb and flow of such religious activities over time has also been linked to the war in Chechnya. Most Arab and Middle Eastern fighters who made their way to Chechnya did so by using Azerbaijan as a transit country. Saudi Arabia, where Salafism is the official state religion, is the main source of this ideology—whose export has been made possible since the 1970s primarily by the country's oil wealth. Many wealthy Saudis, Kuwaitis, and natives of other Persian Gulf states have been donating funds to promote the Salafi interpretation of Islam around the world. Salafi propaganda efforts in Azerbaijan are concentrated in the northern Sunni areas as well as the capital and its outskirts.

Better-organized and more discernible Islamic groups with foreign origin or links are also active in Azerbaijan. The extent of activity of Al Qaeda in the country was discovered in connection with the bombings of the U.S. embassies in Dar es Salaam and Nairobi in August 1998. An hour before the attacks, a fax from Al Qaeda claiming responsibility for the bombings was sent to a London address from a telephone connection in Baku.[38] These attacks helped the government realize the threat posed by foreign radical Islamic movements. Several members of the Egyptian Gama-al-Islami movement, closely connected with Al Qaeda and led by Ayman al-Zawahiri, were arrested in Azerbaijan and extradited to Egypt. Even before the terror attacks of September 11, 2001, the government had found it necessary to crack down on the radical Jeyshaullah movement, which had apparent support from Iran and connections with Hezbollah and plotted subversive actions in the country. The crackdown intensified in 2002. Furthermore, Azerbaijan officially designated the nominally nonviolent Hizb-ut-Tahrir grouping a terrorist organization because its activities had been deemed to be directed against the state system and the sovereignty of Azerbaijan. Several young men believed to belong to this tion were arrested.[39] After the capture in Pakistan of Al Qaeda logistics chief Abu Zubaydah six months after the attacks of September 11, details of a poison attack on European cities were uncovered, with links to the Caucasus. An Al Qaeda operative named Abu Atiya, who was thought to be a veteran of deceased terrorist leader Abu Musab Al-Zarqawi's training camp in Herat, Afghanistan, was apprehended in Baku and turned over to the U.S. Central Intelligence Agency.[40] Azerbaijan's proximity to the North Caucasus, the Middle East, Afghanistan, and Europe appears to have contributed to the country's appeal to transnational terrorists. Being the only Muslim country in the South Caucasus and also having the region's largest metropolis, with wide-ranging air connections to both Europe and the Middle East, Azerbaijan is particularly vulnerable.

Turkey: A Milder Influence

Turkish Islamic activities in Azerbaijan are aimed at a more educated layer of society, and Turkish Islamic movements are based on a considerably more moderate interpretation of Sunni Islam. Unlike its Salafi counterpart, Turkish religious propaganda is neither assertive nor populist, and therefore has less appeal among dissatisfied groups seeking an outlet. Turkish religious activities in Azerbaijan are carried out through both governmental and nongovernmental channels. In both cases, these activities tend to be accommodating toward the state and to observe Azerbaijani laws and other requirements. Government-sponsored activities are conducted under the supervision of the Diyanet Isleri Baskanligi (Government Directorate of Religious Affairs). These activities involve building mosques, which the directorate coordinates with Azerbaijan's State Committee for Work with Religious Organizations, and operating a theology faculty at Baku State University. There are several Turkish mosques in Baku and other major cities.

Turkish Islam is based on the more moderate Hanafi school of Sunni Islam, which has been further transformed under secular Turkish rule, with the emphasis in sermons put on moral, social, and economic issues. Hence, as in Turkey, Turkish imams in Azerbaijan tend to avoid discussions of politics and other controversial topics, focusing instead on general moral and ethical obligations of Muslims. They disapprove of any form of violence and call for order and moderation. There are also official scholarships, provided by the Government Directorate of Religious Affairs, for Azerbaijani students to study theology in Turkey. The level of exchange nevertheless decreased in the early 2000s.

Among Turkish NGOs, the Nurcu (Followers of Light) movement is prominent, also known as Nurcular or Fethullahçılar, after its leader, Fethullah Gülen, a Turkish and theologian born in 1941. The movement was founded at the beginning of the twentieth century. A strong believer in science's role in modern life, Gülen has placed more emphasis on scientific education and has encouraged his followers to open modern Turkish schools around the world. The Nur movement seeks to achieve a balance between materialism and spiritualism, rationalism and mysticism, worldliness and excessive asceticism,[41] and advocates tolerance and interfaith dialogue among Christians, Jews, and Muslims. The philosophy of the Nur movement is rooted in Hanafi Sunni Islam, but incorporates Sufi ideas. The movement could be characterized as representing postmodern Sufism that focuses on improving an individual's moral and religious beliefs and avoids "explicit Islamic propaganda."[42] Nevertheless, since the AKP's coming to power in Turkey, the movement has become increasingly politicized in Turkey, leading to concerns also in Azerbaijan.

The movement's educational activities in Azerbaijan include a network of 10 high schools, an elementary school, a gymnasium, 10 university preparation schools, and Qafqaz University.[43] All of these schools follow the Turkish secular curriculum, approved by the Ministry of Education of Azerbaijan. The primary language of instruction is English; Azerbaijani and Turkish are also used. Established in 1993, Qafqaz University is one of the leading private institutions of higher education in Azerbaijan. In 2001, the university was granted "experimental status" by the Ministry of Education for its successful curriculum, which is based on a Turkish and Western program of studies. Similarly, Turkish high schools in Azerbaijan are known for their achievements in the field of science. Officially, no religious courses are taught at Turkish schools, as Azerbaijan's curriculum does not allow the teaching of religion in public and private schools. The only allowed course, "Morality/Spirituality," deals with moral and ethical issues rather than religion. Although by the time of their graduation many students remain unobservant, the majority of them nonetheless become acquainted with basic information about Islam thanks to informal conversations and discussions with their teachers and peers.

In general, Turkish religious activities in Azerbaijan are concentrated in major cities such as Baku, Gandja, and Sumgait, but also in northern and central provinces that are predominantly Sunni. Turkish Islam is not considered a security threat, being viewed instead as a counterbalance to Salafi Islam. Heydar Aliyev encouraged Turkish Islamic religious activity in the northern provinces, hoping that it would curb increasing Salafi influence imported from Dagestan. But because of the assertive nature of Salafi propaganda and strong links between residents of the northern provinces of Azerbaijan and Dagestan, Turkish Islam has so far failed to counter the more radical manifestations of the Muslim faith.

The State's Relationship to Religion

Religious issues in general and political Islam in particular have not been issues dominating the Azerbaijani government's agenda. All major political forces are committed to secularism and are based, if anything, on a nationalist agenda. That said, religious issues have in recent years acquired higher prominence. The government has created the State Committee for Work with Religious Organizations, and the Ministry of National Security has repeatedly stated that radical Islamic organizations have become its primary concern. Yet while the state has realized the importance of managing the issue of religious organizations, it has not succeeded in approaching it strategically. The most obvious example of this is the conflict that has emerged between two state institutions assigned to regulate religious affairs—the State Committee for Work with Religious Organizations and the Spiritual Directorate of Muslims of the South Caucasus. Likewise, the question of religious education remains to be dealt with.

Responding to the weakness and unpopularity of the Spiritual Directorate, the government in 2001 established a secular institution, the State Committee for Work with Religious Organizations, in an attempt to more effectively monitor and regulate religious activity in the country. The committee, long chaired by well-known scholar Rafiq Aliyev and since 2006 by long-time Aliyev advisor Hidayet Orucov, has been responsible for oversight and registration of religious structures (Islamic and non-Islamic), religious groups, and nongovernmental religious organizations, and their activities in Azerbaijan. Once installed, the State Committee immediately started the process of re-registering nearly 2,000 mosques, churches, and other religious communities and organizations. As of 2006, a total of 341 religious organizations had been registered by the State Committee, 29 of them being groups with non-Islamic affiliations.[44] The number of unregistered structures in service was estimated to be much larger.

The State Committee for Work with Religious Organizations has broad powers to control the importation, publication, and distribution of religious literature, and has the authority to suspend the activities of religious groups violating the law. Relations between the State Committee and the Spiritual Directorate of Muslims of the South Caucasus were from the outset very hostile. This rivalry derived partly from competition for primacy in the decision-making process in the field of religion, but also partly from the personal rivalries between Rafiq Aliyev and Sheikh Pashazade, head of the Spiritual Directorate, as well as from Aliyev's attempts to impose new restrictions and rules on mullahs, especially regarding financial transparency in mosques. This led to public recriminations between the two figures as well as lawsuits and verbal attacks. Rafiq Aliyev, among others, accused the Spiritual Directorate of disseminating illegal and radical literature imported from abroad. The Spiritual Directorate and the State Committee hence quarreled over the right of oversight and seemed to have little influence in stopping the spread of radicalism in some layers of Azerbaijani society. This was primarily due to the fact that neither organization was empowered to guide or direct preachers and the messages delivered by them, being, instead, responsible for overseeing and registering religious organizations, checking for their proper documentation, and appropriating donations whose source could not be accounted for. That limitation, in turn, has revealed a vacuum in Azerbaijan's governing structures that in large part has rendered religion a phenomenon outside the scope of the state. The state hence lacks the right mechanism to tackle issues associated with religion that regularly emerge and that require state guidance. State control over the most acute issues related to religious affairs therefore in practice has moved to a third body: the Ministry of National Security, which conducts surveillance of mosques and religious organizations and raids houses where radical and clandestine Islamic groups assemble for meetings (because state pressure forces some radical groups to meet secretly in private homes). The Ministry of National Security regularly arrests militants from various radical groups, indicating an ability to infiltrate and control such groups, even as they proliferate nationally. According to government officials, the struggle against religious extremism has become an increasing priority. In early 2006, Minister of National Security Eldar Mahmudov publicly stated,

> Religious extremist groups threaten the national security of Azerbaijan and the struggle against them is the priority of the special services. Today we are facing more and more cases of terrorist attempts by religious-extremist groups, with the aim of overthrowing the secular-democratic regime of Azerbaijan and withdraw the country's participation in [the] antiterrorist coalition. As a method for this, they often choose foreign banks, offices, embassies, and other strategic targets. Our experience shows that the basis for such extremist groups [is] young men, usually poorly educated from poor segments of the society or theology students aged 20–25. The most difficult task is to prevent the attraction of young people into such groups and networks. The worst news of the year for us was the information about Al Qaeda trying to recruit young Azerbaijani women into their network.[45]

A major problem lies in the sphere of education. The Ministry of Education is one of the least reformed agencies in the government, and remains plagued by significant corruption at all levels. This is a general problem, but the ministry's lack of efficiency is also visible in the field of religion. There is no religious education in Azerbaijani schools; nor is there a modern humanities curriculum. In other words, the education system lacks modern curricula in the humanities and social sciences, including the history of various religions in Azerbaijan and the country's status as a secular state. Education in the humanities, including the understanding of religious history and the tenets of religion, is a crucial issue, particularly given the surge of spiritual interest in society and the conflict among state institutions regulating religious issues. The seventy years of atheism have left a void in the Azerbaijani population's relationship with religion. The fact that so many Azerbaijanis are unable to tell the difference between Shiite and Sunni Islam is alarming, and exacerbated by the incompetence of official religious structures, because it leaves the playing field open to foreign, radical Islamic groups that are often well versed in religious propaganda, possess substantial resources, and are motivated to conquer new souls. Hence, as the young generation is unable to receive proper and balanced information on what Islam stands for, its members are particularly vulnerable to radical proselytizing.

Civil Society and Media in Azerbaijan

The weakening and collapse of the Soviet Union allowed for the creation of voluntary organizations in Azerbaijan, and, more gradually, for the emergence of independent media outlets. Indeed, the period from 1989 to 1993 was one of great civic activism, most notably in the formation of the various components that became the Azerbaijani Popular Front. The Popular Front's collapse in 1993, and the polarized political atmosphere in the country following Heydar Aliyev's return of to power, slowed the progress toward the development of civil society. Subsequently, civil society and the news media have been under great pressure to align themselves with either the government or the opposition. Adding to that, most issues have come to be considered political in Azerbaijan, in one way or another, and distrust among Soviet-era cadres toward any organizations not controlled by the state have worsened conditions for civil society groups. For all of this, however, Azerbaijan continues to be a country where independent and even oppositional activism is possible.

Civil Society and Voluntary Associations

Foreigners meeting with Azerbaijani civil society leaders are sometimes perplexed by the number of different business cards their interlocutors carry. It is not uncommon for an Azerbaijani intellectual to lead or otherwise be associated with several different NGOs while also holding membership in a political party—most likely an opposition party. This is perhaps a legacy of the political development of the early 1990s. Much of Baku's intelligentsia threw in its lot with the Popular Front, and upon the APF's loss of power, retained their links with the various opposition parties that were subsequently formed. But for most, politics was something that neither put food on the table nor occupied all of their time. As a result, many intellectuals founded organizations, be they research institutes, activist groups, or NGOs. As an elite out of power with superior and language skills and learning, they formed the natural vanguard of eligible grantees for the funds made available by international donors.

An appreciation of this development is fundamental to understanding the problems Azerbaijan's civil society has experienced. While Western donors often took these organizations at face value and funded them on the basis of the proposals they submitted, many government officials were unwilling or unable to differentiate between the political and professional activities of these NGO leaders. An NGO led by a person affiliated with the opposition was seen as an oppositional NGO. As such, it was an enemy of the regime, and therefore an enemy of the state. This characterization is perhaps exaggerated: especially in recent years, many young and Western-educated government officials can and do understand the importance of an independent civil society. Nevertheless, most officials who came of age during the Soviet era cannot shed their instinctive suspicion of such organizations, especially as they have found many of them to be affiliated with the opposition, and thus have assigned guilt by association to those that are not. Yet it is not only the government that has found it difficult to differentiate between politics and civil society. In many cases, the NGO activists themselves have been unable to walk the fine line among their different tasks and duties. Often, they have the same mentality as the government officials, only in mirror image—the leaders of many civil society groups indeed have used these organizations as vehicles for opposition politics. In many cases, this has left Western donors as the only actors taking these groups for what they claim to be—without understanding the deeply political nature of the enterprises they are funding, or at least the widespread perception to that effect.

As a result, little cooperation has developed between civil society and the government. Instead of a mutually fruitful relationship in which civil society groups seek to work with and strengthen government institutions, and government incorporates the views and experiences of NGOs, the relationship has generally been characterized by suspicion. In spite of a certain amount of justification on its part, the government does bear the greatest share of the blame for this mutual wariness, having failed to tap the potential of civil society groups to participate in policymaking and reform. The situation is made worse by the absence of political will to implement reform within many state institutions.

Another element of concern is the question of whether NGOs reflect a Tocquevillean development of voluntary associations, which develop roots in society and build a culture of citizenship, in turn fostering social and political participation. For a number of reasons, it appears that such a process is generally lacking in Azerbaijan. First, seven decades of Soviet rule bequeathed a legacy of deep-seated apathy, which was further entrenched by the failure of the Popular Front. Many ordinary people came to equate democracy with chaos and recession, and, initially at least, embraced the order that followed with the return of authoritarian practices. For the most part, the population continues to remain passive and unaware of its rights. Azerbaijanis often appear to prefer to wait for the government to solve their problems rather than take the initiative themselves. Community mobilization at the local level remains weak, with little communication existing between local authorities and community groups. A second hindrance to the development of participatory politics in Azerbaijan is that, to a great extent, the nation remains plagued by narrow loyalties to kin, region, or group that impede the development of genuine citizenship. Third, the government's attitude toward NGOs and their funding has blocked the development of civil society and also severely curtailed philanthropy in general and the availability of domestic funding for NGOs in particular. Wealthy individuals are simply afraid to contribute to organizations that are perceived as oppositional or independent. Finally, much of the blame goes to the Western donors themselves, who have failed to develop funding policies to reduce the dependence of NGOs on Western funding. As a result, too many NGOs in Azerbaijan (as elsewhere) have turned into virtual businesses, in which entrepreneurs identify the priorities of Western donors and propose to conduct projects on that topic, altering their focus as donor practices change. Such organizations immediately disband once Western funding dries out, leaving little of lasting value to society. At best, they contribute to positive developments in an instrumental manner during their existence; at worst, they take on a role of professional opposition, and, perhaps worse yet, instill in their staff and clients an attitude of condescension toward government employees, who generally have lower salaries and less education than they do. Consequently, these NGOs make the emergence and effective operation of true voluntary organizations all the more difficult. That said, the number of NGOs in Azerbaijan has continued to rise, although it is unclear how many of the registered organizations are actually viable. Most remain personality driven rather than issue driven. As such, many lack skills in internal fundraising, program development, and, not least, adequate reporting and the practices of transparency, being instead fiefdoms controlled by their founders and run in a relatively authoritarian manner.

This is not to say that the development of civil society in Azerbaijan has been of no positive value. To the contrary, many worthwhile movements have been able to establish themselves, with or without Western support. Particularly among women's organizations and environmental groups, development has been remarkable. Moreover, the proliferation of NGOs has provided employment opportunities for a great number of primarily young Azerbaijanis. These jobs have given hundreds, if not thousands, their introduction to modern professional life, and supplied other valuable experience. Especially in the social sector, these organizations undoubtedly have helped great numbers of people deal with the difficulties of transition.

In recent years, several important developments have affected NGOs. For instance, the registration process for NGOs has become much less cumbersome since the late 1990s. A less favorable development occurred in 2004, when the government decided to cancel NGOs' exemption from employment and social security taxes. Aside from this, the government does not interfere in the day-to-day activities of NGOs that do not explicitly articulate an antigovernment agenda. Parts of the state bureaucracy, including the Ministry of Youth and the Ministry of the Environment, actively cooperate with NGOs on joint projects. Also, the Ministry of Justice has created a joint commission with prominent human rights organizations to discuss the issue of political prisoners and the situation in prisons. While government officials' increased willingness to acknowledge the importance of NGOs and engage in dialogue with them may be driven by a desire to gain international legitimacy, there also seems to be interest in accepting the NGOs' involvement in making and implementing public policy, and in influencing the NGO community in general. For the latter purpose, creating pro-governmental NGOs has been an increasingly popular tactic.

A number of opposition youth organizations emerged in Azerbaijan following the participation of large numbers of young people in the opposition group Kmara! during Georgia's Rose Revolution and in a similar group, Pora!, during Ukraine's Orange Revolution. The Azerbaijani groups, most of which were formed in 2005, carried names such as Magam ("It's time"), Dalga ("Wave"), Yox ("No"), and Yeni Fikir ("New thought"). These youth organizations aspired to actively influence the political process, especially concerning elections. The government responded to them warily, however, understanding their potential to destabilize the government. Although President Ilham Aliyev changed the electoral law to allow NGOs to observe elections in late 2005, the youth organizations were subjected to heavy pressure. The leaders of Yeni Fikir were arrested prior to the 2005 elections, some in connection with an incident in which a number of them, in an apparent set-up, were caught accepting money from foreign sources and heard on tape claiming to be preparing for a revolution. Generally, the Azerbaijani youth groups showed less organization, determination, and discipline than their counterparts in Georgia or Ukraine had. The government could thus counter the actions of the youth organizations more swiftly because the weakness of the groups could readily be exploited, which was not the case in Georgia. Youth activists were detained or expelled, or harassed in other ways. Subsequent to the 2005 elections, only Dalga continued to be active at the student level, conducting awareness and education projects.

If the regime sought to neutralize the youth groups, it also countered them by setting up its own such groups. In 2005, the government created Ireli ("Forward"), which grew rapidly to become the largest youth movement in the country, before it was unexpectedly dissolved in late 2008. Beyond youth movements, the emergence of so-called government-oriented NGOs—a phenomenon known as GONGOs in the international NGO community, and which is particularly strong in Russia—can also be observed in Azerbaijan.[46]

In sum, Azerbaijani civil society has a long way to go before it can play a constructive and responsible role, and before it will be able to stand on its own two feet. Government attitudes are changing, though slowly; the government's actions—and, equally, its inaction—remain the most important impediment to the strengthening of civil society. But for the situation to change, revisions in the thinking of the NGOs themselves and of Western donors are necessary.

The Media

A great variety of information is available to Azerbaijan's citizens. However, the freedom and quality of information varies greatly, depending on the form of media that is accessed. Newspapers and the Internet are the least available information sources—newspapers rarely have a print run exceeding a dozen thousand, while the Internet is available mainly to the urban youth and professional communities. It is television that is the major source of information for most of Azerbaijan's population, a whopping 88 percent of Baku residents and 93 percent of those outside the capital in 2005.[47] A poll by the internet publication *Baku Today* found that less than 3 percent of respondents read newspapers regularly, while 70 percent did so seldom or never.[48] And as is the case in most states in the South Caucasus, it is in television that government influence over the media is the most obvious.

Azerbaijan has half a dozen national TV channels, as well as a number of regional ones. Azerbaijan State Television (AZTV) still follows the hoary practice of reporting mainly on the deeds and statements of the president and other high officials—although opposition candidates were granted time on state TV for the first time ahead of the 2005 elections. Several other TV channels are privately owned, such as Lider, ANS, ATV, and Space. While private, most of these are known to be close to or controlled by specific officials within the government. Lider has acquired the doubtful honor of being characterized as the most pro-government of the private channels, both by the Council of Europe and by the nongovernmental Najaf Najafov Fund, which conducts monitoring on the neutrality and bias of Azerbaijani media outlets on contracts from the U.S. Agency for International Development and the Eurasia Foundation.[49] Its survey during and after the 2005 parliamentary elections found a full half of Lider's broadcasts to be biased, putting the channel only ten percentage points behind state mouthpiece AZTV. By contrast, ANS was considered the most objective, with less than 15 percent of its broadcasts being biased. The relatively new public television channel was also found to be less biased.

The experience of ANS illustrates the pressures faced by TV outlets that endeavor to present objective news broadcasting. Following several warnings and a refusal by the controlling authorities to renew the channel's license, it was taken off the air on November 24, 2006, and not allowed to resume broadcast operations until December 12 that year. An additional blow was the prohibition of the broadcasting of the BBC, Voice of America, and Radio Free Europe that entered into force in spite of international protests in January 2009.

The print media in Azerbaijan exhibit much more variation than broadcast outlets, though not necessarily higher quality. Two newspapers published in Russian, *Ekho* and *Zerkalo.* are well esteemed and are considered serious and independent. By contrast, most of the Azerbaijani-language press tends to the tendentious in its reporting, and its newspapers tend to serve either opposition or pro-government factions. The opposition newspapers are able to use harsh antigovernment rhetoric, sometimes crossing the line into vociferous, even slanderous criticism. Yet the opposition media, much like some pro-government outlets, base their reporting on rumors and allegations rather than on fact and serious reporting. The quality of the print media began to deteriorate in 2000, with serious journalism giving way to tabloid-style stories and reporting marred by ad hominem attacks. Indeed, the surveys conducted by the Najaf Najafov Fund found that the opposition newspapers—such as *Yeni Müsavat, Azadliq*, and *Hurriyet*— engaged in strongly biased reporting, surpassing even the bias of the government's print outlets. The raucous nature of the print media has its cost. Libel suits are a frequent tool used by the government against editors and journalists, and opposition journalists have also at times been subjected to beatings and other harassment.

The provision of Internet access has proceeded more slowly in Azerbaijan than in its Caucasian neighbors. This is due in great part to the dominant role of the government, and the complications that ensue from its dual roles as regulator and provider of Internet service. Nonetheless, access is available at very low cost in Azerbaijan's urban areas, mainly through Internet cafés where young people seem to spend most of their time. The price for residential Internet access is much higher, however. In contrast to states with harsher political climates, such as Iran and China, Azerbaijan does not as a matter of general practice restrict access to websites. Indeed, a number of opposition and satirical Internet forums have developed that have significant readership. Yet at times—and in all likelihood more often because of the actions of overzealous lower-level officials than as a matter of state policy—access to specific websites has been curtailed. This became the fate of a Chechen pro-independence website in March 2003, following Russian pressure on the Azerbaijani government. Likewise, the satirical antigovernment website tinsohbeti.com and other sites have occasionally been put off limits to Azerbaijani websurfers. All in all, however, Reporters Without Borders in 2009 considered Azerbaijan's Internet situation to be "middling," the second-best grade on a four-grade scale ranging from good to middling, difficult, and grave.[50]

Downturn in Media Freedom

The murder of opposition journalist Elmar Huseynov in 2005 had a traumatic effect on Azerbaijan's media outlets. The murder case has not been credibly resolved, though most suspicions pointed in the direction of an individual government-associated oligarchs Huseynov was investigating. Authorities at first claimed they sought two Georgian nationals for the crime; in 2006, however, the above-mentioned Haji Mammadov (the former police chief convicted of running a kidnapping and murder gang) took the blame for the crime, which he claimed to have been ordered by deposed former economy minister Farhad Aliyev. Coming from a person already about to be sentenced to life in prison and putting the blame on a person already in jail, it seemed too convenient a confession for many observers, especially as there seemed to be no clear motive for the murder.[51]

From 2006 to 2009, the media situation in the country gradually worsened, as pressure on independent journalists intensified. It did so in two ways: first, the widespread prosecution on journalists on charges that international observers considered to be fabricated; and second, increasing incidents of violence against journalists, which authorities failed to properly investigate.

Following the Huseynov murder, several oppositional journalists have been attacked by apparently random assailants or subjected to violence by law enforcement officers. From 2005 to 2008, eight serious attacks on

---

journalists took place, which remained unresolved, implying that a culture of impunity persisted for violence against journalists.[52]

In the legal domain, defamation charges have been one chief legal instrument used against journalists. That has been the case in spite of President Aliyev instituting a moratorium on defamation lawsuits in 2005—a moratorium that other high officials did not respect.[53] Interior minister Ramil Usubov in particular made frequent use of defamation lawsuits following the Mammadov affair, in response to growing allegations that he had been aware of the kidnapping gang's activities but not intervened.

One major target of legal action was Eynulla Fatullayev, editor of the popular oppositional *Gündelik Azerbaycan* magazine, who had dedicated himself to investigating the murder of Elmar Huseynov. Fatullayev was sentenced to over eight years in prison in 2007, on a variety of charges ranging from tax evasion to defamation, charges that the investigators from the Committee to Protect Journalists found "either unsupported or fabricated."[54] Defamation lawsuits do not only affect oppositional journalists: even normally pro-government journalists seem to draw the ire of individual officials, as two editors of the pro-government daily Ideal were sentenced to jail terms in 2008.[55] Such events are normally the result of government-connected oligarchs seeking to use media outlets to undermine each other.

Given the president's expressed opposition to defamation lawsuits and some movement (though excruciatingly slow) on reforming the defamation law,[56] charges of hooliganism have been employed instead with increasing frequency. In 2007, the editor of the oppositional weekly *Azadlyg* was convicted to four years in prison on charges of hooliganism, after having been attacked on the street by two individuals.[57] The "hooliganism" tactic appears was used in 2009, in a case that was widely covered in the West. After claiming to have been accosted in a café by unknown men and reported the incident to the police, bloggers Adnan Hajizade and Emin Milli were sentenced to over two years each in 2009 for hooliganism. The two bloggers, who had earlier been relatively close to the government but fallen out with it, had been the authors of satirical anti-government videos. The international outcry that resulted, partly because the bloggers were well-connected in international circles, nevertheless seemed to further cate their prospects, occurring at a time when the Azerbaijani authorities felt particular frustration with the West.

In sum, the evolution of the media situation is the perhaps most depressing development in Azerbaijan the past decade. As the Committee to Protect Journalists noted, Azerbaijan was the "second-leading jailer of journalists in Europe and Central Asia. Only Uzbekistan jailed more."[58] The question is why this was the case, since the media situation appeared to be an outlier in the country's general development. While the political situation had not improved in 2005–10, neither had it regressed to that degree in other areas as it did in the realm of the media. Even in the media, Azerbaijan's internet was comparably free, whereas the instances of persecution of journalists made the country stand out. Moreover, even from a government point of view, the type of blatant persecution of journalists that was taking place in the country seemed to make little sense, bringing it more costs than benefits, certainly in the international arena. Indeed, while oppositional journalists were unquestionably the hardest hit, pro-government ones were not exempt from persecution. Indeed, there were a number of events involving government ministers and oligarchs squaring off in proxy struggles in the media. This type of combat between high officials became the most overt illustration of the serious disagreements and conflicts of interest that exist within the government camp.

This begs the question whether the persecution of journalists is a result of a political strategy, or of the lack thereof. Indeed, President Aliyev has at least in his rhetoric claimed an intent to give priority to the freedom of the media, and agreed that the defamation laws do not comply with Azerbaijan's international commitments. Since the situation did not appear to improve, was Aliyev either unwilling or unable to improve the situation? Oppositional forces in Azerbaijan would argue that the President simply does not care about these issues, or that he is purposefully allowing it to happen. Pro-Western forces in the Azerbaijani government, on the other hand, would suggest that the situation is the result of the internal rivalries within the government camp—a direct result of the attempts by the authoritarian-minded old guard's attempts to undermine President Aliyev's position, and his relationship to the West. While this argument could be termed self-serving, conjuring up images of a "good king" and "evil barons," it should not be dismissed out of hand. The fact is that the oppositional *Azadlyq* newspaper and *Turan* news agency were evicted from their premises just days before Azerbaijani First Lady Mehriban Aliyeva was to visit Washington DC, in what was clearly an important visit designed to build relations with the United States following onto Ilham Aliyev's own visit earlier that year. Since the timing was clearly badly chosen, it is a distinct possibility that the occasion was chosen on purpose by forces high up in the state bureaucracy that had little interest in a warming to the West.

A closer look at the cases involved suggests that the truth lies somewhere in between these two scenarios. It is clear that the Azerbaijani governing elite is amorphous and divided, while predatory and corrupt forces have amassed immense wealth and influence. The journalists that were targeted—with some exceptions—could very well have been targeted for their imagined transgressions against individual oligarchs rather than the government as a whole. Minister of Interior Usubov, in particular, sued journalists even after the president had explicitly called for a moratorium on defamation cases. It is therefore logical to assume that the bulk of the persecution of the media is a result of the initiative of high-level officials acting in their personal interest.

In the final analysis, the president would be likely able to prevent the further persecution of journalists, if he made that a priority at the cost of confronting some of the most powerful "barons" in the country. How large that cost would be, and what interest the president would have in actually doing so, remain unanswered questions.

Conclusions

A multitude of influences are driving and shaping Azerbaijan's rapidly developing society as it emerges from the traumatic transition from Soviet rule. But in a regional context, and in spite of the catalog of problems discussed in the present chapter, Azerbaijani society displays elements of an incipient liberal society with great potential for consolidating the democratic values that nearly all the country's political forces espouse, even though they often fail to live up to them. Change will continue, if not at the debilitating pace that characterized the first two decades of independence. Azerbaijan is rapidly becoming integrated into the global economy, sharing the consequences of globalization, both good and bad, with the rest of the world. Located at a civilizational as well as a political crossroads, Azerbaijan is subject to a greater variety of contradictory impulses and influences than most countries. In the social laboratory that is modern Azerbaijan, the most salient questions are how the nation will deal with the role of religion in society, and how it will process its relationship with Western values and norms. This struggle growing out of these two questions, which at its basis concerns the very identity of Azerbaijan, will likely go on for years.

11

Caucasus Context:
Formulating Foreign Policy

As a small state, located in a strategic position among great powers and with complicated relations to its neighbors, Azerbaijan's foreign relations have become crucial not only to the country's security but indeed to its survival. In fact, Azerbaijan is located in a central position along what has been called the "arc of instability," borrowing a cold war-era concept once coined by Zbigniew Brzezinski. It is the only country to border both Russia and Iran, forming a crucial gateway connecting Europe to Central Asia and beyond. This location, and the country's significant energy resources, have made Azerbaijan a geopolitically key country in the intersection of Europe and Asia. That, in turn, has generated much attention from outside powers, to the country's advantage as well as detriment. The most obvious forces are the three traditional power-brokers of the region—Russia, Iran and Turkey—as well as the sole superpower, the United States. But aside from these four and more cautiously the expanding European Union, countries as varied as Israel, Pakistan, Japan and China have shown a keen interest in developing relations with, and having a presence in, Azerbaijan.

More than being in a strategic location, Azerbaijan faces the unpleasant reality of being located in a turbulent part of the world. Its own achievement of independence took place through one of the most dramatic upheavals of the twentieth century, the breakup of the Soviet Union. Whereas this process was peaceful on the whole, it was not in the Caucasus, where it was associated with wars that tore across the region. Even seventeen years into independence, the Russian invasion of Georgia showed that war was very much a factor to be reckoned with in this neighborhood. Aside from its own conflict with Armenia, Azerbaijan from the outset faced suspicious or directly hostile attitudes from its closest neighbors and historical overlords, Russia and Iran.

Far from receding, Azerbaijan's geopolitical importance has increased significantly in the time since its independence. The exploration of Caspian oil resources was a major element in this, and has formed a cornerstone of

Azerbaijani diplomacy. But to the West, the distant events of September 11, 2001, made the importance of Azerbaijan more apparent, including to those that had little interest in the country itself. American strategic planners, unable to rely on either Russia or Iran for planning and prosecuting a war in Afghanistan, were suddenly forced to rely on bases in Central Asia. For access to these bases the relied on a sole secure air corridor that crossed the South Caucasus. Of the countries in the region, Azerbaijan was the only one that could not be avoided; fortunately for the United States and its coalition partners, it was also eager to support the coalition in the war effort.

Events in global politics since have underlined Azerbaijan's enduring importance in regional and world politics. The hype in energy prices in 2006–2008, unlikely to be the last, added importance to Azerbaijan's role in oil markets as a supplier of its own as well as Central Asian oil and natural gas to the West. Moreover, the 2003 war in Iraq and the ensuing controversy over Iran highlighted Azerbaijan both due to its location near those hotspots—in fact just on Iran's border—but also because of its singular symbolic value as a secular, western-oriented and pluralistic Shi'a Muslim society.[1]

This and the four following chapters will discuss Azerbaijan's foreign policy and its main vectors. While this chapter focuses on the context of the formulation of Azerbaijani foreign policy, subsequent ones study the main vectors of its foreign policy in greater detail.

The Domestic and Regional Context of Azerbaijan's Foreign Policy

As Tadeusz Swietochowski aptly notes, Azerbaijan is "quintessentially a borderland many times over—between Europe and Asia, Islam and Christianity, Sunni and Shi'a Islam, Russia and the Middle East, Turkey and Iran."[2] This borderland status is the major determinant of its foreign relations and affects both the external and domestic determinants of Azerbaijan's foreign policy; this geography is together with energy wealth and a neighborhood with contested borders what Brenda Shaffer has termed "permanent factors" in Azerbaijan's foreign policy.[3]

In present-day international politics, the interplay between the domestic and international realms is increasingly blurred by the ever stronger political and economic interdependence between nations. This is especially true for small countries like Azerbaijan, surrounded by great powers that have little qualms interfering in its politics—whether seeking unashamedly to influence its policymaking as in the case of Russia, or having strong opinions about its governance and political system, as in the case of the United States. While many elements of Azerbaijani foreign policymaking are dictated by this external reality, a number of domestic determinants also have great significance, explaining to a considerable extent the stability of Azerbaijani foreign policy since the coming to power of non-communist forces in mid-1992. These link both to Azerbaijan's cultural and national identity, its past, as well as the structure of its state.

Domestic Determinants

Azerbaijani society has multiple cultural and historical elements that link it both to the Muslim world and to Europe. In turn, the countries of the Islamic world to which Azerbaijan is most closely tied have been undergoing deep identity crises. For most of the twentieth century, Turkey and Iran were on parallel processes of modernization and secularization, under the committed secularist leadership of Kemal Atatürk and his legacy, and the Pahlavi dynasty, respectively. Before the rather recent resurgence of political Islam, this was in fact a broader trend in the Islamic world, going as far as Afghanistan, where King Amanullah had a short-lived attempt at modernization and Westernization in the 1920s.

But in both the Turkish and Iranian cases, the process was strongly challenged. In Iran, it was violently reversed with the 1979 Islamic revolution, making Iran very much an antithesis to Turkey, indeed epitomizing a rejection of its secularism and European vocation. In the Turkish case, the process nevertheless continued to develop as the Cold War—and geographic proximity—made the country an increasingly stable part of Europe. But under the surface, Turkish society itself underwent a complicated process that failed to overcome the deep cleavages between Western and traditional religious lifestyles, and whose internal divisions were affected by the global Islamic movement. This process gathered speed particularly since that movement benefited from the huge transfer of wealth from the developed world to the Middle East in the 1970s, wealth that was channeled to Islamic movements around the world, including Turkey. By the late nineties, a gradually moderating form of political Islam grew to become the dominant force in Turkish politics. Under the government of the Islamic conservative Justice and Development Party since 2002, Turkish society and politics have been affected by a gradual but powerful Islamization.

Developments in Turkey and Iran have always had an outsize impact on Azerbaijan. These influences were especially important in the formative periods of Azerbaijani nationalism, in the late nineteenth and early twentieth, as well as in the late twentieth century. However, to this should be added the European influences that Azerbaijan has been exposed to for centuries, mainly through its interaction with Russia. These were at their deepest during the Soviet era, when they permeated society to an unprecedented extent. These forces have combined to shape Azerbaijan's society and political identity in a secular manner, making it more similar in many ways to a European than to an Islamic society. Indeed, Islamic clerics have played only a very limited role in the formation of present-day Azerbaijan. Azerbaijan's own intelligentsia has since the late nineteenth century developed a decidedly secular and liberal orientation; aside from the Elçibey period, Azerbaijani foreign policy has never aligned on the basis of ethnicity or religion, instead following a pragmatic course focused on defending the country's national interests.[4]

All these forces put together make Azerbaijan's society as European as it is Middle Eastern. This is the case despite its Islamic and conservative traditions, as well as pockets within society that, much as in both Turkey and Russia, remain opposed to the Western orientation of society. Interestingly, these include both Soviet-derived communist and Islamist currents, which moreover occasionally interact. These forces nevertheless remain marginal. Thus opinion surveys and sociological studies have repeatedly shown that between two thirds and three quarters of Azerbaijan's population support a Western foreign policy orientation, while minorities support either a Russia-centric or an Iranian, Islamic orientation.[5]

Developments since the first years of independence have not changed the basic orientations of either Azerbaijan's elite or population, although the Karabakh conflict and related developments have prompted an increase in nationalist and religious feelings as well as growing frustration and a sense of betrayal by the Western world.

As viewed in chapter 10, Azerbaijan has been experiencing unprecedented external influences on its society in the post-Soviet period. Western, Russian and Islamic currents of various types and shapes have affected the country, mixing uneasily in the fertile ground of post-Soviet identity formation. The resurgence of Islamic sentiment and growing feeling of disillusionment with the West have served to qualify, but not yet question, the generally pro-Western foreign policy orientation of the country. It should be recalled that Azerbaijan does not have a line drawn in the sand pushing it West as decisively and incontrovertibly as Kemal Atatürk's legacy generated in the Turkish case. And even there, signs of withering are present.

Internal societal forces at play have contributed to shaping an Azerbaijani foreign policy that is mainly Western in its orientation, pledging allegiance—but not always living up to—to the democratic model of a state based on the rule of law, and aspiring to membership in Euro-Atlantic instiutions. This has nevertheless not meant that Azerbaijan has eschewed contact with the Islamic world: indeed, Azerbaijan has sought close contacts with Muslim countries and done so assertively, including chairing the Organization of the Islamic Conference in 2007. This was conditioned very much by the support that most Islamic countries—with the notable exception of Iran—provided Azerbaijan in regard to its conflict with Armenia. Given the West's lukewarm interest and close connections to Armenia, Azerbaijan used links to the Islamic world to put pressure on Armenia, not least through the voting power that these countries possess at the United Nations.

An additional determinant of Azerbaijan's foreign policy has been the country's political system. As a presidential system that provides only a limited role for the legislature, the President has had the prerogative of formulating and implementing the country's foreign policy. Added to that has been the semi-authoritarian character of the political system, which has ensured that the role of the political opposition remained limited. Whatever one may think of this, it has contributed to the stability of Azerbaijani foreign policy, as the President has been able to adopt a long-term approach in setting foreign policy goals and in seeking to achieve them. In addition, especially under Heydar Aliyev's presidency, foreign policy was very much tied to the personality of the leader, his name recognition, charisma, and the authority with which he acted on the international scene.

That does not imply that Azerbaijan's foreign policy has been insulated from society. As the multiple turns in negotiations over Karabakh suggest, Heydar Aliyev was repeatedly compelled to revise his position on a peace deal with Armenia given strong public opposition and opposition activism on the issue. This stands in stark contrast with the foreign policy of other post-Soviet countries, for example Uzbekistan, where President Islam Karimov has performed several dramatic foreign policy U-turns between the West and Russia, without any meaningful involvement of society. In Azerbaijan, such a turn would be much more difficult to perform, given the pluralistic character of Azerbaijani society and the existence of a frank and open debate on foreign policy in the press, broadcast media and in society in general. Hence even though the president's powers are extensive, foreign policy formulation must take into account the popular mood, and ensure that policies formulated have an implicit public legitimacy.

External Determinants: the Politics of the Caucasus

By its geography as well as by its politics, the South Caucasus is a clearly delimited region. It is geographically defined by the Black Sea to the west and the Caspian Sea to the east; as well as by the Caucasus mountains that run between these two seas and forms the spine of the Caucasus, dividing its northern and southern parts. Only to the South, toward Iran and Turkey, is the region's external borders more blurred.

Politically, the South Caucasus consists of three small countries surrounded by the three great powers that have traditionally dominated the area: Iran, Turkey and Russia. The size differential between the three large powers and the three Caucasian states is huge, whether measured in demographic, economic, or military terms. Put together, the three Caucasian states have a population of about fifteen million people—less than a fifth of the population of either Turkey or Iran, and a tenth of Russia's. The fundamental defining condition of the Caucasus is one of the uneasy coexistence of small nations and great powers.

In the post-Soviet era, the Caucasus developed into a turbulent region plagued by multiple layers of security risks and conflict, lacking institutionalized measures for cooperation of any form let alone in terms of security. Indeed, the region has been plagued by a security deficit, which coupled with the widely diverging threat perception of the three states, forms the basic reality in which Azerbaijan's successive governments have developed the country's foreign policy.

The Caucasian Security Deficit: Transcending the National-International Divide

In spite of the manifold security challenges to the region, there are no functioning inter-governmental mechanisms or institutions that help build regional stability or provide for meaningful conflict management. International efforts at conflict resolution, sponsored mainly by the OSCE and UN, have failed to bring results.[6] International security structures, such as NATO's Partnership for Peace program and the Russian-led Collective Security Treaty Organization, have also failed to stabilize the region, while the integration into Euro-Atlantic institutions such as the Council of Europe, NATO, and the European Union has progressed only slowly. Since 2000, NATO's involvement has gradually increased, with PfP being the main vehicle for the intensified relationship between the Atlantic Alliance and the South Caucasus.[7]

The regional security deficit consists of internal, regional, and transnational challenges, which are in turn interlinked. The internal component of the security deficit is the risk of domestic civil and political conflict, which has affected all three states at different stages of their evolution. The second, intra-regional, challenge to security consists of the unresolved territorial conflicts, which form the single most dangerous threat to security in the region and whose perils have been increasing rather than decreasing with time—as showed by the Russian invasion of Georgia in 2008. The third category is an array of transnational, non-state security threats posed mainly by radicalism and organized crime, growing problems in the region. In addition to these intra-regional security challenges, the countries of the South Caucasus are compounded by a fluid and unpredictable array of relations with the regional and great power that have interests in the region. The smaller states try to enlist regional powers to promote their interests in the conflicts, while the great powers use the conflicts to advance their own interests—some of which are static and predictable, while also being prone to fluctuation.

The political balance within and between the three Caucasian states and societies is a fragile one, and the weakness of these states and their various threat perceptions has compelled them to seek foreign patronage and support. The region's own attractiveness has in turn led to a high level of great power interest. The interests of foreign powers therefore deeply affect political processes within the three states, making political forces and leaders in the Caucasus watchful of their relations with foreign powers, in the hope that such relations would give them an advantage in domestic and regional political struggles. Combined with the changing policies and uncertain commitment to the region on the part of the great powers, this increases the instability and unpredictability of South Caucasian political processes.

The Caucasian security deficit, stemming from these interrelated and unregulated security threats, has plagued the region since independence. The growing importance of the South Caucasus in the aftermath of the anti-terrorist operation in Afghanistan and the war in Iraq made its security deficit a threat not only to regional security but to that of Euro-Atlantic interests more broadly, creating a palpable need for institutionalized security arrangements to manage, reduce and if possible resolve the security threats in the region.

The insecurity of the South Caucasus impedes political stability, accountability and democratic development in several ways. Most prominently, insecurity in the early-to-mid 1990s derailed the political liberalization ongoing in the region and legitimized the return of authoritarian rule in all three states, certainly in Azerbaijan. The popular urge for order and stability allowed governing structures to backpedal on institutional reform. Political instability, moreover, followed as a direct consequence of the conflicts, as poor government performance led to the rapid loss of popular legitimacy and encouraged armed political contenders to challenge authorities. Moreover, the weakening of governing structures that resulted from the conflicts facilitated corruption and criminal infiltration of administrative bodies at a national and regional level.

In the economic sense, the conflicts and the insecurity they bred severed regional trade linkages. Fighting brought material destruction and created an economic burden as well as fall in economic output caused in part by the displacement of hundreds of thousands of people. The economic downfall exacerbated problems with corruption and organized crime. Moreover, the loss of licit trade was replaced by illicit trade, which has been partially concentrated to separatist territories outside government control. The most prominently example is South Ossetia, whose Ergneti market functioned as a key point in smuggling of goods from Russia to Georgia until 2004.

The refugee populations have integrated only slowly into the general population, with effects that impact society as a whole, especially in Azerbaijan and Georgia. In addition, the unresolved conflicts are contributing to fanning the flames of nationalism in the region, thereby impeding the development of civic-based identities and democratic political culture.

Threat Perceptions of the States of the Caucasus

Against the background of similar security concerns, the three states of the South Caucasus nevertheless have dramatically diverging perceptions of threat, which in turn lie at the basis for their divergent and contrasting foreign and security policies. Enduring and indeed existential threat perceptions are crucial components of the regional security situation and a component of the instability in the South Caucasus. Partly due to historical experiences and partly to their bilateral relations, the development of common regional policies among the three states has been out of the question. Instead, each regional state has defined its own national interests and threat perceptions with little regard for the impact this has on its neighbors—the only exception here being the Georgian-Azerbaijani relationship. This zero-sum approach has provided a fertile ground for external powers to impose their influence by capitalizing on the threat perceptions of the three weak states of the region.

Armenian and Georgian Threat Perceptions

Armenia's threat perception has been based mainly upon its historical fear of Turkish aggression, going back to the massacres of Armenians in the final decades of the Ottoman Empire—though this has gradually softened as Turkey and Armenia have sought to improve ties. Regaining independence at a time of conflict with Azerbaijan, Turkey's backing of Azerbaijan, the Turkish-Armenian border closure, and attempts to put pressure on Armenia to end its occupation of Azerbaijani territories led to a revival of Armenian fears of Turkish aggression. Diplomatic efforts by the Armenian Diaspora and government are geared toward achieving international recognition of the 1915 massacres as genocide, with possible compensations claims. Turkey denies these accusations, and is fearful of potential territorial claims on territories in eastern Turkey. Armenia's fears may have been unrealistic as Turkey's foreign policy has always been defined by caution, and its actions in the region have been further restricted by diplomatic links to the West and Russia.[8] Yet Armenia's threat perception has been very real, and a strong guiding force in Armenian foreign policy. As a result, in spite of its anti-Moscow stance in the Perestroika era, Armenia rapidly restored its security and military links to Moscow, signing a key treaty already in May 1992. Armenia since relied on Russia as a guarantor of its security, and has been an active participant in the Collective Security Treaty Organization. For most of its independence, Armenia has followed a pro-Moscow foreign policy that has contributed to its relative isolation in the region.

Moscow has regarded Armenia as an important ally in the Caucasus, and most Armenians view a close relationship with Moscow as necessary. Russia currently maintains a large military base in Gumri, as well as a division of S-300 anti-aircraft missiles and a squadron of the Russian air force with MIG-29 fighters. Meanwhile, Armenia has developed close links with Iran, a crucial trading partner whose interest in preventing the rise of a strong Azerbaijan have helped strengthen Iranian-Armenian relations. Finally, Armenia also sought to upgrade its relationship with the U.S. and NATO. Together, this forms Armenia's policy of complementarity, implying a quest for close links with Russia, Iran as well as the West. The large, organized and wealthy Armenian diaspora has been Armenia's main foreign policy asset. In the U.S., it long managed to effectively lobby the U.S.

Congress to secure an earmarked average of $90 million in annual assistance programs for Armenia (including Karabakh) and to ensure parity in U.S. military assistance to Armenia and Azerbaijan—in spite of the Pentagon regularly seeking considerably more for Azerbaijan than for Armenia. Armenia's foreign policy often seems to juggle increasingly difficult and potentially incompatible relationships with considerable success. Yet the viability of Armenia's foreign policy is directly correlated to the state of relations between the U.S. and Russia; and to the level of tension in the relationship between the U.S. and Iran. Simply put, Armenia is dependent on forces that are not necessarily compatible.

Georgia's perception of external threat is well-defined: since independence, Russia has been the main source of concern for the Georgian state. Russian adversarial behavior has included direct pressure, such as refusal to withdraw military bases from the Georgian soil, repeated threats of direct military action, assassination attempts against the country's leadership, as well as economic levers such as the politically-motivated severing of gas supplies. Even more serious, Russia directly supported separatist forces in Abkhazia and South Ossetia for years before invading and effectively annexing these territories in 2008. Unlike in Azerbaijan, the arrival of President Vladimir Putin to power in Russia worsened Russian-Georgian relations, in particular after the Ukrainian Orange revolution, which made the Russian leadership passionately determined to undermine both Georgia and Ukraine. In response, and given its lack of valuable natural resources, Georgia tried to market its position as a gateway between the West and the larger Caspian region in the reconstruction of the ancient Silk Road. Tbilisi therefore reached out to its other neighbors, and has constantly looked to the West in search of alternative economic and political opportunities. Relations with Europe and especially the U.S. have been a priority for Georgia. Georgia's relations with Turkey were marked by historical tensions, but were gradually overcome and in the late 1990s, Georgia forged a strategic partnership with Turkey. In the energy, transportation, political and military sectors, Georgia and Azerbaijan have been at the forefront of creating a Caucasian corridor from Europe and Turkey to the Caspian and Central Asia. Azerbaijan and Georgia hope that economic development and Western investments will ensure their security and stability, and provide conflict resolution and the restoration of their territorial integrity. Working in parallel as enthusiastic members of NATO's Partnership for Peace, the two states share a similar outlook on the world and on relations with their neighbors. In fact, as Vladimir Socor has noted, the security of Georgia and Azerbaijan is inseparable: the two stand or fall together.[9]

Azerbaijan's Threat Perceptions

Dating back prior to independence, Azerbaijan identified Armenian aggression and Russian imperialism, in fact acting in tandem, as the leading threats to its national independence and security.[10] To that was gradually added a rising concern over Iran's attitude to Azerbaijan. Unlike Armenia and Georgia, Azerbaijan does not perceive an acute external existential threat, though many Azerbaijani experts and officials suspect Iran for being opposed in principle to the existence of an Azerbaijani state. Much like Greece's virulent opposition to the creation of a state of Macedonia, Iran was deeply disturbed by the creation of an independent republic of Azerbaijan. Problems were worsened by a series of factors: continued tension in Azerbaijani-Iranian political and economic relations, including over delineation of the maritime boundaries of the Caspian sea; Iranian support for Shi'a extremist groups in Azerbaijan and agitation against Azerbaijan's secular form of government; Iranian concern over U.S.-Azerbaijani relations; and over accusations of Iranian Azerbaijani separatist agitation from the territory of the Republic of Azerbaijan.[11]

The most acute threat perceptions, emanating from Russia and Armenia, led to the gradual formulation of Azerbaijani foreign policy's chief aim: the restoration and consolidation of the country's full sovereignty. This in turn has two aspects: first and foremost, the consolidation of Azerbaijan's independence; and secondly, the imperative to restore Azerbaijan's territorial integrity. The former aim was by no means obvious in the early 1990s, given the memory of the 1918–1920 experience, when a weak Azerbaijani state plagued by conflict with its neighbor succumbed to reintegration into Moscow's empire. Russia's accelerating imperial ambitions from the mid-1990s onward, accelerating in Vladimir Putin's second term in power, made the aim of securing true independence a real and continuous struggle. Indeed, most post-Soviet states experienced renewed Russian efforts to limit their sovereignty in the 2000s. Azerbaijan has gained international recognition of its independence over the past decade and built a solid and independent economic base, leading this concern to abate somewhat. Nevertheless, the great power ambitions seeking to limit the extent of that independence, aiming at incorporating Azerbaijan in structures that limit its freedom of choice, remain very real.

Aside from these major concerns, Azerbaijan also has the problem of territorial disputes with both Turkmenistan and Iran over the delimitation of the Caspian Sea and its legal status; and the development of East-West transport and trade corridors. A smaller, yet real security concern is the threat of externally sponsored Islamic extremism. This has primarily been connected to Iranian ambitions and transnational actors that are outside the control of any state authority. The latter groups in particular are a danger precisely because they are not controlled by a state, implying that the threat cannot be managed through traditional inter-state relations.

Perceiving threats from the south, north and west, Azerbaijani governments since 1992 have reached out to Turkey and the West, particularly the United States, for support as well as economic and trade relations. The Baku government has sought to use its energy resources and strategic location to develop its relations with states and organizations that could be enlisted to pursue the aims of consolidating independence, building a stable and prosperous country through the export of oil, and resolve the Karabakh conflict in a way acceptable to Azerbaijan. As such, aside from the west, sympathetic actors like Israel and Pakistan have also been of importance. Relations with Russia somewhat improved since 1999, but Turkey remained Azerbaijan's key ally in the political, military and economic sectors at least until 2009. Azerbaijan also placed great emphasis on cooperation with the U.S. and NATO, becoming a PfP member in 1994 and contributing to peacekeeping missions in Kosovo, Afghanistan, and Iraq, and was one of the first countries to render assistance to the U.S. after September 11, 2001.

Closer to home, as noted above, the relationship between Baku and Tbilisi has been a major element in the country's foreign policy, particularly during the simultaneous tenure of presidents Heydar Aliyev and Eduard Shevardnadze. Relations strengthened significantly since independence, as both understood that their security was intimately connected. Azerbaijan cannot export its oil without Georgia, which connects it to Turkey and the West; while Georgia partially relies on Azerbaijan's oil exports for its economic and political security and its own geopolitical importance. The two were motors in the GUAM (Georgia Ukraine Azerbaijan Moldova) alliance that developed since 1997 as a counterbalance to Russian hegemonic tendencies within the CIS. The Georgian-Azerbaijani relationship has been instrumental in leaving Armenia outside regional transportation schemes and cooperative efforts, thereby attaching a cost to its hold on Karabakh. Geographically, Azerbaijan and Georgia are better positioned than Armenia as a transport and communications route, as they form the corridor between the Black and the Caspian Seas. Hence, any transport conduit can easily bypass Armenia but not Azerbaijan, a fact that Baku has used to its advantage.

Foreign Policy Formulation: from the Popular Front to Ilham Aliyev

The formulation of Azerbaijani foreign policy has gone through several phases, largely coterminous with the changes in government in the country. Hence the first eight months of independence saw Azerbaijan remaining in the Russian orbit, something that changed dramatically with the Popular Front coming to power. The Front espoused a more nationalistic and ideological foreign policy, and was succeeded by the Aliyev government, which followed the main outlines of the Front's foreign policy, but did so in a more pragmatic and discrete manner, and a in a less antagonistic style, than its predecessors.

The Mutalibov Era: Reluctant Sovereignty

By putting his signature under Azerbaijan's declaration of independence on October 18, 1991, Ayaz Mutalibov was the person to inaugurate Azerbaijan's foreign relations. The content of the declaration of independence itself was uncontroversial, as it reaffirmed the basic principles of international law, the equality of states, respect for territorial integrity, and the inadmissibility of the use of force.[12] If anything, it was significant because of the clearly western nature of the principles espoused there. The Azerbaijani parliament then applied for membership in the United Nations eleven days later, a request that was granted only in March 1992. What was striking in the actual conduct of foreign policy in this period was nevertheless not so much change as continuity. Azerbaijan's diplomacy focused strongly on Russia and Iran, while relations with Turkey and the West carried mainly a formal nature. In Turkey, especially, Mutalibov was received with some distance given his obvious Moscow connection. One of Mutalibov's first steps was to seek membership in the successor organization to the Soviet Union, the Commonwealth of Independent States—in spite of a massive opposition from the public and from the Popular Front, fed by the still very palpable popular anger directed at Russia caused by the January 20, 1990, Soviet military attack on Baku. Meanwhile, Mutalibov made his first foreign trip as president of an independent state to Iran, in a quest to allay Iranian fears of Azerbaijani irredentism, restore economic relations, and to use Iranian territory to link Azerbaijan with Nakhchivan. He found himself in Tehran once again already in February 1992, celebrating the anniversary of the Islamic revolution, having visited Turkey briefly to sign agreements on friendship and cooperation that carried little of the later bond between the two states.[13]

In fact, Mutalibov's foreign policy was clearly Russia-centric. He seems to have stuck to his pre-independence analysis: only Russia could "give" Azerbaijan control over Karabakh back. His worldview did not seem to fully grasp the meaning of the Soviet Union's collapse, seeming to believe that a Russia-centric alliance or union would be rebuilt in one way or another—with the baseline being that Moscow was still the major arbiter of Caucasian affairs. Hence distancing Azerbaijan from Russia would be counter-productive, since it would only anger Russia and make Moscow support Armenia. In the Soviet context, his policy had provided some re-sults—Operation Ring to the north of Karabakh, where Soviet forces sup-ported the disarming or Armenian armed groups and dislocation of some Armenian civilians, perhaps being the main example. The Russia focus of his foreign policy was so strong that in spite of being at war, Azerbaijan did not begin the building of a national army until well into 1992, when Armenian forces were consolidating their grip on Karabakh.

Indeed, the Khojaly massacre of February 1992 led to the foundering of Mutalibov's Russia-centric foreign policy. In spite of his policies, a mili-tary unit under Russian command had participated in a massacre of Azer-baijanis in Karabakh alongside Armenian formations. Khojaly made it plain and obvious that Mutalibov had focused entirely on Russia's benevo-lence, yet Russia was now not only siding with Armenia but actively in-volved in the killing of Azerbaijani civilians. No wonder that Mutalibov tried to cover up the massacre for several days, and later made the ludicr-ous statement that Popular Front armed groupings and not the Armenians had committed this massacre against their own people. Khojaly, of course, was also the event that brought Mutalibov's tenure in power to an end.

In his place came an interim period under "dollar" Mamedov. For ob-vious reasons, Mamedov was less enthusiastic about the CIS and Russia, trying instead to push Azerbaijan toward some fuzzy form of non-aligned status. But Mamedov was an interim President, at a time when power was gradually and very quickly being transferred to the Popular Front, some-thing that was confirmed with the election of Elçibey to the presidency.

The Popular Front Period: Ideological Nationalism

The foreign policy of the Popular Front government had its basis in the Front's January 1992 congress, where a conservative and nationalist for-eign policy concept won over a more liberal, almost neutralist rival concept. It ascribed to the same western principles of international law, but emphasized such concepts as confronting imperialism and developing democracy, and solidarity among the peoples of the Caucasus, including the concept of a "Caucasian home." More importantly, the Front made it clear it would prioritize relations with Turkic nations, primarily Turkey, and also seek to develop relations with Muslim countries.[14] In this sense, the Front pledged allegiance to the Turkist agenda of emphasizing modernity in its quest for membership in the contemporary world; Turkism by prioritizing the ethnic and cultural link among Turkic nations; and Islam in a cultural and secular rather than religious manner by connecting to Islamic culture and civilization.

In his election platform, Elçibey made it clear that Azerbaijan under his rule would have a Western and Turkish orientation, would work to remove Azerbaijan from the Russian orbit, and avoid to come under Iranian influence. He lashed out at both Russia and Iran, especially before his election, when he famously predicted Iran would fall apart just like the Soviet Union, condemned the discrimination of "thirty million Azerbaijanis," and called for the unification of Azerbaijan. While he avoided that type of statements while president, Tehran had gotten the message. Elçibey was no friend of Iran's, and this exacerbated the already existing fears of the Iranian regime, for whom the creation of a state of Azerbaijan was anathema. Hence Iran became much less than helpful on most issues of interest to Baku, primarily Karabakh but also trade and transit to Nakhichevan and Turkey. Conversely, Iran's relations with Armenia improved. As far as Russia was concerned, Elçibey refused to ratify Mutalibov's accession to the CIS, thereby failing the earlier government's commitment to join the organization. In Elçibey's analysis, the CIS was nothing but a thinly veiled attempt at resurrecting the Soviet Union, and hence an incarnation of the evil empire that Azerbaijan needed to escape. If the CIS today seems of little value even to Russia, the early 1990s were different: the adherence of the former Soviet States to the CIS was a central Russian foreign policy objective, seen as a way of preventing the slippage of Russian influence in the former Soviet space. Indeed, forcing Azerbaijan and Georgia into the CIS was one of the major objectives of Russian pressure on these two countries in 1992–94. Given the problems, Elçibey instead placed his bets on solving the conflict with the help of Turkish support and engaging Western institutions like the CSCE.

With the benefit of hindsight, this was as big a miscalculation as Mutalibov's. In spite of early euphoria and some saber-rattling on the Armenian border, Turkey was clearly not willing to challenge Russia to the point of offsetting Russian support for Armenia. Indeed, faced by Russian threats, Turkey limited its support to diplomatic and political efforts that were significant to bring the Azerbaijani cause to the international arena. Yet this changed little on the ground as Azerbaijan was losing territory. As for the West, preoccupied by the crisis in the Balkans and still viewing the Caucasus as Russia's turf, Azerbaijan had little concretely to expect from that quarter. Hence the basic assumptions that formed the basis for the Front's foreign policy proved to be flawed, much like those of Mutalibov.

But it was not only the policies of the Front leadership that had a negative impact on Azerbaijan. Indeed, the ideological aspect of its foreign policy and the leadership style of President Elçibey himself were equally harmful. Indeed, Elçibey's foreign policy lacked long-term strategic objectives and a cool analysis of how those objectives could be achieved in the given situation. Instead, it was mainly declaratory, and did not give much consideration to the consequences of its decisions. Effectively, Azerbaijan was at war with one of its two smaller neighbors, and on a confrontational course with both of its larger ones. This strategy could hardly be termed ideal.

Elçibey's Russia policy did understand the true nature of Russia's interest in the region. However, it showed little insight of the remaining levers available to Moscow to achieve its objectives in the Caucasus. Hence it is conceivable that the Front could have lessened the damages it incurred by pursuing these objectives more discretely, without overtly alienating Moscow. But the Front had a very bad position to begin with. As the Mutalibov era showed, Moscow was not satisfied even with a pliant Azerbaijan, and Russia's antagonistic policies could not have been averted short of a total surrender to Moscow. Indeed, the Huseynov episode as well as the Russian policies in neighboring Georgia showed to what lengths Russia was ready to go to prevent the loss of the South Caucasus. In this sense, the Front charted out a course of Azerbaijani foreign policy that contributed to the military loss of Karabakh in the short term, but that worked to strengthen Azerbaijani independence in the long run. The alternative would have been, perhaps, to capitulate to Moscow, avoid an equally disastrous defeat in Karabakh but still failing to gain the territory back, and effectively lose independence. That would likely have meant exporting Azerbaijani oil through Russia, and deferring to Russia on foreign policy issues, in a way similar to Armenia, Kyrgyzstan or Tajikistan. Even choosing between these alternatives, the latter may not necessarily have been preferable, as it would have put the country in a situation from which it would be extremely difficult to extricate itself.

On the other hand, alienating Iran was an unnecessary irritant for an Azerbaijan that sought to remove itself from the Russian orbit. This was a time where the Russian-Iranian partnership had not yet formed, and Azerbaijan could have made use of potential differences between Russia and Iran had the ideological element in its foreign policy been less pronounced. In particular, the pan-Turkic winds blowing through Elçibey's foreign policy generated great opposition not only in Iran and Russia, but caused alarm inside Azerbaijan as well, as society was not ready for such an unconditional embrace. Meanwhile, Elçibey also alienated the more pragmatic forces determining Turkish foreign policy. Indeed, Turkey's failure to support Azerbaijan more assertively was partly related to a palpable sense in Ankara that both Elçibey's government and the President himself were unstable, excessively ideological, and unreliable.

All that said, the Front government did manage to score a number of concrete international victories in the diplomatic realm. First, Azerbaijan's vehemently anti-Russian policy succeeded in making the country the first former Soviet republic to be freed of Russian troops. The early withdrawal of Russian forces was clearly a stratagem to ensure Huseynov's coming to power, who would in all likelihood have invited Russia back in. But the fact remains that the Front's negotiations, begun almost immediately upon taking over power, managed to ensure the withdrawal of both Russian army and border forces that makes Azerbaijan stand out in comparison to Armenia and particularly Georgia, in light of that country's decade-long struggle to rid itself of Russian military presence, after it effectively surrendered to Russia in 1994.

Secondly, Azerbaijan managed to successfully internationalize the Karabakh conflict, leading to the involvement of the CSCE as a mediator, as well as several UN resolutions condemning the use of force in Karabakh and the occupation of Azerbaijani territory.[15] Though these did not name an aggressor, they served to underline the international community's recognition of Azerbaijan's territorial integrity. Finally, it was also Elçibey who first launched the idea of Azerbaijani-Georgian-Ukrainian cooperation which he would never act on, but which Heydar Aliyev successfully developed to found GUUAM.

The Aliyev Era: Pragmatic Nationalism

With few exceptions, Heydar Aliyev's government built on the foreign policy of the Popular Front. Contrary to expectations, the former Politburo member was no Russian stooge, any more than his colleague Eduard Shevardnadze. But given his experience in Moscow at a union-level political position, Aliyev knew the working of the Russian state extremely well, and was also well-versed in the functioning of international politics in general. Unlike either of his predecessors, he was in a position to make a realistic assessment of Azerbaijan's situation, the policies to be expected from Russia as well as from other powers, and of the policy options available to advance realistically set policy objectives.

In so doing, Aliyev began with a reassessment of the situation. It was clear to him that Azerbaijan needed to normalize relations with Russia and Iran. For that reason, one of his first steps was to bring Azerbaijan into the CIS. Nevertheless, in spite of Russian pressure, he did not allow the return of Russian forces as peacekeepers nor Russian border forces along the Iranian border. With Iran, Aliyev had developed working relations as leader of Nakhchivan, and even received some Iranian assistance. Hence Aliyev could easily use his contacts to calm Iranian concerns spurred by the Elçibey era. Concomitantly, Aliyev took one step back from Elçibey's embrace of Turkey, though in no way downgrading the long-term contents of the relationship.

In fact, the main difference between Elçibey and Aliyev in the realm of foreign policy was style and strategy, not orientation. Where Elçibey appeared erratic and ideological, Aliyev was diplomatic and pragmatic. Where Elçibey aroused strong feelings, Aliyev allayed concerns. But it soon became apparent that Aliyev was pursuing the very same objective that Elçibey was aspiring to: consolidating the independence of Azerbaijan. In so doing, Aliyev had a clear set of priorities. The first was to bring the war in Karabakh to an end. Having understood that the prospects for a military victory were absent during the brief December 2003 counteroffensive, Aliyev settled for a cease-fire. Second, he sought to balance relations with all major powers to decrease the overt and covert pressures on the country, including on his own position in power, while preventing the return of Russian military presence. Third, he worked to speedily sign a contract with multinational oil companies in order to give stakeholders from as varied a group of powers as possible an interest in Azerbaijan and to attract signing fees—the AIOC came to include American, European, Turkish, Russian, Arab, and Japanese companies. Fourth, he built on increased stability in Azerbaijan, oil interests, and the increasing reaction to Armenia's excessive territorial appetite to improve Azerbaijan's standing in the West. This aimed to reverse the pro-Armenian tilt of western leaders, media, and public opinion; to consolidate the existing but nominal Western support for Azerbaijan's territorial integrity; and to build on that to enlist Western powers in supporting the Azerbaijani position on Karabakh.

In retrospect, the policy was largely successful, though it never managed to resolve the Karabakh conflict, although the cease-fire achieved in mid-1994 has largely held. Azerbaijan built working relations with Russia, which improved especially after Putin's coming to power in 1999. With Iran, the oil contract was a setback, since American pressure forced Aliyev to exclude Tehran from the deal. Nevertheless, Iran's meddling in Azerbaijani affairs decreased as the earlier rhetoric in Baku on southern Azerbaijan was stifled. The "Contract of the Century" was signed in October 1994, forming the beginning of Azerbaijan's gradual rise on the international scene. As for relations with the West, Azerbaijan scored a diplomatic victory in the OSCE Lisbon summit of 1996, while Aliyev was invited to Washington in 1997, indicating a dramatic improvement of Azerbaijan's position in world politics in three short years. Azerbaijan also worked as a motor of the GUAM alliance, formalized in 1999, which was important in effectively torpedoing the CIS as an instrument to restore Russian control over the former Soviet Union.

By the beginning of the twenty-first century, Heydar Aliyev had managed to turn Azerbaijan into the only truly independent state of the Caucasus. Unlike Armenia and Georgia, Azerbaijan had no foreign troops on its territory. Unlike Armenia and Georgia, Azerbaijan was not dependent on either Russia or the West for its security. Indeed, although it is usually Armenia that is credited with a foreign policy based on complementarity, this term is in fact more suited to Azerbaijan: Unlike Armenia, Azerbaijan has managed not only to balance the four major powers with influence in the Caucasus, but to remove itself from a situation of dependence on any of them and to formulate it foreign policy independently from them. This became clear in the aftermath of September 11, 2001, when Azerbaijan could, without constraints, formulate its own response to the event, and offer America unconditional assistance without waiting for the Russian reaction, which is exactly what Armenia was forced to do. Conversely, in April 2009, Ilham Aliyev was able to turn down an invitation by President Barack Obama to meet him in Istanbul, given his frustration with Washington's support for then Turkish-Armenian rapprochement.

Ilham Aliyev's Foreign Policy: Caution and Continuity

With the sole but significant exception of the Karabakh conflict, Ilham Aliyev took over the reins of a country with a stable and improving position on the international scene. However, a somewhat unpleasant surprise for the new President was the growing importance of democratization as an element in Western foreign policy. Indeed, the Western reaction to his election, exacerbated by the simplistic image of a dynastic succession in an oil-rich country, showed the constantly changing proportions accorded to strategic and democratic concerns.

The timing coincided with the growing profile of the freedom agenda in President Bush's foreign policy, which became official a year later with the inauguration of Bush's second term. This development, coupled with the peaceful revolutions in Georgia and Ukraine, ironically brought back in a different guise the tight interlinking of domestic and foreign policies that had been characteristic of the early 1990s. This time, however, the linkage was reversed. In the early 1990s, the domestic scene was heavily influenced by the external scene due to the weakness of the state and to the interference of foreign powers into Azerbaijan's affairs. This problem had been alleviated with the state-building process of Heydar Aliyev's decade in power. But now, it was the character of Azerbaijan's domestic politics that colored the country's position in the external realm and affected the policy options available to the government.

Indeed, the geopolitics of Eurasia were rapidly acquiring a strong ideological component. This had been a manageable constraint earlier, but was becoming a defining element in any country's relationship with the West, and therefore a crucial factor in determining policy options. As Uzbekistan's experience showed, a regime intent on preventing democratization at any cost could no longer expect a strong partnership with the West to continue. Domestic politics were therefore securitized in Azerbaijan, since a refusal to compromise on domestic political control would effectively make the country increasingly dependent on Russia and Iran, and lead to a deterioration of relations with both the West and Turkey, which was increasingly closely tied to Europe. In this situation, Ilham Aliyev took a considerably more cautious approach than Uzbekistan's Islam Karimov, who chose to abandon his country's strategic choice for the sake of regime security. Ilham Aliyev, on the contrary, sought to find a middle way, embarking on a gradual liberalization process focused on economics more than politics, while seeking to retain the initiative and enough control over the domestic political scene to safeguard his position in power. In so doing, it became increasingly clear that energy wealth was a key factor enabling the government to retain a level of popularity strong enough to stay in power without jeopardizing its relations with the West. By presiding over a booming economy where wealth trickled down to the population, Ilham Aliyev seemed able to have it both ways.

Nevertheless, his tenure in power also coincided with a decline of the influence of the West in the South Caucasus, with the war in Georgia being a watershed event in the eyes of the Azerbaijani elite. This provided further impetus to a policy of balance and self-reliance in Azerbaijan's foreign relations, one that dictated an attempt to establish good relations with all neighboring powers rather than making the country dependent on any one power or alliance.

Conclusions

Azerbaijan has gradually developed into a stable and independent actor on the regional scene in a turbulent environment, and to that an increasingly influential one in its neighborhood. This increases the strategic importance of the country, particularly to the West, and makes Azerbaijan a pivotal state in Eurasian geopolitics, as Brzezinski put it in 1997.[16] The stability and independence of Azerbaijan are nevertheless not a reason for complacency. Aside from an unresolved territorial conflict of its own, Azerbaijan is located in a region that will almost certainly develop crises that could test the foundations of its foreign policy. Georgia's instability and adversarial relationship with Russia is of utmost concern to Azerbaijan, as is the transformation of Turkey, the increasing anarchy in the North Caucasus, and the international tension surrounding Azerbaijan's closest neighbor, Iran. The bottom line is that Azerbaijan remains a small state, which will continue to be affected by a multitude of developments among and between the larger powers of Eurasia. As Azerbaijan has little influence over these relationships but stands to be affected by them, the risk of being drawn into confrontations that it would prefer to avoid is ever present and will come to require continued statesmanship of successive Azerbaijani governments.

12

Iran and the "Other" Azerbaijan

Though relations with Turkey, Russia, and the West often dominate Azerbaijan's foreign relations, the country with the greatest long-term importance in its foreign policy is arguably Iran. More Azerbaijanis live in Iran than in Azerbaijan, and until and unless the large Azerbaijani population south of the Araks River finds itself in a harmonious relationship with power and statehood—whether in an Iran where their rights are respected, or under any other solution—Azerbaijan will have more at stake in Iran's future than in that of any other state.

Though the term *Azerbaijan* came into use to designate a geographical area on both sides of the Araks River long before the twentieth century, in the 1900s it became the ethnonym of a distinct, self-conscious Azerbaijani people. While estimates vary regarding the distribution of the Azerbaijanis, it is beyond doubt that Azerbaijanis in Iran are at least twice as numerous as their counterparts in the Republic of Azerbaijan. Estimates from sources close to the Iranian government tend to mention the number 15 million; nationalist Azerbaijani sources talk of close to 30 million, or even more. The real number is somewhere between, though intermarriage, migration within Iran, and assimilation into Persian culture all make the quest for a definitive total elusive. The figure of 20 million often mentioned in the literature is likely no exaggeration, making the Azerbaijanis by far the largest minority in Iran, more numerous in all likelihood than the Kurds, Arabs, Turkmens and Baluchis combined.[1] They have also been regarded as the best-integrated minority in the country, based in large part on their long attachment to the Iranian state and the unifying force of Shia Islam, the branch of Islam they have in common with the Persian population. Indeed, conventional wisdom stresses the strength of the Iranian identity of the Azerbaijanis of Iran, and the weakness of their ethnic identity.

To a certain extent the conventional wisdom is true, given the significant representation of Azerbaijanis in the economy, the Shiite clergy (the ulema), and, to a lesser extent, the political sphere in Iran, and considering that at least a third of Tehran's population is ethnically Turkic. Iran's long-ruling Supreme Leader, Ayatollah Ali Khamenei, a native of the town of

Khameneh in East Azerbaijan Province, is known to be half-Azerbaijani, and to speak Azerbaijani Turkish. Another native of Khameneh is Mir Hossein Mousavi, whose ill-fated campaign for the Iranian presidency in 2009 gave rise to the reformist Green Movement of Iran. As the careers of these two men of Khameneh illustrate, the Azerbaijanis in Iran, much like the Kurds in Turkey, are not hampered by their ethnic origin so long as they assume and integrate into the language and culture of the majority population. Large parts of the Tehran Bazaar are in Azerbaijani hands, and Azerbaijanis are numerous in the officer ranks of the Iranian armed forces. The strength of Iranian identity among Azerbaijanis is reinforced by the fact that the Safavid dynasty, which came to power in Iran in the early sixteenth century and made Shia Islam the state religion, was Azerbaijani in origin (see chapter 1).

The continued control of Iran's state and society by a hard-line clerical regime dominated by Persian culture and language ensures that more than two-thirds of the Azerbaijani nation remains under a form of government diametrically opposed to that enjoyed by the one-third who live in the Republic of Azerbaijan. Meanwhile, the U.S.-Iranian confrontation that began in 1979 and the growth of political tensions surrounding Iran's forthrightly anti-Western regime and nuclear ambitions have put Azerbaijan in a complicated position. It would be one of the most directly affected countries should a war break out in Iran—or should the current regime collapse in violence, whether externally induced or not, and whether related to ethnic tensions or not.

The "Azerbaijan Question"—that is, the uncertain status of the huge cohort of Azerbaijanis living in Iran—is complicated by a host of additional issues, including the delimitation of the Caspian Sea and geopolitics in general. Nevertheless, the extent to which relations between Iran and Azerbaijan are strained at any given time can be gauged primarily by how either side is responding to this overarching transnational question.

The Azerbaijan Question and Iranian Policy

The distinct ethnic identity of the Azerbaijanis in Iran has often been neglected by scholarship, which has tended to regard them as identifying strongly with Iran. However, this perception has been challenged recently, especially in the work of Brenda Shaffer, Nasib Nassibli, and Jamil Hasanli.[2] These scholars point to a recurrent political expression of distinct Azerbaijani identity throughout the post–World War II era in Iran. During the 1978–79 revolution, the strong following of the ethnic Azerbaijani Ayatollah Mohammed Kazem Shariatmadari in Tabriz and other parts of Iranian Azerbaijan was linked to a perception among Azerbaijanis that Shariatmadari was a representative of their specific interests.[3] Since the revolution, a separate and distinct Azerbaijani identity has been growing among the residents of northwestern Iran. Many Azerbaijanis initially supported the Islamic Revolution, regarding it as a liberation from what they perceived as the Persian chauvinism of the Pahlavi dynasty, and hoping that it would lead to the establishment of a state where they, as Shiite Muslims, would be first-class citizens on par with the Persians. But this did not happen. Cleric-ruled Iran sustained many of the minority policies of the Pahlavi dynasty, in spite of occasional periods of greater leniency and freedom. Disillusionment with this situation has been a major factor in the increasing inclination of Azerbaijanis in Iran to revisit the issues of their identity and loyalty.

In 1991, the size and economic as well as strategic significance of the Azerbaijani minority did not represent an immediate threat to the Iranian regime, but was certainly an issue Tehran treated with utmost caution. In this context, the emergence of an independent Azerbaijani state from the ruins of the Soviet Union was greeted with dismay in Tehran's ruling circles, already acutely aware of the evaporating revolutionary zeal around the country and growing popular discontent. Whether or not irredentism would grow strong in Baku, the very existence of Azerbaijani statehood would have magnetic appeal for significant numbers of Azerbaijanis south of the border with Iran, and would in the long term ensure that whatever distinct Azerbaijani identity existed in Iran would not wither away, but, to the contrary, gradually grow. Moreover, general disillusionment with the failure of the Islamic Revolution to deliver improved living standards to the population would now have the potential to take on an ethnic dimension in the northwestern regions, particularly as the regime failed to change much of Tehran's minority policies. Acutely aware of the evaporating revolutionary zeal around the country and of growing popular discontent, the clerical regime was instinctively dismayed at the creation of the state of Azerbaijan.

Such a reaction was, of course, by no means unique to Iran. In Europe, the visceral Greek reaction to the creation of an independent republic of Macedonia stands as an example of the jealousy of states toward jurisdictions bearing a name identified with a part of their own territory. To add to Tehran's worries, the nascent Azerbaijani republic was endowed with considerable energy resources relative to its small population, which provided it with the potential to acquire significant wealth—a process that soon enough got under way, then rapidly accelerated in the second decade of independence. Conversely, Iran has experienced an extended period of economic decay attributable to its 1980–88 war with Iraq, a monocultural economy heavily controlled by the state, U.S.-imposed trade sanctions, and international ostracism. Hence, much in the same way that Turkey has made it a foreign policy priority to prevent the establishment of a Kurdish state in northern Iraq, Iran would clearly have preferred the continuation of the arrangement established with the 1828 Treaty of Turkmanchai, namely, the division of Azerbaijan between Russia and Iran.

As the war between Azerbaijan and Armenia over Mountainous Karabakh escalated in the 1990s, Iran was domestically torn in devising a policy. Some religious forces as well as ethnic Azerbaijani groups advocated support of the brethren in Azerbaijan against the Armenian infidel. Meanwhile, the foreign policy establishment saw the weakening of the Republic of Azerbaijan as a boon to Iranian national interests, and therefore pursued a policy that combined official neutrality with growing support for Armenia. Iran's vacillation and hesitation in the first years of the 1990s can be ascribed to this internal division, but within a few years the broad direction of Tehran's policies became obvious. In general, the regime used the conflict to pressure Baku, with the exception of instances when restoring a balance was necessary. An example occurred in mid-1993, when Armenian aggression was throwing the region into chaos, and defeat and suffering in Azerbaijan were raising the possibility that Iranian public opinion would become aroused, forcing the regime to act preventively. At the time, Iran was serving as Armenia's main purveyor of electricity and goods, and once the Armenian conquest of Karabakh had been completed, Iranian trucks began to supply most of the secessionist enclave's needs.

The decisive factor tilting Tehran toward Yerevan was the policies of the Azerbaijani Popular Front (APF) government. As discussed in chapter 11, President Abulfez Elçibey's regime developed a vehemently anti-Russian and anti-Iranian policy. Elçibey himself was a convinced secularist, despised Iran's theocracy, and openly criticized Iran's denial of cultural rights to its Azerbaijani minority. Before ascending to the presidency, Elçibey spoke of Iran as a "doomed state," and flaunted the idea of reunifying Azerbaijan. In a sense, Elçibey and his nationalist policies confirmed Tehran's worst fears, and pushed Iran further toward Armenia. Iranian economic support played an important role in keeping Armenia alive and functioning at a time of economic embargo by Turkey and severed trade links with Azerbaijan. Should Iran have sided with Azerbaijan and joined the embargo on Armenia, the latter would have had to rely exclusively on supplies shipped through Georgia. In this sense, from the Azerbaijani perspective, Iran can be said to have made Armenia's expansionist policies possible.

Iranian Political Changes and the Azerbaijan Question

The group consciousness of the population of Iranian Azerbaijan has grown significantly since the early 1990s. In its response, the Iranian government has oscillated between repression and conciliation. The issue of collective identity first drew attention in 1989, when Azerbaijanis in Nakhichevan tore down border installations in order to reestablish contact with their kin across the Araks River, in defiance of Soviet policies. This brought a first rush of ethnic nationalist sentiment on both sides. The subsequent dissolution of the Soviet Union and emergence of the state of Azerbaijan enabled contacts across the river to develop at much greater speed. Cultural and family linkages multiplied. Despite these developments, trade relations between Azerbaijan and Iran remained limited.

At least as important, the population of northern Iran has come into much closer cultural and economic contact with Turkey, partly through increasing trade and partly through the effect of Turkish satellite television. Iran's theocratic regime ensures that state TV programming holds little appeal for the Iranian population; furthermore, broadcasts are almost exclusively in Persian. Hence, the Azerbaijani population of northern Iran has gravitated toward Turkish culture, the languages being close enough for Azerbaijanis to get quickly accustomed to the Turkish dialect. In fact, in Iran as in the Republic of Azerbaijan, the Azerbaijani language has itself been subjected to change: a number of Turkish conjugations, words, and expressions have entered the language, most obviously in regions of Iran bordering Turkey.

Exposure to Turkish culture has also affected the self-perception of the Iranian Azerbaijanis. Historically, the dominance of Persian culture and its dismissive attitude toward Turkic culture had the effect of socializing many Azerbaijanis into the former, perceived as the "high culture" in Iran. Contact with Turkey has nevertheless publicized that country's far higher level of social and economic development, and in turn boosted the ethnic self-consciousness and identity of Iranian Azerbaijanis—in many ways erasing the feeling of cultural inferiority the Persian elite had long sought to instill in the ethnic minorities of Iran.

The political repercussions of these developments in terms of identity have nevertheless remained limited. An organization called the National

Liberation Movement of South Azerbaijan (NLMSA) has been created, though its political strength appears limited, as does its following. Azerbaijani nationalism in Iran has remained relatively poorly organized, partly as a result of Iranian repression. But the perhaps most important impediment to its development has been a lack of consensus on what it wants to achieve. Politically motivated Azerbaijanis are torn among those desiring mainly increased representation and greater cultural rights within the Iranian state; those seeking political autonomy within Iran; those seeking the creation of an independent southern Azerbaijani state; those seeking unification with the Republic of Azerbaijan; and those seeking a confederation embracing Turkey and both northern and southern Azerbaijan.

Despite such differences, which can be easily observed, not least among the Iranian Azerbaijani diaspora, the increase in the political expression of Azerbaijani nationalism is unmistakable. The number of protests against the Iranian state, and violent repression of these protests, have both increased since the late 1990s. Tabriz University has been a focal point for the organization of protest activities, including a large movement active in the summer of 2003.[4]

Members of the NLMSA are regularly arrested and imprisoned, and occasionally put to death. The honorary chairman of the NLMSA and leader of the Azerbaijani community in Iran, Dr. Mahmudali Chehregani, was repeatedly prevented from standing for election to the Majlis, the Iranian parliament. He was arrested, denied medical treatment, and suffered torture that resulted in partial paralysis.[5] Chehregani left Iran for the United States in 2002. Azerbaijani-language newspapers are, like all oppositional media in Tehran and elsewhere in the country, repeatedly closed down.[6]

In parallel with the liberalization of Iranian society that occurred in the late 1990s during the presidency of Mohammed Khatami, a change in political atmosphere also took place regarding minorities. This included the easing of restrictions on music and social activities, and among the beneficiaries was the Azerbaijani minority. Hence, while the government continued to harshly repress any political expression of Azerbaijani identity, it sought to liberalize cultural rights as a way of removing some of the popular base of the growing protest movement. A larger number of Azerbaijani-language publications and academic programs were allowed.[7]

This policy nevertheless did not seem to take any of the steam out of the rising Azerbaijani consciousness. Indeed, it may have had the opposite effect, much as perestroika and glasnost did north of the Araks River during the late Soviet period. In the mid-1990s, the Azerbaijan Question was still in many respects taboo in Tehran.[8] An Azerbaijani-speaking Iranian government official told the present author in 1998 that he had learned the language in Turkey—despite the obvious fact that he spoke in the jani dialect, not the Turkish one.[9] By 2003, however, Azerbaijani could be heard spoken freely between Iranian government officials in private, and political activity, including scholarly writing on ethnic issues in Iran, was tolerated. Of course, Azerbaijani remained banned from official settings. Moreover, the onset of the presidency of hard-line conservative Mahmoud Ahmadinejad in 2005 does not appear to have led to a backlash, as expressions of Azerbaijani identity appeared unproblematic in Iran, including in official circles. For instance, in 2009, when meeting an Iranian deputy minister of foreign affairs in his Tehran office, the present author was introduced as an Azerbaijani-speaker, whereupon the minister immediately switched to Azerbaijani with great joy.

While it is difficult to determine whether this liberalization has worked as a safety valve, there continues to be a palpable sense among the Azerbaijani minority of continuing discrimination in the political, economic, and cultural fields.

If Ahmadinejad's government has not restricted displays of ethnic identity, the gradual reduction of the democratic aspect of Iran's political system has certainly exacerbated feelings of discrimination and voicelessness. The countermove against Khatami's relatively liberal rule began with the overtly manipulated Majlis elections in February 2003, well before Ahmadinejad became president. From then on, Supreme Leader Khamenei and other members of Iran's clerical leadership worked meticulously to marginalize and exclude the reformist forces in society from decision-making positions. The uneasy "cohabitation" that had existed between Khamenei the hard-liner and Khatami the reformer was over. Iran was then pointedly characterized as the only country in the world where the president was also the leader of the opposition. But the extent to which Khamenei would go to prevent such a situation from recurring was put on display to the entire world in 2009 with the highly questionable reelection to the presidency of the incumbent Ahmadinejad, and the state's truculent reaction to the protests that followed.

The counterreformation certainly did not ease matters in Iranian Azerbaijan. Indeed, the largest demonstrations in many years took place in Tabriz in the summer of 2004. Azerbaijani sources reported that several hundred thousand people participated in the rally, which was kept under control by no less than 40,000 Iranian police.[10] Protests over the continued rejection of instruction in the Azerbaijani language in schools led to renewed protests and clashes in September 2004, with several people injured as a result and a dozen arrested.[11]

In May 2006, Iranian Azerbaijan finally exploded. The trigger was something as ostensibly harmless as a newspaper cartoon that could be understood as depicting Azerbaijanis as cockroaches. This led to massive rallies across northern Iran, especially in Tabriz and Orumiyeh, gathering hundreds of thousands in largely peaceful protests.[12] The authorities responded with overwhelming force, killing an estimated 100 people and jailing an estimated 11,000—including, in what looked like a preemptive action, known Azerbaijani nationalist intellectuals. Most of the detainees were subsequently released, but it is clear that the systematic raids crippled the awakening in Iranian Azerbaijan, at least temporarily.

In 2009, as is well known, ethnic Azerbaijani Mir Hossein Mousavi was in all likelihood robbed of his election to Iran's presidency—or at least to a second round against the incumbent Ahmadinejad—by what amounted to a coup against the electoral components of the Iranian system by a coalition consisting of Ahmadinejad himself, Supreme Leader Khamenei, and the Islamic Revolutionary Guard Corps. According to official figures, Ahmadinejad won by a landslide in Iranian Azerbaijan—a highly illogical result given the natural tendency to vote en masse for a native son.

Following the crackdown on the Green Movement of Iran, the Iranian regime could no longer depend on enjoying an implicit public legitimacy, as had largely been the case until the summer of 2009. Instead, the regime now appeared to be upheld solely by brute force.

In the wake of the events of 2009, it seemed apparent that the increasing hard-liner control over Iranian state institutions and increased repression could lead to an intensification of polarization on an ethnic basis. This would affect Azerbaijan considerably, but there would be little Baku could do to affect the situation.

The Regional Context

Developments in Iran have been occurring against the backdrop of a rapidly changing regional environment. This is perhaps best illustrated by the feelings of isolation and encirclement by the United States experienced by the Iranian regime following the U.S. invasions of Afghanistan and Iraq.

The initial outcome of Operation Enduring Freedom was positive for Iran: it removed a vehemently anti-Iranian and anti-Shia government from neighboring Afghanistan. Iran itself had had a standoff with the Taliban regime on the Iranian-Afghan border in 1998, caused by the killing of several Iranian consular officials in Afghanistan by the Taliban movement. Having the Taliban next door had become, for the Iranians, an apt illustration of the precariousness of Iran's geographic location. Iranian representatives liked to argue that they were "sandwiched between the Taliban and Saddam Hussein."[13] Benefits likewise accrued with the U.S. overthrow of Saddam Hussein in Iraq eighteen months later, which removed a significant threat to Iran and greatly increased Tehran's influence in Iraq. Iran took an ambivalent position in regard to both conflicts, however, indicating that it had little problem with the deposing of either the Taliban or Saddam Hussein, but was worried about what would come afterward: a long-term American presence on its doorstep. Having been included in President George W. Bush's "axis of evil," the Tehran hard-liners increasingly perceived a direct threat of American military action against them that only increased after U.S. operations in Iraq and the intensifying debate over Iran's nuclear program. Tehran also worried about the unrest and instability that would result in the region if American intervention did not stabilize its two neighbors.

Consequently, toward the Caucasus Tehran has followed a policy of defensive caution and limited containment of the United States on its borders. Iran has strengthened its already close relationship with Russia, which has meant the enlisting of Russian diplomatic support for the acquisition of weaponry and crucially important nuclear technology—mainly of Russian origin.[14] The Russian link has gained increased importance in Tehran as the regime frantically seeks to achieve nuclear weapons capability. The cost of this policy has, however, come in the realm of Iranian policy in the former Soviet sphere. Indeed, it seems to be an unwritten rule that Iran's role in the Caucasus and Central Asia is circumscribed by deference to Russian domination—as Iran's policies toward Chechnya and the civil war in Tajikistan suggest. In other words, Iran's policy seldom interferes with or contradicts Russian policy in these regions.

Issues in Azerbaijan's Relations with Iran

After getting off to a good start in 1991 with the presidential tenure of Ayaz Mutalibov, relations between Azerbaijan and Iran cooled to the freezing point during Abulfez Elçibey's time as president. This change could be attributed to several issues. Paramount was the question of southern Azerbaijan, described in detail in the preceding section of the present chapter. Other points of contention included the Karabakh conflict and Armenia's relations with Iran, the status of the Caspian Sea, U.S.-Azerbaijani relations, and Iranian support for Shiite radicalism in Azerbaijan.

Southern Azerbaijan

Most acute during Elçibey's tenure, the southern Azerbaijan issue has slipped into the background since the beginning of the Aliyev era in 1993. Nevertheless, it persists as a background irritant and cause of suspicion in bilateral relations.

President Elçibey's anti-Iranian stance was never hidden, as his pronouncements on behalf of the cultural rights of Azerbaijanis in Iran and on the theocratic political system in Iran remained vivid in the memories of Iranian leaders. Since moving into opposition, the parties that have been formed out of the Azerbaijan Popular Front have continued to raise the issue regularly, much to Iran's dismay. The fact that these parties coordinate with anti-Iranian activists among the Azerbaijani diaspora is an added concern on the Iranian side. On the part of the Azerbaijani government, the policy since Aliyev's accession to power has been clear: the government officially underlines its respect for Iran's territorial integrity, and to the extent possible steers clear of discussing the situation of ethnic Azerbaijanis in Iran publicly. Meanwhile, elements of anti-Iranian groups from southern Azerbaijan such as the NLMSA are active on Azerbaijani territory. When the NLMSA's honorary chairman, Mahmudali Chehregani, was allowed to leave Iran in early 2002, he traveled to Baku, where he made several presentations on the plight of Azerbaijanis in Iran, talked of a nationalist resurgence.[15]

In general, Baku's policy has been to tolerate the presence of such groups as long as they keep a low profile and avoid embarrassing the government or creating disputes with Tehran; thus, they are not allowed to open offices, and Azerbaijan is restrictive in granting citizenship to Iranian Azerbaijanis. Nevertheless, Tehran's perception of Baku's toleration of these forces has led to recurrent Iranian protests, and more. On August 22, 2001, at the height of the crisis between Iran and Azerbaijan over the Caspian Sea (see below, under "The Delimitation of the Caspian Sea"), the leader of the NLMSA, Piruz Dilanci, survived an assassination attempt in his Baku residence.[16] Given the Iranian government's well-known systematic efforts to assassinate opposition forces in exile, suspicion naturally fell on Tehran.

The Azerbaijani government's attempts to coordinate, organize, and influence the Azerbaijani diaspora, including the regular convocation of the

World Azerbaijani Congress in Baku, have created tensions with Iran, as these diaspora groups include organizations with a southern agenda. For example, presentations by European-based Iranian Azerbaijanis at the March 2006 gathering covered human rights violations in Iranian Azerbaijan and the possibility of the unification of northern and southern Azerbaijan. This led to a diplomatic row. The Iranian government, including its ambassador in Baku, termed these speeches interference in Iran's internal affairs. Historical sensitivities were also raised as the Iranian ambassador referred to famous poets considered part of the Azerbaijani heritage as "Iranian poets," prompting an immediate reaction from the Azerbaijani writers' union.[17]

While Iran bristles at any mention of southern Azerbaijan, Iranian voices have not been less provocative. On various occasions, different Iranian figures have endorsed a reunification of Azerbaijan, but emphasized that it should occur as the "return" of the presently independent Azerbaijan to its historical motherland, Iran. For instance, in 1996 Ayatollah Mohsen Shabestary, the Khamenei-appointed Friday prayer leader in Tabriz, stated that "the Azerbaijan Republic was once ours. So, if there is any talk of unification of the two Azerbaijans, it is they who should come back to Iran."[18] On a 2000 visit to the city of Qerm, near the border with Azerbaijan, Khamenei himself told a local crowd that "beyond this border there are Muslim brothers like you who love Islam, the clergy, and the Islamic Republic."[19] In 2001, the secretary of the influential Expediency Discernment Council, Mohsen Rezai, stated that "Azeri officials should govern their country in such a manner that the Iranian people do not demand the return of Azerbaijan to Iran."[20] Given that the Expediency Discernment Council is a consultative body that advises the Supreme Leader and has a mandate to resolve differences between the Majlis and the Guardians Council (which is empowered to vet legislation), there can be little doubt that the statement constituted an official warning. In sum, Tehran's position has been simple: if Azerbaijan encourages—or even tolerates—activism targeted at Iranian Azerbaijan, Baku might get reunification, but under the rule of *Tehran*. As Azerbaijani identity grows more palpable in Iran and increasingly vexing to the Iranian government, it will remain a sore spot, at best, and a deep source of tension, at worst, in relations between the two countries.

Karabakh and Iranian-Armenian Relations

The Karabakh war was the most direct northern threat to Iran's national security emanating since the 1940s.[21] Fighting around Karabakh threatened to spill into Iran at several occasions, notably in the fall of 1993. Because both adversaries are Iran's neighbors, the conflict directly affects Iran's security, even when, as in recent times, there is little actual fighting. At an early stage—virtually as soon as the two belligerents became independent—Iran offered its good offices to help bring about a peaceful solution to the conflict, though ultimately to no avail. A cease-fire was negotiated in Tehran in March 1992, with the signing of a "Tehran declaration," though it soon proved abortive. On May 7, another Iranian-brokered cease-fire was signed, but the very next day Armenian forces conquered Shusha Province. The two failed cease-fires showed that Iranian mediation efforts carried no weight on the Armenian side, and that Russia's ambition to dominate peacemaking in the Caucasus would keep Iran on the sidelines. Indeed, the occupation of Shusha was followed by the conquest of the Lachin corridor just as Yerevan entered into a military alliance with Moscow. Iranian hardliners, for once agreeing with Elçibey, condemned Armenia for using the cease-fires brought about by Iranian diplomacy as an opportunity to rearm. Even had Tehran not met these setbacks to its peacemaking efforts, the advent of the Popular Front government in Baku and Russia's return to the South Caucasus would have made further Iranian diplomatic forays impossible.[22]

As the fighting over Karabakh erupted into full-scale war in 1992, Iran switched from attempting conflict resolution to using the conflict to pressure Azerbaijan. This was most commonly done through different forms of support for Armenia. Perhaps most important, Iran served as a purveyor of goods and electrical power to Azerbaijan's adversary. This was crucial because transport was difficult through war-torn Georgia, Armenia's only other trade conduit. Iran's support went beyond these merely commercial relations, as reports have indicated that Tehran allowed weapons en route to Armenia to transit Iran.[23] After the 1994 cease-fire, Iran developed ever closer economic relations with Armenia, for instance building a gas pipeline to strengthen Armenia's energy security. Tellingly, Yerevan has repeatedly praised Tehran's "balanced policy toward the Karabakh conflict."[24]

All that said, it should also be noted that whenever the conflict threatened to spill into Iran, Tehran would pressure Armenia as well. For instance, in Fall 1993, Iran made a joint appeal with Turkey to the UN Security Council to condemn the Armenian occupation of territories outside Karabakh. In September 1993, when Nakhichevan was under threat of an Armenian attack, Iranian troops crossed the Araks River into the Azerbaijani enclave, which was enough to intimidate Armenia, Russia's strong

protests to Tehran notwithstanding. Armenia's foreign minister subsequently assured Tehran that there would be no more attacks on Nakhichevan.[25]

Whereas Iranian-Armenian cooperation has blossomed in the political,
economic, scientific and cultural spheres, Iranian-Azerbaijani relations
have never been characterized by the same warmth. Even after Abulfez
Elçibey's overthrow and Heydar Aliyev's assumption of the presidency,
relations only improved on the surface. Until 2004, Tehran resisted the
creation of an Azerbaijani consulate in Tabriz, although Iran kept a consulate in Nakhichevan. In 1999, Iran's ambassador to Baku stated that the
issue of opening a consulate would be resolved only after a package of
proposals from Iran had been accepted—hardly standard diplomatic proce-
dure.[26] Heydar Aliyev himself was not loath to express his frustration with
Iranian policies on Karabakh. In March 2001, he walked out of a meeting
with a visiting Iranian minister after the latter informed him of Iran's plans
to restore a bridge over the Araxes between Iran and Armenian-occupied
territories in Azerbaijan.[27]

Its handling of the Karabakh issue dealt a strong blow to any ambitions
on Iran's part to appear as a power acting in solidarity with the people of
Azerbaijan. Indeed, Karabakh continues to be one of the most important
factors generating mistrust of Iran in Azerbaijan.

Delimitation of The Caspian Sea

With the collapse of the Soviet Union, Iran promptly became a passionate
opponent of the sectoral delimitation of the Caspian Sea. With little oil in
its would-be sector of the Caspian, Tehran argued that the Law of the Sea
was not applicable to the body of water since it was in fact not a sea but a
giant lake. Yet the oil companies seemed less than disturbed by Moscow
and Tehran's stance, and moved on with the exploitation projects. Of
course, the participation of the Russian state-owned company Lukoil in a
consortium the Russian Foreign Ministry deemed illegal played a role in
attenuating the fears of oil multinationals.[28] To a lesser extent, Iranian
companies have also participated in international consortia in the Caspian,
including the large Shah-Deniz gas project, in Azerbaijani waters. However, Moscow's position on the Caspian Sea gradually weakened, and in mid-
1998 Russia accepted the division of the bottom and subsoil of the Caspian,
in a separate agreement with Kazakhstan.[29] This left Iran alone defending
"proportional exploitation" and "fair sharing" of the wealth, principles the
Iranian government has consistently reiterated.[30]

During 2000 and 2001, Russia made separate diplomatic agreements with Kazakhstan and Azerbaijan stipulating the division of the Caspian seabed but joint exploitation of the waters. A subsequent Azerbaijani-Kazakhstani treaty ensured that the entire northern Caspian was covered by a legal regime. But the southern Caspian, primarily of interest to Iran, Azerbaijan, and Turkmenistan, was not, as Iran continued to reject such a solution. According to standard methods of median line delimitation, Iran would receive jurisdiction over the smallest sector of the Caspian, which would amount to about 13 percent of its surface. Moreover, the Iranian sector would consist mostly of deep-sea waters, where exploration and drilling typically are costly. Hence, Iran seemed to be hedging its bets on achieving a larger share of the sea. Indeed, Tehran hinted that it would consider an "equitable" division granting it 20 percent of the Caspian.[31] Moreover, Iran was showing an increased level of activism. Whereas for reasons of economics and principle it had not attempted to exploit its Caspian waters until then, starting in 2001 Iran unilaterally began to explore the sea for oil and gas—in areas that would not necessarily fall within the Iranian sector, depending on what percentage that sector would ultimately comprise. The rationale for these activities seemed decidedly political—after all, Iran could drill for oil in the Persian Gulf at a fraction of the cost it would incur in the deep-water southern Caspian.[32] Iranian policy seemed to be replicating the stance taken successfully by Azerbaijan and Kazakhstan in the early 1990s: exploring and drilling for oil unilaterally in what they considered their sector of the Caspian. Iran's oil minister, Bijan Namdar-Zanganeh, stated in 2001 that Iran would not "wait for other littoral states to find a legal status and [would] start exploring for oil and gas itself."[33] Tehran then began drilling for oil within the disputed area of the sea—indeed, only a mile from an area where Azerbaijan and Royal Dutch Shell were planning to drill.[34]

In fact, Iranian policy went through a qualitative change in 2001. For unclear reasons, a much more aggressive stance toward Azerbaijan developed during that year, nearly coming to the point of open conflict. After diplomatic efforts during the spring failed to bring about a resolution of the Caspian Sea legal dispute, Iran unilaterally claimed 20 percent of the surface area of the Caspian, focusing its legal efforts mainly on the energy-rich waters claimed by Azerbaijan and less on the energy-poor areas in the Iranian-Turkmen border zone. In August, an Iranian warship suddenly forcibly evicted an Azerbaijani-flagged but BP-owned exploration vessel carrying out research on the Sharq-Alov oil field. With the international reaction muted, Iran continued its gunboat diplomacy against Azerbaijan, initially conducting daily overflights above Azerbaijani-claimed waters, then, in the absence of objections other than Baku's protests, over Azerbaijani villages in parts of the country bordering Iran. The attempt on the life of NLMSA leader Piruz Dilanci also occurred at this time. It took Turkish intervention to ratchet down the increasing Iranian pressure on Azerbaijan. The chief of staff of the Turkish armed forces, Hüseyin Kıvrıkoğlu, visited Baku in early September, attending the graduation ceremony of the first group of Turkish-trained Azerbaijani cadets to complete studies at the Azerbaijani military academy. As ten Turkish F-5 fighter jets performed air shows over Baku, to the awe of the biggest crowd seen in the capital since the largest anti-Soviet demonstrations of the late 1980s, Kıvrıkoğlu told President Aliyev that the Turkish and Azerbaijani skies were one common sky. Iranian overflights of Azerbaijani territory were discontinued.

The full reasons behind the Iranian activism of 2001 remain unclear. One possibility is that Iran sought to destabilize Azerbaijan and prevent the Baku-Tbilisi-Ceyhan oil pipeline project from proceeding. Another, perhaps related reason may have been Iranian fears of the rapidly developing relations among Israel, Turkey, Georgia, and Azerbaijan.[35] In any event, the episode was soon overshadowed by the attacks of 9/11, and the controversy petered out. Iran had to shift its attention eastward and southward, in response to the tumultuous changes unfolding in Afghanistan and, later, Iraq.

Though off the radar screen for the time being, the problem of Caspian Sea delimitation remained unresolved.

U.S.-Azerbaijani Relations

The relations between Baku and Washington have been yet another factor aggravating tensions between Iran and Azerbaijan, especially at times when U.S.-Azerbaijani ties have seemed particularly close. Problems began when Azerbaijan welcomed American oil companies to the Caspian, something both Iran and Russia resisted, correctly seeing such a move as bringing increasing American political attention to the region. The deal that led to creation of the Azerbaijan International Operating Company (AIOC) was a case in point, not least because Iran was cut out of it at the United States' request—which made Tehran understand perfectly clearly where Azerbaijan's priorities lay. Of course, Baku did not cut Iran out only at the U.S. request as there was no great desire to have Theran play a role in the project, but it was nevertheless an important factor. As Azerbaijan moved closer to NATO in the late 1990s, participating in NATO-led peacekeeping missions and upgrading bilateral military ties with the United States, Tehran's concerns grew that Azerbaijan would be used to insert U.S. military forces into the Caspian region.

Rumors in summer 2003 and again in 2006—originating, predictably, in the Russian news media—that Azerbaijan would be used as a launching pad for a U.S. invasion of Iran, and that Baku had consented to this, led to thinly veiled Iranian threats of military action and violations of Azerbaijani airspace by Iranian jets. In 2004, persistent rumors of the impending establishment of a U.S. military base in Azerbaijan prompted renewed Iranian pressure on Azerbaijan. The rumors were at least partly attributable to U.S. defense secretary Donald Rumsfeld's frequent visits to Baku since 9/11.[36]

Azerbaijan hence found the U.S.-Iranian confrontation to be a test of its balanced foreign policy, with both Washington and Tehran in effect trying to force Baku to take sides. As one observer noted, Azerbaijan found itself in "a very uncomfortable situation, trying to maneuver within the limited space available."[37] Iran and Azerbaijan subsequently signed a nonaggression pact, in May 2005. It was widely interpreted as being an Iranian device to prevent the use of Azerbaijani territory for a U.S. military action against Iran.[38] Azerbaijan's inability to escape being affected by the relationship among the four great powers in the Caucasus is nowhere more obvious than in the U.S.-Iranian case.

Since the resignation in November 2006 of Secretary of Defense Rumsfeld, however, no cabinet-level U.S. official visited Azerbaijan until his successor, Robert Gates, visited in June 2010. Indeed, America's gradual loss of interest in the Caucasus had the inadvertent effect of easing Iranian-Azerbaijani relations somewhat. As Baku became increasingly estranged from Washington in the late Bush and early Obama administrations, the likelihood of U.S. military bases in Azerbaijan decreased considerably—as did the prospect that Baku would allow the use of its territory for an attack on Iran.

Iran and Shiite Radicalism in Azerbaijan

Since Azerbaijan's independence, Iran has to varying degrees supported radical Shiite Islamic movements in Azerbaijan. This is perhaps no surprise, given the theocratic character of the Iranian regime. In their early phase, Iran's activities were not particularly covert. Iranian mullahs were sent to Azerbaijan to proselytize, hoping to find fertile ground in a land starved of religion for decades. The focus of activities lay in what traditionally had been the most strongly Shiite areas of Azerbaijan, including the area near the Iranian border and localities north of Baku on the Apsheron Peninsula. Though the Iranian mullahs were barred after several years, this only resulted in a change in tactics, as Iran began training Azerbaijani religious students who were later sent back to Azerbaijan. Iranian groups have been especially active among internally displaced persons in Azerbaijan's southern provinces, where most of the refugees from the Karabakh war are encamped.

In addition, Tehran has given support to Islamic political forces in Azerbaijan. First and foremost among these is the Islamic Party of Azerbaijan, which draws most of its core support from villages on the Apsheron Peninsula. The party is a supporter of ousted president Ayaz Mutalibov. Tehran has also hedged its bets by supporting the secular Social Democratic Party, whose Internet address, tellingly, is mutalibov.org. The onetime president in fact only joined the party in 2003.[39] The Social Democratic Party's representatives, such as Zardusht Alizade, have been among the most pro-Iranian forces in Azerbaijani politics. Iran has also been funding madrassas, Islamic schools where children are instructed in the virtues of the Islamic regime and the Iranian Revolution. These often operate without documentation, and the government has closed down a number of them.[40]

More serious perhaps has been the covert Iranian support for violent groups such as the Jeyshaullah movement and Hezbollah, which have both been active in Azerbaijan (see chapter 10). Jeyshaullah's actions have included the assassination of historian and academician Ziya Bunyatov, and the movement has been included on the U.S. State Department's list of terrorist organizations. As discussed in chapter 10, the threat from foreign-sponsored religious groups, especially those of Iranian origin, was the primary impetus behind creation of the State Committee for Work with Religious Organizations, which has gradually been able to gain a measure of control over the religious situation in the country.

Starting in 2005, Iranian support for religious activism seemed to diminish, as Tehran tried a different tack—developing better relations with Ilham Aliyev's government in order to safeguard Iranian interests and avoid pushing Azerbaijan even deeper into the American camp. Perhaps an insight developed that Iran's policies had failed, as evidenced by the strengthening of the Azerbaijani state, and indeed had been counterproductive in terms of Iran's own interests. Nevertheless, Iran continues to maintain the ability to switch its support for radicalism in Azerbaijan on or off, depending on its political objectives.

Conclusions

In spite of all the existing and potential problems, the governments of Azerbaijan and Iran have worked to develop a modus vivendi since about 2005.[41] Indeed, a flurry of bilateral visits began to take place after Iranian president Khatami visited Baku in August 2004—a visit that led to the end to the long-standing Iranian opposition to establishment of an Azerbaijani consulate in Tabriz.[42] Ilham Aliyev then visited Tehran in January 2005 to sign nine agreements on various aspects of bilateral relations.[43] In December of the same year, Aliyev and new Iranian president Mahmoud Ahmadinejad inaugurated construction of pipelines that would make the provision of natural gas to Nakhichevan possible by means of a gas-swapping arrangement between their two countries.[44] In August 2007 Ahmadinejad made his first trip to Baku, which Aliyev reciprocated in March 2009 on the sidelines of the Economic Cooperation Organization summit.[45] A series of other ministerial-level delegations have also concluded numerous practical agreements over the years. Perhaps most important, Iran unilaterally canceled visa requirements for Azerbaijani citizens in November 2009.[46]

These moves all point to an improving relationship, at least on the surface. But there is little doubt that relations between the countries remain tenuous at best, due to the fundamentally different external orientations, and social and political models, espoused by the two. Azerbaijan's continued dependence on Iran for access to Nakhichevan, while creating the potential for cooperation, is also a factor, not to mention Iran's vexatious relationship with the West.

Key among the continuing sources of mistrust between Tehran and Baku will be the problem of Iranian Azerbaijan. The national awakening that is taking place in the territory may be slow, and generally peaceful, but it is a fact, and one that the Iranian government has been unable to address constructively. As this situation develops, and potentially becomes unruly, there will be repercussions upon Azerbaijan.

The combination of internal Iranian and regional developments leaves both the Republic of Azerbaijan and Iranian Azerbaijan in a precarious situation. On the external front, given Azerbaijan's relations with the United States, the Iranian posture toward Azerbaijan, which has at times been overtly hostile, could become so again. Tehran's determined quest for nuclear capability, and the fact that Azerbaijan will inevitably be affected by a conflict over Iran's nuclear program, adds to the potential for sustained tensions. The outlook is further complicated by the strengthening of hardliner control over the Iranian state, as well as increasing discord and a vicious circle of protests and violent repression in Iranian Azerbaijan. The feeling of encirclement felt within the Iranian ruling elite has already led to intensification of the cycle of internal protest and repression, which was concentrated in the Azerbaijani and Kurdish areas of the country before spreading to Tehran in 2009.

The Iranian government's conspiratorial worldview seems to cause it to regard all protests as the products of foreign machinations to undermine the Islamic regime. This perspective, in turn, carries the risk of exacerbating the repressive and counterproductive policies of the Iranian government both generally and in Iranian Azerbaijan. In this sense, internal developments in Iran, especially as they concern the Azerbaijani community, cannot be dissociated from the regional politics of Iran's neighborhood—even though the troubles in Iranian Azerbaijan are entirely homegrown. Azerbaijani nationalists have so far received precious little support from either Turkey, Azerbaijan, or the United States, with such backing being limited to fringe nationalist groups in the two former countries and a segment of the right wing in the latter.

The Iranian Azerbaijan issue was important in the formulation of Azerbaijani nationalism in the Soviet period, with the "literature of longing" and the building of the image of a divided Azerbaijani nation. This characterization remains a powerful factor in the minds of the Azerbaijani intelligentsia, as well as in the imagination of the Azerbaijani diaspora, among whose members the North-South division tends to be mitigated by a common culture and language, distance from home, and the need for cooperation to achieve common goals.

That is not to say that most Azerbaijanis are enthusiastic about the idea of reunification. Indeed, the prospect of the state tripling in population to include 20 million or more coethnics who have endured two centuries of Persian, not Russian, rule, and the different social norms and mores that would follow from that, is a cause for worry among many Azerbaijanis of the North. Indeed, the prospect of being drowned by the southern brethren, who are much more religious and, at least in the eyes of the Northerners, less modern and developed, has sharply reduced the urge for reunification within Azerbaijan itself. But this is not to say that there is no sense of solidarity, or a lack of support for the aspirations of Iranian Azerbaijanis to live in harmony, with respect for their cultural and political rights—a situation that is manifestly not the case at present.

In the final analysis, it is very difficult for Baku to have a significant positive impact on developments in Iran; it is condemned to do no more than seek to minimize adversity. Obviously, the ideal solution for Baku would be a peaceful and democratic development in Iran that would lead to Iranian Azerbaijan existing harmoniously in an arrangement within Iran's borders, while interacting freely and to mutual benefit with the Republic of Azerbaijan. Such a development unfortunately does not seem to hold great promise of materializing anytime soon. Consequently, Baku would be right to expect trouble in southern Azerbaijan and to prepare for that eventuality.

13

Russia, the Resurgent Imperialist

Azerbaijan's 200-year history as a Russian colony continues to color relations between the two countries. But for several reasons, this was no typical colonial relationship. First, because Russia was a land empire, Azerbaijan and its other colonies lay on its borders. Second, because of the peculiar nature of Soviet communism and the unique context in which it took hold, Soviet Russia's profound cultural, economic, and social effects on its dependent territories included elements of traditional colonialism as well as more beneficial impacts. Finally, unlike the former colonial powers of the West, Russia has not repudiated its imperialist past. These three factors have been crucial in ensuring the persistence of a strong Russian presence—psychological, if not always physical—in Azerbaijan and the other Caucasus states.

Some observers, mainly optimistic Turkic nationalists, thought that the collapse of the Soviet Union would mean a Russian retreat from the lands of Turan. But that did not happen. Quite to the contrary, after a short interlude Russia returned with a vengeance in the former Soviet space, seeking to reestablish its preeminence before any other state or alliance stepped in to replace it.

Nowhere has the Russian reassertion been more vigorous and more arduous than in the Caucasus. Russia has used a variety of mainly coercive strategies, ranging from fomenting ethnic conflict and supporting separatist forces to using economic leverage and outright military force, to ensure that the region does not slip from its control. This energetic pursuit of regional hegemony has become one of the most compelling factors framing Azerbaijan's diplomatic relations and international goals. The bilateral relationship with Moscow naturally has remained one of the most important to Baku, simply because of the influence and power Russia has shown itself able and willing to leverage in the region. Russia remains a determinant, and a potential spoiler, of many of Azerbaijan's goals and ambitions, regionally and even globally.

Russian Political Thinking on the Caucasus

While their intensity has fluctuated with Russia's political and economic power, Russian policies in the Caucasus have been remarkably consistent since the early 1990s.[1] Once the Russian state became consolidated, Moscow sought to sustain its preeminent influence in the region, jealously guarding its interests there and overtly seeking to establish an acceptance—not only regionally but internationally—that the Caucasus was within Russia's sphere of influence. This imperial tendency in Russian thinking, initially dominant in the military and security structures, was elevated to the highest state hierarchies with the arrival to power of Vladimir Putin in 1999.

The most direct regional consequence of the dissolution of the Soviet Union was the achievement of national independence of three states: Armenia, Azerbaijan, and Georgia. Much as in 1918, the South Caucasus was set free largely because Moscow was preoccupied with domestic problems and issues. In 1918, the Bolshevik Revolution needed to be consolidated before the new leadership could embark on a *reconquista* of the territories that had been ruled by czarist Russia. Likewise, in 1991, a new Russian state needed to be built and consolidated, a process that necessitated a loosening of the grip on the periphery. On both occasions, Moscow recognized the independence of the three states, and for a short period restrained its outright ambitions to reclaim them. But in both 1920 and 1993, that is, less than two years after the respective declarations of independence of the South Caucasian states, a drive to reassert control over the region grew powerful in Moscow. Of course, while similarities abound between the two periods, the differences between them are equally important. While Bolshevik Russia overran the Caucasian states militarily during 1920–21 and incorporated them forcibly into the emerging Soviet Union, Russia was neither able or willing to do the same in the post–Cold War era. By 2008 it had resolved to absorb—for all practical purposes—two Georgian provinces, while maintaining, much as in the Soviet period, that these satellites were independent states. Yet even that concession to regional and international niceties failed to temper the centrifugal tendencies of the region.

Ruling circles in Russia have yet to accept the independence of the South Caucasian states, and while Russia has not sought an all-out conquest of the South Caucasus, it has employed a wide range of instruments at its disposal to sustain and expand its influence and control over the region. In the years since the dissolution of the Soviet Union, Russian foreign policy toward the South Caucasus has gone through several major phases.

First was the immediate reaction to the dissolution of the Soviet empire: a state of confusion that lasted though the initial stage of the building of the Russian state.[2] Indeed, Russia needed to define itself before defining any policy orientation toward its former dominions. Therefore, Moscow relinquished control over the three South Caucasian republics both politically and militarily, much as it had done in 1917. During 1991–92, reformers associated with Boris Yeltsin dominated Russian thinking. They believed that Russia needed to learn from the European experience in order to resolve the country's pressing domestic problems.[3] Russian foreign policy during the first year after the Soviet collapse had a set of priorities that made it introspective and pro-Western, and that accorded precious little concern to the rest of what had been the Soviet Union. In a sense, it was still the foreign policy of a republic that was trying to assert its own identity distinct from that of the Soviet Union.[4]

Russia's first foreign minister, Andrei Kozyrev, seemed to envision the future of the former Soviet Union along the lines of the European Union: voluntary integration to promote peace and prosperity would replace the imposed ideological base, and a modern and prosperous Russia would form the natural attraction of this new union, around which former satellites would willingly coalesce.[5] But Russia did not develop into the prosperous and modern vision of its leaders in the early 1990s, instead turning into an increasingly troubled, unstable, and corrupt oligarchy in which the state was extremely weakly institutionalized.[6] Russia therefore failed to make itself an attractive partner to the other former Soviet republics, which in turn gradually gave priority to developing their foreign relations with other powers. Russia's leaders consequently concluded that a coercive approach would be necessary.

Minister Kozyrev's liberal vision, which in truth had never gone undisputed, was soon overridden by the conservative forces that dominated the parliament, the military, and the powerful security establishment—actually, most state institutions other than the Russian (as opposed to Soviet) Ministry of Foreign Affairs. Fond hopes for an EU-style integration of the former Soviet space gave way to a neo-imperial perspective.[7] These institutionally based conservatives believed that the success of Russia's transition depended upon the restoration of Russia's role in the world. The initial emphasis on relations with the West and the ensuing neglect of the Middle East, Asia, and especially the rest of the former Soviet Union were rejected as concessions to the United States, Europe, and their allies.[8] The neo-imperialists also rejected the idea that international politics had fundamentally changed, arguing instead that geopolitics as a defining factor of international relations was very much alive. Proponents of this particular view-point included Yevgeny Primakov, head of the security services, who subsequently served as Russian foreign minister and as prime minister.

Policies began to shift as early as 1992, as Russia began to rebuild ties to the Middle Eastern countries, not least Iran.[9] In November 1993, a new military doctrine was promulgated that asserted "a sphere of influence that coincides with the one maintained by the USSR."[10] This intention was made clear by provisions that called for the Russian military to deploy troops on the territories of member states of the Commonwealth of Independent States (CIS), "either together with units of another state or as exclusively Russian formations at their own separate bases."[11] In addition, ensuring the continued CIS membership of surrounding states was made a policy priority, along with insistence on having their "external" borders controlled by Russian border troops—in the case of the states of the South Caucasus, their borders with Iran and Turkey, not with each other or with Russia.[12] These policies enjoyed some success, though Russia's military defeat in 1996 at the hands of separatists in Chechnya, created a situation in which the states of the South Caucasus could slip gradually from Russian control.

With Vladimir Putin's accession to the presidency in 1999, the process of rebuilding Russia's place in the world, beginning in the post-Soviet space, gained new traction. More than anything else, President Putin sought to make Russia a strong and functioning state. Marking a sharp contrast with the chaos of the Yeltsin era, he strived to bring the state hierarchy, the unruly regions, and the oligarchs of the economy under control under what he termed a "vertical of power."[13] By a methodical process and aided by windfall profits from oil and gas exports, he succeeded in rebuilding the state and restoring its primacy over society, without necessarily solving many of Russia's underlying problems. The rebuilding of the state took place at the cost of political freedoms and democracy: Russia slipped ever more into autocracy, but with the added benefits of large oil incomes and a close symbiosis between the state and the large energy conglomerates among which Gazprom, Transneft, and RAO-UES were the most prominent.[14] Energy became one of Moscow's most called-upon tools in the restoration of its great-power status, with control over the westward export of Caspian Sea energy resources an important component.

With the "color revolutions" in Georgia (2003) and Ukraine (2004), Russia's policies toward its neighbors grew considerably more aggressive. Indeed, in addition to geopolitical competition, an ideological element entered Eurasian politics. Moscow now fervently sought to prevent the spread of democratically minded governments on its borders, viewing them as a threat not only to Russia's influence but to its own system of government. As political scientist Thomas Ambrosio has observed, Moscow formulated a five-prong strategy to counteract the spread of democracy in its neighborhood: "insulate, redefine, bolster, subvert, and coordinate."[15] "Insulate" characterizes the domestic aspect, the Kremlin's attempt to ensure the impossibility of a democratic upheaval at home through a variety of mainly repressive means. "Redefine" refers to Russia's rhetorical attempts to defend its own system, including inventing terminology such as "sovereign democracy" and questioning the democratic credentials of the West itself. "Bolster" describes the Kremlin's attempts to support authoritarian tendencies in neighboring countries, while "subvert" encapsulates the Kremlin's systematic attempts to undermine democracy and security, particularly in Georgia and Ukraine. Finally, "coordinate" sums up the Kremlin's efforts to synchronize its policies with those of other nondemocratic states, such as Iran and China, to balance the West's support for democracy.

The Russian efforts to undermine the security and statehood of democratizing countries in the region, to bolster authoritarian regimes, and to continue to dominate energy transport routes all should be seen as interconnected, and related to the priority Russia gives to preventing the emergence on its western flanks of democratic and sovereign states that are willing to integrate with the rest of Europe.

Moscow and the Caucasus in the 1990s: Russian Policy in Action

In the late 1980s, the Caucasus—both North and South—began slipping out of Moscow's control.[16] Nationalist forces had come to dominate politics in both Armenia and Georgia. This development had few external implications, but nationalist agitation was also mounting in Azerbaijan, which had special importance to Moscow as the largest of the Caucasian republics and the only one with kinship ties to external powers such as Turkey and Iran. Brutal Soviet crackdowns in Tbilisi on April 9, 1989, and in Baku on January 20, 1990, only served to bolster anti-Soviet and nationalist feeling among the populations of Georgia and Azerbaijan.

Dissolution and Independence, then the Reconquista

The independence of the South Caucasian states meant an imminent and very tangible loss of Moscow's control over the Caucasus.[17] Furthermore, a fourth republic, north of the Caucasus Mountains, had declared independence in the same period: under the leadership of former air force general Jokhar Dudayev, Chechnya aspired to membership in the community of independent nations, thereby seceding not only from the Soviet Union but also from the Russian Federation. In spite of this direct challenge to Russian statehood, Moscow initially ignored Chechnya for almost three years, focusing its energy instead on reasserting control over the South Caucasus. This response exactly paralleled Russian priorities in the nineteenth century: Russia achieved control of the South Caucasus through wars with Iran and Turkey in 1812 to 1813 and from 1827 to 1828, but the struggle continued in the North Caucasus for more than three decades, rebellions there not being subdued completely until 1864.

Russia's modern-day *reconquista* of the South Caucasus began almost immediately after the dissolution of the Soviet Union. Moscow was heavily involved in the conflict over the separatist province of South Ossetia, threatening military action against Georgia on more than one occasion, and played an important role in all conflicts of the region, displaying its ability—and readiness—to provide arms to various fighting factions. In practice, Moscow first succeeded in asserting control over Armenia. This was logical, given Yerevan's rapidly developing involvement in warfare on the territory of Azerbaijan. Turkey's increasingly pro-Azerbaijani stance and economic embargo on Armenia compelled Yerevan to accept any support that might come its way, and Russia was more than forthcoming. The de facto price of a military agreement in May 1992 was Yerevan's submission to Moscow's three principal demands: CIS membership, the stationing of Russian troops on the country's external borders, and the installation of Russian military bases inside Armenian territory. (These requirements would become an important part of Russia's "sphere of influence" military doctrine, issued the following year.

Russian policy then turned to Georgia. In July 1992, Moscow put in force a cease-fire agreement between Georgia and South Ossetia that led to South Ossetia's de facto independence and the interposition of Russian troops on the administrative border separating parts of the region from the rest of Georgia. Russia had repeatedly offered Georgia military assistance in return for its acquiescence to Russia's three demands, but Georgian leader Eduard Shevardnadze nevertheless refused.[18]

As the guns went silent in South Ossetia, turmoil began in Georgia's other autonomous republic, Abkhazia. Its leaders displayed a self-confident attitude, asserting that Abkhazia was "strong enough to fight Georgia"—a peculiar claim, given the Abkhazians' overwhelming numerical inferiority:

they numbered only about 100,000, whereas the Georgians totaled more than four million.[19] When Abkhazia declared independence, in July 1992, undisciplined Georgian paramilitary forces invaded the breakaway republic, looting and burning as they went. But in October, Georgian forces came up against a well-armed Abkhazian counteroffensive, supported by North Caucasian volunteers, heavy artillery, and air support. The origin of these weapons was obviously Russian. Later in the war, Russia's direct involvement was blatantly exposed when an unmarked fighter aircraft was shot down, whose pilot turned out to be a Russian air force officer in full uniform.[20] By October 1993 Georgian forces had been evicted from Abkhazia, and more than 200,000 ethnic Georgian civilians had fled its territory. During the entire conflict, Moscow offered Georgia military support should it consent to the three demands already so familiar to Armenia. As he had in the case of South Ossetia, Shevardnadze at first demurred, but a large-scale mutiny in the Georgian military following the loss of Abkhazia that threatened the total disintegration of the Georgian state prompted the president to accept Russia's demands. Russian forces then swiftly moved in, crushing the mutiny as quickly as it had emerged. Russia then took control of Georgia's Turkish border, established four military bases in strategic locations around Georgia, and was granted a *droit de regard* over the Georgian security, defense, and interior ministries. But crucially, Tbilisi's surrender to Moscow did not lead to any Russian support for the resolution of the conflicts in Abkhazia and South Ossetia. Only with the coming to power of Mikheil Saakashvili in 2004 would Georgia begin to extricate itself from Moscow's embrace.

The Push for Azerbaijan and the Chechen War

With Georgia subdued, the focus of events moved to Azerbaijan in mid-1993. As described in chapter 4 of the present volume, military commander Surat Huseynov had withdrawn his troops from the front in the war with Armenia, a move that resulted in the Azerbaijani loss of Kelbajar Province, and retreated to his native Gandja, barracking near the Russian 104th Airborne Regiment's base. The Azerbaijani Popular Front government had managed in 1993 to secure a Russian agreement to close the Gandja base by the end of the year, despite Russian assurances that if the 104th were granted permission to maintain a long-term presence, it could be very useful to Azerbaijan in the war with Armenia.

As is described in chapter 4, the 104th Airborne Regiment suddenly departed Azerbaijan in late May 1993, leaving the better part of its armaments to Huseynov, whose ensuing rebellion led to the collapse of the Popular Front government and the loss of four provinces to the east and south of Mountainous Karabakh, and almost gave Huseynov power in Baku. Only the arrival of Heydar Aliyev prevented this. Aliyev led Azerbaijan into the CIS, and promised substantive discussions on basing rights and border troops, but demanded that the talks wait until the war in Karabakh ended. Aliyev was thereby able to obtain the release of armaments from Soviet military depots, and could now thwart the Armenian offensive and even regain some lost ground before the May 1994 cease-fire agreement was concluded.

Heydar Aliyev proved to be a master negotiator, never allowing Russia to introduce border troops or military bases into Azerbaijan. Instead, he focused on developing the oil resources of the Caspian Sea, and accelerated negotiations with foreign, mainly American, oil companies. Thus, unlike Armenia and Georgia, Azerbaijan began slipping away even before Moscow managed to get a grip on it. The development of oil resources with American and other Western companies would not only bring Azerbaijan economic benefits, but would also increase Western interest in the country. Russia remained adamantly opposed to Azerbaijan's unilateral exploitation of Caspian oil resources; only days after the signing of the "contract of the century" (see chapter 4), Huseynov attempted another coup, this time to unseat Aliyev. When it failed, Huseynov fled Azerbaijan, initially seeking sanctuary in the Qabala radar station north of Baku, the sole remaining Russian facility in the country. Moscow's efforts to take control of Azerbaijan, the most important state in the Caucasus, had failed.

Moscow's chief remaining tool for controlling Azerbaijan was the export route for Azerbaijani oil resources. The only operational pipeline able to carry Azerbaijani oil to world markets until 1999 ran from Baku to Novorossiysk, a Russian port on the Black Sea. In trying to identify the best transport route for the Azerbaijani oil, oil companies found themselves inclined to prefer the existing Russian route (see chapter 9), which could be upgraded at a reasonable cost to carry the anticipated amounts of oil. Unfortunately, the Baku-Novorossiysk route passed through Chechnya, where Jokhar Dudayev was presiding over a self-proclaimed independent state that the oil companies would hardly entrust their wealth to. Whereas Moscow would have preferred to establish control over the South Caucasus before dealing with the problems in the North—just as in the previous century—Russian control over Azerbaijan had now become directly related to control of Chechnya. Numerous other factors undoubtedly intervened, but a major reason for the timing and the imperative to invade Chechnya in late 1994 was Azerbaijan's oil.

The Slipping Away of the Caucasus, 1996–99

If Russia had succeeded in subduing Chechnya, it is fairly likely that it would also have succeeded in remaining the dominant power in the South Caucasus. However, that did not happen. After months of fighting that revealed the incompetence and brutality of the Russian armed forces, Chechen rebels managed to regain control of the breakaway republic's capital, Grozny, in August 1996. This was perhaps the most important development in the Caucasus since the dissolution of the Soviet Union.

The Chechen victory and the humiliation of the Russian military dramatically changed the entire regional situation. Azerbaijan intensified its pro-Western orientation, and investments in its oil industry grew at a rapid clip, in spite of the 1998 economic crisis that led to a plunge in oil prices. Azerbaijan was joined by Georgia, which, despite the presence of Russian bases and border guards on its territory, developed an equally strong (if not stronger) pro-Western attitude in adamant opposition to Russian imperialism. In Central Asia, Uzbekistan joined the chorus, with President Islam Karimov denouncing, perhaps more harshly than anyone, the imperial policies of the Kremlin. Western attention grew commensurately. The Clinton administration declared its strong interest in the region by early 1997, and the European Union pledged to sponsor the Transport Corridor Europe-Caucasus-Asia (TRACECA) program, most forthrightly at a 1998 gathering in Baku fittingly titled the "International Conference on the Restoration of the Historic Silk Route." After the miscalculations of the early 1990s, Turkey now reengaged with the Caucasian states, supporting the restructuring of the Azerbaijani military and rapidly developing its ties to Georgia to the level of a strategic partnership.

By 1998 Georgia and Azerbaijan were speaking openly of the possibility of membership in the North Atlantic Treaty Organization, Azerbaijan even going so far as to float the idea of NATO military bases on its territory.[21] Meanwhile, Russia desperately hung on to its regional anchor, Armenia, for instance delivering complimentary arms shipments worth more than US$1 billion to the country in the late 1990s.[22] But by 1999, even Armenia had begun to question its heavy dependence on Russia, and Armenian leaders became frequent visitors to Western capitals. Imminent headway in negotiations over Karabakh threatened to deprive Russia of its Caucasian anchor, as peace with Azerbaijan would also in all likelihood lead to the partial normalization of Turkish-Armenian relations, and thereby dramatically reduce Armenia's dependence on Moscow.

1999: Putin Turns the Tide

By 1999, Moscow's deteriorating position in the region was obvious. To Russian observers, its roots must have been equally easy to identify: the defeat in Chechnya. The war in Chechnya had illustrated Russia's slippage from superpower status to that of a second-rate power. Chechnya's success had emboldened anti-Russian and pro-Western forces in the South Caucasus and Central Asia. It had extinguished the prospects of the Baku-Novorossiysk pipeline and made the Baku-Tbilisi-Ceyhan (BTC) pipeline increasingly feasible, in spite of its exorbitant cost. In fact, it was the defeat in Chechnya that prevented Moscow from projecting its influence in the South Caucasus while other powers increasingly did so. Only by addressing the problem at its roots, obliterating the source of instability and restoring firm control over the North Caucasus, could Russia reclaim its lost ground in the South. The logic of the nineteenth century was now stood on its head: Moscow needed to restore control in Chechnya in order not to lose the South Caucasus.

Initially, the policy seemed to pay off. The Russian military had learned from its past mistakes, and with Russian advances in Chechnya, the rhetoric emanating from Tbilisi, Baku, and Tashkent softened dramatically. Everyone understood that if Chechnya succumbed to Russian arms, Moscow's *reconquista* would not stop there. President Putin also showed that his diplomatic skills were superior to his predecessor's: he managed to recast the brutality in Chechnya and the restoration of authoritarian rule in Russia in ways that attracted, or at least did not diminish, the support of Western governments. For instance, after 9/11, Putin adroitly placed the Chechen issue in the context of the global war on terrorism, thereby for all practical purposes dissipating American criticism.[23]

Putin also knew how to time his policies with America's electoral cycles. It is hardly a coincidence that Moscow's first bout of arm-twisting on Georgia, in early 2001, featuring the cutting of energy supplies and the introduction of a discriminatory visa regime, occurred precisely when world attention was concentrated on the hung presidential election in the United States. (In 2008 Putin would capitalize on the lame duck status of President George W. Bush by invading Georgia.)

Some believe that a newly deft Russian touch was also on display in Armenia in the fall of 1999, when the killing of Prime Minister Vazgen

348 AZERBAIJAN SINCE INDEPENDENCE

Sarkissian and seven other people inside the Armenian Parliament brought a halt to the peace process between Armenia and Azerbaijan and made Robert Kocharyan the sole power broker in Armenian politics. As discussed in chapter 6 of this volume, no evidence of Russian involvement has been found, yet the suspicion on the part of regional observers of Russian involvement was only heightened by revelations to that effect by former Russian intelligence officer Aleksandr Litvinenko, who was himself murdered by the Russian intelligence services in London in 2006 (see chapter 7).

Following its setback in Chechnya, Moscow embarked on a new offensive in the South Caucasus, focusing especially on Georgia. There were vociferous Russian allegations that both Azerbaijan and Georgia supported Chechen separatists, including claims that a thousand Taliban fighters had crossed Azerbaijani and Georgian territory to get to Chechnya. Nothing to corroborate this charge was ever produced, but Moscow followed up its allegations by gradually increasing its pressure on Georgia, with a mix of economic and subversive levers that were to get ever harsher, especially following the 2003 Rose Revolution. In 2006, for example, Russian energy supplies to Georgia were cut just at the time of the Russian-Ukrainian energy crisis after mysterious explosions on Russian territory destroyed the pipelines and power lines carrying gas and electricity to Georgia. Even more serious was the increasingly unabashed Russian support for Abkhazia and South Ossetia. Moscow began to extend Russian citizenship illegally to the residents of the two separatist regions, then started claiming a right to defend the interests of Russian citizens abroad, a theme that would be the main pretext for Russia's invasion in 2008. Moscow also staffed the governments in Abkhazia and South Ossetia with active-duty Russian security service personnel.

Russian foreign policy developed into an increasingly assertive campaign to reassert control over the entire CIS. A key element was the gradual tightening of economic levers, especially energy, as a tool of Russian policy. In tandem with Gazprom for natural gas and RAO-UES for electricity, Moscow eventually developed a near monopoly on the transport and export of natural gas in the former Soviet Union. This entailed using political pressure to acquire long-term deals to buy Central Asian producers' gas, which Russia would then use to free up export capacity for gas sold to Europe. As for electricity, RAO-UES managed to acquire control over production as well as distribution of electricity in most CIS countries, often using debt-for-asset swaps, in which state debts to Russia would be written off in exchange for controlling stakes in strategic enterprises, including, for example, Armenia's nuclear power plant.[24]

Moscow's thirst for hegemony was exacerbated by the revolutions in Georgia and Ukraine, which brought pro-Western forces to power, alarmed the Russian leadership into thinking that it was rapidly losing influence, and introduced an ideological element into the geopolitics of Eurasia—one that Russia sought to manipulate by offering to protect the regime security of concerned authoritarian leaders faced with ever stronger Western calls for democracy. By 2005, Russia had helped convince Uzbekistan's leadership to close a U.S. base in that country at Kharshi-Khanabad.[25] In Moldova, Russia continued to support the Transnistrian separatist region, which remained outside Moldovan control, while exerting pressure on Ukraine to resist strong Western encouragement to impose customs controls on its border with Transnistria.[26]

The evolution of Russian policy in the former Soviet space, then, has been relatively linear. Putin's Russia has moved decidedly in a nationalistic and neo-imperialist direction, and sought to prevent Western encroachment in what it views as its backyard. In the Baltic states and Ukraine, not to mention Georgia and Moldova, Russia has used unconventional methods to safeguard its interests and prevent the slippage of these countries into what Moscow views as a Western sphere of influence. Moscow has blatantly interfered in the internal affairs of these countries, taking advantage of their economic dependence on Russia and manipulating territorial conflicts to undermine their stability, development, and freedom to formulate policy. The purpose of the Russian strategy seems obvious: to maintain the dependence of the CIS countries on Russia, and thus make Russia the primary and, ideally, sole arbiter of the international politics of Eurasia. In 2008, the evolution of Russian foreign policy reached a logical conclusion as tensions with Georgia boiled over, and Moscow launched a well-planned invasion of the country that led to the Russian occupation of Abkhazia and South Ossetia.

Azerbaijan and Russia: A Tense Working Relationship

In view of the clear tendencies observable in Russia's relationship with the countries of the former Soviet space, Azerbaijan stands out as an exception. Azerbaijan does not have Russian military installations on its soil, and is not a member of the Russian-sponsored Collective Security Treaty Organization, having withdrawn from what was then the CIS's Collective Security Treaty in 1999. Baku has not allowed Russia to monopolize its energy assets, and maintains an independent foreign policy line. In spite of this, Azerbaijan and Russia have since 1999 experienced a great improvement in relations, which runs counter to the experience of other independently minded states such as Georgia, Moldova, and Ukraine. Indeed, Azerbaijan stands out as one of the few CIS countries that managed to have mainly cordial relations with Russia without acquiescing in Russian domination of their economy, politics, and foreign policy. The contrast with Georgia could not be starker, given the price that Tbilisi has paid for its vigorously independent foreign policy. Indeed, as one observer put it during Vladimir Putin's 2006 visit to Baku,

> [Russia's policy] appears somewhat contradictory. Azerbaijan has been at least as pro-Western as Georgia in the last decade and has certainly done more than Georgia to break Moscow's geostrategic grip on the region. The Baku-Tbilisi-Ceyhan oil pipeline, built with U.S. backing and soon to be followed by the Baku-Tbilisi-Erzurum gas pipeline, has vastly increased the economic independence of both Azerbaijan and Georgia.[27]

In fact, Vladimir Putin's arrival to power provided the impetus for an improvement of relations with Azerbaijan. This development, while seemingly puzzling, actually has several reasons behind it. To begin with, the improvement in the bilateral relationship stemmed from the personal rapport Putin struck up with Heydar Aliyev. The two leaders seemed to build on a common background in the security services. Indeed, both spoke about their past in the KGB with pride throughout their presidencies. Aliyev was a general in the KGB and Putin a colonel; in this sense, not only did Aliyev have a similar background but was Putin's superior and senior. In the personality-focused politics of the former Soviet Union, such issues matter very much, and Aliyev knew how to use this to his favor. Indeed, during Putin's first official visit to Azerbaijan, in January 2001, Aliyev had the Russian president visit the Martyr's Lane, dedicated to the victims of the Soviet Union's Black January crackdown of 1990.[28] Yet personal connections only matter so much, and Russian-Azerbaijani relations have continued to improve since the coming to power of Ilham Aliyev, which Putin strongly endorsed. Thus, several other factors of a more pragmatic nature seem also to have been at play.

Putin's ascension to the Russian presidency signaled that the Kremlin had adopted a policy based on realpolitik. Moscow identified Georgia as a weak state that could be influenced by a variety of factors. By contrast, Azerbaijan appeared to be the strongest state in the Caucasus, and hence one where pressure and overt efforts at manipulation would yield little, and even be counterproductive. Following the Karabakh war, few levers remained to the Russians in regard to Azerbaijan. Minorities could not easily be mobilized, as in Georgia, given Azerbaijan's rather harmonious relations with its (non-Armenian) minorities. Efforts in the early 1990s to stir minority discontent had yielded only limited results. The more inclusive national concept embraced by the Aliyev government meant that minorities, in spite of some problems, were not a major source of instability. In terms of governance, Aliyev in the mid-1990s did what Putin himself would do a few years later: rebuild the state and its coercive—as well as economic—functions. In contrast with Georgia, where many areas were outside state control, corruption was both rampant and anarchic, and government institutions dysfunctional, in Azerbaijan Aliyev managed to restore control over the national territory, give corruption a controllable and hierarchical structure, and sustain state institutions that were accountable to him, if not yet to the people. In sum, Azerbaijan was a functioning state, Georgia was not, and therefore the opportunities for mischief were considerably greater in Georgia. In addition, differing social structures mattered. A culture of individualism and resistance to authority made Georgia, ironically, more susceptible to outside interference than Azerbaijan, with its tradition of hierarchical leadership and respect for authority. Consequently, it was easier for Aliyev to maintain control of society, and to install a functioning and loyal intelligence service, something Eduard Shevardnadze never succeeded in doing. Finally, in economic terms Azerbaijan was also ahead of Georgia, as the structural reforms of the mid-1990s had paid off and investments in the oil industry had allowed the government to gradually improve living conditions and the infrastructural base. Following the Rose Revolution, the ideological element also amplified the differences. Mikheil Saakashvili's democratic credentials only strengthened Moscow's determination to undermine Georgia; Aliyev's semi-authoritarianism was more amenable to Putin's interests.

Similarities could be found in Moscow's relations with the Central Asian states, where Putin decided to use charm and carrots instead of sticks. With Uzbekistan in particular, Moscow embarked on a campaign to woo the country away from the United States, seeking to portray itself as a much more reliable partner, one that was in the region for the long haul, unlike the United States, whose focus was diverted following the Iraq war and did not recover. This policy eventually paid off, after a series of American mistakes and general lack of attention with regard to Uzbekistan.[29] Concerning Azerbaijan, Putin followed a similar line, trying to capitalize on the cold shoulder Ilham Aliyev had received in the West. Moscow thus assessed Georgia and Azerbaijan differently: Georgia was understood as the most vociferously anti-Russian country in the CIS, where there was no point seeking to persuade the leadership to ally with Moscow. Azerbaijan seemed a different matter entirely, especially given Baku's growing disenchantment with the West and, starting in 2008, with Turkey—a disenchantment Moscow sought to capitalize upon in both cases.

The differing foreign policy styles of Georgia and Azerbaijan were also a factor. Where Georgia pursued a frankly confrontational policy toward Russia, Azerbaijan's policy was light on theatrics but much more concentrated on action. This implied that from an emotional perspective, Georgian politicians continually irritated Russia by declarative statements and provocations. Azerbaijan's policies were often similar, but discrete, and therefore did not attract the ire of Moscow.

Another factor was the cultural relationship between Russia and the two Caucasian states. For Moscow, it was easier to countenance the independent line followed by Azerbaijan, a Muslim country with close links to Turkey and Iran. Georgia, on the other hand, being Orthodox Christian, was understood to be a state that should look up to Moscow. The feeling was not mutual, of course, but this led to a perception in Moscow that Georgia's independence and pro-Western stance were tantamount to treason, whereas Azerbaijan's situation was not so perceived.

Ilham Aliyev's focus on trade and economic issues also played a role, given the increasing importance of economic interests in Russian foreign policy. Indeed, Putin's February 2006 visit to Baku was interpreted as a shift in the focus of the bilateral relationship toward economic and trade issues.[30] As a result, relations with Russia have come to include several potential issues of economic interest to Azerbaijan. The project to build a "North-South Transport Corridor" connecting Europe and Russia to Iran and the Indian Ocean via Azerbaijan and the Caspian Sea is one of these. While the North-South Corridor is clearly a rival project to the proposed East-West axis connecting Central Asia to Europe via the South Caucasus, the Black Sea, and Turkey, it is not necessarily so for Baku.[31] Indeed, with Western interest in the East-West corridor waning, opportunities for North-South trade are increasingly welcomed by Baku: participation in the North-South Corridor would only enhance Azerbaijan's geostrategic position and help build its economy. In sum, Azerbaijan found that it could do business with Russia, and that the resultant deals did not always come with strings attached.

Indeed, Russia's embrace of Azerbaijan has been such that Ilham Aliyev visited Moscow more or less on a yearly basis from 2003 to 2010. Against this backdrop, what is significant is not that Azerbaijan's relations with Russia have improved, but how slight the tilt toward Russia has been in its foreign policy. Azerbaijan has kept its distance from Russian positions that have been in conflict with those of the West, even at times of relentless pressure from Moscow. The most significant instance occurred during the Orange Revolution, when Putin vigorously supported the candidacy of incumbent prime minister Viktor Yanukovich, then urged all CIS governments to congratulate Yanukovich on his fraudulent victory in order to quickly consolidate some international legitimacy for Putin's preferred candidate. Several leaders, including Armenian president Kocharyan, obliged. In spite of strong Russian pressure on Baku,[32] Ilham Aliyev refused, implicitly following the European and American line that the elections were illegitimate.[33] Four years later, Ilham Aliyev was confronted with an even more acute crisis in his immediate vicinity: Russia's invasion of Georgia. On this occasion, Aliyev had the fortune of finding himself attending the 2008 Olympic Games in Beijing. He did not return prematurely to Baku; nor did he make any statements on the war. His foreign minister, Elmar Mamedyarov, pointedly did not officially cancel his vacation. When the presidents of Poland, Ukraine, Estonia, Latvia, and Lithuania appeared in Tbilisi on August 12, standing on the steps of the Georgian Parliament in a show of support of Georgia and defiance of Russia, Aliyev was not present. This suggested that in the years between the Ukrainian crisis and the Georgian war, Baku's calculus had changed. Baku did not see the West's partnership as serious enough to risk alienating Moscow; the West's failure to prevent the war, and its weak response to it, certainly strengthened the imperative toward caution on the part of Azerbaijani decision makers. Nevertheless, that did not mean Azerbaijan abandoned its close neighbor and partner, Georgia. The same five presidents who found their way to the Georgian capital in the middle of a war did so by landing in Gandja, site of the closest airport to the Georgian capital, whose own airport was not operational. This clearly would not have happened without presidential approval.

Russia and Karabakh

A central issue in Azerbaijan's relationship with Russia is Moscow's role in the Karabakh conflict. Indeed, for most of the 1990s international experts as well as Azerbaijani representatives viewed Russia as perhaps the single greatest impediment to a resolution of the conflict—while acknowledging Russia's centrality to any solution. Azerbaijani representatives even lamented Russia's position as cochair of the Minsk Group, perhaps understanding the necessity of bringing in Russia but simultaneously pointing out the absurdity of a mediator that was also in a military alliance with one of the parties to the conflict.[34] Indeed, as one Azerbaijani observer put it,

> Russia has done everything possible to convince Azerbaijan that peace in Karabakh will come from the maternal arms of Moscow—and all Azerbaijan has to do is return to Russia for protection.... Baku would first have to accept that only Russia could guarantee the peace process. Many believe it is that attitude that has contributed to what they see as the Armenians' rigid position.[35]

The improvement of Russian-Azerbaijani relations after 1999 brought with it a seemingly new approach to the conflict in Russian foreign policy. Indeed, Western diplomats involved in the Minsk Group process noted a more constructive attitude on the part of the Russian leadership.[36] This was one factor that led the U.S. government to invest political capital in the failed Key West negotiations of 2001 (see chapter 7). Again in 2006 and in 2009, it was a sense that Russia was not actively impeding the negotiations that led to the investment of American and French political capital in the talks. Ahead of the inconclusive talks at Rambouillet in France in 2006 (see chapter 7), Russia's new approach seemed to conform well with the Western analyses of Russia's best interests: with trouble in the North Caucasus spreading out of Chechnya, Moscow ought to support the resolution of problems in the South Caucasus in order to avoid an unstable and explosive situation next door. Likewise in 2009, the West assumed that Moscow wanted to improve its international image, and thus concluded that increased support for a resolution to the Karabakh conflict would fulfill that purpose.[37]

Western diplomats, then, took Moscow's protestations of constructive engagement at face value. And they were right to do so, since the new Russian approach provided perhaps the best chance for an improvement of the situation. Yet there was, in truth, little reason to see why Russia's real ambitions would have changed. To begin with, Moscow's constructiveness on Karabakh did not fit with the general tendency of Russian policy in Russia's self-proclaimed "near abroad," nor with the underlying principles of that policy. Indeed, Moscow's rhetoric and all of its policies vis-à-vis Georgia, Moldova, Ukraine, and Central Asia appeared to serve the purpose of restoring Russia's primacy in the post-Soviet space and ensuring that no other power, particularly the United States, could challenge Russian influence in the area. This led Russia to work ever more relentlessly to undermine Georgian stability and prevent a resolution of Georgia's territorial conflicts, all as a direct consequence of Tbilisi's pro-Western policies. In this context, a resolution of the Karabakh conflict that involved a strong international component would be severely detrimental to that interest. Indeed, if Moscow went to war in Georgia to sustain its sphere of influence, would not a peace deal in Karabakh counter that very purpose? A peace deal would free Armenia of much of its dependence on Russia, and would facilitate what Moscow did not want: growing Western—and possibly Turkish—influence in the region.

But by 2009 the regional calculus had shifted somewhat, thanks in great part to Moscow's own actions in the region. The war in Georgia sent shock waves throughout Europe, whose implications would take several years to clarify. Most immediately, the war energized Turkish regional policy, which had been dormant for several years, and added impetus to the emerging Turkish-Armenian rapprochement. Moscow had initially been wary of this development, given that warmer relations between Ankara and Yerevan had the potential to add options to Armenia's foreign policy. But gradually, the Russian leadership came to endorse it, for several reasons. First, doing so enabled Moscow to portray itself as a constructive force in the region following the war in Georgia. Second, the war had led to logistical problems for Moscow, which could not apply the full force of economic coercion against Georgia without also hurting Armenia. As such, a Turkish-Armenian rapprochement would ease Armenia's situation and enable Moscow to squeeze Georgia without hurting its ally. (That said, by early 2010 Turkish officials complained of feeling cheated as Moscow failed to live up to promises to support Turkey's demand that progress in Karabakh talks should be linked to the Turkish-Armenian normalization process[38]) Of much greater consequence, indeed, was that Russian leaders had observed the rapid deterioration of Turkish-Azerbaijani relations that the diplomatic honeymoon between Ankara and Yerevan had precipitated. From a geopolitical perspective, that was at least as significant a development as the improvement of Turkish-Armenian relations, and one that Moscow believed it could capitalize upon. Hence, for the first time in two decades, Azerbaijan's reorientation from a pro-Western policy to a more Russian-aligned one seemed a real possibility, at least from Moscow's perspective.

From all these developments emerges the crucial question: under which circumstances would Russia support and help implement a peace deal between Armenia and Azerbaijan? Clearly, the answer is that Russia would support peace in Karabakh only if it were to be the sole, or at least dominant, arbiter of such a deal—that is, if it could be assured that Armenia and Azerbaijan would not use the newly found peace to escape Russia's orbit and consolidate their integration into Euro-Atlantic institutions, especially NATO. From Azerbaijan's perspective, therefore, nothing has changed in twenty years: the price of a beneficial settlement of the Karabakh conflict under Moscow's leadership remains no less than the independence of Azerbaijan. Until the trust between Baku and Moscow reaches entirely different levels, Azerbaijan is unlikely to jeopardize its independence as part of such a deal.

Energy Games and the Return of Russia

The end of the first decade of the twenty-first century brought an altered regional picture in terms of the geopolitics of energy. From an unswerving focus on oil in the 1990s, both producer and consumer states shifted their attention in the 2000s to natural gas. From Azerbaijan's perspective, this meant mainly the export of the output from the second phase of development of the Shah-Deniz deposit. Baku's overarching priority in this regard had been to export its natural gas in the same direction as its oil, to the West. But the South Caucasus pipeline brought Azerbaijani gas only as far as Erzurum, in eastern Turkey. For the small quantities produced during Shah-Deniz 1, the first phase of the deposit's development, that was not a problem. But using Erzurum as the pipeline terminus would be a totally inadequate arrangement for Shah-Deniz 2, which on its own would yield up to 15 billion cubic meters (bcm) per year of natural gas.[39] Therefore, further infrastructural development would be needed for the production of gas to pick up; indeed, until infrastructure was put in place, Azerbaijan would not be able to begin developing the deep-sea gas resources of the Azeri-Chirag-Guneshli oil field. In the short term, Baku worked with Turkish officials to build a low-capacity link of about 4 bcm eventual annual capacity called the Turkey-Greece-Italy interconnector, inaugurated in 2007, which was to be expanded to carry up to 8 bcm by 2012.

Given the inadequacy of what were no more than provisional arrangements (especially in light of Azerbaijan's strategic goal of becoming a corridor for the movement of eastern Caspian Sea gas to Europe), the main focus for the long run was on the Nabucco pipeline, an EU-supported project that would connect eastern Turkey to the Austrian gas hub at Baumgarten, with an annual capacity of 31 bcm. But, as shown in chapter

15 of the present volume, the European Union and the United States failed to translate their nominal support for the Nabucco project into concrete action, while Turkey failed to offer Azerbaijan a transparent and commercial transit agreement. As a result, by 2009 the lack of progress on the Nabucco pipeline project had forced Azerbaijan and its partner companies—BP and Statoil—to delay the development of Shah-Deniz 2.

Russia, which had done more than any other party to sow doubts about the feasibility of the Nabucco project, was now well placed to move in and offer Azerbaijan an alternative. Gazprom's chief executive officer, Alexei Miller, traveled to Azerbaijan repeatedly in 2008 and 2009, offering to buy Azerbaijan's entire gas production at European netback prices, minus the cost of transportation. (The netback price is the price a commodity could receive in its refined, marketable form or forms, minus processing costs.) At a time when Turkey was seeking a continuation of a deal that allowed it to buy Azerbaijani gas at US\$120 per thousand cubic meters (a price that was not only less than half of what it was paying for Russian gas, but less than half of what Azerbaijan would receive from Russia), Miller's proposal became increasingly appealing to Azerbaijani decision makers even before the deterioration of Turkish-Azerbaijani relations in 2009.

By early 2010, Baku had agreed to reverse the gas pipeline connecting Azerbaijan to Russia, thus laying the groundwork for Azerbaijani gas exports to Russia. Nevertheless, Baku agreed only to sell Russia 0.5 bcm per year (and eventually up to 1 bcm) of the State Oil Company's own gas, not gas from Shah-Deniz. Even as Azerbaijani frustration with Turkey and the West reached new heights, the leadership in Baku remained unwilling to fall into the Russian "trap." This wariness is perhaps best illustrated by the argument made by high-level officials in late 2009 that Azerbaijan could sell its gas to Iran or even China.[40] Indeed, Azerbaijani president Aliyev told Western oil company officials in 2010 that the gas would either be sold to the West or kept in the ground.[41]

Even though Azerbaijan's leadership grew increasingly alienated from Turkey and the West during 2008–10, Moscow's efforts to seize the opportunity to "flip" a Western ally (as it had done with Uzbekistan in 2006) bore little fruit. Russia's flirtations on both the Karabakh issue and energy exports notwithstanding, there was no major shift on Baku's part. The two leading tenets of Azerbaijani foreign policy remained firmly in place: first, maintain a strong focus on the country's national interests; and second (here the contrast with Uzbekistan was particularly sharp), always proceed with caution and avoid rash action.

Conclusions: Russia's Reluctant Adaptation to Reality

As the largest and most powerful country in Azerbaijan's vicinity, Russia will remain indefinitely at the forefront of Baku's foreign policy considerations. Russia's looming presence in the Caucasus also means that Azerbaijan will continue to be strongly affected by the state of Russia's relations with the West. If Russia and the West are on good terms, this facilitates Azerbaijan's efforts to pursue a policy of integration with the West while maintaining good relations with its giant neighbor. But trouble in Russia's relations with the West creates the prospect of a squeeze on Azerbaijan and the crimping of its ability to formulate its own foreign policy. Hence, when the Putin administration sought to attract Azerbaijan instead of pressuring it, in the course of Russia's attempts to restore its influence in the Caucasus, this tactic was to a great extent related to the difficulties in Azerbaijan's relations with the West.

The core of the problem, of course, is that Russia has not fundamentally consented to the loss of empire. Since 1991, Russian regional policies have consisted of what Dmitri Trenin calls a "reluctant adaptation to the reality" of the independence of the former Soviet Union's republics and Russia's gradual loss of influence in the region. This reluctance has taken rather serious forms, as illustrated by Russia's meddling in internal conflicts, interference in the domestic affairs of the regional states, and use of economic leverage to pressure other states to follow its foreign policy priorities. Russia's neo-imperial tendency is clearly understood in Baku, but its implications are less obvious. Indeed, even as Azerbaijan seeks to escape Russian domination and consolidate its true independence, Georgia's travails must be a chilling reminder of the cost of confronting Russia. All the same, Azerbaijani leaders understand that Russian pressure on Georgia is only part of a larger agenda of undermining the independence of all states in the region, Azerbaijan included.

Azerbaijan will likely continue to walk a fine line, seeking to maximize its independence while avoiding unnecessary confrontations with Russia. In doing so, Azerbaijan is dependent on the policies of other major powers to which it looks for alliance and support. Among these, Turkey and the United States are inescapably the most prominent—the fitfulness of relations between the government in Baku and its counterparts in Ankara and Washington notwithstanding.

14

Turkey, Best Neighbor or Big Brother?

When Azerbaijan began developing its foreign relations in the 1990s, the nationalism characteristic of a newly independent state pulled it away from its erstwhile colonial overlord, Russia. The secular nature of Azerbaijani nationalism and the dominance of language in conceptualizing the nation meant that independence also did not lead to particularly pro-Iranian feelings. Instead, it was a feeling of kinship with Turkey that most strongly engaged Azerbaijani intellectuals and government officials. This feeling that there was a special tie with Turkey proved especially important in the first decade of independence, when Azerbaijan was cultivating a sense of itself as a state and figuring out its place in the world. However, since the second decade of Azerbaijan's independence, both Turkey and Azerbaijan have changed. Turkey came under the rule of an Islamic conservative party that had little enthusiasm for Turkic brotherhood, while Azerbaijan gained increasing self-confidence as its independence consolidated and its economy boomed. This naturally affected the relationship between the two countries, once famously aphorized by Heydar Aliyev, in a 1995 address to the Turkish parliament, as "one nation, two states." Like any pair of siblings, Baku and Ankara have found that their pragmatic interests do not always comport with the solidarity that might be expected in such a close relationship, notably in key areas such as energy politics and relations with Armenia. The relationship therefore has been continuously redefined, with many of the changes driven by the competing appeals of pragmatism and emotion.

A Sense of Brotherhood Awakens

The linguistic proximity of Turkey and Azerbaijan, whose national tongues are essentially dialects of a single Western Turkic language, made Baku uniquely receptive to societal, economic, and political links with Turkey. As Azerbaijanis could understand Turkish with relative ease, the legacy of seven decades of Soviet-imposed isolation was relatively easy to overcome. Wealthier Azerbaijanis found it a simple matter to travel to Turkey and interact with the population, while ordinary Azerbaijanis, even poor villagers, soon got hooked up to Turkish television networks, and became intimate with Turkey's celebrity gossip, soap operas, and soccer league. Turkish businesspeople were singularly well positioned to take advantage of Azerbaijan's opening to the world. They knew the workings of the market economy and were accustomed to operating in environments riddled with corruption and complicated regulations; and of course, they also spoke the language. It therefore came naturally to many large international firms to use their Istanbul offices as stepping-stones to the establishment of operations in Azerbaijan, as well as the rest of the Caucasus region.

As the 1990s progressed, Turkish businesspeople swarmed into Baku, taking full advantage of this unique opportunity. With truckers from Turkey becoming an increasingly common sight on Azerbaijan's highways, the Turkish commercial presence was not limited to the capital city. Azerbaijanis' conversancy with Turkey's language and popular culture also grew more and more widespread. Turkey was playing an exceptionally important role in the development of contemporary Azerbaijan, and seemed likely to continue to do so regardless of how the political winds blew.

Turkey's societal model was also one that appealed not only to most Azerbaijani leaders but to the Azerbaijani people in general. The Turkey created by Mustafa Kemal Atatürk was neither the Soviet Union nor Iran: it was staunchly secular, seeking to keep religion out of politics and to reduce its influence on the public sphere. But the Turkey of Atatürk was never atheist, and did not interfere in private religious matters as long as they stayed private. Turkey, moreover, had evolved into a modern and increasingly democratic society with close ties to Europe, which seemed a workable model for Azerbaijan that provided hope of integration with the most advanced countries of the world.

A fortunate development for these hopes was Turkey's development into Azerbaijan's most important supporter. After some early doubts about which side to take, Turkey took a stand just as the war between Armenia and Azerbaijan over Mountainous Karabakh escalated. Though the Turkish government refrained from direct intervention, it became Azerbaijan's staunchest backer in the international arena, especially during the presidency of Suleyman Demirel (1993–2000). Turkey initiated what has become a long-term training commitment to the Azerbaijani military, and protestations of brotherhood and indivisibility were repeatedly made by both sides. Two instances are particularly memorable. One occurred during President Heydar Aliyev's speech to the Turkish Parliament in 1995, when he coined the phrase expression "one nation, two states" to characterize his nation's relationship with Turkey. The second was during a summer 2001 visit to Baku by the Turkish chief of staff, General Hüseyin Kıvrıkoğlu. Speaking in the context of a tense period in relations between Azerbaijan and Iran, General Kıvrıkoğlu declared that "Azerbaijan's and Turkey's skies are one common sky."

For all that ties them together, there are also differences between Turkey and Azerbaijan, which stem from their differences in size and historical experience. Perhaps the main point of friction is the widespread perception in Azerbaijan that Turkey regards itself as a "big brother" to the much smaller Azerbaijan. Azerbaijanis in general react very negatively to this perceived attitude of superiority, which is attributed in part to Turkey's long history as the seat of the Ottoman Empire. For their part, Azerbaijanis perceive their society as more advanced in many ways than Turkey's. For example, Azerbaijan's rates of literacy and secondary education are considerably higher than Turkey's, and certain Western cultural traditions introduced by the Russian Empire, such as classical music, opera, and theater, are more highly developed. The growing domination of Baku's small and medium-level business activity by Turkish entrepreneurs has also generated some resentment, which was already palpable as early as the end of the first decade of independence.

Meanwhile, the increasingly confessional tone of Turkish society and politics has, in turn, affected Turkish perceptions of Azerbaijan. Indeed, the importance accorded to Azerbaijan varies greatly among Turkey's political forces, among which three basic groups can be distinguished. The first is the thoroughly Westernized elite, which perceives itself as European and sees Turkey as part of the West. While this group has nothing against Azerbaijan per se, it views the Turkic nations of the East—much as it does the Middle East—as mere distractions from Turkey's main ambition, to become part of the West. This secular stratum, relatively important in the 1990s, has since been gradually marginalized—while growing increasingly anti-Western.

The second group is the secular center-right, for which the country's Turkish identity is very important. To varying degrees, this group espouses some form of nationalism, and therefore feels strong cultural affinities with Azerbaijan and other Turkic nations. For this large segment of society, including the political class, it is natural for Turkey to keep close ties with Azerbaijan and actively support its interests and its independence. The secular center-right dominated Turkish politics in the 1990s, with Suleyman Demirel as its main representative, but was then pushed aside some-what by the rise of the Islamic conservative movement.

The third group consists of the Islamic conservatives. For them, religious identity is more important than ethnicity or nationality; their most compel-ling association is with the *umma* (the greater Muslim community), not with other Turks or Turkic speakers. Moreover, Islamic-minded Turks tend to view Muslims from the former Soviet Union with suspicion, perceiving their faith as corrupted by Soviet atheism and Russian rule. The less abste-mious attitude toward alcohol and pork attributed to Muslims from the former Soviet space is pointed out in support of this charge. The domin-ance of Sunni Islam among Turkey's Islamic conservatives compounds their skepticism toward the Muslims of Azerbaijan, most of whom are Shia. Turkey's Islamic conservatives consequently have displayed little interest in Azerbaijan or other Turkic republics save for proselytizing ef-forts—mainly by the modernist Islamic community of Turkish preacher Fethullah Gülen—and have been much more consumed with developing Turkey's ties to the Islamic Middle East. At times when Islamic conserva-tives have dominated Turkish politics—as during 1996–97 and again start-ing in 2002—this perspective led to a downgrading of the importance at-tached to Azerbaijan. During 2008–09, this had dramatic implications for bilateral relations, when the Turkish government moved ahead with an attempt to normalize relations with Armenia (see "The Armenia Border Issue," below).

From Neglect to Euphoria: The Early 1990s

At the time of the Soviet Union's collapse in 1991, both the Turkish gov-ernment and Turkish society had spent seven decades in isolation from the Turkish people's ethnic "cousins" in Azerbaijan and Central Asia. On Tur-key's part, this extended separation contributed to an early neglect and ignorance of these two areas to its east, which had a significant influence on Turkish policy in the region, especially toward Azerbaijan. First, the poor understanding of the region led to an ill-conceived euphoria regarding future Turkic unity, which had as its backdrop the 1989 rejection of Tur-key's request for admission to the European Community. The Karabakh conflict and Turkey's inability to influence the course of the war soon enough shattered this euphoria.

Turkish Policy in the Soviet Era

Except for a few short periods, the Ottoman Empire (ca. 1300–1922) seldom controlled the territory of present-day Azerbaijan. Yet the early Turkish nationalist thinking that eventuated in the founding of the Turkish republic did ascribe significant importance to Azerbaijan. Atatürk himself reportedly stated that "Azerbaijan's joy is our joy and Azerbaijan's sorrow is our sorrow."[1] As discussed in chapter 1 of the present volume, the Ottoman push to the Caucasus in 1917 and 1918, as the empire was dying, was crucial to the establishment of Azerbaijan's initial effort at representative government, the First Republic of 1918–20.

But in opposition to Enver Pasha's dreams of empire in Asia, the Republic of Turkey, created in 1923, abstained totally from rekindling this surge to the East, even though Turkish nationalism was one of the six principles of the Kemalist ideology. Atatürk's brand of nationalism was neither ethnically based, exclusivist, nor aggressive. Rather, it was an inclusive civic variant whose principal function was to forge a new nation within the borders of a multi-ethnic Turkish republic. Concomitant with the project of putting a civic stamp on Turkish nationalism, Turkey's foreign policy was guided by Atatürk's maxim *"Yurtta Sulh, Cihanda Sulh"* (Peace at home, peace in the world). In practice, this made Turkey an inward-looking country, and it gave up all plans to expand its influence in its eastern neighborhood.

With the exception of right-wing nationalists and émigré organizations of Caucasian or Central Asian peoples, and small groups of scholars, Turkey effectively forgot its linguistic and ethnic cousins. This was all the more remarkable given the emphasis placed by the republic's historiographers on the Central Asian roots of Turkish civilization. An important factor in this lapse of historical memory was Bolshevik Russia's role as an ally against the imperialist powers during Atatürk's war for the liberation of Turkey. Beyond sharing enemies, the new governments in Ankara and Moscow were brought closer by being revolutionary forces that had toppled their respective anciens régimes, and by being internationally isolated.

The cordial Kemalist-Bolshevik relations of the early 1920s would have repercussions much later, in helping to shape the post-Soviet Caucasus. Indeed, the Soviet territorial delimitation in the South Caucasus was undertaken with some regard to Turkish interests—the primary example being the overt guarantor status over Nakhichevan granted to Turkey. Moreover, concern for Turkey may have been a factor in the Soviet decision to consign Karabakh to Azerbaijan after it became a Soviet republic. Turkish-

Soviet relations remained cordial on the surface until World War II, but the Soviet Union then became a distinct threat to Turkey, given Soviet claims to a right to control the Bosporus and the Dardanelles—a direct cause of Turkey's decision to join the North Atlantic Treaty Organization.[2] In subsequent decades, Turkey's NATO membership prevented Ankara from formulating an independent foreign policy with regard to the Soviet Union, and caused it to allocate little time, effort, or resources to pursuing an active policy toward the Turkic peoples of the Soviet Union. The disastrous experience of 1918 was a contributing reason for this. As Mustafa Aydın has written,

> Ever since the establishment of the Turkish nation-state…the Republican leaders, conscious of the dangers of any kind of pan-Turkish adventures such as had characterized the policies of the last days of the Ottoman empire, had been quite consistently categorical in their denial to express any interest in the so-called "outside Turks," especially those within the Soviet Union.[3]

A singular ignorance thus developed, even among informed circles in Turkey, regarding the culture, language, and history of the Turkic peoples of Central Asia and the Caucasus. For instance, in the early 1990s many Turks thought that the Chechens and Abkhaz—who did have large diasporas in Turkey—were Turkic peoples, only to learn that these two ethnic groups understood hardly a word of Turkish. Likewise, many Turks were surprised to find out that the kindred Kazakh and Kyrgyz languages were not readily comprehensible to Turkish-speakers.

Exceptions existed, though: right-wing nationalists kept up an interest in the Turkic world, as did some on the center-right. It is no coincidence that Süleyman Demirel, a constant advocate of an active Turkish policy in the region in the 1990s, visited Tashkent and Baku in 1967. He was reportedly warmly greeted by crowds that had obviously not forgotten their Turkic origins.[4] Nevertheless, when the Soviet Union started falling apart in the early 1990s, the "complete indifference [to] Turkic heritage in the Soviet Union"[5] on the part of Turkish policymakers led them to confront a situation they were unprepared to handle. Particularly illustrative is President Turgut Özal's 1989 reply to an American journalist asking him what Turkey's stance was toward the Karabakh dispute. His answer, which came back to haunt him repeatedly, was that being Shiite Muslims, the Azerbaijanis were "closer to Iran than to us."[6] More than a clumsy remark, the comment implied that religious affiliation was more important than ethnolinguistic ties, and demonstrated Özal's own penchant toward religion as a source of identity. But most of all, it showed the mental distance between Turkey and the developments in the Caucasus in the late Soviet period. Given its entrenched stance (a consequence of its NATO membership) in regard to the Cold War, Ankara was until very late 1991 reluctant to abandon its strategy of dealing with the Soviet Union as if it were a unified whole.

A Sudden, Brief Euphoria: 1991–93

When everything in Moscow came tumbling down, Turkish foreign policy in a very short time underwent a spectacular change. Turkey had built its geopolitical place in the world on its role in the Cold War; the end of the Cold War led to fears that Turkey's importance to the West was disappearing. Ankara also saw its traditional role in regional politics withering away. It needed to find itself a new role if it wanted to remain relevant both internationally and regionally. Several reasons converged—both internal and external—to make Ankara opt for an embrace of the newly independent Turkic states of the former Soviet Union, Azerbaijan in particular.

Baskın Oran has argued that the primary external factor that "pushed Turkey towards these new countries" was the United States, which saw Turkey as a model for these freshly independent Muslim states, and a counterforce to the spread of Iranian influence in the region.[7] Influence in the new states of Eurasia was also a way to regain the strategic importance Turkey had enjoyed during the Cold War. The internal dynamics had economic, political, and psychological elements. The new states of Eurasia presented a new market for Turkish exports, as well as new sources of energy. Politically, following the European Community's rejection of Turkey's application for membership in 1989, some in Ankara saw a possible new role as the leader of a Turkic community of states. Internally, the right-wing nationalist political movement, which regularly polls around 10 percent of the vote (and has been growing recently) was very active in pressuring the center-right government to pursue a more active policy. An additional factor was the Caucasian diaspora populations, which numbered some eight to ten million people and were represented at high levels of government, with considerable clout on state policy. Finally, an important psychological element of the time was the feeling of isolation in Turkey at the end of the Cold War. The discovery of a possible new community of friendly nations, with which Turkey had ties of kinship, created excitement at both the popular and elite levels, and had significant consequences for policymaking.

As Turkic leaders from the former Soviet Union began arriving in Ankara with requests for assistance in late 1991, many Turkish policymakers became euphoric. Prime Minister Demirel declared in February 1992 that a "gigantic Turkish world" was being created, from the Adriatic Sea to the Great Wall of China.[8] Turkish dreams of the twenty-first century being a "century of the Turks" were also entertained by President Nursultan Nazarbayev of Kazakhstan.[9] Indeed, to a certain degree the leaders of the Turkic states—not least Azerbaijani president Abulfez Elçibey—initially echoed pan-Turkic sentiments. But in its euphoria, Turkey tended to take on the role of an older brother: despite Turkish assurances that cooperation would be on an "equal basis," the attitude of many Turkish policymakers hinted otherwise. In late 1993, Ambassador Umut Arik, head of Turkey's Agency for International Development, told students of Ankara's Middle East Technical University that "the languages of the Turkic peoples of the east are not sufficient to be state languages; they must be replaced with Istanbul Turkish."[10] The reactions of the Azerbaijani students present at the occasion can easily be imagined.

To Turkey, Azerbaijan was from the outset the most important country in the South Caucasus, and the Turkish government recognized Azerbaijan several weeks before it recognized the other newly independent states in the region. Azerbaijan was both geographically and culturally the closest of the Turkic republics. Strategically, it was the only Caucasus state on the Caspian Sea, and was thereby crucial to Turkish access to Central Asia; Azerbaijan also had substantial energy reserves. As outlined by Süha Bölükbaşı, Turkey's policy toward Azerbaijan was guided by five priorities: support for Azerbaijan's independence; support for Azerbaijan's sovereignty over Karabakh; a desire to prevent or limit a Russian return to the South Caucasus; participation in Azerbaijani oil production and the export of Azerbaijani oil through Turkey; and preservation of a friendly, though not necessarily pan-Turkist, government in Baku.[11]

Even though Turkey became the first state to recognize Azerbaijan's independence, on November 9, 1991, relations were slow to develop until the forced resignation of Azerbaijani president Ayaz Mutalibov in spring 1992. Mutalibov had been decidedly cautious in building ties to Turkey. When Abulfez Elçibey came to power, his fancy for the "Turkish model" of governance, his militant secularism, and his strongly anti-Iranian views may have aligned well with what many leading Turks privately believed. But Elçibey's erratic style did not align with the traditional cautiousness of Turkish foreign policy. Indeed, Elçibey was a bit too pan-Turkic even for Ankara's taste, and certainly too indiscreet a pan-Turkist. Elçibey's lack of political tact caused influential circles in Turkey to see him as a destabilizing factor, unfit to govern, as well as an impediment to Turkey's regional objectives. For his part, Prime Minister Demirel had a much warmer relationship with Heydar Aliyev, still in Nakhichevan at the time, than with Elçibey. By contrast, the nationalist faction in Turkey vigorously supported Elçibey even long after his forced retirement, and came to despise the more pragmatic Aliyev. When the Elçibey government was ousted in June 1993, this development was seen on the surface as a Turkish loss and a Russian gain. Observers in both Turkey and the West detected an inability on Ankara's part to keep a friendly regime in power. In Turkey itself, Elçibey's fall was interpreted by some to mean the end of the Turkish model.[12] Though the episode did reaffirm Russia's ability to interfere in the internal affairs of the Caucasian states, Turkey was actually intimately involved in bringing Aliyev to power. As Thomas Goltz has shown, the situation in Azerbaijan had deteriorated so much by early 1993 that Ankara "started looking out for alternative horses to back."[13] To Demirel, that meant his friend Heydar Aliyev. As Goltz has related, Demirel on three occasions in the spring of 1993 pushed Aliyev to assume a more active role in propping up the Elçibey regime. Aliyev refused to be associated with the government, but in June, Demirel prompted Elçibey to ask Aliyev to come to Baku. In this sense, Ankara played a crucial role in thwarting Moscow's plan to put insurgent commander Surat Huseynov in power in Elçibey's place.

Unlike Elçibey, who gave principled priority to Turkey, Aliyev played the Turkish card whenever it suited his purposes, but showed that he could also turn his back on Ankara if necessary. In September 1993 he annulled many agreements that had been signed between Elçibey's government and Turkey, ordered Turkish nationals to seek visas before entering Azerbaijan, and dismissed 1,600 Turkish military advisers serving in the country.[14] Yet only a year later, when his domestic position was consolidated, Aliyev again courted Ankara and expressed his confidence in the brotherhood between the two countries. Aliyev, hence, saw Turkey as one of Azerbaijan's partners, not as its sole partner. He purposefully broadened Azerbaijan's links with the West as well as the Muslim world, focusing on establishing better relations with the United States and Iran, but also countries such as Pakistan and Saudi Arabia.[15]

For Turkey, the replacement of Elçibey with Aliyev meant a less devoted but more pragmatic regime in Baku. Aliyev also made a point of showing that the relationship was a two-way street: it was not only Azerbaijan that needed Turkey; Turkey also needed Azerbaijan. From a relative position of strength, then, Aliyev could address the Turkish Parliament in 1995 and state that "we are one nation but two states."

Karabakh: Turkey's Wake-Up Call

By 1994, Turkey was waking up from its Turkic euphoria. More than anything else, the Karabakh conflict (and Turkey's inability to affect its course) punctured dreams of a dominant Turkic role in the region.

Turkish Policies on Karabakh

Whatever assistance programs Turkey set up for Azerbaijan in the early 1990s, these efforts paled in comparison with the importance of Turkey's role in the Karabakh conflict, which more than anything determined Azerbaijani views on Turkey. Initially, Ankara tried to present itself as a mediator between the parties. Although Armenia was wary of Turkish involvement from the beginning, it did not immediately denounce Ankara's efforts. Hence, Turkish diplomats, especially foreign minister Hikmet Çetin, embarked on several rounds of shuttle diplomacy in the region and among several European capitals.[16] Turkey helped bring the issue to the agenda of the Conference on Security and Cooperation in Europe.[17] Furthermore, Çetin used Turkish connections in the West to try to bring the conflict to the attention of Western governments, notably by personally telephoning U.S. secretary of state James Baker regarding the issue.[18] Demirel defended the cautious policy by arguing that there was no legal basis for a Turkish intervention, and that in any case Azerbaijan had not asked for it.[19]

The Turkish attempt at mediation was not destined to last long. After the Khojaly massacre of Azerbaijani civilians, large anti-Armenian demonstrations were held in Turkey, with tens of thousands of people demonstrating in favor of a military intervention on Azerbaijan's behalf. The Turkish government could not disregard these public demands, and most Turkish leaders had feelings of solidarity with Azerbaijan. Turgut Özal himself on several occasions stated that the Armenians should be "frightened a little,"[20] sending shock waves through Armenia and the Armenian diaspora, and enabling both to accuse Turkey, however frivolously, of planning new atrocities against Armenians.

As Armenian military advances on Azerbaijani territory intensified, Turkey rapidly adopted a more pro-Azerbaijani stance. The Turkish press was filled with criticism of the government's mild stance on the Armenian drive, and of Turkey's feeble performance in the Caucasus and Central Asia compared to its aim of becoming a regional leader.[21]

The government also came under heavy opposition criticism for standing idly by while the Turkish people's Azerbaijani brethren were being massacred. The most visible critic was the head of the Nationalist Movement Party, Alparslan Türkeş, who as early as February 1992 had argued for a Turkish military intervention, since, he said, "Turkey cannot stand idly by while Azerbaijan's territory is being occupied."[22] The senior statesmen and Democratic Left Party chairman Bülent Ecevit argued that the failure to demonstrate unambiguous support for Azerbaijan could undermine Turkey's prestige in Azerbaijan and Central Asia—which, in hindsight, is exactly what happened.[23] But the mightiest challenge to the government came from the main opposition leader, Mesut Yılmaz. In March 1992, he argued for troops to be deployed along the Armenian border and maintained that Turkey held a guarantor status over Karabakh.[24] On several occasions, Yılmaz reiterated his belief that Turkey should deploy troops near the Armenian border and Nakhichevan to deter Armenian advances.[25]

In March 1992, Demirel's government announced that it would inspect airplanes headed for Armenia that would be passing over Turkish airspace, in an effort to implement an arms embargo.[26] Turkey then helped enforce Azerbaijan's economic embargo on Armenia, refusing to allow aid or trade destined for that country to transit Turkish territory. In an interview with the *Washington Post* later in March, Demirel stated that he was under severe pressure to take more decisive action, and did not rule out a Turkish military intervention.[27] However, there were too many forces constraining Turkey from pursuing a truly independent policy on Karabakh.

Constraints on Turkish Policy in the Karabakh Conflict

Despite Turkey's overtly pro-Azerbaijani stance during 1992–93, Ankara did not supply Baku with anything that could have helped it turn the tide of the Karabakh war. Some retired Turkish army officers were sent to help train the Azerbaijani army; Armenian sources claim that Turkey provided weapons, but if such shipments took place, these weapons were insignificant, given the readily available Soviet weaponry in the region. Turkey's policy on Karabakh illustrates the profound restraint exercised by Turkish leaders, who very likely would have wished to do much more for Azerbaijan. Why, then, did Ankara hold back? It is possible to discern at least seven factors that constrained Ankara in the formulation and implementation of its policy toward Armenia and Azerbaijan in the early days of the fighting.

First, the doctrine of Kemalism explicitly prohibits military adventurism abroad: Turkey is to get involved in a conflict only if it is directly threatened. (The long-standing dispute over Cyprus indeed resulted in a Turkish intervention in 1974, which was attributable primarily to Turkey's treaty-based guarantor status in relation to the island). Given that Azerbaijan was an independent and sovereign country, Turkey's traditional foreign policy doctrine held that Ankara should not meddle in the conflict between Azerbaijan and another independent state. Ankara had a guarantor status regarding Nakhichevan that was similar to its arrangement concerning Cyprus— and indeed, Armenia avoided targeting Nakhichevan.

Second, a domestic balance between opposing opinions neutralized any impulse toward strong action. A clear divide emerged between elected officials and political appointees, on the one hand, and the career military and civil service establishment, on the other.[28] As politicians in government as well as the opposition outbid one other in expressing pro-Azerbaijani statements, the establishment was not about to let elected leaders drag the country into a war in the Caucasus. It is hence doubtful whether the military would have followed orders of direct intervention, had these been given.

Third, Turkey's freedom to act was tightly limited by its ties to the West; indeed, this was perhaps its most important constraint. Turkish involvement would have increased the risk of an escalation of the conflict and a consequent face-off pitting Turkey against Russia and Iran. Thus, Turkey's NATO partners were insistent that Turkey rein itself in. In addition, the proven influence of the Armenian lobby in the U.S. Congress made a ban on U.S. military aid to Turkey seem a realistic consequence of a Turkish intervention in Karabakh. Moreover, an intervention would likely undermine Turkey's case for EU membership, one of its most ardently sought international objectives.

The fourth factor was Russia. Every time Turkey signaled its intention to increase its involvement in Karabakh, Moscow responded promptly. An illustrating example of this occurred in April 1993, when Armenian forces seized Kelbajar Province (see chapter 4). When President Özal denounced Russia for supporting the Armenians and announced that Turkey would provide Azerbaijan with arms,[29] Russian defense minister Pavel Grachev warned Ankara in rather undiplomatic terms to stay out of Azerbaijan.[30] If Turkish policymakers had thought Russia was weakened by the collapse of the Soviet Union, some rethinking clearly took place in Ankara. In June

1994, the chief of staff of the Turkish armed forces, General Doğan Güreş, was reported to have said that "Russia is now posing a greater threat to Turkey than it used to during the Cold War."[31] Azerbaijan's fate was hence not dear enough to Ankara to justify jeopardizing Turkey's relations with Russia.

Fifth, the legacy of the 1915 massacres of eastern Anatolia's Armenian population was a powerful disincentive for any intervention against Armenia. The stigma that Armenian communities in the West have succeeded in attaching to Turkey made it difficult for Ankara to put action behind its verbal support for Azerbaijan. Indeed, Prime Minister Demirel stated in early 1993 that a Turkish intervention on Azerbaijan's side would only result in the whole world getting behind Armenia.[32]

Sixth, Turkey in the early 1990s was hardly a harmonious and peaceful society: its military was fighting the most vicious and powerful Kurdish insurgency in decades, and during 1992–93 the government effectively did not control large swaths of southeastern Turkey where the presence of the separatist Kurdistan Workers' Party (PKK) was particularly strong. The situation there improved only in 1995, long after the cease-fire in Karabakh; under such conditions, Turkey could hardly have afforded a second military operation in the Caucasus.

Finally, the international reaction that Turkey faced after invading Cyprus in 1974 had imparted a lesson. For thirty years, Cyprus had been a persistent irritant in Turkey's relations with Europe and the United States. Clearly, Ankara feared that any deeper intervention in Karabakh could result in a similar situation.

Azerbaijan's Reaction

Azerbaijan's reaction to Turkey's measured support was twofold. The convoys of humanitarian aid from the West that Ankara, acceding to heavy Western pressure, allowed to pass through the otherwise-closed border to Armenia triggered a widespread feeling of deceit and betrayal on the popular level. If the Azerbaijani people had hoped that Turkey would present itself as their country's main protector, it soon became clear that Turkey lacked both the capacity and the will to assume such a role. Among the Azerbaijani leadership, however, there was more of an understanding of Turkey's constraints. Turkey's position as a member of NATO, its own turmoil in its Kurdish areas, and Russia's resurgence all provided understandable reasons why there was little prospect that Turkey would support Azerbaijan more actively.[33]

This understanding on the part of the leadership did not mitigate the reality that Turkey lost significant prestige in Azerbaijani eyes and to a certain extent began losing its privileged position in the country. Yet Azerbaijan was faced with the fact that, for all its shortcomings, Turkey was still the only state it could count on as an ally against Armenia.

A More Pragmatic Policy: 1997–2003

Turkey's Low Point

Turkey's post-Karabakh relations with Azerbaijan began with an embarrassing coup attempt. As described in chapter 5 of the present volume, the 1994 action by members of the special-purpose police force known as OMON, acting under the direction of Deputy Minister of the Interior Rovshan Javadov, set off a crisis in Turkish-Azerbaijani relations when the involvement of high-level Turkish figures was uncovered. To this day, the Azerbaijani government claims that figures in the Turkish Embassy in Baku were involved, as well as high-level intelligence officials. Heydar Aliyev repeatedly alleged that the coup makers had been in direct contact with Prime Minister Tansu Çiller. The prime minister herself traveled to Baku to apologize for the activities of an "uncontrollable right-wing group."[34] President Aliyev evidently found Çiller's statement unconvincing; in 1998, he told a Turkish television audience that Çiller was involved in the coup.[35] This view was supported by a leaked report prepared by the Turkish National Intelligence Organization (MIT). The MIT stated that the Turkish state minister responsible for relations with other Turkic republics, Ayvaz Gökdemir, planned the coup with Çiller's approval, but that the MIT—and possibly officials at the Turkish Embassy in Baku—informed President Demirel, and thus contributed substance to a warning he arranged to have sent to Aliyev.[36] The exact details of the event have never been fully unearthed, but the evidence of high-level Turkish involvement is significant.

This episode rocked relations between Azerbaijan and Turkey to the core. It was only the personal relationship between Aliyev and Demirel, and the fact that Demirel had warned Aliyev about the coup, that prevented a sharp break in Turkish-Azerbaijani relations. But even if relations were saved, the events damaged Turkey's standing in Azerbaijan even further. That high government officials in a brotherly country had staged a coup against the Azerbaijani government was a wake-up call to Baku that it could truly trust no one. By 1995, Turkish policy toward the Caucasus, and specifically toward Azerbaijan, was hitting a low point. As Mustafa Aydın has put it, problems in Turkish policy toward Central Asia and the Caucasus included Turkey's "frequent euphoric pronouncements, empty valor, overconfident but miscalculated grand designs, as well as a disorganized attempt to carve out a zone of influence in the region."[37]

In the wake of the coup debacle, Turkey's domestic political affairs were likewise descending into disarray. The simmering tension between the secularist and Islamist factions grew more intense when the Islamist-oriented Welfare Party narrowly emerged as the winner in the December 1995 National Assembly elections. So fragmented were Turkish electoral politics that a mere 21 percent of the vote was sufficient to position the party to lead a new government. During the Welfare Party's brief tenure as the senior partner in a coalition government, Turkish foreign policy rapidly reoriented itself toward the Middle East. From Baku's perspective, Turkey was now run by an Islamist prime minister with little regard for Azerbaijan, and a foreign minister (Tansu Çiller) whom Heydar Aliyev held responsible for the 1995 coup attempt.

Once the Welfare Party was forced out of power in 1997, a thoroughgoing reevaluation of Turkish policy toward the South Caucasus gradually occurred. By the end of the 1990s, Turkey had built up a position of strength in the region, bolstered by its close cooperation with the United States on regional matters.

The Return of Geopolitics

Turkey's renewed engagement in the South Caucasus took place in spite of the country's continued domestic instability, and a political vacuum that was the result of the self-destruction of the country's major political parties. This vacuum allowed the military, the foreign policy establishment, and President Demirel to step in to take the lead in determining policy toward the Caucasus. By this time, the Turkish military had come around to espousing many of former president Özal's ideas about international relations, in practice if not in name. The General Staff was now advocating and driving a more assertive foreign policy, the most important element of which was the alliance with Israel. Aside from this alliance, which revolutionized the geopolitics of the Middle East, this renewed assertiveness had the effect of suppressing the PKK insurgency in southeastern Turkey and forcing Syria and Iran to curtail their support for the Kurds and other separatist elements operating inside the country. Turkey began to see itself as a regional power in its own right. In spite of having had his own bouts with the military throughout his long career, President Demirel was now acting very much in unison with the top brass. Turkey refined its policies toward the East, and began to put increasing emphasis on the Caucasus, including a bolstered strategic partnership with Georgia. A pragmatic understanding of the region developed in Ankara in place of the emphasis on ethnic ties that had dominated previously.

Ankara saw the South Caucasus in strategic terms, and defined Georgia and Azerbaijan as the key countries whose independence needed to be supported if Turkey were to project its influence eastward, and if the movement of Caspian Sea energy resources through Turkey were to be possible. The Baku-Tbilisi-Ceyhan pipeline, in particular, was key to the region's development, and a concrete issue around which multilateral cooperation among Turkey, Azerbaijan, Georgia, and the United States could grow. With Turkey's alliance with Israel, there was ample discussion of a U.S.-supported Israel-Turkey-Georgia-Azerbaijan axis developing, countered by a Syria-Iran-Armenia-Russia axis. The geopolitics of the former Soviet space were becoming increasingly linked to the Middle East.

In large part because of diplomatic activity related to the transport of Caspian energy resources, the security of the Caucasus became an increasingly hot issue in 2001. Iranian pressure on Azerbaijan, possibly with a view to preventing the Baku-Tbilisi-Ceyhan pipeline from being realized, was stepped up in the first half of the year (see chapter 12). Turkey's response to the July 23 incident in which an Iranian warship forced an Azerbaijani-flagged research vessel away from a Caspian Sea oil field in waters claimed by Azerbaijan (and Iran's subsequent violations of Azerbaijani airspace) showed very clearly where Turkish foreign policy toward the Caucasus was being formulated. Indeed, whereas the Turkish foreign ministry stopped at issuing press releases, it was the General Staff that acted, by dispatching Chief of General Staff Hüseyin Kıvrıkoğlu and ten fighter jets to Baku. Ankara publicly maintained that the visit had nothing to do with Iran, and had long been planned to mark the graduation of Azerbaijani officers from the Turkish-run military academy in Azerbaijan. Yet the implication of the visit was perfectly clear: the Turkish military had stepped in with a show of force to counter Iran's threats against Azerbaijan. In fact, this was the first—and so far only—time that Ankara stepped in to put action behind its rhetoric of brotherhood and support for Azerbaijan. Footage showing Kıvrıkoğlu's deadly serious face as he told Heydar Aliyev that Turkey's and Azerbaijan's skies were one and the same was duly noted throughout the region. The complete cessation of aggressive Iranian moves against Azerbaijan after Kıvrıkoğlu's Baku visit proved the effectiveness of the move. Tehran had challenged Western support for Azerbaijan, and Ankara had called the bluff while Europe and the United States remained silent. Of course, if Ankaracame out of the episode with strengthened prestige, Iran kept one golden nugget: a decade later, the disputed field was still untouched by any oil company. In sum, Tehran continues to hold future Azerbaijani oil development hostage.

Islamic Conservative Rule and Neglect of the Caucasus

A Period of Regional Disengagement

General Kıvrıkoğlu's stalwart stand in Baku notwithstanding, the decade that followed his visit could best be characterized by a gradual Turkish retreat from the South Caucasus, at least until 2008. Three factors combined to produce this disengagement, which has been described as resulting in the "end of the honeymoon" between Turkey and Azerbaijan.[38] The first was the financial crisis of 2000–2001, which intensified Turkey's focus on domestic issues while, in regard to foreign affairs, orienting it more toward Europe. The second factor was the election to power of a government led by the Justice and Development Party. The third was the end of Suleyman Demirel's term as president and his replacement by the chairman of the Constitutional Court, Ahmet Necdet Sezer.

The Turkish military's stiff stance on Azerbaijan in 2001 was especially significant because of the dire straits in which Turkey found itself at the time. Between November 2000 and February 2001, the worst financial crisis in the country's modern history hit Turkey. Large segments of the banking sector collapsed, and the Turkish lira lost 40 percent of its value, plunging the country into chaos as millions lost the value of their savings. The unemployment rate soared.[39] These events set off a political crisis, as the public ran out of patience with the bickering among Turkish politicians. In the November 2002 parliamentary elections, called eighteen months early, all of the parties that had been elected to Parliament just three years earlier were thrown out, all having failed to cross the 10 percent threshold for representation. In effect, the entire Turkish political class was voted out.

The main beneficiary of the parliamentary clean sweep was the Justice and Development Party (Adalet ve Kalkınma Partisi—AKP), which won 363 of 550 seats with slightly over 35 of the vote, a disproportional representation because only two parties crossed the 10 percent threshold. The AKP had been formed when, in the run-up to the elections, Turkey's Islamist political movement split in two. The orthodox core formed the Felicity Party, while more progressive and moderate forces led by Istanbul mayor Recep Tayyıp Erdoğan and former Welfare Party minister Abdullah Gül established the AKP. With its self-proclaimed moderate agenda, the party sought to break with the Islamist and authoritarian past; moreover, Erdoğan's record as a successful manager during his tenure as Istanbul's mayor made the AKP acceptable to many Turks who would never have otherwise considered voting for Islamists. Seeing the writing on the wall, many members of the collapsing liberal and conservative secular parties rallied to the AKP in advance of the elections, and some were included on its list. Despite this broadening, the party remained controlled by a tightly knit core group of leaders around Erdoğan, with an affiliation to the Nakşibendi [Naqshbandiyya], the largest of the religious brotherhoods in Turkey.

Among other things, Suleyman Demirel's retirement also meant the loss of statesmanship and vision in Turkish foreign policy. The leadership vacuum in foreign policy created by a sequence of coalition governments had been filled by Demirel, who used his age, the respect he commanded, and his personal relationships with many world leaders, including Heydar Aliyev, to put Turkey on the map. Sezer, by contrast, was a lawyer, who made a point of doing no more and no less than the constitution prescribed. He took few initiatives in foreign policy, and his foreign visits, such as to Baku in early 2006, were primarily of symbolic importance. For Azerbaijan, the personal link between Demirel and Aliyev had been the cornerstone of the bilateral relationship. In the absence of such ties, the relationship subsequently suffered.

The AKP's coming to power affected Turkey's policies toward the Caucasus both directly and indirectly, and mainly to the detriment of the country's interests. The situation was reminiscent of the Welfare Party's short tenure in power in the mid-1990s. With its roots in a subculture that had little interest in Turkic fraternity, the AKP leadership emphasized affiliation on a religious rather than ethnic basis. There was therefore little enthusiasm in Ankara for the Caucasus, but there were no major deviations from the general outlines of earlier Turkish policies either, other than a somewhat greater emphasis on business relations that mirrored the rise of Turkey's economy. Complying with recent tradition, Erdoğan made his first trip abroad after the election to Azerbaijan, Kazakhstan, and Turkmenistan, with his discussions focusing on business and trade development.[40]

The new government focused on political and economic reforms, on Turkey's integration with Europe, and, with gradually increasing intensity, on building relations with the Islamic world. One of the ways in which the AKP differed substantially from the anti-European Welfare Party was that it gave Turkey its most ardently pro-European government ever—for the first three years of its tenure. Unlike political parties of the secularist establishment, the AKP did not have the same attachment to the strong state of the Kemalist tradition, which, the party believed, was an impediment to its reform agenda aimed mainly at opening up religious liberties in the country. Moreover, the ironic lesson from the Welfare Party's time in government was that only integration into the EU could reduce the Turkish army's role in politics and therefore make it possible to pursue Islamic politics in Turkey. The AKP hence set a rapid pace of reform that resulted in the onset of negotiations on EU membership in 2004. For pragmatic reasons, the AKP government focused much of its foreign relations on Europe during its first term in power, 2002 to 2007. But the AKP also gave increasing attention to the Middle East. This particular emphasis had its pragmatic element, but idelogical considerations played a large part as well. The U.S. invasion of Iraq took place just months after the AKP won power, and was a formative experience for the new government, indeed, the dominant regional issue during its first term. The issues of national, cultural, and religious identity raised by the invasion and subsequent war also enabled the AKP to develop its presence in the Middle East in a manner consistent with the party's political instincts.

Relations with the United States and the Greater Middle East

During the AKP government's first term, the gap between Ankara and Washington widened, affecting the cooperation between Turkey and the United States toward the greater Middle East, as well as the Caucasus. Turkish public opinion was strongly opposed to the invasion of Iraq, and, despite existing commitments to Washington, the Turkish Parliament failed to pass a resolution that would make Turkey a part of the military effort. From that point, Turkish-American relations deteriorated sharply. Matters were worsened by Turkish fears of a Kurdish state emerging in northern Iraq, and by generally accurate Turkish perceptions that the United States was reluctant to hit PKK targets in that area. Only when U.S. efforts to stabilize Iraq began to bear fruit in 2007 did the United States agree to share intelligence with Turkey on a more systematic basis and to allow Turkish military operations against the PKK on Iraqi territory.

Beyond Iraq, Turkish-American relations soured on account of the changes in Turkish society that took place during the tenure of the AKP. As Zeyno Baran has shown in a recent study, a key factor was the strong realignment of opinions and identities taking place in Turkey.[41] In 1999, a little over a third (36 percent) of Turks identified as Muslims first; by 2006, that segment had grown to almost half (46 percent). Concomitantly, support for secularism declined. Almost three-quarters (73 percent) of Turks agreed that religion should be restricted to the private sphere in 2002; five years later, the figure had dropped to just over half (55 percent). Negative views of Jews developed in parallel: In 2004, such views were espoused by nearly half (49 percent) of those surveyed; more than three quarters (76 percent) expressed such views in 2008.

These findings suggest the growing penetration of Turkish society by the Islamic conservative worldview, through the growing impact of pro-Islamic media outlets and the example set by the political leadership. This also had foreign policy consequences: primarily, the steep rise of anti-Americanism, which some government officials endorsed. Paradoxically, the widespread perception in secular circles that the West was supporting the AKP as an experiment with "moderate Islam" also led to increased anti-Americanism among those in opposition to the AKP. As a result, whereas over half of Turks had been favorably disposed toward the United States in 2000, by 2007 less than a tenth were so inclined—making Turkey the most anti-American country surveyed by polling organizations such as Pew or the German Marshall Fundäs Transatlantic Trends. The numbers improved, but only marginally, with the accession to the U.S. presidency of Barack Obama. The growth of anti-Americanism was mirrored by a gradual rise in favorable ratings for Iran.

These changing perceptions were paralleled by a shift in Turkish foreign policy. Especially during the AKP's second term, which began in 2007, Prime Minister Erdoğan developed increasingly close ties with the Hamas leadership in Gaza, and strongly ratcheted up his anti-Israeli rhetoric. In general, Turkey disassociated its foreign policy in the Middle East from that of the West. While Turkey was by no means considering leaving NATO or abandoning its EU bid, it did move to make its foreign policy toward the Middle East independent of Western policies. Thus, Ankara showed little interest in supporting Western initiatives with regard to Iran, Syria, or Sudan. Indeed, Ankara effectively helped Syria escape from its international isolation, became a defender of Iran's position on the nuclear issue, and developed cordial ties with the rulers of Sudan, explicitly ignoring the violence in Darfur, even embracing the war-crime indicted Sudanese leader Omar Al Bashir. In addition, the AKP government improved its relationship with Moscow and joined with Russia in blocking planned NATO maneuvers in the Black Sea.[42] Ankara's ties with Tehran improved substantially under the AKP, leading Erdoğan to refer to Iranian president Mahmoud Ahmadinejad as his "friend."[43] This raises the question how Ankara would react to a renewed Iranian confrontation with Azerbaijan of the type that occurred in 2001. With the AKP in power and enjoying a warm relationship with Iran, it seemed highly unlikely that Ankara would step in to support Azerbaijan the way it did in 2001.

Azerbaijan, conversely, was largely supportive of U.S. initiatives. It was one of only three Muslim-majority countries (the others being Kazakhstan and Albania) to contribute troops to the Iraq operation, and Baku made closer ties with Washington a priority in its foreign policy. Thus, the changes in Turkey caused much friction between Ankara and Baku. In sum, a divergence of worldviews developed between the governments in Baku and Ankara, and a growing mental distance emerged between them. As a result, Azerbaijani leaders no longer felt kindred to Turkish leaders the way they had in the 1990s. Indeed, in terms of lifestyle and worldview, the tables had been turned: the Azerbaijani leadership was now effectively more "Western" than its Turkish counterpart, whose outlook increasingly resembled that commonly found in the capitals of the Middle East.

The Decline of the Turkish-Azerbaijani Relationship

The growing differences of the first decade of the new century prepared the ground for a rapid unraveling of Turkish-Azerbaijani relations. The unraveling began when Ankara reactivated its regional role in the aftermath of Russia's 2008 war against Georgia—but did so with a set of priorities entirely different from those that had characterized Turkish activism in the 1990s. A combination of the Turkish response to the Georgian war, Turkey's energy policy, and its rethinking of relations with Armenia all contributed to the imperiling of the alliance that had developed between Turkey and Azerbaijan.

The Georgian War

When Russia invaded Georgia, in August 2008, Turkey's reaction showed the conflicting pressures and instincts guiding its decision making. On the one hand, the AKP government paid lip service to Turkey's Western alignment and the joint projects it has been pursuing with the West for years; but on the other hand, it launched an initiative that explicitly shut out the West.

Following the crisis, the Turkish government did not object when U.S. warships, most significantly the flagship of the U.S. Navy's Mediterranean fleet, the USS *Mount Whitney*, transited the Turkish straits and entered the Black Sea. Though the Montreux Convention did not leave Turkey much choice, the absence of resistance to the *Mount Whitney*'s presence showed that Ankara was sensitive to Western policies and had stood up to Russian criticism. Indeed, Moscow imposed sudden and arbitrary restrictions on Turkish trade at the time as a warning. Likewise, Turkey was among the first countries to provide logistical support and other assistance to Georgia. These actions were directly in line with Turkey's long-term interests in the region, and consistent with policies of the past decade. In fact, Ankara's main accomplishment in the region had been the realization of the South Caucasus energy corridor, which was part and parcel of a plan to make Turkey an energy and transportation hub for Europe. Russian policies in Georgia were widely interpreted to threaten the future of the energy and transportation corridor, and were therefore regarded as a major blow to Turkish interests. This strategic picture would logically have provided an impetus for a strengthening of the Turkish-American coordination on South Caucasus affairs, which was launched in the late 1990s but had been in-creasingly moribund since the U.S. invasion of Iraq in 2003.

When Prime Minister Erdoğan launched a stability initiative for the South Caucasus in the middle of the Georgian war, however, the format and proposed membership of the initiative raised important questions as to Ankara's intentions. The initiative included the three Caucasian states, Turkey, and Russia—but not the United States, the EU, or Iran. Further-more, Turkey's Western partners were neither consulted not informed ahead of the move, and the logic behind this particular membership struc-ture was never explained. In effect, although a Turkish initiative, such a mechanism would create a structure dominated by Russia, with Turkey playing a secondary role. Given Russia's overt claims to a sphere of inter-est of its own in the South Caucasus, it was unclear what role Moscow would see for Turkey in the region, other than that of a secondary power legitimizing Russian dominance. While China had counterbalanced Rus-sian influence in Central Asia through the Shanghai Cooperation Organiza-tions, Turkey did not have enough clout to play a similar role on its own in the Caucasus. Instead, the creation of a regional body that had no members from the West contradicted the ambitions of Euro-Atlantic integration dear to Azerbaijan and Georgia. Therefore, the proposed structure flew in the face of these two states' national interests, and both Tbilisi and Baku privately voiced their concerns regarding the initiative.

The launch and format of the stability initiative clearly illustrated the changes in Ankara's perception of its northern and eastern neighborhoods. It showed that Russia had gained more and more importance in Turkish foreign policy, while that of the West had weakened. In times past, a crisis between Russia and the West such as that brought on by the Georgian war would have found Turkey standing resolutely with the Western alliance. Yet Ankara's reaction in 2008 was different: carving out a role for itself in coordination with Russia but not with the West, not to mention Azerbaijan.

Ankara's moves put Azerbaijan in a difficult position. While Baku had duly noted the growing distance between itself and Ankara, there had not yet been any concrete implications for Azerbaijan's security or national interests. Relations had had their ups and downs in the past, but the Azerbaijani leadership considered Turkey its most reliable ally. But crises test friendships, and the Georgian war was the greatest crisis in the South Caucasus since independence. And during this crisis, Ankara's behavior reinforced, to an alarming extent, the existing Azerbaijani fears over Turkey's drift.

The Downturn in Energy Cooperation

Trade and energy had always been key elements in the Turkish-Azerbaijani relationship. Indeed, the connections among Azerbaijan, Georgia, and Turkey grew in the 1990s to form the centerpiece of the infrastructure system dubbed the "east-west superhighway" (see chapter 9 of the present volume). The system's flagship project, the Baku-Tbilisi-Ceyhan oil pipeline, had the greatest geopolitical significance. Other important projects included the South Caucasus gas pipeline linking Baku and Erzurum, and the Kars-Akhalkalaki-Baku rail project. Development of highway infrastructure alongside these developments completed the picture.

From the start, energy and transportation relations have had economic, strategic, and cultural implications for the bilateral Turkish-Azerbaijani relationship. In economic terms, the development of energy and transportation infrastructure has gradually strengthened trade ties between Turkey and Azerbaijan. Turkish truckers and bus drivers, already accustomed to traveling long distances across their large home country, have not found it difficult to extend their routes to include smaller neighbors such as Azerbaijan and Georgia. Reasonably good infrastructure and easy border-crossing procedures have made it all the easier to integrate the Azerbaijani and Georgian economies with the growing Turkish economy, which, because it is becoming more integrated with the European economy, enables the European economic integration of the two South Caucasus states as well. As Western business practices take root in Turkey, the integration of the Caucasus with Turkey will accelerate the implementation of such practices in Azerbaijan. As Azerbaijan has become an important potential transit country for East Caspian resources, its strategic importance to Turkey's business and political relations with Central Asia has grown as well. Energy was a key area of cooperation in the 1990s, but in the late 2000s it became an area of discord. This discord focused mainly on the second stage of the development of Azerbaijani natural gas exports to and through Turkey. Indeed, when phase two of development of the Shah-Deniz oil field was poised to get under way, this meant that the South Caucasus pipeline needed to be upgraded—just as Turkey was sorting out the conflicting objectives underlying its ambition to become an energy hub. Central to that ambition is the Nabucco pipeline, the leading project to bring Caspian Sea and Middle Eastern gas to Europe via Turkey. The longest stretch of the pipeline by far—longer than the segments in all other participating countries combined—is scheduled to pass through Turkey. Hence, Turkey could be termed the key state in the project—as well as the key to any prospects for transporting gas from the Caspian to the EU, given the expensive nature of alternative routes through the Black Sea. The transit issue has been a major complicating factor and sore point in Turkish-Azerbaijani relations, with Ankara's confusing and changeable demands causing much concern in Baku.

The planning or construction of several energy projects that would require the involvement of Turkey—not only the Baku-Tbilisi-Ceyhan pipeline but also Iraqi energy projects, a proposed pipeline linking Ceyhan with the Black Sea port city of Samsun, and the Nabucco project—boosted Turkish self-confidence and strengthened Turkey's chances of becoming an energy hub. Yet Turkey's own intransigence has, paradoxically, helped undermine that very prospect. Turkey has demanded the right to purchase 15 percent of the gas at discounted prices and to resell the gas that enters its territory, and has voiced various claims regarding transit fees. Turkey's insistence that it continue to benefit from the flow of cheap gas from Azerbaijan's Shah-Deniz field—gas that it acquired at well below market prices, indeed, at levels about a third of what it pays for Russian gas (see chapter 13)—has upset Baku as well as gas-producing companies.

Turkish policies have been driven by three factors: Turkey's need to consider both domestic consumption and transit politics, its wish to keep domestic prices low, and its attempts to turn itself into a regional energy hub rather than a mere transit country. The first and second issues are rather straightforward: Turkey's large and growing domestic market remains heavily dependent on Russian gas. Being the main transit country for alternative gas supplies to Europe would be a risky position, given Russia's history of politically motivated supply interruptions. Thus, Turkish negotiators have sought to acquire rights to divert gas from transit pipelines into its domestic market, should the need arise. The main problem has been finding the formula and pricing for such a mechanism.

Turkey's hub ambitions are more complex. At times, certain policymakers in Ankara have appeared to toy with the idea of turning Turkey into a "second Gazprom"—by buying gas at low prices at its eastern borders and reselling at higher prices on its the western borders—rather than have it function as a transit state operating according to market principles and European business practices. While obviously bad for producers such as Azerbaijan, this idea was ill fated for at least two other reasons. First, under such conditions, Western governments and companies would be unwilling to make the investments Turkey would need in order to realize these projects. Indeed, the corridor through Turkey has become attractive precisely because it operates under European market conditions, something that would change should Turkey turn into a "gas hub." Second, such Turkish ambitions were effectively killed by Russia's decision to offer Caspian Sea producers much higher prices than it had set earlier—very much in order to undermine Turkey's chances of becoming a major transit state. More generally, Turkish policymakers have tended to use energy projects as bargaining tools *before* they are actually built, a practice that discourages partners and in fact undermines these very projects, reducing their likelihood of being built and thus of Turkey benefiting from them. The low point came in February 2009, when Prime Minister Erdoğan made comments at a speech in Brussels that suggested that Turkey's support for Nabucco and energy issues more generally had become a matter for negotiation in the talks on EU accession.[44]

A key problem was that Turkey appeared to lack a coherent strategy until 2009. In reality, Turkey lacked a *coordinated* energy policy, not to mention a diplomatic strategy linked to energy policy. The leadership of the Ministry of Energy, often at odds with the Ministry of Foreign Affairs, was a leading impediment during the tenure of Hilmi Güler as energy minister. The appointment of a new minister, Taner Yıldız, in mid-2008 appeared to be an improvement. Well versed in energy affairs compared to his predecessor, Yıldız espoused a more realistic view of Turkey's role in European energy supplies. In particular, Yıldız regarded as unrealistic the prospect of Turkey becoming a gas hub. He favored instead making Turkey a transit country, a role that could provide long-term geostrategic benefits.[45] Nevertheless, such ideas appeared to continue to be entertained by Prime Minister Erdoğan. Given the increasingly authoritarian manner in which Erdoğan ran his government, the energy minister was not really the issue. No agreement was reached between Azerbaijan and Turkey on transit rights during 2009. This effectively blocked development of the second phase of the Shah-Deniz project. Officials of StatoilHydro, the commercial operator of Shah-Deniz, confirmed that production from phase two would be postponed until 2016, explicitly citing the absence of a transit agreement.[46]

Meanwhile, Russia was not slow in capitalizing on the discord between the two Turkic states, as Gazprom moved in and offered to buy all of Azerbaijan's gas at European netback prices—in other words, three times what Turkey was paying. In what was more a symbolic move than anything else, Baku agreed in 2009 to supply half a billion cubic meters of natural gas per year to Russia—a small quantity, but nonetheless a signal to Turkey and the West that Azerbaijan had options and was running out of patience. Indeed, Baku was now torn between economic and political considerations. Russia's offer was financially lucrative—if genuine—but politically dangerous, it being clear that it was geostrategically and not economically motivated, since Russia would not profit from reselling Azerbaijani gas to Europe if it paid European prices to Azerbaijan. The politically favorable option, Nabucco, on the other hand, failed to materialize, and appeared increasingly distant on account of European indecision and Turkish confusion.

The Armenian Border Issue

The most divisive of all issues in Turkish-Azerbaijani relations has been the Armenian border issue. Since the late 1990s, the United States and Europe have exerted mounting pressure on Turkey to open economic relations with Armenia, an action that would have the effect of breaking the embargo Turkey imposed in solidarity with Azerbaijan following the occupation of Kelbajar Province in 1993. Azerbaijan, of course, adamantly objects to such a move as long as Armenia occupies almost a sixth of its territory, urging Turkey to refrain from caving in to Western importuning.[47]

Nonetheless, Western pressure (along with lobbying by business groups in eastern Turkey) has been the main reason for Turkish leaders to consider opening the border with Armenia. Given the European focus of Turkish foreign policy during the first term of the AKP government, and the growing distrust between Baku and Ankara, Azerbaijani leaders increasingly feared a Turkish "sellout" on the issue. On several occasions during the 2000s, rumors of Turkish openings toward Armenia sparked anxiety in Baku, but nothing actually happened until 2008.

Strong forces in Turkey in fact had resisted a unilateral opening to Armenia, and not only out of solidarity with Azerbaijan. Suspicious of Armenian irredentist designs, advanced most prominently by the Armenian diaspora, Ankara wanted Yerevan to recognize the border between the two countries. Arguing that the initiation of diplomatic relations would imply the mutual recognition of borders, Armenian leaders refused to make what they termed a "superfluous statement" to that effect.[48] As for the diaspora, groups such as Armenian National Committee of America overtly opposed Yerevan's recognition of the border with Turkey, arguing it would constitute "renouncing the rightful return of Armenian lands."[49] Since 1998, moreover, campaigning to have the 1915 massacres of Armenians in the Ottoman Empire recognized as genocide had become official policy in Yerevan, bringing the Armenian government in alignment with the diaspora groups and irritating Ankara further.

Turkey's consistent approach since the mid-1990s had been to make the normalization of Turkish relations with Armenia an element in the peace process between Armenia and Azerbaijan—essentially offering to open its border with Armenia at some point in a coordinated sequence of events that would contribute to resolution of the conflict. Turkey refused to take that step unilaterally, demanding prior Armenian concessions in the conflict; to do otherwise, the logic went, would lead to abandonment of the remaining leverage on Armenia to vacate occupied territories, and essentially to acquiescence in the ethnic cleansing of Azerbaijanis. This logic continues to command strong public support in Turkey. Thus, linking the Turkish-Armenian relationship with the Armenian-Azerbaijani conflict remained conventional wisdom in both Turkey and Azerbaijan. But Western officials and pundits—especially the International Crisis Group—had other ideas.[50] Delinking the processes, they argued, would render Armenia more secure, as it would not have to fear Turkey; it would also reduce Armenia's dependence on Russia and, therefore, would make Armenia more willing to compromise on the Karabakh issue. What this line of reasoning failed to do, of course, was offer any reason why Armenia would find it in its interest to compromise on Karabakh once it improved its relations with Turkey. Indeed, an equally logical conclusion would be that a safer Armenia—ruled by a leadership with deep roots in Karabakh—would hold on ever more strongly to Karabakh. In sum, the dominant Western view neglected the fact that Armenia did not hold on to Karabakh out of fear, but because it thought the world would eventually accept its military conquest.

Until 2008, the prospects for Turkish-Armenian normalization seemed remote, as the calculus of Turkish national interest spoke against unilateral Turkish action. As long as political forces sensitive to Turkic solidarity were strong in the Turkish government—for which such a move would constitute a sellout of Turkey's closest ally—it would have only slim chances of becoming actual government policy. Even leaving aside the cultural linkages, Turkey hardly stood to gain from a unilateral opening to Armenia, because a delinking of the Armenian border issue from the Armenian-Azerbaijani conflict would inevitably alienate Azerbaijan. Azerbaijan's population is almost three times Armenia's, and its gross domestic product almost four times larger. Azerbaijan has extensive energy resources that are delivered to—or at least through—Turkey, and it is strategically located as Turkey's gateway to Central Asia. If winning over Armenia meant losing the privileged relationship with Azerbaijan, that seemed like a bad trade. The fact that the closed Armenia border was an irritant in Turkey's relations with the EU and United States was, in the balance, something Turkish officials were willing to put up with. If the EU proved itself serious about Turkish accession, the policy could always be changed.

Ankara's calculus nevertheless changed in 2008, for three reasons. First, the AKP's retention of a parliamentary majority in the 2007 elections emboldened the party in its foreign and domestic policies. Its foreign policy doctrine, formulated by Erdoğan's chief adviser and subsequent foreign minister, Ahmet Davutoğlu, featured a "zero-problem" policy toward Turkey's neighbors. Resistance to an opening toward Armenia was hence weakened. Second, the war in Georgia shook the fragile status quo in the South Caucasus and spurred greater domestic activism on the part of the Turkish government. Turkey's stability initiative was well received in Yerevan. Indeed, the shift in Turkish policy, which appeared to imply acceptance of a position as "junior partner" to Russia in the South Caucasus, opened the way for further contacts with Armenia and reduced Russian opposition to Turkish moves in the region. The third—and by far most important—factor was Barack Obama's election to the presidency of the United States in November 2008. Obama had made it clearer than any major presidential candidate in modern history that, if elected, he intended to recognize the Armenian massacres as genocide, a position that caused acute concern in Ankara. Rapprochement with Armenia was one of the few remaining ways that Turkey could get President Obama off the hook domestically on that commitment by candidate Obama—and that was precisely what the Obama administration demanded from Turkey. Everyone understood that American recognition of the massacres as genocide would kill any chances of a Turkish-Armenian rapprochement. Thus, the prospect of exactly such a rapprochement could influence both the Obama administration and moderate elements in the Armenian diaspora to desist from pressing for Obama's recognition. Indeed, arguing for one would now appear foolhardy, as it would sabotage the best opportunity in years to improve Armenia's regional situation.

These factors all combined to bring about the "soccer diplomacy" that began when Abdullah Gül, now president of Turkey, traveled to Yerevan in early September 2008 at the invitation of his Armenian counterpart to attend a qualifying game between the national teams of the two countries, complemented by a flurry of diplomatic exchanges and meetings. By late March, plans for a normalization of relations beginning in early April were unofficially announced and leaked to the media—but these plans fudged the question of whether Ankara had actually delinked its normalization of relations with Armenia from the Armenian-Azerbaijani conflict.

Baku's outrage did not register in Turkish media and politics until after the local elections of March 2009, in which the AKP did much worse than expected. The media and main opposition parties in Turkey now took up this issue, castigating the government for selling out Azerbaijan. Ilham Aliyev then pulled out from a planned trip to the high-profile Istanbul summit of the Alliance of Civilizations. Turkish efforts to secure his attendance failed, as did two telephone calls from Secretary of State Hillary Clinton, including one promising a meeting with President Obama.

The Turkish government had not expected Azerbaijan's reaction to be so strong; nor had it foreseen the domestic uproar that followed, including in the ruling party's own ranks. Thus, the AKP regime was forced to backpedal, making it clear that Armenian concessions on Karabakh remained a prerequisite for the ratification of any Turkish-Armenian agreement. Prime Minister Erdoğan traveled to Baku and made clear in his address to the Azerbaijani Parliament that the Turkish-Armenian border would remain closed until a mutually acceptable solution to the Karabakh conflict was found. In effect, he had reverted to Turkey's long-standing policy of linking its relationship to Armenia with the Armenian-Azerbaijani conflict.

On August 31, 2009, the Turkish and Armenian foreign ministers nevertheless signed diplomatic protocols not only on the establishment of diplomatic relations but on broader bilateral ties. This was likely due to strong

American pressure not to let the initiative die out, as well as the cabinet shakeup that elevated Ahmet Davutoğlu to the post of foreign minister, allowing him to emphasize his "zero-problem" approach to regional foreign policy. In fact, after successive rapprochements with formerly antagonistic neighbors including Greece and Syria, the state of affairs between Turkey and Armenia was the main antagonistic relationship left to sort out.

Ankara's problem was that as long as the Armenian-Azerbaijani conflict remained unresolved and Azerbaijani internally displaced persons were unable to return to their homes, Turkish policy toward Armenia could not be dissociated from relations with Azerbaijan. In the context of the officially supported maxim "one nation, two states," any unilateral opening to Armenia that was perceived as detrimental to Azerbaijan would be explosive stuff. This conundrum was reflected in the AKP government's contradictory statements. In signing the protocols, Ankara effectively committed to opening the border within two months of ratification. But in statements making explicit reference to the border opening, foreign minister Davutoğlu and other officials also stated that no move injurious to the interests of Azerbaijan would be made.

The only way these conflicting statements could be reconciled would be through progress in the parallel process of conflict resolution between Armenia and Azerbaijan. Ankara's hope lay in the conclusion of a preliminary deal between Baku and Yerevan envisaging the withdrawal of Armenian forces from the five occupied provinces of Azerbaijan outside Karabakh itself. Thus, the AKP government made itself dependent on forces that it could not control; even though there were positive signals in 2009, there was no obvious reason to assume that a deal of any kind was imminent. By placing its hopes on the prospect of a Karabakh deal, Ankara once again risked having to choose between reneging on its commitment to normalize ties with Armenia and fulfilling it at the cost of causing a breakdown in its relations with Azerbaijan—neither option being particularly consistent with the "zero-problem" policy. In either situation, Ankara would lose.

The Turkish Parliament's role in this process should not be underestimated. Indeed, it is very doubtful that the AKP, despite its large parliamentary majority, could have gotten the votes for an opening of the Armenian border without progress on Karabakh. Indeed, loud voices within the party were in strong disagreement with the leadership. In this sense, the situation was reminiscent of the 2003 vote on the Iraq war. Then, the party leadership had allowed members to vote according to their consciences, thereby avoiding the need to enforce party discipline on an unwilling parliamentary group—and thus giving itself an exit strategy. The same strategy could well be used if the Armenian protocols ever got to Parliament. However, the Armenian Constitutional Court's January 2010 ruling on the protocols, which Ankara interpreted as changing their meaning, appeared to provide another exit strategy. Indeed, the court's caveats in interpreting the Protocols not to mean any end to Armenia's quest for recognition of the 1915 massacres as genocide, emphasizing the de-linking of the Turkish-Armenian relationship from the Karabakh issue, and murky legalistic language on the common border all offered the Turkish leadership an opportunity to lambast Armenia for changing the game.

No matter the outcome of the Turkish-Armenian rapprochement, the strategic calculus in Baku was profoundly altered by this episode. For all practical purposes, the privileged relationship Azerbaijan had enjoyed with Turkey was over—at least as long as the AKP stayed in power. Not only was the relationship over: as one senior Azerbaijani diplomat put it, "We are no longer allies."[51] Azerbaijan could no longer count on Turkey, while the singularly adamant American push for Turkey to move on the Armenian opening also bred disillusionment with the West. No event of the previous fifteen years had made Azerbaijani policymakers feel as isolated as the Turkish-Armenian rapprochement.

Turkey and Azerbaijan Today

During the first decade of Azerbaijan's independence, Turkey was the country's main foreign ally and in many ways its mentor. But under the fraternal veneer, the relationship was never uncomplicated. The product of two vastly different historical experiences, the size disparity, and sheer national interest, these complications were most evident in the 1995 coup attempt against Heydar Aliyev and in the tensions during 2008–09 over energy transit and Armenia.

However, the real strength of the long-term relationship between Azerbaijan and Turkey lies not in the political elites but at the societal level, stemming from the close ethnolinguistic ties between the two countries and the considerable economic, cultural, and educational exchanges between the two societies. Aside from the substantial trade ties between them, Turkish popular culture has permeated Azerbaijan deeply. Turkish popular and traditional music artists regularly perform in Azerbaijan and attract huge crowds. Likewise, the successes of the Turkish soccer team have generated a huge following in Azerbaijan. Witness this enthusiastic account:

> Traffic was forced to stop in major streets of Baku for many hours on June 16 and 22 [2002] as thousands of people poured into the streets and Baku's main Azadliq Square to cheer for their team and its unexpected success. The police [were] shocked and caught off guard and all they could do was to helplessly watch the chaos developing in the streets of the usually calm center of Baku. People were shouting slogans like "Türkiye," "Türkiye and Azerbaijan," "Türkiye, Victory," carrying Azerbaijani and Turkish flags and painting their faces and bod[ies] in red...red, the color of Turkism![52]

Pan-Turkism may not be a viable political ideology, but Turkic solidarity does remains a societal factor. Especially during times of pressure, a sense of brotherhood with Turkey has shown itself to be a powerful emotion among Azerbaijanis. The largest crowd ever recorded in post-Soviet Azerbaijan also had a Turkish connection: the air show by Turkish air force jets at the time of General Kıvrıkoğlu's summer 2001 visit drew several hundred thousand people into the streets of Baku. This points to a deep cultural connection between Turkey and Azerbaijan that will continue to form the backbone of the relationship for the foreseeable future.

However, this sense of solidarity is much more deeply rooted in Azerbaijan than it is in Turkey. That may be a natural consequence of the great size and power disparity between the two countries: Turkey will always be more important to Azerbaijan than Azerbaijan is to Turkey. Furthermore, as Islamic solidarity increasingly rivals Turkic solidarity in Turkey, this is likely to further temper the intensity of the relationship on the Turkish side. But it is also possible that as Azerbaijan becomes wealthier and more self-conscious, its population may not continue to acquiesce in being treated as the neglected younger brother. As Azerbaijan matures as an independent nation, its ties to Turkey may very well become less emotional and more pragmatic.

Even as some signs point to a more dispassionate relationship, the two countries' commonly held Muslim faith is opening new avenues of solidarity. Turkish religious groups—in particular the Nurcu movement of Fethullah Gülen (see chapter 10)—have spent two decades building a base of support in Azerbaijan. Especially through its schools, the Gülen movement has helped create a tight network of young Azerbaijanis who exhibit strong loyalty to Turkey—but in the form of an attachment to the leader of the movement, Fethullah Gülen, and his brand of "moderate Islam," not to traditional republican Turkish values. Gülen's adherents have already come to play a role in Azerbaijan—for example, exerting pressure (though unsuccessfully) in 2009 on the Azerbaijani government to be more agreeable in regard to Turkey's plan to open its border with Armenia.

As the saying goes, in foreign affairs there are no eternal friends, only eternal interests. That appears to be increasingly true in Turkish-Azerbaijani relations, and it may in fact be in Azerbaijan's interest to begin treating Turkey more as it treats its other foreign partners. Indeed, when the crisis that resulted from Turkey's opening to Armenia broke out in 2008, Azerbaijan realized that it had taken Turkey for granted: it had never even bothered building a serious lobbying presence in Ankara. Precisely because the relationship was built largely on emotions and protestations of brother-hood, the impact of the crisis went very deep in Baku, to the point where the Turkish-Armenian efforts toward rapprochement were understood in some quarters as a betrayal.

The challenge for the future, for both Ankara and Baku, will be to reassess the aphorism that has long encapsulated the two countries' relationship: "one nation, two states." Indeed, there is a logical contradiction in this declaration: considering Azerbaijan and Turkey as one nation implies that they share an unbreakable bond. It follows naturally from this that their respective interests should be identical and joint. But states identify their interests separately, not jointly, through calculation and political processes. In the case of Azerbaijan and Turkey, there is no formal mechanism for consultation that regulates any linkage between their respective political processes. And as long as Azerbaijan and Turkey remain distinct states—and no one seriously expects that to change—their interests, as defined by their respective leaderships, will not always align. The contradiction between the claim of belonging to a single nation and the realities of two states is therefore likely to continue to be the main feature of Turkish-Azerbaijani relations.

15

Azerbaijan and the West

Since independence, Azerbaijan's foreign policy has been remarkably stable, as has its generally western orientation. But an underlying question is whether Azerbaijan is a *part of* the West, or a state that merely has the West as its major foreign partner? Ambivalence on both sides ensures that this question remains unanswered. Azerbaijani leaders are ambivalent toward the commitments required for full integration with the West, while leading Western powers are ambivalent as to whether the South Caucasus in general—and Azerbaijan in particular—could or should form part of the West.

The consistent priority of Azerbaijan's foreign policy has been to consolidate the independence and sovereignty of the country. In this endeavor, Baku has regarded the economic and political norms and institutions of the Western-led international system as supportive of this goal—particularly the international system's advocacy of the equality of states and of the market-based economic principles that have allowed Azerbaijan to build its economic independence through energy sales.

But Azerbaijan has also grown increasingly doubtful of both the ability and the willingness of the West to engage with the South Caucasus region, particularly in regard to security. Given the rising political price that Moscow (and, to a lesser extent, Tehran) has exacted from countries in the region that seek Euro-Atlantic integration, the logic that impelled the West's expansion into Central and Eastern Europe in the 1990s cannot automatically be applied in the South Caucasus. Azerbaijan's relations with the West therefore cannot be understood simply in terms of integration, but should be seen, rather, from the perspective of an increasingly independent state that pursues such relations, but not at the cost of disregarding the realities dictated by geography and the real political balances in its neighborhood. Even as it has striven for balance in its foreign policy, Azerbaijan has often found itself pushing for greater Western engagement with the South Caucasus, extolling the region's importance to the West.

A comparable level of interest cannot be said to exist on the part of the West. Over time, and among the various Western powers, there have been significant shifts in priorities and attention levels in their approaches to Azerbaijan and the rest of the South Caucasus. In retrospect, the period from about 1997 to 2004 stands out as the pinnacle of Western engagement in Azerbaijan and the South Caucasus. Since then, the West—particularly the United States—seems to have gradually lost interest in both Azerbaijan and the region. That may seem understandable, given that the United States has had its hands full in Iraq and Afghanistan, Europe has been preoccupied by internal divisions and the organizational restructuring of the European Union, and the West in general has been struggling to restore economic stability in the wake of the 2008 financial crisis. But from another perspective, the West's waning interest can be regarded as a sign of strategic myopia, given the importance of Azerbaijan and the South Caucasus in general to some of the most pressing issues facing the West, from energy security to Afghanistan and Iran.

One area of discord among Western actors in regard to Azerbaijan has been concern over the country's domestic political situation. Again, a comparison with the experience of Central and Eastern Europe is relevant. Former Soviet bloc states such as Hungary and Romania largely accepted Western terms on how their polities were to be structured and governed, in view of the greater benefits that would accrue in both economic and security terms from membership in the EU and the North Atlantic Treaty Organization. But exactly because Azerbaijani leaders have never been convinced that they have a realistic chance of gaining either EU or NATO membership, the logic that worked in Central and Eastern Europe has not worked in Azerbaijan. In fact, Azerbaijani leaders have been increasingly skeptical of the sincerity of Western attempts at democracy promotion in their country.

By 2010, Azerbaijan's Western orientation was being seriously tested. Years of declining Western interest, combined with the changes in the global balance of power and Azerbaijan's own meteoric economic rise, fed skepticism in Baku about the primacy of the West, which had seemed so obvious back in the 1990s. In parallel, intensifying Russian courtship of Azerbaijan and the accelerating de-secularization going on next door in Turkey had begun to change the calculus on the ground. Meanwhile, Azerbaijan's political reform agenda had ground to a halt, further slowing the pace of integration with the West. Simply put, in 2010 a Western orientation appeared to be only one of Azerbaijan's many options. To understand the prospects of Azerbaijan's ties with the West, it is worth studying in greater detail the bases of both sides of the relationship.

The Issues Underlying Azerbaijan's Western Orientation

Since 1991, when Azerbaijan became independent, relations with the West have developed and broadened greatly in all fields. These relations can be grouped into three "baskets of issues": governance and democratization, energy and trade, and security cooperation. Over time, these three areas have been accorded varying degrees of importance.

Governance and Democratization

Governance and democratization has always been the most complicated among the three baskets of issues. By virtue of its stated purpose of integration with Euro-Atlantic institutions—that is, subscribing to Western values and principles—Baku made commitments to political reform that Middle Eastern and Central Asian states generally did not. When efforts to live up to these commitments were found wanting, Western countries and organizations often issued strong and occasionally scathing criticism of Azerbaijan's record concerning democracy and human rights. Yet despite this criticism, and the rising frustration it generated, the Azerbaijani government never wavered from its stated course of closer ties with Europe, and never joined the growing Russian-led efforts in the first decade of the new century to coordinate resistance to Western pressure among authoritarian regimes.

Azerbaijan's stance became most evident after 2004, as the "color revolutions" in Georgia and Ukraine injected an ideological element into the geopolitical competition that had long existed in the former Soviet space. Calls for democracy took center stage in Western policies toward the region, and many post-Soviet rulers grew worried—some to the brink of paranoia—about "foreign-sponsored" revolutions. Led by President Vladimir Putin, Russia quickly seized the initiative, seeking to play the role of protector of these authoritarian governments.[1] Moscow then succeeded in enlisting, to varying degrees, most post-Soviet states in condemnation of the Western agenda. In July 2004, for example, Russia convinced eight post-Soviet states—Armenia, Moldova, Belarus, and Ukraine, plus four Central Asian states—to sign a letter criticizing the Organization for Security and Cooperation in Europe (OSCE) for excessively focusing on human rights, applying "double standards," and in general failing to respect the sovereignty of its post-Soviet member states.[2]

From a superficial viewpoint, Azerbaijan would have seemed just the type of regime to come under Moscow's wing. But rejecting paranoia and refusing to follow Moscow's lead, Baku chose to stake out a middle course, emphasizing its commitment to an evolutionary model under which political development would occur in tandem with economic development. For example, Baku refused to endorse the fraudulent 2004 election that would have granted Viktor Yanukovich the presidency of Ukraine, as well as the so-called Tulip Revolution in Kyrgyzstan in 2005, which President Ilham Aliyev dismissed to a senior Western academic as a "primitive coup, not a revolution."[3]

Of course, as shown in chapter 6 of the present volume, the leadership in Baku did take extra security precautions during Azerbaijan's 2005 parliamentary elections, while seeking to deflect criticism of its domestic affairs by playing upon the country's increasing strategic importance in terms of energy issues and international security. Moreover, in recent years Azerbaijani leaders have turned to arguments similar to ones used by Russia in terming Western calls for democratization a form of interference in its internal affairs, especially at times when Baku felt that the West was not helpful on issues close to its heart, such as energy exports or the conflict in Mountainous Karabakh. The point, however, is that the higher levels of government never seemed overly concerned by the growing ideological element in Eurasian geopolitics, and never allowed it to affect the country's foreign policy choices. This is evidenced by the increasingly warm relations President Aliyev developed with the new revolutionary leaders of Georgia and Ukraine, Mikheil Saakashvili and Viktor Yushchenko.

Governance and democracy has decidedly not been Baku's favorite basket of issues in its dealings with the West. The regime has sought to walk a fine line, sticking to its Western orientation while seeking to withstand pressure for further political reform. In the view of Azerbaijani leaders, the areas of energy and trade and security cooperation have offered much better return on its efforts to foster mutually beneficial relations with the West.

Energy and Trade

As Europe grew more concerned over its dependence on Middle Eastern oil and Russian natural gas, Azerbaijan was able to astutely carve a niche for itself as an energy-producing country that sought to play by Europe's rules, thereby providing an opportunity for the diversification Europe so desperately needed and which the United States so strongly supported. Azerbaijani leaders played the energy trump card to build the country's stature both regionally and globally, attracting Western interest that—or so Baku hoped—would result in growing support among Western states for Azerbaijan's independence, security, and territorial integrity. The fact that the country's international position and ties with the West have both improved enormously since the mid-1990s can be clearly attributed to Baku's strategic decision at that time to link its diplomacy to its energy resources.

There are two reasons why Azerbaijan was able to leverage what are—from a global perspective—its relatively limited reserves of oil and gas so as to establish itself as a player on the European stage. First, its geographic position—west of the Caspian Sea and close to Europe—was much more advantageous than that of the Central Asian states. Furthermore, once Georgia stabilized, that neighbor to the west was able to provide reliable access to the Black Sea and Turkey. But second, as noted in chapter 9 of the present volume, Azerbaijan made a point of being a trustworthy supplier and commercial partner. Unlike Russia and Kazakhstan, Azerbaijan did not seek to renegotiate major contracts with Western oil companies. Many officials in Baku felt, like their Kazakh counterparts, that the Production Sharing Agreements (PSAs) were unduly beneficial to the multinational companies and had been signed at a time of national weakness. Nevertheless, Baku did not seek to renegotiate the PSAs, in keeping with its priority of building a reputation for reliability, which provided the basis for the strategic anchoring of the country to the West in economic and political terms.[4]

Heydar Aliyev built oil diplomacy into a smoothly executed strategy. He understood that oil was Azerbaijan's only means of positioning itself on the international scene and consolidating its independence. Handing out oil concessions, in the form of participation in PSAs, allowed Aliyev to make it in the interest of the major powers to support Azerbaijan—and to support his own government, an arrangement that provided stability while some opposition groups spoke of renegotiating contracts.

First on the list of powers to be cultivated was the United States, followed by Russia, Turkey, Europe, Iran, and Japan. Once American oil companies were enlisted, they also helped provide access to senior political figures and influential lobbying firms in Washington.[5] A number of former high U.S. officials began taking an interest in Azerbaijan, giving attention partly to the country's strategic location but also to the oil industry. The U.S.-Azerbaijan Chamber of Commerce, created in 1995, has counted among its advisory council former U.S. National Security Advisors Henry Kissinger, Brent Scowcroft, and Zbigniew Brzezinski, as well as former secretary of state James Baker III, as well as former secretary of defense Dick Cheney (who left the board when he became vice president) and Richard Armitage, who would go on to be Deputy Secretary of State. This suggests the success, in remarkably quick order, of Azerbaijan's campaign to enlist support in the United States. Heydar Aliyev's efforts were crowned with a state visit to Washington in 1997, which was presented to the Azerbaijani public as a major foreign policy achievement, and was broadcast in smallest detail over and over again on national television—signaling the importance accorded by Aliyev's government to relations with the United States.

Azerbaijan also built increasingly close ties with Israel, and when Turkey and Israel consolidated relations in the 1990s, Azerbaijan became, de facto, the "northern flank" of this alliance, at least from Jerusalem's perspective. Hence, the pro-Israeli lobby in the U.S. Congress began supporting Azerbaijan's cause alongside Turkey's.[6] Though the Turkish-Israeli relationship deteriorated once the Islamic conservative Justice and Development Party took power in Turkey in 2002, this only lent further impetus to the Azerbaijani-Israeli relationship.

Making the most of its carefully nurtured relationships with its regional and Western partners, Azerbaijan saw to completion the major infrastructural projects that now link the country to Turkey and the West and make it a supplier of both oil and natural gas to the EU. From Azerbaijan's perspective, the natural follow-up to the Baku-Tbilisi-Ceyhan and Samsun-Ceyhan projects was the Nabucco gas pipeline, which would bring large quantities of Azerbaijani gas to the EU. Indeed, it is notable how long Azerbaijan eschewed all other options for gas sales, including sales to both Russia and Iran. In spite of divisions in Europe on Nabucco, decreasing American engagement in regional energy diplomacy, and Russian pressure, Azerbaijan stuck to its commitment even as delays on the project began to affect the production schedules for the Shah-Deniz project. Only after relations with Turkey soured and Moscow offered prices 50 percent higher than those Turkey seemed ready to pay did Baku agree to sell small quantities of gas to Russia. Even in 2010, President Ilham Aliyev kept urging European leaders to take the Nabucco project seriously—an indication of the durability of the Western orientation of Azerbaijan's foreign policy in the energy field.

Security Cooperation

Given Azerbaijan's location, security has been one of the country's major concerns, and a driving force in its relationship with the West. Moreover, security has very often interacted significantly with energy; in part, energy has served as an instrument to increase Azerbaijan's security.

Baku's goals in engaging with the West on security issues have derived from its threat perceptions, involving both the conflict with Armenia (where Azerbaijan seeks to overturn the status quo) and the geopolitical threats emanating primarily from Russia and Iran. These goals have included building support for Azerbaijan's independence, engaging Western powers in becoming constructively involved with the Karabakh conflict, and, more broadly, achieving recognition of Azerbaijan's importance in regional and international security affairs, as a means of obtaining Western commitments—formal or informal—to the country's security.

Azerbaijan has thus walked a fine line between being a consumer and a provider of security. As a consumer of security, it is most concerned with meeting its needs in regard to its unresolved conflict with Armenia and regional geopolitical challenges. In appeals to the West, it has targeted the norms and principles that govern Western policies with regard to the right of a small country to independence, but especially with regard to the Karabakh conflict, in which Azerbaijan has consistently depicted itself as an aggrieved party seeking to have international law upheld. On the other hand, it has used its oil and gas exports and its contributions to the international coalition against terrorism and to various peacekeeping operations to portray itself as a provider of security. In doing so, Azerbaijan has appealed to the self-interest of the West, notably in terms of energy and the struggle against terrorism. In the 1990s, energy was Azerbaijan's main instrument for gaining cooperation in the security field. This policy worked remarkably well, as evidenced by the growing Western (and especially American) engagement with the country, and the fact that Azerbaijan became increasingly stable and secure as an independent state. In 2001, Azerbaijan was able to add a dimension to this: whereas there had been only limited scope for it to claim credibly to provide added value in terms of security for the West, that changed with the terrorist attacks of September 11. President Heydar Aliyev's immediate and positive response contributed significantly, but most important was Azerbaijan's geographic position, crucial to any logistical link between NATO and Afghanistan. Baku capitalized on this, and took the extra step of sending a symbolic number of soldiers to Iraq following the 2003 U.S. invasion. Azerbaijan also has continued to provide intelligence and other support in the global struggle against terrorism. In later years, after withdrawing from Iraq in 2008, Azerbaijan increased the size of its contingent in Afghanistan, and sought to contribute to the supply logistics of the U.S. effort there by building a transport corridor, in cooperation with Georgia.

The Development of Western Interests

The West was just as unprepared for the independence of the post-Soviet republics as the states surrounding the erstwhile Soviet space. Western scholarship and expertise on the Soviet Union was heavily focused on the Russian-speaking world, whereas the Caucasus and Central Asia were, with some notable exceptions, hardly studied in their own right.[7] For this reason, attributable to inertia, as well as general confusion about the direction of world politics following the end of the Cold War, Western interests in the region were hardly obvious to anyone in the early 1990s, and awareness of the debilitating conflicts besetting the region was sketchy, at best. These were—and to a large extent remain—areas that Western leaders considered troublesome, that they understood poorly, that were of uncertain importance to them, and from which they sought to maintain a healthy distance.

One possible explanation for this blend of wariness and apathy was the focus of Western attention on the conflicts in the Balkans. But it also betrayed an implicit perception, lingering to this day, that these territories were part of Russia's "turf." Politically, the United States took the early lead in making the protection of the independence and sovereignty of the Soviet successor states a policy priority. This was hugely significant, as it constituted a symbolic statement of solidarity with newly independent nations consistent with America's own tradition of anticolonialism. By contrast, European countries were much slower to defend the sovereignty of these new states, and remain much more tolerant toward Russian dominance there.

Acknowledgment of the significance of the region has grown more widespread in recent years, in particular with the increasing importance of energy security and strategic access to the Caucasus and Central Asia. To this should be added the development in the West of considerable expertise on this part of the world. Academic and research institutions in the West, especially in the United States, possess resources and capabilities that far surpass those of their counterparts in Iran, Russia, China, and Turkey. Many Western colleges and universities now offer courses on the region, enabling students—that is, future decision makers—to take advantage of the developing expertise. Dozens if not hundreds of Western students in the social sciences and humanities have written or are writing dissertations on

Central Asia and the Caucasus. Consequently, the onetime scarcity of knowledge of the region has given way to a significant and expanding body of research. Expanding this knowledge even further have been the hundreds if not thousands of diplomats and businesspeople who have acquainted themselves with the region.

Governance and Democracy

The West has continuously stated its interest in the development in the former Soviet Union of sovereign, democratic states based on the rule of law, respectful of human rights, and supportive of market economics. Given that liberal democracy developed into the morally and—in the 1990s—politically dominant norm in world politics, nearly all post-Soviet states, including Azerbaijan, pledged allegiance to these basic principles of governance—if not in practice, then at least as a goal. The Azerbaijani Popular Front government had a strongly stated democratic ideology, which formed what effectively became a kind of benchmark against which subsequent governments were compared. The Popular Front's brief time in power (1992–93) was plagued by chaos and anarchy, with the short-lived rulers learning that unchecked freedom and democracy made the country ungovernable. Nevertheless, flawed as the Popular Front era was, it drew a line in the sand, restoring continuity with the democratic principles established in 1918 with the First Republic.

When Heydar Aliyev came back to power in 1993, Azerbaijan was a considerably different place than it had been in early 1992, and certainly very different from the Central Asian republics of the former Soviet space. Its society had had a taste, if ever so imperfect, of openness, and going back to overtly authoritarian rule was not on the agenda. Moreover, Aliyev presided over a weak state that needed support to consolidate independence, and the West was the only force capable of providing a balance to Russian and Iranian schemes. This meant that Azerbaijan's ruling elite not only had to pay lip service to a pluralistic society, but would also have to live up to certain elements of participatory governance and human rights in order to be able to attract Western support for its security. Western states and organizations would also be comparing developments in Azerbaijan to the widespread perception of the Popular Front's rule as a democratic, if ill-fated, period.

As a result, a peculiar type of dance has developed over the years. Azerbaijan has proved responsive to Western criticism, but in fact has fulfilled its commitments only gradually and partially. The story of Azerbaijan's interaction with the international community is one of numerous last-minute concessions ahead of elections, machinations by elites to maintain influence in spite of steps taken to liberalize the political system, and occasional outright flouting of commitments when that was perceived as necessary to the ruling elite's political survival.

As for the West, it has had serious problems with the delivery of its message, and this is not specific to Azerbaijan. Too often, Western representatives come as the bearers of a gospel, preaching to local leaders about their flaws and faults in a manner often perceived as hectoring and condescending, if not neo-colonial. Moreover, most Western governments and organizations have focused excessively on elections as the central element of democratization, thereby neglecting institution-building processes, particularly at the provincial and local levels.[8] Whereas provincial cities and towns see little Western interest throughout the year, during election times Western election observers descend like locusts a day or two prior to the vote, only to disappear again after the international press conference. Moreover, Western diplomats and representatives of various organizations often live out of touch with the local population. They, and the Western-educated local civil society elite they foster and fund, typically outshine the poor, badly educated, and resource-deprived local government officials they interact with. While this situation is common to most developing countries, it has particular bearing in a conflict-ridden country such as Azerbaijan.

Azerbaijani officials and observers have been struck by the depth of Western emotion about their system of governance, while the Westerners seemed considerably less interested in other lofty principles, including concern for the plight of destitute refugees or the condemnation of ethnic cleansing and territorial conquest. In 2009, Ilham Aliyev's moderate and progressive foreign policy adviser, Novruz Mammedov, epitomized this reaction, stating that the West had cared more about the jailing of two bloggers than about the hundreds of thousands of refugees who had yet to return to their homes.[9] Such feelings are widespread, and strengthen the impression in Azerbaijan that the West is guided by double standards. Western representatives are seen as promoting democracy not necessarily in an honest manner but to advance their own interests in the region, however vaguely defined. As Mammedov put it, "We consider this as a tool of pressure on Azerbaijan."[10] Invidious comparisons tied to the "color revolutions," in particular, have raised the hackles of Azerbaijani officials. Where Georgia appeared to pursue an embrace of democracy with the Rose Revolution, Azerbaijan's development was seen in the West as exactly the opposite: an undemocratic "dynastic succession" from father to son, involving ugly crackdowns on the opposition. Whether or not this characterization was fair, it definitely remained compelling among Western elites, forming a substantial impediment to better strategic relations between Azerbaijan and the West. The inability of the government to handle the transfer of power without police brutality in both 2003 and 2005 was a serious and unnecessary setback in the government's attempts to gain international legitimacy.

In light of Azerbaijan's vigorous economic recovery, spectacular double-digit growth, and, since 2003, increasing political consolidation, Azerbaijani officials have become more confident in their own strength, and less patient with Western lecturing on democracy. For instance, while he has not gone so far as to join Russia's antidemocracy coalition within the OSCE, President Aliyev has repeatedly made clear that he does not view Western pressure for democratization as sincere. The salience of energy issues in the mid- and late 1990s somewhat quieted Western criticism, as did the primacy of security concerns in the aftermath of 9/11. Then, around the time of the Iraq invasion, there was a resurgence of the freedom agenda among American and European policymakers that had the result of greatly complicated Ilham Aliyev's relations with the West after his election in 2003. But the wheel kept turning, and by 2010 surging energy prices, problems over Iran, and a certain amount of disillusionment with "color revolutions" helped diminish concern with democracy promotion. Such shifts in emphasis have only served to heighten the Azerbaijani leadership's skepticism regarding the sincerity of the West.

Energy and Trade

Azerbaijan's place in the world is greatly conditioned by its energy resources. It was the Caspian oil rush in the mid-1990s that put Azerbaijan on the map; it was oil interests that helped Azerbaijan acquire a lobby in Washington in the late 1990s; and it was oil that built Azerbaijan's ties with Great Britain, perhaps its most important Western European relationship.

The 1994 "contract of the century" sparked Azerbaijan's development as an important energy-producing state. In the wake of this mammoth deal with energy multinationals, Heydar Aliyev's oil diplomacy helped Azerbaijan build relations with Western leaders and market itself as an alternative energy producer to the Middle East. While the groundwork was laid in the late 1990s, it was not until 2000 to 2005 that this policy came to fruition.

During this period, oil diplomacy became increasingly integral to the advancement of Baku's security interests. Two trends in international politics combined to underline Azerbaijan's importance as a player in the energy sector. The first was the deterioration of the West's relationship with the Muslim world after 9/11, which sparked concerns in the West about over-reliance on Middle Eastern oil resources. The second trend was the rapid growth of energy consumption in the huge and booming Chinese and Indian economies, which coincided with a decrease in the growth of global oil production. This led to fears of the irreversible peak in global oil production occurring earlier than previously anticipated.[11] These two trends converged to drive oil prices over $75 per barrel in 2006 and to $150 before the 2008 financial crisis. A related factor was Europe's growing realization of the negative consequences of its dependence on Russian natural gas.

With the completion of the Baku-Tbilisi-Ceyhan pipeline, Azerbaijan was able to market itself as a producer of significant quantities of oil that would be coming online for the European market. Azerbaijan's one million barrels of oil per day amount to one-twentieth of Europe's consumption, but make up a much larger fraction of Europe's imports, and loom even larger in any accounting of oil reserves available in areas adjacent to the European market. Azerbaijan also gradually became a potential natural gas supplier to Europe, thanks to the Shah-Deniz gas field and the South Caucasus gas pipeline. Moreover, Azerbaijan was important not only as a producer but also as a gateway to the even larger resources of Central Asian oil and gas that Europe began looking to for diversification of its energy supplies—something that nevertheless was not widely understood in the West.

The timing of Azerbaijan's return to the global energy markets hence could hardly have been better. In his 2006 meeting with Ilham Aliyev, President George W. Bush noted that Azerbaijan had "a very important role to play" in energy security.[12]

Aside from energy, Azerbaijan's location at the crossroads of Europe and Asia has also given it a key role in the trade routes that slowly began to develop in the aftermath of the Soviet Union's collapse. As discussed in chapter 9 of the present volume, competing north-south and east-west transportation corridors have been advocated by various players. The one thing these corridors have in common is that they cross Azerbaijani territory, and thus add another dimension to Azerbaijan's potential as an energy transit and production area.

Security

The third area of importance in Western relations with Azerbaijan is security. In the late 1990s, the U.S. government concluded that it had significant though nonvital interests at stake in Central Asia and the Caucasus. At the time, Europe had not even come to pose the question in those terms. Yet some strategic thinkers, most notably Zbigniew Brzezinski, were already identifying Azerbaijan as a "strategic pivot,"[13] given its geographic location between Russia and Iran, and the troubles brewing in the areas surrounding the country. Azerbaijan's secular Muslim nature added a symbolically important element to this very practical geopolitical assessment. If the country's key role was gradually being realized on an abstract level in the late 1990s, the events of the early twenty-first century would work brutally to turn it into a concrete reality for strategic planners in the West. By stepping forward and agreeing to grant transit rights to Western forces, Azerbaijan became indispensable to the coalition that was formed to topple Taliban rule in Afghanistan in late 2001. In the years that followed, the war in Iraq and the confrontation between the West and Iran only brought the focus of world politics closer to Azerbaijan's door. Western leaders did not always connect the dots and realize the importance of this small country, but Azerbaijan's capacity to play a major role in some of the major foreign policy issues facing Western leaders was certainly present.

But pursuing this opportunity was not without dangers for Baku. If deciding to participate in the Afghanistan war seemed an obvious choice to Heydar Aliyev, subsequent choices were less clear-cut—for example, Azerbaijan's decision, as the first Muslim-majority country and one of only three to do so, to send troops to Iraq, though the benefits appeared to far outweigh the costs. The West's brewing confrontation with Iran was an entirely different matter, however, given that it would make Azerbaijan a frontline state if hostilities broke out—and could endanger the very existence of the leadership in Baku. As a neighbor that had been subjected to Iranian strong-arm tactics before, Azerbaijan had more to gain than most other stakeholders from the halting of the Iranian nuclear program. But Azerbaijan's leaders were also acutely aware of the potential consequences in terms of Iranian retaliation, something Iranian officials made painfully clear. Given the poor record of the West in standing by its faraway allies in times of need, Azerbaijani leaders felt that supporting an operation against Iran would be a bridge too far.

In the first decade of the twenty-first century, Azerbaijan's strategic importance was made clear by its location at a crossroads of Eurasian geopolitics, its growing role in helping to secure Western energy security, the credibility and forward position it could bring to the war on terror, and its decision to commit to supporting Western endeavors in the Greater Middle East and Eurasia. For better or worse, the direction of world politics was increasingly making Azerbaijan a state that would enjoy the benefits of long-term strategic significance—but also have to live with the costs.

U.S. Relations with Azerbaijan

In the first years after the Soviet collapse, the United States' main concern in the post-Soviet space was economic reforms in Russia and nuclear nonproliferation. There was little proactive U.S. policy towards the southern rim of the former Soviet Union. Basic "working guidelines" were established, which stipulated some basic U.S. interests. Yet as one policymaker would later put it, "A preoccupation with the four 'nuclear successor states' prevented the Caucasus and Central Asian states from getting much serious attention until 1994."[14] The administration of President Bill Clinton did formulate three modest policy goals for the Newly Independent States, as the region came to be known. First, the United States declared its support for their independence, seeking to prevent the restoration of Russian control or Iranian influence. Second, it vowed to support the establishment of liberal democratic regimes. Third, it supported the export of Caspian Sea energy resources by a route that would not entail exclusive dependence on Russia, and, most important, that would not cross Iranian territory.[15] These principles were to lay the ground for more assertive policies come the late 1990s, when the United States identified increasingly clear interests in the Caucasus.

Section 907a and the Role of the Armenian Lobby

America's role in the Caucasus, in particular its relations with Azerbaijan, was greatly affected by the inclusion of an obscure paragraph in the Freedom Support Act of 1992, a federal law enacted to support long-term economic assistance to the Soviet successor states. Section 907a of the Freedom Support Act prohibited all government-to-government assistance by the United States to Azerbaijan. Specifically, it stipulated that "United States assistance… may not be provided to the Government of Azerbaijan until the President determines, and so reports to the Congress, that the Government of Azerbaijan is taking demonstrable steps to cease all blockades and other offensive uses of force against Armenia and Nagorno-

Karabakh."[16] In including this language in the legislation, the U.S. Congress implicitly defined Azerbaijan as the aggressor in the conflict. Section 907a was placed in the bill thanks to the efforts of the Armenian lobby, which had contributed to the rapid establishment of relations between Armenia and the United States.[17] At the time, in early 1992, Georgia was gripped by civil war and Azerbaijan was ruled by the unreformed Communist government of Ayaz Mutalibov. It is in this context that the Armenian lobby was able to portray Armenia as the most progressive state in the region in terms of fostering a democratic political environment.[18] Mutalibov's Russia-first policy made Azerbaijan uninterested in the West, while internal squabbles between Mutalibov's regime and the Popular Front further distracted an already war-torn Azerbaijan from pursuing a coherent foreign policy. Azerbaijan was unable to even make the Azerbaijani side of events in Karabakh reach news desks in the West; thus, Armenian communities in America and France were able to depict Azerbaijan as an aggressor in the conflict, creating a characterization that required years of effort on the part of Azerbaijani diplomats to roll back.

Section 907a of the Freedom Support Act was drafted by senator and later Democratic presidential nominee John F. Kerry, though Armenian Americans have subsequently confided that Senator Kerry knew little of the actual facts of the conflict. By the time the act became law, the situation described in section 907a (i.e., the alleged "blockades and other offensive uses of force against Armenia and Nagorno-Karabakh") bore little resemblance to reality. Indeed, it never had. Azerbaijan had never had any ability to impose a blockade on Armenia, given that a blockade is an effort to prevent a country from trading with other countries. Azerbaijan had an embargo on Armenia, but did not and could not prevent it from trading with other neighbors. Armenia had, incidentally, itself imposed an embargo on Nakhichevan. More important, well before President George H.W. Bush's signature on the Freedom Support Act had dried, Azerbaijani citizens were fleeing Armenian military campaigns on Azerbaijan's own territory. As early as mid-1993 the UN Security Council—which includes the United States as a permanent member—was characterizing Armenian actions in the conflict as aggression, even as a federal law remained on the books in the United States implicitly defining *Azerbaijan* as the aggressor.

It should be noted that successive U.S. administrations were opposed to section 907a, correctly perceiving it as an impediment to a constructive American role in the Caucasus, in particular to the United States' ability to act as an evenhanded mediator between the warring parties. In spite of this, no president has found it worth the expenditure of political capital to actively seek removal of the item from U.S. law. Pro-Azerbaijani members of Congress have managed to "nibble away" at the edges of section 907a, for example, by granting Azerbaijan access to the Overseas Private Investment Corporation and the Trade Development Agency.[19] Only in 2002, in the wake of 9/11, which brought a realization of the need for military cooperation with Azerbaijan, did Congress grant the president the authority to issue an annual waiver of the offending item, a prerogative presidents Bush and Obama have both consistently exercised.

Section 907a had a profound effect on America's relations with Azerbaijan. Its most important impact was on the level of public opinion, as Azerbaijanis responded with disbelief and a feeling that they had been deceived and humiliated, which caused their once highly favorable view of the United States to gradually change. The impact of Section 907a on Azerbaijani public opinion is most strongly felt among the displaced persons from the conflict area, who on the whole take a much more negative view of the United States than is held by the population in general. In retrospect, it is remarkable that America has been able to retain relatively high approval ratings in Azerbaijan, higher than those it receives in many Western European countries. Contrary to the general view in Washington, the waiver of Section 907a did little to help matters. While Azerbaijani diplomats and politicians are somewhat content with the waiver, many Azerbaijanis are now acutely aware that they are subject to this yearly ritual of judgment, which they understand as a form of blackmail: by keeping section 907a on the books, the United States retains a form of leverage against the Azerbaijani government whose apparent purpose is to ensure that it does not engage in an effort to restore its territorial integrity unilaterally and by force. In practice, the issue is losing relevance since Azerbaijan, with its financial strength, does not need U.S. assistance. The symbolic effect nevertheless remains.

The Middle Years: Evolution of Relations

Gradually, other players in American policymaking developed an interest in Azerbaijan. The two most prominent were the oil industry and the Department of Defense. Both would play a major role in restoring the balance in U.S. treatment of Azerbaijan and Armenia.

It has been said that, at least until September 2001, oil was the major issue driving U.S. interest in the Caspian region. Yet the role of the defense establishment as one of the early promoters of a U.S. role there should not be underestimated. As Elizabeth Sherwood-Randall observed in 1998,

"The importance of Transcaucasian oil in driving American policy has been exaggerated. From the perspective of the Department of Defense, the biggest concern was with the role of the new post-Soviet military establishments in the Caucasian republics."[20] As early as 1994, the Defense Department began arguing for closer engagement with the countries of the South Caucasus because of their strategic location, notably their proximity to Russia and Iran.

That said, the influence of the energy issue is incontrovertible. By the mid-1990s, the U.S. government had developed a doctrine of "multiple pipelines," in an effort to ensure that Caspian Sea energy resources were exported westward.[21] This was a strategic move, dictated not by any illusions of Caspian oil feeding U.S. markets but by an understanding of the role of energy in the building of independent states and of these states' role in regional and global energy security. This strategy sought to prevent Iran from becoming a transit corridor for Caspian oil, and to avert a Russian monopoly over transit routes. Significantly, it did not seek to marginalize Russia: one U.S.-supported project was the Caspian Consortium pipeline link between Kazakhstan's Caspian Sea coast and the Russian Black Sea port of Novorossiysk. The policy was thus anti-monopolistic—in that it sought to prevent Russian dominance over Caspian exports—but not anti-Russian. This strategy, the earliest evidence of a long-term goal for the region actively supported by U.S. policies, led to the development of an interest in Azerbaijan, the source of a significant portion of Caspian oil, and in the potential transit corridor to the West for Kazakhstani and Turkmenistani energy resources, for which the United States sought construction of a trans-Caspian pipeline.

The major Western oil companies found themselves supporting many of the Azerbaijani government's objectives. The Caspian Sea's status was one example: Russia and Iran sought a condominium of riparian states over the sea's resources and wanted foreign companies out. The Azerbaijani and Kazakhstani stance, that the sea should be segmented into national sectors, was much more in line with the interests of the oil companies, which preferred working with governments that needed their presence, and therefore accorded the companies concessions under what turned out to be very advantageous conditions. Likewise, the instability in the Caucasus was a threat to the companies' long-term operations there, which led them to push their home governments to help stabilize the region and aid in its economic development.

Though the Russian defeat in the war in Chechnya in 1996 did not directly affect Azerbaijan, it had immense implications for the South Caucasus. It weakened Russia's ability to project power in the region, and emboldened independent-minded leaders such as Heydar Aliyev and Georgia's Eduard Shevardnadze. Equally important, it changed American and European perceptions of Russia as a great power, with the Caucasus as its natural backyard. These changes of perception accelerated America's engagement with the region. In January 1996, the United States took up the position of permanent co-chair of the Minsk Group, thereby becoming the leading force in seeking a resolution to the Karabakh conflict. In March, President Clinton's National Security Advisor, Samuel Berger, singled out China, Turkey, and the Caucasus as areas of special emphasis and stressed Washington's intention to step up its involvement in the Caucasus and Central Asia.[22] In July, Deputy Secretary of State Strobe Talbott stated that the South Caucasus and Central Asia constituted "a strategically vital region" for the United States, and that what happened there "matter[ed] profoundly" to America.[23] That month also marked a milestone in Azerbaijani diplomacy, as President Aliyev was invited to the United States on an official visit to the Clinton White House.

Official statements regarding U.S. policy toward the region now formally acknowledged energy development and the creation of an east-west energy transport corridor, as well as security cooperation, as explicit American interests aside from the building of democratic institutions and conflict resolution.[24] In 1999, support for U.S. engagement with the region took legislative form in the Silk Road Strategy Act, sponsored by Republican senator Sam Brownback.[25] Azerbaijan was also singled out in Zbigniew Brzezinski's 1997 volume *The Grand Chessboard* as one of five strategically pivotal countries in Eurasia, along with Ukraine, Turkey, Uzbekistan, and Iran.[26]

By 2000, it was apparent that U.S. policy had evolved considerably since 1992. Armenia's cordial ties with Iran, its close relationship with Moscow, and its foreign and security dependence on Russia meant that it was unwilling or unable to pursue the type of pro-Western policies preferred by Azerbaijan and Georgia. Even when Armenia did so, it was with greater hesitancy than was shown by its two neighbors, as in the Kosovo conflict. Indeed, Baku had begun to make itself useful to the United States, starting with small steps such as contributing to Western efforts in the Kosovo conflict and being an example of a secular Muslim state that had good relations with Israel. These efforts ensured a sound footing for the spike in the quality of relations that would occur after September 11, 2001.

America and Azerbaijan in the Post-9/11 World

For the South Caucasus, the immediate effect of the terrorist attacks of 9/11 was to make security issues the focus of U.S. policy, and to inaugurate an intensive but short-lived period of positive and productive relations with Azerbaijan.

Following 9/11, Azerbaijan was one of the first countries to extend support to the United States and to offer full access to its facilities. This drove home the point that the level of independence among post-Soviet states was directly correlated to their response to 9/11. Countries with independent foreign policies such as Azerbaijan, Georgia, and Uzbekistan reacted rapidly and positively, whereas those dependent on Russia, such as Armenia, were constricted by the need to consult Moscow before determining what kind of support they would offer America.

In concrete terms, Azerbaijan played an indispensable part in supporting the U.S. military campaign against the Taliban and Al Qaeda in Afghanistan. Without U.S. access to Azerbaijan's airspace, prosecution of the war would have been severely impeded. Transit from NATO countries through Iran was a nonstarter, and Russia offered only limited transit rights. The situation seemed to confirm Brzezinski's notion of Azerbaijan as a pivotal state for U.S. strategic interests, and brought an immediate benefit: the waiver of Section 907a was passed by the U.S. Congress in early 2002. The Bush administration then sought to end the parity in military aid to Azerbaijan and Armenia, intending to send four times as much aid to Azerbaijan, although Congress usually prevented that, keeping parity between the two belligerents in spite of Pentagon requests.

The honeymoon in U.S.-Azerbaijani relations lasted well into the Iraq war, as Azerbaijan was one of only half a dozen Muslim countries to take part in the so-called coalition of the willing, and one of only three Muslim-majority countries (the other being Albania and Kazakhstan) to contribute troops to the Iraq operation. The Bush administration also continued to support the east-west transportation corridor and the building of the Baku-Tbilisi-Ceyhan pipeline, though less fervently than its predecessor.

The U.S.-Azerbaijani relationship nevertheless soon became marred by the familiar problem of governance and democracy. This time, developments in both the United States itself and Azerbaijan combined to sour relations. At issue in the United States was the growing conviction that democracy was the best long-term antidote to terrorism. Indeed, in his second term, President George W. Bush would make the "freedom agenda" an increasingly important part of his foreign policy. This trend in American foreign policy coincided with the "color revolutions" in Georgia and Ukraine, which had important implications for Azerbaijan. As discussed in chapter 6 of the present volume, the peaceful revolution that made Georgia an exemplar of democratic transition in Western eyes coincided with the handover of power from Heydar Aliyev to Ilham Aliyev, which was widely understood, simplistically, as nothing more than a dynastic succession. The succession prompted stereotypes of Heydar Aliyev that focused on his Politburo and KGB past; Ilham Aliyev also suffered from negative characterizations by the Western news media.

Prior to the 2003 Rose Revolution, Georgia under Eduard Shevardnadze had looked chaotic in comparison to Azerbaijan, which had a reasonably orderly and relatively pluralistic sociopolitical environment. Consequently, the Azerbaijani leadership had been able to prevent governance issues from rising to the top of the agenda in relations with the United States. Had the Rose Revolution not occurred, it is doubtful whether the American reaction to the transition of power in Azerbaijan, which also took place in 2003, would have been as enduring as it was. In any case, the conjecture of events made Azerbaijan look bad at a moment when one of its next-door neighbors was looking very good.

This period of turmoil in regional politics also coincided with the growing difficulties that beset the Bush administration's Iraq adventure, which led it to accord less attention to Central Asia and the Caucasus. One of the first clearly attributable outcomes of this development was the deterioration and collapse of the U.S.-Uzbekistani strategic partnership in 2005. While Uzbekistan is clearly not comparable to Azerbaijan, having a much more authoritarian system, the dynamics of the relationship itself do bear some resemblance. In both cases, American policy lost track of the multiple interests at stake, allowing the establishment of an emphasis on governance and democracy, while strategic and energy issues were allowed to slide into the background. Moreover, in both cases the Russian leadership was quick to pick up where America left off, enticing each country's leadership with offers of political and military support that would include backing against presumed domestic revolutionary challengers. In Uzbekistan, this combination of events led to a drastic reorientation of the country's foreign policy, but also to an equally visible deterioration of the already problematic domestic situation.

America succeeded in avoiding such an outcome in Azerbaijan, despite persistent Russian courting of Heydar Aliyev and, later, Ilham Aliyev, and strong pressure by the "old guard" within the government to move closer to Moscow. Baku did hedge its bets by improving relations with both Moscow and Tehran, but did not react emotionally and downgrade its U.S. relations. Yet Washington's messages to Baku were increasingly contradictory. Secretary of Defense Donald Rumsfeld visited Baku repeatedly, assuring the Azerbaijani leadership of the importance the United States assigned to Azerbaijan in its regional policies. Meanwhile, an entirely different stance was taken by the State Department, which focused on issues of governance and democratization as prerequisites for improved relations.

It was anticipated that the 2005 parliamentary elections would burnish Azerbaijan's democratic credentials in a way that would restore relations to the previously enjoyed level. Yet in spite of improvements that, arguably, made the 2005 process more pluralistic than past votes, the remaining irregularities, especially in ballot counting, led the U.S. leadership to question whether Azerbaijan had indeed shown a commitment to political reform.

Ilham Aliyev finally received a symbolically important invitation to Washington in spring 2006. This likely was extended in great part because of the Uzbekistan debacle and Washington's realization that it was losing ground in the strategic arc comprising the post-Soviet states of the South Caucasus and Central Asia. The visit's reverberations were comparable to those of Heydar Aliyev's 1997 visit in conferring a sense of international legitimacy on Ilham Aliyev's presidency. More important, the visit allowed for the restoration of a dialogue on many fronts that had been left lagging, and a renewed American engagement on the entire span of issues forming the U.S.-Azerbaijani relationship. This process would have been crowned by a resolution to the Karabakh conflict, which American diplomats worked hard to achieve, but this was not to be.

Another Transitory Renewal of U.S. Interest

The 2006 renewal of U.S. attention to Azerbaijan proved temporary. Especially after the Republican Party lost control of both houses of Congress in the 2006 U.S. congressional elections, the Bush administration seemed to lose steam on most foreign policy issues, focusing almost exclusively on staving off failure in Iraq. The "surge"—the increase in the number of U.S. troops in the country that began in early 2007—succeeded in helping to stabilize the security situation, but meanwhile, conditions in Afghanistan continued to deteriorate. In the South Caucasus, U.S. efforts to resolve the conflict over Karabakh lost momentum, as did American involvement in energy politics and in diplomatic consultations in general with regional states. The November 2006 departure of Secretary Rumsfeld, a strong advocate of the region's importance within the U.S. government, had much to do with this disengagement. Rumsfeld's successor, Robert Gates, showed little interest in the region until visiting Baku in 2010, preferring to focusing solely on Afghanistan and Iraq.

The Bush administration belatedly turned its attention to two remaining issues concerning Eastern Europe: recognition of the sovereignty of Kosovo, and the inclusion of aspiring members Georgia and Ukraine to the NATO Membership Action Plan at the April 2008 NATO summit in Bucharest. Guided perhaps by the remnants of the freedom agenda, these efforts seemed to constitute an effort to consolidate the gains during Bush's presidency and improve security in Eastern Europe. While Baku strongly disagreed with the Kosovo decision, the move to put Georgia and Ukraine on the path to NATO membership was positive from an Azerbaijani perspective. The effort in Bucharest failed, however, as Washington failed to enlist the support of major European allies, chiefly among them Germany. An important and tragic consequence was the stimulation of Moscow's long-standing ambition to subdue Georgia, which it did in its August 2008 invasion.[27] The slow-coming, ineffectual U.S. reaction to the war—Washington left the handling of the crisis to the EU and did very little to support its chief ally in the South Caucasus, Georgia—sent shock waves throughout the region, and had important implications for Azerbaijani strategic thinking. In summary, these implications were that Russia was both willing and able to use outright military force to accomplish its foreign policy objectives; that no player, particularly not the West, was willing or able to prevent such behavior; that the West was therefore not a reliable partner in the issues that mattered most to post-Soviet states, that is, independence, security, and sovereignty; and finally, that initiating democratic reforms in Russia's backyard was a very dangerous enterprise.[28] As such, the events vindicated Baku's policy of avoiding dependence on any single great power and its efforts to build positive relations with Russia and Iran; but at the same time, it undermined much of the basis for Azerbaijan's foreign policy and its reliance on a Euro-Atlantic orientation as the best way for the country to secure its independence.

Matters deteriorated even further during the first year of the presidency of Barack Obama. To begin with, the Obama administration showed a distinct lack of interest in European affairs, especially those of Eastern Europe. This was seen most clearly in its decision to unilaterally shelve plans for the deployment of missile defense programs in Poland and the Czech Republic, and in the relatively tepid American support for Georgia—including deferring to Moscow in implementing a de facto arms embargo on Georgia. In the context of the "reset" diplomacy with Russia and a singular focus on arms control issues, Washington's interest in the Caspian region in general and Azerbaijan in particular dropped to historic lows.

As if that were not bad enough, the administration's only real initiative in the region was a slap in the face to Azerbaijan. As detailed in chapter 14 of the present volume, the administration exerted strong pressure for the opening of the Turkish-Armenian border, largely as a way of extricating itself from candidate Obama's promises to recognize the 1915 massacre of Armenians as genocide. While this was a laudable project in itself, the U.S. government did not in parallel increase its efforts to resolve the Armenian-Azerbaijani conflict. Quite to the contrary, the administration explicitly put that issue on the back burner, strongly urging the delinking of the two processes, something that was clearly contrary to Azerbaijani interests. There was hardly even a serious effort to engage Baku in the process or to keep it informed of events involving Turkey and Armenia. Only after Baku's protests had forced a correction of Turkey's stance in the matter, and Ilham Aliyev had cancelled his attendance at the summit of the Alliance of Civilizations in Istanbul in April 2009, did Secretary of State Hillary Clinton call President Aliyev to seek to obtain his attendance, promising a meeting with President Obama. In an indication of the level to which U.S.-Azerbaijani relations had deteriorated, Aliyev declined.

In 2010, the Administration's failure for almost a year to nominate an ambassador to Azerbaijan exacerbated the relationship further, leading Azerbaijani officials to overtly criticize the United States, while the analytical community in Washington began sounding alarm bells the the U.S. was losing an important ally. Finally, in spring 2010, the Administration seems to have pushed the damage control button, as Secretary of Defense Robert Gates traveled to Baku to shore up the relationship, carrying a letter from President Obama. The visit was followed up by a visit by Secretary of State Clinton, indicating the understanding in Washington that the relationship was important. Still, the Administration seemed mainly preoccupied by Azerbaijan's importance for the logistics of the Afghanistan operation. Whether the newfound interest in Azerbaijan would be sustained remained to be seen as this book went to press.

Europe and Azerbaijan: The EU Continues to Punch Below Its Weight

The Washington-Baku relationship clearly has experienced ups and downs in the nearly two decades since Azerbaijan's independence. Nevertheless, it is clear that American thinking on Azerbaijan has developed over time, and that a constituency of American officials, businesspeople, and scholars knowledgeable about the country has emerged.

As far as Europe is concerned, despite the proximity of Azerbaijan, a policy has yet to develop. Though Europe has gradually moved to take a more active role in the South Caucasus, its presence in the region remains limited. In a sense, because of its inability to pool its considerable resources, Europe has continued to punch below its weight in the region two decades after the Soviet republics of the South Caucasus became independent states. This weak performance relates, of course, to the slow development of a common European foreign policy in general. But it is also linked to the weaker nature of strategic thinking in Europe as compared to America, and to a stronger desire in many European capitals not to step on Russia's toes. Because Europe is made up, in large part, of former colonial powers, Russian neocolonial and neo-imperial policies are met with greater tolerance in Europe than in the United States, itself a onetime European colony.

Impediments to a Coherent European Strategy

Given Europe's economic strength and the power of attraction that the European integration project has inspired, it is little wonder that Europe should be understood in regions such as the South Caucasus as a unitary entity, with ensuing expectations. The EU's role in the turnaround of the countries of Eastern and Central Europe, with which the South Caucasus shared many similarities only a decade ago, only serves to intensify these expectations. But, as elsewhere, there is confusion as to what the EU really is. Is it an emerging federal superstate or an international organization? This confusion, coupled with Europe's own mixed messages, not only has contributed to growing expectations of a European role in the region, but has prompted speculation about eventual EU membership for the countries of the South Caucasus.

The EU has an ambition to be a global economic and political powerhouse. In spite of setbacks such as the Balkan wars in the 1990s, Europe is still seen by many of its own residents and politicians as both a partner and a counterweight to the United States. Its ambitious project of simultaneously widening and deepening the EU in the early 2000s testified to this. This, in turn, has contributed to Europe being viewed, from the South Caucasus, as an entity somehow comparable to the United States, with its geographic proximity being an added factor in its regional regard.

Yet the weakness of European foreign and security policy and the difficult adjustment to an EU consisting of twenty-seven member states has crippled Europe's ability to play a coherent role in the region. The result is a kind of limbo status for the EU. Until the Treaty of Lisbon took effect at the end of 2009, Europe's internal divisions and bureaucratic consensus mechanisms made proactive policies in foreign affairs the exception rather than the rule. Except in times of acute crisis, Europe was unlikely to take initiatives; inertia was the standard mode. Even with the Lisbon treaty having gone into effect, it will likely take several years for the new decision-making system mandated in the treaty to be fully implemented. Second, the 2004–07 expansion from fifteen to twenty-seven member states took a toll on the EU. Coinciding with the Iraq war, it exposed the differences between the Union's old member states and its new, predominantly eastern members. As they (and some old members) sided with Washington rather than the Paris-Berlin axis, it became painfully clear that a twenty-seven-member EU was too large and unruly for even a powerful Franco-German alliance to dominate. This realization contributed significantly to the aversion to enlargement that developed, and to cautious if not hostile views toward European engagement in the South Caucasus. Especially among the oldest member states of the EU, there is now a sense of a need to restore Europe's core institutions before moving to taking on a greater role in the East.

Enlargement of the EU (along with NATO expansion) nonetheless brought long-term tangible benefits to the countries of the South Caucasus, including Azerbaijan. The new EU members were considerably more Atlanticist than "old Europe," and showed a much greater interest in—and understanding of—the predicament of the nations of the South Caucasus. Moreover, the new members seemed to possess a greater capacity to view Europe's role in the region in strategic terms. Poland, the Baltic states, and Romania stood out as countries pushing back against the policies of the EU and NATO in the region. The first indication of the role these states would play was shown in the European reaction to the 2004 disputed Ukrainian election: the states of Eastern and Central Europe took a leading role in alerting EU institutions to the ramifications of the events in Ukraine. Indeed, it is unlikely that Europe's reaction would have been as strong if these states had not been members. For the long term, the 2004–07 cadre provides the countries of the South Caucasus with an emerging core constituency in the EU that will gain in strength and importance as its members integrate fully into Union institutions. The inauguration in 2008 of the

Eastern Partnership, an EU effort to build multilateral relations with former Soviet republics within continental Europe, is one proof of that.

Europe's role in the region is nevertheless likely, even in the longer term, to remain marred by the lack of a coherent strategy, and by the difficulties of bringing its member states to act in unison in a region where their interests sometimes diverge. These structural impediments to an EU role in the region need to be thoroughly understood—not in order to belittle European activities in the Caucasus, but in order to view them as a backdrop to the slowly evolving European role in the region.

The Development of European Policies

In the first decade after the collapse of the Soviet Union, the Caucasus did not have an important place among Europe's perceived interests. In the early 1990s, the European states and the EU as a whole remained wary of involvement, the exception being the consecutive roles of Italy, Sweden, and Finland in the OSCE Minsk Group on the Armenian-Azerbaijani conflict. European states nevertheless gradually did become important donor countries to the South Caucasus in terms of development cooperation, primarily assisting Georgia and Armenia. For instance, the EU launched a visionary though eventually unrealized transport infrastructure development project, Transport Corridor Europe-Caucasus-Asia (TRACECA), as well as the Interstate Oil and Gas Transport to Europe (INOGATE) project, which fared somewhat better. France became cochair of the OSCE Minsk Group in 1997, a role that gave it the opportunity to play a part in the process surrounding conflict resolution in Karabakh, and British corporate interests in Azerbaijan's energy sector, led by BP, made London an important player in the region. But despite these steps, which should not be minimized, Europe's approach remained cautious and tentative. During the 1990s, Europe was hampered by crises that were much more urgent and much closer to home, primarily the Balkan wars, and by the absence of a common European foreign and security policy—a structural problem that makes comparison with the United States less than fair. Indeed, the Balkan experience showed the difficulties that prevented European states from acting rapidly and in unison to manage serious crises in Europe's own neighborhood. As far as the Caucasus was concerned, Europe did not feel that it had important interests at stake in the region, and therefore remained largely aloof.

By the dawn of the twenty-first century Europe itself had changed, with an ambition to act more cohesively in the external arena. Moreover, the need for a more visible presence in the Caucasus had come to be recognized in many quarters, even though the skeptics remained numerous.[29] War was once again raging in Chechnya, European corporate concerns had interests in the Caspian Sea energy resources, and the European focus on democratization and good governance in its neighborhood was being increasingly emphasized in the South Caucasus. Georgia joined the Council of Europe in 1999, and Armenia and Azerbaijan followed suit in 2001. The military operations in Afghanistan in late 2001 increased not only American but also European perceptions of the strategic value of the Caucasus corridor to Central Asia. During the 2001 Swedish presidency of the EU, the EU troika, led by Anna Lindh, made its first-ever visit to the three countries of the South Caucasus. Once consigned to oblivion, the South Caucasus was slowly becoming an "issue" in Europe. Successive EU presidencies groped for a way to deal with the conflict-ridden and elusive region, yet each never managed to accord the South Caucasus a priority position in its six months of fame. It became clear that, unlike other areas, the South Caucasus did not have important member state "sponsors" who could bring the region up to a prominent position on the EU agenda.

Moreover, the three states of the South Caucasus had differing agendas regarding Euro-Atlantic integration. Georgia was the most vocal and ambitious, desiring both NATO and EU membership. Azerbaijan was more discreet but nonetheless committed, while Armenia, though forced to consider its dependence on Russia, gradually and significantly accelerated its interaction with NATO and the EU.

The South Caucasus' lack of a strong sponsor within the EU turned out to be a serious drawback when the "Wider Europe" framework was being designed by the EU to provide a form of cooperation with neighboring countries. In spring 2003, when the EU launched the European Neighborhood Policy, under which it offered adjacent states "a privileged relationship, building upon a mutual commitment to common values (democracy and human rights, rule of law, good governance, market economy principles, and sustainable development),"[30] the South Caucasus countries were literally reduced to a footnote in the document.[31] Countries such as Libya and Syria were included in the initiative, even though they were not members of Euro-Atlantic institutions such as the Council of Europe or NATO's Partnership for Peace, and had foreign policies with much less of a European vocation. Such treatment of the South Caucasus caused consternation in the region, and came rapidly to be understood as a mistake even in Brussels.

A New Wind?

A series of events combined to make the EU shift positions and decide, in spring 2004, to incorporate the South Caucasus into the European Neighborhood Policy.

First of all, in July 2003 the Union appointed an EU special representative to the South Caucasus, Finnish diplomat (and onetime Minsk Group co-chair) Heikki Talvitie. Talvitie was based in Helsinki, not Brussels; his mission was financed with Finnish funds; and he was given a limited mandate. This appointment showed the evolution of European intent, but betrayed the lack of institutional readiness on the part of the EU to take a serious role in the region.

The outbreak of Georgia's Rose Revolution in late 2003 brought the South Caucasus further attention within the EU, just as expansion of the Union was creating a constituency of member states with an interest in the region. With its impressive reforms following the revolution, Georgia put the region's best foot forward; nonetheless, the South Caucasus as a whole was experiencing impressive economic growth and reform that further whetted European interest. Azerbaijan's world-leading economic progress led the way, but all three states of the South Caucasus were among the top ten economies in the world in terms of growth of gross domestic product for the period 2005–08. Such findings signaled a substantial change from the economic free fall of the mid-1990s. Economic reforms made the regional states credible economic and trade partners in spite of enduring problems with armed conflict, excessive bureaucracy, and corruption. The Caucasus was no longer just a trouble spot, but a region with potential. In late 2004, the Orange Revolution in Ukraine further emphasized the changing character of the wider Black Sea region, of which the South Caucasus is a part.

Finally, in 2006, the opening of the Baku-Tbilisi-Ceyhan pipeline could not have been better timed, occurring as it did in a period of increasing European concern over Russia's reliability as an energy supplier, following Moscow's increasingly blatant use of energy as a political lever against Ukraine, Moldova, and Georgia. Before the Ukrainian gas crisis of 2006, which prompted Europe to take energy security issues more seriously, Azerbaijan was seen mainly as a troublesome member of the Council of Europe. By spring 2006, however, Azerbaijani officials detected a positive change in European attitudes, focusing mainly on the possibility of importing Azerbaijani gas from the Shah-Deniz field to Europe via the Nabucco pipeline, then under construction.

European institutions began to rise to the challenge. Swedish diplomat Peter Semneby was appointed to succeed Heikki Talvitie as the EU's special representative to the South Caucasus in 2006, and was granted an expanded mandate so as to enable a more active Union role in the Caucasus.

That said, EU efforts toward the South Caucasus remained ad hoc, depending largely on the interests of individual European politicians rather than institutional processes. Moreover, the growing tensions in Russian-Georgian relations led Georgia to consume the overwhelming majority of Europe's attention toward the region, though as the events of August 2008 showed, this was not without reason. Nevertheless, the Georgian focus meant that Azerbaijan largely fell outside the European purview, since European leaders seemed inclined to intervene reactively to contain crises rather than take a proactive and holistic approach to the South Caucasus as a region. The French EU presidency's intervention to mediate a cease-fire in the Russian-Georgian war is the most prominent example. The war showed that the South Caucasus was indeed part of Europe in security terms, and that a crisis in the region would land in the EU's lap whether it wanted it or not.

In late 2008, partly in response to the war in Georgia, the EU launched the Eastern Partnership, an instrument to improve relations with six states on its eastern periphery, including the three South Caucasus countries. Initially underfunded, the Eastern Partnership nonetheless had great potential significance. It provided the possibility for Azerbaijan to integrate with the EU at a pace of its own choosing. In the longer term, the possibility of obtaining visa-free travel to Europe and deep free-trade agreements with the EU would enable countries in the EU's eastern neighborhood to harmonize the overwhelming portion of their regulations and institutions with those of the Union. It has been estimated that a deep free-trade agreement would entail the incorporation of about 60 percent of the EU *acquis communautaire* (i.e., the rights, and responsibilities that constitute EU membership). That, in turn, would pave the way for possible membership if and when the political winds in the EU were once again amenable to enlargement.

There was a twofold problem with the Eastern Partnership, however: it lacked a membership perspective, and it did not address the main concern of the regional states, namely security issues. Only in terms of the soft security that closer integration with the EU would provide could the Eastern Partnership be said to play a role. As for membership, the question was left open. Neither did the instrument foresee the provision of major financial resources of the kind that had been made available to East-Central

Europe in the 1990s, though the Swedish presidency of late 2009 managed to secure substantial additional funding for the European Investment Bank's activities in the region. Clearly, the condition of the world economy in 2008–10 did not make the prospects of large financial packages likely. Thus, the Eastern Partnership mainly constituted an opportunity to engage in tedious reforms in decidedly dull areas such as the harmonization of phytosanitary standards for food and agriculture, competition law, and public procurement—without the carrot of membership that had mobilized reformist zeal in East-Central Europe.

In spite of these shortcomings, Georgia and Ukraine jumped at this opportunity, while Azerbaijan was initially more cautious. The question for Baku was whether it had the political will to conduct the reforms needed for closer integration with the EU under the aegis of the Eastern Partnership. For Azerbaijan, with its oil economy, the temptation to refrain from these deep reforms and remain an energy partner to Europe was clearly present. As it became increasingly clear that Europe was moving away from an interest in security affairs along its eastern periphery, and as the EU itself failed to mobilize consensus on the Nabucco pipeline, the cost-benefit analysis of closer integration with Europe was by no means producing a clear-cut outcome for the Azerbaijani leadership. Although such integration would undoubtedly benefit the Azerbaijani economy as a whole over the longer term, not least in regard to economic diversification, the incentive structures were not yet strong enough to lead to action.

Azerbaijan's European Prospects

As that rara avis, a secular Muslim country seeking integration with Euro-Atlantic institutions, Azerbaijan faces uncertain but enticing prospects. Azerbaijan and Europe are developing an increasingly close trading relationship, highlighted by the westward movement of Azerbaijani energy supplies. Beyond that, however, the relationship's development is uncertain, and dependent on the direction of both Azerbaijani and European politics. Given the weaker nature of strategic thinking in Europe, when compared to that in the United States, the governance and democratization factor is likely to remain more central to Europe's attitude to Azerbaijan, even in the face of growing European energy needs. A countervailing interest in a strategic presence in the Caucasus is not equally visible in Europe.

Perhaps the best indication of Azerbaijan's view of its relationship with Europe is provided by Turkey. President Ilham Aliyev and independent

Azerbaijani observers have kept a keen eye on EU-Turkish relations. Simply put, if the Union rejects Turkey's membership application, and this decision is perceived as being based on the country's cultural identity, Azerbaijan will lose any remaining hope of eventual integration with the West. If, on the other hand, the EU eventually embraces Turkish membership, Azerbaijan will conclude that Europe's gates may be open to it as well, and, moreover, that Europe is indeed built on common values and is not the proverbial "Christian club."

In the meantime, the Azerbaijani leadership maintains a healthy level of skepticism. Starting with the president—who experienced this firsthand in his parliamentary work in the Council of Europe—Azerbaijani officials see themselves as being held at a greater distance than their two South Caucasus neighbors, with Armenia and Georgia receiving preferential treatment on account of their shared Christian background. Perhaps this perception will change with greater exchanges between Azerbaijan and Europe, but this will depend more on the course of European politics than on Azerbaijan itself.

Euro-Atlantic Institutions and Azerbaijan

An important aspect of the Euro-Atlantic community's presence in the South Caucasus is the role of multilateral institutions such as the Council of Europe and NATO, and to some degree the OSCE. Compared to the EU, the Council of Europe and NATO have been present in the South Caucasus to an extent not often sufficiently acknowledged, and have played an important role in the development of Azerbaijan's relationship with the West. Indeed, these two organizations have, with the United States, been the leading forces of progress and democratization in the South Caucasus.

Azerbaijan joined the Council of Europe in 2002. Though some Azerbaijani officials may initially have seen membership mainly in symbolic terms, as a token of membership in the European family, the actual importance Baku attached to its participation is best illustrated by the decision, during Heydar Aliyev's rule, to have Ilham Aliyev lead Azerbaijan's delegation to the Parliamentary Assembly of the Council of Europe. Yet aside from symbolic value, membership turned out to have immense practical importance, to a degree that Azerbaijani officials had perhaps not envisaged. Indeed, Azerbaijan subjected itself to unrelenting scrutiny of its efforts to meet the conditions of membership while its application was under consideration. Subsequently, the Council of Europe has become a participant in the day-to-day process of institutional reform in Azerbaijan.

As for NATO, it is often viewed as a defense alliance. Yet especially since the end of the Cold War, the political element that is actually an essential part of this alliance has become increasingly important. Indeed, NATO membership is based on the same democratic values that form the base for the Euro-Atlantic community in general, and NATO enlargement has gone forward in tandem with EU enlargement in terms of driving institutional and democratic reform. The standards required for NATO membership are perhaps less stringent than those set by the EU, yet NATO's appeal lies partly in its membership being more attainable than EU membership, and in the cooperative instrumentality of the Partnership for Peace. Indeed, the Partnership for Peace has grown into a formidable tool for stabilization and security, because it allows partner countries to tailor their participation with NATO in the form of Individual Partnership Action Plans.

Among countries of the Black Sea region, Azerbaijan has been one of the most active participants in the Partnership for Peace. Moreover, it has participated in peacekeeping operations under NATO's umbrella in Kosovo and Afghanistan, as well as in Iraq. And following its expansion into eastern and southeastern Europe in 2004, NATO has increasingly come to focus on relations with countries of the Black Sea basin. This focus is related to its role as leader of the allied military operation in Afghanistan, and has manifested itself in the decision to conduct an "intensified dialogue" with Ukraine and Georgia.

Until 2004, Azerbaijan and Georgia were comparable as regards the degree of their relations with NATO. Both contributed strongly to the Partnership for Peace, and they were seen as being on comparable tracks to integration with the alliance. Since then, however, as part of the move toward more Western-style governance that followed the Rose Revolution, Georgia has embarked on a much more ambitious quest for NATO membership. Baku itself has not scaled back its commitment to a cooperative relationship with NATO, which has continued to prosper within the framework of its Individual Partnership Action Plan. However, it has refrained from Georgian-style expressions of enthusiasm for stepping onto the membership fast track. Azerbaijan's more measured pace of reform and its ambition to keep cordial relations with both Iran and Russia have certainly been key elements in this divergence. Where Georgia saw NATO membership as a guarantee of its security in the face of constant and excruciating Russian pressure, Azerbaijan concluded that it could find a working language with Russia and Iran that did not prevent it from pursuing its core national interests, and that seeking NATO membership, a long shot in the first place, would change that. Deputy Minister of Foreign Affairs Araz Azimov made this point openly in November 2009, stating that "the countries that express a desire to enter into NATO encounter a certain jeopardy," and urging NATO to issue security guarantees to its partner countries, especially in the wake of the war in Georgia.[32]

Conclusions: A Reorientation Away From the West?

During 2009 there were growing signs of Azerbaijan's frustration with the West, spurring speculations of an Uzbek-style reorientation of Azerbaijani foreign policy toward Russia. Indeed, there has been a tendency on the part of the West to take Azerbaijan for granted, which has been manifested in combination with an apparent disengagement from the South Caucasus. At the same time, Russia has forcefully reasserted its influence in the region.

A reorientation of Azerbaijani foreign policy is not impossible, and certainly gained support among the country's elites in the wake of the Russian war against Georgia. Nevertheless, such a turn of events is unlikely, especially if Western policies regain some direction. As the present chapter has shown, Azerbaijan's commitment to a pro-Western foreign policy is based not on whims but on rational calculations deriving from the long-standing perceptions of threats and interests outlined in chapter 11. As successive Azerbaijani leaders have continuously stated, this foreign policy choice has a strategic and long-term character.

While Azerbaijan's relations with the West in this sense resemble Georgia's, there are fundamental differences. Of greatest importance is that Azerbaijan has worked to keep itself from becoming dependent on Western support and protection to the degree that Georgia did. Thus, Baku developed relations with both Russia and Iran in order to reduce the threats from its larger neighbors. And whereas Georgia's leadership, under immense pressure from Moscow, used highly public actions and rhetoric to display its Western vocation, Azerbaijani leaders have operated much more discreetly.

Skepticism toward the West has developed among the Azerbaijani leadership: there is simply a lack of trust that the West will genuinely embrace a Turkic, Muslim nation such as Azerbaijan and integrate it into its institutions—and a reluctance to implement the reforms that would be needed.

Azerbaijan thus finds itself in a position curiously similar to Turkey's. Europe, in President Ilham Aliyev's own words, is the only model for its political and economic development.[33] This shows an awareness of the precarious geopolitical environment Azerbaijan finds itself in, and a distaste for the political systems of some of its neighbors—particularly Iran's. But Aliyev's assessment also shows a peculiar similarity to the logic behind Kemal Atatürk's embrace of the West, which he defined as the "level of contemporary civilization." As Atatürk put it, "It is nonsense to talk of our civilization and your civilization; at the present time there is only one civilization that is alive and advancing. We either join that or we are uncivilized."[34]

The West is attractive to Azerbaijan in great part because it offers a successful model of development, and because Azerbaijani society does not find either an Iranian model or—more broadly speaking—an Islamic model relevant. Nor does Russia provide a viable alternative. The West has an added attraction, namely that affiliation would be voluntary, and would necessarily involve relations at something of a distance, as opposed to the Iranian and Russian models, with their connotations of compulsion and imperialism. Azerbaijani leaders may criticize the West for advancing its interests by advocating intrusively on behalf of a very particular political system. But given Azerbaijan's history, social makeup, and location, its elite has—much like its Turkish counterpart, in spite of reservations regarding the Islamic movement in Turkey—drawn the conclusion that Western-style democracy is clearly the best alternative available. There may be differences on the pace and extent of any adoption of the Western form of social and political organization. But there appears to be agreement on the strategic implications of a closer integration with the West, which is seen as a crucial factor in making Azerbaijan's independence irreversible.

This is not only an elite project. Indeed, it could be argued that the European vocation is more deeply rooted in Azerbaijan than it is in Turkey. Russian colonization and Soviet rule were considerably more effective than the Kemalist revolution in inculcating European ways of life, most obviously in bringing universal literacy. Moreover, as shown in previous chapters of the present volume, Azerbaijan's native intelligentsia is itself clearly and overwhelmingly European in orientation; even before Soviet rule, the clergy played next to no role in public debate. Similarly, polls measuring support for democratic values among the population show Azerbaijan aligning very clearly with countries in Central and Eastern Europe—and distancing itself ideologically from Russia, where support for strong leaders and authoritarian rule remains widespread.

Azerbaijan is likely to continue to integrate with the West, though this process will probably witness both setbacks and successes. Setbacks, when they occur, will stem from Azerbaijan's own process of development and from political currents in the West. Most important will be the ability of both parties to move forward in dealing with the three major baskets of issues in tandem, while not allowing progress on any one of the three—whether it be security cooperation, energy and trade, or governance and democratization—either to flag or to occur with undue speed.

Even more fundamental than the question of whether Azerbaijan will be a partner of the West is the question of whether Azerbaijan will be a *part* of the West. The answer, to borrow from Tadeusz Swietochowski, is that the country will always be quintessentially a borderland.[35] As such, part of its identity definitely lies in Europe and the West. How big that part is can be debated, and certainly will be affected by the policies adopted by the leaders of both Azerbaijan and the West. A heavy burden lies on the shoulders of Western leaders: if Azerbaijan is lost, it will be because the West has lost it. Given the direction of international affairs, Azerbaijan's role as a secular and somewhat pluralistic Muslim society is likely only to grow in importance for the West. Azerbaijan's strategic location on the doorstep of Central Asia and the Middle East should warrant a rising level of attention in Western capitals, while its energy resources, now online rather than simply projected, are making Azerbaijan a more equal partner with the West.

Turkey's relationship with the West will bear immense importance for Azerbaijan. But Turkey's European vocation has a much stronger ideological element to it, dating to the Ottoman reforms and the Kemalist revolution, which are the main reason why Turkey has pushed ahead with its ambitions of European integration in spite of continuous setbacks and European resistance. Turkish leaders for decades made the European vocation and acceptance as a full member of the European family a part of the very identity of modern Turkey. Paradoxically, though Azerbaijan's society may be more deeply European than Turkey's, there is less of an identity factor at play. Azerbaijan is in the process of building its distinct national identity, and does not have the Kemalist heritage. As such, Azerbaijan's identity could survive without the West much better than Turkey's could. But that prospect should be of no comfort to Azerbaijan—nor to the West.

Epilogue

The ambition of this book has been to shed light on the emergence of independent Azerbaijan. It tells a story that includes many painful episodes, setbacks and challenges. Yet considering the starting point of independence less than two decades ago and taking into account the regional context in which Azerbaijan finds itself, the story is a remarkably positive one.

Less than twenty years ago, Azerbaijan faced war, the fragmentation of the newborn country, a collapsed economy and political chaos. In the intervening years, much has happened in Azerbaijan's neighborhood. To the north, there is deepening chaos in the Russian North Caucasus that has only been exacerbated by two wars in Chechnya. To the south, an increasingly beleaguered Iranian regime is challenging the world with its nuclear weapons program while brutally suppressing its own population. To its west, Georgia has engendered many hopes with its rapid transformation, but also suffered a devastating invasion by its powerful northern neighbor.

Azerbaijan still suffers from the fallout of one externally fomented conflict, that over Nagorno-Karabakh, which truly forms a shadow over the country. But as traumatic and costly as that conflict has been, it remains geographically contained. Most importantly, that conflict did not prevent the development and consolidation of Azerbaijan's state and economy. Indeed, in less than twenty years, many if not most of the essential institutions of statehood have been built. Moreover, Azerbaijan can be termed the only state in the South Caucasus whose sovereignty is unquestioned, given Russia's influence over Armenia and its military challenge to Georgia's independence.

Many have directed criticism at the needlessly heavy hand that the Azerbaijani authorities wield in domestic affairs, and the slow pace of political reform in the country. Much of this criticism is warranted, and this heavy hand has been widely publicized thanks to international and Azerbaijani watchdog groups. Less publicized has been the factors that underlie these problems. As this book has sought to show, Azerbaijan's political system is one where formal institutions, such as the presidency and the governing bodies, have yet to fully replace informal forces as the true locus of authority. The authority of informal groupings traces its prominence back to pre-Soviet Azerbaijan's Khanates; yet the late Soviet period and

427

the unruly transition to independence permitted the consolidation and entrenchment of forces that are nominally loyal to the formal institutions of power, but which in reality exclusively pursue their own narrow interests. These forces are dominated by holdovers from the Soviet past, and help delay a generational shift in the country's elites. These forces, who incidentally lend themselves to being manipulated by outside forces, contribute greatly to an environment in which capricious actions are taken, and where the rule of law is undermined. Thus, one of the greatest challenges for Azerbaijan and a prerequisite for its political development is whether the strength of informal power structures can be tamed and subjugated to formal and accountable institutions.

Azerbaijan's newfound prosperity has presented the country, and its population, with numerous opportunities. As unseemly as it may seem to criticize a country's growing prosperity, it must be pointed out that oil and gas remain among the worst ways to achieve prosperity. The fact that scholars, based on the experience of the twentieth century, routinely talk of a "resource curse" suggests that the potential liabilities of oil-driven prosperity can be as substantial as the benefits. The fact that large chunks of the country's economy remain in the hands of the informal power wielders mentioned above is cause enough for concern, as is the dearth of examples of countries that have successfully managed a mainly oil-driven economy. Yet Azerbaijan's oil and gas resources are clearly also the chief factor that has enabled it to emerge as the strong and independent state that it is today. While Azerbaijan's leadership has continuously indicated an awareness of the problems associated with oil-led growth, the question is to what extent these problems can be—and are being—successfully mitigated.

The development of Azerbaijan's politics and economy are, of course, strongly related to the many social issues that confront the country. The perhaps most important one is whether the state in the long term embraces or ignores the rural population. Given the size of Baku and its economic activity compared to the rest of the country, the risk that Baku would effectively swallow Azerbaijan cannot be ignored. Bridging the divide between the city and the rest of the country will be a key challenge in the country's development. The future of the Karabakh issue will have a decisive effect: should Azerbaijan get the chance to begin redeveloping the large Western areas of the country currently under occupation, that may generate a substantial push for rural and regional development.

In Azerbaijani society, the rise of the Azerbaijani language and the cultural affirmation of Azerbaijani identity is one of the most noteworthy developments of the period since independence. The work of Azerbaijani scholars to reclaim the country's history, otherwise written mainly by conquerors and neighbors, remains a work in progress. Yet the process of cultural reassertion has taken place in a generally benign manner, with little of the overt chauvinism that often accompanies such processes. Azerbaijani society is struggling to determine its own identity in relation both to its own rich history, and a multitude of external cultural forces, among which the West, Turkey, Russia, and the global Islamic culture are all making their mark.

The realm of foreign policy—incidentally one where the informal power brokers have comparatively little influence—is one that Azerbaijan's leaders have handled deftly, at least since 1994, with the single-minded purpose of consolidating Azerbaijan's independence and integrating it with the world. This success is an indication of what the country's leaders are able to achieve when unfettered from the informal power networks that wield such influence on domestic affairs.

In the process of building itself up as an independent state, Azerbaijan has sought to align itself with the West. Yet as this book has discussed, there is a growing tendency for Azerbaijan's leaders to lean toward a balanced or "multi-vectoral" foreign policy akin to the model that Kazakhstan pioneered a decade ago. The reasons for this tendency to emphasize relations with powers in all direction at the expense of a focus on integration with the West are many. Yet it is clear that the perception of Western disengagement from the South Caucasus, exemplified by the watershed effect of the war in Georgia, has greatly reduced the West's appeal in Azerbaijan.

The evolution of Azerbaijan's foreign relations in the longer terms will be greatly intertwined with the evolution of Azerbaijan's society and identity, as well as its political system. The country's two closest geographic and cultural neighbors—Iran and Turkey—are certain to have an outsize impact, not least because of the serious flux that both are experiencing, though in very different ways: while Turkey has been gravitating toward Islamic conservatism in the past decade, the theocracy in Iran appears increasingly fragile. Looking ahead, the future of Iran could well be the single most important external factor affecting Azerbaijan, given the intimate connections across the Araks river.

Bibliographical Note

This book draws on a wealth of publications on Azerbaijan, ranging from news reports and articles in academic and policy journals to books. These sources are cited in the endnotes to the text. In place of simply replicating these references in a bibliography, this short bibliographic note aims to provide the reader with a guide to appropriate sources on Azerbaijan in the English language. The sources available are widely spread out; there are few book-length studies of Azerbaijan, and only a limited number of book chapters and academic articles on the country. Therefore, readers seeking further analysis on a particular subject will often need to consult a variety of sources.

A number of guidebooks are available on Azerbaijan. The best is Mark Elliott's *Azerbaijan with Excursions to Georgia*, published by Trailblazer press. The guidebook is richly illustrated with the author's own hand-drawn maps, provides much detail and useful suggestions for travelers both to Baku and the outlying regions of the country. A fourth edition was published in 2010.

Those seeking news and analysis of current events in Azerbaijan can consult several sources. One is the *Central Asia-Caucasus Analyst* (www.cacianalyst.org) edited by this author, which publishes biweekly analyses and field reports on the region. The Jamestown Foundation (jamestown.org) publishes the *Eurasia Daily Monitor*, which features regular updates on Azerbaijan. So does the Open Society Institute's *Eurasianet.org* website, as well as a numer of Baku-based news agencies and internet portals including today.az, news.az and Trend.

The best literary introduction to the Caucasus and Azerbaijan is a novel, *Ali and Nino,* by Kurban Said, originally published in 1938. It is available in many editions and translations. Set in early twentieth century Baku, this geopolitical love story between an Azerbaijani boy and Georgian girl of noble origins captures the essence of the Caucasus in a way unsurpassed by subsequent works, and holds relevance to this day. The mystique and debate surrounding the authorship of the novel only adds interest to the book.

On the history of Azerbaijan, the work of Polish-American historian Tadeusz Swietochowski stands out. The most accomplished scholar writing on Azerbaijan's history, Swietochowski is the author of numerous articles but especially two books: *Russian Azerbaijan 1905–1920: The Shaping of National Identity in a Muslim Community* (Cambridge University Press, 1985), and *Russia and Azerbaijan: A Borderland in Transition* (Columbia University Press, 1995). He also co-authored, with Brian Collins, the *Historical Dictionary of Azerbaijan*, published by Scarecrow Press in 1999. In 2011, his *Azerbaijan: Legacies of the Past and the Trials of Independence* is scheduled to be published by Routledge. To this should be added Audrey Altstadt's major history of Azerbaijan, *The Azerbaijani Turks: Power and Identity Under Russian Rule* (Hoover Institution Press, 1992), whose publication coincided with the emergence of independent Azerbaijan, and which provides a detailed overview not least of the Soviet era. A valuable study of the emergence of the first Azerbaijani republic in 1918 is Firuz Kazemzadeh's, *The Struggle for Transcaucasia, 1917–21* (New York: Philosophical Library, 1951, reprinted in 2008 by Anglo-Caspian press).

Readers interested in an Azerbaijani perspective of the country's history can consult several works. The memoirs of Naki Keykurun, an Azerbaijani nationalist forced into exile following the Bolshevik revolution, *The Memoirs of the National Liberation Movement in Azerbaijan*, were published in 1998 by the Azerbaijan Society of America. Historian Yaqub Mahmudlu's *Azerbaijan: Short History of Statehood* has been made available to English-speakers through a translation published in Pakistan (Leaf publiccations, and available on the website of Azerbaijan's embassy in Pakistan, www.azembassy.com.pk). Two Azerbaijani scholars turned parliamentarians also deserve mention. Nasib Nassibli's pioneering work on the 1918–20 period has unfortunately not been translated into English. However, English-speakers can now consult Jamil Hasanli's work, *At the Dawn of the Cold War: The Soviet-American Crisis over Iranian Azerbaijan, 1941–1946* (Rowman and Littlefield, 2006).

There are unfortunately few book-length studies of post-Soviet Azerbaijan. A work that stands out is the unique eyewitness document by the American journalist, adventurer and scholar Thomas Goltz, who found himself living through the war-torn emergence of this country. His first-person account was published by this book's publishers, M.E. Sharpe, in 1998 as *Azerbaijan Diary: A Rogue Reporter's Adventures in an Oil-Rich, War-Torn Post-Soviet Republic*. In 2000, Curzon Press published journalist Charles van der Leeuw's *Azerbaijan: A Quest for Identity*. It is an often entertaining overview of Azerbaijan's recent history, but would have required a more rigorous fact-checking before publication, as it is riddled by factual errors. On Iranian Azerbaijan, however, there is a growing body of literature, most notably represented by Brenda Shaffer's *Borders and Brethren: Iran and the Challenge of Azerbaijani Identity* (MIT Press, 2002).

Several volumes have been published on Azerbaijan's economy and society. No coverage of Azerbaijan's economy compares with the long and detailed studies conducted by World Bank experts, and made available at the Bank's website. Azerbaijan is also prominently featured in *The Economics and Politics of Oil in the Caspian Basin: The Redistribution of Oil Revenues in Azerbaijan and Central Asia*, edited by Boris Najman, Richard Pomfret, and Gaël Raballand. The energy industry and its impact is the subject of several studies, including *The Baku-Tbilisi-Ceyhan Pipeline: Oil Window to the West*, edited by S. Frederick Starr and the present author, as well as Norwegian scholar Daniel Heradstveit's *Democracy and Oil: The Case of Azerbaijan* (Reichert Verlag, 2007). Thanks to Norway's energy ties with Azerbaijan, some of the best work on the country has been conducted by a number of scholars connected to Norway's international affairs institute (NUPI).

Azerbaijan's politics and foreign policy have been the subject of numerous short articles, primarily published in policy journals, but few deep analytical studies. Many of these are referenced in the endnotes to the relevant chapters in this volume. Studies of Azerbaijan's politics tend to be written more from the perspective of identifying and publicizing deficits in democratization than seeking to understand the workings of the political system. In this vein, Freedom House's *Nations in Transit* series, which features yearly reports on Azerbaijan, is probably the most useful. As for Azerbaijan's foreign relations, the bulk of the literature is regional, concerning the geopolitics of the Caucasus, and has a strong tendency to view the small, local states as objects rather than subjects of foreign relations. An exception is *Azerbaijan in Global Politics: Crafting Foreign* Policy, edited by Alexandros Petersen and Fariz Ismailzade, published by the Azerbaijan Diplomatic Academy in 2009. Much reflection on Azerbaijan's relations with the United States is provided in the book published by Azerbaijan's first Ambassador to Washington, Hafiz Pahayev: *Racing Up Hill* (Global Scholarly Publications, 2006). Some academic articles have recently been published putting Azerbaijan's own foreign policy in focus, such as Nazrin Mehdiyeva's "Azerbaijan and Its Foreign Policy Dilemma" (*Asian Affairs*, November 2003) and Pınar Ipek's "Azerbaijan's Foreign Policy and Challenges for Energy Security" (*Middle East Journal*, Summer 2009). The prolific writings of young Azerbaijani scholars Fariz Ismailzade, Taleh

Ziyadov, Tabib Huseynov and Anar Valiyev also deserve mention in this regard.

Two subjects feature most prominently as concerns scholarly interest in Azerbaijani society: the role of Islam and the position of women. The role of Islam has attracted the interest of many scholars, not least German scholar of religion Raoul Motika, who nevertheless publishes mainly in German. In English, notable works include Arif Yunusov's *Islam in Azerbaijan*, published by the Friedrich Ebert foundation in 2004, and Sofie Bedford's *Islamic Activism in Azerbaijan: Repression and Mobilization in a Post-Soviet Context* (Stockholm University, 2009). Gender relations in Azerbaijan is the subject of one of few monographs on the country: Ferideh Heyat's *Azeri Women in Transition: Women in Soviet and Post-Soviet Azerbaijan* (Routledge, 2002).

Given the outsize impact of the Karabakh conflict on Azerbaijan and the region, the conflict is the subject of a large portion of published literature on the country. Background on the conflict can be found in Thomas de Waal, *Black Garden: Armenia and Azerbaijan Through Peace and War* (New York University Press, 2003); and Michael P. Croissant, *The Armenian-Azerbaijani Conflict: Causes and Implications* (Praeger, 1998). Other useful sources include David D. Laitin and Ronald Grigor Suny, "Armenia and Azerbaijan: Thinking a Way out of Karabakh," *Middle East Policy*, January 1999; and Dov Lynch, *Engaging Eurasia's Separatist States: Unresolved Conflicts and De Facto States* (Washington, D.C.: U.S. Institute of Peace Press, 2004). This author's contributions include *The Nagorno-Karabakh Conflict* (Uppsala University, 1999, available online) and pp. 61–141 in *Small Nations and Great Powers: A Study of Ethnopolitical Conflict in the Caucasus* (Curzon Press, 2001).

This bibliographic note does not aspire to be exhaustive, and makes no claim to include all the numerous valuable writings on Azerbaijan that have appeared—for this, the reader is urged to consult the endnotes to this book. Nor does this author necessarily agree with the arguments made in the works cited in this note. Nevertheless, it should serve as a guide for further reading.

Notes

Chapter 1

1. Charles van der Leeuw, *Azerbaijan: A Quest for Identity* (Richmond, UK: Curzon Press, 2000), p. 26.

2. Solomon Nigosian, *The Zoroastrian Faith: Tradition and Modern Research* (Montreal: McGill-Queen's Press), 1993, p. 17; I. Khlopin, "Zoroastrianism – Location and Time of its Origin," *Iranica Antiqua*, vol. 27, 1992: 96–116.

3. Though sometimes confusing, van der Leeuw's account of this period (pp. 25–89) is detailed and most entertaining.

4. Audrey Altstadt, *The Azerbaijani Turks: Power and Identity Under Russian Rule* (Stanford, CA: Hoover Institution Press, 1992), p. 4.

5. Peter B. Golden, "The Turkic Peoples and Transcaucasia," in *Transcaucasia, Nationalism, and Social Change*, ed. Ronald Grigor Suny (Ann Arbor: University of Michigan Press, 1996), pp. 45–67.

6. Geoffrey Lewis (trans.), *The Book of Dede Korkut* (Harmondsworth, UK: Penguin, 1974). See, alternately, Faruk Sumer, Ahmet Uyusal, and Warren Walker (trans. and eds.), *The Book of Dede Korkut: A Turkish Epic* (Austin: University of Texas Press, 1991). See also H.B. Paksoy, "Introduction to Dede Korkut," *Soviet Anthropology and Archaeology* 29, no. 1 (1990)

7. Brenda Shaffer, *Borders and Brethren: Iran and the Challenge of Azerbaijani Identity* (Cambridge, MA: MIT Press, 2002), pp. 19–20.

8. Altstadt, *Azerbaijani Turks*, p. 17.

9. Altstatdt, *Azerbaijani Turks*, p. 17; Tadeusz Swietochowski, *Russia and Azerbaijan: A Borderland in Transition* (New York: Columbia University Press, 1995), pp. 12–14.

10. Swietochowski, *Russia and Azerbaijan*, pp. 10–11.

11. Ibid., p. 15.

12. Altstadt, *Azerbaijani Turks*, p. 21.

13. Swietochowski, *Russia and Azerbaijan*, p. 17.

14. Terry Adams, "Back to the Future: Britain, Baku Oil, and the Cycle of History," *Azerbaijan International* 6, no. 3 (1998).

15. Swietochowski, *Russia and Azerbaijan*, p. 20.

16. See discussion in Altstadt, *Azerbaijani Turks*, ch. 3.

17. Ibid., p. 32.

18. Ibid., p. 36.

19. Kari Eken Strømmen, *Tyrker, Muslim og Sovjetborger: Utvilking av azerbajdsjansk nasjonal identitet under sovjetregimet* [Turk, Muslim, and Soviet Citizen: The Development of Azerbaijani National Identity Under the Soviet Regime] (Oslo: Norwegian Institute of International Affairs, Report No. 245, 1999), p. 35.

20. Altstadt, *Azerbaijani Turks*, p. 43.

21. Swietochowski, *Russia and Azerbaijan*, p. 39, quoting Armenian sources reaching the same conclusion, e.g., Sarkis Atamian, *The Armenian Community: The Historical Development of a Social and Ideological Conflict* (New York: Philosophical Library, 1959), pp. 114–15.

22. Shaffer, *Borders and Brethren*, p. 25.

23. Ibid., pp. 22–25.

24. Tadeusz Swietochowski, *Russian Azerbaijan 1905–1920: The Shaping of National Identity in a Muslim Community* (New York: Cambridge University Press, 1985), p. 23.

25. Hasan Javadi, *Satire in Persian Literature* (London: Associated University Press, 1988), p. 258.; Shaffer, *Borders and Brethren*, p. 26.

26. Strømmen, *Tyrker, Muslim og Sovjetborger*, p. 40.

27. Adeeb Khalid, *The Politics of Muslim Cultural Reform: Jadidism in Central Asia* (Berkeley: University of California Press, 1998).

28. Shaffer, *Borders and Brethren*, p. 27.

29. Volker Adam, "Auf der Suche nach Turan: Panislamismus und Panturkismus in der aserbaidschanischen Vorkriegspresse," [In Search of Turan: Pan-Islamism and Pan-Turkism in the Azerbaijani Pre-War Media] in *Caucasia Between the Ottoman Empire and Iran, 1555–1914*, eds. Raoul Motika and Michael Ursinus (Wiesbaden, Germany: Reichert Verlag, 2000), pp. 189–206.

30. Altstadt, *Azerbaijani Turks*, p. 70.

31. Ziya Gökalp, *Principles of Turkism*, trans. Robert Devereux (Leiden, Netherlands: E. J. Brill, 1968). Originally published in Turkish as *Türkçülüğün Esasları*, 1923.

32. A. Holly Schissler, *Between Two Empires: Ahmet Agaoglu and the New Turkey* (New York: I.B. Tauris, 2003).

33. Swietochowski, *Russian Azerbaijan*, p. 32.

34. Altstadt, *Azerbaijani Turks*, p. 70.

35. For an overview of Azerbaijan's "firsts," see "Famous People From Azerbaijan," compiled by Adil Baguirov. Available at www.zerbaijan.com/azlist.htm, downloaded June 9, 2009.

36. Strømmen, *Tyrker, Muslim og Sovjetborger*, pp. 41–45.

37. Swietochowski, *Russian Azerbaijan*, p. 64.

38. Ibid., p. 38.

39. Ibid., p. 42.

40. Naki Keykurun (Sheykhzamanli), *The Memoirs of the National Liberation Movement in Azerbaijan* (Clifton, NJ: Tomris Azeri, Azerbaijan Society of America, 1998), p. 16. Originally published in Turkish as *Azerbaycan İstiklal Mücadelesinden Hatıralar*, 1964. The English translation is available online at www.zerbaijan.com/azeri/tomris book1.htm (downloaded June 9, 2009).

41. Shaffer, *Borders and Brethren*, pp. 32–33.

42. Ibid., p. 35.

43. Cengiz Çağla, *Azerbaycanda Milliyetçilik ve Politika* [Nationalism and Politics in Azerbaijan] (Istanbul, Turkey: Bağlam, 2002), pp. 58–60.

44. Swietochowski, *Russian Azerbaijan*, pp. 48–49.

45. This dilemma of identity is best illustrated in *Ali and Nino* (1938), by Kurban Said [pseudonym of Lev Nussimbaum]. Various editions in numerous languages have been published. Currently, one of the most widely sold English-language editions is a translation by Jenia Graman (Garden City, NY: Anchor, 2000).

46. Swietochowski, *Russian Azerbaijan*, p. 76.

47. Ibid., pp. 78–79.

48. Micñael A. Reynolds, "Buffers, not Brethren: Young Turk Military Policy in the First World war and the Myth of Panturanism," *Past and Present*, no. 2003, May 2009: 137–179.

49. Altstadt, *Azerbaijani Turks*, pp. 78–79; Keykurun's memoirs (see note 39) are a vivid example of this.

50. Swietochowski, *Russian Azerbaijan*, p. 83.

51. Altstadt, *Azerbaijani Turks*, p. 75.

52. Stephen Jones, *Socialism in Georgian Colors: The European Road to Social Democracy, 1883–1917* (Cambridge, MA: Harvard University Press, 2005).

53. Altstadt, *Azerbaijani Turks*, p. 100.

54. Keykurun, *Memoirs*, p. 60; Ronald Grigor Suny, *The Baku Commune, 1917–1918: Class and Nationality in the Russian Revolution* (Princeton, NJ: Princeton University Press, 1972), pp. 86–87.

55. Swietochowski, *Russian Azerbaijan*, pp. 89–91.

56. Firuz Kazemzadeh, *The Struggle for Transcaucasia, 1917–21* (New York: Philosophical Library, 1968), pp. 49–50; Swietochowski, *Russian Azerbaijan*, p. 96.

57. Jörg Baberowski, *Der Feind ist überall: Stalinismus im Kaukasus*, [The Enemy is Everywhere: Stalinism in the Caucasus] (Munich: Deutsche Verlags-Anstalt, 2003), p. 63.

58. Ibid., p. 102.

59. Keykurun's memoirs (see note 39) include vivid accounts of this process.

60. Altstadt, *Azerbaijani Turks*, p. 87, cites Shaumian's own recollections: "We exploited the opportunity of the first armed assault on our cavalry unit and began an attack on the whole front."

61. Suny, *Baku Commune,* p. 218.

62. Altstadt, *Azerbaijani Turks*, p. 86; Kazemzadeh, *Struggle for Transcaucasia*, p. 76; Swietochowski, *Russian Azerbaijan*, pp. 116–18; the quote is from Suny, *Baku Commune*, p. 224.

63. Baberowski, *Der Feind ist überall*, pp. 132–33. (Translation from German by the present author.)

64. Kazemzadeh, *Struggle for Transcaucasia*, p. 88.

65. Baberowski, *Der Feind ist überall*, p. 142; Kazemzadeh, *Struggle for Transcaucasia*, quote is from p. 105.

66. Kazemzadeh, *Struggle for Transcaucasia*, p. 114.

67. Quoted in Swietochowski, *Russian Azerbaijan*, p. 129.

68. Ibid., p. 145.

69. Ibid., p. 148.

70. Kazemzadeh, *Struggle for Transcaucasia*, pp. 223–24.

71. Ibid., p. 222.

72. Swietochowski, *Russian Azerbaijan*, p. 132.

73. Suny, *Baku Commune,* p. 218.

74. Lionel C. Dunsterville, *The Adventures of Dunsterforce* (London: Edward Arnold, 1920), p. 219.

75. Keykurun, *Memoirs*, p. 94.

76. Kazemzadeh, *Struggle for Transcaucasia*, p. 228.

77. Swietochowski, *Russian Azerbaijan*, p. 174.

78. Ibid., p. 176.

79. Ibid., quoted on p. 177.

80. Ibid., p. 183.

81. Swietochowski, *Russia and Azerbaijan*, pp. 100–101.

Chapter 2

1. Brian Peace, ed., *To See the Dawn, Baku, 1920: First Congress of the Peoples of the East* (New York: Pathfinder, 1993).

2. Häsän Häsänov, *Näriman Närimanovun Milli Dövletçilik Baxışları vä Fäaliyyäti* [Nariman Narimanov's Views on National Statehood and Activities] (Baku, Azerbaijan: Elm, 2005), p. 66.

3. Gerhard Simon, *Nationalism and Policy Toward Nationalities in the Soviet Union: From Totalitarian Dictatorship to Post-Stalinist Society*, trans. Karen Forster and Oswald Forster (Boulder, CO: Westview, 1991), p. 135.

4. Tadeusz Swietochowski, *Russian Azerbaijan, 1905–1920: The Shaping of National Identity in a Muslim Community* (New York: Cambridge University Press, 1985), p. 112.

5. Terry Martin, "An Affirmative Action Empire: The Soviet Union as the Highest Form of Imperialism," in *A State of Nations: Empire and Nation-Making in the Age of Lenin and Stalin*, eds. Ronald Grigor Suny and Terry Martin (New York: Oxford University Press, 2001), p. 67.

6. Simon, *Nationalism and Policy*, p. 24, quoting KPSSv rezoliutsiiakh i resheniakh sezdov, konferentsii i plenumov CK, vol. 2 (Moscow, 1970), p. 252.

7. Ian Bremmer, "Reassessing Soviet Nationalities Theory," in *Nations and Politics in the Soviet Successor States*, eds. Ian Bremmer and Ray Taras (New York: Cambridge University Press, 1993), p. 5.

8. Simon, *Nationalism and Policy*, p. 42.

9. Ibid., pp. 31–34.

10. Ibid., p. 22.

11. Hélène Carrère d'Encausse, "Determinants and Parameters of Soviet Nationality Policy," in *Soviet Nationality Policies and Practices*, ed. Jeremy R. Azrael (New York: Praeger, 1978), p. 48.

12. Audrey Altstadt, *The Azerbaijani Turks: Power and Identity Under Russian Rule* (Stanford, CA: Hoover Institution Press, 1992), p. 110.

13. Ibid., p. 121.

14. Ibid., pp. 131–32.

15. Tadeusz Swietochowski, *Russia and Azerbaijan: A Borderland in Transition* (New York: Columbia University Press, 1995), pp. 115–16.

16. Altstadt, pp. 140–41.

17. Swietochowski, *Russia and Azerbaijan*, p. 125.

18. Ibid., p. 127.

19. Altstadt, p. 150.

20. Ibid., p. 151.

21. Ibid.; see also Vagif Agayev, Fuad Akhundov, Fikrat T. Aliyev, and Mikhail Agarunov, "World War II and Azerbaijan," *Azerbaijan International* 3, no. 2 (1995).

22. Altstadt, p. 154.

23. Swietochowski, *Russia and Azerbaijan*, p. 133, citing Joachim Hoffman, *Kaukasien 1942–43: Das Deutsche Heer und die Orientvolker der Sowjetunion* [Caucasus 1942–43: The German Army and the Eastern Peoples of the Soviet Union] (Freiburg: Rombach, 1991), p. 220.

24. Brenda Shaffer, *Borders and Brethren: Iran and the Challenge of Azerbaijani Identity* (Cambridge, MA: MIT Press, 2002), pp. 53–58.

25. Swietochowski, *Russia and Azerbaijan*, p. 175.

26. Altstadt, *Azerbaijani Turks*, pp. 164–69; Shaffer, *Borders and Brethren*, pp. 66–67; Swietochowski, *Russia and Azerbaijan*, pp. 175–77.

27. Swietochowski, *Russia and Azerbaijan*, p. 179.

28. Gertrude Schröder, "Transcaucasia since Stalin: the Economic Dimension," in Romald G. Suny, *Transcaucasia, Nationalism and Social Chance: Essays in the History of Armenia, Azerbaijan and Georgia* (Ann Arbor, MI: Michigan Slavic Publications, 1983.)

29. Irfan Ülkü, *Bağımsızlıktan sonra Azerbaycan* [Azerbaijan after Independence], (Istanbul: Doğan Kitapçılık, 2000), p. 80.

30. Thomas Goltz, *Azerbaijan Diary* (New York: M.E. Sharpe, 1998), p. 67.

31. Georgi Derluguian, "Azeri Orientalists as Mirror of the Postsoviet Revolution," *21st Century* (Noravank Foundation), no. 2, 2007: 48.

32. Altstadt, *Azerbaijani Turks*, p. 182.

33. Derluguian, "Azeri Orientalists": 50.

34. Audrey Altstadt, "Azerbaijanis Reassess Their History," *Report on the USSR*, Radio Liberty, August 18, 1989.

35. Yasin Aslan and Elizabeth Fuller, "Founder of Independent Azerbaijani Republic Rehabilitated," *Report on the USSR*, Radio Liberty, June 30, 1989; Annette Bohr and Yasin Aslan, "Independent Azerbaijan, 1918–1920: Call to Reevaluate History of Former Nation-State," Radio Liberty, *Report on the USSR,* August 18, 1988.

36. Altstadt, *Azerbaijani Turks*, p. 191.

37. Ülkü, *Bağımsızlıktan sonra Azerbaycan*, pp. 71–73.

38. Swietochowski, *Russia and Azerbaijan*, p. 183.

39. Ülkü, *Bağımsızlıktan sonra Azerbaycan*, p. 105.

40. Swietochowski, p. 183, and Richard Owen, "Rise of the Southern Soviet Republics," *Times* of London, November 29, 1982.

Chapter 3

1. Interview with Chingiz Sultansoy, Baku, 1999.

2. Brenda Shaffer, *Borders and Brethren: Iran and the Challenge of Azerbaijani Identity* (Cambridge, MA: MIT Press, 2002), pp. 125–26.

3. Author's Interview by the author with Sabir Rustamhanli, October 2005.

4. Mark Malkasian, *"Gha-ra-bagh!" The Emergence of the National democratic Movement in Armenia* (Detroit, MI: Wayne State University Press, 1996).

5. *L'Humanité*, November 18, 1987.

6. Mikhail Gorbachev, *Memoirs* (New York: Doubleday, 1996), pp. 333–40.

7. *Los Angeles Times*, April 19 1988; Igor Nolyain, "Moscow's Initiation of the Armenian-Azerbaijani Conflict," *Central Asian Survey*, vol. 13, no. 4, 1994: 541–63.

8. Gary Lee, "Protests in Azerbaijan Planned to Coincide with Expected Decision Later This Week," *Washington Post*, March 21, 1988.

9. *Krasnaya Zvezda*, November 26, 1988.

10. *The Guardian*, November 28, 1988.

11. *Izvestiya*, November 26, 1988.

12. "Moscow Purge in Azerbaijan," *The Guardian*, December 27, 1988.

13. Audrey Altstadt, *The Azerbaijani Turks: Power and Identity Under Russian Rule* (Stanford, CA: Hoover Institution Press, 1992), pp. 204–5.

14. Nasib Nasibzade, "Müsavatçılıq keçmişte ve indi" [Müsavatism in the past and present] in *Bölünmüş Azärbaycan, Birleşik Azärbaycan* [Divided Azerbaijan, United Azerbaijan] (Baku, Azerbaijan, Ay-Ulduz, 1997).

15. Program of the Azerbaijani Popular Front, 1989, first general principle.

16. Bill Keller, "Nationalist in Azerbaijan Win Big Concessions from Party Chief," *New York Times*, October 13, 1989.

17. Altstadt, *Azerbaijani Turks*, p. 213.

18. Excellent comprehensive coverage of January 20 is provided in Altstadt, *Azerbaijani Turks*, pp. 213–19. See, in particular, p. 214, n. 152.

19. Mark Saroyan, "The 'Karabakh Syndrome' and Azerbaijani Politics," *Problems of Communism* 39 (September/October 1990): 14–29.

20. Radio Liberty, February 20, 1990, cited in Altstadt, *Azerbaijani Turks*, p. 219.

21. Michael Dobbs, "Soviets Say Troops Used to Avert Coup in Baku: Nationalists Said to Plan Seizure of Power," *Washington Post*, January 27, 1990.

22. Radio Liberty, *Report on the USSR,* March 12, 1990.

23. Altstadt, *Azerbaijani Turks*, p. 220.

24. Elizabeth Fuller, "Azerbaijani Central Committee Elects New First Secretary," Radio Liberty, *Report on the USSR*, February 2, 1990.

25. David E. Murphy, "Operation 'Ring'— the Black Berets in Azerbaijan," *Journal of Soviet Military Studies*, vol. 5, no. 1, March 1992: 80–96.

26. Aydin Balayev, *Azerbaidjanskoye natsionalnoye dvijenie: ot Moussavata do Narodnova Fronta* [The Azerbaijani National Movement: From Müsavat to the National Front] (Baku: Elm, 1992), p. 65.

27. Nazim Cafersoy, *Elçibey dönemi Azerbaycan dis politikasi* [Azerbaijani Foreign Policy in the Elçibey Period] (Ankara: ASAM, 2001), p. 30.

Chapter 4

1. *Azadlıq* (Baku, Azerbaijan), January 14 and 21, 1992.

2. Nazim Cafersoy, *Elçibey Dönemi Azerbaycan Dış Politikası* [Azerbaijani Foreign Policy in the Elçibey Period] (Ankara, Turkey: ASAM, 2000), p. 36.

3. A fact pointed out to the author by Thomas Goltz in 1999.

4. Thomas Goltz, *Azerbaijan Diary* (Armonk, NY: M.E. Sharpe), 1998, p. 122.

5. Goltz, *Azerbaijan Diary*, pp. 117–30; Goltz, "Nagorno-Karabakh Victims Buried in Azerbaijani Town," *Washington Post*, February 28, 1992; Goltz, "Armenian Soldiers Massacre Hundreds of Fleeing Families," *Sunday Times* (London), March 1, 1992; Anatol Lieven, "Corpses Litter Hills in Karabakh," *The Times* (London), March 2, 1992; "Massacre by Armenians Being Reported," *New York Times*, March 3, 1992; Hugh Pope, "600 Azerbaijanis Slain at Khojaly, Investigator Says," *Los Angeles Times*, June 12, 1992.

6. Thomas de Waal, *Black Garden: Armenia and Azerbaijan through Peace and War* (New York: NYU Press, 2004), p. 172.

7. Goltz, *Azerbaijan Diary*, p. 132.

8. Portions of the videos are available at In Memory of Chingiz Mustafayev, "Video Archive," www.chingizmustafayev.com/video_arxiv.php (downloaded July 2, 2009).

9. Goltz, *Azerbaijan Diary*, p. 135.

10. "New Republican Party First Secretary Elected in Azerbaijan," Radio Liberty RL 487/82, December 6, 1992.

11. Translation by Goltz, *Azerbaijan Diary*, p. 146. The statement is available in the original Azeri in Irfan Ülkü, *Bağımsızlıktan sonra Azerbaycan* [Azerbaijan after Independence] (Istanbul: Doğan Kitapçılık, 2000), p. 117.

12. Abdollah Ramazanzadeh, "Iran's Role as Mediator in the Nagorno-Karabakh Crisis," in *Contested Borders in the Caucasus*, ed. Bruno Coppieters (Brussels: VUB Press, 1996).

13. Audrey Altstadt, "Azerbaijan's Struggle Toward Democracy," in *Conflict, Cleavage, and Change in Central Asia and the Caucasus*, eds. Karen Dawisha and Bruce Parrott (New York: Cambridge University Press, 1997), p. 126.

14. Goltz, *Azerbaijan Diary*, p. 135; Altstadt, "Azerbaijan's Struggle," p. 126.

15. This episode is vividly recounted by Goltz in *Azerbaijan Diary*, 195–98.

16. Ibid., p. 226.

17. Ibid., p. 70.

18. Ibid., pp. 212–14.

19. Cafersoy, *Elçibey Dönemi*, p. 51.

20. Aryeh Vasserman, "A Year of Rule by the Popular Front of Azerbaijan," in *Muslim Eurasia: Conflicting Legacies*, ed. Yacoov Ro'I (London: Frank Cass, 1995), p. 143.

21. Cafersoy, *Elçibey Dönemi*, pp. 53–54.

22. Hendrik Fenz, "Transformation in Aserbaidschan: Nationalismus als Brücke zur Demokratie?" [Transformation in Azerbaijan: Nationalism as Bridge to Democracy?] (Ph.D. dissertation, Hamburg University, 2003), p. 163.

23. Arif Yunusov, "Azerbaydzhan v postsovietski period: Problemy a vozmozhnye puti razvitiya," in *Severniy Kavkaz-Zakavkaze: Problema stabilnosti i perspektivy razvitya*, [North Caucasus-South Caucasus: Problems of Stability and Perspectives for Development] eds. O. Vornukova and I. Iskandarian (Moscow, 1997).

24. Goltz, *Azerbaijan Diary*, p. 256.

25. Interview with Abulfez Elçibey, conducted by the author, Baku, October 1998.

26. Cafersoy, *Elçibey Dönemi*, p. 59.

27. For an overview of foreign policy in the Popular Front period, see Cafersoy, *Elçibey Dönemi*, pp. 65–159.

28. Dilip Hiro, "The Azerbaijan Question," *The Nation*, September 14, 1992.

29. See Hafiz Pashayev, *Racing Up Hill: Selected Papers of Azerbaijan's First Ambassador to the United States of America*, (Albany, NY: Global Scholarly Publications, 2006.)

30. "Azerbaijani Army Commander Dismissed over Battlefield Setbacks," *BBC Summary of World Broadcasts*, February 25, 1993.

31. *Nezavisimaya Gazeta*, February 23, 1993.

32. Hugh Pope, "40,000 Flee Armenian Offensive," *The Independent* (London), April 7, 1993.

33. Goltz, *Azerbaijan Diary*, p. 256.

34. Ibid., p. 399.

35. *Transition Report 1995* (London: European Bank for Reconstruction and Development, 1995); *Statistical Handbook 1993* (Washington, D.C.: World Bank, 1994).

36. Altstadt, "Azerbaijan's Struggle," pp. 136–38.

37. Anna Matveeva and Clem McCartney, "Policy Response to an Ethnic Community Division: Lezgins in Azerbaijan," *International Journal on Minority and Group Rights* 5, no. 3 (1998): 227–28.

38. Personal communication from Azerbaijani official, 1999.

39. Elizabeth Fuller, "Azerbaijan's June Revolution," *RFE/RL Research Report* 2, no. 32 (1993), p. 26.

40. This is according to Thomas Goltz, one of the first independent observers to come to the scene. See Goltz, *Azerbaijan Diary*, pp. 356–61.

41. Goltz, *Azerbaijan Diary*, p. 392.

42. Thornike Gordadze, "Russian-Georgian Relations in the 1990s," in *The Guns of August 2008: Russia's War in Georgia*, eds. Svante E. Cornell and S. Frederick Starr (Armonk, NY: M.E. Sharpe, 2009).

43. Ülkü, *Bağımsızlıktan sonra Azerbaycan*, pp. 117–33; see also Goltz, *Azerbaijan Diary*, pp. 366–69.

Chapter 5

1. John P. Willerton, *Patronage and Politics in the USSR* (New York: Cambridge University Press, 1991), 196.

2. Charles H. Fairbanks Jr., "The Postcommunist Wars," *Journal of Democracy* 6, no. 4 (1995): 18–34.

3. Nasser Sagheb and Masoud Javadi, "Azerbaijan's 'Contract of the Century,'" *Azerbaijan International* 2, no. 4 (1994).

4. Irfan Ülkü, *Bağımsızlıktan sonra Azerbaycan* [Azerbaijan after Indepdence] (Istanbul: Doğan Kitapçılık, 2000), p. 223.

5. Ibid., pp. 233–34.

6. Ibid., p. 228.

7. Laura le Cornu, *Azerbaijan's September Crisis: An Analysis of the Causes and Implications*, Former Soviet South Briefing no. 1 (London: Royal Institute of International Affairs, 1995), p. 3.

8. Thomas Goltz, *Azerbaijan Diary* (Armonk, NY: M.E. Sharpe, 1998), p. 448; Ülkü, *Bağımsızlıktan sonra Azerbaycan*, pp. 225–34; le Cornu, *Azerbaijan's September Crisis*, p. 3.

9. Le Cornu, *Azerbaijan's September Crisis*, p. 3.

10. In *Bağımsızlıktan sonra Azerbaycan*, Ülkü devotes a long chapter, (pp. 235–62), to what he terms a "black page in Turkey's history."

11. For a fuller account see Svante Cornell, *Small Nations and Great Powers: A Study of Ethnopolitical Conflict in the Caucasus* (London: Curzon Press, 2001), pp. 300–302, and Goltz, *Azerbaijan Diary*, pp. 451–52.

12. Armen Bayburtian, Armenian deputy minister of foreign affairs, in an interview with the author in Yerevan, September 1998.

13. For a detailed sequence of events, see Cornell, *Small Nations*, pp. 102–7.

14. Azer Kerimov, "Azerbaijan React to Armenian Election, as Karabakh Cease-Fire is Violated," *Central Asia-Caucasus Analyst*, March 5, 2008.

15. Mehran Kamrava, "State-Building in Azerbaijan: The Search for Consolidation," *Middle East Journal* 55, no. 2, Spring 2001: 228.

16. Cornell, *Small Nations and Great Powers,* pp. 372–87.

17. Marina S. Ottaway, *Democracy Challenged: The Rise of Semi-Authoritarianism* (Washington, D.C.: Carnegie Endowment for International Peace, 2003), p. 3.

18. Daniel Heradstveit and Kari Eken Strømmen, *Nation-Building in Azerbaijan: Democracy and Human Rights*, Occasional Paper no. 248 (Oslo, Norway: Norwegian Institute of International Affairs, 1999), pp. 48–52.

19. See, e.g., interviews in the Turkish daily *Sabah*, September 6, 1998, and in *Azerbaijan International* 5, no. 3 (1997), quoted by Heradstveit and Strømmen.

20. Aliyev spoke at a forum sponsored by the United States–Azerbaijan Chamber of Commerce at Georgetown University, Washington, D.C., on July 30, 1997. Among other sources, the text of this address appears in *Azerbaijan International* 11, no. 4 (2003).

21. Svante E. Cornell and Fariz Ismailzade, "Azerbaijan," in Adrian Karatnycky, Alexander Motyl, and Amanda Schnetzer, eds., *Nations in Transit 2002* (New York: Freedom House, 2002), pp. 80–93.

22. Svante E. Cornell and Fariz Ismailzade, "Azerbaijan," in Adrian Karatnycky, Alexander Motyl, and Amanda Schnetzer, eds., *Nations in Transit 2003* (New York: Freedom House, 2002), pp. 100–122.

23. See, e.g., *Statement of the National Democratic Institute for International Affairs (NDI) International Election Observer Delegation to Azerbaijan's October 11, 1998, Presidential Election*, (Washington D.C.: National Democratic Institute, October 13, 1998).

24. Office of Democratic Institutions and Human Rights, Republic of Azerbaijan: Review of the Law on Parliamentary Elections (Warsaw, Poland: Organization for Security and Cooperation in Europe, 2000).

25. The episode is discussed at greater length in Svante E. Cornell, "Democratization Falters in Azerbaijan," *Journal of Democracy* 12, no. 2 (2001): 118–31.

26. Michael Wyzan, "Azerbaijan's Economy Grows but Problems Loom," *Asia Times Online*, May 14, 1999 (available at www.atimes.com/c-asia/AE14Ag02.html).

Chapter 6

1. Elin Suleymanov, "The 1990s End in Azerbaijan, as the Nation Mourns Its Patriarch," *Central Asia–Caucasus Analyst*, December 17, 2003.

2. Narmina Mamedova, "Azerbaijan: One Party, Two Candidates," *Central Asia–Caucasus Analyst*, July 2, 2003.

3. Significantly, in his cover letter to the State Department, U.S. ambassador to Azerbaijan Reno Harnish added three words, causing a key portion of one sentence to read as follows: "affected the legitimacy *of the results* of the election" [emphasis added]. These words, not included in his staff's report, provoked an outburst of criticism in

Washington, in particular from Senator John McCain, Republican of Arizona, on the U.S. Senate floor.

4. Author's conversations with several Azerbaijani opposition sympathizers confiding they or their like-minded friends had voted for Ilham Aliyev. Baku, Spring 2004.

5. Charles H. Fairbanks Jr., "Georgia's Rose Revolution," *Journal of Democracy* 15, no. 2 (2004): 110–24.

6. Leila Amirova and Zarema Velikhanova, "Ilham Aliev's Uncertain Rise," Institute of War and Peace Reporting, Caucasus Reporting Service (Report No. 199, October 9, 2003), www.iwpr.net/index (accessed August 19, 2009).

7. Author's interview with Ilham Aliyev, Baku, October 2005.

8. Elin Suleymanov, "New Foreign Minister to Revitalize Azerbaijan's Diplomacy?" *Central Asia–Caucasus Analyst*, April 21, 2004.

9. Vladimir Socor, "Will Azerbaijan's Opposition Choose Turmoil as a Strategy?" *Eurasia Daily Monitor*, November 16, 2005.

10. Author's interview with President Ilham Aliyev, October 2005.

11. The report of the international monitoring mission, and especially the presentation of the results at a Baku press conference on November 7, 2005, was cheered by the opposition, but significantly, several members of the observation mission of the Parliamentary Assembly of the Council of Europe (PACE) were disturbed by the fact that the report did not correspond to the discussions their observation mission had had earlier the same day, when a considerably more balanced assessment had dominated. As one member of the PACE observation mission told this author, the heads of the four delegations (OSCE, the Council of Europe, the North Atlantic Treaty Organization, and the European Parliament) met in closed chambers to draft the report, which delegation members did not see until it was later disclosed to the general public at the press conference—at which point it emerged in a tone that was generally negative and almost entirely failed to acknowledge the progress that had been made relative to previous elections.

12. Asim Mollazade, "The Emerging Political Life in Azerbaijan," presentation at the Central Asia-Caucasus Institute Forum, Washington D.C., December 6, 2006. Also quoted in Tim Wall, "Hillary Clinton of Azerbaijan Gets Elected," *St. Petersburg Times*, November 15, 2005.

13. Associated Press, "Protest in Azerbaijan Disappoints," November 10, 2005.

14. See Reporters without Borders website at http://www.rsf.org/en-rapport91-id_rubrique948-Azerbaijan.html.

15. "Finding Elmar's Killers," Committee to Protect Journalists, September 16, 2008, http://www.cpj.org/reports/2008/09/azerbaijan-elmar.php.

16. Organization for Security and Cooperation in Europe, "OSCE media freedom representative welcomes release of imprisoned journalists, urges legal reform in Azerbaijan," Press Release, April 21, 2009. http://www.osce.org/item/37290.html.

17. Shahin Abbasov, "Azerbaijan: Baku Can Leapfrog over Ukraine, Georgia for NATO Membership—Source," *Eurasianet.org*, http://eurasianet.org/departments/insig htb/articles/eav060409.shtml (posted June 4, 2009).

18. OSCE Office of Democratic Institutions and Human Rights, Press Release, October 16, 2008, http://www.osce.org/odihr/item_1_34400.html.

19. See e.g. Larry Diamond, "Thinking about Hybrid Regimes," *Journal of Democracy* 13, no. 2, April (2002): 21–35.

20. See Fareed Zakaria, *The Future of Freedom* (New York: W.W. Norton, 2003).

Chapter 7

1. For an overview of the war and its background, see Svante E. Cornell and S. Frederick Starr, eds., *The Guns of August 2008: Russia's War in Georgia* (Armonk, NY: M.E. Sharpe, 2009).

2. Background on the conflict can be found in Svante E. Cornell, *The Nagorno-Karabakh Conflict* (Uppsala, Sweden: Uppsala University, Department of East European Studies, Report No. 46, 1999), available at www.silkroadstudies.org/new/inside/publications/1999_NK_Book.pdf; Svante E. Cornell, *Small Nations and Great Powers: A Study of Ethnopolitical Conflict in the Caucasus* (Richmond, England: Curzon Press, 2001), pp. 61–141; Thomas de Waal, *Black Garden: Armenia and Azerbaijan Through Peace and War* (New York: New York University Press, 2003); and Michael P. Croissant, *The Armenian-Azerbaijani Conflict: Causes and Implications* (New York: Praeger, 1998). Other useful sources include an issue of the international journal *Accord* (no. 17, 2005) titled *The Limits of Leadership: Elites and Societies in the Nagorny Karabakh Peace Process* (Laurence Broers, ed.), which provides short articles on aspects of the conflict; David D. Laitin and Ronald Grigor Suny, "Armenia and Azerbaijan: Thinking a Way out of Karabakh," *Middle East Policy* 7, no. 1 (1999): 145–76; and Dov Lynch, *Engaging Eurasia's Separatist States: Unresolved Conflicts and De Facto States* (Washington, D.C.: U.S. Institute of Peace Press, 2004).

3. John Greenway, "Europe's Forgotten People: Protecting the Human Rights of Long-Term Displaced Persons," Report to the Parliamentary Assembly of the Council of Europe, p. 21.

4. Interview with Ilham Aliyev, conducted by the author, Baku, Azerbaijan, October 2005.

5. Tabib Huseynov, "A Karabakh Azeri Perspective," *Accord* no. 17 (2005): 26.

6. Gerard Libaridian, "The Elusive 'Right Formula' at the 'Right Time,'" *Accord* no. 17 (2005): 36.

7. Security Council resolutions on Karabakh included Resolutions 822 (April 30, 1993), 853 (July 29, 1993), 873 (October 14, 1993), and 884 (November 11, 1993). The UN General Assembly also passed a resolution on November 19, 1993.

8. John J. Maresca, "Agony of Indifference in Nagorno-Karabakh," *Christian Science Monitor*, June 27, 1994, p. 19.

9. See e.g. Charles Fairbanks et al., *Strategic Assessement of Central Eurasia*, Washington: CACI and Atlantic Council of the United States, 2001.

10. BBC Monitoring Service, January 1, 1994.

11. David Hoffman, "Karabakh Smoothens Its Lifeline," *Washington Post*, September 19, 1996.

12. Vicken Cheterian, *Little Wars and a Great Game: Local Conflicts and International Competition in the Caucasus* (Working Paper No. 32) (Berne, Switzerland: Swiss Peace Foundation, 2001), p. 34.

13. Hrach Melkumian and Emil Danielyan, "Aide Says Next President Should be 'Karabakhstsi', *RFE/RL Caucasus Report*, vol. 7 no. 23, June 10, 2004, http://www.rferl.org/content/article/1341775.html.

14. John J. Maresca, "Lost Opportunities in Negotiating the Conflict over Nagorno-Karabakh," *International Negotiation* 1, no. 4 (1996): 472.

15. Personal communication from Heikki Talvitie, Stockholm, Sweden, November 1997.

16. Gerard Libaridian, "Time Is on Neither Side," in Gerard Libaridian and Arif Yunusov, *New Approaches to Nagorno-Karabakh: A Window of Opportunity?* EastWest Institute Policy Brief no. 3, 1998.

17. "OSCE Summit Unable to Overcome Karabakh Stalemate," *Jamestown Monitor* 2, no. 226 (December 4, 1996), available at www.jamestown.org/archives/monitor/m1996; *Turkish Daily News* (Ankara), December 3, 1996; "Karabakh Rebuffs OSCE," *Jamestown Monitor* 2, no. 223 (December 13, 1996), available at www.jamestown.org/archives/monitor/m1996.

18. This was made clear to the author by Armen Baibourtian, deputy foreign minister of Armenia, in an interview in Yerevan in October 1998.

19. "OSCE Offers to Defer Nagorno's Status," Radio Free Europe/Radio Liberty, www.rferl.org/content/Article/1086707.html (posted September 29, 1997); Roland Eggleston, "Armenia/Azerbaijan: Negotiators Try New Approach," Radio Free Europe/Radio Liberty, www.rferl.org/content/Article/ 1086522.html (posted September 30, 1997).

20. *Newsline*, October 1 and 20, 1997, Radio Free Europe/Radio Liberty, available at www.rferl.org/archive/en-newsline.

21. *Armenia Report*, November 12, 1997, Radio Free Europe/Radio Liberty.

22. As stated in an editorial in the Armenian daily *Hayastani Hanrapetutyun*, November 5, 1997 (cited in *Armenia Report*, November 5, 1997, Radio Free Europe/Radio Liberty).

23. Lawrence Sheets, "OSCE Karabakh Proposals," Reuters, November 9, 1998.

24. Vladimir Socor, "Russian Input Distorts OSCE Mediation in Karabakh Conflict," *Jamestown Monitor* 4, no. 210 (November 12, 1998), available at www.james town.org/archives/monitor/m1998.

25. *Noyan Tapan* News Agency, November 11 and 12, 1998; "OSCE Proposals Welcomed by Armenia, Karabakh," *Jamestown Monitor* 4, no. 211 (November 13, 1998), available at www.jamestrown.org/archives/monitor/m1998.

26. "OSCE and the Karabakh Conflict: Failure of a Mission," *Jamestown Monitor* 4, no. 222 (December 2, 1998), available at www.jamestrown.org/archives/monitor/m 1998.

27. *Eurasia Daily Monitor* 4, no. 221 (December 1, 1998), available at www. jamestown.org/archives/monitor/m1998.

28. Emil Danielyan, "Armenia/Azerbaijan: New Efforts To Solve Nagorno-Karabakh Dispute," Radio Free Europe/Radio Liberty, www.rferl.org/content/Article/ 1091380. html (posted May 24, 1999).

29. See, e.g., "Armenian, Azerbaijani Presidents Meet," *Newsline*, October 12, 1999, Radio Free Europe/Radio Liberty, available at www.rferl.org/content/Article/1142011. html.

30. For a further discussion of 1999 in the Caucasus, see Svante E. Cornell, "The Caucasus Under Renewed Russian Pressure," *Analysis of Current Events* 13, no. 3(2001).

31. Zeyno Baran, *Georgia Under Worst Pressure Since Independence* [Georgia Update Monograph Series] (Washington, D.C.: Center for Strategic and International Studies, January 10, 2001).

32. Miriam Lanskoy, "Azerbaijan Under Pressure," *The NIS Observed: An Analytical Review* 4, no. 17 (November 1999), available at http://www.bu.edu/ iscip/digest/vol4/ ed0417.html.

33. Tofiq Zulfugarov, "Obstacles to Resolution: An Azerbaijani Perspective," *Accord,* no. 17 (2005): 41.

34. Fariz Ismailzade and Jason Pellmar, "Marking Time," *Transitions Online*, January 14, 2000, available at http://www.bu.edu/iscip/digest/vol4/ed0417.html.

35. Zulfugarov, "Obstacles to Resolution": 41.

36. See "Shooting of Armenian Parliament Was Organized by Russian Special Services," *Azg* daily, May 3, 2005, available at http://www.azg.am/EN/2005050307; Ruzanna Stepanian, "Armenian Officials Deny Russian Role in 1999 Parliament

Carnage," *Armenia Report*, May 4, 2005, Radio Free Europe/Radio Liberty, available at http://www.armeniandiaspora.com/forum/showthread.php?t=26001.

37. Libaridian, "The Elusive 'Right Formula'": 37.

38. Caspian Studies Program, Harvard University, *Negotiations on Nagorno-Karabakh: Where Do We Go from Here?* (transcript of a panel discussion conducted April 23, 2001), available at http://ksgnotes1.harvard.edu/BCSIA/SDI.nsf/web/ CSPevents.

39. Gerard Libaridian has repeatedly pointed this out. Personal conversation, Tbilisi, February 2005.

40. "Azerbaijan's Military Budget to Double in 2006: Aliyev," Agence France Presse, September 9, 2005; Taleh Ziyadov, "Public Mood in Azerbaijan Points to a New War," *Eurasia Daily Monitor* 2, no. 184 (October 3, 2005), available at www.jamestown.org/programs/edm/single; "Azerbaijan Announces Fifty-three Percent Rise in Army Spending," Reuters, April 15, 2008.

41. "Baku: President Chairs Meeting on Army-Building," Armenian Diaspora, www.armeniandiaspora.com/forum (posted September 20, 2005).

42. Personal communication to the author from Robert Kocharyan, February 2006.

43. The complete text of the statement can be found on the website of *The Armenian Reporter*, at http://www.reporter.am/go/article/2009-07-10-presidents-of-united-states-russia-and-france-issue-karabakh-statement (posted July 10, 2009).

44. See former Armenian foreign minister Vartan Oskanian's interview with Radio Liberty, August 4, 2009, at www.civilitasfoundation.org.

45. Libaridian, "The Elusive 'Right Formula'": 37.

46. "Karabakh: For Whom the Time Works? Interview with Armenian President Robert Kocharyan," Regnum News Agency, March 3, 2006, available at http://www.regnum.ru/english/599743.html.

47. Libaridian, "Time Is on Neither Side," available at http://www.ciaonet.org/ pbei/ewi/ewi02/index.html.

48. Fariz Ismailzade, *The OSCE Minsk Group and the Failure of Negotiations in the Nagorno-Karabakh Conflict*, Caspian Brief No. 23, April 2002 (Washington: Cornell Caspian Consulting, 2002), p. 5.

49. Following a Hague seminar session on the conflict where this author had discussed the frustration in the region surrounding the Minsk Group's lack of momentum, Jacolin approached the author and insisted, "On ne peut pas forcer un âne à boire" (personal communication, The Hague, April 2004).

50. "Quotation of the Week," *RFE/RL Caucasus Report*, vol. 5, no. 10, March 14, 2002.

51. S. Frederick Starr, *Resolving Karabakh: Strategic Options for the U.S. Government* (Washington, D.C.: Central Asia–Caucasus Institute, 2004).

52. Personal communication to the author from Vafa Gulizade, Azerbaijani presidential adviser, Ankara, Turkey, 1995.

53. S. Neil MacFarlane and Larry Minear quote a "leading foreign ministry official" in Stepanakert as follows: "There are many different levels of autonomy, the highest being independence. Azerbaijan had to decide which one it was talking about. Was it Bosnia, Tatarstan, or what? The problem is that they are unwilling to concretize their proposal." S. Neil MacFarlane and Larry Minear, *Humanitarian Action and Politics: The Case of Nagorno-Karabakh*, Occasional Paper No. 25 (Providence, RI: T. J. Watson Institute for International Studies, 1997), p. 88. This conclusion is also based on conversations between the author and Tofiq Zulfgarov, foreign minister of Azerbaijan, Baku, and Armen Baibourtian, deputy foreign minister of Armenia, Yerevan, both in October 1998.

54. Pervane Sultanova, "İlham Əliyev: 'Azərbaycanın qüdrətli dövlətə çevrilməsinə çalışmalıyıq'" [Ilham Aliyev: we should work to turn Azerbaijan into a powerful state] *525ci Qazet*, March 17, 2006. Author's translation from Azerbaijani.

55. Personal communication from Minsk Group co-chair, Washington D.C., 2006.

56. For information on Ehud Barak's thinking on the issue, see Benny Morris, "Camp David and After: An Exchange—An Interview with Ehud Barak," *New York Review of Books*, June 13, 2002, available at www.nybooks.com/articles/15501.

Chapter 8

1. S. Frederick Starr, *Clans, Authoritarian Rulers, and Parliaments in Central Asia,* Silk Road Paper (Washington, D.C.: Central Asia–Caucasus Institute Silk Road Studies Program, June 2006), available at www.silkroadstudies.org.

2. James Sherr, *The Implications of Russia's Elections: Relations with the "Near Abroad,"* Policy Paper, (Stockholm, Sweden: Institute for Security and Development Policy, April 2008), p. 23, available at www.isdp.eu/files/publications.

3. Svante Cornell and Niklas Swanström, "Kyrgyzstan's 'Revolution': Poppies or Tulips?" *Central Asia–Caucasus Analyst*, May 18, 2005, available at www.cacianalyst. org; Erica Marat, *The State-Crime Nexus in Central Asia,* Silk Road Paper (Washington, D.C.: Central Asia–Caucasus Institute Silk Road Studies Program, October 2006), available at www.silkroadstudies.org.

4. Fariz Ismailzade, "Toward a Two-Party System in Azerbaijan?" *Central Asia–Caucasus Analyst*, February 9, 2005, available at www.cacianalyst.org.

5. Julie A. Corwin, "CIS: A Dirty Trick That Has Proved Exportable," *Azerbaijan Report*, Radio Free Europe/Radio Liberty, October 11, 2005, available at www.rferl.org/content/article/1062036.html.

6. Thomas Carothers, "The End of the Transition Paradigm," *Journal of Democracy* 13, no. 1 (2002): 5.

7. Ibid.: 8–9.

8. Interview with Ilham Aliyev, conducted by the author, Baku, Azerbaijan, October 2005.

9. Ray Takeh, "Close, but No Democracy," *The National Interest* no. 78 (Winter 2004/2005): 61.

10. Fareed Zakaria, *The Future of Freedom: Illiberal Democracy at Home and Abroad* (New York: Norton, 2003).

11. Ibid.

Chapter 9

1. Michael Ross, "The Political Economy of the Resource Curse," *World Politics* 51, no. 2 (1999): 297–322; Mary Kaldor, Terry Lynn Karl, and Yahia Said, eds., *Oil Wars* (London: Pluto Press, 2007).

2. Audrey Altstadt, *The Azerbaijani Turks: Power and Identity Under Russian Rule* (Stanford, CA: Hoover Institution Press, 1992), p. 164.

3. Ibid., p. 165.

4. Tadeusz Swietochowski, *Russia and Azerbaijan: A Borderland in Transition* (New York: Columbia University Press, 1995), p. 179.

5. Ibid., p. 182.

6. Vagif Agayev, Fuad Akhundov, Fikrat T. Aliyev, and Mikhail Agarunov, "World War II and Azerbaijan," *Azerbaijan International* 3, no. 2 (1995): 50–55.

7. Robert Barylski, "Russia, the West, and the Caspian Energy Hub," *Middle East Journal* 49, no. 2 (1995): 217–32.

8. Jonathan Hemming, *The Implications of the Revival of the Oil Industry in Azerbaijan,* CMEIS Occasional Paper No. 58 (Durham, England: University of Durham, 1998), p. 7, available at http://eprints.dur.ac.uk/archive/00000141/01/58DMEP.pdf.

9. *Poverty Reduction Strategy Paper* (Baku: Republic of Azerbaijan, May 2001), p. 2.

10. Ibid., p. 3.

11. Operations Evaluation Department, *Azerbaijan: Reconstruction of an Economy,* Evaluation Brief No. 4 (Washington, D.C.: World Bank, July 28, 1999), available at http://lnweb90.worldbank.org/oed/oeddoclib.nsf.

12. U.S. Attorney, Southern District of New York, "U.S. Announces Charges in Massive Scheme to Bribe Senior Government Officials in the Republic of Azerbaijan," Press Release, October 6, 2005, available at http://www.justice.gov/usao/nys/ pressreleases/October05/kozenyetalindictmentpr.pdf.

13. Luke Johnson, "The Maverick: The Spectacular Rise and Fall of a Hyperactive Privatiser," *The Telegraph*, April 2, 2006.

14. David Glovin, "Bourke Convicted of Bribery in Kozeny's Azerbaijan Oil Deal," *Bloomberg News*, July 11, 2009.

15. Michael Ross, "Azerbaijan's Energy Windfall: Boon or Curse?" presentation at U.S. Government seminar, 2006. Presentation provided courtesy of its author.

16. See, e.g., *Annual Report of the National Bank of Azerbaijan for 2005* (Baku: National Bank of Azerbaijan, 2005), pp. 27–29.

17. "Boom and Gloom: Azerbaijan's Economy, Drunk on Oil, Is Suffering Rapid Inflation," *Economist*, March 8, 2007, available at http://www.economist.com/display Story.cfm?story_id=8819945&fsrc=RSS.

18. Pirouz Khanlou, "Construction? Destruction! Blueprint of Baku's Urban Development," *Azerbaijan International* 13, no. 3 (2005): 38–47; Thomas Goltz, "The New Baku: A Disaster in the Making," *Azerbaijan International* 13, no. 3 (2005): 28–31. Both articles are available at http://azer.com/aiweb/categories/magazine.

19. See, for example, speech by Norwegian Foreign Minister Jonas Gahre Støre at the Azerbaijani State University of Languages, April 29, 2008, available at http://www.regjeringen.no/nb/dep/ud/aktuelt/taler_artikler/utenriksministeren/2008/add ress_baku.html?id=509327.

20. Hemming, *Implications of the Revival*, p. 17.

21. David I. Hoffman, "Oil and Development in Post-Soviet Azerbaijan," *Energy, Wealth, and Development in Central Asia and the Caucasus* 10, no. 3 (1999): 5–28.

22. Jonathan Elkind, "Economic Implications of the Baku-Tbilisi-Ceyhan Pipeline," in *The Baku-Tbilisi-Ceyhan Pipeline: Oil Window to the West*, eds. S. Frederick Starr and Svante E. Cornell (Washington, D.C.: Central Asia–Caucasus Institute and Silk Road Studies Program, 2005), p. 45, available at www.silkroadstudies.org/BTC.htm.

23. See, e.g., PriceWaterhouseCoopers, *Introducing the National Oil Companies* (presentation at the Global Energy, Utilities, and Mining Conference, November 2005), available at www.pwc.com/extweb/industry.nsf/docid/49f2db1ed1eb0236852571c6005 adc63/$file/tom-collins-noc-presentation-for-website.pdf. See also the yearly *BP Statistical Review of World Energy*.

24. Dan Morgan and David B. Ottaway, "Azerbaijan's Riches Alter the Chessboard," *Washington Post*, October 4, 1998.

25. Ibid.; on Remp, see Paul Klebnikov, "The Quietly Determined American," *Forbes*, October 24, 1994, p. 48.

26. Elkhan Polukhov, "Contract of the Century: The Problem in an Historical Perspective," *Caucasian Regional Studies* 2, no. 1 (1997), available at http://poli.vub.ac.be/ publi/crs/eng/0201-05.htm.

27. Ibid.

28. Thane A. Gustafson, Aleksey Reteyum, and Laurent Ruseckas, *The Caspian Sea: Whose Waters? Whose Oil?* (Cambridge, MA: Energy Research Associates, 1995).

29. Kamyar Mehdiyoun, "Ownership of Oil and Gas Resources in the Caspian Sea," *American Journal of International Law* 94, no. 1 (2000): 186.

30. Abraham S. Becker, *Russia and Caspian Oil: Moscow Loses Control* (Santa Monica, CA: RAND, 1998).

31. For a thorough overview of the development of the negotiations, see Yusin Lee, "Toward a New International Regime for the Caspian Sea," *Problems of Post-Communism* 52, no. 3 (2005): 37–48.

32. Jan Kalicki and Jonathan Elkind, "Energy Transportation Futures," in *Energy and Security: Toward a New Foreign Policy Strategy*, eds. Jan Kalicki and David Goldwyn (Washington, D.C.: Woodrow Wilson Center Press and Johns Hopkins University Press, 2005), pp. 149–174.

33. Morgan and Ottaway, "Azerbaijan's Riches."

34. Elkind, "Economic Implications," p. 46.

35. Terry Adams, "Baku Oil Diplomacy and 'Early Oil' 1994–1998: An External Perspective", in Alexandros Peterson and Fariz Ismailzade, eds., *Azerbaijan in Global Politics: Crafting Foreign Policy* (Baku: Azerbaijan Diplomatic Academy, 2009), 244–45.

36. "Shah-Deniz Signed: Third Major Contract in Caspian," *Azerbaijan International* 4, no. 3 (Autumn 1996): 35, available at http://azer.com/aiweb/categories/magazine/43_folder/43_articles/43_shah.html.

37. John Bradbury, "First Gas Has Been Produced," posted December 18, 2006, by Offshore247.com, at www.offshore247.com/news/article.asp?Id=6628.

38. S. Frederick Starr, "The Baku-Tbilisi-Ceyhan Pipeline: School of Modernity," in Starr and Cornell, *Baku-Tbilisi-Ceyhan Pipeline*, p. 8.

39. Andreas Andrianopoulos, "The Economics and Politics of Caspian Oil," *Southeast European and Black Sea Studies* 3, no. 3 (2003): 79.

40. Tamam Bayatly, "BTC Pipeline Embarks on Construction Phase," *Azerbaijan International* 10, no. 3 (2002): 88–89, available at http://www.azer.com/aiweb/categories/magazine/ai103_folder/103_articles/ 103_bp_de velopment.html.

41. Adams, "Baku Oil Diplomacy…", in Peterson and Ismailzade, eds., *Azerbaijan in Global Politics*, 234–35.

42. Richard M. Auty, *Sustaining Development in Mineral Economies: The Resource Curse Thesis* (London: Routledge, 1993); Jeffrey D. Sachs and Andrew M. Warner, *Natural Resource Abundance and Economic Growth*, NBER Working Paper No. 5398 (Cambridge, MA: National Bureau of Economic Research, 1995).

43. "Decree of the President of the Republic of Azerbaijan On establishment of the State Oil Fund of the Republic of Azerbaijan," Decree no. 240, signed by President Heydar Aliyev, available at http://www.oilfund.az/print.php?id=28.

44. The latest figures are available at the State Oil Fund website, http://www.oil fund.az/en/content/15.

45. Extractive Industries Transparency Initiative, "Group Launched to Lead International Transparency Initiative," press release, July 1, 2005.

46. Available at http://www.oilfund.az/az/content/25/164.

47. This analysis is perhaps best argued by Michael L. Ross, in "Does Oil Hinder Democracy?" *World Politics* 53, no. 3, (2001): 325–61.

48. Francis Fukuyama, *State-Building: Governance and World Order in the Twenty-First Century* (Ithaca, NY: Cornell University Press, 2004).

49. today.az News Site, March 13, 2007.

50. *Economist*, "Boom and Gloom."

51. "Analysis: Azerbaijan Grapples with Rising Inflation," *Caucasus Report*, Radio Free Europe/Radio Liberty, April 18, 2008, available at www.rferl.org/content/article/1109595.html.

52. "Ali Abbasov Meets with Caspian Integration Business Club Members," today.az, 15 February 2007, available at http://www.today.az/news/business/36505.html.

53. Newsletter of the Azerbaijani Embassy in Washington, vol. 2 no. 2, January 23, 2009.

54. "Minister Announces Plans for Financing of Regional Innovation Zone," *Israel-Azerbaijan Business News* (October 2007), p. 2, available at http://baku.mfa.gov.il/mfm/Data/123904.pdf.

55. Poverty Reduction Strategy Paper (Interim Report), Ministry of Economic Development. May 2001, available at http://poverty.worldbank.org/files/azerbaijaniprsp.pdf.

56. World Bank, *Azerbaijan Survey of Living Conditions* (Washington: World Bank, 1995).

57. APA News Agency, March 13, 2009.

58. Fariz Ismailzade, "Is Aliyev Government Meddling in Azerbaijan's Business Sector," *Eurasia Daily Monitor*, vol. 3, no. 7, January 10, 2006.

59. Fariz Ismailzade, "Regional Development on Top of Aliyev's Agenda," *Eurasia Daily Monitor*, vol. 4, no. 34, February 15, 2007.

60. S. Frederick Starr, ed., *Partnership, Trade, and Development in Greater Central Asia* (Washington, D.C.: Central Asia–Caucasus Institute, 2007).

61. For a thorough overview of Azerbaijan's place in Eurasian trade, see Taleh Ziyadov, "Azerbaijan at the Crossroads of East-West and North-South Transportation Corridors," in *Greater Central Asia and the New Silk Roads*, ed. S. Frederick Starr (Wash-

ington, D.C.: Central Asia–Caucasus Institute and Silk Road Studies Program, 2007), pp. 303–334.

62. Ibid.

63. *Republic of Azerbaijan: Preparing for Southern Road Corridor Improvement Project (Alyat-Astara Road)*, Technical Assistance Report, Project No. 39176–01 (Manila: Asian Development Bank, November 2005).

64. "Azerbaijan to Allocate U.S.$100m for Baku-Tbilisi-Kars Railway," news.am, January 30, 2010, available at http://news.am/en/news/13247.html.

65. Ziyadov, "Azerbaijan at the Crossroads," p. 18.

Chapter 10

1. Shahbaz Muradov, "Demographic Trends in Azerbaijan on the Threshold of the Twenty-First Century," *Sociological Research* 40, no. 3 (2001): 34.

2. Ibid.: 35–37.

3. Ibid.: 39.

4. *Lost Generation: Section 907 and the Refugees in Azerbaijan* was the title of a 1998 documentary on the refugee children made by APCO Worldwide for Frontera Resources. The film won the ITVA Best Take Award in 1999.

5. *Project Appraisal Document, Education Reform Project, Azerbaijan Republic* (Washington, D.C.: World Bank, 1999); Paul Temple and Georgy Petrov, "Corruption in Higher Education: Some Findings from the States of the Former Soviet Union," *Higher Education Management and Policy* 16, no. 1 (2004): 91.

6. Mark S. Johnson, "Trends in Secular Educational Development in Azerbaijan and Central Asia: Implications for Social Stability and Regional Security," *NBR Analysis* 15, no. 5 (2004): 20–21.

7. Eric Lepisto and Elmina Kazimzade, "Coercion or Compulsion? Rationales Behind Informal Payments for Education in Azerbaijan," *European Education* 40, no. 4 (2008–09): 74.

8. Johanna Popjanevski, *Minorities and the State in the South Caucasus: Assessing the Protection of National Minorities in Georgia and Azerbaijan*, Silk Road Paper (Washington, D.C., and Uppsala, Sweden: Central Asia–Caucasus Institute Silk Road Studies Program, September 2006), p. 60, available at www.silkroadstudies.org.

9. Nasib Nasibzade, *Azerbaycanin xarici siyaseti (1918–1920)* (Baku: Ay-Ulduz, 1996); Jamil Hasanli, *At the Dawn of the Cold War: The Soviet-American Crisis over Iranian Azerbaijan, 1941–1946* (Lanham, MD: Rowman and Littlefield, 2006).

10. Transparency International, *Corruptions Perceptions Index 2009*, available at http://www.transparency.org/policy_research/surveys_indices/cpi.

11. *Anticorruption in Transition: A Contribution to the Policy Debate* (Washington, D.C.: World Bank, 2000), pp. 1–14.

12. James H. Anderson and Cheryl W. Gray, *Anticorruption in Transition 3: Who Is Succeeding... and Why?* (Washington, D.C.: World Bank, 2006), p. 8.

13. *Country Corruption Assessment: Public Opinion Survey in Azerbaijan* (Baku: Transparency International Azerbaijan, 2004), available at http://www.transparency-az.org/files/25.pdf.

14. Ibid., p. 15.

15. Ibid., pp. 26–30.

16. Ibid., p. 23.

17. Svante E. Cornell, "Narcotics and Armed Conflict: Interaction and Implications," *Studies in Conflict and Terrorism* 30, no. 3 (2007): 207–227; Svante E. Cornell and Niklas L.P. Swanström, "The Eurasian Drug Trade: A Challenge to Regional Security," *Problems of Post-Communism* 53, no. 4 (2006): 10–28.

18. *Review of Legal and Institutional Framework for Fighting Corruption: Azerbaijan* (Paris: Organization for Economic Cooperation and Development, 2004), available at http://www.oecd.org/dataoecd/51/1/37228539.pdf.

19. This section is based on a monograph by the author, *The Politicization of Islam in Azerbaijan*, Silk Road Paper (Washington, D.C. and Uppsala, Sweden: Central Asia–Caucasus Institute Silk Road Studies Program, October 2006). Fariz Ismailzade provided assistance with this monograph, and some of the findings are based on interviews and other research he conducted.

20. *United States v. Usama Bin Laden*, No. S(7) 98 Cr. 1023, 5440, U.S. District Court, Southern District of New York, May 2, 2001.

21. Tair Faradov, *Religiosity in Post-Soviet Azerbaijan: Peculiarities, Dynamics, and Tendencies—A Sociological Analysis* (Baku: International Institute for the Study of Islam in the Modern World, 2001).

22. Zerkalo, March 3, 2006.

23. Fariz Ismailzade, "The Rise of Islam in Azerbaijan," *Institute for the Analysis of Global Security*, March 28, 2005.

24. Interview with Nasib Nasibli, chairman, Foundation for Azerbaijani Studies, conducted by Fariz Ismailzade, Baku, July 2006. See Svante E. Cornell, *The Politicization of Islam in Azerbaijan*, Silk Road Paper (Washington, D.C.: Central Asia-Caucasus Institute, October 2006), p. 24.

25. Mark Elliot, *Azerbaijan with Georgia* (Hindhead: Trailblazer, 1999).

26. Farideh Heyat, *Azeri Women in Transition: Women in Soviet and Post-Soviet Azerbaijan* (London: Routledge, 2002).

27. Amiram Barkat, "Azerbaijani Jews Worried over Increasing Radical Islamists," *Ha'aretz*, February 15, 2006.

28. Megan Levy, "Embassy Terror Attack 'Foiled' in Azerbaijan," *Daily Telegraph*, October 29, 2007.

29. Yossi Melman, "Hezbollah, Iran Plotted Bombing of Israel Embassy in Azerbaijan," *Ha'aretz*, May 31, 2009.

30. Sofie Bedford, *Islamic Activism in Azerbaijan: Repression and Mobilization in a Post-Soviet Context* (Stockholm: Stockholm University Studies in Politics 129, 2009), pp. 99–100.

31. See Cornell, *Politicization of Islam in Azerbaijan*, pp. 63–64.

32. Igor Rotar, "Islamic Fundamentalism in Azerbaijan: Myth or Reality?" *Jamestown Prism* 6, no. 8 (August 31, 2000), available at http://www.jamestown.org/single/?no_cache=1&tx_ttnews[tt_news]=27947.

33. Field work in Azerbaijan, September 2006. See Cornell, *Politicization of Islam*, p. 61.

34. Interview with Huddam Meshedi Tair Abbas Ali-oglu, deputy imam of Gandja's largest mosque, Shah Abbas, conducted by Fariz Ismailzade, August 2006.

35. Rafiq Aliyev, interviewed on ANS TV, January 21, 2002.

36. For a discussion of the different factions in the Iranian political elites, see Eva Rakel, "Paradigms of Iranian Policy in Central Eurasia and Beyond," *Perspectives on Global Development and Technology* 2, nos. 3–4 (2002): 549–71.

37. Interview with Huddam Meshedi Tair Abbas Ali-oglu.

38. *United States v. Usama Bin Laden.*

39. Interview with Azerbaijani scholar Nariman Gasimoglu, September 2006.

40. David S. Cloud, "Long In U.S. Sights, A Young Terrorist Builds Grim Résumé on Journey to Iraq, Zarqawi Forged Ties with Al Qaeda, Attracted Own Followers; An Amputation in Baghdad," *Wall Street Journal*, February 10, 2004.

41. George W. Gawrych, review of *Turkish Islam and the Secular State: The Gülen Movement,* eds. Hakan Yavuz and John Esposito, *Journal of Church and State* 46, no. 3 (2004): 650–651.

42. Lester R. Kurtz, " Gülen's Paradox: Combining Commitment and Tolerance," *The Muslim World* 95, no. 3 (2005): 379.

43. For more information, see http://www.cag.edu.az/.

44. *Day.az*, February 16, 2006. See http://www.day.az/news/society/41826.html

45. Day.az News site, March 17, 2006.

46. See "Disinformation; Old and New Information Tricks (An Old Friend Comes Back)," *The Economist* (August 3, 2006), on the emergence of the GONGO phenomenon in Russia.

47. This is according to a Najaf Najafov Fund survey cited by Rufat Abbasov and Mina Muradova in "Azerbaijan: Television Is a Campaign Battleground," *Eurasianet.org Weekly Bulletin* (October 28, 2005), available at http://eurasianet.org.

48. Liz Fuller, "Azerbaijan: Authorities Intensify Pressure on Independent Media," *RFE/RL News Analysis* (November 29, 2006), available at www.rferl.org/content/article/1073092.html.

49. The results of these surveys are posted at the website of the Najaf Najafov Fund, http://www.najafovfund.org.

50. See Reporters Sans Frontières page on Azerbaijan, available at http://arabia.reporters-sans-frontieres.org/article.php3?id_article=10667.

51. See Committe to Protect Journalists, "Attacks on the Press 2006: Azerbaijan," available at http://cpj.org/2007/02/attacks-on-the-press-2006-azerbaijan.php.

52. See Committe to Protect Journalists, "Attacks on the Press 2008: Azerbaijan," available at http://cpj.org/2009/02/attacks-on-the-press-2008-azerbaijan.php.

53. OSCE Baku office, "Memorandum on the Draft Law of the Republic of Azerbaijan on Defamation," May 2007, available at http://www.article19.org/pdfs/analysis/azerbaijan-defamation-osce.pdf.

54. Nina Ognianova, "Finding Elmar's Killers," Committee to Protect Journalists Special Report, September 2008, available at http://www.cpj.org/reports/2008/09/azerbaijan-elmar.php.

55. "Relatives of Ideal Newspaper Founder Nazim Guliyev Arrested," *today.az*, November 21, 2008, available at http://www.today.az/print/news/society/49153.html.

56. OSCE, "Memorandum on Draft..."; "Azerbaijan Needs Law on Defamation," *news.az*, November 16, 2009, available at http://www.news.az/articles/2561.

57. Simon Tisdall, "Trouble in Nowhere Land," *The Guardian*, November 29, 2007.

58. Committe to Protect Journalists, "Attacks on the Press 2008...".

Chapter 11

1. For a discussion of the factors guiding Azerbaijani foreign policy, see the chapter by Foreign Minister Elmar Mammadyarov, ""The Foreign Policy of Azerbaijan: Affecting Factors and Strategic Priorities," in Alexandros Peterson and Fariz Ismailzade, eds., *Azerbaijan in Global Politics: Crafting Foreign Policy* (Baku: Azerbaijan Diplomatic Academy, 2009) 11–21.

2. Tadeusz Swietochowski, "Azerbaijan: A Borderland at the Crossroads of History," S. Frederick Starr, ed., *The Legacy of History in Russia and the New States of Eurasia* (New York: M.E. Sharpe, 1994) p. 296.

3. Brenda Shaffer, "Permanent Factors in Azerbaijan's Foreign Policy," in Peterson and Ismailzade, eds., *Azerbaijan in Global Politics*, 67–84.

4. Shaffer, "Permanent Factors," p. 81.

5. Leila Alieva, "The Institutions, Orientations, and Conduct of Foreign Policy in Post-Soviet Azerbaijan," Adeed Dawisha and Karen Dawisha, eds., *The Making of*

Foreign Policy in Russia and the New States of Eurasia (Armonk: M.E. Sharpe, 1995) pp. 286–308.

6. Istvan Szönyi, "The False Promise of an Institution: Can Cooperation between OSCE and NATO be a Cure?" *Center for International Security and Arms Control*, January 1997. John J. Maresca, "Resolving the Conflict Over Nagorno-Karabakh: Lost Opportunities for International Conflict Resolution," in *Managing Global Chaos: Sources of and Responses to International Conflict*, eds., Pamela Aall, Chester A. Crocker, and Fen Osler Hampson (Washington D.C.: United States Institute of Peace Press, 1996), pp. 255–276; Rexane Dehdashti, *Gewaltminderung und Konfliktregelung in ethnosozialen Konflikten. Möglichkeiten und Grenzen internationaler Akteure in der Kaukasusregion*, unpublished dissertation (Frankfurt am Main 1997). Rexane Dehdashti, *Internationale Organisationen als Vermittler in Innerstaatlichen Konflikten: Die OSZE und der Berg Karabach-Konflikt* (Frankfurt: Studien der Hessischen Stiftung Friedens und Konfliktforschung, 2000).

7. Svante Cornell, Roger McDermott, William O'Malley, Vladimir Socor, and Frederick Starr, *Regional Security in the South Caucasus: The Role of NATO* (Washington D.C.: Central Asia-Caucasus Institute Policy Paper, April 2004).

8. See Malik Mufti, "Daring and Caution in Turkey's Foreign Policy," *Middle East Journal*, vol. 52 no. 1, Winter 1999: 32–50.

9. Vladimir Socor, "A Tale of Two Post-Post-Soviet Countries," *Wall Street Journal Europe*, December 19, 2003.

10. See also discussion in Mammadyarov, "The Foreign Policy of Azerbaijan".

11. "Harsh Words between Iran and Azerbaijan," *Moscow News*, April 7, 1996; "President Aliyev Says Iranian Relations with Armenia Offend Azerbaijan," *Turan* news agency, Baku, August 3, 1999 (BBC Summary of World Broadcasts); "Iranian Diplomat's Stance Makes Azeri President Interrupt Meeting," ANS TV, Baku, March 29, 2001; "Azeri Paper Details Iranian Intelligence Activities during Month of Muharram," *BBC Monitoring Service*, April 7, 2001.

12. As printed in *Khalq Qezeti*, November 7, 1991.

13. Nazim Cafersoy, *Elçibey dönemi Azerbaycan dis politikasi* (Ankara: ASAM, 2001), pp. 67–68.

14. Cafersoy, p. 70.

15. Ibid., pp. 97–99.

16. Zbigniew Brzezinski, *The Grand Chessboard: American Primacy and Its Geostrategic Imperatives* (New York: BasicBooks, 1997).

Chapter 12

1. Brenda Shaffer estimates the number to 14–21 million out of a population of 71 million. *Borders and Brethren: Iran and the Challenge of Azerbaijani Identity* (Cambridge, MA: MIT Press, 2002), pp. 222–223. The U.S. Marine Corps Intelligence Activity's Cultural Field Guide estimates Azerbaijanis to number 20 million or 31 percent of Iran's population, compared to 35 million Persians. "Cultural Field Guide—Cultural Intelligence for Military Operations: Iran," U.S. Marine Corps Intelligence Activity Unclassified (Quantico, VA: U.S. Marine Corps).

2. Among foreign scholars' work, Brenda Shaffer's *Borders and Brethren: Iran and the Challenge of Azerbaijani Identity* deserves special mention. Noteworthy works by Azerbaijani scholars include Nasib Nassibli, *Iranda Azérbaycan Mésélési* [The Azerbaijan Question in Iran] (Baku, Azerbaijan: Ay-Ulduz Néshriyatí, 1997); Nassibli, "The Azerbaijan Question in Iran: A Crucial Question for Iran's Future," *Caspian Crossroads*, Winter 1998; Alireza Ashgarzadeh, "The Rise and Fall of South Azerbaijan Democratic Republic (1945–46): A Look at Hegemony, Racism, and Center-Periphery Relations in Contemporary Iran" (paper presented at a seminar on race and racism, University of Toronto, Canada, December 1999); Jamil Hasanli, *At the Dawn of the Cold War: The Soviet-American Crisis over Iranian Azerbaijan, 1941–1946* (Lanham, MD: Rowman & Littlefield, 2006; published in Turkish as Cemil Hasanli, *Soğuk Savaşın İlk Çatışması İran Azerbaycanı*, Istanbul, Turkey: Bağlam, 2005).

3. Brenda Shaffer, "The Formation of Azerbaijani Collective Identity in Iran," *Nationalities Papers* 28, no. 3 (2000): 449–78.

4. "Recent Unrest in Iran Shows Iranian Azerbaijan Is Awakening—Azeri Paper," *BBC Monitoring International Reports*, July 5, 2003; "Iran Aims to Prevent Ethnic Azeri Politicians from Influencing Protests," *BBC Monitoring International Reports*, June 25, 2003. After the summer 2003 demonstrations, the Iranian government cracked down on student as well as nationalist organizations. A 19-year-old Azeri girl was executed by Iranian authorities in July 2003 for her role in the protests ("Ethnic Azeri Student Leader Killed in Iran—Paper," *BBC Monitoring International Reports*, July 22, 2002). In an earlier incident, in January 2000, Iranian forces had opened fire on a demonstration in Tabriz ("Azeri TV Says Iranian Police Opened Fire During Rally in Tabriz," *BBC Summary of World Broadcasts*, January 10, 2000). A commemoration of a historical Azeri hero that drew 8,000 participants was broken up by Iranian authorities in August 2002 ("Ethnic Azeri in Iran Gets Prison Sentence Following March to Fort—Azeri Paper," *BBC Monitoring International Reports*, August 25, 2002).

5. "Tehran Cracks Down on Azerbaijanis of Iran," *Iran Report*, Radio Free Europe/Radio Liberty, December 13, 1999.

6. "Head of Banned Tabriz Weekly Appeals Against Sentence—Azeri Report," *BBC Monitoring International Reports*, April 19, 2002; [title of article], *Yeni Müsavat* (Baku, Azerbaijan), April 3, 2003.

7. Interviews with Azerbaijani activists, Tehran, December 2003.

8. Experience from author's discussions in Iran in April 1998.

9. Author's discussions with Iranian officials, 1998.

10. "Paper Reports High Turnout in Azeri March in Iran," *BBC Monitoring International Reports*, July 4, 2004.

11. "Five Injured, Ten Arrested as Ethnic Azeris Clash with Police in Iran—TV," *BBC Monitoring International Reports*, September 26, 2004.

12. Karl Rahder, "Iran: Stifling the Azeri Minority," *Security Watch*, April 26, 2007, available at www.isn.ethz.ch/.

13. Communication from Seyed Kazem Sajjadpour, Director-General of the Iranian Institute for Political and International Studies, Uppsala, Sweden, 2000.

14. Robert E. Freedman, "Russian-Iranian Relations in the 1990s," *Middle East Review of International Affairs* 4, no. 2 (2000), available at http://meria.idc.ac.il/JOURNAL/2000/issue2/jv4n2a5.html.

15. Robert Olson, "The 'Azeri' Question and Turkey-Iran Relations, 2000–2002," *Nationalism and Ethnic Politics* 8, no. 4 (2002): 73.

16. Robert Olson, "Turkey-Iran Relations, 2000–2001," *Middle East Policy* 9, no. 2 (2002): 119.

17. Fariz Ismailzade, "New Tensions Complicate Relations Between Baku and Tehran," *Eurasia Daily Monitor* (March 30, 2006), available at www.jamestown.org/single/?no_cache=1&tx_ttnews%5Btt_news%5D=31532.

18. *Sobh* (Tehran), May 28, 1996, quoted in Human Rights Watch, *Iran: Religious and Ethnic Minorities: Discrimination in Law and Practice* (New York: Author, 1997), available at www.unhcr.org/refworld/docid/3ae6a8240.html.

19. Agence France Presse, July 27, 2000.

20. "Iran Might Be Pushed to Recover Azerbaijan, Says High-Ranking Official," *Iran Press Service*, July 30, 2001, available at www.iran-press-service.com/articles_2001/ jul_2001/iran_azerbaijan_dispute_30701.htm.

21. Edmund Herzig, *Iran and the Former Soviet South* (London: Royal Institute for International Affairs, 1995), p. 30.

22. Abdollah Ramezanzadeh, "Iran's Role as Mediator in the Nagorno-Karabakh Crisis," in *Contested Borders in the Caucasus*, ed. Bruno Coppeiters (Brussels, Belgium: VUB Press, 1996).

23. Fred Halliday, "Condemned to React, Unable to Influence: Iran and Transcaucasia," in *Transcaucasian Boundaries*, eds. John F. Wright, Suzanne Goldenberg, and Richard Schoefield (London: UCL Press, 1996), p. 84.

24. "Iranian Delegation Visits Armenia," *Iran Report*, Radio Free Europe/Radio Liberty, December 17, 2002.

25. Ramezanzadeh, "Iran's Role as Mediator."

26. ANS TV (Baku, Azerbaijan), July 30, 1999.

27. "Iranian Diplomat's Stance Makes Azeri President Interrupt Meeting," ANS TV (Baku, Azerbaijan), March 29, 2001.

28. Russia's influential Ministry of Fuel and Energy has constantly pushed for a "more realistic" approach to the Caspian Sea, in order to ensure the participation of Russian companies in oil deals that would be implemented unilaterally anyway. See Robert Barylski, "Russia, the West, and the Caspian Energy Hub," in *Middle East Journal* 49, no. 2 (1995): 217–232. For an analysis of Russian policy and Caspian oil, see Svante E. Cornell, *Small Nations and Great Powers: A Study of Ethnopolitical Conflict in the Caucasus* (Richmond: Curzon Press, 2001), pp. 359–61.

29. "Kazakhstan, Russia Sign Agreements on Caspian, 'Eternal Friendship,'" *NIS Observed* (August 3, 1998), available at http://www.bu.edu/iscip/digest/vol3/ed0311.html.

30. Xinhua News Agency, "Iran Reiterates Stance on Legal Regime of Caspian Sea," March 28, 2001.

31. Ibid.

32. "Iran's Caspian Oil Finds Will Require Deep Drilling," *Middle East Economic Digest*, September 1, 2000.

33. "Iran Against Caspian Summit Until Clarification of Legal Regime," Deutsche Presse-Agentur, March 18, 2001.

34. Personal communication by Azerbaijani official to the author, March 2001.

35. Olson, "Turkey-Iran Relations."

36. Fariz Ismailzade, "Azerbaijan Under Iranian and Russian Pressure on Relations to U.S.," *Central Asia–Caucasus Analyst* (November 3, 2004), available at www.cacianalyst.org/?q=node/2536.

37. Taleh Ziyadov, "U.S. Troops in Azerbaijan? Moscow Says No, but Baku Says Maybe," *Eurasia Daily Monitor* (August 15, 2005), available at www.jamestown.org/single/?no_cache=1&tx_ttnews%5Btt_news%5D=30786.

38. Stephen Blank, "New Military Trends in the Caspian," *Central Asia–Caucasus Analyst*, (June 1, 2005), available at www.cacianalyst.org/?q=node/3072.

39. Liz Fuller, "Analysis: Azerbaijani Election Alignment Takes Place," Radio Free Europe/Radio Liberty, January 13, 2005.

40. Interview with Rafiq Aliyev, ANS TV (Baku, Azerbaijan), January 21, 2002. See also Svante E. Cornell, *The Politicization of Islam in Azerbaijan*, Silk Road Paper (Washington, D.C.: Central Asia–Caucasus Institute Silk Road Studies Program, October 2006).

41. Hooman Peimani, "Iran and Azerbaijan: Toward Normal Relations?" *Central Asia–Caucasus Analyst*, (January 26, 2005), available at www.cacianalyst.org/?q=node/2738.

42. "Results of Iranian President's Baku Trip 'Very Modest,'" *Ekho* (Baku, Azerbaijan), August 11, 2004.

43. "Azerbaijan, Iran Sign Nine Cooperation Accords in Tehran," *BBC Monitoring International Reports*, January 26, 2005.

44. "Presidents Inaugurate Iran-Azerbaijan Gas Swap Project," *Tehran Times*, December 21, 2005.

45. Rovshan Ismayilov, "Iran-Azerbaijan Summit: 'Brotherly' Feelings, Without Results," *Eurasia Insight* (August 24, 2007), available at www.eurasianet.org/departments/insight/articles/eav082407.shtml; "Azerbaycan'la Iran Arasinda büyük isbirligi" [Large cooperation between Azerbaijan and Iran], *Hürriyet* (Istanbul) (March 10, 2009).

46. "Iran, Azerbaycan vatandaslarindan artik vize talep etmeyecektir" [Iran will no longer require visas for Azerbaijani citizens], Islamic Republic News Agency (November 12, 2009), available at www2.irna.ir/fa/news/view/line-111/0911125430122212.htm.

Chapter 13

1. The consistency of Russian policy is discussed in greater depth in "Russia: A Retreating Hegemonic Power," chapter 9 in Svante Cornell, *Small Nations and Great Powers: A Study of Ethnopolitical Conflict in the Caucasus* (Richmond: Curzon, 2001), pp. 333–90.

2. Vera Tolz, "Forging the Nation: National Identity and Nation Building in Post-Communist Russia," *Europe-Asia Studies* 50, no. 6 (1998): 993–1022.

3. Roman Laba, "How Yeltsin's Exploitation of Ethnic Nationalism Brought Down an Empire," *Transition* 2, no. 1 (1996): 5–13, quoting an interview with Gennady Burbulis that was published in the official daily of the Russian government, *Rossiiskaia Gazeta* (Moscow), on April 20, 1991, while Burbulis was a Yeltsin aide.

4. Mohiaddin Mesbahi, "Russian Foreign Policy and Security in Central Asia and the Caucasus," *Central Asian Survey* 12, no. 2 (1993): 184–85.

5. Johan Matz, "Constructing a Post-Soviet International Political Reality: Russian Foreign Policy Towards Newly Independent States 1990–95" (doctoral dissertation, Uppsala University, Sweden, 2001). See also "An Interview with Russian Foreign Minister Andrei Kozyrev," *RFE/RL Research Report* (July 15, 1994), p. 36.

6. Peter J. Stavrakis, *Shadow Politics: The Russian State in the Twenty-First Century* (Carlisle, PA: U.S. Army War College, Strategic Studies Monograph, 1997).

7. Hannes Adomeit, "Russia as a 'Great Power' in World Affairs: Images and Reality," *International Affairs* 71, no. 1 (1995): 35–68.

8. Stanislav Lunev, "Russia's Ominous New Military Doctrine," *Jamestown Prism* (December 1, 1995), available at www.jamestown.org/single/?no_cache=1&tx_ttnews %5Btt_news%5D=19158&tx_ttnews%5BbackPid%5D=217.

9. Robert O. Freedman, "Russia and Iran: A Tactical Alliance," *SAIS Review* 17, no. 2 (1997): 95.

10. Richard F. Staar, "Moscow's Plans to Restore Its Power," *Orbis* 40, no. 3 (1996): 376; *Krasnaya Zvezda* (Moscow), the official newspaper of the Russian Ministry of Defense, provided an abridged version of the doctrine on November 19, 1993.

11. Staar, "Moscow's Plans": 376.

12. "Moscow Presses Baku on Border Troops," May 30, 1995; "More Russian Troops for Ajaria," July 10, 1995; "Russian Officers Command Kyrgyz Troops on Kyrgyzstan Border," June 14, 1995. (All three articles were published in the *Eurasia Daily Monitor* and are available at http://jamestown.nvmserver.com/m1995/.)

13. Lilia Shevtsova, *Putin's Russia* (Washington, D.C.: Carnegie Endowment for International Peace, 2003), pp. 7–67.

14. Theresa Sabonis-Helf, "Power, Influence, and Stability: The Unified Energy Systems of Russia in the Southern Tier FSU," *Central Eurasian Studies Review* 4, no. 1 (2005): 24–29, available at www.cesr-cess.org/CESR_contents.html.

15. Thomas Ambrosio, *Authoritarian Backlash: Russian Resistance to Democratization in the Former Soviet Union* (Burlington, VT: Ashgate, 2009).

16. This section of the present chapter builds on an earlier piece, "The Caucasus Under Renewed Russian Pressure: Realities on the Ground and Geopolitical Imperatives," *Analysis of Current Events* 13, no. 3 (2001).

17. For a detailed account of Russian policy in the Caucasus, see Cornell, "Russia: A Retreating Hegemonic Power."

18. Interviews conducted by the author with high-level Georgian government officials, Tbilisi, 1998. See also Thornike Gordadze, "Georgian-Russian Relations in the 1990s," in *The Guns of August 2008: Russia's War in Georgia,* eds. Svante E. Cornell and S. Frederick Starr (Armonk, NY: M.E. Sharpe, 2009): pp. 28–48.

19. "Georgia: Abkhazia 'Strong Enough to Fight Georgia,'" *BBC Monitoring International Reports,* July 30, 1992.

20. Irakli Kakabadze, "Russian Troops in Abkhazia: Peacekeeping or Keeping Both Pieces?" *Perspectives on Central Asia* 2, no. 6 (1997), available at www.eisenhowerinstitute.org; Thomas Goltz, "Letter from Eurasia: The Hidden Russian Hand," *Foreign Policy,* Fall (1993): 108.

21. As stated by presidential adviser Vafa Guluzade to *Nezavisimaya Gazeta* (Moscow), February 27, 1999.

22. This was revealed by a federal investigation conducted by General Lev Rokhlin, then chairman of the Russian Duma's defense committee, in April 1997. See "Rokhlin Details Arms Supplied to Armenia," *Sovetskaya Rossiya* (Moscow), April 3, 1997.

23. Svante E. Cornell, "The War Against Terrorism and the Conflict in Chechnya: A Case for Distinction," *Fletcher Forum of World Affairs* 27, no. 2 (2003): 167–84, available at www.silkroadstudies.org/new/docs/publications/Fletcher.pdf.

24. Tajikistan participated in a US$250 million debt-for-asset swap in 2004; Armenia took part in one that was almost as large, during 2002–03.

25. Vladimir Socor, "The Unfolding of the U.S.-Uzbekistan Crisis," in John C.K. Daly, Kurt H. Meppen, Vladimir Socor, and S. Frederick Starr *Anatomy of a Crisis: U.S.-Uzbekistan Relations, 2001–2005*, Silk Road Paper (Washington, D.C.: Central Asia–Caucasus Institute & Silk Road Studies Program, 2006), pp. 44–65, available at www.silkroadstudies.org/new/inside/publications/0602Uzbek.pdf.

26. "Ukraine Blockades Export from Transnistria," *Kommersant* (Moscow), March 6, 2006.

27. Robert Parsons, "Analysis: Putin Seeks to Draw Azerbaijan Back into Russian Orbit," Radio Free Europe/Radio Liberty, February 21, 2006, available at www.rferl.org/content/article/1066011.html.

28. Assa-Irada Press, January 10, 2001.

29. This is covered extensively in Daly, Meppen, Socor, and Starr, *Anatomy of a Crisis: U.S.-Uzbekistan Relations, 2001–2005*.

30. Rovshan Ismayilov, "Trade, Investment Take Center Stage at Russia-Azerbaijan Summit," Eurasianet.org, February 28, 2006, available at www.eurasianet.org/departments/business/articles/eav022806.shtml.

31. Regine A. Spector, "The North-South Transport Corridor," *Central Asia–Caucasus Analyst*, July 3, 2002, available at www.cacianalyst.org/?q=node/165/print.

32. The existence of this very strong pressure from the highest levels of Russia's state authorities was related to this author by several high-level Azerbaijani officials in interviews in Baku, October 2005.

33. Elin Suleymanov, "The South Caucasus: Where the U.S. and Turkey Succeeded Together," *Turkish Policy Quarterly* 4, no. 1 (2005): 113–20. The Azerbaijani opposition leaders grudgingly recognized Aliyev's decision; see Könül Şamilqızı, "Bele Getse, Azerbaycan xalqı da öz fedakarlığını nümayiş etdirmeli olacaq," *Yeni Musavät* (Baku), December 22, 2004.

34. Interviews conducted by the author with officials in the Azerbaijani foreign ministry and presidential office, Baku, 1997–1999.

35. Seymur Selimov, "Frozen in Time," *Transitions Online*, April 9, 2001, available at www.tol.org/client/article/712-frozen-in-time.html.

36. Personal communications, U.S. co-chairs of the Minsk Group, Washington D.C., 2003–8.

37. Personal communications, EU diplomats covering the South Caucasus, Tbilisi, Spring 2009.

38. Personal communication, Member of the Foreign Affairs Committee of the Turkish Parliament for the ruling Justice and Development Party, Stockholm, February 2010.

39. John C.K. Daly, "Gazprom Covets Azeri Natural Gas," UPI, June 6, 2008, available at www.upi.com/Science_News/Resource-Wars/2008/06/06/Gazprom-covets-Azeri-natural-gas/UPI-47361212802581/; John Roberts, *The Role of Azerbaijan in European Gas Supply and the Greek Interest*, Policy Brief 15 (Athens, Greece: International Center for Black Sea Studies, May 2009), available at website of the International Relations and Security Network, www.isn.ethz.ch/isn/Digital-Library/Publications/Detail/?ots591=0C54E3B3-1E9C-BE1E-2C24A6A8C7060233& lng=en&id=104881.

40. Alexandros Petersen, "Will Azerbaijani Gas Exports to China Scuttle the Southern Corridor?" *Central Asia–Caucasus Analyst*, December 9, 2009, available at www.cacianalyst.org/?q=node/5234.

41. Personal communication, Western oil company officials, Brussels, March 2010.

Chapter 14

1. *Cumhuriyet*, November 12, 2005.

2. Mehmet Tütüncü, "The Caucasus Policy of Turkey (1990–97): An Evaluation," in *Caucasus War and Peace: The New World Disorder and Caucasia*, ed., Mehmet Tütüncü (Haarlem, Netherlands: SOTA, 1998), p. 183.

3. Mustafa Aydın, "Turkey and Central Asia: Challenges of Change," *Central Asian Survey* 15, no. 2 (1996): 160.

4. Kemal Karpat, "Turkish-Soviet Relations," in Kemla Karpat, ed., *Turkey's Foreign Policy in Transition, 1950–1974*, (London: Brill, 1975), pp. 73–107.

5. Tütüncü, "The Caucasus Policy of Turkey," p. 183.

6. *Cumhuriyet*, January 19, 1990.

7. Baskin Oran, "The Turkish Approach to Transcaucasia and Central Asia," in *Contrasts and Solutions in the Caucasus*, eds., Ole Høyris and Sefa Martin Yürükel (Århus, Denmark: Århus University Press, 1998), pp. 462–63.

8. *Cumhuriyet*, February 24, 1992.

9. Aydın, "Turkey and Central Asia": 160–61.

10. Recorded by the author on location in Ankara, 1993.

11. Süha Bölükbasi, "Ankara's Baku-Centered Transcaucasia Policy: Has It Failed?" *Middle East Journal* 50, no. 1(1997): 80–94.

12. Gün Kut, "Elçibey'in sonu, Türkiye modelinin sonudur" [The end of Elçibey is the end of the Turkish model], *Cumhuriyet*, June 24, 1993.

13. Thomas Goltz, *Azerbaijan Diary: A Rogue Reporter's Adventures in an Oil-Rich, War-Torn Post-Soviet Republic* (Armonk, NY: M.E. Sharpe, 1998), p. 367.

14. Foreign Broadcast Information Service, Central Eurasia Series (hereafter FBIS-CEA), September 8, 1993, quoting *Aydınlik*, September 5, 1993.

15. Joseph A. Kechichian and Theodore W. Karasik, "The Crisis in Azerbaijan: How Clans Influence the Politics of an Emerging Republic," *Middle East Policy* 4, no. 1 (1995): 57–72.

16. Foreign Broadcast Information Service, Western Europe Series (hereafter FBIS-WEU), March 9, 1992, quoting Türkiye Radiyolari, March 6, 1992.

17. *Le Monde* (Paris), February 27, 1992; FBIS-WEU, March 9, 1992, quoting TRT Television, March 7, 1992. On the view of the Conference on Security and Cooperation in Europe on Turkey's role, see FBIS-WEU, March 11, 1992, quoting TRT Television, March 10, 1992.

18. FBIS-WEU, March 9, 1992, quoting Türkiye Radiyolari, March 8, 1992.

19. FBIS-WEU, March 10, 1992, quoting TRT Television, March 9, 1992.

20. FBIS-WEU, March 5, 1992, quoting the Anatolia News Agency, same date.

21. This view was typically expressed in the conservative religious dailies *Türkiye* and *Zaman,* both based in Istanbul. For an example in English, see FBIS-WEU, March 5, 1992, quoting *Türkiye*, March 1, 1992.

22. FBIS-WEU, February 27, 1992, quoting the Anatolia News Agency, February 25, 1992.

23. Elizabeth Fuller, "Nagorno-Karabakh: Can Turkey Remain Neutral?" in *Radio Free Europe/Radio Liberty Research Report* 1, no. 14 (1992), p. 37, quoting *Handelsblatt*, March 11, 1992.

24. FBIS-WEU, March 5, 1992, quoting the Anatolia News Agency, March 4, 1992.

25. FBIS-WEU, March 13, 1992, quoting Türkiye Radyolari, March 12, 1992.

26. FBIS-WEU, March 3, 1992, quoting TRT Television, March 2, 1992.

27. *Washington Post*, March 19, 1992.

28. Mustafa Aydın, "Foucault's Pendulum: Turkey in Central Asia and the Caucasus," *Turkish Studies* 5, no. 2 (2004): 1–22.

29. *New York Times*, April 15, 1993.

30. *The Independent*, July 1, 1993.

31. FBIS-WEU, June 6, 1994, quoting *Hürriyet*, June 5, 1994.

32. For an example of Demirel's statements explaining the Turkish government's Karabakh policy, see FBIS-WEU, March 10, 1993, quoting TRT Television, March 9, 1993.

33. Interview by the author with Memmed Novruzoglu, Azerbaijan's Ambassador in Ankara, June 1996.

34. Gareth Winrow, "Turkey and the Newly Independent States of Central Asia and the Transcaucasus," *Middle East Review of International* Affairs 1, no. 2 (1997), available at http://meria.idc.ac.il/journal/1997/issue2/jv1n2a5.html.

35. "Çiller, darbecilerle irtibat halindeydi," [Çiller was in communication with the coup-makers] *Hurriyet* (Istanbul), February 27, 1998.

36. As reported in the Turkish MIT's report to the Prime Minister, according to the newspaper *Cumhuriyet*, July 19, 1998.

37. Aydın, "Foucault's Pendulum": 9–10.

38. Fariz Ismailzade, "Turkey-Azerbaijan: The Honeymoon Is Over," *Turkish Policy Quarterly* 4, no. 4 (2005), available at http://www.turkishpolicy.com/images/stories/2005-04-neighbors/TPQ2005-4-ismailzade.pdf.

39. Fatih Özatay and Güven Sak, "Banking Sector Fragility and Turkey's 2000–01 Financial Crisis," in *Brookings Trade Forum: 2002*, eds., Susan M. Collins and Dani Rodrik (Washington, D.C.: Brookings Institution Press, 2002), pp. 121–60.

40. Mevlut Katik, "Turkish Party Leader Seeks Favor in Central Asia," Eurasianet.org, January 14, 2003, available at www.eurasianet.org/resource/turkey/articles/index.shtml.

41. For a detailed discussion of these changes, see Zeyno Baran, *Torn Country: Turkey between Secularism and Islamism* (Stanford, CA: Hoover Institution Press, 2010).

42. Fiona Hill and Ömer Taşpınar, "Turkey and Russia: The Axis of the Excluded," *Survival* 48, no. 1 (2006): 81–92.

43. Robert Tait, "'Iran Is Our Friend' Says Turkish PM Recep Tayyip Erdogan," *The Guardian*, October 26, 2009.

44. Saban Kardas, "European Energy Security and Nabucco Occupy a Central Place in Erdoğan's Brussels Trip," *Eurasia Daily Monitor* (January 20, 2009), available at www.jamestown.org/single/?no_cache=1&tx_ttnews%5Btt_news%5D=34377.

45. M.K. Kaya and Svante E. Cornell, "Ankara's Growing Realism on the Nabucco Project," *Turkey Analyst* (May 22, 2009), available at www.silkroadstudies.org/new/inside/turkey/2009/090522B.html.

46. Vladimir Socor, "Shah-Deniz Phase Two Postponement Officially Confirmed," *Eurasia Daily Monitor* (May 1, 2009), available at www.jamestown.org/single/?no_cache=1&tx_ttnews%5Btt_news%5D=34935&tx_ttnews%5BbackPid%5D=7&cHash=e5b127d293.

47. Araz Aslanlı, "Türkiye-Ermenistan Sınırı Açılmalı Mı?" [Should the Turkish-Armenian border be opened?] *Panorama* Magazine, Istanbul (May 2004), available at http://www.ermenisorunu.gen.tr/turkce/makaleler/makale59.html.

48. Statement by Armenian Foreign Minister NN, Swedish Institute of International Affairs, Stockholm, 1996.

49. This wording is taken from the ANCA document "The Turkey-Armenia Protocols Explained," issued following the signing of the Protocols in August 2009, available at http://www.anca.org/assets/pdf/misc/protocols_explained.pdf. "This provision serves the longstanding aim of the Turkish government to secure the fruits of its genocidal crime against the Armenian people by pressuring the Republic of Armenia to officially renounce the rightful return of Armenian lands and property illegally and forcibly seized as a result of the Armenian Genocide. This provision not only forfeits the Republic of Armenia's claims, under the Treaty of Sevres and other international agreements, but also prejudices the rights of Diasporan Armenian in a just resolution of the Armenian Genocide. This provision violates the core principle of international that a nation cannot be held accountable for the terms and conditions of illegally negotiated and illegitimate third party treaties."

50. International Crisis Group, *Turkey and Armenia: Opening Mind, Opening Borders*, Europe Report no. 199, April 14, 2009.

51. Personal communication to author from Senior Azerbaijani diplomat, February 2010.

52. Fariz Ismailzade, "Is Pan-Turkism Still Alive?" *Central Asia-Caucasus Analyst* (July 31, 2002).

Chapter 15

1. Thomas Ambrosio, *Authoritarian Backlash: Russian Resistance to Democratization in the Former Soviet Union* (Burlington, VT: Ashgate, 2009).

2. Ibid., pp. 58–59. (The text of the statement is available on the website of the President of Russia, at http://eng.kremlin.ru/text/docs/2004/07/74223.shtml.)

3. Personal communication from senior Western academic, March 2005.

4. William Partlett, "Enforcing Oil and Gas Contracts Without Courts: Reputational Constraints on Resource Nationalism in Russia and Azerbaijan," *Demokratizatsiya: The Journal of Post-Soviet Democratization* 18.1 (2010): 74–93.

5. Peter H. Stone, "Caspian Wells Come In for K Street," *National Journal*, March 13 (1999): 680.

6. Ilya Bourtman, "Israel and Azerbaijan's Furtive Embrace," *Middle East Quarterly* 13, no. 3 (2006): 47–57.

7. In Azerbaijan's case, two notable exceptions were historians Tadeusz Swietochowski and Audrey Altstadt.

8. This argument is developed by Svante E. Cornell and Anna Jonsson in "Expanding the European Area of Stability and Democracy to the Wider Black Sea Region," in *The Wider Black Sea Region in the Twenty-First Century*, eds., Daniel Hamilton and Gerhard Mangott (Washington, D.C.: SAIS Center for Transatlantic Relations, 2008): pp. 225–50.

9. Shahin Abbasov, "Azerbaijan: Baku Upset over Lack of Karabakh Progress, Steps Up Anti-Western Rhetoric," *Eurasianet*, December 4, 2009, available at http://www.eurasianet.org/departments/insight/articles/eav120409a.shtml; Yeni *Müsavat*, 24 November 2009.

10. Ibid.

11. See, e.g., Kenneth S. Deffeyes, *Hubbert's Peak: The Impending World Oil Shortage* (Princeton, NJ: Princeton University Press, 2001); Richard C. Duncan and Walter Youngquist, "Encircling the Peak of World Oil Production," *Natural Resources Research* 8, no. 3 (1999): 219–32; David Francis, "Has Global Oil Production Peaked?" *Christian Science Monitor*, January 29, 2004.

12. The White House, "President Bush Welcomes President Aliyev of Azerbaijan to the White House," news release, April 28, 2006.

13. Zbigniew Brzezinski, *The Grand Chessboard: American Primacy and Its Geostrategic Imperatives* (New York: Basic Books, 1997).

14. Elizabeth Sherwood-Rendall, "U.S. Policy and the Caucasus," in *Contemporary Caucasus Newsletter* 5 (1998).

15. Paul Goble, "From Myths to Maps: American Interests in the Countries of Central Asia and the Caucasus," *Caspian Crossroads* 3, no. 1 (1997): 30–32.

16. Freedom Support Act of 1992, Oct. 24, 1992, Pub. L. 102–511, 106 Stat. 3320 (22 U.S.C. 5801 *et seq.*).

17. For more on the Armenian lobby and its influence, see David King and Miles Pomper, "The U.S. Congress and the Contingent Influence of Diaspora Lobbies: Lessons from U.S. Policy Toward Armenia and Azerbaijan, *Journal of Armenian Studies* 8, no. 1 (2004): 72–98.

18. Jim Nichol, *Transcaucasus Newly Independent States: Political Developments and Implications for U.S.* Interests, Congressional Research Service Issue Brief (Washington, D.C.: Library of Congress, 1996).

19. King and Pomper, "The U.S. Congress": 89.

20. Sherwood-Rendall, "U.S. Policy and the Caucasus."

21. Thomas Friedman, "Foreign Affairs; Pipeline Politics," *New York Times*, September 13, 1995.

22. James MacDougall, "A New Stage in U.S.–Caspian Sea Basin Relations," *Central Asia and the Caucasus* no. 5 (1997), available at www.ca-c.org/dataeng/st_04_dougall.shtml.

23. K.P. Foley, "Niyazov Makes First Official Visit To U.S.," *Turkmenistan Report*, Radio Free Europe/Radio Liberty, April 20, 1998.

24. House Committee on International Relations, "U.S. Policy Toward the Caucasus and Central Asia." (Testimony by Stephen Sestanovich, ambassador at large and special advisor to the Secretary of State for the New Independent States, 105th Cong., 2nd sess., April 30, 1998.)

25. Silk Road Strategy Act of 1999, Nov. 29, 1999, Pub. L. 106–113, 113 Stat. 1535, 1501A–123.

26. Brzezinski, *The Grand Chessboard.*

27. For further detail on the Bucharest summit and the U.S. failure there, see Ron Asmus, *The Little War That Shook the World* (Basingstoke, England: Palgrave Macmillan, 2010).

28. For a detailed discussion, see Svante E. Cornell, "The Caucasus and the Obama," in *Russia and Eurasia: A Realistic Policy Agenda for the Obama Administration* [Special Report 49], ed., Ariel Cohen (Washington, D.C.: Heritage Foundation, 2009), pp. 23–26.

29. See Dov Lynch, "The EU: Toward A Strategy," in *The South Caucasus: A Challenge for the EU*, Chaillot Paper 65, ed., Dov Lynch (Paris: European Union Institute for Security Studies, 2003), pp. 181–82, for perhaps the most eloquent description of the evolution of EU thinking on the Caucasus.

30. European Commission, *The Policy: What Is the European Neighbourhood Policy?* December 12, 2009, available at http://ec.europa.eu/world/enp/policy_en.htm.

31. It was stated that "given their location, the Southern Caucasus ... fall outside the geographical scope of this initiative for the time being." See *Wider Europe— Neighbourhood: A New Framework for Relations with our Eastern and Southern Neighbours* (Brussels, Belgium: Commission of the European Communities, 2003), p. 4, available at http://ec.europa.eu/world/enp/policy_en.htm.

32. "Azerbaijan Demands Security Guarantees from NATO," ABC.az, November 19, 2009, available at http://abc.az/eng/news_19_11_2009_40367.html.

33. Author's interview with President Ilham Aliyev, Baku, 2006.

34. As quoted by Bernard Lewis, speaking on March 26, 2002. See Bernard Lewis and Joanna J. Myers, "What Went Wrong? Western Impact and Middle Eastern Response" (transcript), available at website of the Carnegie Council for Ethics in International Affairs, www.cceia.org/resources/transcripts/131.html.

35. Tadeusz Swietochowski, *Russia and Azerbaijan: A Borderland in Transition* (New York: Columbia University Press, 1995).

Index

Svante E. Cornell is Research Director of the Central Asia-Caucasus Institute & Silk Road Studies Program, a Joint Research and Policy Center affilated with the School for Advanced International Studies (SAIS) at Johns Hopkins University, Washington D.C., and the Stockholm-based Institute for Security and Development Policy (ISDP), of which he is a co-founder and Director.

Cornell was educated at the Middle East Technical University, Ankara, and received his Ph.D. in Peace and Conflict Studies from Uppsala University in 2002. He was awarded an honorary doctoral degree by the Behmenyar Institute for Law and Philosophy of the Azerbaijani Academy of Sciences in 1999. Cornell has academic affiliations as Associate Research Professor at SAIS, and as Associate Professor of Government at Uppsala University. He is a Research Fellow with the Brussels-based Center for European Studies, and previously served as Course Chair of Caucasus Advanced Area Studies at the U.S. State Department's Foreign Service Institute.

Since 2001, he has been the Editor of the Joint Center's biweekly journal, The Central Asia-Caucasus Analyst (www.cacianalyst.org). His main areas of expertise are security issues, broadly defined, and state-building in the Caucasus, Turkey, and Central Asia. He is the author, among other works, of *Small Nations and Great Powers: A Study of Ethnopolitical Conflict in the Caucasus* (Curzon Press, 2001), the first comprehensive study of the post-Soviet Caucasus, and is co-editor, with S. Frederick Starr, of *The Guns of August 2008: Russia's War in Georgia* (M.E. Sharpe, 2009).